iOS
Apprentice
Eighth Edition

By Joey deVilla, Eli Ganim & Matthijs Hollemans

iOS Apprentice

Joey deVilla, Eli Ganim & Matthijs Hollemans

Copyright ©2019 Razeware LLC.

ISBN: 978-1-942878-97-1

Table of Contents

Book License

By purchasing *iOS Apprentice*, you have the following license:

- You are allowed to use and/or modify the source code in *iOS Apprentice* in as many apps as you want, with no attribution required.

- You are allowed to use and/or modify all art, images and designs that are included in *iOS Apprentice* in as many apps as you want, but must include this attribution line somewhere inside your app: "Artwork/images/designs: from *iOS Apprentice*, available at www.raywenderlich.com".

- The source code included in *iOS Apprentice* is for your personal use only. You are NOT allowed to distribute or sell the source code in *iOS Apprentice* without prior authorization.

- This book is for your personal use only. You are NOT allowed to sell this book without prior authorization, or distribute it to friends, coworkers or students; they would need to purchase their own copies.

About the Authors

Joey deVilla is an author of this book. Joey is a developer turned accordionist turned tech evangelist turned developer cat-herder. A Canadian turned Tampanian, he works at Fintech, blogs at globalnerdy.com and joeydevilla.com, and does what he can to avoid becoming a "Florida Man" news story.

Eli Ganim is an author of this book. He is an iOS engineer who's passionate about teaching, writing and sharing knowledge with others. He lives in Israel with his wife and kids.

Matthijs Hollemans is an author of this book. He is a mystic who lives at the top of a mountain where he spends all of his days and nights coding up awesome apps. Actually he lives below sea level in the Netherlands and is pretty down-to-earth but he does spend too much time in Xcode. Check out his website at www.matthijshollemans.com.

About the Editor

Adam Rush is the final pass editor for this book. He is a passionate iOS developer with over 7 years of commercial experience, contracting all over the UK & Europe. He's a tech addict and #Swift enthusiast. When he's not writing code, he enjoys watching sports and spending time with his family. You can reach him by @adam9rush

About the Artist

 **Vicki Wenderlich** is the designer and artist of the cover of this book. She is Ray's wife and business partner. She is a digital artist who creates illustrations, game art and a lot of other art or design work for the tutorials and books on raywenderlich.com. When she's not making art, she loves hiking, a good glass of wine and attempting to create the perfect cheese plate.

Dedications

"To my loved ones: Moriah, Lia and Ari."

— *Eli Ganim*

"To my family: Megan, Dexter and Aubrey."

— *Adam Rush*

Book Source Code & Forums

If you bought the digital edition

This book comes with the source code for the starter and completed projects for each chapter. These resources are shipped with the digital edition you downloaded here:

- https://store.raywenderlich.com/products/ios-apprentice.

If you bought the print version

You can get the source code for the print edition of the book here: https://store.raywenderlich.com/products/ios-apprentice-source-code.

And if you purchased the print version of this book, you're eligible to upgrade to the digital editions at a significant discount! Simply email support@razeware.com with your receipt for the physical copy and we'll get you set up with the discounted digital edition version of the book.

Forums

We've also set up an official forum for the book here:

- https://forums.raywenderlich.com/c/books/ios-apprentice.

This is a great place to ask questions about the book or to submit any errors you may find.

Digital book editions

We have a digital edition of this book available in both ePUB and PDF, which can be handy if you want a soft copy to take with you, or you want to quickly search for a specific term within the book.

Buying the digital edition version of the book also has a few extra benefits: free updates each time we update the book, access to older versions of the book, and you can download the digital editions from anywhere, at anytime.

Visit our *iOS Apprentice* store page here:

- https://store.raywenderlich.com/products/ios-apprentice.

Print Book Edition

You're reading the print edition of *iOS Apprentice*. This edition contains all of sections 1—3 and the first half of Section 4. Due to print size limitations, the final chapters are available to you as part of the downloadable source code materials.

You can download the source code materials here: https://store.raywenderlich.com/products/ios-apprentice-source-code.

About the Cover

Striped dolphins live to about 55-60 years of age, can travel in pods numbering in the thousands and can dive to depths of 700 m to feed on fish, cephalopods and crustaceans. Baby dolphins don't sleep for a full a month after they're born. That puts two or three sleepless nights spent debugging code into perspective, doesn't it?

Section 1: Getting Started with SwiftUI

This section introduces you to the first of the five apps you'll build throughout this book: *Bullseye*. It's a simple game that challenges the user to move a slider to a specific position without any hints or markers. While it won't make you an App Store millionaire, the exercise of writing it will introduce you to the basics of writing iOS apps.

This section will introduce you to several things you'll use when coding apps. You'll be introduced to Xcode, the integrated development environment for writing programs for Apple devices. You'll also be introduced to Swift, Apple's programming language, which has grown to become one of the most popular among programmers because it's simple, powerful, and fun.

Finally, you'll get your first taste of something that even the most experienced iOS developers haven't had much time to try: SwiftUI. It's the new way to build user interfaces for Apple platforms, and like the programming language from which it takes its name, it's simple and powerful. The first two apps that you'll make in this book will give you a great head start in building interfaces with SwiftUI.

This section aims to be beginner-friendly, and you may be tempted to skip it. Please don't, especially if you're new to iOS development. You'll need the fundamentals introduced in this section for later parts of the book, and you'll miss out on the basics of the all-new SwiftUI.

This section contains the following chapters:

1. Introduction: Welcome to **The iOS Apprentice!** In this book, you're about to deep dive into the latest and greatest Swift and iOS best practices. Throughout this five-section book, you will build four iOS projects using both UIKit and SwiftUI. Good luck!

2. The One-Button App: Take the first step of building a SwiftUI game by creating your iOS project, add some interactivity with a UIButton and learn all about the anatomy of an app.

3. Slider & Labels: Bullseye is all about the slider, get sliding in this chapter by using the Slider control and learn all about different Swift data types.

4. A Basic Working Game: In this chapter, you'll be well on your way to a working game. Learn all about generating random numbers and how best to improve your code afterward.

5. Rounds & Score: A fully working Game: It's all about winning; in this chapter learn how best to score each game and introduce one more round functionality.

6. Refactoring: At this point, you have created a fully functional game, wow! It's time to take a step back and look at best practices in the industry. It's time to clean up some code and make it more readable for the future!

7. The New Look: Apps are known for their clean and simple UI. We will spice up the artwork in this chapter and make it look like a *real* game. We will also make improvements to landscape orientation.

8. The Final App: To finish our game we will add some animations, an icon, and display name ready for the App Store!

Chapter 1: Introduction

Joey deVilla

Hi, welcome to *The iOS Apprentice: Beginning iOS Development with Swift, Eighth Edition*, the swiftest way (pardon the pun) to iOS development mastery!

In this book, you'll learn how to make your own iPhone and iPad apps using Apple's Swift programming language, Xcode 11, and the SwiftUI and UIKit user interface frameworks. You'll do this by building four interesting iOS apps.

The apps you'll make in The iOS Apprentice

Everybody likes games, right? So you'll start by building a simple but fun iPhone game named *Bullseye* that will teach you the basics of iPhone programming. The other apps will build on what you learn there.

Taken together, the four apps that you'll build cover everything you need to know to make your own apps. By the end of the book, you'll be experienced enough to turn your ideas into real apps that you can put on the App Store!

If you've never programmed before or you're new to iOS, don't worry. You should be able to follow along with the step-by-step instructions and understand how to make these apps. Each chapter has a ton of illustrations to keep you from getting lost. Not everything might make sense right away, but hang in there and all will become clear in time.

Writing your own iOS apps is a lot of fun, but it's also hard work. If you have the imagination and perseverance, there's no limit to what you can make your apps do. It's my sincere belief that this book can turn you from a complete newbie into an accomplished iOS developer, but you do have to put in the time and effort. By writing this book, I've done my part. The rest is up to you...

About this book

The iOS Apprentice will help you become an excellent iOS developer, but only if you let it. Here are some tips that will help you get the most out of this book.

Learn through repetition

You're going to make several apps in this book. Even though the apps are quite simple, you may find the instructions hard to follow at first — especially if you've never done any computer programming before. You'll be facing a lot of new concepts.

It's OK if you don't understand everything right away, as long as you get the general idea. As you proceed through the book, you'll go over many of those concepts again and again until they solidify in your mind.

Follow the instructions yourself

It's important that you not just read the instructions, but also actually **follow them**. Open Xcode, type in the source code fragments and run the app in the simulator as instructed. This helps you to see how the app develops, step by step.

Even better, play around with the code and with the Xcode settings. Feel free to modify any part of the app and see what the results are. Make a small change to the code and see how it affects the entire app. Experiment and learn! Don't worry about breaking stuff — that's half the fun. You can always find your way back to the beginning. But better still, you might even learn something from simply breaking the code and learning how to fix it.

If you try everything but are still stuck, drop by the forums for this book at forums.raywenderlich.com. I'm around most of the time and will be happy to answer any questions related to the book and issues you might have run into.

Don't panic — bugs happen!

You'll run into problems, guaranteed. Your programs will have strange bugs that will leave you stumped. Trust me, I've been programming for 30 years and that still happens to me, too. We're only humans and our brains have a limited capacity to deal with complex programming problems. In this book, I'll give you tools for your mental toolbox that will allow you to find your way out of any hole you've dug for yourself.

Understanding beats copy-pasting

Too many people attempt to write iOS apps by blindly copy-pasting code that they find on blogs and other websites, without really knowing what that code does or how it should fit into their programs.

There's nothing wrong with looking on the web for solutions — I do it all the time — but I want to give you the tools and knowledge to understand what you're doing and why. That way, you'll learn more quickly and write better programs.

This is hands-on, practical advice, not a bunch of dry theory (although we can't avoid *some* theory). You're going to build real apps right from the start, and I'll explain how everything works along the way, with lots of images to illustrate what is going on.

I'll do my best to make it clear how everything fits together, why we do things a certain way and what the alternatives are.

Do the exercises

I'll also ask you to do some thinking of your own — yes, there are exercises! It's in your best interest to actually do these exercises. There's a big difference between knowing the path and walking the path... And the only way to learn programming is to do it.

I encourage you to not just do the exercises but also to play with the code you'll be writing. Experiment, make changes, try to add new features. Software is a complex piece of machinery and to find out how it works, you sometimes have to put some spokes in the wheels and take the whole thing apart. That's how you learn!

Have fun!

Last but not least, remember to have fun! Step by step, you'll build your understanding of programming while making fun apps. By the end of this book, you'll have learned the essentials of Swift, the iOS Software Development Kit (SDK) and both the SwiftUI and the UIKit frameworks. More importantly, you should have a pretty good idea of how everything goes together and how to think like a programmer.

This book has one ultimate goal: That by the time you reach the end, you'll have learned enough to stand on your own two feet as a developer. We're confident that, eventually, you'll be able to write any iOS app that you want as long as you understand the basics. You still may have a lot to learn but, when you're through with *The iOS Apprentice*, you can do it without the training wheels.

Is this book right for you?

Whether you're completely new to programming or you come from a different programming background and want to learn iOS development, this book is for you!

If you're a complete beginner, don't worry — this book doesn't assume you know anything about programming or making apps. Of course, if you do have programming experience, that helps. Swift is a new programming language but, in many ways, it's similar to other popular languages such as Python, C# or JavaScript.

If you've tried iOS development before with the old language, Objective-C, then its low-level nature and strange syntax may have put you off. Well, there's good news: Now that we have a modern language in Swift, iOS development has become a lot easier to pick up.

This book can't teach you all the ins and outs of iOS development. The iOS SDK is huge and grows with each new release, so there's no way we can cover everything. Fortunately, we don't need to. You just need to master the essential building blocks of Swift and the iOS SDK. Once you understand these fundamentals, you can easily figure out how the other parts of the SDK work and learn the rest on your own terms.

The most important thing I'll teach you is how to think like a programmer. That will help you approach any programming task, whether it's a game, a utility, a mobile app that uses web service or anything else you can imagine.

As a programmer, you'll often have to think your way through difficult computational problems and find creative solutions. By methodically analyzing these problems, you'll be able to solve them, no matter how complex. Once you possess this valuable skill, you can program anything!

iOS 13 and later only

The code in this book is written exclusively for iOS version 13 and later. Each new release of iOS is such a big departure from the previous one that it doesn't make sense to keep developing for older devices and iOS versions. Things move quickly in the world of mobile computing!

Most iPhone, iPod touch and iPad users are quick to upgrade to the latest version of iOS anyway, so you don't need to be too worried that you're leaving potential users behind.

Owners of older devices may be stuck with older iOS versions, but this is only a tiny portion of the market. The cost of supporting these older iOS versions for your apps is usually greater than the handful of extra customers it brings you.

It's ultimately up to you to decide whether it's worth making your app available to users with older devices, but my recommendation is that you focus your efforts where they matter most. Apple, as a company, relentlessly looks towards the future — if you want to play in Apple's back yard, it's wise to follow its lead. So back to the future it is!

What you need

It's a lot of fun to develop for the iPhone and iPad but, like most hobbies (or businesses!), it will cost some money. Of course, once you get good at it and build an awesome app, you'll have the potential to make that money back many times.

You'll have to invest in the following.

An **iPhone, iPad or iPod touch.** I'm assuming that you have at least one of these. iOS 13 runs on the following devices:

- iPhone 6s or newer

- iPad Pro (any generation)

- iPad 5th generation or newer

- iPad Air 2 or 3rd generation

- iPad Mini 5th generation

- iPod Touch 7th generation

If you have an older device, then this is a good time to think about getting an upgrade. But don't worry if you don't have a suitable device: You can do most of your testing on iOS Simulator.

> **Note**: Even though this book is about developing apps for the iPhone, everything within applies equally to the iPad and iPod touch. Aside from small hardware differences, these devices use iOS or its close cousin iPadOS and you program them in exactly the same way. You should also be able to run the apps from this book on your iPad or iPod touch without problems.

A **Mac computer with an Intel processor**: Any Mac that you've bought in the last few years will do, even a Mac mini or MacBook Air. It needs to have at least macOS 10.14.4 Mojave, and I strongly recommend that you use macOS 10.15 Catalina, especially when building apps with SwiftUI.

Xcode, the development environment for iOS apps, is a memory-hungry tool. These days, even the most inexpensive MacBook Air in the Apple Store comes with 8GB of RAM. You should consider this the minimum RAM for development. Keep this general rule in mind: The more RAM, the better. A smart developer invests in good tools!

With some workarounds, it's possible to develop iOS apps on a Windows or a Linux machine, or on a regular PC that has macOS installed (a "Hackintosh"). If you're up for a challenge, you can try iOS development on these machines, but you'll save yourself a lot of time and hassle by just getting a Mac.

If you can't afford to buy the latest model, then consider getting a second-hand Mac from eBay or some other resale vendor. It should be a Mac that dates from mid-2012 or later; just make sure it meets the minimum requirements (Intel CPU, preferably with more than 4 GB RAM). If it helps, you should know that the code for the SwiftUI portions of this book was written using a mid-2014 MacBook Pro with 16GB of RAM. Should you happen to buy a machine that has an older version of macOS, you should upgrade to the latest version of the operating system from the online Mac App Store for free.

Eventually, an **Apple Developer Program account**: You can download all the development tools for free and you can try out your apps on your own iPhone, iPad or iPod touch while you're developing, so you don't have to join the Apple Developer Program just yet. But to submit finished apps to the App Store, you'll have to enroll in the paid Developer Program. This will cost you $99 per year.

See developer.apple.com/programs/ for more info.

Xcode

The first order of business is to download and install Xcode and the iOS SDK.

Xcode is the development tool for iOS apps. It has a text editor where you'll type your source code and a visual editor for designing your app's user interface.

Xcode transforms the source code that you write into an executable app and launches it in the iOS Simulator or on your iPhone. Because no app is bug-free, Xcode also has a debugger that helps you find defects in your code. Unfortunately, it won't automatically fix them for you; that's still something you have to do yourself.

You can download Xcode for free from the Mac App Store (apple.co/2wzi1L9). This requires at least macOS High Sierra (10.14.4). If you're still running an older version of macOS, you'll first have to upgrade to the latest version of macOS (also available for free from the Mac App Store). Get ready for a big download, as the full Xcode package is almost 8 GB.

Important: You may already have a version of Xcode on your system that came pre-installed with your version of macOS. That version could be hopelessly outdated, so don't use it. Apple puts out new releases on a regular basis and you always want to develop with the latest Xcode and the latest available SDK on the latest version of macOS.

This revision of the book was written using **Xcode version 11** and the **iOS 13** SDK on **macOS Catalina (10.15)**. By the time you read this, the version numbers might have gone up again.

We'll do our best to keep the PDF versions of the book up-to-date with new releases of the development tools and iOS versions, but don't panic if the screenshots don't correspond 100% to what you see on your screen. In most cases, the differences will be minor.

Many older books and blog posts (anything before 2010) talk about Xcode 3, which is radically different from Xcode 11. If it predates the iPad, it's seriously out of date.

More recent materials may mention Xcode versions 4 through 10, which are similar to Xcode 11 but differ in many of the details. Xcode 11 also introduces a new framework, SwiftUI, and you won't find anything about it in older tutorials.

If you're reading an article and you see a picture of Xcode that looks different from yours, the author might be writing about an older version. You may still be able to get something out of those articles, as the programming examples are still valid. It's just Xcode that is slightly different.

What's ahead: An overview

The iOS Apprentice is spread across four apps, and moves from beginning to intermediate topics. You'll build each app from start to finish, from scratch! Let's take a look at what's ahead.

Building apps with SwiftUI

You'll build the first two apps using the newly-announced SwiftUI framework. Announced in 2019 at Apple's WWDC (World Wide Developer Conference), it's a completely different way for developers to design apps. Since it looks like SwiftUI will eventually become the preferred way to build apps, we decided to introduce it to you with your first two apps.

App 1: Bullseye

You'll start by building a game called *Bullseye*. You'll learn how to use Xcode, Swift and SwiftUI in a way that's easy to understand.

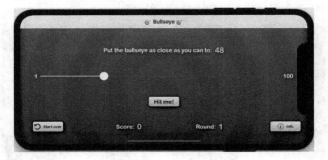

App 2: Checklist

For your next trick, you'll create your own to-do list app. You'll learn more about SwiftUI, the fundamental design patterns that all iOS apps use, data structures, sharing information between objects, and saving the user's information. Now you're making apps for real!

Building apps with UIKit

From the very first iPhone OS and all the way up to iOS 12, iOS apps were written using Apple's original user interface framework, UIKit. With over a decade's worth of UIKit-based code, documentation and tutorials, today's iOS developers can't rely on SwiftUI alone – they'll have to know both user interface frameworks. That's why you'll build the next two apps with UIKit.

App 3: MyLocations

For your third app, you'll develop a location-aware app that lets you keep a list of spots that you find interesting. In the process, you'll learn about UIKit, Core Location, Core Data, Map Kit and much more!

App 4: StoreSearch

Mobile apps often need to talk to web services, and that's what you'll do in your final app. You'll make a stylish app that lets you search for products on the iTunes store using HTTP requests and JSON.

Let's get started and turn you into a full-fledged iOS developer!

The language of the computer

The iPhone may pretend that it's a phone, but it's really a pretty advanced handheld computer that happens to have the ability to make phone calls. Like any computer, the iPhone works with ones and zeros. When you write software to run on the iPhone, you somehow have to translate the ideas in your head into those ones and zeros so that the computer can understand you.

Fortunately, you don't have to write any ones and zeros yourself. That would be a bit too much to ask of the human brain. On the other hand, everyday English — or any other natural human language — just isn't precise enough to use for programming computers.

So you'll use an intermediary language, Swift. It's a little bit like English, and reasonably straightforward for us humans to understand. At the same time, it's ordered and structured enough so that it can be easily translated into something the computer can understand as well.

This is an approximation of the language that the computer speaks:

```
Ltmp96:
        .cfi_def_cfa_register %ebp
        pushl   %esi
        subl    $36, %esp
Ltmp97:
        .cfi_offset %esi, -12
        calll   L7$pb
L7$pb:
        popl    %eax
        movl    16(%ebp), %ecx
        movl    12(%ebp), %edx
        movl    8(%ebp), %esi
        movl    %esi, -8(%ebp)
        movl    %edx, -12(%ebp)
        movl    %ecx, (%esp)
        movl    %eax, -24(%ebp)
        calll   _objc_retain
        movl    %eax, -16(%ebp)
        .loc    1 161 2 prologue_end
```

Actually, what the computer sees is this:

```
0001100101001111010010001100111110010101
0010100010011110101101110011101011010010
0101000111001111101011101100001110000110
1001000001110001010011010011111001100111
```

The movl and calll instructions are part of what's called *assembly language*, which is just there to make machine code more readable for humans. I don't know about you, but for me, it's still hard to make much sense out of it.

It certainly is possible to write programs in that arcane language. In the days of 8- and 16-bit computers, if you were writing a videogame or some other app that had to eke the most performance out of those slow machines, you had to. Even today, programmers who need to work at the system level or need maximum performance from minimal hardware will write some assembly language. I'll take having my apps run fractions of a second slower if I can write programs that I can follow because they look like this:

```swift
func handleMusicEvent(command: Int, noteNumber: Int, velocity:
Int) {

  if command == NoteOn && velocity != 0 {
    playNote(noteNumber + transpose, velocityCurve[velocity] /
127)

  } else if command == NoteOff ||
        (command == NoteOn && velocity == 0) {
    stopNote(noteNumber + transpose, velocityCurve[velocity] /
127)

  } else if command == ControlChange {
    if noteNumber == 64 {
      damperPedal(velocity)
    }
  }
}
```

The above code snippet is from a sound synthesizer program. It looks like something that almost makes sense. Even if you've never programmed before, you can sort of figure out what's going on. It's almost English.

Swift is a hot new language that combines traditional object-oriented programming with aspects of functional programming. Fortunately, it has many things in common with other popular programming languages, so if you're already familiar with C#, Python, Ruby or JavaScript, you'll feel right at home with Swift.

Swift isn't the only option for making apps. Until recently, iOS apps were programmed in Objective-C, which first appeared in 1984. Objective-C is an object-oriented extension of the tried-and-true C programming language, which was first released in 1972. Objective-C comes with a lot of '70s and '80s baggage and doesn't have a lot of the niceties that modern developers have come to expect. That's why Apple created a new language.

Objective-C will still be around for a while, but the future of iOS development is Swift. All the cool kids are using it already.

C++ is another language that adds object-oriented programming to C. It's very powerful but, as a beginning programmer, you probably want to stay away from it. I only mention it because you can also use C++ to write iOS apps. There's also an unholy marriage of C++ and Objective-C named Objective-C++ that you may come across from time to time. If you see it, back away slowly and don't make eye contact.

I could have started *The iOS Apprentice* with an in-depth exploration of the features of Swift, but this is a tutorial, not a sleep aid! So, instead, I'll follow the adage of "Show, don't tell" and explain the language as we go along, very briefly at first, but in more depth later.

In the beginning, the general concepts — what is a variable, what is an object, how do you call a method, and so on — are more important than the details. Slowly but surely, all the arcane secrets of the Swift language will be revealed to you!

Are you ready to begin writing your first iOS app?

Chapter 2: Getting Started with SwiftUI

Joey deVilla

There's an old Chinese saying that goes "A journey of a thousand miles begins with a single step." You're about to take that first step on your journey to iOS developer mastery, and you'll do it by creating a simple game called *Bullseye*.

This chapter covers the following:

- **SwiftKit and UIKit**: These are two ways to build apps and user interfaces, and you'll learn both.

- **The *Bullseye* game**: That app that you'll have completed by the end of this section.

- **Getting started**: Enough preamble — let's create a new project!

- **Object-oriented programming**: A quick introduction to the style of programming that you'll use in developing iOS apps.

- **Adding interactivity**: An app that just sits there is no fun. Let's make it respond to the user!

- **State and SwiftUI**: What is "state," and what does it have to do with SwiftUI?

- **Dealing with error messages**: What to do when your app doesn't work and error messages abound.

- **The anatomy of an app**: A brief explanation of the inner workings of an app.

SwiftUI and UIKit

There's another saying (erroneously) attributed to the Chinese: "May you live in interesting times." Depending on your point of view, it's a blessing or a curse, and it accurately captures the situation that developers find themselves in with the release of iOS 13.

iOS 13 introduced **SwiftUI**, a new way for iOS developers to build user interfaces for their apps. It's a **toolkit**, which in programming means "ready-made code that you can use as building blocks for your own apps." Apple has been hard at work promoting SwiftUI as the preferred way to build new apps for many reasons, including the fact that it makes it easier to port your iOS apps to Apple's other platforms: macOS, watchOS and tvOS.

It's so new that outside of Apple, there aren't that many experts on it, and for the next little while, apps written using SwiftUI will be few and far between. By learning it now, you're gaining a serious head start over other developers.

UIKit is SwiftUI's long-standing predecessor. It's been around since iOS 2.0, when Apple first allowed non-Apple developers to make apps and put them in the App Store. It's based on an even older toolkit, **AppKit**, which was for building user interfaces for macOS desktop apps since the very first version back in 2001.

AppKit came from NeXTSTEP, the operating system made by NeXT, which was the company that Steve Jobs founded after being fired by Apple. Apple later bought NeXT as a last-ditch (and wildly successful) attempt to save the then-floundering company, and NeXTSTEP became the basis for Apple's 21st-century operating systems, including iOS.

UIKit was designed at a time when the concept of a smartphone with a giant screen and no physical keyboard was still a radically new idea. Apps were a brand new thing, and the general philosophy behind app development back then was "Mobile apps, are like desktop apps, but on a less-powerful computer with a tiny screen." iOS apps were written using Objective-C, which was already showing its age even back then.

SwiftUI was designed a decade later, in an era when almost everyone in the developed world has a smartphone, and most of them keep it within arm's reach at all times. Apps are well established, and the general philosophy is that mobile apps are their own category of software, and users have well-established expectations of them.

The preferred language for writing iOS apps is now Swift. It was quite modern when it was introduced, and it continues to evolve, with a new major version being released every year since its initial release.

Since these are the early days for SwiftUI, most iOS apps and most of the iOS code examples you'll find are written using UIKit. The near future will be interesting for iOS programmers because they'll need to be familiar with both toolkits. That's why this book covers SwiftUI *and* UIKit.

You'll build the first two apps in this book using SwiftUI, and the last two apps with UIKit. Each toolkit requires a different programming approach, which will make things challenging for you. We also hope that learning both will be rewarding and fun!

The Bullseye game

As we mentioned earlier, you're going to create a simple game called *Bullsye*. Here's what it'll look like when you're finished:

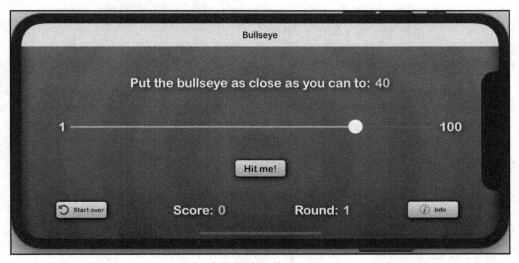

The finished Bullseye game

The objective of the game is to put the bullseye as close to the target as you can. The bullseye is on a slider that goes from 1 to 100, and the target value is randomly chosen. In the screenshot above, you're challenged to put the bullseye at 40. Since you can't see the current value of the slider and there aren't any markings to help you, you have to "eyeball" it.

When you're confident of your estimate, you press the **Hit Me!** button and a pop-up will tell you what your score is:

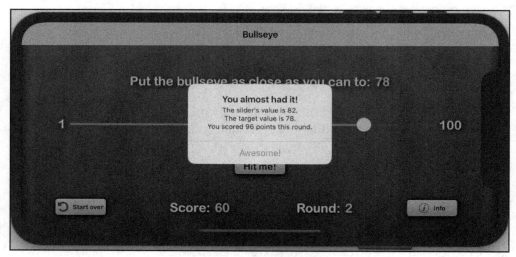

An alert pop-up shows the score

The closer to the target value you are, the more points you score. After you dismiss the alert pop-up by pressing the **OK** button, a new round begins with a new random target. The game repeats until the player presses the **Start Over** button (the one near the bottom-left corner), which resets the score to 0 and the round to 1.

This game probably won't make you an instant millionaire on the App Store, but it will show you the basics of making an app and building user interfaces with SwiftUI. Hey, even future millionaires have to start somewhere!

Making a programming to-do list

Now that you've seen what the game should look like, and what the gameplay rules are, make a list of all the things that you think you'll need to do in order to build this game. It's okay if you draw a blank, but try it anyway.

Here's an example:

The app needs to put the "Hit Me!" button on the screen and show an alert pop-up when the user presses it.

Try to think of other things the app needs to do. It doesn't matter if you don't actually know how to accomplish these tasks. The first step is to figure out *what* you need to do. *How* to do these things isn't important yet.

Once you know what you want, you can also figure out how to do it, even if you have to ask someone or look it up. But the *what* comes first.

You'd be surprised at how many people start writing code without a clear idea of what they're actually trying to achieve. No wonder they get stuck! Whenever you start working on a new app, it's a good idea to make a list of all the different pieces of functionality you think the app will need. This will become your programming to-do list. Having a list that breaks up a design into several smaller steps is a great way to deal with the complexity of a project.

> **Note**: If you ever need a fancy way of saying that you're breaking down a big complex task into a set of smaller, simpler tasks, just say that you're performing *functional decomposition.*

You may have a cool idea for an app, but when you sit down to write the program it can seem overwhelming. There is so much to do, and there's always the question: "Where do I begin?" By cutting up the project into small steps, you make it less daunting. You may find that some of those small steps can be divided into even smaller steps. You can always find a step that is simple and small enough to make a good starting point and take it from there.

Don't worry if you find this exercise challenging. You're new to all of this! As you gain more programming experience, you'll find it easier to identify the different parts that make up a design and become better at splitting it into manageable pieces.

Here's an example of a to-do list based on the description of *Bullseye*:

- Put a button on the screen and label it "Hit Me!"

- When the player presses the "Hit Me!" button, the app has to show a pop-up that shows the player a score indicating how close they were to the target.

- Put text on the screen, such as "Score:" and "Round:". The score increases as the player earns more points, and the number of rounds increases with each attempt by the player.

- Put a slider on the screen with a range between the values 1 and 100. The player moves the slider as closely to the target value as they can.

- Come up with the target value at the start of each round and display it on the screen. This needs to be a random number between 1 and 100, inclusive.

- Determine the value of the slider (based on its position) after the player presses the "Hit Me!" button.

- Compare the value of the slider to the target value and calculate a score based on how far off the player is. Show this score in the alert pop-up.

- Put a "Start Over" button on the screen. Make it reset the score to zero and round to one.

- Put the app in landscape orientation.

- Make it look pretty.

There may be a detail or two missing from this list, but it's a good starting point. Even for a game as basic as this one, there are quite a few things you need to do. Making apps is fun, but it's definitely a lot of work, too!

Getting started

The first two items on the *Bullseye* to-do list are, essentially:

1. Put a button on the screen.

2. Show a pop-up when the player presses the button.

You'll start by building an app that does only these two things. Once you've done this, you'll build the rest of *Bullseye* on this foundation.

This initial app will look like this:

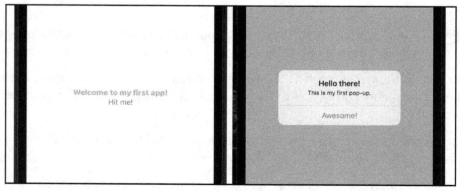

The app contains a line of text and a single button (left) that shows an alert when pressed (right)

Time to start coding! To follow the coding exercises in this book, you'll need:

- **Coding tools.** The exercises in this book require **Xcode 11.0** or later, which you can download for free using the **App Store** on your Mac. Xcode 11 requires **macOS 10.15**, also known as "Catalina". It won't run on prior versions of macOS. The differences between Xcode 11 and earlier versions are so big that we don't recommend using an earlier version.

- **Optionally — but *ideally* — a device.** The apps you'll make will run on an iPhone running **iOS 13.0** or later, or an iPad running **iPadOS 13.0** or later. If you don't have a device, you can make do with the **Simulator**, an application that runs on your Mac and acts as if it were an iPhone, iPad, Apple Watch, or Apple TV. It allows you to test the apps you write without having to deploy it to a device. You can do the exercises in this book without a device with a few limitations, but there's no substitute for the real thing.

Creating a new project

➤ Launch **Xcode**. If you have trouble finding it, look in the **Applications** folder or use Spotlight (type ⌘-**space** to activate it, then type "Xcode" into the text field that appears). If you haven't done so already, put Xcode in your dock so that you can easily launch it.

You'll see the "Welcome to Xcode" window when it starts:

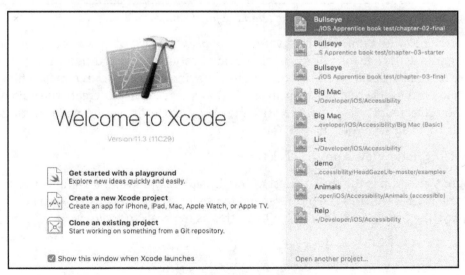

Xcode bids you welcome

➤ Choose **Create a new Xcode project**. The main Xcode window appears with an assistant that lets you choose a template:

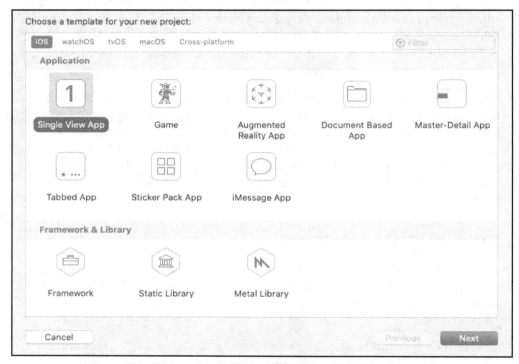

Choosing the template for the new project

Xcode comes with templates for a variety of app styles, each of which is pre-configured with code for a different kind of application. When you choose one of these templates, Xcode creates a new project that includes the **source files** — files containing the code that make up an app — that are necessary to create the kind of app you selected. These templates are handy because they're ready-made starting points that can save you a lot of effort.

➤ Select **Single View App** and click **Next**.

Single View App is the the simplest of the iOS app templates. It's a simple app with a single view — which is the term we tend to use for "screen" or "page" — that displays the text "Hello World". You'll use this as the basis for *Bullseye*.

You'll be shown a pop-up where you enter options for your new project.

Configuring the new project

➤ Fill out these options as follows:

• **Product Name**: Enter **Bullseye** here.

• **Team**: If you're already a member of the Apple Developer Program, this will show your team name. For now, it's best to leave this set to **None**. We'll cover this in more detail later on.

• **Organization Name**: Put your own name or the name of your company here.

• **Organization Identifier**: You should fill this with something that uniquely identifies you or your organization. The standard practice is to enter your personal or organization domain name in reverse here. For example, if your domain name is *mydomain.com*, enter **com.mydomain** into this field. If you don't have your own domain name, enter **com.example**. Don't worry too much about what you enter here right now, it doesn't really matter until you submit your app to the App Store, and you can always change this setting later.

- **Language**: Make sure that this is set to **Swift**. All the exercises in this book are in Swift.

- **Use SwiftUI**: Make sure that this is selected. You'll use SwiftUI to create the user interface for *Bullseye*.

- **Use Core Data**, **Include Unit Tests**, and **Include UI Tests**: Make sure that these are *not* selected. You won't use any of these features in this project.

➤ Press **Next**. Now, Xcode will ask where to save your project:

Choosing where to save the project

➤ Choose a location for the project files. For example, the Desktop or your Documents folder.

Xcode will automatically make a new folder for the project using the Product Name that you entered in the previous step, **Bullseye** in this case, so you don't need to make a new folder yourself.

At the bottom of the File Save dialog, there is a checkbox labeled **Create Git repository on My Mac**. You can ignore this for now. You'll learn about the Git version control system later on.

➤ Click **Create** to finish.

Xcode will now create a new project named "Bullseye," based on the Single View Application template, in the folder you specified. When it is done, the screen should look something like this:

The main Xcode window at the start of your project

There may be small differences between the screenshot above and what you see on your own computer. As long as you're running Xcode version 11.0 or later, any differences you see should only be superficial.

Important: Before you continue, examine the list of files on the left side of the Xcode window. If you see a file named **ContentView.swift**, your project is set up properly and you can proceed to the next step. If you don't see a file named **ContentView.swift** in the list, but instead see **ViewController.swift**, it means that you forgot to check the **UseSwiftUI** checkbox when choosing the options for the project. If you see files with the names **ViewController.h** and **ViewController.m**, then you picked the wrong language (Objective-C) when you created the project. In either case, start over and be sure to check the **UseSwiftUI** checkbox and choose **Swift** as the programming language.

Now, let's take a closer look at your project.

Looking at the Editor

The first thing you should look at is the **Editor**, which takes up most of the left side of the Xcode window:

The Editor in a newly created Single View Application project

You'll spend a lot of time in the Editor, as it's where you enter — and as its name implies; *edit* — code. Right now, it's displaying the source code inside the **ContentView.swift** file. This file defines what goes into and what happens on the app's single "screen" or "page," which is also referred to in programming terms as a *view*.

For now, you should concern yourself with the part of the code that actually determines what the app does. It's the middle section, shown below:

```swift
import SwiftUI

struct ContentView : View {
  var body: some View {
    Text("Hello World")
  }
}
```

Don't worry if this makes no sense to you right now, we'll review this line-by-line later in this chapter. However, here's a quick sneak peek if you're especially curious:

The first line, `import SwiftUI`, is an instruction to make use of the SwiftUI toolkit. SwiftUI provides a lot of features that you can call on to make user interfaces and respond to user actions.

The rest of the code defines the app's single view (remember, in this case, when we say "view", you should think "screen" or "page"). It says that there is a thing called `ContentView` and this it's a `View`. It also says that `ContentView` contains a single `Text` object that displays the text "Hello World".

Note that the source code above leaves out the part at the beginning: The handful of bluish-gray lines of text ending with a copyright notice. This is a block of *comments*, which are notes intended for people who will read the code. They have no effect on the app or how it runs. We'll discuss comments in more detail in the following chapter.

The source code above also leaves out the part at the end that starts with the line `struct ContentView_Previews:`. This code is responsible for drawing a preview of your app, and we'll play around with it later.

Looking at the Canvas

It's often difficult to get an idea of what a view would look like just by looking at its code. That's what the **Canvas** is for. It's located just to the right of the Editor and looks like this:

The Canvas pane at the start

The Canvas pane shows the message **Automatic preview updating paused** in its upper left corner. This means that it's currently *not* updating its contents to show the visual results of the code in the Editor. Let's un-pause it so that you can see what the view should look like.

> **Note**: If you don't see the Canvas in the Xcode window, click the **Editor Options** button. A menu will appear; select **Canvas**:

The Editor Options button and menu

➤ Click **Resume** (in the upper right corner of the Canvas pane) to see a preview of the app's view.

A spinning progress indicator will appear in the Canvas pane and, after a few moments, you should see this:

The Canvas pane after pressing the Resume button

The canvas is a much easier way to visualize your user interface, especially as your views become more complicated. As you'll learn later, you can edit your user interfaces in the canvas too!

Running your project

Now, let's bring your project to life by running it in the Simulator.

Once again, the Simulator is a macOS application that pretends to be various Apple devices: iPhones, iPads, Apple Watches, and Apple TVs. It's useful for running quick tests of your apps and for trying it out on devices that you don't have. In the beginning, you'll run your apps on the Simulator. Later on, you'll learn how to deploy them to a device.

➤ Click on the device picker near the top-left corner of the Xcode window:

The device picker

➤ In the menu that appears, under the section marked **iOS Simulators**, select **iPhone 11**:

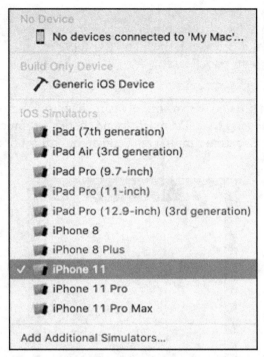

The device picker menu with iPhone 11 selected

➤ Click the **Run** button near the top-left corner of the Xcode window, to the left of the device picker:

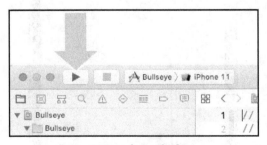

Press Run to launch the app

Note: If this is the first time you're using Xcode, it may ask you to enable developer mode. Click **Enable** and enter your password to allow Xcode to make these changes. Also, make sure that you do not have your iPhone or iPad plugged into your computer at this point. Otherwise, Xcode might try to run the app on the actual device instead of the Simulator. Since you're not yet set up for running on a device, this could result in errors that might leave you scratching your head. Stick with the Simulator for now; you'll learn how to deploy the app to your phone later.

Xcode will labor for a bit, and will eventually launch your brand new app in the Simulator. The app doesn't look like much — and there's not much you can with it, either. That said, it's an actual running app, and an important first milestone in your journey!

What an app based on the Single View Application template looks like

If the app doesn't run and Xcode says **Build Failed** or **A build only device cannot be used to run this target** when you click the Run button, make sure that **iPhone 11** (or any other iPhone model listed under **iOS Simulators** in the device picker's menu) — not **Generic iOS Device** — is selected in the device picker:

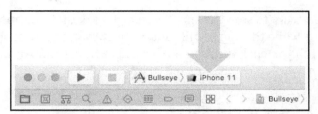

Making Xcode run the app on the Simulator

Until you press **Stop**, Xcode's Activity viewer at the top says, "Running Bullseye on iPhone 11":

The Xcode activity viewer

➤ Click the **Stop** button to exit the app:

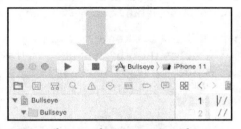

Press the stop button to stop the app

On your phone, or in the Simulator, you'd use the Home button to exit an app. On the Simulator, you could also use the **Hardware ▸ Home** item from the menu bar or use the handy ⇧+⌘+**H** shortcut), but that won't actually terminate the app. It will disappear from the Simulator's screen, but the app stays suspended in the Simulator's memory, just as it would on a real iPhone.

It's not really necessary to stop the app. You can go back to Xcode and make changes to the source code while the app is still running. However, these changes won't become active until you click **Run** again. This will terminate any running version of the app, build a new version and launch it in the Simulator.

What happens when you click *Run*?:

Xcode will first *compile* your source code — that is, translate it from Swift into executable binary code. Languages like Swift, which are called *high-level languages*, are for human programmers, who are better at things like creativity and the overall design and logic of the application that they're creating. Executable binary code — also called machine code — is a *low-level language*; it's for processor chips like the one in the iPhone (and the simulated one in the Simulator), which are better at things like performing up to trillions of math calculations in a second. As you might expect, human and machine languages are quite different, and so a translation step, called *compilation*, is necessary.

The *compiler* is the part of Xcode that converts your Swift source code into machine code. It also gathers all the other components that go into an app, which can include things such as images, icons, and sounds, and puts them into the *application bundle*. The application bundle contains everything the app needs to run.

This entire process is also known as *building* the app. If there are any errors come up during compilation (spelling mistakes in your code are a common cause of these), the build will fail. If compilation finishes without any errors, Xcode creates the application bundle, and then copies to its target — either the iPhone or the Simulator — and launches the app. All that happens with a single press of the **Run** button!

Changing the text

It's a long-time computer programming tradition to write a program that simply displays "Hello, world!" when learning how to program in a new language or for a new platform. That's why Apple made it part of the Single View Application template. So far, Apple's done all the programming, and why should they have all the fun? Let's take the app they've provided and use it to make your own.

Let's update the text and make it a little less generic.

➤ In the Canvas, click on "Hello World":

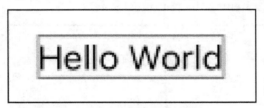

'Hello World', highlighted in both the Editor and the Canvas

Notice that "Hello World" is highlighted in both the Canvas and the Editor. In the Canvas, the highlighting looks like a fine blue rectangle drawn around "Hello World":

Hello World

'Hello World', highlighted in the Canvas

And in the Editor, the line Text("Hello World) is highlighted:

```
struct ContentView: View {
    var body: some View {
        Text("Hello World")
    }
}
```

'Hello World', highlighted in the Editor

"Hello World" is highlighted in both because they're different ways of looking at the same things. The Editor shows you the user interface in the form of code, while the Canvas shows you the user interface as it will appear to the user.

Let's make changes to the text using both the Canvas and the Editor.

➤ In the Canvas, Command-click on "Hello World". A pop-up menu appears, listing a number of actions you can take:

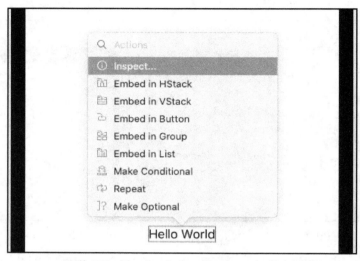

Hello World, after being Command-clicked

➤ Click the **Inspect...** item in the pop-up menu:

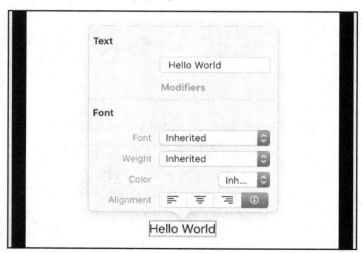

'Hello World' and the inspector

This brings up the Inspector, which displays the properties of "Hello World" and lets you change them. It may not be immediately apparent, but the Inspector is bigger than it appears.

If you scroll while the cursor is over the Inspector, you can see all the properties:

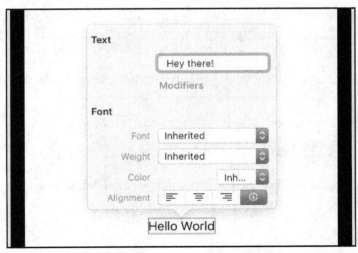

Scrolling the Inspector to the bottom

➤ Make sure the Inspector is scrolled to the top and enter "Hey there!" into the text field just below the **Text** heading:

Editing the text to say 'Hey there!'

➤ Click anywhere on the Inspector to dismiss it.

'Hey there', highlighted in the Editor and Canvas

"Hello World" is now "Hey there!" The change you made in the Canvas is reflected in the Editor. The line that once read `Text("Hello World")` now reads `Text("Hey there!")`.

> **Note**: If the Canvas hasn't updated itself to show the the new text, click the **Resume** button near the upper-right corner of the Canvas.

This ability to edit works both ways. Let's try another change to the text, this time using the code.

➤ In the Editor, change `Text("Hey there!")` to the following:

```
Text("Welcome to my first app!")
```

The section of code near the line you just changed should now look like this:

```
struct ContentView : View {
  var body: some View {
    Text("Welcome to my first app!")
  }
}
```

The change you made in the Editor is reflected in the Canvas:

'Welcome to my first app!' in the Editor and Canvas

➤ Click the **Run** button.

You should see your changes when the app starts in the Simulator:

Welcome to my first app!

Simulator displaying Welcome to my first app!

Making the text bolder

The text needs some sprucing up. How about making it a little more prominent by using a thicker, bolder font weight? Let's try to do that, using both the Canvas and the Editor.

In the Canvas, Command-click on "Welcome to my first app!" and select **Inspect…** from the pop-up menu.

'Welcome to my first app!' and the Inspector

➤ In the **Weight** menu, select **Semibold**:

Choosing a new font weight for 'Welcome to my first app!

➤ Click anywhere on the Inspector to dismiss it.

'Welcome to my first app!' with semibold font weight, in the Editor and Canvas

➤ Click the **Run** button. "Welcome to my first app!" is now a little more pronounced:

'Welcome to my first app!' with semibold font weight, in the Simulator

Once again, the change you made in the Canvas has a matching change in the Editor. The line that defines the text now reads like this:

```
Text("Welcome to my first app!")
  .fontWeight(.semibold)
```

The newly added `.fontWeight(.semibold)` is a **method** that changes the **Weight** property of "Welcome to my first app!". You'll look at methods in a little more detail soon, but in the meantime, think of them as small pieces of code that belong to an object which make that object perform a specific task.

You use a method by *calling* it. This is done by first specifying the name of the object whose method you want to call, followed by a period (`.`), followed by the name of the method.

> **Hint:** Any time you see the `.` character in Swift code, think of it as being shorthand for "Use this method on the object I just mentioned". For example, you should read `Text().fontWeight()` as "Use the `fontWeight` method of my `Text` object."

`fontWeight` is one of many methods that belong to the `Text` object. It changes the weight of its `Text` object's font to the setting you provide it with. In this particular case, that setting is `.semibold`, which is a pre-defined value describing a font weight best described as "bold, but not too bold."

> **Note:** `.semibold` is the short version for the font weight setting. Its full name is `Font.Weight.bold`. Swift lets us get away with omitting the `Font.Weight.` part is because it knows that the only kind of settings you can provide the `fontWeight()` method are the `Font.Weight` kind.

Swift considers `.fontWeight(.semibold)` to be part of the same line as `Text("Welcome to my first app!")`. However, adding it as its own indented line makes it easier to read. The indentation is a convention that programmers use to say "this line is a continuation of the previous one," and the Swift compiler simply ignores it.

> **Note:** If you're in an experimental mood, try editing the code for the text so that it's all in a single line:
>
> ```
> Text("Welcome to my first app!").fontWeight(.semibold)
> ```
>
> and then press the **Run** button. The app still works, which means that Swift didn't find anything wrong with the change. Once you've confirmed that the code works, change it back to its original formatting.
>
> You're probably asking "Why use formatting that the compiler's going to ignore, anyway?" The answer is best summed up by notable MIT computer science professor Harold Abelson, who wrote "Programs must be written for people to read, and only incidentally for machines to execute."

> The compiler doesn't care about the how the code is formatted, but a little formatting makes it easier for humans to read, understand, make changes to, and more easily find errors in code.

Now that you've made a change to the font weight of "Welcome to my first app!" in a graphical way, it's time to try it in code.

➤ In the Editor, change the lines of code starting with `Text` so that the font weight is black instead of semibold:

```
Text("Welcome to my first app!")
    .fontWeight(.black)
```

If you made the change by entirely deleting `.semibold`, a pop-up appeared when you typed in the `.`:

Code completion appearing when changing the font weight

This is Xcode being helpful with its *code completion* feature. It knows that what values you can put into `.fontWeight` modifier and provides them for you in a handy list. If Xcode presented this to you, choose **Font.Weight black** from the list.

Once you've made the change to the code, you'll see a matching change in the Canvas. (If you don't, click the Canvas' **Resume** button.)

➤ Click the **Run** button. "Welcome to my first app!" is even more pronounced:

'Welcome to my first app!' with black font weight, in the Simulator

Changing the text's color

Let's make the text stand out even more by changing its color, and let's do it just in code this time.

➤ In the Editor, change the lines of code starting with Text so that it looks like the following:

```
Text("Welcome to my first app!")
  .fontWeight(.black)
  .foregroundColor(.green)
```

While entering the code, as you type the . character that comes before color, Xcode will try to help you by presenting a code completion pop-up. It will present a list of features of the Text object that you might want to use:

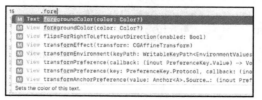

Code completion appearing adding a new modifier to 'Welcome to my first app!'

You should either choose or type in the color() method, which sets the color of the Text object's text to the color you specify. You specify that color between the parentheses — the (and) characters.

When you type the `.` inside these parentheses, Xcode presents a different list:

```
15              .foregroundColor(.g)
16        }         Color  green
17  }             Color  gray
18              M  Color  init(red: Double, green: Double, blue: Doubl
19  #if DEBUG    M  Color  init(colorSpace: Color.RGBColorSpace, red: D
20  struct ContentV:  Color  orange
21      static var   M  Color  init(hue: Double, saturation: Double, bright
22          Content  M  Color  init(hue: Double, saturation: Double, bright
23        }
```

Code completion appearing adding specifying a color for 'Welcome to my first app!'

Choose or type in `.green`, and then check the Canvas to confirm that "Welcome to my first app!" is now green. Once again, you might need to click the **Resume** button near the upper right corner of the Canvas.

➤ Click the **Run** button. Just like the Canvas, "Welcome to my first app!" is now green in the app.

Object-oriented programming

Before you continue with the app, it's time to look a little more closely at the topic of **object-oriented programming**. You may not realize it, but you've already been doing it!

Objects

Object-oriented programming is an approach that tries to manage the complexity of writing programs by dividing them into *objects*. Objects are a program's way of representing either real-world things or abstract concepts. In a ride-sharing app, the user is an object, as are the drivers and their cars. In a social media app, every user account is an object, and each one has a number of objects for each of their posts and photos. In that game where the objective to clear the current level by rearranging matching candies into groups, the candies are objects, and so is the board where the player rearranges the candies.

In your app, you've already been working with a number of objects, both in the code and on the screen:

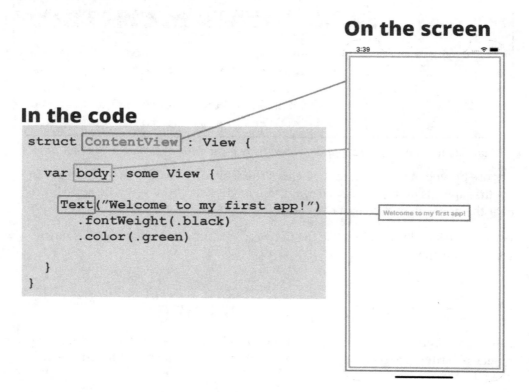

The objects

Let's take a look at the code that defines one of these objects: the `ContentView`. We've looked at this once before, but this time we'll go into more detail.

```
struct ContentView : View {
```

The whole line, translated from Swift to plain language, means "This is the definition of a `struct` named `ContentView`, and it's a `View`."

This translation is still a little technical, and could use some further explanation. The word `struct` is short for *structure*, which is a description of a kind of object in Swift. Swift has other kinds of objects that you'll learn about later in this book, such as `class`.

A View is a kind of object that comes built-in with SwiftUI, and it represents anything that's drawn onscreen, including the screen itself. Views can contain other views.

Since ContentView is a View, it has the same properties and can have the same methods that View has. Any properties and methods defined inside ContentView is *in addition to* any properties and methods it gets from being a View.

> **Hint:** Any time you see the : character in Swift code, think of it as being shorthand for "is a". For example, you should read ContentView : View as "ContentView *is a* view."

Now that you have a rough idea on how to define objects, let's move on to discussing how you can make them **know things** and **do things**: By discussing properties and methods.

Properties and methods

Objects are made up of at least one of these two kinds of things:

1. **Properties**: Without data, computer programs have nothing to work with. Properties are where objects store their data. To continue with the ride-sharing app example, the user objects have properties such as the user's name and current location. Each car object would have properties that store the make, model and year of the car, as well as its current location, and if applicable, the current passenger (which would be a user object). **Properties are the things that objects *know*.**

2. **Methods**: These are groups of code that perform actions, often on the data in the object. In the example of the ride-sharing app, the user object might have a method to update the user's current location. Each car object may have a method to update the car's current location, or calculate its distance from a given user. That user, once again, would be a user object, and the calculation would require the current location data from that user object. Remember, to call a method, you first specify the name of the object whose method you want to call, followed by a period (.), followed by the name of the method. **Methods are the things that objects *do*.**

Let's go back to reviewing the code. You'll see that it already includes examples of both properties and methods!

Let's start with properties. Right now, `ContentView` defines a property in addition to the properties it gets from being a `View`. That property is body, and it's an object that acts as the container for all the objects on the screen that `ContentView` represents.

```
var body: some View {
```

This line, translated from Swift to plain language, means "This is the definition of a variable named body, and it's a `some View`." Basically, this is letting `ContentView` know what to display as its main body: The text field.

`var` is short for *variable*, which means two things:

1. It's a container for data.

2. Its contents can change.

Unlike `ContentView`, whose definition says that it's a `View`, the definition of body says that it's a `some View`. The `some` in front of `View` broadens the possibilities for body. Without getting into too much detail for now, it means that body can contain either a `View` or something that *behaves like* a `View` (meaning that it's an object *isn't* a `View`, but can has the same properties and methods as `View`.

The contents of body are currently defined by these lines, which also include some examples of calling methods:

```
Text("Welcome to my first app!")
    .fontWeight(.black)
    .color(.green)
```

The first line creates a `Text` object, which is a piece of read-only text that gets drawn on the screen. It also sets the `Text` object's content — which is one of its properties — to the text "Welcome to my app!"

The next two lines are examples of calling methods. Specifically, they call two methods on the `Text` object:

1. The first line calls the `Text` object's `fontWeight()` method, and provides it with a value representing the font weight black. In response to the message, `fontWeight()` applies the requested change in font weight to the original `Text` object, creating a new, bolder `Text` object.

2. The second line calls the new, bolder `Text` object's `color()` method, and provides it with a value representing the color green. In response to the message, `color()` applies the requested change in color to the new, bolder, `Text` object, creating an even newer green `Text` object with the same font weight.

This is the final Text object, which is drawn in the view.

This process is illustrated in the diagram below:

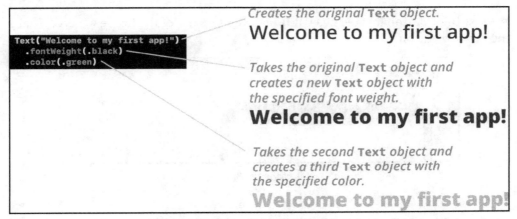

Method chaining explained

The process of applying two or more methods to an object, one after the other, is called *method chaining*. If you've done programming in JavaScript, you've probably seen this before.

You've already done some object-oriented programming up to this point:

- You've created — or as programmers would say, *instantiated* — a Text object that says "Welcome to my app!".

- You called on the Text object's methods to perform tasks: fontWeight() to make its text bold, and color() to change its color.

Phew — that was a lot to cover. Don't worry if you don't get everything right away or if you have trouble remembering everything; there's a lot concepts here that may be brand new to you. We'll review these concepts again and again through the book until they feel like second nature. Again: it's all about **learning via repetition**.

Adding interactivity

Right now, the app simply displays text and then just sits there. That simply won't do: It's time to add some interactivity! You'll do this by adding a button labeled "Hit me!", which was one of the key items on the to-do list for the app.

You could add the button by adding code into the Editor, but you should also learn how to add user interface items the drag-and-drop way, using the Library and Canvas.

➤ Press the + button located near the upper right corner of the Xcode window. That's the **Library** button:

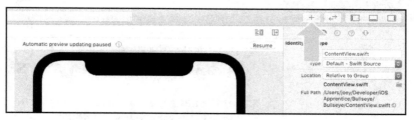

The Library button

The window for the **Library** will appear:

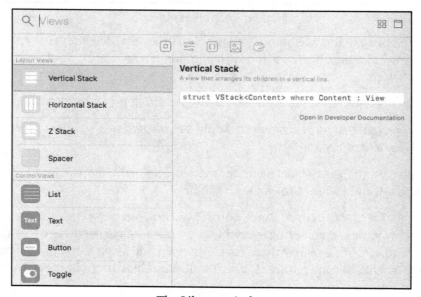

The Library window

The Library is a collection of useful pre-made resources that you can drag and drop into your projects. These resources are divided into five major categories — Views, Modifiers, Snippets, Media, and Color — with one tab for each. It's good for experimenting with ideas, and in a number cases, can save you some typing.

➤ With the Library window in view, make sure that the **Views** tab (the leftmost one, with the square-within-a-square icon) is selected. Remember, a view is anything that can be drawn on the screen, which means that a button is a view. Highlight the **Button** item in the Library list:

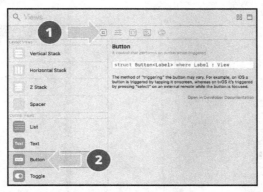

The Library window, with the Button view selected

➤ Click and start dragging the **Button** item from the Library list and onto the Canvas. Drag it to just below the "Welcome to my first app!" text. A blue line should appear just below the text, and a pop-up window that reads **Add Button to a new Vertical Stack along with existing Text.** should appear at the bottom of the Canvas:

Dragging a button onto the view

If you look at the Editor, you'll notice some new code has appeared in the Editor. (Once again, you might need to click the **Resume** button near the upper-right corner of the Canvas.) Xcode should look like this:

The Editor and Canvas, with the button added

Take a closer look at the code in the Editor:

```
struct ContentView : View {
  var body: some View {
    VStack {
      Text("Welcome to my first app!")
        .fontWeight(Font.Weight.black)
        .color(Color.green)
      Button(action: {}) {
          Text("Button")
      }
    }
  }
}
```

A couple of new elements have been added by dragging a button onto the Canvas. First, let's take a look at the new `Button` object:

```
Button(action: {}) {
    Text("Button")
}
```

You may have noticed a couple of things about `Button`:

• In its parentheses, there's `action:`, followed by braces. You'll put code that responds to the `Button` being pressed inside these parentheses.

Remember that in Swift, : means "is a", and braces mark a group of lines of code, or mini-program. You might want to read `action: {}` as "action is a mini-program."

- `Button` contains a `Text` object, and that object determines what the button says.

The other new element is a `VStack`, which is short for *vertical stack*, which is a view that acts as a container for many views, and it arranges them in a vertical line. Before we look more closely at the `VStack` code, let's format it so that it's easier to see what it does.

➤ Change the indentation of the lines relating to the button so that the `VStack` code looks like the code below:

```
VStack {
    Text("Welcome to my first app!")
        .fontWeight(Font.Weight.black)
        .color(Color.green)
    Button(action: {}) {
        Text("Button")
    }
}
```

With the code formatted this way, it's easy to see that the `VStack` contains two views: a `Text` and a `Button`. Since the `Text` appears first, it is positioned at the top of the `VStack`, with the `Button` just below it.

The diagram below shows the relationship between the `VStack` code and what you see in the Canvas:

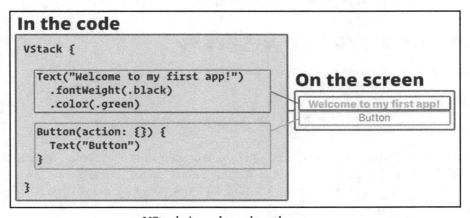

VStack, in code and on the screen

According to the to-do list, the `Button` should say "Hit me!" and not "Button", so let's fix that.

➤ Change the line defining the `Text` inside `Button` so that it reads like this:

```
Button(action: {}) {
  Text("Hit me!")
}
```

➤ Click the **Run** button.

You should see the following in the Simulator:

The app, with the Hit me! button added

➤ In the app, click the **Hit me!** button.

Nothing happens when you click the button. That's to be expected, because you haven't yet defined what should happen when the button is clicked.

Responding to button clicks

Let's go back to the code that defines the button:

```
Button(action: {}) {
  Text("Hit me!")
}
```

As mentioned earlier, any code that should be executed when `Button` being is clicked should go inside the braces that follow `action:`. Let's try some quick experimentation as a first step towards the goal of creating a pop-up when then user presses the button.

➤ Edit the code for the `Button` so that it looks like this:

```
Button(action: {
  print("Button pressed!")
}) {
  Text("Hit me!")
}
```

You'll see what `print()` does in a moment.

Harnessing the power of print()

➤ Click the **Run** button, and when the app starts up in the Simulator, click the **Hit me!** button a couple of times.

You may initially be disappointed when clicking **Hit me!** seems to do nothing. But if you take a look at Xcode, you'll see that a pane has opened at the bottom of its window, and every time you click **Hit me!** in the Simulator, a new "Button pressed!" appears in the pane:

The debug pane, displaying 'button pressed'

`print()` is a *function*, which is a kind of method, except that it's not attached to any object. Not being attached to an object means that you can use it without having to name an object first.

> **Hint:** In Swift, any time you see a name that starts with a lowercase letter that's immediately followed by parentheses, such `fontWeight()` or `print()` — you're probably looking at the name of a function or method. The difference is that methods are preceded by the object they belong to (for example, `Text("Hello").fontWeight(.black)`), which functions don't belong to obejcts and simply appear on their own (for example, `print("Hi")`).

The `print()` function takes some text and then *prints* it in Xcode's Console, which is the pane that appeared when you pressed **Hit me!** in the Simulator. The Console is a read-only text area that displays messages from the compiler and other Xcode systems, as well as messages from your own apps via `print()`.

`print()` is a *debugging* tool. This means that its purpose is to help the programmer figure out what's going on in their program, and it's often used to determine the cause of bugs (hence the name). You only see its results in Xcode, and only in apps that are run from Xcode in the Simulator or on devices that are connected to your computer. In apps that have been installed on a device and run on their own instead of Xcode, `print()` has no effect. It's there only for the benefit of you, the programmer.

As you continue programming, you'll find yourself using `print()` as an indicator to check that specific pieces of code are being executed, or to check on some value that your program has stored. In the code you just wrote, you're using `print()` as a signal that control of the program had reached a specific point: the `action:` code for the `Button`.

The fact clicking **Hit me!** in the app causes `print()` to print "Button pressed!" in the Console is a good sign. It means that you can respond to a button being clicked. Congratulations — you've just written some interactive code!

You're not done yet. Since `print()` is a debugging tool, users *never* see their results. From their point of view, clicking **Hit me!** still does nothing. You still have to make the button provide a response that the user can see. In order to do that, we need to go over the concept of *state*.

State and SwiftUI

A key part of programming SwiftUI is *state*. Rather than start with the computer science definition of state, let's go with something that might be a little more familiar: the dashboard of a car.

The dashboard of a car

The gauges and odometers are usually the most noticeable parts of a dashboard. They show the car's current speed, fuel level, engine temperature and distance traveled, each of which is some kind of numerical quantity.

Dashboards also have warning lights, such as the "check engine" light, the low oil pressure warning light, the "it's time to take the car to the shop for overpriced regular maintenance" light and the "someone's not wearing their seat belt and will be very sorry if there's an accident" light. Each of these lights is either on, indicating that there's a problem that needs the driver's attention, or off. This "on/off", "yes/no" information can be described as *binary*.

The information on a car's dashboard — speed, fuel level, whether on not someone in the car likes to live dangerously without a seat belt and so on — taken all together, is that car's *state*.

The driver's actions can change the car's state, and the new state is immediately shown in the dashboard. For example, if the driver presses on the accelerator pedal, the car's speed increases, which in turn causes the speedometer to display the car's new speed. If the driver then presses on the brake pedal, the car slows down, and the speedometer automatically and immediately shows the new, slower speed.

Internal circumstances can also change the car's state, and once again, this new state is shown in the dashboard instantly. As the car uses up fuel, the fuel gauge moves away from F and towards E. When the driver fills the tank, the fuel gauge immediately goes back to F.

Another example is the "maintenance" light. When a pre-determined amount of time passes or the car has traveled a pre-determined distance since it was last brought in for maintenance, the car's state changes from not needing maintenance to needing it, and the "maintenance" light turns on. Once the car has been brought to the dealership or a mechanic for maintenance, the car's state changes back to not needing maintenance and the light turns off.

There's a term for every possible combination of every possible value of those things that make up the car's state: the *state space*. With all the possible combinations of things that make up the car's state — speed, fuel level, engine temperature, distance traveled, and so on — a car has a really large state space.

The one-button app's state space

Unlike our car example, the one-button app you're building has a much smaller state space. In case you've forgotten, let's take a second look at what the app will look like by the end of this chapter:

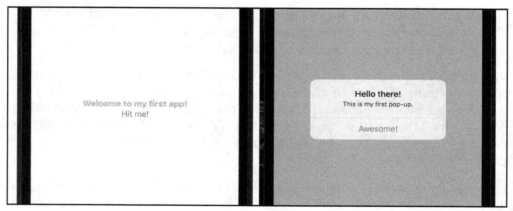

What the app will look like by the end of this chapter

It turns out that the app has only two states:

1. **Welcome**: Simply displaying the "Welcome to my first app!" screen that you've already seen. This is what the user should see when they haven't pressed the **Hit me!** button.

2. **Alert**: Displaying the alert pop-up. This is what the user should see when they press the button.

The app's state space is so small that it's possible to draw it out in a *state diagram*:

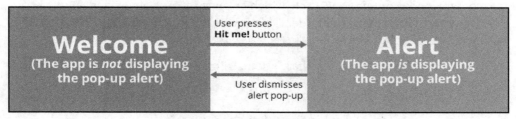

State diagram for the one-button app

The rectangles represent the app's two states. The arrows are *transitions*, which are the ways to get from one state to another. Written beside each transition arrow is the reason for the change in state, formally known as a *transition condition*. The app has two transitions:

1. From **Welcome** to **Alert**. This transition happens when the user presses **Hit me!**.

2. From **Alert** to **Welcome**. This transition happens when the user dismisses the alert pop-up.

SwiftUI and state space

Coding a user interface in SwiftUI is similar to drawing a state diagram. Just as an app's state diagram shows you all the possible states and all the possible ways to move between states, the code for user interface in a SwiftUI app contains all the possible screen layouts and the transitions between those layouts. It's the state diagram for the user interface, in code form.

Let's review the code for the user interface as it is right now:

```
struct ContentView : View {
  var body: some View {
    VStack {
      Text("Welcome to my first app!")
        .fontWeight(.black)
        .color(.green)
      Button(action: {
        print("Button pressed!")
      }) {
        Text("Hit me!")
      }
    }
  }
}
```

Remember, the body property of `ContentView` defines the layout of the screen. At the moment, body contains a `VStack`, which arranges a `Text` object and a `Button` object in a vertical stack, in that order. This covers the **Welcome** state. We're missing the layout for the **Alert** state.

We'll define that layout soon, but there's something we need to take care of first: the app's state.

Representing state in the app with a variable

Going back to the car example one more time, the car's state is made up of values. Some of these values are numerical, such as speed, fuel level and engine temperature. Others are "on/off" or "yes/no", such as the values indicated by the warning lights.

A program's state is also made up of values, and these values are stored in variables. Variables allows the app to remember things. Think of them as temporary storage containers, each one storing a single piece of data. A variable — or more often, many variables — is the perfect place to store an application's state.

You've already seen a variable in action: body, which contains everything that your app's single screen displays — the "Welcome to my first app" text, and the **Hit me!** button. Now you're going to create a variable to represent the app's state.

The variable that represents the app's state needs to store two possible values:

1. A value representing the state where the app *is not* displaying the alert pop-up.

2. A value representing the state where the app *is* displaying the alert pop-up.

This sounds like an "on/off", "yes/no" value. In Swift and many other programming languages, such values are expressed as `true` and `false` and are called *Boolean values*, after English mathematician and logician George Boole.

Let's create a variable that holds a Boolean value to keep track of whether or not the alert pop-up should be visible. We'll give it the name `alertIsVisible`. When the app starts, the alert pop-up should *not* be displayed, which means that `alertIsVisible`'s initial value should be `false`.

➤ Add a line to the code for `ContentView` so that it looks like the following:

```
struct ContentView : View {
   @State var alertIsVisible: Bool = false

   var body: some View {
```

```
    VStack {
      Text("Welcome to my first app!")
        .fontWeight(.black)
        .color(.green)
      Button(action: {
        print("Button pressed!")
      }) {
        Text("Hit me!")
      }
    }
  }
}
```

Let's look at the newly-added line, `@State var alertIsVisible: Bool = false`.

- You've already seen the keyword `var`, which means "This is a variable named…" It's followed by the name of the variable `alertIsVisible`.

- The variable `alertIsVisible` is followed by `:`, which means "is a", and `Bool`, which is Swift for "Boolean". This means that `alertIsVisible` can contain one of two possible values, `true` or `false`.

- Finally, the `= false` part means that `alertIsVisible` is initially set to the value `false`. Being a variable, you can expect this value to change at some point.

That unfamiliar new keyword, `@State`, needs a little more explaining. You've probably figured out that it marks `alertIsVisible` as a variable that stores information about the app's state. It also tells Swift to watch for any changes to the contents of this variable and be ready to take action when that happens.

When the app starts, `alertIsVisible`'s value is `false`. It will stay that way forever unless we add code to change its value to `true`. We want that to happen when the user presses **Hit me!**.

➤ Change the code for `ContentView` so that it reads as follows:

```
struct ContentView : View {
  @State var alertIsVisible: Bool = false

  var body: some View {
    VStack {
      Text("Welcome to my first app!")
        .fontWeight(.black)
        .color(.green)
      Button(action: {
        print("Button pressed!")
        self.alertIsVisible = true
      }) {
        Text("Hit me!")
```

```
        }
      }
    }
  }
```

You've just added a line that sets `alertIsVisible` to `true`, and you've done it inside `Button`'s block of code marked `action:`, which gets executed when the user presses the button.

You might be wondering about the keyword `self`, which got tacked on to the beginning of `alertIsVisible`. `alertIsVisible` is a feature of the `ContentView` object, and in code *outside* `ContentView`, you access it with the code `ContentView.alertIsVisible`. However, you're *inside* `ContentView`, so you access it with the code `self.alertIsVisible` instead.

Defining the layout for the other state

It's worth repeating: In SwiftUI, you define the layout for all possible states. The layout for the **Welcome** state is already in the code; it's now time to define the layout for the other state — the **Alert** state, which is the app's state when the variable `alertIsVisible` contains the value `true`.

The state of the app is now updated whenever the user presses the button. It's time to write code to respond to that change in state.

The alert pop-up should appear when the user clicks the button. Fortunately, one of the methods that comes built into the `Button` object is called `alert()`, and it makes an alert pop-up appear if a given state variable's value is `true`.

Rather than *tell* you how it works, it's simpler (and more fun!) to *show* you:

➤ Change the code for `ContentView` so that it reads as follows:

```swift
struct ContentView : View {
  @State var alertIsVisible: Bool = false

  var body: some View {
    VStack {
      Text("Welcome to my first app!")
        .fontWeight(.black)
        .color(.green)
      Button(action: {
        print("Button pressed!")
        self.alertIsVisible = true
      }) {
        Text("Hit me!")
```

```
        }
        .alert(isPresented: self.$alertIsVisible) {
          Alert(title: Text("Hello there!"),
                message: Text("This is my first pop-up."),
                dismissButton: .default(Text("Awesome!")))
        }
      }
    }
  }
```

➤ Press the **Run** button, and when the app starts up in the Simulator, press the **Hit me!** button.

You should see the following:

The alert pop-up

Let's take a closer look at the code you just added:

```
.alert(isPresented: self.$alertIsVisible) {
  Alert(title: Text("Hello there!"),
        message: Text("This is my first pop-up."),
        dismissButton: .default(Text("Awesome!")))
}
```

alert() is a method on Button that presents an alert to the user. It requires two *arguments*, which is just computer science talk for "things that you provide to a method or function when you call it so that it can do its job." Arguments can be either data or instructions (or in other words, code). In this case, you're providing two pieces of data:

1. **A *binding*, or two-way connection to a Boolean state variable.** In this case, that variable is alertIsVisible, and the two-way connection means that alertIsVisible's value and the alert pop-up are tied together. Changing alertIsVisible to true causes the alert pop-up to appear, and the user

dimissing the pop-up causes `alertIsVisible`'s value to be set to `false`. The `$` in `$alertIsVisible` tells Swift that this is a *two-way binding*: changes to `alertIsVisible` affect the alert pop-up, and changes to the alert pop-up — affect `alertIsVisble`.

2. **An `Alert` object.** This defines what the alert pop-up should contain.

The `Alert` object needs to be provided wth three things:

1. **`title`:** This is the bold text at the top of the alert pop-up. You typically want this to be short — no more than a handful of words. The argument is a `Text` object, which you initialize with another argument: "Hello there!"

2. **`message`:** This is the text below the title. You can make this a little longer than the title, but you shouldn't make it longer than a sentence or two. As with the `title`, the argument is also a `Text` object that you initialize with "This is my first pop-up." (Feel free to change any of these.)

3. **`dismissButton`:** This is the button at the bottom of pop-up. It dismisses the pop-up when the user presses it. The argument a method that creates a button with the text "Awesome!"

Congratulations, you've just written your first iOS app! What you just did may have seemed like gibberish to you, but that shouldn't matter. We'll take it one small step at a time.

You can strike off the first two items from the to-do list already: Putting a button on the screen and showing an alert when the user taps the button.

Take a little break, let it all sink in and come back when you're ready for more! You're only just getting started...

> **Note:** Just in case you get stuck, the complete Xcode projects have been included in the files that come with this book. They're snapshots of the project as they would appear at the beginning and end of each chapter. That way, you can compare your version of the app to the book's, or — if you really make a mess of things — continue from a known working version.

You can find the project files for each chapter in the corresponding folder.

Dealing with error messages

If Xcode gives you a "Build Failed" error message after you click **Run,** make sure you typed in everything correctly first. Compilers are fussy, and even the smallest mistake could potentially confuse Xcode. It can be quite overwhelming at first to make sense of the error messages that Xcode spits out. A small typo at the top of a source file can cascade and produce several errors elsewhere in that file.

One common mistake is differences in capitalization. The Swift programming language is case-sensitive, which means it sees Alert and alert as two different names. Xcode complains about this with a "<something> undeclared" or "Use of unresolved identifier" error. When Xcode says things like "Parse Issue" or "Expected <something>" then you probably forgot a brace } or parenthesis) somewhere. Not matching up opening and closing brackets is a common error.

Tip: In Xcode, there are multiple ways to find matching braces to see if they line up. If you move the editing cursor past a closing brace, Xcode will highlight the corresponding opening brace, or vice versa. You could also hold down the ⌘ key and move your mouse cursor over a line with a brace and Xcode will highlight the full block from the opening curly brace to the closing brace (or vice versa) — nifty!

You can see the block, here:

```
var body: so       '        {
   VStack {
      Text("We           first app!")
         .fontWeight(.black)
         .foregroundColor(.green)
      Button(action: {
         print("Button pressed!")
         self.alertIsVisible = true
      }) {
         Text("Hit me!")
      }
      .alert(isPresented: self.$alertIsVisible) {
         Alert(title: Text("Hello there!"),
               message: Text("This is my first pop-up."),
               dismissButton: .default(Text("Awesome!")))
      }
   }
}
```

Xcode shows you the complete block for braces

Tiny details are very important when you're programming. Even one single misplaced character can prevent the Swift compiler from building your app.

Fortunately, such mistakes are easy to find:

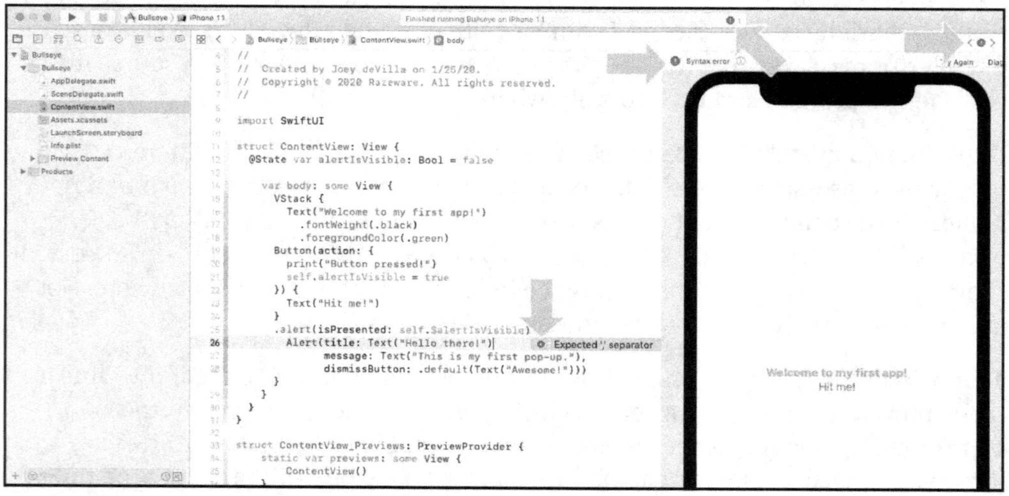

Xcode makes sure you can't miss errors

When Xcode detects an error, it switches the pane on the left from the Project navigator, to the **Issue navigator**, which shows all the errors and warnings that Xcode has found. (You can go back to the project navigator using the small icons along the top.)

The screenshot above shows an intentional error: a missing comma between the `title` and `message` parameters of the `Alert()` view that should appear whenever `alertIsVisible` is true.

Click on the error message in the Issue navigator and Xcode takes you to the line in the source code with the error. It's often not clear what went wrong when your build fails. For certain kinds of errors, Xcode lends a helping hand, suggests a fix and even offers to make the fix for you:

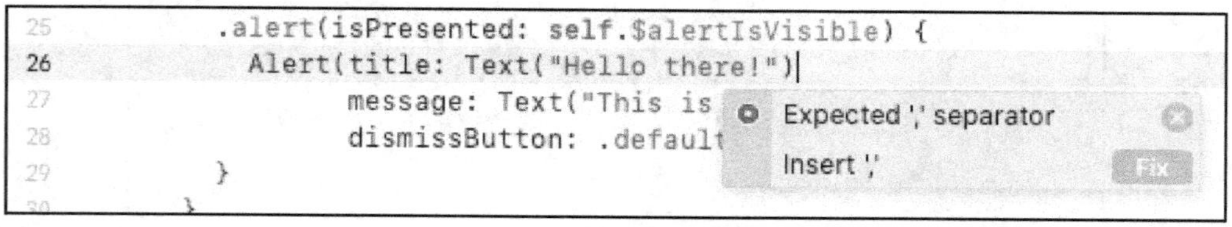

Fix-it suggests a solution to the problem

In this case, clicking the **Fix** button has Xcode follow its suggestion and insert the missing comma...

```
25              .alert(isPresented: self.$alertIsVisible) {
26                  Alert(title: Text("Hello there!"),
27                      message: Text("This is my first pop-up."),
28                      dismissButton: .default(Text("Awesome!")))
29              }
```

Fix-it implements its solution

...and with the fix made, all the error indicators vanish. You have a working app again!

Errors and warnings

Xcode makes a distinction between errors (red) and warnings (yellow). Errors are fatal. If you get one, you cannot run the app until the error is fixed. Warnings are informative. Xcode just says, "You probably didn't mean to do this, but go ahead anyway."

In the previous screenshot showing all the error locations via arrows, you'll notice that there is a warning (a yellow triangle) in the Issue navigator. We'll discuss this particular warning and how to fix it later on.

Generally though, it is best to treat all warnings as if they were errors. Fix the warning before you continue and only run your app when there are zero errors and zero warnings. That doesn't guarantee the app won't have any bugs, but at least they won't be silly ones!

The anatomy of your app

Let's finish this chapter by looking at what goes on behind the scenes of your app.

You've already been introduced to the concept of *objects*, which are the building blocks of the app. The key objects in the app so far are:

• ContentView: An object representing the app's main screen.

You've also been introduced to the idea of *state*, which you can think of as a snapshot of the app's current circumstances. Right now, the app has two possible states, which are represented by the contents of the alertIsVisible variable, which holds a Boolean value (that is, it contains either true or false):

1. The **Welcome** state, where the user sees the main screen, with the "Welcome to my first app!" message. This is the app's state when alertIsVisible is set to false.

2. The **Alert** state, where the main screen is obscured by the alert pop-up. This is the app's state when alertIsVisible is set to true.

In SwiftUI, apps work by having its objects and state affect and be affected by each other. An object can react to some external stimulus — which could come from the user, the operating system, another object, or a change in state — which then causes the object to change the app's state.

Changing the state can affect objects, which perform some action or change some data in response, which in turn can affect the state.

As strange as it may sound, an app spends most of its time doing...absolutely nothing. It just sits there waiting for something — an *event* — to happen. We say that iOS apps are *event-driven*, which means that apps' objects constantly listen for certain events to occur, and when they do, the objects respond as programmed.

When the user taps the screen, the app springs into action for a few milliseconds and then it goes back to sleep until the next event arrives.

Your part in this scheme is that you're writing the source code that ties SwiftUI objects and state together, so that objects respond to changes in state, and make the appropriate changes to the state, which in turn causes the objects to respond, and so on.

The diagram below shows how the app that you've just completed works "under the hood":

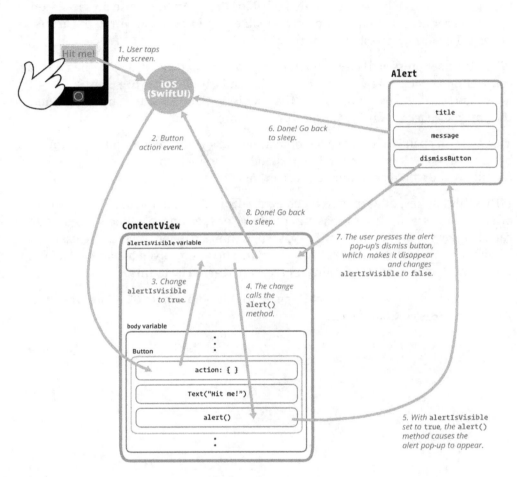

The anatomy of your app

When the user presses the **Hit me!** button on the screen, its corresponding Button object executes the code in its action: method, which sets the contents of the alertIsVisible variable to true. alertIsVisible is a state variable, which means that it can affect objects in the app.

The Button object also calls its alert() method, which has a two-way binding to alertIsVisible. This means that this method is called every time alertIsVisible changes. The alert() method also defines an Alert view that should appear if alertIsVisible is set to true, which is the case when the button is pressed.

With the alert pop-up now displayed onscreen, the app returns back to what it does most of the time: waiting for the next user interaction. Since the alert is *modal* — that's user interface jargon for "completely blocking everything else on the screen until the user deals with it" — the only possible user interaction within the app is to dismiss the alert by pressing its button.

When the user presses the **Awesome!** button on the alert to dismiss it, the two-way connection between the visibility of the alert and `alertIsVisible` causes `alertIsVisible` to be set to `false`. The user is now back on the main screen, and the app goes back to waiting for the next user interaction.

This app will spend more than 99% of its time waiting for input events — in this case, button presses — from the user. It will spend a very small amount of time, measured in milliseconds, on responding to those events.

WHile this app responds only to touch events from the user, the user can provide other events as well, such as shaking the device or speaking. The operating system can also provide events that notify apps when things happen, such as the user receiving an incoming phone call, or when the app has received incoming data from the internet, and so on. Everything apps do is triggered by events.

You can find the project files for the app up to this point under **02 - The One-Button App** in the **Source Code** folder.

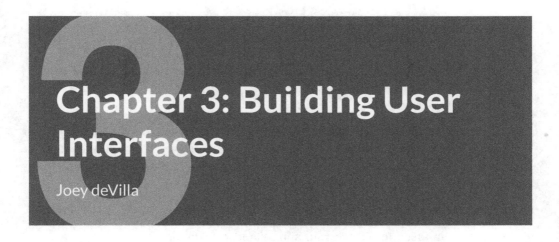

Chapter 3: Building User Interfaces

Joey deVilla

Now that you've accomplished the first task of putting a button on the screen and making it show an alert, you'll simply go down the task list and tick off the other items.

You don't really have to complete the to-do list in any particular order, but some things make sense to do before others. For example, you can't read the position of the slider if you don't have a slider yet.

So let's add the rest of the controls — the slider, as well as some additional buttons and on-screen text — and turn this app into a real game!

When you've finished this chapter, the app will look like this:

The game screen with standard SwiftUI controls

Hey, wait a minute… that doesn't look nearly as pretty as the game I promised you! The difference is that these are the standard controls. This is what they look like straight out of the box.

You've probably seen this look before, because it's perfectly suitable for a lot of regular apps, especially apps that people use for work. However, the default look is a little boring for a game. That's why you'll put some special sauce on top later, to spiff things up.

In this chapter, you'll cover the following:

- **Portrait vs. landscape**: Switch your app to landscape mode.

- **Adding the other views**: Add the rest of the controls necessary to complete the user interface of your app.

- **Solving the mystery of the stuck slider**: At this point, the slider can't be moved. Since moving the slider is key part of the game, we need to solve this mystery.

- **Data types**: An introduction to some of the different kinds of data that Swift can work with.

- **Making the slider less annoyingly precise**: We don't need the slider to report its position with six-decimal precision, but to the nearest whole number.

- **Key points**: A quick review of what you learned in this chapter.

Portrait vs. landscape

Notice that in the previous screenshot, the **aspect ratio** — the ratio of width to height — of the app has changed. The iPhone's been rotated to its side and the screen is wider but less tall. This is called **landscape** orientation.

Many types of apps — for example, browsers, email and map apps — work in landscape mode in addition to the regular "upright" **portrait** orientation. Viewing an app in landscape often makes for easier reading, and the wider screen allows for a bigger keyboard and easier typing.

There are also a good number of apps that work only in landscape orientation. Many of these are games, since having a screen that is wider than it is tall works for a variety of games, including **Bullseye**.

Right now, the app works in both portrait and landscape orientations. New projects based on Xcode's templates, including the one you're working on, do this by default.

➤ Build and run the app. If you've been following the steps in this book up to this point, it should look like this in the simulator:

The app so far, in portrait orientation

The simulator defaults to portrait orientation, right side up, since this is the usual way people hold their phones. You can simulate the action of turning your phone to its side — or even upside down — in a couple of different ways:

- You can change the simulator's orientation by opening its **Hardware** menu and using the **Rotate Left** and **Rotate Right** options in that menu to rotate the simulator 90 degrees left or right.

- You can also use keyboard shortcuts. Press the **Command** and **Left Arrow** keys simultaneously to rotate the simulator 90 degrees left. Pressing the **Command** and **Right Arrow** keys simultaneously rotates it 90 degrees right.

- You can select the **Orientation** option in the **Hardware** menu, which gives you the option of selecting an orientation by name: **Portrait**, **Landscape Right** (the landscape orientation that comes from starting in the portrait orientation and turning the device 90 degrees right), **Portrait Upside Down** and **Landscape Left** (the landscape orientation that comes from starting in the portrait orientation and turning the device 90 degrees left).

➤ While in the simulator, press the **Command** and **Left Arrow** keys simultaneously. You should see this:

Welcome to my first app!
Hit me!

The app so far, in landscape orientation

One of the advantages that SwiftUI has over the old way of building iOS user interfaces — UIKit — is that it adjusts automatically to changes in orientation without requiring much work from the programmer. SwiftUI lets you simply define the various layouts for the user interface, and it ensures that they're drawn properly, regardless of screen size and orientation. Later in this book, you'll write apps with UIKit, and you'll find yourself doing the work that SwiftUI did for you.

Converting the app to landscape

The **Bullseye** game works best in landscape orientation, since landscape allows for the widest slider possible. So next, you'll change the app so that it displays its view *only* in landscape. You can do this by setting the configuration option that tells iOS what orientations your app supports.

➤ In the Navigator section of Xcode, which is the leftmost column in the Xcode window, make sure that you've selected the Project navigator, whose icon looks like a file folder. Click the blue **Bullseye** project icon at the top of the Project navigator's list. The Editor and Canvas will disappear and panes that let you change your project's configuration will replace them.

➤ Make sure that you've selected the **General** tab:

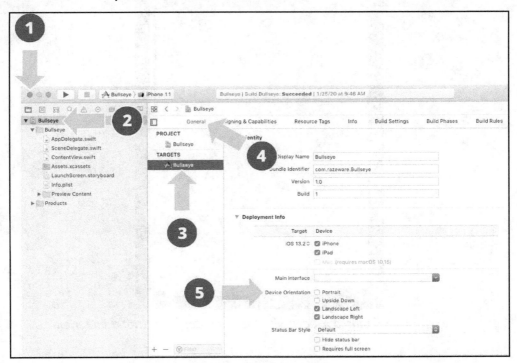

The settings for the project

In the **Deployment Info** section, there are a number of checkboxes in an area marked **Device Orientation**.

➤ Make sure that you've unchecked **Portrait** and **Upside Down**, and that you've checked **Landscape Left** and **Landscape Right**.

➤ Build and run the app. You'll see that no matter which way you rotate the simulator, the app always stays in landscape orientation:

The app, set to landscape only, with the simulator in portrait orientation

Adding the other views

You're going to see the word "view" a lot in this book, so take a moment to quickly go over what "view" means. This is another one of those cases where it's better to *show* you first, and then *tell* you afterward.

Once again, here's what the **Bullseye** screen will look like at the end of the chapter, this time with all the *apparent* views highlighted and labeled:

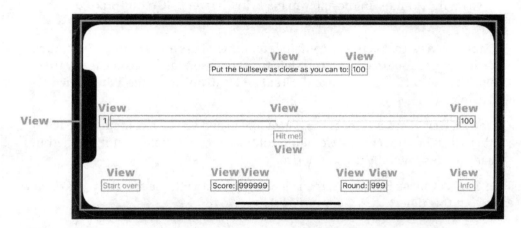

The game screen, with all the views highlighted

Some of the views are invisible; you'll learn more about them soon.

A view is *anything* that gets drawn on the screen. In the screenshot above, it seems that everything is a view: The text items, the buttons and the slider are all views. In fact, every user interface control is a view.

Some views can act as containers for other views. The biggest view in the screenshot is one of these: It's the view representing the screen, and it contains all the other views on the screen: The text items, the buttons and the slider.

Different types of views

There are different types of views. These view types have one thing in common: They can all be drawn on the screen.

What makes each type different is a combination of *what they look like* and *what they do*. So far, you've worked with a few of them:

- **Text**: A view that displays one or more lines of read-only text. The "Welcome to my first app!" message in the app you made in Chapter 2, "Getting Started with SwiftUI" is a **Text** view.

- **Button**: A view that performs an action when triggered. In iOS, a user triggers a button when they complete a button press by releasing the button after pressing down on it. "Hit me!" in the app you made in Chapter 2, "Getting Started with SwiftUI" is a **Button** view.

- **VStack**: A view that acts as a container for other views and arranges them into a vertical stack. You used this to arrange the screen so that "Welcome to my first app!" is above "Hit me!". Unlike the **Text** and **Button** views, the **VStack** view is invisible.

- **View**: A view that represents the entire screen and acts as a container for all the other views on the screen. I wouldn't call this view "invisible", but it's something that the user generally doesn't notice.

Take a look at those **Bullseye** screen views again, but with the specific types of views called out this time:

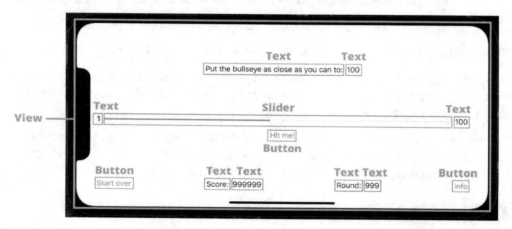

The different kinds of views in the game screen

You may have noticed a control you haven't worked with before: The **Slider**. This control lets a user enter a number by sliding a control, which is called a **thumb**, along a straight track where one end represents a minimum value and the other end represents a maximum value.

> **Note**: In most apps, you wouldn't make the user enter a precise number value using a slider. However, for a game like **Bullseye**, the slider makes the game challenging. After all, we don't want to make it too easy for the player!

As I mentioned earlier, some of the views that will go on the game screen are invisible. One of them is a **VStack**, which you've already used. You'll continue to use it to arrange the views into rows. The screenshot below shows the rows that you'll create using the **VStack**:

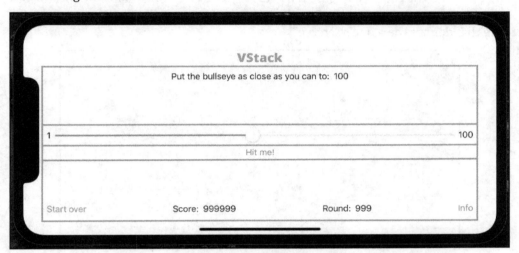

The VStack in the game screen

You'll also need to arrange some rows side by side. To do this, you'll use a new control, **HStack**, which acts as a container for other views and arranges them into a horizontal stack (hence the name). You'll use three **HStack** views, and you'll put each one inside a **VStack** cell, as shown below:

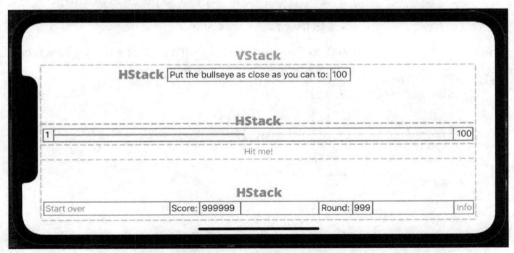

The HStacks in the game screen

Reviewing what you've built so far

Let's look at the code for the app as it is right now. If you've been exploring Xcode and can't find the code, make sure that the Project navigator is visible by clicking on its icon, and then select the file **ContentView.swift**. This is the file that contains the code that defines the game's screen:

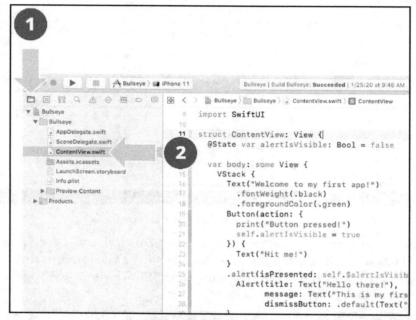

Getting back to the code

Here's the part of the code that you've been working with to define the game screen:

```swift
struct ContentView: View {
  @State var alertIsVisible: Bool = false

  var body: some View {
    VStack {
      Text("Welcome to my first app!")
        .fontWeight(.black)
        .foregroundColor(.green)
      Button(action: {
        print("Button pressed!")
        self.alertIsVisible = true
      }) {
        Text("Hit me!")
      }
      .alert(isPresented: self.$alertIsVisible) {
```

```
        Alert(title: Text("Hello there!"),
            message: Text("This is my first pop-up."),
            dismissButton: .default(Text("Awesome!"))))
      }
    }
  }
}
```

We've gone over this code before, but here's a quick review of how this all works:

ContentView is the view representing the screen. The first line of the code begins with struct ContentView : View, and it tells you that ContentView is a **View**. Remember, any time you see a : character in Swift, you should read it as "is a".

ContentView is an object, and objects can have **properties**, which are things that an object *knows* and **methods**, which are things that an object *does*. Right now, ContentView doesn't have any methods, but it does have two properties. Each of these properties is a var, which means "variable":

1. **alertIsVisible**: This property is true if the app is currently displaying the alert pop-up, and false otherwise. It's false by default, but changes to true when the user presses the **Hit me!** button, and then changes back to false when the user dismisses the alert pop-up. @State marks it as a variable that Swift should watch, and tells Swift that it should be ready to take action if its contents change.

2. **body**: This property defines the content, layout and behavior of the contents of ContentView. Right now, ContentView contains a **VStack** of two views: The "Welcome to my first app!" **Text** view and the **Hit me! Button** view.

Notice that the definition of body starts with the line body: some View. You should read this as "body is a some View." The grammar of that sentence is a little strange, but it means that the body property can hold either a plain **View** or some other type of **View**, such as **Text, Button** or in this case, a **VStack**.

The definition of body implies that it can hold only one view at a time. That would normally make for very simple, very boring apps except for the fact that there are some views that can hold other views. VStack, HStack and even View are examples of these. For **Bullseye**, we'll fill body with a **VStack**, and fill that **VStack** with the other views that make up the game.

Formatting the code to be a little more readable

In order to make the code easier to work with, you're next going to space it out add some comments. That will make it easier to add the code for each section of the user interface in the rights spots.

➤ Edit the code in **ContentView.swift** so that it looks like the code shown below. You won't be deleting anything or changing any existing lines. You'll be simply be adding lines — some of which are blank, and some of which begin with the // characters:

```swift
import SwiftUI

struct ContentView: View {

  // Properties
  // ==========

  // User interface views
  @State var alertIsVisible: Bool = false

  // User interface content and layout
  var body: some View {
    VStack {

      // Target row
      Text("Welcome to my first app!")
        .fontWeight(.black)
        .foregroundColor(.green)

      // Slider row
      // TODO: Add views for the slider row here.

      // Button row
      Button(action: {
        print("Button pressed!")
        self.alertIsVisible = true
      }) {
        Text("Hit me!")
      }
      .alert(isPresented: self.$alertIsVisible) {
        Alert(title: Text("Hello there!"),
              message: Text("This is my first pop-up."),
              dismissButton: .default(Text("Awesome!")))
      }

      // Score row
      // TODO: Add views for the score, rounds, and start and
```

```
info buttons here.
      }
   }

   // Methods
   // =======
}


// Preview
// =======

struct ContentView_Previews: PreviewProvider {
    static var previews: some View {
        ContentView()
    }
}
```

➤ Run the app. You shouldn't notice any changes.

The changes you made don't affect the way the program works, and as a result, they won't make a difference to the user. They *will* make a difference to *you*, because they affect the way the code *reads*. Even with relatively simple apps like **Bullseye**, it code can quickly get complex. Anything you do to make the code easier to read and understand will help you write better, more error-free code.

The lines beginning with // are *comments*. Like blank lines, they also don't perform any action or make any changes. Unlike blank lines, they contain text, but anything after the // characters and up to the end of the line is ignored. Comments are notes that programmers add to code to provide additional information about it. Programmers use comments for a number of purposes, including:

- Indicating who wrote the code and when. That's what the comments at the start of the **ContentView.swift** are. Comments like this are often put at the start of the file, and Xcode automatically does this with all its source code files.

- Explaining what sections of code are for. That's what you're doing with these comments. They mark the different sections of the code, such as where the properties and methods of the ContentView object go, the individual rows in the user interface, and so on.

- Providing a summary of what the code does, especially in cases where it might otherwise be difficult to understand.

- Giving additional background information that's not made clear in the code.

- Acting as a reminder to either fix something broken in the code or to add something missing to the code. In this sort of comment, many developers add words like TODO or HACK so that they can find these reminders again easily with a "search" function. You added a couple of TODO comments in the body variable to note that you need to add code to define the slider and score rows in the user interface.

Laying out the target row

Let's start with the text at the top of **Bullseye**'s screen (highlighted below), which tells the user the target value they're aiming for:

The target text

This text challenges the user to move the slider to a specific value. You could use a single Text object with both the challenge and the target value, but we'll go with *two*: One for the challenge and one for the target value.

You want to lay these two **Text** objects out side by side, which sounds like an opportunity to use an **HStack**. Here's a screenshot with some extra graphics showing how the **Text** objects and **HStack** fit together:

The HStack containing the target text's Text views

There are a couple of ways to create this **HStack**. One way is to type the necessary code into the Editor. But instead, you'll do it another way: By using the Canvas. You'll embed the existing "Welcome to my first app!" text into an **HStack**, and then you'll change its text.

➤ If the **Resume** button is visible in the upper-right corner of the Canvas, press it.

➤ In the Canvas, command-click on **Welcome to my first app!**. Select **Embed in HStack** from the menu that appears:

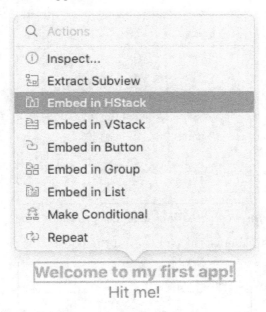

Embedding the 'Welcome to my first app!' Text view into an HStack

This embeds the "Welcome to my first app!" view into an HStack. If you look at the Editor, you'll see that the code in the **Target row** section has been updated to reflect what you did on the Canvas:

```
// Target row
HStack {
  Text("Welcome to my first app!")
    .fontWeight(.black)
    .foregroundColor(.green)
}
```

Next, you'll do even more with the Canvas. It's time to change the text.

➤ In the Canvas, command-click on **Welcome to my first app!**. Select **Inspect...** from the menu that appears:

Inspecting the 'Welcome to my first app!' view

➤ Use the inspector to change the text to "Put the bullseye as close as you can to:":

Editing the 'Welcome to my first app!' view

This changes the **Text** view, and will also update the code in the editor:

```
// Target row
HStack {
  Text("Put the bullseye as close as you can to:")
    .fontWeight(.black)
    .foregroundColor(.green)
}
```

➤ We don't want the "Put the bullseye as close as you can to:" text to be green and bold, so remove the calls to the Text view's fontWeight() and foregroundColor() methods so that the code in the *Target row* section looks like this:

```
// Target row
HStack {
  Text("Put the bullseye as close as you can to:")
}
```

The next step is to add a new **Text** view to the **HStack**, to the right of the "Put the bullseye as close as you can to:" view. Use the library and the editor to do this.

➤ Open the library — remember, you do this by pressing the **Library** button, which is the + button located near the upper-right corner of the Xcode window:

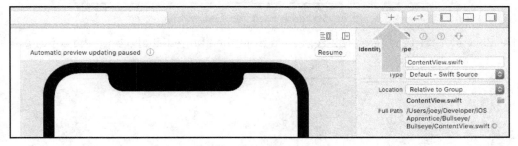

The Library button

➤ The Library window will appear. Make sure that you've selected the **Views** tab, which is the leftmost one, with the square-within-a-square icon, then highlight the **Text** item in the Library list:

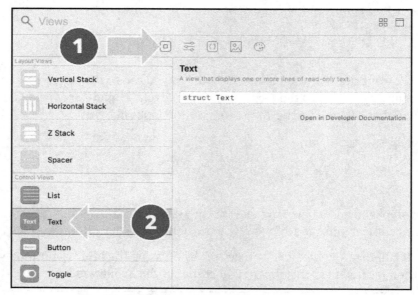

The library window, with the Text view selected

➤ Click and start dragging the **Text** item from the library list and onto the editor as shown below:

```
23      // Target row
24      HStack {
25          Text("Put the bullseye as close as you can to:")
26      }                                                      Text   Text
27
```

Dragging a text view from the library into the editor

➤ As you drag the item onto the editor, a blank line should appear below the
Text("Put the bullseye as close as you can to:") line. When this blank line
appears, drop the item. A new **Text** object will appear in the code, which will now
look like this:

```
// Target row
HStack {
  Text("Put the bullseye as close as you can to:")
  Text("Placeholder")
}
```

➤ Change the placeholder text (literally "Placeholder") in the newly-added **Text** view to **100**. The code for the Target row should now look like this:

```
// Target row
HStack {
  Text("Put the bullseye as close as you can to:")
  Text("100")
}
```

➤ Build and run the app. You'll see that the two **Text** views have replaced the "Welcome to my first app!" message:

The app with the Target row added

The target value in the second **Text** view, **100**, is a placeholder. You're using 100 because this text view will eventually contain a random number between 1 and 100. 100 is the largest — and more importantly, *widest* — text that will go into this view.

Laying out the slider row

Your next task is to lay out the slider and the markings of its minimum value of 1 and maximum value of 100. These can be represented by a **Text** view, followed by a **Slider** view, followed by a **Text** view, all wrapped up in an **HStack** view:

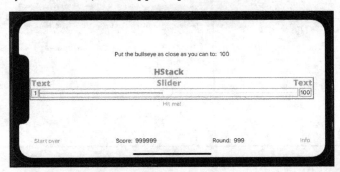

The slider and accompanying text, with the Slider and Text views and HStack pointed out

This time, try setting this up by writing some code. After all, you have some examples of using HStack and Text in code already!

➤ In the *Slider row* section, replace the `// TODO: Add views for the slider row here.` line so that code looks like this:

```
// Slider row
HStack {
  Text("1")

  Text("100")
}
```

This defines the **1** and **100** Text views that are on the left and right sides of the slider, respectively. You could also type in the code to create the slider, but first, take a look at one more feature of the library.

➤ Open the library (press the + button near the upper right corner of the Xcode window). Make sure that you've selected the **Views** tab, which is the leftmost one, with the square-within-a-square icon, then type **slider** into the library's search text field, which is just to the right of the magnifying glass icon. As you type, the library's views in the library's list will disappear until only the slider remains.

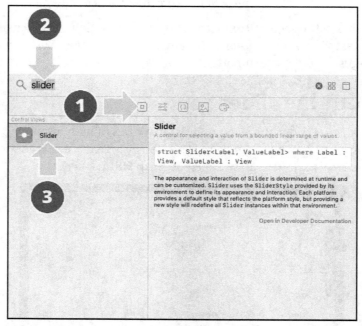

The Slider in the library, after using the Search text field

➤ Drag the **Slider** view from the library list onto the editor, and drop it in the empty line in the //Slider row section of the code between the Text("1) line and the Text("100) line:

```
29          // Slider row
30          HStack {
31              Text("1")
32                      Slider
33              Text("100")
34          }
```

Dragging the Slider from the library and onto the code

The code for the Slider row should now look like this:

```
// Slider row
HStack {
    Text("1")
    Slider(value: .constant(10))
    Text("100")
}
```

➤ Build and run the app. The Slider row is now visible:

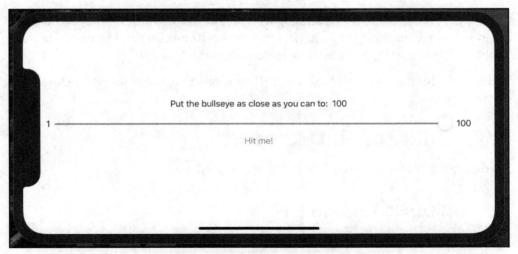

Put the bullseye as close as you can to: 100

1 ————————————————————————————— 100

Hit me!

The app with the Slider row added

If you tried to move the slider, you probably noticed that it's stuck on the right side. This has something to do with the .constant(10) that you gave as the **Slider**'s value: argument.

This is a good time to look at a useful Xcode feature that allows you to find out more about just about anything in the code that has a name.

➤ While holding down the **option** key, move the cursor over the `.constant` in the line `Slider(value: .constant(10))`. The word `constant` should change color and the cursor's shape should change to a question mark (**?**). Click on `constant` and a pop-up window will appear with more details about it:

```
29          // Slider row
30          HStack {
31            Text("1")
32            Slider(value: .constant(10))
33            Text("100")
```

Summary
Creates a binding with an immutable value.

Declaration

```
static func constant(_ value: Value) -> Binding<Value>
```

Open in Developer Documentation

The app with the Slider row added

The summary text — "Creates a binding with an immutable value" — may sound like meaningless techno-babble to you now, but the words **binding** and **immutable** should be hints that it has something to do with **state**.

You'll deal with the mystery of the stuck slider soon enough, but you'll finish setting up the controls first.

Laying out the Button row

Here's a little gift for you: The Button row's already done!

Laying out the Score row

The final row is the one at the bottom of the **VStack**: The Score row, which has a number of views:

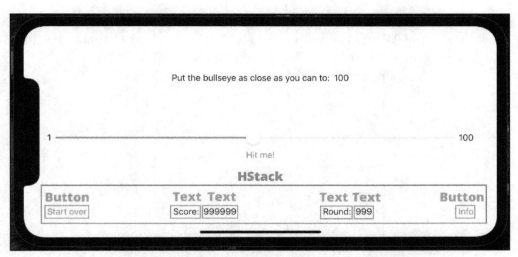

The Score row, with the Button and Text views pointed out

These views are:

- A **Button** view labeled **Start over**: The user will press this button to start a new game. It will reset the score to 0 and the round to 1.

- Two **Text** views for the score: One containing the text "Score" and one containing the score value. For now, the score will be set to a placeholder value of 999999.

- Two **Round** views: One containing the text "Round", and one containing the number of the current round. For now, this number will be set to a placeholder value of 999.

- A **Button** view labeled **Info**: The user will press this button to get more information about the game. It will take the user to another screen, where they'll see the additional information.

Don't forget that these should be all in a row, which means that you need an **HStack**, so start with that.

➤ In the *Score row* section, replace the `// TODO: Add views for the score, rounds, and start and info buttons here.` with a blank line.

➤ Open the library (once again, press the + button near the upper right corner of the Xcode window). Make sure that you've selected the **Views** tab (the leftmost one, with the square-within-a-square icon), then find the **Horizontal Stack** view:

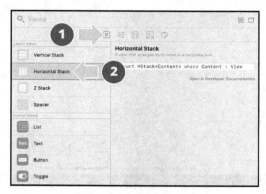

HStack in the Library

Drag this view onto the editor and drop it into the blank line after `// Score row`:

```
49        // Score row
50            Horizontal Stack
51        }
52    }
```

Dragging the HStack from the library onto the code

The code starting at `// Score row` should now look like this:

```
// Score row
HStack {
  Text("Placeholder")
}
```

Notice that Xcode didn't just give you an **HStack**; it also included a **Text** view. You didn't ask for it, so try removing it by deleting the `Text("Placeholder")` line.

Here's what happens:

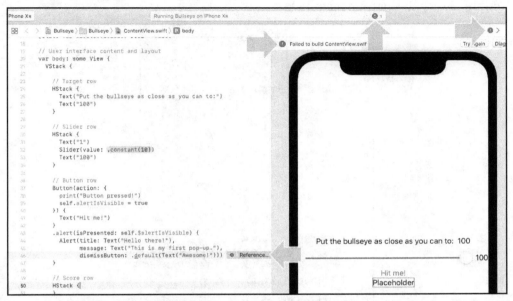

Xcode showing error indicators everywhere after being presented with an empty HStack

Xcode is diligent about alerting you to errors in your code, and it turns out that an empty **HStack** is an error. An **HStack** must contain at least one view, so Xcode did a little preemptive error prevention by throwing in a "free" **Text** view when creating the **HStack**. You've probably figured out that the same rule applies to **VStack** views.

➤ If you got experimental and tried removing the **Text** view from the **HStack**, try undoing the change. If that doesn't work, simply type in code so that the code starting at `// Score` row looks like this:

```
// Score row
HStack {
  Text("Placeholder")
}
```

Since **Button** views contain **Text** views, Xcode has included a useful feature that takes advantage of this.

➤ Command-click on the Text keyword in the `// Score` row section of the code. You should see this pop-up menu:

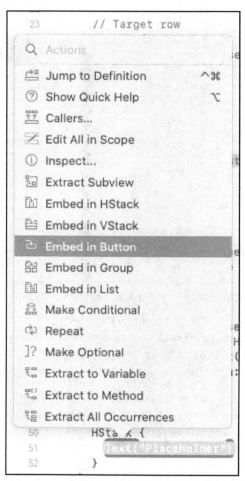

Command-clicking on Text to reveal the pop-up menu and selecting 'Embed in Button'

➤ Scroll down the menu and select **Embed in Button**. Xcode will embed the **Text** view inside a **Button** view and the code will now be:

```
// Score row
HStack {
  Button(action: {}) {
    Text("Placeholder")
  }
}
```

➤ Copy the Button code and paste it so that the code becomes the following:

```
// Score row
HStack {
  Button(action: {}) {
    Text("Placeholder")
  }
  Button(action: {}) {
    Text("Placeholder")
  }
}
```

➤ Change the **Text** view in each **Button** view so that the first one becomes the **Start over** button and the second one becomes the **Info** button. The code should now look like this:

```
// Score row
HStack {
  Button(action: {}) {
    Text("Start over")
  }
  Button(action: {}) {
    Text("Info")
  }
}
```

By now, you're probably beginning to get the hang of creating user interfaces the SwiftUI way. Next, add the remaining **Text** views between the **Button** views.

➤ Add **Text** views so that the `// Score row` code becomes this:

```
// Score row
HStack {
  Button(action: {}) {
    Text("Start over")
  }
  Text("Score:")
  Text("999999")
  Text("Round:")
  Text("999")
  Button(action: {}) {
    Text("Info")
  }
}
```

➤ Build and run the app. The Simulator should display this:

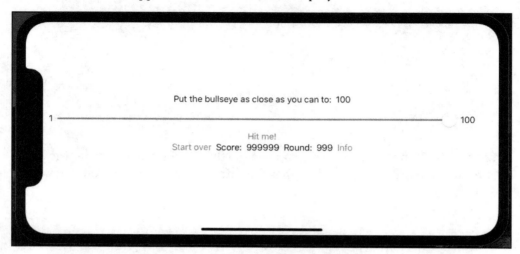

Put the bullseye as close as you can to: 100

1 ———————————————————————————————————— 100

Hit me!
Start over Score: 999999 Round: 999 Info

The app with all the views, running in the Simulator and looking compressed

All the controls are there, but the app looks somewhat compressed. In the next section, you'll fix that.

Introducing spacers

It's time to bring some **Spacer** views into your app. As their name implies, these views are designed to fill up space.

When you put a **Spacer** view into an **HStack**, it expands to fill up the remaining horizontal space.

A spacer in an HStack, sandwiched between two views

Next, see what happens when you use a spacer in the *Score row*.

➤ Add **Spacer** views to the *Score row* code so that it looks like this:

```
// Score row
HStack {
  Button(action: {}) {
    Text("Start over")
  }
  Spacer()
  Text("Score:")
  Text("999999")
  Spacer()
  Text("Round:")
  Text("999")
  Spacer()
  Button(action: {}) {
    Text("Info")
  }
}
```

➤ Build and run the app. The Score row should look a lot less compressed:

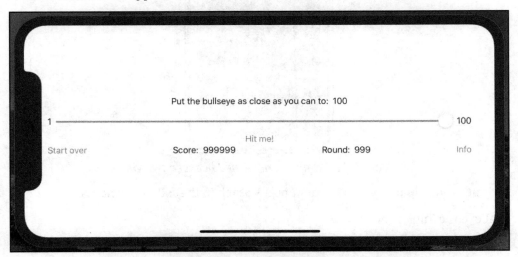

The app with Spacer views added to the Score row

Spacer views also work in **VStack** views. There, they expand to fill up the remaining vertical space.

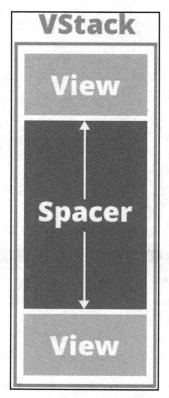

A spacer in a VStack, sandwiched between two views

Let's put some **Spacer** views in your app's **VStack** in the following places:

- Above the Target row.

- Between the Target row and the Slider row.

- Between the Slider row and the Button row.

- Between the button row and the Score row.

➤ Change the code for ContentView so that it looks like this:

```
struct ContentView: View {

  // Properties
  // ==========
```

```swift
// User interface views
@State var alertIsVisible: Bool = false

// User interface content and layout
var body: some View {
  VStack {
    Spacer()

    // Target row
    HStack {
      Text("Put the bullseye as close as you can to:")
      Text("100")
    }

    Spacer()

    // Slider row
    HStack {
      Text("1")
      Slider(value: .constant(10))
      Text("100")
    }

    Spacer()

    // Button row
    Button(action: {
      print("Button pressed!")
      self.alertIsVisible = true
    }) {
      Text("Hit me!")
    }
    .alert(isPresented: self.$alertIsVisible) {
      Alert(title: Text("Hello there!"),
            message: Text("This is my first pop-up."),
            dismissButton: .default(Text("Awesome!")))
    }

    Spacer()

    // Score row
    HStack {
      Button(action: {}) {
        Text("Start over")
      }
      Spacer()
      Text("Score:")
      Text("999999")
      Spacer()
      Text("Round:")
      Text("999")
      Spacer()
      Button(action: {}) {
```

```
            Text("Info")
          }
        }
      }
    }

    // Methods
    // =======
}
```

➤ Run the app. It's looking a whole lot better!

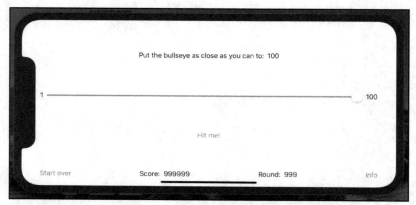

The app with Spacer views added to the Score row and between rows

There's just one last little change you need to make to the app's layout: The Score row is a little too close to the bottom. In the next section, you'll find out how to fix that.

Adding padding

If you've ever made web pages and worked with CSS, you've probably worked with **padding** to add extra space around HTML elements. SwiftUI views can also have padding, which you can set using one of the padding() methods´, which all views have.

In this case, we want to add some padding to the bottom of the Score row. You can do this by calling the padding() method for the **HStack** containing the Score row.

➤ Add the following to the end of the *Score row* code, so that it ends up looking like this:

```
// Score row
HStack {
  Button(action: {}) {
    Text("Start over")
  }
  Spacer()
  Text("Score:")
  Text("999999")
  Spacer()
  Text("Round:")
  Text("999")
  Spacer()
  Button(action: {}) {
    Text("Info")
  }
}
.padding(.bottom, 20)
```

The `padding()` method takes two arguments:

1. The set of edges to pad. There are a number of options for this argument including `.bottom` (which you just used), `.leading` and `trailing` (for the leading and trailing edges, respectively), `.top`, `.horizontal` (which pads both leading and trailing edges), `.vertical` (which pads both top and bottom edges) and `.all`.

2. The amount of padding. This is a number of screen distance units called **points**, which you'll cover a little later on.

➤ Build and run the app. It looks a whole lot better!

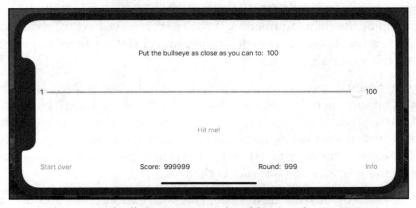

The app with all the spacers and padding on the Score row

Solving the mystery of the stuck slider

Let's get back to why the slider doesn't work. As mentioned earlier, it has to do with **state**.

Store with two signs: 'Open' and 'Sorry we're closed'. Creative Commons photo by "cogdogblog" — Source: https://www.flickr.com/photos/cogdog/7155294657/

If you've ever gone to a restaurant where the sign said they were open, only to find that they were closed when you tried to enter, you've experienced what happens when a user interface, in this case the "Open" sign, doesn't match the state (the place was actually closed).

This kind of problem happens when the user interface and state aren't connected. In the restaurant example, keeping the "open/closed" sign in sync with the restaurant's actual open/closed state means that someone has to make sure that the sign is always providing the right information. If you've ever worked in the food service industry, you know that the kind of dedication and reliability needed to make sure that the sign is always right is rare.

You may have seen this sort of thing in software as well. One example is the user interface of an email app that tells you that you have a new message, but when you check, it turns out that you'd already read it. You've probably seen other examples of user interfaces that were wrong about their application's state. As apps grow, their state becomes more complex, and it's all too easy to forget to update some part of the user interface when some state detail changes.

SwiftUI solves the problem of the mismatch between user interface and application state by creating bindings between them. In a SwiftUI application, when you update some property that's part of its state, any user interface elements bound to that property automatically update to reflect the change.

You can also choose to make two-way bindings, where if the user changes the value of some user interface element that's bound to some state property by pressing a button, entering a value into a text field or moving a slider, that property is automatically updated.

This means that in SwiftUI, user interface controls have to be connected to some kind of value. Sometimes, that value is a constant, which is often the case with **Text** views:

```
Text("This is a constant value")
```

The code that currently sets up the slider in **Bullseye** is similar:

```
Slider(value: .constant(10))
```

In this case, the slider is bound to a state property that is set to 10 and can't be changed; therefore the slider's position can't be changed, either.

Making the slider movable

The solution to the mystery of the stuck slider is to connect it to a state variable, whose value *can* change. So now, declare one. You'll call it sliderValue and set its initial value to 50.

➤ Add a declaration for the sliderValue variable to the *Properties* section of ContentView, so that the lines starting with the // User interface views comment look like this:

```
// User interface views
@State var alertIsVisible: Bool = false
@State var sliderValue: Double = 50.0
```

Remember, @State marks the variable as part of the application's state and tells Swift to watch it for changes to its value. The var sliderValue: Double = 50 part is Swift for "The variable sliderValue is a Double, and its value is 50.0"

Note: A **Double** is a Swift data type that represents numbers with decimal points really, really, *really* precisely. We're using it because that's the kind of value that sliders work with. We'll talk more about data types soon.

Now that there's a state variable for the slider, it's time to connect the two together!

➤ Change the line where the slider is set up to the following:

```
Slider(value: self.$sliderValue, in: 1...100)
```

This code creates — or in programmer-speak, **instantiates** — a **Slider** view. Here's what the three parameters do:

- **value**: Specifies the *binding* that connects a state variable to the slider. If you think of sliderValue as the value of the slider's current position, $sliderValue (note the $) is the two-way connection between the slider and the sliderValue. Changing the value of sliderValue affects the position of the slider's thumb (the thing on the slider that moves), and moving the thumb on the slider changes the value in sliderValue. Since $sliderValue is a property of the object that you're in, you precede it with self..

- **in**: Specifies the range of values that the slider covers. 1...100 represents the range of values starting at 1 at its minimum and ending and including 100 at the maximum.

➤ Build and run the app. The initial value of sliderValue is 50.0, which means that the slider's initial position is midway between the left and right ends. You can also move the slider now!

Reading the slider's value

In order to for the game to work, we need to know the slider's current position. Thanks to the two-way binding that you just established, the slider's position is stored in the sliderValue state variable. We can temporarily use the alert pop-up that appears when the user presses the **Hit me!** button to display this value.

Here's the code for the Button row:

```
// Button row
Button(action: {
  print("Button pressed!")
  self.alertIsVisible = true
}) {
  Text("Hit me!")
}
.alert(isPresented: self.$alertIsVisible) {
  Alert(title: Text("Hello there!"),
        message: Text("This is my first pop-up."),
        dismissButton: .default(Text("Awesome!")))
}
```

Now, change the argument that you provide to the `message:` parameter so that it displays the slider's current value.

➤ Change the call to the **Button**'s `presentation()` method to:

```
.alert(isPresented: self.$alertIsVisible) {
  Alert(title: Text("Hello there!"),
        message: Text("The slider's value is \
(self.sliderValue)."),
        dismissButton: .default(Text("Awesome!")))
}
```

➤ Build and run the app, move the slider anywhere you like, then press the **Hit me!** button. The alert pop-up will appear, and it'll give you a painfully precise readout of the slider's value:

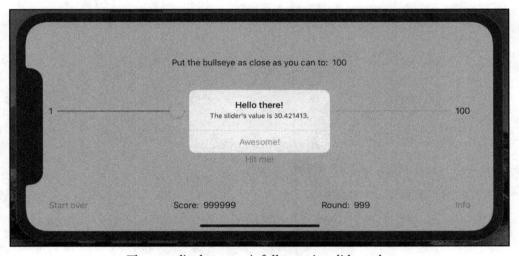

The app displays a painfully precise slider value

Take a closer look at the Text view that was passed to the alert pop-up's `message:` parameter:

```
Text("The slider's value is \(sliderValue).")
```

The alert pop-up uses the text before and after `\(sliderValue)` — "The slider's value is " and ".". On the other hand, `\(sliderValue)` is replaced by the value in the `sliderValue` variable. Think of the `\( ... )` as a placeholder: "The slider's value is *X*", where *X* will be replaced by the value of the slider.

Data types

Before doing more work on the app, take a moment to consider **data types** in Swift. These classify the different kinds of data that Swift can work with.

Strings

You've already done a fair bit of work with **strings,** which represent text information. Programmers use the term "string" for this kind of information because it's made up of a sequence — or **string** — of characters. Think of characters in a string as being like pearls on a necklace:

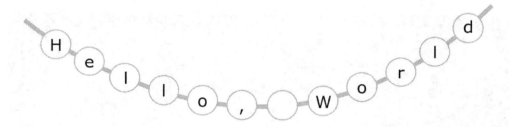

A string of characters

Here are some the strings you've used so far:

- `"Welcome to my first app!"`
- `"Hit me!"`
- `"Awesome!"`
- `"The slider's value is \(sliderValue)."`

You used the first three when making **Text** views, and the last one to display the slider's value in the alert pop-up.

Creating a string is simple in Swift: Just put text between a pair of "double quote" characters ("). Other languages let you create strings by using either "single quote" characters (') or double quotes, but Swift doesn't. Strings should be **delimited** — that's computer-science fancy-talk for "started with and ended with" — by double quotes. And they must be plain double quotes, not typographic "smart quotes".

To summarize, this is the proper way to make a Swift string...

```
"I am a good string"
```

...and these are wrong:

- `'I should have double quotes'`
- `''Two single quotes do not make a double quote''`
- `"My quotes are too fancy"`

Inserting variables' values into strings

Anything between the characters \(and) inside a string is special — instead of taking that information literally, Swift evaluates whatever is between those characters and turns the result into a string.

You used this in the alert pop-up to display the value of the slider's current position, which is stored in the state variable `sliderValue`. You did it by using this string to create the alert pop-up:

```
"The slider's value is \(sliderValue)."
```

If you run the app and press the **Hit me!** button without moving the slider (which means its value will be 50), the pop-up *doesn't* display this text:

The slider's value is \(sliderValue).

Instead, it says:

The slider's value is 50.000000.

Inside a string, Swift treats the \(and) as markers for the beginning and ending of something it should evaluate, converts that thing into a string, and then inserts it into the rest of the string.

This feature isn't limited to numerical variables — you can also put string variables between \(and). Suppose a variable named `weather` contains the value **sunny**. Swift interprets the string `"We expect the weather to be \(weather) today."` as **We expect the weather to be sunny today**.

You can even put calculations between \(and). Swift interprets the string `"Your answer, \(1 + 2), is correct."` as **Your answer, 3, is correct**.

Filling in the blanks this way is a very common way to build strings in Swift and is known as *string interpolation*.

Numbers

Swift has a number of ways to represent numerical values. The two that you'll probably use the most are:

- **Double**: This is short for **double-precision floating-point number**, which is a fancy computer-science way of saying "painfully precise number." It's accurate to 15 or 16 digits, which should be more than enough precision for most calculations. It also has a large range, being able to represent numbers as small as 10-345 and as large as 10308. You'll use these when you need to store and work with numbers with decimal points.

- **Int**: This is short for **integer**, which simply means "whole number". You'll use these when you need to store and work with numbers without decimal points.

You've already worked with a Double when you created the sliderValue variable to store the position of the slider. The slider reports its position as a Double, so that's what we use to store its value.

Booleans

You'll often have to store values of the "yes/no" or "on/off" kind. That's what Bool variables — short for "Boolean" — are for. They can store only two values: true and false.

Boolean values, which are often referred to simply as **Booleans**, are often used in programs to make decisions. You'll soon learn about the if statement, which performs a set of instructions if some condition is true, and another set of instructions (or no instructions) if the condition is false.

Variables

If you're new to programming, it's important to remember that programs are really made of just two things:

1. **Data**, which is information that we want to manage, process and perform calculations with.

2. **Instructions**, which tell the computer to how to manage, process and perform calculations with the data.

Programs store their data in variables. So far, **Bullseye** stores its data in just two variables — one to keep track of the slider's position, and one to keep track of whether or not the alert pop-up is visible. The previous chapter told you to think of variables as temporary storage containers, each one storing a single piece of data. Just as there are containers of all shapes and sizes, data also comes in all kinds of shapes and sizes, which we call **data types**. You've just looked at a few data types: Strings, Ints, Doubles and Bools.

The idea is to put the right shape in the right container. The container is the variable and its type determines what "shape" fits. The shapes are the possible values that you can put into the variables. You might want to think of variables as being like children's toy blocks:

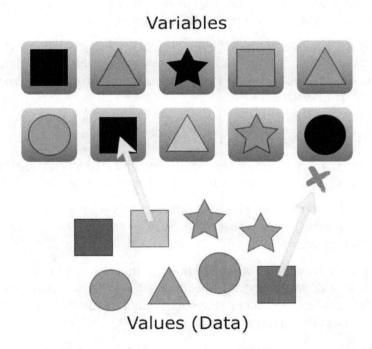

Variables are containers that hold values

You won't just put stuff in the container and then forget about it. You'll often replace the contents with a new value. When the thing that your app needs to remember changes, you take the old value out of the box and put in the new value. That's the whole point behind variables: They can *vary*.

For example, sliderValue will change every time the user moves the slider, and you'll change the value of alertIsVisible to true every time the user presses the

Hit me! button. The size of the storage container and the sort of values the variable can remember are determined by its **data type**, or just **type**.

You specified the `Double` type `sliderValue` variable, which means this container can hold very precise numbers. `Double` is one of the most common data types. There are many others though, and you can even make your own.

The idea is to put the right shape in the right container. The container is the variable and its type determines what "shape" fits. The shapes are the possible values that you can put into the variables.

You can change the contents of each box later, as long as the shape fits. For example, you can take out a blue square from a square box and put in a red square — the only thing you have to make sure of is that both are squares.

But you can't put a square in a round hole: The data type of the value and the data type of the variable have to match. You can't put a string value into an integer variable, and you can't put an integer value into a string variable. The type of the value has to match the variable.

How long do variables last?

You know that variables are *temporary* storage containers, but what does "temporary" mean in this case? How long does a variable keep its contents?

Unlike meat or vegetables, variables won't spoil if you keep them for too long. A variable will hold onto its value indefinitely, until you put in a new value or destroy the container altogether.

Each variable has a certain lifetime, also known as its **scope**, which depends on exactly where in your program you defined that variable. In the case of **Bullseye**, both `alertIsVisible` and `sliderValue` stick around for just as long as their owner, `ContentView`, does. Their fates are intertwined.

`ContentView` exists for the duration of the app, and therefore so do `alertIsVisible` and `sliderValue`. They don't get destroyed until the app quits. Soon, you'll also see variables that are short-lived (also known as **local variables**).

Making the slider less annoyingly precise

There *is* such a thing as too much precision. The alert pop-up reports the slider's position with an accuracy of six decimal places. We want the game to be challenging, but not *that* challenging! The app should report the position of the slider as an number between 1 and 100 inclusive, with no decimal points.

The Slider reports its position as a Double, which is a very precise number with a decimal point. Right now, the app simply takes this number and displays it in the alert pop-up. We want the pop-up to round the position to the closest whole number and report the position as an Int.

Rounding a Double to the nearest whole number

Every Swift data type comes with a set of methods to act on that data. Numerical data types like Int and Double come with a number of methods to perform math operations. Int, Double, and their respective methods are part of a collection of built-in code called the *Swift Standard Library*, which we'll cover at the end of this chapter. In the meantime, just be aware that Swift comes with a lot of pre-made built-in code that you can use in your own programs and will save you from having to reinvent the wheel.

The Double type has methods that are useful for working with numbers with decimal points. One of these is rounded(), which takes the original value and gives back — or as we say in programming, **returns** — a rounded version of the value. For example, if you call rounded() on a Double variable containing the value **4.2**, it will return the value **4.0**.

rounded() uses "schoolbook rounding," which means that if the fractional part of the number is **0.5** or larger, it rounds up to the higher value. It rounds **4.5** up to **5.0**, **4.4999** to **4.0**, and **-4.5** to **-5.0**.

➤ Update the code for the Button row so that it looks like the following:

```
// Button row
Button(action: {
  print("Button pressed!")
  self.alertIsVisible = true
}) {
  Text("Hit me!")
}
.alert(isPresented: self.$alertIsVisible) {
  Alert(title: Text("Hello there!"),
        message: Text("The slider's value is \
(self.sliderValue.rounded())."),
        dismissButton: .default(Text("Awesome!")))
}
```

➤ Build and run the app. Move the slider wherever you like, and then press **Hit me!**. You should see something like this:

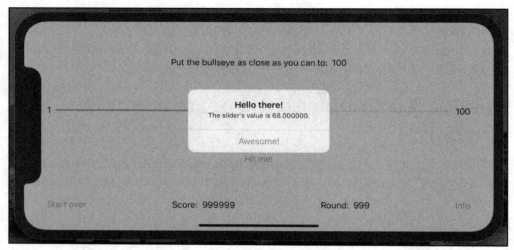

The app displays a rounded, but still painfully precise slider value

This is an improvement, but there's still the matter of those trailing zeros. There are a couple of ways to remove them:

• One way is to format the number to show only the digits before the decimal point.

• Another way would be to convert the number into an integer (an Int) and display that value.

Later on in the development of **Bullseye**, we're going to generate a target number, which will be a whole number that the user will have to match by positioning the slider. This means that the target number will be an Int. We'll need to compare the target number to the value of the slider's position, so the second approach sounds like the better one.

The simplest way to convert a Double value into an Int value is to create a new Int value and use the Double's value to **initialize** it.

➤ Update the code for the Button row so that it looks like the following:

```
// Button row
Button(action: {
  print("Button pressed!")
  self.alertIsVisible = true
}) {
  Text("Hit me!")
}
```

```
.alert(isPresented: self.$alertIsVisible) {
   Alert(title: Text("Hello there!"),
         message: Text("The slider's value is \
(Int(sliderValue.rounded()))."),
         dismissButton: .default(Text("Awesome!")))
}
```

➤ Build and run the app. Move the slider wherever you like, then press **Hit me!**. You should see something like this:

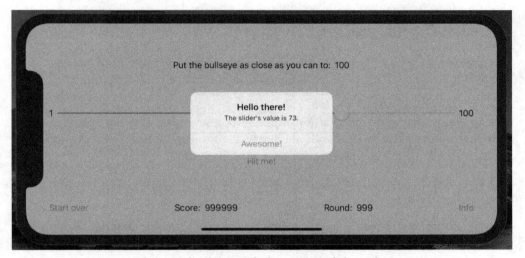

The app displays a whole number slider value

Here's the part that's changed:

```
message: Text("The slider's value is \
(Int(sliderValue.rounded())).",
```

In this code, sliderValue.rounded() is being fed into Int(). This tells Swift to create a new Int using sliderValue.rounded(), which is the value of the slider rounded to the nearest whole number.

Any time you see a capitalized word followed by parentheses ((and)), braces ({ and }) or both, it usually means that something new is being created — or in programming terms, **instantiated** — using the things between the parentheses and braces. You've already seen many examples of this. Here's one:

```
Text("Here is some text.")
```

This instantiates a new **Text** view containing the text "Here is some text."

Here's a more complex example:

```
VStack {
  Text("Here is some text.")
  Text("And here's more text!")
}
```

This instantiates a new **VStack** view, and inside it, two **Text** views are also instantiated.

The Swift Standard Library

You could've written a method to round a `Double` to the nearest whole number, but you didn't have to. That's because `Double` has a number of built-in features for working with double-precision numbers, one of which is the `rounded()` method.

`Double`, `rounded()`, and many other similar goodies are part of a large collection of code that make up the Swift Standard Library. It contains a lot of useful pre-made functionality that you can use in your own apps, including:

- Data types, including the ones you worked with in this chapter: `Int`, `Double`, `String`, and `Bool`.

- Methods that go with each of those data types, which let you do more things with them. You've already used one of them: `Double`'s `rounded()` method. In the next chapter, you'll use a couple more Standard Library methods to generate a random number and remove the "minus sign" from a negative number.

- Functions, such as `print()`.

- Other more advanced features, all of which can serve as the building blocks for your apps that you don't need to write yourself.

It's pretty much impossible to do any Swift programming without making use of something in the Swift Standard Library — that how useful it is. It does more than just provide useful features. It will also save you so much time because it contains all sorts of things that you'd otherwise have to code yourself. Better yet, all the features it provides have the advantage of having been throroughly tested — and not just by Apple's quality assurance team, but by the entire Swift developer community who use it regularly (and who complain loudly when it's not working as they expect).

You'll use the Swift Standard Library as often as you use Xcode, so it's worth reviewing it regularly as you learn Swift and iOS programming. It evolves with each version of Swift, so even experienced developers, looking at its online documentation from time to time to see what changed.

To see everything that the Swift Standard Library has to offer, visit the Swift Standard Library home page, located in Apple's developer documentation site at https://developer.apple.com/documentation/swift/swift_standard_library.

Key points

So far, you've done the following:

- Set up all of **Bullseye**'s basic user interface elements.

- Made the slider work

- Converted the original alert pop-up to report the slider's position value.

Along the way, you've learned a lot, including:

- What portrait and landscape orientations are and how to and make an app landscape-only.

- Different types of views.

- A little more about state and variables.

- Data types.

In the next chapter, you'll take the app and turn it into a functioning game!

You can find the project files for the app up to this point under **03 - Slider** in the **Source Code** folder.

Chapter 4: Swift Basics

Joey deVilla

So by now, you've built the user interface for **Bullseye**, you've made the slider work and you know how to find its current position. That already knocks quite a few items off your to-do list. In this chapter, you'll take care of a few more items on that list. Here's what this chapter will cover:

- **Generating and displaying the target value**: Select the random number that the player will try to match using the slider and display it onscreen.

- **Calculating the points scored**: Determine how many points to award to the player based on how close they came to positioning the slider at the target value.

- **Writing methods**: You've used some built-in methods so far, but built-in methods can't cover everything. It's time to write your own!

- **Improving the code**: Make the code more readable so that it's easier to maintain and improve and less error-prone.

- **Key points**: A quick review of what you learned in this chapter.

Generating and displaying the target value

First, you need to come up with the random number that the user will try to match using the slider. Where can you get a random number for each game's target value?

Generating (sort of) random numbers

Random numbers come up a lot when you're making games because games need to have an element of unpredictability. You can't get a computer to generate numbers that are truly random and unpredictable, but you can employ a **pseudo-random number generator** to spit out numbers that at least appear to be random.

To make random numbers, pseudo-random generators typically start with a **seed value**, a number derived from an event that isn't easy to predict. Some examples include the number of milliseconds the system has been running, the user's most recent keyboard input, mouse clicks and other events. They feed this seed value into a mathematical formula that creates a list of wildly different numbers that *appear* random.

If you were to run a pseudo-random number generator that always started with the same seed value, it would always generate the same set of numbers in the same order. But it's pretty unlikely that the events Swift uses for its seed values will be exactly the same each time, so the random number generators built into Swift are good enough for everyday applications like games.

> **For the curious:** macOS and iOS constantly update a file named **/dev/random** with hard-to-predict values from the system's device drivers, and you can use that file as a source of seed values for pseudo-random number generators. You can see what it contains by opening the **Terminal** app and entering od -d / dev/random on the command line. You'll see a stream of numbers, which you can stop by typing **control+c**.

Generating a random target number

Swift's data types for numbers, which include Int and Double numeric types, have a method that lets you generate random numbers in a given range.

➤ Add the following line to the start of **ContentView.swift**:

```
@State var target: Int = Int.random(in: 1...100)
```

The set of @State variables should now look like this:

```
@State var alertIsVisible: Bool = false
@State var sliderValue: Double = 50.0
@State var target: Int = Int.random(in: 1...100)
```

Take a closer look at the line you just added.

The first half of the new line, @State var target: Int, doesn't include anything that you haven't already seen. It says that you're declaring a variable named target that holds Int (i.e., integer, or whole number) values, and that target makes up part of the state for ContentView. As a state variable, Swift will watch target for changes to its value, then take any necessary action when that value changes.

The second half of the line, = Int.random(in: 1...100), might be new to you. It assigns an initial value to target, and that value is a random number between 1 and 100 inclusive. The random number comes from the random() function built into the Int data type to get a pseudo-random integer between 1 and 100. The 1...100 part is a **closed range**, which you should read as "all the numbers between 1 and 100, including 1 and 100." The ... part indicates that you want the range to include the last number (100) as part of the range.

You could also use a **half-open range**, which you specify with these characters: ..<. 1..<100 is an example of a half-open range, and you should read it as "all numbers between 1 and 100, including 1, *excluding* 100." If you wanted to specify a range of numbers from 1 to 100 inclusive using a half-open range, you'd do it with 1..<101.

With this single line, the app now generates a new random target value every time it starts. Your next step is to make that target value visible to the user.

Displaying the target value

➤ Scroll down to the part of the body variable that begins with the comment line Target row:

```
// Target row
HStack {
  Text("Put the bullseye as close as you can to:")
  Text("100")
}
```

This code defines the text near the top of the screen, which tells the user what the target value is:

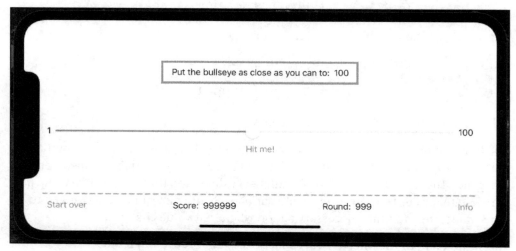

The app screen, with the target text highlighted

Right now, the text that displays the score value holds the placeholder text "100":

```
Text("100")
```

➤ Change it so that it displays the value inside target, the state variable you just created:

```
Text("\(self.target)")
```

You've just replaced the 100 with \(self.target). As you learned in the previous chapter, the characters \(and) have a special meaning when used inside a string. They mark the beginning and end of something that Swift should evaluate, convert into a string and then insert into the rest of the string.

In this case, the object between \(and) that Swift needs to evaluate is self.target. Remember that any time you see code in the form of **object.feature**, you should read it as code that makes use of an object's feature. In this case, the object is self, which is Swift for "the object that this code lives in." In this case, self refers to ContentView. The feature is target, which is one of ContentView's variables... the one you just created.

Since `target` is a state variable (because you marked it with the keyword `@State`), the `Text` object will always display the current value of `target`, even when `target` changes. You'll see this in action in the next chapter, when you incorporate multiple rounds into the game.

➤ Build and run the app. There's only a 1 in 100 chance that your target will be to put the bullseye as close as possible to 100:

The app screen, now with a random target value

➤ Stop the app and run it again, then do that again a few more times. 99% of the time when you restart the app, the target value will be different from the previous one.

Calculating and displaying the points scored

Now that you have both the target value *and* a way to read the slider's position, as you learned from the previous chapter, you can calculate how many points the player scored.

How close is the slider to the target?

The closer the slider is to the target when the player presses the **Hit me!**, the more points they should receive. To calculate the score for each round, you look at how far the slider's value is from the target:

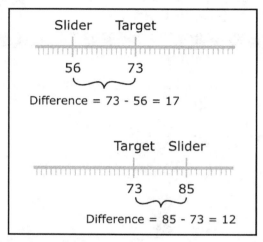

Calculating the difference between the slider position and the target value

A simple approach to finding the distance between the target and the slider is to subtract sliderValue from target.

Unfortunately, that gives a negative value if the slider is to the right of the target because now sliderValue is greater than target.

You need some way to turn that negative value into a positive value — or you end up subtracting points from the player's score (unfair!).

Doing the subtraction the other way around — sliderValue minus target — won't always solve things either because, then, the difference will be negative if the slider is to the left of the target instead of the right.

Hmm, it looks like you're in trouble here...

> **Exercise**: How would you frame the solution to this problem if you wanted to solve it in natural language? Don't worry about how to express it in code for now. Just think it through in plain language.

I came up with something like this:

- *If the slider's value is greater than the target value, then the difference is: Slider value minus the target value.*

- *However, if the target value is greater than the slider value, then the difference is: Target value minus the slider value.*

- *Otherwise, both values must be equal, and the difference is zero.*

If you prefer to think in pictures, here's the solution in flowchart form:

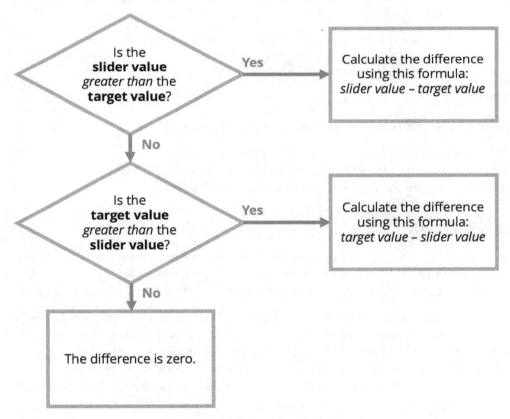

Calculating the difference, in flowchart form

This will always lead to a difference that is a positive number, because you always subtract the smaller number from the larger one. Do the math to test it out:

- If the slider is at position 60 and the target value is 40, then the slider is to the right of the target and has a larger value. The difference is 60 − 40 = 20.

- However, if the slider is at position 10 and the target is 30, then the slider is to the left of the target and has a smaller value. The difference is 30 – 10 = 20.

Calculating the points scored

The number of points the player receives should depend on the difference between the slider value and the target value:

- When the slider is right on top of the target, the difference between the slider value and the target value is 0. In this case, the player should receive the maximum number of points for getting a bullseye.

- When the slider is as far as possible from the target, it means that the slider is at one end and the target is at the opposite end. In this case, the player should receive the minimum number of points for being way off.

For now, we'll use a simple formula:

points* = 100 - *difference between slider value and target value

With this formula, the player earns 100 points for placing the slider right at the target value. In the case where the slider is at one end and the slider is at the opposite end, the player scores one point, just for showing up.

Algorithms

In coming up with a way to calculate the score, you've come up with an **algorithm**. That's a fancy term for a process or series of steps to follow to perform a calculation or solve a problem. This algorithm is very simple, but it's an algorithm nonetheless.

There are many algorithms that you can adapt for use in your own programs. As you gain more experience programming, you might run into well-known ones such as **quicksort**, for sorting a list of items, and **binary search**, for quickly searching a sorted list. The academic field of computer science centers around studying algorithms and finding better ones. You can find these algorithms in books or online and you can use them in your own programs, saving you from having to reinvent the wheel.

Although there are many published algorithms, you'll still have to come up with your own algorithms to fit the specific needs of the program you're writing. Some will be as simple as the one above; others will be complex and might cause you to throw up your hands in despair. That's part of the fun of programming.

You can describe any algorithm using plain language or diagrams — use whatever method works better with the way you think. Remember that an algorithm, no matter how complex it is or how fancy a result it produces, is just a set of steps to follow.

If you ever get stuck and you don't know how to make your program calculate something, step away from the computer and think the steps through. Take out a piece of paper — still one of the best software engineering tools out there — and try to write or draw out the steps. Ask yourself how would you perform the calculation or solve the problem by hand. Once you know how to do that, converting the algorithm to code should be a piece of cake.

Writing your own methods

Back near the start of Chapter 2, you read about the concept of functional decomposition, which is the process of tackling a large project by breaking it into sub-projects, and possibly breaking the sub-projects into even smaller sub-projects until they are manageable.

Whenever you find yourself thinking something along the lines of, "At this point in the app, I need to tackle this sub-project," that's a sign that you need to create a method to perform that task. Once you have a method, you can simply activate it by calling it by name.

You've already made use of a pre-defined method: `rounded()`, which comes built-in with the `Double` data type. You used it to round the slider's current value to the nearest whole number:

```swift
// Button row
Button(action: {
  print("Button pressed!")
  self.alertIsVisible = true
}) {
  Text("Hit me!")
}
.presentation(self.$alertIsVisible) {
  Alert(title: Text("Hello there!"),
        message: Text("The slider's value is \
(Int(self.sliderValue.rounded()))."),
        dismissButton: .default(Text("Awesome!")))
}
```

There couldn't possibly be a built-in method for every purpose, but that's not a problem because you can write your own. Start by writing a method to calculate how many points the player should receive.

Implementing a basic method for calculating the points to award the player

In building a method to calculate how many points to award to the player, you're going to use an approach called **stepwise refinement**. This means starting by building the simplest thing that could possibly work and then refining it over a number of steps until you get the desired result.

The first version of this method will simply award 100 points to the player, no matter where the player positioned the slider. At this point, you want it to simply report a number.

➤ Add the following to the end of ContentView, after the **Methods** comments and before ContentView's closing brace (}):

```
func pointsForCurrentRound() -> Int {
  return 100
}
```

Now, take a look at this new method, starting with the first line:

```
func pointsForCurrentRound() -> Int {
```

This line is the method's **signature**, which specifies three things:

1. The name of the method.

2. The information that the method must receive.

3. The information that the method provides as a result.

Just like structs and vars, methods start with a keyword that specifies what kind of thing you're defining. For methods, this keyword might surprise you: it's func, which is short for **function**. You use this keyword because methods are a kind of function, which is a general term for a block of code that you can call by name and which may or may not return a value at the end.

The name of the method follows the func keyword. In this case, it's pointsForCurrentRound().

You've probably noticed that method names end with parentheses (the ( ) characters). That's a convention borrowed from the way you write mathematical functions. That's how you can tell whether something's a variable or a function: Function names end with parentheses, while variable names don't.

Some methods require additional information before they can perform their task. You've already used such a method, rounded(), which requires a rounded number. If you were defining a method that required additional information, you would put that information within the parentheses. Since pointsForCurrentRound() doesn't require additional information, you don't have to put anything between the parentheses.

After the parentheses comes this symbol: ->. It doesn't mean "minus" followed by "greater than." Rather, you should interpret it as an arrow pointing rightward, and should read it as "returns a value of the following data type." This is immediately followed by Int. This means that when pointsForCurrentRound() has completed its task, it should give back — or as we say in programming, **return** — an integer value.

After the method signature comes the **body** of the method, which goes between braces (the { and } characters). The body of the method specifies what the method does.

The body of the pointsForCurrentRound() method is a single line:

```
return 100
```

The return keyword defines the result that the method provides. return 100 makes the method provide a result of 100 when called.

So you've completed your first step, reporting a number that you've set! Now that you have a basic method for calculating the points to award the player, you can see it in action.

Calling the method and viewing its result

To see how it works, use print to show what pointsForCurrentRound() returns.

➤ Change the print statement in the **Button row** section so that it displays the results of pointsForCurrentRound(). The result should look like this:

```
// Button row
Button(action: {
  print("Points awarded: \(self.pointsForCurrentRound())")
  self.alertIsVisible = true
}) {
  Text("Hit me!")
}
.alert(isPresented: self.$alertIsVisible) {
  Alert(title: Text("Hello there!"),
```

```
        message: Text("The slider's value is \
  (Int(self.sliderValue.rounded())).").
        dismissButton: .default(Text("Awesome!")))
  }
```

➤ Build and run the app and press the **Hit me!** button a few times, keeping an eye on the Xcode's debug console. You should see a line that says **Points awarded: 100** for each press of the **Hit me!** button:

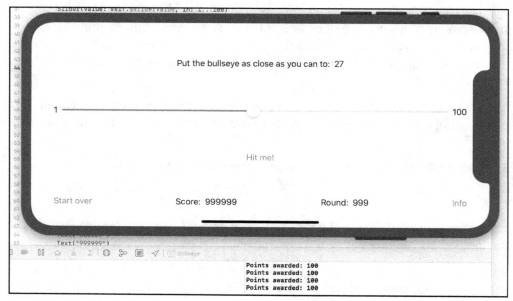

Seeing the points awarded in the debug console

pointsForCurrentRound() returns the number that you set, but that's not the *correct* one. Next, you'll fix that so the game awards the right number of points.

Making pointsForCurrentRound() actually calculate points

Now that pointsForCurrentRound() returns a value and the alert pop-up displays that value, it's time to change the value to the actual number of points that the player should receive.

➤ Replace the code in `pointsForCurrentRound()` so that the method looks like this:

```
func pointsForCurrentRound() -> Int {
  var difference: Int
  if self.sliderValue.rounded() > self.target {
    difference = self.sliderValue.rounded() - self.target
  } else if self.target > self.sliderValue.rounded() {
    difference = self.target - self.sliderValue.rounded()
  } else {
    difference = 0
  }
  return 100 - difference
}
```

You've now replaced the code that simply awards the player 100 points no matter how well they played with code that implements the algorithm you created earlier.

The code may *look* right, but Xcode will take exception:

```
func pointsForCurrentRound() -> Int {
  var difference: Int
  if self.sliderValue > self.target {                    ⊘ Binary operator '>' cannot be applied to operands of type 'Double' and 'Int'
    difference = self.sliderValue - self.target          ⊘ Binary operator '-' cannot be applied to operands of type 'Double' and 'Int'
  } else if self.target > self.sliderValue {             ⊘ Binary operator '>' cannot be applied to operands of type 'Int' and 'Double'
    difference = self.target - self.sliderValue          ⊘ Binary operator '-' cannot be applied to operands of type 'Int' and 'Double'
  } else {
    difference = 0
  }
  var awardedPoints: Int = 100 - difference
  return 999
}
```

Xcode complaining loudly

The error messages show what the problem is: You're attempting to compare and subtract two different kinds of things:

- `sliderValue.rounded()`, which is a `Double`.

- `target` which is an `Int`.

To us humans, both `Double` and `Int` values are just numbers, and differentiating between them seems like nitpicking. However, computers represent `Double` and `Int` values very differently, and the compiler treats them as very different things. A computer can't make sense of it.

To compare `sliderValue` and `target` and perform arithmetic on them, you'll need to convert one of them to the same type as the other. Since you're only using a `Double` because sliders use that data type to report their values, we'll convert `sliderValue.rounded()` into an `Int`.

➤ Update `pointsForCurrentRound()` so it looks like this:

```
func pointsForCurrentRound() -> Int {
  var difference: Int
  if Int(self.sliderValue.rounded()) > self.target {
    difference = Int(self.sliderValue.rounded()) - self.target
  } else if self.target > Int(self.sliderValue.rounded()) {
    difference = self.target - Int(self.sliderValue.rounded())
  } else {
    difference = 0
  }
  return 100 - difference
}
```

The error messages should be gone now. Before running the app, take a moment to review this new code.

The first line should be familiar:

```
var difference: Int
```

This declares a new variable, `difference`, which you'll need to store the difference between the slider's current position and the target value. Since the difference will be a whole number, it's an `Int`.

Note that you haven't assigned a value to `difference`, you've simply declared it's an `Int`. That's because you'll assign a value to it in the lines of code that follow.

What follows the first line is new:

```
if Int(self.sliderValue.rounded()) > self.target {
  difference = Int(self.sliderValue.rounded()) - self.target
} else if self.target > Int(self.sliderValue.rounded()) {
  difference = self.target - Int(self.sliderValue.rounded())
} else {
  difference = 0
}
```

The `if` construct allows your code to make decisions, and it works much as you expect:

```
if something is true {
  then do this
} else if something else is true {
  then do that instead
} else {
  do something when neither of the above are true
}
```

Basically, you put a **logical condition** after the if keyword. If that condition turns out to be true, like if sliderValue is greater than target, then the code in the block between the { } brackets executes.

However, if the condition isn't true, then the computer looks at the else if condition and evaluates that instead. There may be more than one else if, and code execution moves one by one from top to bottom until one condition proves to be true.

If none of the conditions are found to be valid, then the code in the final else block executes.

In the implementation of this little algorithm, you compare sliderValue.rounded() against the target. Remember that the slider (and therefore sliderValue) is precise to about 6 decimal places, so we're rounding its value to the nearest whole number.

First, you determine if sliderValue.rounded() is greater than target:

```
if self.sliderValue.rounded() > self.target {
```

The > is the **greater-than** operator. The condition self.sliderValue.rounded() > self.target is true if the value stored in sliderValue is at least one higher than the value stored in target. In that case, the following line of code executes:

```
difference = self.sliderValue.rounded() - self.target
```

Here, you subtract the smaller value, target, from the larger one, sliderValue.rounded(), and store the result in difference.

Notice how the variable names clearly describe what type of data they contain. Often, you'll see code that's harder to understand, like this:

```
a = b - c
```

It's not immediately clear what's happening here, except that some arithmetic is taking place. The variable names a, b and c don't give any clues as to their purpose or what kind of data they contain. That makes it harder to maintain your code in the future.

Now, go back to the `if` statement. If `sliderValue` is equal to or less than `target`, the condition is untrue (or `false` in computer-speak) and execution will move on to the next condition:

```
} else if self.target > self.sliderValue.rounded() {
```

The same thing happens here as before, except now you've reversed the roles of `target` and `sliderValue`. The computer will only execute the following line when `target` is the greater of the two values:

```
difference = self.target - self.sliderValue.rounded()
```

This time, you subtract `sliderValue.rounded()` from `target` and store the result in the `difference` variable.

There is only one situation you haven't handled yet: When `sliderValue.rounded()` and `target` are equal. If this happens, the player has put the slider exactly at the position of the target random number, a perfect score. In that case, the difference is 0:

```
} else {
  difference = 0
}
```

By now, you've already determined that one value is not greater than the other, nor is it smaller. You can only draw one conclusion: The numbers must be equal!

Once you know the difference between the slider and the target values, calculating the number of points to award to the player is simple. It's 100 minus the difference, and the method returns that value:

```
return 100 - difference
```

Now that you've reviewed everything, you're probably eager to see the method in action!

➤ Build and run the app and play a few rounds: Move the slider, press **Hit me!**, and look at Xcode's debug console to see how you scored each time:

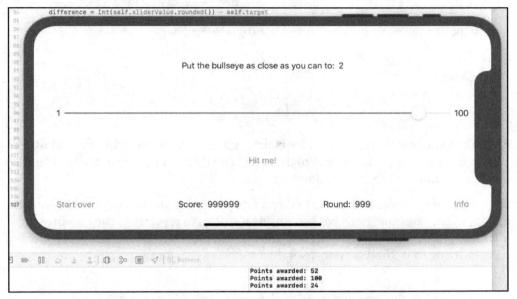

The first working points calculations

Displaying the points

Now that `pointsForCurrentRound()` properly calculates the points the player earned, it's time to display them. So next, you'll make a change to the alert pop-up so that it displays the results of `pointsForCurrentRound()`.

➤ Scroll up to the **Button row** section and change the `message:` parameter of the `Alert` so that the section looks like this:

```swift
// Button row
Button(action: {
  print("Points awarded: \(self.pointsForCurrentRound())")
  self.alertIsVisible = true
}) {
  Text("Hit me!")
}
.alert(isPresented: self.$alertIsVisible) {
  Alert(title: Text("Hello there!"),
        message: Text("The slider's value is \
(Int(self.sliderValue.rounded())).\n" +
                      "The target value is \(self.target).\n" +
                      "You scored \
```

```
(self.pointsForCurrentRound()) points this round."),
        dismissButton: .default(Text("Awesome!"))))
}
```

Take a look at the `message:` parameter for the `Alert` view:

```
message: Text("The slider's value is \
(Int(self.sliderValue.rounded())).\n" +
          "The target value is \(self.target).\n" +
          "You scored \(pointsForCurrentRound()) points this
round."),
```

The first thing that you should notice is that you made a longer string by "adding" strings together with the + sign. Programmers call this **string concatenation**, and you'll see it quite often in programming.

The next thing to note is that the first two lines end with \n, but they don't seem to appear in the pop-up. That's because inside a string, \n represents the **newline** character, which ends the current line and starts a new one. You're using it to break a run-on string into three easy-to-read lines.

Note: In Swift, as in many other programming languages, the appearance of the \ character inside a string marks the start of an **escape sequence**, which is a sequence of characters that Swift should translate into another character or a sequence of characters.

You use escape sequences to represent things that would be hard or impossible to represent directly inside a string.

The final thing you should notice is that each of the strings that you concatenate uses the \(and) characters to include values from a property or method:

```
"The slider's value is \(Int(self.sliderValue.rounded())).\n"
```

```
"The target value is \(self.target).\n"
```

```
"You scored \(pointsForCurrentRound()) points this round."
```

Remember that you use the \(and) characters for string interpolation, and you now know that the \ marks the beginning of an escape sequence. As an escape sequence, this code is not interpreted literally; it's a signal to Swift that anything between \ (and) is first evaluated, then converted into a string, and then included along with the rest of the string.

➤ Build and run the app. Move the slider and press **Hit me!**, and you'll see the new and improved alert pop-up:

The alert pop-up displaying the slider value, target value and points earned

Improving the code

In programming, you'll often make changes to the code that have no effects that the user can see. These are changes to the app's internal structure, and they're visible only to the programmer — that is, *you*.

But that doesn't mean that they aren't worth doing. There are many reasons for making these changes, such as making the code easier to read, understand and maintain, and making it less likely that you'll introduce bugs into the code. Programmers call the process of making these kinds of changes **refactoring**. That's what you're going to do in this section.

Using a constant to DRY your code

Take a look at the `if` statement inside `pointsForCurrentRound()`:

```
if Int(self.sliderValue.rounded()) > self.target {
  difference = Int(self.sliderValue.rounded()) - self.target
} else if self.target > Int(self.sliderValue.rounded()) {
  difference = self.target - Int(self.sliderValue.rounded())
} else {
  difference = 0
}
```

The repeated use of `Int(self.sliderValue.rounded())` makes it more difficult to read. It's also a calculation that runs *four times*, even though the result is the same each time. That sort of repetition is nothing to a computer, but the programmer who has to read it — and that's probably you — has to take a moment to figure out what that code is trying to do... *four times*.

In case you've forgotten, the code takes the slider's current value, rounds it to the nearest whole number, and then uses that result to create a new `Int` value.

You can improve this code by performing the calculation once and storing its result for later use. You can even give the storage place a meaningful name that makes the code easier to read. To do this, create a new variable, `sliderValueRounded`, to hold the result of `Int(self.sliderValue.rounded())`. You can then use it to make the `if` statement much easier to read.

➤ Make changes to `pointsForCurrentRound()` so that its code reads like this:

```
func pointsForCurrentRound() -> Int {
  var sliderValueRounded = Int(self.sliderValue.rounded())
  var difference: Int
  if sliderValueRounded > self.target {
    difference = sliderValueRounded - self.target
  } else if self.target > sliderValueRounded {
    difference = self.target - sliderValueRounded
  } else {
    difference = 0
  }
  return 100 - difference
}
```

The `if` statement is a lot easier to read now.

You've just changed code that performed a calculation that gave the same answer four times into code that performs the same calculation only once, stores its answer, and uses that answer when needed.

This is an approach that programmers call "Don't Repeat Yourself," or **DRY**.

The rationale behind DRY is that it makes code easier to read and to change, and makes it less prone to errors by reducing unnecessary redundancy. You just saw how much easier the code is to follow with the changes you made. If you decided later that you wanted to change the way that you convert the slider's value, you'd have to do it only once with your new DRY code, instead of *four times* with the previous code.

➤ Build and run the app to confirm that it still works and that the changes you made aren't visible to the player.

You may have noticed that even though the program works, Xcode has a suggestion:

Xcode says that sliderValueRounded was never mutated

"Variable 'sliderValueRounded' was never mutated?" Why would anyone want to mutate a variable?

Introducing let and constants

If you're into science fiction, you probably read "mutated" and thought of it as meaning "exposed to radiation or chemicals and turned into a horrible monster." However, in programming, "mutated" simply means "changed".

Take a look at the if statement in pointsForCurrentRound(), where you use the variable sliderValueRounded:

```
if sliderValueRounded > self.target {
  difference = sliderValueRounded - self.target
} else if self.target > sliderValueRounded {
  difference = self.target - sliderValueRounded
} else {
  difference = 0
}
```

In this code, sliderValueRounded is compared to self.target, subtracted from self.target, or has self.target subtracted from it. At no point does the value of sliderValueRounded ever change once it's set. It's not really a variable because it doesn't *vary*.

Xcode is suggesting that since sliderValueRounded never changes, you should change it from a variable into a constant by using the let keyword instead of var.

You use let to declare **constants**, which are like variables except that their values can be set only once; after that, they can't be changed. If you try to change the value of a constant after its value is set, it causes an error.

Take Xcode's suggestion but this time, instead of manually changing the code, make Xcode do the work for you.

➤ Click on the icon beside the suggestion, which Xcode calls "warnings". The warning pop-up will expand and you'll see a suggested fix: Replace var with let.

```
func pointsForCurrentRound() -> Int {
  var sliderValueRounded = Int(self.sliderValue.rounded())
  var difference: Int
  if sliderValueRounded > self.target {
                                            ⚠ Variable 'sliderValueRounded' was never mutated; consider changing to 'let' constant   ⚙
    difference = sliderValueRounded - sel      Replace 'var' with 'let'                                                              Fix
  } else if self.target > sliderValueRounded {
    difference = self.target - sliderValueRounded
  } else {
    difference = 0
  }
  return 100 - difference
}
```

Expanding the warning reveals Xcode's suggested fix

➤ Click on the **Fix** button to let Xcode take this action and make the fix itself. The code will now look like this:

```
func pointsForCurrentRound() -> Int {
  let sliderValueRounded = Int(self.sliderValue.rounded())
  var difference: Int
  if sliderValueRounded > self.target {
    difference = sliderValueRounded - self.target
  } else if self.target > sliderValueRounded {
    difference = self.target - sliderValueRounded
  } else {
    difference = 0
  }
  return 100 - difference
}
```

➤ Build and run the app again. You'll see that it still works just like before and that no changes are noticeable to the player.

Since changing sliderValueRounded from a variable to a constant had no noticeable effect on the app, you might be asking "What was the point? Why should Xcode care if a variable never changes and suggest that I use a constant instead?"

The answer is that using a constant here helps prevent bugs. Many coding errors happen because the programmer thinks a variable holds a certain value, only to discover that some other code has changed that value.

This is true in the simple sort of programming you're doing right now, where you only have to worry about one thing happening at a time. In **parallel programming**, where you have many pieces of code running at the same time, or **asynchronous programming**, where you have many pieces of code running independently at unpredictable times and all communicating with each other, it's even easier for code to change data that it shouldn't be changing.

This is why there's a general rule that says whenever possible, use a constant instead of a variable. If you need to store the result of a calculation for later use, you'll often find that the result never changes so you can store it as a constant.

Xcode is good at spotting opportunities to turn variables into constants, but it's not perfect. Take another look at the complete code for pointsForCurrentRound(), paying particular attention to how `difference` is set:

```
func pointsForCurrentRound() -> Int {
  let sliderValueRounded = Int(self.sliderValue.rounded())
  var difference: Int
  if sliderValueRounded > self.target {
    difference = sliderValueRounded - self.target
  } else if self.target > sliderValueRounded {
    difference = self.target - sliderValueRounded
  } else {
    difference = 0
  }
  return 100 - difference
}
```

The computer science term for the different actions taken as the result of things like the `if` statement is **branches**. In the code above, there are three branches and in each one, `difference` is set to a different value. However, no matter which branch the code takes, the value of `difference` never changes after it's set, so it should be turned into a constant. Remember that a constant is like a variable, except that its value can be set only once.

➤ Change the line:

```
var difference: Int
```

to:

```
let difference: Int
```

➤ Build and run the app. Once again, you'll see that it still works, with no noticeable changes.

Another attempt to DRY some code

Since you've defined the sliderValueRounded constant in pointsForCurrentRound(), try using it in ContentView's body to make it more DRY. Scroll up to the **Button row** section and pay particular attention to message::

```
// Button row
Button(action: {
  print("Button pressed!")
  self.alertIsVisible = true
}) {
  Text("Hit me!")
}
alert(isPresented: self.$alertIsVisible) {
  Alert(title: Text("Hello there!"),
        message: Text("The slider's value is \
(Int(self.sliderValue.rounded())).\n" +
                       "The target value is \(self.target).\n" +
                       "You scored \(pointsForCurrentRound())
points this round."),
        dismissButton: .default(Text("Awesome!")))
}
```

That unwieldy Int(self.sliderValue.rounded()) that you got rid of in pointsForCurrentRound() is in the string that displays the slider value. Since you've already defined sliderValueRounded in pointsForCurrentRound(), try using it there.

➤ Change the code that defines the alert pop-up so that it looks like this:

```
alert(isPresented: self.$alertIsVisible) {
  Alert(title: Text("Hello there!"),
        message: Text("The slider's value is \
(sliderValueRounded).\n" +
                       "The target value is \(self.target).\n" +
                       "You scored \(pointsForCurrentRound())
points this round."),
        dismissButton: .default(Text("Awesome!")))
}
```

While it seems as if this change would make your code more readable, Xcode has issues with it:

```
.alert(isPresented: self.$alertIsVisible) {
  Alert(title: Text("Hello there!"),
        message: Text("The slider's value is \(sliderValueRounded).\n" +   ⊙  Use of unresolved identifier 'sliderValueRounded'
                    "The target value is \(self.target).\n" +
                    "You scored \(self.pointsForCurrentRound()) points this round."),
        dismissButton: .default(Text("Awesome!")))
}
```

Xcode displays an error message about sliderValueRounded

"Use of unresolved identifier 'sliderValueRounded'" is Xcode's robotic way of saying "I have no idea of what sliderValueRounded is."

To figure out why you are getting this warning, you'll change your code back and then you'll look at why you got an error.

➤ Change the code that defines the alert pop-up back to this:

```
alert(isPresented: self.$alertIsVisible) {
  Alert(title: Text("Hello there!"),
        message: Text("The slider's value is \
(Int(self.sliderValue.rounded())).\n" +
                    "The target value is \(self.target).\n" +
                    "You scored \(pointsForCurrentRound())
points this round."),
        dismissButton: .default(Text("Awesome!")))
}
```

The lives and times of variables and constants

If you look at the code in ContentView, you'll see that there are variables and constants in two places:

1. Inside ContentView but outside everything else in ContentView.

2. Inside pointsForCurrentRound().

Take a look at the code for `pointsForCurrentRound()` again:

```
func pointsForCurrentRound() -> Int {
  let sliderValueRounded = Int(self.sliderValue.rounded())
  let difference: Int
  if sliderValueRounded > self.target {
    difference = sliderValueRounded - self.target
  } else if self.target > sliderValueRounded {
    difference = self.target - sliderValueRounded
  } else {
    difference = 0
  }
  return 100 - difference
}
```

`pointsForCurrentRound()` has two constants: `sliderValueRounded` and
`difference`. They come into being the moment they are declared within the method
(which happens at the `let` statement), and they vanish from existence at the end of
the method. You can only refer to them after they've been declared, and they exist
only inside `pointsForCurrentRound()`. This restriction would also apply if they
were variables.

When you declare constants and variables inside a method, you can only refer to
them within that method. This is why programmers call them **local** constants and
variables.

Now look at the start of `ContentView`:

```
struct ContentView : View {
  @State var alertIsVisible: Bool = false
  @State var sliderValue: Double = 50.0
  @State var target: Int = Int.random(in: 1...100)

  var body: some View {

    ...
```

When the app starts, it creates an instance of `ContentView`. You'll learn more about
what happens when an app starts later on in this book. Upon the creation of
`ContentView`, its variables: `alertIsVisible`, `sliderValue`, `target` and body also
come into being. Since these variables belong to the `ContentView` instance,
programmers call them **instance variables**.

Instance variables are accessible from anywhere within the object they belong to.
That's why `ContentView`'s methods (`pointsForCurrentRound()`), references
(`sliderValue` and `target`) and variables (other instance variables) can reference
them.

When a variable exists and you can reference it, it's **in scope**. A good general rule to follow is that a variable is in scope only inside the braces where you declared it. For example:

```
{
  var a = 30  // a is in scope here

  // (More code goes here)
  {
    var b = a + 1  // Both a and b are in scope here

    // (More code goes here)
  }
  // b is no longer in scope.

  print("The value of a is \(a).")  // a is still in scope
}

  // Both a and b are no longer in scope.
```

In case you'd forgotten: the // characters mark the start of a comment, which the compiler ignores. You can read about them in more detail below.

Comments

You've probably noticed the green text that begins with // a few times now. As I explained earlier, these are comments. You can write any text you want after the // symbol, and the compiler will ignore any text from the // to the end of the line.

```
// I am a comment! You can type anything here.
```

The best use for comment lines is to explain how your code works. You should try to write your code in a self-explanatory way, but sometimes a little extra explanation can go a long way.

Unless you have the memory of an elephant, you'll probably have forgotten exactly how your code works when you look at it six months later; this is where comments are useful. As I've said before, you want to write code so that the next programmer can easily understand it, because that next programmer might be *you*!

There's another style of comment that covers more than one line. Anything between the /∗ and ∗/ markers is a comment:

```
/*
  I am also a comment!
  I can span multiple lines.
*/
```

The /∗ ∗/ comments are good for longer comments. They also have another common use: temporarily disable whole sections of source code, which is helpful when you're trying to hunt down a pesky bug.

Remember, the compiler ignores comments, so you can make it ignore one or more lines of code by putting them into a comment. This practice is known as **commenting out**.

Xcode makes it simple to comment out one or more lines of code. Use the **Command**-/ keyboard shortcut to comment/uncomment any currently-selected lines, or if you have nothing selected, the current line.

A second attempt at DRYing some code

Right now, two different places in ContentView make use of the same calculation to get the value of the slider: Round it to the nearest whole number and convert it into an Int.

You use that calculation in the part of the body instance variable that defines the alert pop-up:

```
Alert(title: Text("Hello there!"),
      message: Text("The slider's value is \
(Int(self.sliderValue.rounded())).\n" +
                    "The target value is \(self.target).\n" +
                    "You scored \(pointsForCurrentRound())
points this round."),
      dismissButton: .default(Text("Awesome!"))))
}
```

It's also used in the pointsForCurrentRound() method:

```
func pointsForCurrentRound() -> Int {
  let sliderValueRounded = Int(self.sliderValue.rounded())
  let difference: Int
  if sliderValueRounded > self.target {
    difference = sliderValueRounded - self.target
  } else if self.target > sliderValueRounded {
```

```
      difference = self.target - sliderValueRounded
   } else {
      difference = 0
   }
```

Ideally, you'd like to have a "single source of truth" for the slider's current position as an integer value, and you'd like to make it accessible from anywhere inside `ContentView`.

There are a couple of ways you could make this happen. One way would be to define a new method. It would look like this (don't type this one in; just read it):

```
func sliderValueRounded() -> Int {
   return Int(sliderValue.rounded())
}
```

This new method would make a rounded, whole-number value for the slider position available from anywhere within `ContentView`. If a method were the only way you could do this, you'd use it.

However, there's another way to get this value: a **computed property**, which is a property that acts like a method. In cases where you need a simple calculation based on a property, it's often better to use a computed property instead of a method. We explain the differences between property types in Chapter 26 in Section 3 of the book.

➤ Add the following to the end of the **User interface views** part of `ContentView`'s **Properties** section, immediately after the line where you declare `target`:

```
var sliderValueRounded: Int {
   Int(self.sliderValue.rounded())
}
```

Declaring a computed property is like declaring an ordinary property in that it begins with `var` or `let` followed by the property name and the property's data type. The difference is that computed properties have a body which defines the value in the property. In the case of the `sliderValueRounded` property, the body contains `Int(self.sliderValue.rounded())`.

Now that you have the computed property, you can use it.

➤ Change the code that defines the alert pop-up to the following:

```
Alert(title: Text("Hello there!"),
      message: Text("The slider's value is \
(self.sliderValueRounded).\n" +
```

```
                    "The target value is \(self.target).\n" +
                    "You scored \(self.pointsForCurrentRound())
    points this round."),
        dismissButton: .default(Text("Awesome!")))
```

➤ Change `pointsForCurrentRound()` to the following. Since `ContentView` now has a `sliderValueRounded` property, there's no longer a need for a `sliderValueRounded` constant within the method:

```
func pointsForCurrentRound() -> Int {
  let difference: Int
  if self.sliderValueRounded > self.target {
    difference = self.sliderValueRounded - self.target
  } else if self.target > self.sliderValueRounded {
    difference = self.target - self.sliderValueRounded
  } else {
    difference = 0
  }
  return 100 - difference
}
```

➤ Build and run the app. It still works in the same way, but underneath, the code is now easier to read and to maintain.

Simplifying the Alert code

`ContentView`'s body defines the user interface; as a result, it's big and can be unwieldy. For example, consider the code in body that generates the alert pop-up:

```
Alert(title: Text("Hello there!"),
      message: Text("The slider's value is \
(self.sliderValueRounded()).\n" +
                    "The target value is \(self.target).\n" +
                    "You scored \(pointsForCurrentRound())
    points this round."),
        dismissButton: .default(Text("Awesome!")))
```

The `message:` parameter has a big chunk of text in it. This is a good place to make use of a method to simplify things.

➤ Add the following method in `ContentView`'s **Methods** section, just below the `pointsForCurrentRound()` method:

```
func scoringMessage() -> String {
  return "The slider's value is \(self.sliderValueRounded).\n" +
         "The target value is \(self.target).\n" +
         "You scored \(self.pointsForCurrentRound()) points this
```

```
round."
}
```

You should note a couple of things about this method:

- Because this method returns a result, it has a name that describes that result.

- This method returns a `String` instead of an `Int`. Methods aren't limited to only returning numbers; they can return all kinds of data, as you'll see in the exercises in this book.

➤ Incorporate the new `scoringMessage()` method into the alert pop-up code:

```
Alert(title: Text("Hello there!"),
      message: Text(self.scoringMessage()),
      dismissButton: .default(Text("Awesome!"))))
```

That's a lot cleaner.

➤ Once again, build and run the app. Again, you won't see any noticeable changes, but you'll feel the warm glow of satisfaction that you've done a good job refactoring the code.

Removing redundancies

Take a look at the **Properties** section of `ContentView`, particularly the part marked **User interface views**:

```
@State var alertIsVisible: Bool = false
@State var sliderValue: Double = 50.0
@State var target: Int = Int.random(in: 1...100)
var sliderValueRounded: Int {
  Int(self.sliderValue.rounded())
}
```

Remove the data types from the first three properties so that the code looks like this:

```
@State var alertIsVisible = false
@State var sliderValue = 50.0
@State var target = Int.random(in: 1...100)
var sliderValueRounded: Int {
  Int(self.sliderValue.rounded())
}
```

Note that Xcode doesn't display any error messages after this change.

➤ Build and run the app to confirm that it still works, even though you've removed the information about those properties' data types.

Why does the code still work? It's because Swift is smart enough to deduce, or as we say in programming, **infer**, the type of a variable or constant based the value you assign to it.

Consider the first property:

```
@State var alertIsVisible = false
```

By assigning the value `false` to `alertIsVisible`, Swift infers that `alertIsVisible`'s data type is `Bool`.

Here's the next property:

```
@State var sliderValue = 50.0
```

Assigning `sliderValue` with the value **50.0** — a number with a decimal point — causes Swift to infer that the variable's data type is `Double`, the preferred data type for numbers with decimal points.

And then comes this property:

```
@State var target = Int.random(in: 1...100)
```

`Int.random(in: 1...100)` is a method that returns a random integer between 1 and 100 inclusive. By assigning it to `target`, Swift infers that `target` is an `Int` property.

Whenever possible, you should let Swift infer the type of variables and constants. There *are* times when Swift can't do that, though. Here's an example, taken straight from `pointsForCurrentRound()`

```
let difference: Int
if self.sliderValueRounded > self.target {
  difference = self.sliderValueRounded - self.target
} else if self.target > self.sliderValueRounded {
  difference = self.target - self.sliderValueRounded
} else {
  difference = 0
}
return 100 - difference
```

`difference` isn't assigned a value until after it's declared, which means that Swift doesn't have anything to use to infer `difference`'s type. In circumstances like this,

Swift *has* to be told what data type difference is. Swift also has to be told the data type of computed properties. If you try to change the declaration of sliderValueRounded to the following...

```
var sliderValueRounded: {
  Int(self.sliderValue.rounded())
}
```

...Xcode will complain quickly by throwing a very short error message: "Expected type". This is where computed properties are more like methods; they can get so complex that Swift can't infer their data type.

Key points

In this chapter, you added the following features to your app:

• The game now displays the target value at the top of the screen.

• It also calculates the points that the player earned based on the difference between the slider and the target values, then displays those points.

You also learned about:

• Generating pseudo-random numbers

• Algorithms

• Writing your own methods

• Making decisions with the if statement

• Adding strings using concatenation and representing special characters with escape sequences.

• Refactoring

• The let statement and constants

• The scope of variables and constants

• Computed properties

You have the basic elements of a working game, but it can only play a single round right now. In the next chapter, you'll make the game fully functional with rounds and scorekeeping. You can find the project files for the app up to this point under **04 - Outlets** in the **Source Code** folder.

Chapter 5: A Fully Working Game

Joey deVilla

You've made a lot of progress on the game, and the to-do list is getting shorter! You have a basic version of the game running, where you can generate and display the target value, and you can also calculate and show the player the number of points they've scored in the current round.

It's now time to make a fully-working game, where the player can play multiple rounds and the game keeps a running score. We'll also give the player the ability to start a new game.

This chapter covers the following:

- **Improving the `pointsForCurrentRound()` algorithm**: Simplifying how the the number of points awarded to the player is calculated.

- **What's the score?**: Calculate the player's total score over multiple rounds and display it onscreen.

- **One more round...**: Implement updating the round count and displaying the current round on screen.

- **Key points**: A quick review of what you learned in this chapter.

Improving the pointsForCurrentRound() algorithm

Let's do a little more refactoring of `pointsForCurrentRound()`, the method that calculates how many points to award to the player based on the difference between the target value and where they put the slider. Here's its code at the moment:

```
func pointsForCurrentRound() -> Int {
  let difference: Int
  if self.sliderValueRounded > self.target {
    difference = self.sliderValueRounded - self.target
  } else if self.target > self.sliderValueRounded {
    difference = self.target - self.sliderValueRounded
  } else {
    difference = 0
  }
  return 100 - difference
}
```

Most of the code in this method is devoted to making sure that `difference` — the difference between the slider value and the target value — is always positive. This is done by making sure that the smaller value is always subtracted from the larger value.

"Absolute" power

There's a simpler way to do this, and it comes from one of the many math functions built into the Swift Standard Library: The abs() function. Given a number, which can be an `Int`, a `Double` or any other Swift data type that represents a number, it returns the *absolute value* of that number, which is the value of that number, but ignoring the sign.

Here are some examples of abs() in action:

- abs(5) returns 5

- abs(-5) returns 5

- abs(-5.25) returns 5.25

➤ Let's use abs() to simplify the code in pointsForCurrentRound(). Change its code to the following:

```
func pointsForCurrentRound() -> Int {
    let difference = abs(self.sliderValueRounded - self.target)
    return 100 - difference
}
```

Note that you didn't have to specify difference's data type. That's because Swift can infer it from the code on the right side of the = sign: self.sliderValueRounded and self.sliderValueRounded are both Ints, subtracting the latter from the former also yields an Int and the absolute value of that result is also an Int. Based on this, Swift infers that difference is an Int.

➤ Run the app and click **Hit me!**. It works as before, without any changes that the player will notice, but with much less code:

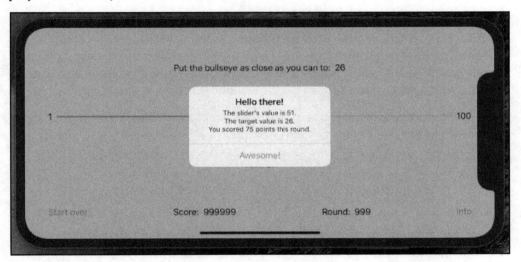

Good code is simple and readable, and this often translates to less code. If you can get the same result using less code, you get not only the benefits of simplicity and readability, but fewer lines of code makes it less likely to introduce bugs.

Removing a "magic number"

Here's the current code for `pointsForCurrentRound()`:

```
func pointsForCurrentRound() -> Int {
  let difference = abs(self.sliderValueRounded - self.target)
  return 100 - difference
}
```

If you've worked on the code recently, it's probably quite obvious to you what the **100** in `return 100 - difference` is for. It's the maximum possible score, which happens when the player positions the slider right at the target value.

However, if you spend some time away from *Bullseye's* code and then return to it, you might have forgotten where the **100** comes from. You might also decide to change this value at a later point.

There's a programming term for numbers like this that appear in code: *magic numbers*. They're called magic because they're just there, without any explanation or context; they just "magically" appear in the code. In programming, we strongly discourage the use of magic numbers, and recommend that you replace them with a constant with a name that explains what the number is for.

➤ Let's define a new constant, `maximumScore`, to replace the magic number. Change the code for `pointsForCurrentRound()` to this:

```
func pointsForCurrentRound() -> Int {
  let maximumScore = 100
  let difference = abs(self.sliderValueRounded - self.target)
  return maximumScore - difference
}
```

Once again, you don't have to specify `maximumScore`'s data type. Based on the value of **100** assigned to it, Swift will infer that `maximumScore` is an `Int`.

➤ Run the app. Once again, it works as it did before the change.

You've replaced a number without context — **100** — with the constant `maximumScore`, which both holds the value 100 *and* explains what it's for. Even with this additional line, you still have a `pointsForCurrentRound()` that's less than a third the size of the original.

What's the score?

Now that you have a lean, mean pointsForCurrentRound() and know how far off the slider is from the target, it's time to keep track of the player's score.

The first thing you'll need is a place to store the score. Think about the nature of the score:

- It should have a name that makes its use and purpose clear: score.

- It's a whole-number value. This means that it should be an Int. It should have an initial value of **0**.

- It's part of the state of the game. Thus means that it should be marked with the @State keyword.

➤ Add the new variable just before the *User interface views* section of ContentView's properties, starting with a comment that shows that this variable, along with some others, will contain the game stats, as shown below:

```
// Properties
// ==========

// Game stats
@State var score = 0

// User interface views
@State var alertIsVisible = false
```

Now that there's a score variable, there needs to be code to add the points that the player earned to it. The player earns points when they tap the **Hit me!** button, so that seems like a logical place to calculate the total score.

The code for the **Hit me!** button is in the body variable, in the *Button row* section:

```
// Button row
Button(action: {
  print("Points awarded: \(self.pointsForCurrentRound())")
  self.alertIsVisible = true
}) {
  Text("Hit me!")
}
.alert(isPresented: self.$alertIsVisible) {
  Alert(title: Text("Hello there!"),
        message: Text(self.scoringMessage()),
        dismissButton: .default(Text("Awesome!")))
}
```

The code in the `Button` view's `action:` parameter is executed whenever it's tapped. Right now, that code is:

```
print("Points awarded: \(self.pointsForCurrentRound())")
self.alertIsVisible = true
```

This code does the following:

- It outputs the points that the player has earned for the current attempt on Xcode's console. This only happens with the Simulator, or on a connected device that's running the app from Xcode, and will only be seen by the programmer. The user never sees this.

- It sets the `alertIsVisible` property to `true`, which causes the alert pop-up to appear.

Let's add to this code. We should add the points that are being awarded to the player for this round to the total score.

➤ Change the code for the `Button` view so that it looks like the following:

```
// Button row
Button(action: {
  print("Points awarded: \(self.pointsForCurrentRound())")
  self.alertIsVisible = true
  self.score = self.score + self.pointsForCurrentRound()
}) {
  Text("Hit me!")
}
.alert(isPresented: self.$alertIsVisible) {
  Alert(title: Text("Hello there!"),
        message: Text(self.scoringMessage()),
        dismissButton: .default(Text("Awesome!")))
}
```

There's now a place in which to store the score, and there's a way to add to the score when the player taps **Hit me!**. It's now time to display the score.

Since `score` is a `@State` variable, it means that Swift constantly watches it for changes, and immediately updates any user interface elements that make use of it when those changes happen. Let's set up that user interface element.

➤ Scroll down to the part of the body variable marked *Score row* and change it to the following:

```
// Score row
HStack {
  Button(action: {}) {
```

```
    Text("Start over")
  }
  Spacer()
  Text("Score:")
  Text("\(self.score)")
  Spacer()
  Text("Round:")
  Text("999")
  Spacer()
  Button(action: {}) {
    Text("Info")
  }
}
.padding(.bottom, 20)
```

Note the change. You've replaced this hard-coded score:

```
Text("999999")
```

With:

```
Text("\(self.score)")
```

➤ Run the app. When it starts, you'll see something like this:

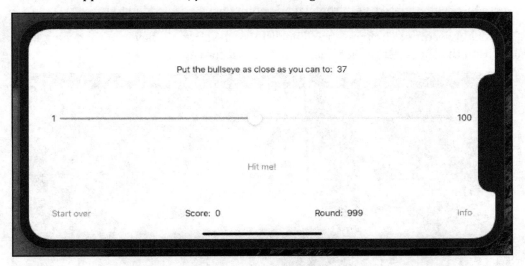

Note that the player's score is no longer 999999, but 0, which is the initial value assigned to score. The Text view now displays the score, which is always up to date because score is a @State variable.

➤ Click **Hit me!** The pop-up will appear:

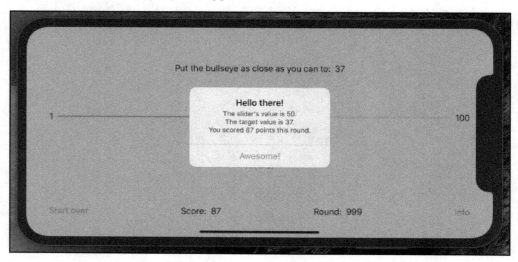

The pop-up acts as you'd expect, displaying the slider's value, the target value, and the number of points the player scored.

What's new is the score. If you look at the bottom of the screen, you'll see that the score has been updated, with the player's points have been added to it.

➤ Click **Awesome!** The pop-up will be dismissed, and you'll have another change to position the slider. Move the slider, and click **Hit me!** again:

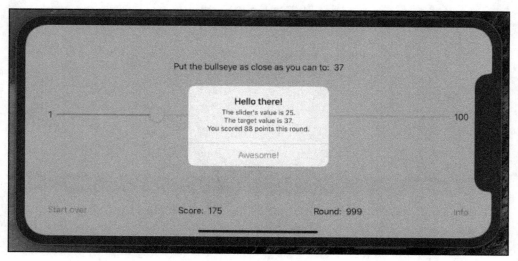

Once again, the pop-up appears, along with value, the target value, and the number of points the player scored. And once again, if you look at the bottom of the screen, you'll see that the score has been updated.

There's just one problem now: The target never changes. We'll fix that by starting a new round.

One more round...

Once the player has tapped **Hit me!** and been awarded their points, the game should present the player with a new target. This means coming up with a new random value for target. That part is easy:

```
self.target = Int.random(in: 1...100)
```

The trickier part is figuring out *where* to put this code.

The most obvious place is inside the action: parameter of the Button view. Right now, code in this parameter causes the pop-up to appear and updates the score. It looks like a good place to generate a new target value.

➤ Change the code in body at the start of the *Button row* section so that it looks like the following:

```
// Button row
Button(action: {
  print("Points awarded: \(self.pointsForCurrentRound())")
  self.alertIsVisible = true
  self.score = self.score + self.pointsForCurrentRound()
  self.target = Int.random(in: 1...100)
}) {
```

➤ Run the app and make a note of the target value — don't do anything else just yet:

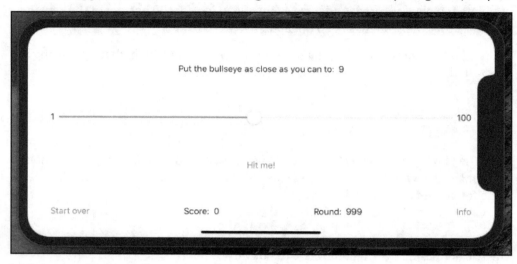

In the example above, the target value is 9.

➤ Click **Hit me!**. 99 times out of 100, you'll see that the target value has changed!

The target value was 9 before you clicked **Hit me!**, and changed — both on the main screen and in the pop-up — to 94.

The player was awarded 56 points, and if you do the math:

- Take the maximum score of **100**,

- the new target value of **94** and the slider position of **50**, making a difference of **44**,

- which makes for **56** points, which comes from 100 - 44.

How did this happen?

Asynchronous code execution

You probably know that computers — your iOS device included — can perform several tasks at the same time, either by actually performing tasks simultaneously, or combining careful scheduling with their millisecond speed to make it appear as if they're multitasking.

Let's look at the Button code again:

```
// Button row
Button(action: {
    print("Points awarded: \(self.pointsForCurrentRound())")
    self.alertIsVisible = true
    self.score = self.score + self.pointsForCurrentRound()
    self.target = Int.random(in: 1...100)
}) {
```

The multitasking starts when alertIsVisible is set to true. The program follows two paths:

1. The program continues to execute the rest of the code in Button's action parameter.

2. Setting the state variable alertIsVisible to true triggers Button's .presentation() method and causes the alert pop-up to appear.

These two paths of execution happen over a span of milliseconds, and practically simultaneously.

The diagram below might make it easier to understand what's happening:

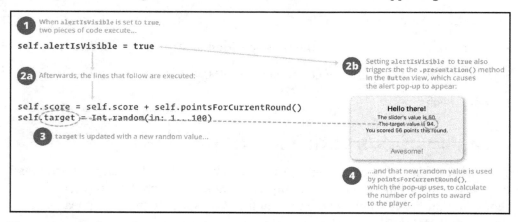

The series of events that causes the alert pop-up to appear happens right away, but the code in the action: parameter has already updated the score and generated a new target number before the alert pop-up has even finished drawing itself onscreen.

In programmer-speak, alerts work *asynchronously*. We'll talk much more about that in a later chapter, but it means that you should keep in mind that a lot of code that updates the user interface based on changes to state variables often gets executed at the same time. Clearly, we'll need to take another approach.

➤ Change the code in body at the start of the *Button row* section so that the only code in the button's action: parameter sets alertIsVisible to true. The section should end up like this:

```
// Button row
Button(action: {
  print("Points awarded: \(self.pointsForCurrentRound())")
  self.alertIsVisible = true
}) {
  Text("Hit me!")
}
.alert(isPresented: self.$alertIsVisible) {
  Alert(title: Text("Hello there!"),
        message: Text(self.scoringMessage()),
        dismissButton: .default(Text("Awesome!")))
}
```

Finding a better place to start a new round

The problem with our first approach is that it tried to start a new round in response to the player tapping **Hit me!**, which is *before* the alert pop-up gets displayed. The new round should start in response to the player dismissing the alert pop-up, which happens when they tap the pop-up's **Awesome!** button.

It turns out that the `Alert` object, which is initialized at the end of the button row section of code...

```
Alert(title: Text("Hello there!"),
      message: Text(self.scoringMessage()),
      dismissButton: .default(Text("Awesome!")))
```

...accepts an optional extra parameter *after* `dismissButton:`, and that parameter is code to be executed when the alert pop-up is dismissed.

➤ Change the code in bodys *Button row* section so that it looks like this:

```
// Button row
Button(action: {
  print("Points awarded: \(self.pointsForCurrentRound())")
  self.alertIsVisible = true
}) {
  Text("Hit me!")
}
.alert(isPresented: self.$alertIsVisible) {
  Alert(title: Text("Hello there!"),
        message: Text(self.scoringMessage()),
        dismissButton: .default(Text("Awesome!")) {
          self.score = self.score + self.pointsForCurrentRound()
          self.target = Int.random(in: 1...100)
      })
}
```

Note: You may have noticed that objects and methods seem to expect some of their parameters inside parentheses (()) and some of them inside braces ({}). We'll explain why this is so later in this book, and it will all make sense. For now, just trust in the code that we're showing you.

➤ Run the app, and, once again, make a note of the target value first:

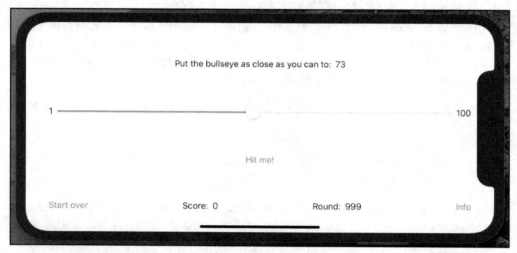

In the example above, the target value is 73.

➤ Click **Hit me!**. This time, you'll see that the target value is still 73, and that the points earned this round are based on that value:

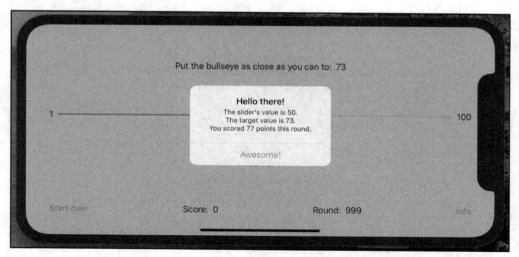

You should also note that the score hasn't been updated yet — it's still 0.

➤ Dismiss the pop-up by pressing **Awesome!**, and make a note of the target value and score:

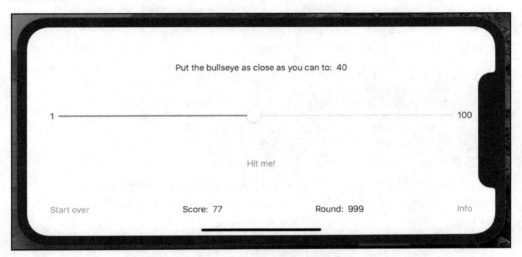

The target value is new, and the score has been updated. Now it's time to properly display the current round.

Showing the current round

Just as there's a designated place to store the score, there also needs to be a place to store the number of the current round.

Think about what this variable should be like:

- It should have a name that makes its use and purpose clear: round.

- It's a whole-number value. This means that it should be an Int. It should have an initial value of **1**.

- It's part of the state of the game. Thus means that it should be marked with the @State keyword.

➤ Add the new variable to the *Game stats* section of ContentView's properties. The section should look like this at the end:

```
// Game stats
@State var score = 0
@State var round = 1
```

Now that we have the round variable, we need code to increase its value by 1 — or in programmer-speak; *increment* it — at the start of a new round. A new round starts when the player dismisses the alert pop-up, so that's where this code should go.

The code for the **Hit me!** button is in the body variable, in the button row section:

➤ Change the code at the end of bodys *Button row* section so that it looks like this:

```
Alert(title: Text("Hello there!"),
      message: Text(self.scoringMessage()),
      dismissButton: .default(Text("Awesome!")) {
         self.score = self.score + self.pointsForCurrentRound()
         self.target = Int.random(in: 1...100)
         self.round = self.round + 1
   })
```

There's now a place in which to store the number of the current round, and that number is incremented when the player dismissed the alert pop-up. It's now time to display it.

As with score, round is a state variable, it means that Swift constantly watches it for changes, and changes cause any user interface elements that make use of it to be updated. Let's set up that user interface element.

➤ Scroll to the part of the body variable marked *Score row* and change it to the following:

```
// Score row
HStack {
  Button(action: {}) {
    Text("Start over")
  }
  Spacer()
  Text("Score:")
  Text("\(self.score)")
  Spacer()
  Text("Round:")
  Text("\(self.round)")
  Spacer()
  Button(action: {}) {
    Text("Info")
  }
}
.padding(.bottom, 20)
```

Note the change. You've replaced this hard-coded count of rounds:

```
Text("999")
```

With:

```
Text("\(self.round)")
```

➤ Run the app. When it starts, you'll see something like this:

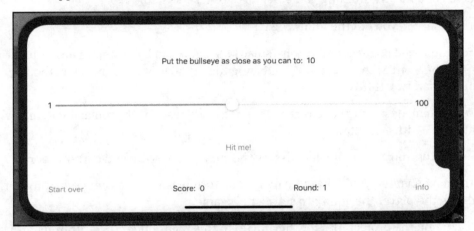

Note that the starting round is no longer 999, but 1, which is the initial value assigned to round. The Text view now displays the correct round, which is always up to date because round is a @State variable.

➤ Click **Hit me!**, and then dismiss the alert pop-up when it appears. You'll see something like this:

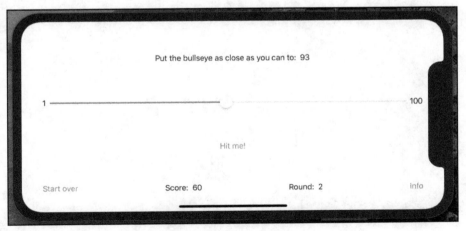

The screen shows that you're now on round 2.

All the display elements work now!

Key points

You've got a mostly-working game; feel free to take a victory lap.

In this chapter, you did the following:

- You improved `pointsForCurrentRound()`'s algorithm by using the `abs()` function from the Swift Standard Library, reducing the number of lines in the method by more than two-thirds.

- You also made `pointsForCurrentRound()` more readable by replacing a "magic number" with a constant.

- Added the ability to store and display the cumulative score and current round.

In the next chapter, you'll do some more refactoring, tweak the game to improve it, and give the player the ability to start a new game.

You can find the project files for the app up to this point under **05 — Rounds and Score** in the Source Code folder. If you get stuck, compare your version of the app with these source files to see if you missed anything.

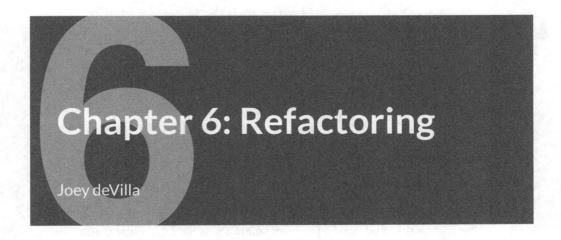

Chapter 6: Refactoring

Joey deVilla

At this point, your game is fully playable. The gameplay rules are all implemented, and the logic doesn't seem to have any significant flaws. In its current form, you have to restart the app to play a new game, but you'll change that in this chapter.

As far as we can tell, there aren't any bugs. That said, there's still some room for improvement!

This chapter will cover the following:

- **Improvements**: Small UI tweaks to make the game look and function better.

- **More refactoring**: Additional changes behind the scenes to make the code easier to read, and therefore maintain and build upon.

- **Starting over**: Resetting the game to start fresh.

- **Making the code less self-ish**: The keyword self is used all over the code. Are they all necessary?

- **Key points**: A quick review of what you learned in this chapter.

Improvements

While the game isn't very pretty yet — and don't worry, you'll fix that in the next chapter — there are still a couple of tweaks that you can make to improve its user experience.

The alert title

Unless you've already changed it, the title of the alert pop-up still says "Hello there!". That's something leftover from back when it was a single-button app. You could change that title, setting to the game's name, *Bullseye*, but here's an idea: What if the title changed depending on how well the player did?

Here are the details:

- If the player is either really lucky or has a very good eye and puts the slider right on the target, the alert's title could say "Perfect!"

- If the player didn't put the slider right on the target but got really close to the target but not quite there, say under five units away, the alert's title could say "You almost had it!"

- A close-ish attempt, say 10 or fewer units away, could be rewarded with the title "Not bad."

- In all other cases, the alert gives the player a little tough love with "Are you even trying?"

Here's a flowchart that illustrates the process:

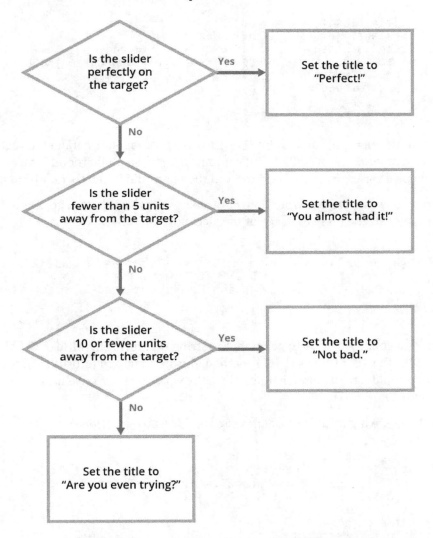

Flowchart illustrating how the alert title is determined

Exercise: Think of a way to accomplish this. How would you program it? Hint: There are an awful lot of "if's" in the preceding sentences.

Before we write the code to set the alert pop-up's title based on how close the slider and target are, let's figure out where this code should go.

Let's look at the code that defines the alert pop-up:

```
Alert(title: Text("Hello there!"),
    message: Text(self.scoringMessage()),
    dismissButton: .default(Text("Awesome!")) {
      self.score = self.score + self.pointsForCurrentRound()
      self.target = Int.random(in: 1...100)
      self.round = self.round + 1
    }
)
```

The title of the alert pop-up is defined by the `Alert`'s `message:` parameter. Right now, the `Text` view that it's filled with contains the string "Hello there!". We need a way to change this string based on how well the player did in the current round.

In the previous chapter, we wrote the `scoringMessage()` method to generate the string that forms the main message of the alert pop-up:

```
func scoringMessage() -> String {
  return "The slider's value is \(self.sliderValueRounded).\n" +
         "The target value is \(self.target).\n" +
         "You scored \(self.pointsForCurrentRound()) points this
round."
}
```

We'll write a similar method to generate the string that forms the title of the alert pop-up. Like the `scoringMessage()` method, this new method returns a value and therefore should have a name that describes the value it returns. We'll call it `alertTitle()`.

➤ Add the following to the end of `ContentView`'s *Methods* section, just after `scoringMessage()`:

```
func alertTitle() -> String {
  let difference: Int = abs(self.sliderValueRounded -
self.target)
  let title: String
  if difference == 0 {
    title = "Perfect!"
  } else if difference < 5 {
    title = "You almost had it!"
  } else if difference <= 10 {
    title = "Not bad."
  } else {
    title = "Are you even trying?"
  }
  return title
}
```

This code first calculates `difference`, the difference between the slider position and the target. It then creates a string constant named `title`, which will contain the title that this method returns. As you can see, most of this method is taken up by an `if` statement that runs through different possibilities to select a title.

The `if` statement has four different *clauses*. Here's the first one:

```
if difference == 0 {
   title = "Perfect!"
```

It says if the difference between the slider and the target is 0, set the value of `title` to **Perfect!**.

You're probably wondering what the == means. There's a critical difference between it — two "equals" signs in a row — and a single "equals" sign:

- The single equals sign, =, means "Set this variable or constant to a given value." To take an example from the code above, `title = "Perfect!"` means "Set `title` to **Perfect!**."

- The double equals sign, ==, means "is equal to." To take an example from the code above, `difference == 0` means "`difference` is equal to **0**", a statement that is either `true` or `false`.

When you start programming, you may find yourself using = in when you should really be using ==. Watch for this, especially when Xcode gives you an error message related to an `if` statement.

Here's the `if` statement's second clause:

```
} else if difference < 5 {
   title = "You almost had it!"
```

If the first clause doesn't apply, and `difference` is less than 5, `title` is set to **You almost had it!**.

The `if` statement reads as follows:

```
} else if difference <= 10 {
   title = "Not bad."
```

If the first and second clause don't apply, and `difference` is 10 or less, `title` is set to **Not bad**.

At the end of the if statement comes the else clause:

```
} else {
    title = "Are you even trying?"
```

This handles the case when none of the other clauses apply. In this case, title is set to **Are you even trying?**.

Now that we have the alertTitle() method, it's time to make use of it.

➤ Change the code in body that defines the alert pop-up to the following:

```
Alert(title: Text(alertTitle()),
      message: Text(scoringMessage()),
      dismissButton: .default(Text("Awesome!"))) {
        self.score = self.score + self.pointsForCurrentRound()
        self.target = Int.random(in: 1...100)
        self.round = self.round + 1
    }
```

Note the change. You've replaced this hard-coded message:

```
Text("Hi there!")
```

With:

```
Text(scoringMessage())
```

➤ Run the app. When it starts, you'll see something like this:

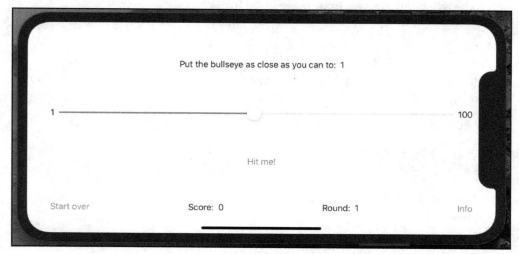

The game, with a target value of 1

The example is a really lucky one because a target of 1 is very easy to hit — you move the slider all the way to the left. Here's what the alert pop-up looked like after doing so:

The alert pop-up, where the slider is right on the target, with the title 'Perfect!'

Here's what the alert looks like if **Hit me!** is pressed when the slider is positioned far from the target:

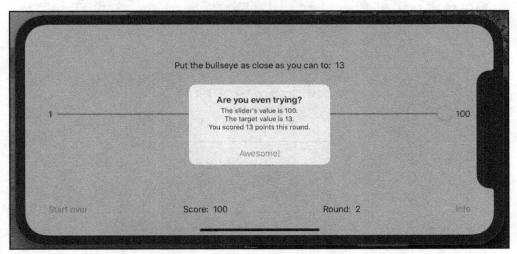

The alert pop-up, where the slider is way off the target, with the title 'Are you even trying?'

Here's the alert when the slider is fewer than 5 units away from the target:

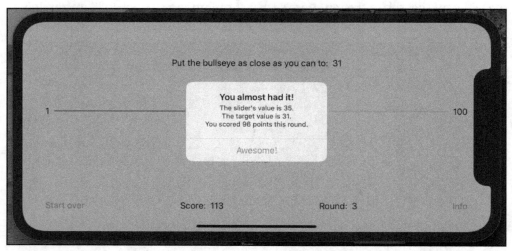

The alert pop-up, where the slider is 4 units away from the target, with the title 'You almost had it!'

And finally, if the player presses **Hit me!** after putting the slider a "not bad" distance (between 5 and 10 units) from the target, they see this:

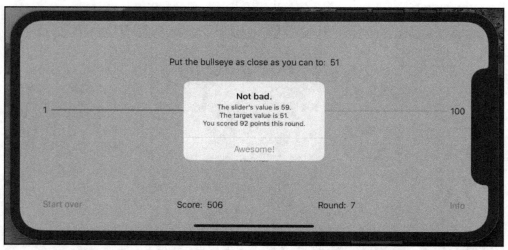

The alert pop-up, where the slider is 8 units away from the target, with the title 'Not bad.'

Bonus points

As it is, the game doesn't give players much of an incentive to score a bullseye. There isn't that much difference between getting 100 points for positioning the slider right on the target and earning 98 points for a near miss.

What if the game awarded bonuses for accuracy — say, 100 points for a bullseye and 50 points for being off by one?

Here's a flowchart showing the bonus process:

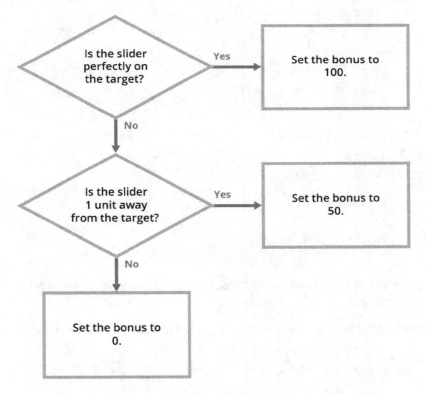

Flowchart illustrating how the bonus is determined

Exercise: Before you continue reading and look at the code that follows, think about how you'd implement this bonus rule.

The `pointsForCurrentRound()` method calculates how many points to award to the player, so it's probably where you should make the change.

➤ Update `pointsForCurrentRound()` to this:

```
func pointsForCurrentRound() -> Int {
  let maximumScore: Int = 100
  let difference = abs(self.sliderValueRounded - self.target)

  let bonus: Int
  if difference == 0 {
    bonus = 100
  } else if difference == 1 {
    bonus = 50
  } else {
    bonus = 0
  }

  return maximumScore - difference + bonus
}
```

Here's the code that determines if the player has earned a bonus:

```
let bonus: Int
if difference == 0 {
  bonus = 100
} else if difference == 1 {
  bonus = 50
} else {
  bonus = 0
}
```

The `let bonus: Int` line declares a constant named bonus, where the calculated bonus will be stored.

The `if` statement that follows has three different *clauses*. Here's the first one:

```
if difference == 0 {
  bonus = 100
```

It says that if the difference between the slider and the target is 0, set the value of bonus to 100.

Here's the `if` statement's second clause:

```
} else if difference == 1 {
  bonus = 50
```

If the first clause doesn't apply, but this one does, bonus is set to 50. The clause applies only if difference is equal to 1.

The else clause at the end handles all the other cases not handled by the first or second clause:

```
} else {
  bonus = 0
}
```

➤ Run the app to see if you can score some bonus points!

With the newly-added code for calculating a bonus score, here's what players will see when they position the slider perfectly at the target value:

The pop-up showing that the player got 200 points for positioning the slider perfectly

If they're off by one, they won't get the 100-point bonus, but they'll get the 50-point consolation bonus:

The pop-up showing that the player got 149 points for missing the target by one unit

More refactoring

Back in Chapter 4, I introduced you to the concept of refactoring. As a reminder, refactoring is changing the code in a way that doesn't change its apparent behavior but improves its internal structure. Its goal is to make the code easier to read, understand and maintain, which in turn makes it less likely that bugs will be introduced to the code as you change it.

Let's do some more refactoring now.

Refactoring the bonus algorithm

You may have noticed a couple of things about the bonus algorithm, either by looking carefully at its code or from playing the game and getting a perfect or off-by-one score:

- The player is always awarded 200 points for perfectly positioning the slider on the target value. This is because you can only get the 100-point bonus when you earn 100 points.

- If the player misses the target by one, they're always awarded 149 points. This comes from the fact that being off by one earns 99 points, and adding the 50-point bonus yields a not-quite-round 149 points.

Let's change the algorithm so that:

- If the slider value is equal to the target, give the player 200 points.

- If the slider value is not equal to the target but off by one, give the layer a nice round 150 points.

- If neither of the above applies, give the player the standard number of points, which is an arbitrary maximum value minus the difference between the slider value and the target value.

For those of you who like to think in pictures, here's the algorithm in flowchart form:

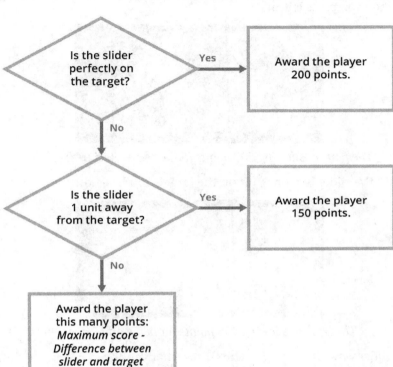

The pop-up showing that the player got 149 points for missing the target by one unit

➤ Let's implement this revised algorithm. Change `pointsForCurrentRound()` so that it looks like this:

```
func pointsForCurrentRound() -> Int {
  let maximumScore = 100
  let difference = abs(self.sliderValueRounded - self.target)

  let points: Int
  if difference == 0 {
    points = 200
  } else if difference == 1 {
    points = 150
  } else {
    points = maximumScore - difference
  }

  return points
}
```

➤ Run the app and try to put the slider right on the target value. You'll see this message when you press **Hit me!**:

The pop-up showing 200 points for perfectly placing the slider

➤ Try to put the slider just one unit off the target. You'll see this:

The pop-up showing 150 points for being off by one unit

➤ Set the slider way off the target, and this is what you'll get:

The pop-up showing the score being calculated the usual way

DRYing up the code

The `pointsForCurrentRound()` method calculates the number of points to award to the user by looking at the difference between the slider's value and the target. It does so with this line of code:

```
let difference: Int = abs(self.sliderValueRounded - self.target)
```

The `alertTitle()` method determines the title that appears in the alert pop-up based on the difference between the slider's value and the target. Here's the line of code that used to do this, and it should give you a sense of *déjà vu*:

```
let difference: Int = abs(self.sliderValueRounded - self.target)
```

This code isn't DRY — Don't Repeat Yourself — because we're repeating ourselves! You might even say that it's WET — Write Everything Twice!

If you decide to change the way that the difference between the slider value and the target is calculated, you'll have to change it in *two* places. This increases the likelihood that you might forget to update one of those places or introduce an error by unintentionally varying how the difference is calculated.

Let's remove this redundancy by calculating the difference between the slider and target in just once place. This can be done with a method or a computed property. Since the difference is a simple calculation based on two properties — `sliderValueRounded` and `target` — it makes sense to use a computed property.

➤ Add the following computed property to the end of the *User interface views* part of `ContentView`'s *Properties* section:

```
var sliderTargetDifference: Int {
  abs(self.sliderValueRounded - self.target)
}
```

➤ Now that you have this method, use it in `pointsForCurrentRound()`...

```
func pointsForCurrentRound() -> Int {
  let maximumScore = 100
  let points: Int
  if self.sliderTargetDifference == 0 {
    points = 200
  } else if self.sliderTargetDifference == 1 {
    points = 150
  } else {
    points = maximumScore - self.sliderTargetDifference
  }
  return points
}
```

➤ ...then use it in `alertTitle()`:

```
func alertTitle() -> String {
  let title: String
  if self.sliderTargetDifference == 0 {
    title = "Perfect!"
```

```
    } else if self.sliderTargetDifference < 5 {
      title = "You almost had it!"
    } else if self.sliderTargetDifference <= 10 {
      title = "Not bad."
    } else {
      title = "Are you even trying?"
    }
    return title
  }
```

➤ Run the app. It works, without any changes that the player will notice. Once again, you've improved the underlying code without affecting the user experience.

Starting over

The **Start over** button at the lower-left corner of the screen does nothing at the moment. Let's make it active! When the player presses it, the following should happen:

• The score should reset to 0.

• The round should reset to 1.

• The slider should return to its original midway position of 50.

• A new random target value between 1 and 100 inclusive should generate.

The code that does this should go into the action: parameter for the Button view for the **Start over** button. We could put some code directly in there, but the body variable is already pretty cluttered. Let's put the steps listed above into a method and then call that method from the action: parameter.

This method won't return a value; it will merely perform some actions. For this reason, we'll give it a name that describes what it does: startNewGame.

➤ Add the following method to the end of ContentView's *Methods* section:

```
func startNewGame() {
  self.score = 0
  self.round = 1
  self.sliderValue = 50.0
  self.target = Int.random(in: 1...100)
}
```

➤ Now that we have the `startNewGame()` method, let's use it. Scroll to the *Score row* section of the body variable and change it so that it looks like the following:

```
// Score row
HStack {
  Button(action: {
    self.startNewGame()
  }) {
    Text("Start over")
  }
  Spacer()
  Text("Score:")
  Text("\(self.score)")
  Spacer()
  Text("Round:")
  Text("\(self.round)")
  Spacer()
  Button(action: {}) {
    Text("Info")
  }
}
.padding(.bottom, 20)
```

➤ Run the app, play a round or two, and then press the **Start over** button. You'll start a new game, with the slider restored to its original position.

More DRYing

Just as we put the code for starting a new game into its own method to declutter the body variable, let's do the same for the code that starts a new round. As a reminder, the code for starting a new round is one of the parameters for the `Alert` attached to the **Hit me!** button:

```
Alert(title: Text(alertTitle()),
    message: Text(self.scoringMessage()),
    dismissButton: .default(Text("Awesome!")) {
        self.score = self.score + self.pointsForCurrentRound()
        self.target = Int.random(in: 1...100)
        self.round = self.round + 1
  })
```

Let's put the code from the last parameter listed above into its own method, which we'll name `startNewRound()`.

➤ Add the following method to the end of `ContentView`:

```
func startNewRound() {
  self.score = self.score + self.pointsForCurrentRound()
```

```
      self.round = self.round + 1
      self.sliderValue = 50.0
      self.target = Int.random(in: 1...100)
  }
```

Note we're also resetting the slider to the midpoint at the start of a new round. Just as we do when starting a new game.

➤ Let's make use of the startNewRound() method. Scroll to the *Button row* section of the body variable and change it so that it looks like the following:

```
// Button row
Button(action: {
  print("Points awarded: \(self.pointsForCurrentRound())")
  self.alertIsVisible = true
}) {
  Text("Hit me!")
}
.alert(isPresented: self.$alertIsVisible) {
  Alert(title: Text(alertTitle()),
        message: Text(self.scoringMessage()),
        dismissButton: .default(Text("Awesome!")) {
           self.startNewRound()
    })
}
```

➤ Run the app and play a couple of rounds to confirm that the changes you made are working properly.

The methods you most recently added, startNewGame() and startNewRound() are at the end of ContentView:

```
func startNewGame() {
  self.score = 0
  self.round = 1
  self.sliderValue = 50.0
  self.target = Int.random(in: 1...100)
}

func startNewRound() {
  self.score = self.score + self.pointsForCurrentRound()
  self.round = self.round + 1
  self.sliderValue = 50.0
  self.target = Int.random(in: 1...100)
}
```

Both startNewGame() and startNewRound() end with the same two lines! We can DRY up this code by taking those two lines and putting them in their own method.

➤ Change the methods to look like this:

```
func startNewGame() {
  self.score = 0
  self.round = 1
  self.resetSliderAndTarget()
}

func startNewRound() {
  self.score = self.score + self.pointsForCurrentRound()
  self.round = self.round + 1
  self.resetSliderAndTarget()
}

func resetSliderAndTarget() {
  self.sliderValue = 50.0
  self.target = Int.random(in: 1...100)
}
```

➤ Once again, run the app to confirm that the changes you made work properly.

Making the code less self-ish

If you look at the code you've written so far, you'll see the keyword `self` all over the place. What does `self` mean, anyway?

`self` is Swift's way of saying "the current object." In this case, that object is `ContentView`. Any time you've had to refer to one of `ContentView`'s properties, you've prefaced it with `self`. For example, to reset the slider's position back to 50, you did it with this code:

```
self.sliderValue = 50.0
```

This is how you say "Set the `sliderValue` property of the current object to 50.0" in Swift.

It's the same for calls to `ContentView`'s methods — you also prefaced them with `self`. For example, to call the method that resets the slider and target values, you did it with this code:

```
self.resetSliderAndTarget()
```

Most of the time, when referring to the properties or methods of an object from within that object, `self` isn't necessary. This is another one of those cases where Swift is smart enough to infer what you mean.

Let's declutter the code and make it easier to read (and therefore easier to maintain and expand upon) by removing the unnecessary instances of self. We'll start with the methods:

➤ Remove all the instances of self from the *Methods* section so that it looks like this:

```
// Methods
// ========

func pointsForCurrentRound() -> Int {
  let maximumScore = 100
  let points: Int
  if sliderTargetDifference == 0 {
    points = 200
  } else if sliderTargetDifference == 1 {
    points = 150
  } else {
    points = maximumScore - sliderTargetDifference
  }
  return points
}

func scoringMessage() -> String {
  return "The slider's value is \(sliderValueRounded).\n" +
         "The target value is \(target).\n" +
         "You scored \(pointsForCurrentRound()) points this
round."
}

func alertTitle() -> String {
  let title: String
  if sliderTargetDifference == 0 {
    title = "Perfect!"
  } else if sliderTargetDifference < 5 {
    title = "You almost had it!"
  } else if sliderTargetDifference <= 10 {
    title = "Not bad."
  } else {
    title = "Are you even trying?"
  }
  return title
}

func startNewGame() {
  score = 0
  round = 1
  resetSliderAndTarget()
}

func startNewRound() {
  score = score + pointsForCurrentRound()
```

```
  round = round + 1
  resetSliderAndTarget()
}

func resetSliderAndTarget() {
  sliderValue = 50.0
  target = Int.random(in: 1...100)
}
```

➤ Run the app to confirm that removing all those instances of `self` didn't break it.

Now it's time to work on the properties, starting with those that *aren't* body. That's a really big property, and we'll look at it on its own in a moment.

➤ Remove all the instances of `self` from the `User interface views` part of the *Properties* section so that it looks like this:

```
// User interface views
@State var alertIsVisible = false
@State var sliderValue = 50.0
@State var target = Int.random(in: 1...100)
var sliderValueRounded: Int {
  Int(sliderValue.rounded())
}
@State var score = 0
@State var round = 1
var sliderTargetDifference: Int {
  abs(sliderValueRounded - target)
}
```

➤ Once again, run the app to confirm that removing those additional instances of `self` didn't break it.

For the body property, let's work on it in sections.

➤ Remove any instances of `self` from the *Target row* and *Slider row* sections so that they look like this:

```
// Target row
HStack {
  Text("Put the bullseye as close as you can to:")
  Text("\(target)")
}

Spacer()

// Slider row
HStack {
  Text("1")
  Slider(value: $sliderValue, in: 1...100)
```

```
    Text("100")
}
```

➤ Run the app to confirm that it still works with these changes.

It's time to work on the *Button row* section. Here's what it looks like at the moment:

```
// Button row
Button(action: {
  self.alertIsVisible = true
}) {
  Text("Hit me!")
}
.alert(isPresented: self.$alertIsVisible) {
  Alert(title: Text(alertTitle()),
      message: Text(self.scoringMessage()),
      dismissButton: .default(Text("Awesome!")) {
        self.startNewRound()
      }
  )
}
```

➤ Change the button's `action:` parameter so that it no longer includes the `self` keyword:

```
// Button row
Button(action: {
  alertIsVisible = true
}) {
```

Within a second or two of making this change, Xcode shows this error message:

```
// Button row
Button(action: {
  alertIsVisible = true      ⊘  Reference to property 'alertIsVisible' in closure requires explicit 'self.' to make capture semantics explicit
}) {
```

Xcode shows an error message after you remove the first 'self' in the button row

The error message is cryptic: "Reference to property 'alertIsVisible' in closure requires explicit 'self.' to make capture semantics explicit." What does that mean?

The first unfamiliar word in the error message is *closure*. You could look up its meaning in Wikipedia, but it's so dense with esoteric computer science terminology that you might know *less* about closures after reading it!

Instead of worrying about what the technical definition of a closure is, think of closures as code that you can put into variables or pass to methods and functions to be executed at a later time. That's what the button's `action:` parameter is a closure: it's code for the button to execute whenever it's pressed.

As a closure, the code in the button's `action:` parameter isn't part of `ContentView`, but separate from it. That means that they have no sense of the object they may be in or any of its properties or methods. However, they *can* access — or, as Xcode puts it, *capture* — the local variables around them.

That's what the "capture" in the error message refers to. Inside an object, the `self` variable is available anywhere, and the closure captures it.

Simply put, closures need to use `self` when referring to the properties or methods of the object they're in.

➤ With what you now know about closures and `self` in mind, remove only those instances of `self` from the *Button row* section that aren't inside closures. The resulting code should look like this:

```
// Button row
Button(action: {
  print("Points awarded: \(self.pointsForCurrentRound())")
  self.alertIsVisible = true
}) {
  Text("Hit me!")
}
.alert(isPresented: $alertIsVisible) {
  Alert(title: Text(alertTitle()),
        message: Text(scoringMessage()),
        dismissButton: .default(Text("Awesome!")) {
            self.startNewRound()
    })
}
```

➤ Run the app to confirm that it still works with these changes.

> Note: In the beginning, it may not always be clear when you can drop the `self` keyword and when it's absolutely necessary to use it. Until you get the hang of it, you can always err on the side of *not* using `self` and rely on Xcode's error messages to tell you when you need to include it.

➤ And finally, remove any instances of `self` from the *Score row* section that aren't in closures. This should be the result:

```
// Score row
HStack {
  Button(action: {
    self.startNewGame()
  }) {
```

```
    Text("Start over")
  }
  Spacer()
  Text("Score:")
  Text("\(score)")
  Spacer()
  Text("Round:")
  Text("\(round)")
  Spacer()
  Button(action: {}) {
    Text("Info")
  }
}
.padding(.bottom, 20)
```

➤ Run the app to confirm that it still works with these changes.

You've now removed all the unnecessary instances of `self` from the code. It's much easier to read now!

A couple more enhancements

After so many "behind the scenes" changes, it's time for enhancements that the player *can* see! These will be easy to add, but they'll also enhance the player experience.

Randomizing the slider position at the start of each round

Rather than reset the slider to the midpoint at the start of each round, let's move it to a random position instead. Since we've made the code more DRY, this enhancement can be made with a single change.

➤ Update `resetSliderAndTarget()` to the following:

```
func resetSliderAndTarget() {
  sliderValue = Double.random(in: 1...100)
  target = Int.random(in: 1...100)
}
```

Remember that the slider is so precise that its values are `Double`, not `Int`. That's why its value is randomized using `Double.random()` instead of `Int.random()`.

Randomizing the slider position when the game launches

When the game launches, the target and slider values are determined by their initial values, which are set when their variables are declared:

- The slider is set to 50.0.

- The target is set to a random whole number between 1 and 100 inclusive.

After the very first round, the game uses the `resetSliderAndTarget()` method to set the slider and target values. `resetSliderAndTarget()` is called by two different methods:

- `startNewRound()`: Called when the player dismisses the alert pop-up.

- `startNewGame()`: Called when the player presses the **Start over** button.

To make the game more consistent, it should call `startNewGame()` when the game launches. Luckily, there's a way to do that.

Every `View` object has a built-in set of methods that get called when certain view-related events happen. One of these events is when the view first appears. The method that gets called when this happens is called `onAppear()`. You provide `onAppear()` with the code that should be executed when the view appears.

All the onscreen elements in the game appear when the game launches, so you can use the `onAppear()` method for any of the views in `ContentView`'s body property. Since the `VStack` in body acts as the container for all the onscreen elements, we'll use its `onAppear()` method.

The call to `onAppear()` will look like this:

```
.onAppear() {
  self.startNewGame()
}
```

It will be called only once: the very first time that the `VStack` is drawn on the screen, which will happen only when the game is launched.

➤ Change the end of body so that it looks like this. I've included a lot of the surrounding code so because it can be hard to tell where the code should go:

```
// Score row
HStack {
```

```
        Button(action: {
          self.startNewGame()
        }) {
          Text("Start over")
        }
        Spacer()
        Text("Score:")
        Text("\(score)")
        Spacer()
        Text("Round:")
        Text("\(round)")
        Spacer()
        Button(action: {}) {
          Text("Info")
        }
      }
      .padding(.bottom, 20)
    }
    .onAppear() {
      self.startNewGame()
    }
  }

  // Methods
  // =======
```

➤ Run the app. The slider position will now be randomized at the very start, instead of always starting at 50.0.

Key points

In this chapter, you did the following:

- You enhanced the message that appears when the player does particularly well.

- You also made improvements to the way points and bonuses are awarded.

- You enabled the **Start over** button.

- You did a fair bit of refactoring, which included removing redundant and unnecessary code.

- You learned about closures.

- You learned about views' onAppear() method and used it to automatically perform a task when the app is first launched.

At this point, *Bullseye* is pretty polished, and your task list is getting shorter. In the next chapter, you'll transform the game from its plain look and feel into something a little more polished.

You can find the project files for the current version of the app under **06 - Refactoring** in the Source Code folder.

Chapter 7: The New Look

Joey deVilla

Bullseye is looking good! The gameplay elements are complete and there's one item left in your to-do list: "Make it look pretty."

As satisfying as it was to get the game working, it's far from pretty. If you were to put it on the App Store in its current form, very few people would get excited to download it. Fortunately, iOS and SwiftUI make it easy for you to create good-looking apps. So, let's give *Bullseye* a makeover and add some visual flair.

This chapter covers the following:

- **Landscape orientation revisited**: Making changes to the project to improve its support for landscape oreintation.

- **Spicing up the graphics**: Adding custom graphics to the app's user interface to give it a more polished look.

- **The "About" screen**: It's time to make the "Info" button work, which means that pressing it should take the player to *Bullseye's* "About" screen.

Landscape orientation revisited

Let's revisit another item in the to-do list — "Put the app in landscape orientation." Didn't you already do this?

You did! By changing the project settings so that the app supported only the **Landscape Left** and **Landscape Right** orientations. There's one last bit of cleaning up that you need to do to make landscape orientation support complete.

Apps in landscape mode don't display the iPhone status bar — the display at the top of the screen — unless you tell them to. That's great for *Bullseye*. Games require a more immersive experience and the status bar detracts from that.

The system automatically handles hiding the status bar for your game. But, you can improve the way *Bullseye* handles the status bar by making sure that it's always hidden, even when the app is launching.

➤ Go to the **Project Settings** screen and scroll down to **Deployment Info**. In the section marked **Status Bar Style**, check **Hide status bar**.

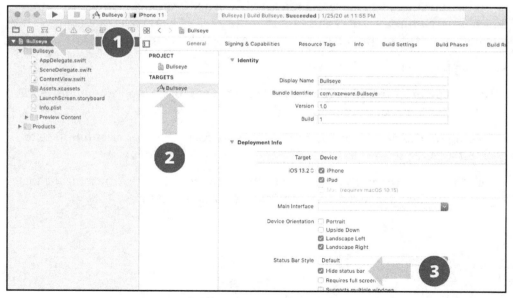

Hiding the status bar when the app launches

It's a good idea to hide the status bar while the app is launching. It takes a few seconds for the operating system to load the app into memory and start it up. During that time the status bar remains visible unless you hide it using this option.

It's only a small detail, but the difference between a mediocre app and a great one is the small details.

➤ That's it! Run the app and you'll see that the status bar is history.

Info.plist

Most of the options from the **Project Settings** screen, such as the supported device orientations and whether the status bar is visible during launch, are stored in a configuration file called **Info.plist**.

The information in **Info.plist** tells iOS how the app will behave. It also describes certain characteristics of the app that don't fit anywhere else. Such as the app's version number.

In earlier versions of Xcode, you often had to edit **Info.plist** by hand. This was a tedious and sometimes error-prone process. With the latest versions of Xcode, this is hardly necessary anymore. You can make most of the changes directly from the **Project Settings** screen.

Even with the changes to Xcode that minimize the amount of time you have to work directly with **Info.plist**, it's still good to know of its existence and what it looks like.

➤ Go to the **Project navigator** and select the file named **Info.plist** to take a peek at its contents.

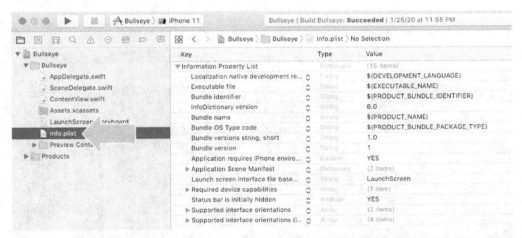

The **Info.plist** file is a list of configuration options and their values. Most of these may not make sense to you, but that's OK. They don't always make sense to many experienced developers either.

Notice the option **Status bar is initially hidden**. It has the value YES. This is the option that you just changed.

Spicing up the graphics

Getting rid of the status bar is only the first step. We want to go from this...

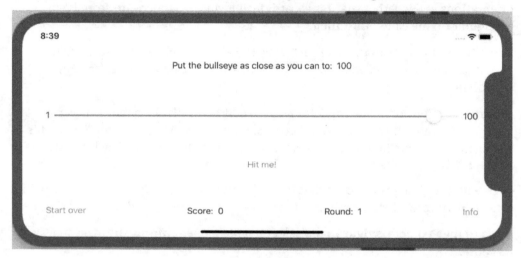

Yawn...

...to something that's more like this:

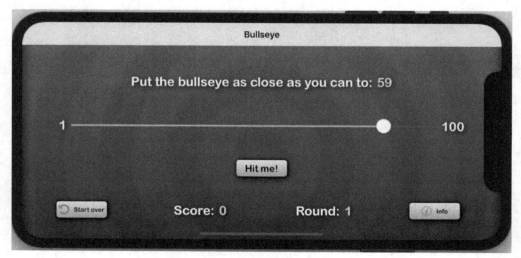

How the app will look in the end

The actual controls won't change. You'll simply be using images to spruce up their look. You'll also adjust the user interface's colors and typefaces.

You can put an image in the background, on the buttons, and even on the slider, to customize the appearance of each. The images you use should generally be in PNG format, though JPG files would work too.

Adding the image assets

If you're artistically challenged, then don't worry: we've provided a set of images for you. But if you do have *mad Photoshop skillz,* then by all means feel free to design and use your own images.

The **Resources** folder that comes with this book contains a subfolder named **Images**. You'll import these images into the Xcode project.

➤ In the **Project navigator**, find **Assets.xcassets** and click on it.

This item is the app's *asset catalog*, which stores all the images that go into it. Right now, it's empty and contains a placeholder for the app icon. You'll add an icon and images soon:

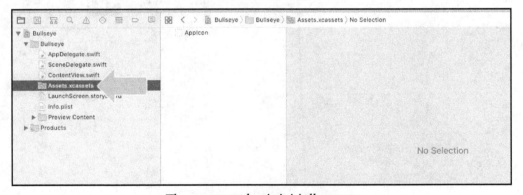

The asset catalog is initially empty

➤ Open the **Resources** folder that comes with this book, the open the subfolder named **Images**. Drag the files within into the Xcode project:

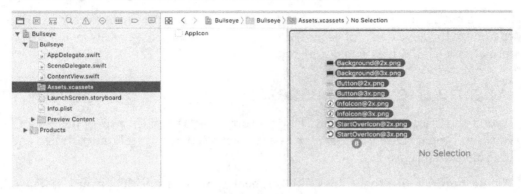

Dragging files into the asset catalog

Xcode will copy all the image files from the **images** folder into the project's asset catalog:

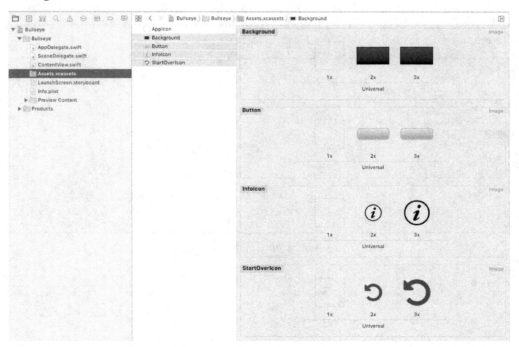

The images are now inside the asset catalog

> **Note**: If Xcode added a folder named **Images** instead of the individual image files, then try again. This time, make sure that you drag the files inside the **Images** folder into Xcode rather than the folder itself.

1x, 2x, and 3x displays

For each image you dragged into the asset catalog, you created an **image set**. Image sets allow an app to support different devices with different screen resolutions. Each image set has a slot for the **1x**, **2x** and **3x** version of the image:

- **1x** images are for low-resolution screens, with pixels that seem big and chunky by today's standards. Only the first iPhones — the original, 2G, 3G, and 3GS — have these screens. None of these devices can run a version of iOS released after 2012. You're pretty unlikely to write apps that use **1x** graphics.

- **2x** images are for high-resolution Retina screens. As the name implies, they're drawn with twice the number of pixels as a **1x** image. A wide range of iPhones — from the iPhone 4 through 8 and the iPhone 11 — and iPads and late-model iPods these screens.

- **3x** images are for high-resolution Retina HD screens, which come with the iPhone X, the iPhones that followed, and any iPhone with a "+" in its name. These images are drawn with three times the number of pixels as a **1x** image.

When an app displays an image, iOS tries to use the version of the image that best matches the device's screen resolution. If that's not available, it uses the next best version.

When you dragged the images into the asset catalog, Xcode used their filenames to determine which image set and slot to drop them into. For example, the images in the **Background@2x.png** and **Background@3.png** files go into the **Background** image set. The **Background@2x.png** image goes into the **2x** slot and the **Background@3x.png** image goes into the **3x** slot. Had there been a **Background.png** file, it would go into the **Background** image set's **1x** slot. Any file whose name doesn't end with **2x** or **3x** is assumed to be a **1x** image.

If you'd rather determine which images are **1x**, **2x** and **3x**, you can also drag and drop invididual images into their respective slots.

Putting up the wallpaper

Let's begin by replacing *Bullseye*'s drab white background with the more appealing
Background image that you added to the app's asset catalog:

SwiftUI makes it easy to change the background of any view. This is done using
view's background() method, which lets you specify another view to use as the
background. In this case, we'll create an Image view containing the **Background**
image asset and use it as the background for the main screen.

Remember that ContentView's body property contains all the user interface
elements on the app's screen. If you look at its contents, you can see that it contains
a VStack. This, in turn, contains all other user interface elements:

```
var body: some View {
  VStack {
    Spacer()

    // Target row
...
```

We'll use the background() method of this VStack to set its background image.

➤ Scroll to the end of the VStack at the end of the body property and change it so
that it looks like this. Add the call to the VStack's background() method on the line
after the call the onAppear() method:

```
    // Score row
    HStack {
      Button(action: {
        self.startNewGame()
```

```
    }) {
        Text("Start over")
    }
    Spacer()
    Text("Score:")
    Text("\(self.score)")
    Spacer()
    Text("Round:")
    Text("\(self.round)")
    Spacer()
    Button(action: {}) {
        Text("Info")
    }
    }
    .padding(.bottom, 20)
    }
    .onAppear() {
        self.startNewGame()
    }
    .background(Image("Background"))
}
```

The line of code that you just added, `.background(Image("Background"))`, creates an `Image` view and fills it with the appropriate **Background** image from the asset catalog. This is either the **2x** or **3x** version, depending on the device it's running on. The code then makes it the background view for the `VStack`.

➤ Let's see what this code does. Run the app.

Here's what the app looks like on the Simulator when it's simulating the iPhone 11, which uses the **3x** background:

The 3x background on the iPhone 11

Let's try the app on a smaller device without the "notch". We'll use the iPhone 8, which uses the **2x** background.

➤ Select **iPhone 8** and run the app:

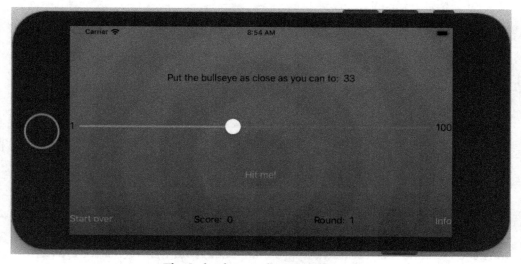

The 2x background on the iPhone 8

That takes care of the background. Let's work on the text.

Changing the text

Now that *Bullseye* has its new background image, the black text is now nearly illegible. We'll need to change it so that it stands out better. Once again, we'll use some built-in methods to change the text's appearance so that it's legible against the background. Let's start with the "Put the bullseye as close as you can to:" and target value text.

➤ Scroll to the part of the body property marked *Target row* and change it so that it becomes the following:

```
// Target row
HStack {
  Text("Put the bullseye as close as you can to:")
    .font(Font.custom("Arial Rounded MT Bold", size: 18))
    .foregroundColor(Color.white)
    .shadow(color: Color.black, radius: 5, x: 2, y: 2)
  Text("\(target)")
    .font(Font.custom("Arial Rounded MT Bold", size: 24))
    .foregroundColor(Color.yellow)
```

```
        .shadow(color: Color.black, radius: 5, x: 2, y: 2)
  }
```

On both Text objects, three methods are being called in a chain:

- font(), which specifies the typeface that the Text object should use. It expects a Font object, and we're using its custom method to create one with a specified typeface — Arial Rounded MT Bold — and size in points. We'll make the target value a little bigger for emphasis. font()'s output is a new Text object in the specified typeface, which is then immediately fed to…

- foregroundColor(), which specifies the color that the Text object should be. It expects a Color object. We're using two built-in values: Color.white for the instruction text and Color.yellow for the target value text. Its output is a Text object in the new color, which is passed to…

- shadow(), which draws a shadow behind the Text object. It expects the size of the shadow's radius (how far it spreads) and its x and y-offsets in points. Its output is a Text object with a shadow, and this is the object that's drawn onscreen.

➤ Switch the Simulator back to **iPhone 11** and run the app. You should be able to read the instructions and the target value now:

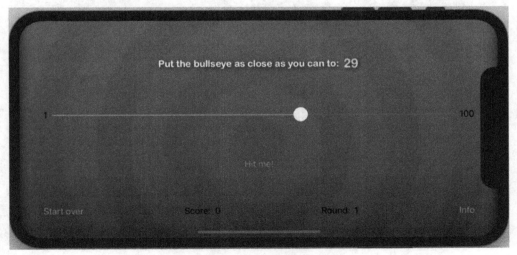

The target row, with styled text

Let's apply similar changes to the "1" and "100" on either side of the slider.

➤ Scroll to the part of the body property marked *Slider row* and change it so that it becomes the following:

```
// Slider row
HStack {
  Text("1")
    .font(Font.custom("Arial Rounded MT Bold", size: 18))
    .foregroundColor(Color.white)
    .shadow(color: Color.black, radius: 5, x: 2, y: 2)
  Slider(value: $sliderValue, in: 1...100)
  Text("100")
    .font(Font.custom("Arial Rounded MT Bold", size: 18))
    .foregroundColor(Color.white)
    .shadow(color: Color.black, radius: 5, x: 2, y: 2)
}
```

➤ Run the app. The numbers on either side of the slider should be legible:

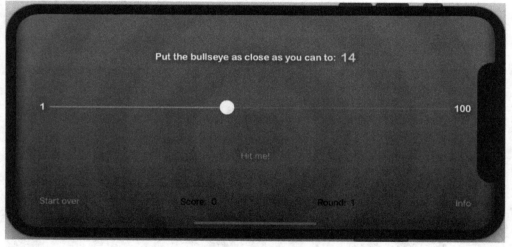

The target and slider rows, with styled text

At the bottom of the screen are the text elements that display the score and round. We'll give this row the same treatment as the target row: white text for titles, and larger yellow text for values.

➤ Scroll to the part of the body property marked *Score row* and change it so that it becomes the following:

```
// Score row
HStack {
  Button(action: {
    self.startNewGame()
  }) {
```

```
    Text("Start over")
  }
  Spacer()
  Text("Score:")
    .font(Font.custom("Arial Rounded MT Bold", size: 18))
    .foregroundColor(Color.white)
    .shadow(color: Color.black, radius: 5, x: 2, y: 2)
  Text("\(score)")
    .font(Font.custom("Arial Rounded MT Bold", size: 24))
    .foregroundColor(Color.yellow)
    .shadow(color: Color.black, radius: 5, x: 2, y: 2)
  Spacer()
  Text("Round")
    .font(Font.custom("Arial Rounded MT Bold", size: 18))
    .foregroundColor(Color.white)
    .shadow(color: Color.black, radius: 5, x: 2, y: 2)
  Text("\(round)")
    .font(Font.custom("Arial Rounded MT Bold", size: 24))
    .foregroundColor(Color.yellow)
    .shadow(color: Color.black, radius: 5, x: 2, y: 2)
  Spacer()
  Button(action: {}) {
    Text("Info")
  }
}
.padding(.bottom, 20)
```

➤ Run the app to see all the text changes. It will look like this:

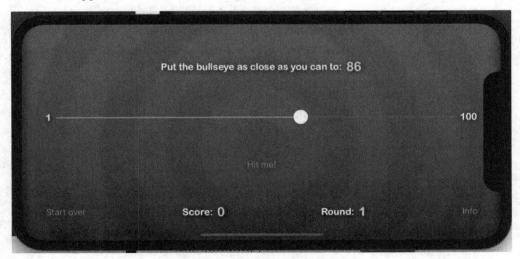

The app, with all its text styled

The app's looking a lot better now. Let's work on those buttons next!

Making the buttons look like buttons

Let's make the buttons look more like buttons.

Just as we used the background() method to change the background of the VStack that contains the app's user interface, we'll do the same for the buttons. We'll do so by using each Button view's background() method and the image in the asset catalog named **Button**:

The button image

We'll also use the font() and color() methods of the Text objects contained within those buttons to customize their typeface and color, and the shadow() method on the button's Image object.

Let's update the appearance of the **Hit me!** button with the button background image and the Arial Rounded MT Bold typeface at size 18.

➤ Scroll to the part of the body property marked *Button row* and change it so that it becomes the following:

```
// Button row
Button(action: {
  print("Points awarded: \(self.pointsForCurrentRound())")
  self.alertIsVisible = true
}) {
  Text("Hit me!")
    .font(Font.custom("Arial Rounded MT Bold", size: 18))
    .foregroundColor(Color.black)
}
.background(Image("Button")
  .shadow(color: Color.black, radius: 5, x: 2, y: 2)
)
.alert(isPresented: $alertIsVisible) {
  Alert(title: Text(alertTitle()),
      message: Text(scoringMessage()),
      dismissButton: .default(Text("Awesome!")) {
        self.startNewRound()
  })
}
```

➤ Run the app to see the **Hit me!** button's new look:

The 'Hit me!' button's mew look

You're probably getting physically and mentally tired from all that typing, especially since you've been entering the same code over and over. Let's do something about that.

Introducing ViewModifier

If you look at body in its current state, you'll see a lot of repetition. For starters, there are *five* instances where the following methods are called on a Text view:

```
.font(Font.custom("Arial Rounded MT Bold", size: 18))
.foregroundColor(Color.white)
```

There are also *three* instances where the following methods are called on a Text view:

```
.font(Font.custom("Arial Rounded MT Bold", size: 24))
.foregroundColor(Color.yellow)
```

And there are *nine* instances where this method is called on Text and Image views to give it a shadow:

```
.shadow(color: Color.black, radius: 5, x: 2, y: 2)
```

If there was some way to DRY up body's code and put these repeated calls to these methods into a package that can be called again and again, it might help the compiler get past its stumbling block.

Fortunately for us, there *is* a way: The ViewModifier protocol. Remember the definition for "protocol" from a couple of chapters back: It's a set of properties and methods that an object agrees to include as part of its code.

The ViewModifier protocol states that any object that adopts it agrees to furnish a method named body(), which accepts some content. That content can then have a number of calls to any number of `View` methods made on it. We're going to create some objects that adopt the `ViewModifier` protocol and use them to create packages of methods that we'll use to style different parts of the user interface.

It might be easier to show you how to use `ViewModifier` instead of explaining it.

➤ Add the following in the space between the end of `ContentView` and the start of the preview code:

```
// View modifiers
// ===============

struct LabelStyle: ViewModifier {
  func body(content: Content) -> some View {
    content
      .font(Font.custom("Arial Rounded MT Bold", size: 18))
      .foregroundColor(Color.white)
      .shadow(color: Color.black, radius: 5, x: 2, y: 2)
  }
}
```

The most important part of this object it its `body()` method. The `body()` method accepts a single piece of information, `content`, which contains the content of the view that called it. It then calls a set of specified methods on that content.

In the case of `LabelStyle`, it calls the `font()`, `foregroundColor()` and `shadow()` methods on the content to change its font to Arial Rounded MT Bold with a size of 18 points, its color to white and with a shadow. We'll use this to style the `Text` objects that display the instructions, as well as the labels for the slider, score, and number of rounds.

➤ Add the following in the space between the end of `LabelStyle` and the start of the preview code:

```
struct ValueStyle: ViewModifier {
  func body(content: Content) -> some View {
    content
      .font(Font.custom("Arial Rounded MT Bold", size: 24))
      .foregroundColor(Color.yellow)
      .shadow(color: Color.black, radius: 5, x: 2, y: 2)
  }
}
```

`ValueStyle` is almost identical to `LabelStyle`. The key difference is its calls to `font()` and `foregroundColor()` change the content's font to Arial Rounded MT Bold with a size of 24 points, and its color to yellow. We'll use this to style the `Text` objects that display the game values: the target, score, and number of rounds.

If you've done some web development, this should feel familiar. It's not all that different from defining a CSS style.

Now that we have these two objects that adopt the ViewModifier protocol — LabelStyle and ValueStyle — we can use them to style the views in ContentView's body property.

➤ Change the *Target row* section of ContentView's body property to the following:

```
// Target row
HStack {
  Text("Put the bullseye as close as you can
to:").modifier(LabelStyle())
  Text("\(target)").modifier(ValueStyle())
}
```

The code's a lot simpler! Instead of calling a chain of font(), foregroundColor() and shadow methods on the Text objects in this row, we're using View's modifier() method to style them. The modifier() method takes a single argument — an object that has adopted the ViewModifier protocol — and uses that object to style its View.

In the code above, `modifier()` uses `LabelStyle` to style the "Put the bullseye as close as you can to:" text, and `ValueStyle` to style the displayed value of `target`.

➤ Change the *Slider row* section of `ContentView`'s body property to the following:

```
// Slider row
HStack {
  Text("1").modifier(LabelStyle())
  Slider(value: $sliderValue, in: 1...100)
  Text("100").modifier(LabelStyle())
}
```

Again, we're using `modifier()` and `LabelStyle`, this time to style the text on either side of the slider. This leaves us with one more row to update.

➤ Change the *Score row* section of `ContentView`'s body property to the following:

```
// Score row
HStack {
  Button(action: {
    self.startNewGame()
  }) {
    Text("Start over")
  }
  Spacer()
  Text("Score:").modifier(LabelStyle())
  Text("\(score)").modifier(ValueStyle())
  Spacer()
  Text("Round").modifier(LabelStyle())
  Text("\(round)").modifier(ValueStyle())
  Spacer()
  Button(action: {}) {
    Text("Info")
  }
}
.padding(.bottom, 20)
```

➤ It's time to see if all these changes worked. Run the app. You'll see that all the text and button styling has taken effect:

Some refactoring and more styling

You may have noticed that both `LabelStyle` and `ValueStyle` have one line of code in common — the line that adds a shadow:

```
.shadow(color: Color.black, radius: 5, x: 2, y: 2)
```

You also may have noticed that this method is also called on the `Image` views inside the `Button` views. This repetition suggests that we do some DRYing and put this code in a single place where we can call it. It's time to create a `ViewModifier` for shadows!

➤ Add the following after `ValueStyle` and before the start of the preview code:

```
struct Shadow: ViewModifier {
  func body(content: Content) -> some View {
    content
      .shadow(color: Color.black, radius: 5, x: 2, y: 2)
  }
}
```

Before we continue, take a look at the signature of the body method of every `ViewModifier` object:

```
func body(content: Content) -> some View
```

This says that the body method returns either a `View` or something that behaves like a `View`. If you couple this with the fact that `View` objects use `ViewModifier` objects by way of the `modifier()` method, it means that `ViewModifiers` can use other `ViewModifiers`!

➤ Change `LabelStyle` and `ValueStyle` so that they incorporate `Shadow`:

```
struct LabelStyle: ViewModifier {
  func body(content: Content) -> some View {
    content
      .font(Font.custom("Arial Rounded MT Bold", size: 18))
      .foregroundColor(Color.white)
      .modifier(Shadow())
  }
}

struct ValueStyle: ViewModifier {
  func body(content: Content) -> some View {
    content
      .font(Font.custom("Arial Rounded MT Bold", size: 24))
      .foregroundColor(Color.yellow)
      .modifier(Shadow())
```

```
    }
  }
```

➤ Run the app to confirm that these changes work.

Now that there's a `ViewModifier` for shadows, we can use it on the button image in the button row.

➤ Scroll to the part of the body property marked *Button row* and change it so that it becomes the following:

```
// Button row
Button(action: {
  print("Points awarded: \(self.pointsForCurrentRound())")
  self.alertIsVisible = true
}) {
  Text("Hit me!")
    .font(Font.custom("Arial Rounded MT Bold", size: 18))
    .foregroundColor(Color.black)
}
.background(Image("Button")
  .modifier(Shadow())
)
.alert(isPresented: $alertIsVisible) {
  Alert(title: Text(alertTitle()),
        message: Text(scoringMessage()),
        dismissButton: .default(Text("Awesome!")) {
            self.startNewRound()
    })
}
```

It's time to make the buttons in the score row look like buttons, complete with shadows.

➤ Scroll to the part of the body property marked *Score row* and change it so that it becomes the following:

```
// Score row
HStack {
  Button(action: {
    self.startNewGame()
  }) {
    Text("Start over")
  }
  .background(Image("Button")
    .modifier(Shadow())
  )
  Spacer()
  Text("Score:").modifier(LabelStyle())
  Text("\(score)").modifier(ValueStyle())
```

```
  Spacer()
  Text("Round").modifier(LabelStyle())
  Text("\(round)").modifier(ValueStyle())
  Spacer()
  Button(action: {}) {
    Text("Info")
  }
  .background(Image("Button")
    .modifier(Shadow())
  )
}
.padding(.bottom, 20)
```

➤ Run the app and marvel at its complete set of buttons:

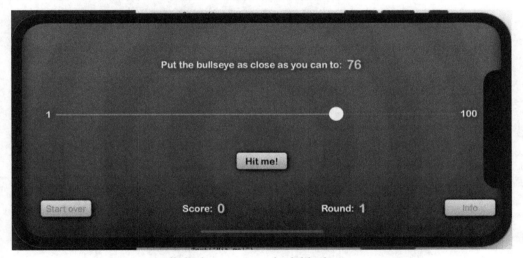

All the buttons now look like buttons

Let's create some ViewModifiers for the button text. We'll create one with larger text called ButtonLargeTextStyle for the **Hit me!** button, and one with smaller text called ButtonSmallTextStyle for the **Start over** and **Info** buttons.

➤ Add the following after Shadow and before the start of the preview code:

```
struct ButtonLargeTextStyle: ViewModifier {
  func body(content: Content) -> some View {
    content
      .font(Font.custom("Arial Rounded MT Bold", size: 18))
      .foregroundColor(Color.black)
  }
}

struct ButtonSmallTextStyle: ViewModifier {
```

```
func body(content: Content) -> some View {
  content
    .font(Font.custom("Arial Rounded MT Bold", size: 12))
    .foregroundColor(Color.black)
  }
}
```

With these new ViewModifiers, we can style the button text.

➤ Scroll to the part of the body property marked *Button row* and update it to the following:

```
// Button row
Button(action: {
  print("Points awarded: \(self.pointsForCurrentRound())")
  self.alertIsVisible = true
}) {
  Text("Hit me!").modifier(ButtonLargeTextStyle())
}
.background(Image("Button")
  .modifier(Shadow())
)
.alert(isPresented: $alertIsVisible) {
  Alert(title: Text(alertTitle()),
        message: Text(scoringMessage()),
        dismissButton: .default(Text("Awesome!")) {
          self.startNewRound()
    })
}
```

➤ Scroll to the part of the body property marked *Score row* and update it to the following:

```
// Score row
HStack {
  Button(action: {
    self.startNewGame()
  }) {
    Text("Start over").modifier(ButtonSmallTextStyle())
  }
  .background(Image("Button")
    .modifier(Shadow())
  )
  Spacer()
  Text("Score:").modifier(LabelStyle())
  Text("\(score)").modifier(ValueStyle())
  Spacer()
  Text("Round").modifier(LabelStyle())
  Text("\(round)").modifier(ValueStyle())
  Spacer()
  Button(action: {}) {
```

```
      Text("Info").modifier(ButtonSmallTextStyle())
    }
    .background(Image("Button")
      .modifier(Shadow())
    )
  }
  .padding(.bottom, 20)
```

➤ Run the app. It's looking pretty nice now!

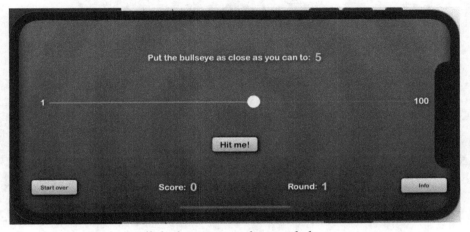

All the buttons now have styled text

Putting images inside buttons

Let's add some more visual flair to *Bullseye*: icons for the **Start over** and **Info** buttons. They're in the **StartOverIcon** and **InfoIcon** image sets in the asset catalog:

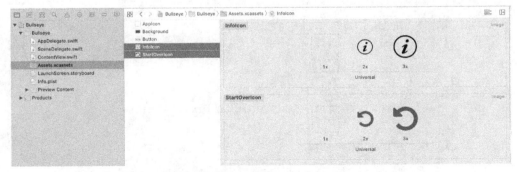

InfoIcon and StartOverIcon in the asset catalog

Button objects are a kind of View, and like all views, they can contain other views. This makes it possible to create buttons that contain more than a single line of text.

We'll customize the **Start over** button by combining an `Image` view and a `Text` view inside an `HStack`, as shown below:

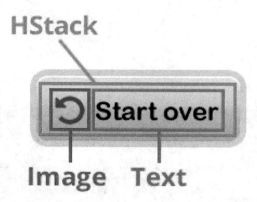

➤ Change the *Score row* section of `ContentView`'s body property to the following:

```
// Score row
HStack {
  Button(action: {
    self.startNewGame()
  }) {
    HStack {
      Image("StartOverIcon")
      Text("Start over").modifier(ButtonSmallTextStyle())
    }
  }
  .background(Image("Button")
    .modifier(Shadow())
  )
  Spacer()
  Text("Score:").modifier(LabelStyle())
  Text("\(score)").modifier(ValueStyle())
  Spacer()
  Text("Round").modifier(LabelStyle())
  Text("\(round)").modifier(ValueStyle())
  Spacer()
  Button(action: {}) {
    HStack {
      Image("InfoIcon")
      Text("Info").modifier(ButtonSmallTextStyle())
    }
  }
  .background(Image("Button")
    .modifier(Shadow())
  )
}
.padding(.bottom, 20)
```

➤ Run the app to see the changes:

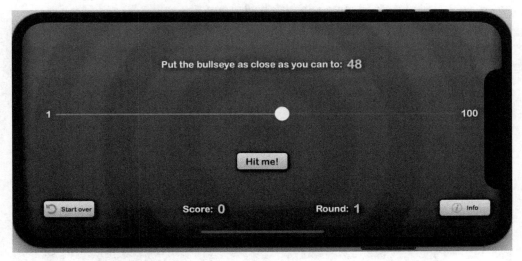

Adding accent colors

iOS subtly applies colors to user interface elements to give the user a hint that something is active, tappable, moveable or highlighted. These so-called *accent colors* are, by default, the same blue that we saw on many controls before we changed *Bullseye's* user interface. Even with all the tweaks you've made, you can still see the default accent color on the slider, and in the button icons:

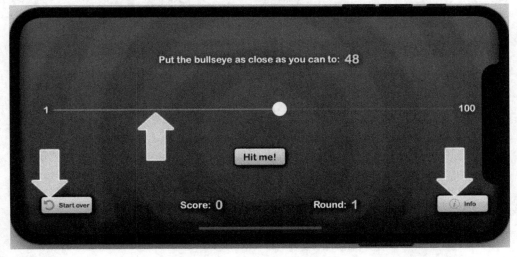

You can change a view's accent color, along with the accent color of any views it contains, using the `accentColor()` method. Let's change the slider's accent color to green, which should stand out against its background.

➤ Change the *Score row* section of `ContentView`'s body property to the following:

```
// Slider row
HStack {
  Text("1").modifier(LabelStyle())
  Slider(value: $sliderValue, in: 1...100)
    .accentColor(Color.green)
  Text("100").modifier(LabelStyle())
}
```

➤ Run the app. You'll now see the slider's accent color, which highlights the left side of its track, is now green:

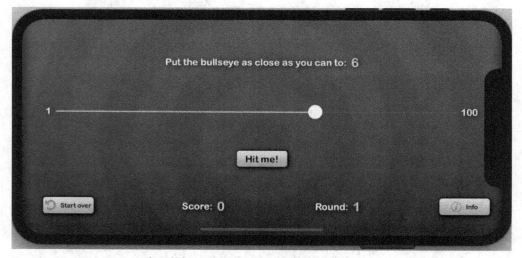

The slider, with its new custom accent color

You're not limited to using pre-defined colors. Let's create a custom color, midnight blue, and use it as the accent color for the **Start over** and **Info** buttons.

First, we need to define what midnight blue is. If you're familiar with web development, you probably know the RGB (red, green and blue) color model. If not, you specify colors as a combination of three numbers representing red, green and blue on a scale of 0 through 255.

We'll define midnight blue as this color:

Midnight blue

In web development, you specify RGB colors as a set of three hexadecimal (base 16) numbers. The color we're calling midnight blue is defined by these values:

- **red**: 0 in hexadecimal, which is also 0 in decimal.

- **green**: 33 in hexadecimal, which is 51 in decimal.

- **blue**: 66 in hexadecimal, which is 102 in decimal.

When you instantiate a Color object in SwiftUI, it expects to get the values for red, green and blue on a scale of 0 to 1. Converting the decimal values for midnight blue to this scale is simple: Divide each one by 255, which gives us:

- **red**: 0

- **green**: 0.2

- **blue**: 0.4

First, you need to define midnight blue.

➤ Add the following to the start of ContentView, just before the *Game stats* properties:

```
// Colors
let midnightBlue = Color(red: 0,
                         green: 0.2,
                         blue: 0.4)
```

Now that we have defined midnightBlue, let's apply it to the HStack containing the score row. This will set the accent color for all the views contained within.

➤ Change the *Score row* section of `ContentView`'s body property to the following:

```
// Score row
HStack {
  Button(action: {
    self.startNewGame()
  }) {
    HStack {
      Image("StartOverIcon")
      Text("Start over").modifier(ButtonSmallTextStyle())
    }
  }
  .background(Image("Button")
    .modifier(Shadow())
  )
  Spacer()
  Text("Score:").modifier(LabelStyle())
  Text("\(score)").modifier(ValueStyle())
  Spacer()
  Text("Round").modifier(LabelStyle())
  Text("\(round)").modifier(ValueStyle())
  Spacer()
  Button(action: {}) {
    HStack {
      Image("InfoIcon")
      Text("Info").modifier(ButtonSmallTextStyle())
    }
  }
  .background(Image("Button")
    .modifier(Shadow())
  )
}
.padding(.bottom, 20)
.accentColor(midnightBlue)
```

➤ Run the app. The accent color for the **Start over** and **Info** buttons is now midnight blue.

The "About" screen

Your game looks awesome and your to-do list is done. Does this mean that you are done with *Bullseye*?

Not so fast! Remember the **Info** button at the lower right corner of the screen? Try tapping it. Does it do anything? No?

Ooops! Looks as if we forgot to add any functionality to that button! It's time to rectify that — let's add an "About" screen to the game. It'll appear whenever the player presses **Info**.

Here's what it will look like at the end:

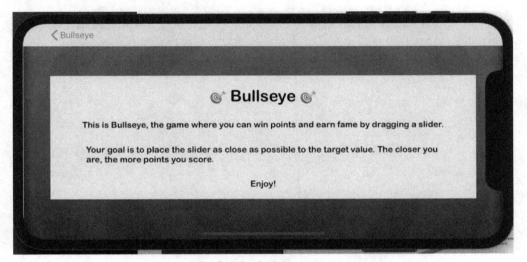

The finished About screen

Most apps, even very simple games, have more than one screen. This is as good a time as any to learn how to add additional screens to your apps.

It's worth repeating: The term "view" can refer to any element on a screen in an app, but also the screen itself. Views can contain other views, and the screen is a view that contains all the views on that screen.

ContentView is the name that Xcode assigns to the single view (or screen) when it creates a single view app. When Xcode created it, it also created the file that contains it: **ContentView.swift**.

Xcode makes it easy to create additional views and their containing files. Let's

Xcode automatically created the main `ViewController` object for you. But you'll have to create the view controller for the About screen yourself. Fortunately, it's pretty easy to do this.

Adding a new view

➤ Go to Xcode's **File** menu and choose **New ▸ File…**. In the window that pops up, choose the **SwiftUI Views** template (if you don't see it then make sure **iOS** is selected at the top).

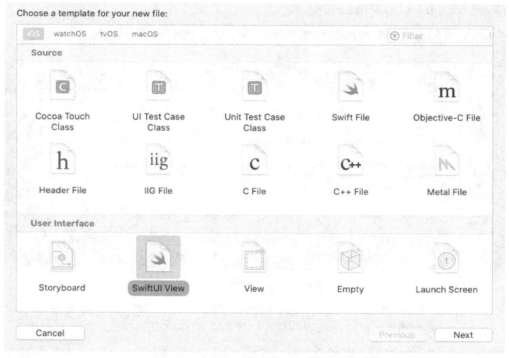

Choosing the file template for SwiftUI View

➤ Click **Next**. Xcode will ask you what to name this new view file and where to save it. You'll either see this...

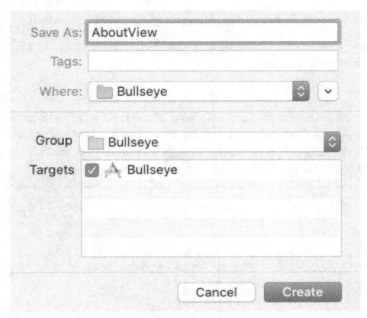

The options for the new file

...or this:

The options for the new file

➤ In either case, change the contents of the **Save As:** field to **AboutView**, then click the **Create** button.

➤ Choose the **Bullseye** folder (this folder should already be selected).

Also make sure **Group** says **Bullseye** and that there is a checkmark in front of **Bullseye** in the list of **Targets**.

➤ Click **Create**.

Xcode will create a new file and add it to your project. As you might have guessed, the new file is **AboutView.swift**. Xcode will show you the contents of that new file. You should have a sense of *deja vu*: this is what **ContentView.swift** looked like at the start of Chapter 2. You've come a long way:

```swift
//
//  AboutView.swift
//  Bullseye
//
//  Created by Joey deVilla on 1/25/20.
//  Copyright © 2020 Joey deVilla. All rights reserved.
//

import SwiftUI

struct AboutView: View {
    var body: some View {
        Text("Hello, World!")
    }
}

struct AboutView_Previews: PreviewProvider {
    static var previews: some View {
        AboutView()
    }
}
```

The newly-created AboutView

Connecting the "Info" button to AboutView

It's time to make the **Info** button on ContentView do its thing!

➤ Switch back to editing **ContentView.swift** by clicking on it in the Project Navigator:

```
Spacer()
Text("Round").modifier(LabelStyle())
Text("\(round)").modifier(ValueStyle())
Spacer()
Button(action: {}) {
  HStack {
    Image("InfoIcon")
    Text("Info").modifier(ButtonSmallTextStyle())
  }
}
.background(Image("Button")
  .modifier(Shadow()))
    )
  }
}
.padding(.bottom, 20)
.accentColor(midnightBlue)|
}
.onAppear() {
  self.startNewGame()
}
.background(Image("Background"))
}
```

Back to ContentView

The simplest way to navigate between views is to make use of a NavigationView. It's a special kind of view with just one purpose: To make it simple to navigate back and forth between other views.

We're going to take ContentView and put it inside a NavigationView. Doing this causes a couple of things to happen automatically:

• It sets up a *Navigation Bar* at the top of the view. This can house buttons that allow the user to easily navigate between views.

• It sets up ContentView so that it's easy to navigate to other views. It also returns back to ContentView with a **Back** button that appears in the navigation bar.

Let's add a NavigationView to ContentView.

➤ Scroll to the start of `ContentView`'s body property and select everything starting with `VStack` and ending with the `.background(Image("Background"))`. The start of your selection should look like this:

```
36    // User interface content and layout
37    var body: some View {
38        VStack {
39            Spacer()
40
41            // Target row
42            HStack {
43                Text("Put the bullseye as close as you can
                        to:").modifier(LabelStyle())
44                Text("\(target)").modifier(ValueStyle())
45            }
46
47            Spacer()
48
49            // Slider row
50            HStack {
51                Text("1").modifier(LabelStyle())
52                Slider(value: $sliderValue, in: 1...100)
53                    .accentColor(Color.green)
54                Text("100").modifier(LabelStyle())
55            }
56
57            Spacer()
58
```

The start of your selection

And the end of your selection should look like this:

```
80        // Score row
81        HStack {
82            Button(action: {
83                self.startNewGame()
84            }) {
85                HStack {
86                    Image("StartOverIcon")
87                    Text("Start over").modifier(ButtonSmallTextStyle())
88                }
89            }
90            .background(Image("Button")
91                .modifier(Shadow())
92            )
93            Spacer()
94            Text("Score:").modifier(LabelStyle())
95            Text("\(score)").modifier(ValueStyle())
96            Spacer()
97            Text("Round").modifier(LabelStyle())
98            Text("\(round)").modifier(ValueStyle())
99            Spacer()
100            NavigationLink(destination: AboutView()) {
101                HStack {
102                    Image("InfoIcon")
103                    Text("Info").modifier(ButtonSmallTextStyle())
104                }
105            }
106            .background(Image("Button")
107                .modifier(Shadow())
108            )
109        }
110        .padding(.bottom, 20)
111        .accentColor(midnightBlue)
112    }
113    .onAppear() {
114        self.startNewGame()
115    }
116    .background(Image("Background"))
117    }
```

The end of your selection

➤ With that code still selected, press ⌘+] to indent your selection one level.

➤ Scroll to the start of body and add a `NavigationView` so that it looks like this:

```
// User interface content and layout
var body: some View {
  NavigationView {
    VStack {
      Spacer()

      // Target row
      ...
```

➤ Scroll to the end of body and close the `NavigationView` with a closing brace and a couple of methods. The end result should look like this:

```
      .onAppear() {
        self.startNewGame()
      }
      .background(Image("Background"))
    }
    .navigationViewStyle(StackNavigationViewStyle())
  }
```

➤ Run the app. It now displays a navigation bar at the top of the screen:

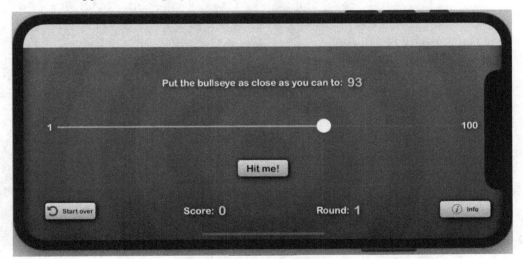

The navigation bar appears

By putting `ContentView` inside a `NavigationView`, it's now possible to make use of controls to take the user to a different view. We're going to replace the `Button` that was used for **Info** and replace it with a `NavigationLink`.

The `NavigationLink` link won't be all that different from a `Button`. It will still contain an `HStack` the button icon and text, and it will still use the button background image. However, instead of giving it code to perform when it's pressed, you specify a destination view.

➤ Go to the *Score row* section of `ContentView`'s body property and change this line...

```
Button(action: {}) {
```

...to this:

```
NavigationLink(destination: AboutView()) {
```

The section should now look like this:

```
// Score row
HStack {
  Button(action: {
    self.startNewGame()
  }) {
    HStack {
      Image("StartOverIcon")
      Text("Start over").modifier(ButtonSmallTextStyle())
    }
  }
  .background(Image("Button")
    .modifier(Shadow())
  )
  Spacer()
  Text("Score:").modifier(LabelStyle())
  Text("\(score)").modifier(ValueStyle())
  Spacer()
  Text("Round").modifier(LabelStyle())
  Text("\(round)").modifier(ValueStyle())
  Spacer()
  NavigationLink(destination: AboutView()) {
    HStack {
      Image("InfoIcon")
      Text("Info").modifier(ButtonSmallTextStyle())
    }
  }
  .background(Image("Button")
    .modifier(Shadow())
  )
}
.padding(.bottom, 20)
.accentColor(midnightBlue)
```

➤ Run the app and press the **Info** button. You'll be taken to AboutView, which will look like this:

AboutView

➤ Press the **Back** button in the navigation bar. You'll be returned back to ContentView.

Now that the player can navigate between views, it's time to fill AboutView.

➤ Switch to **AboutView.swift** in Xcode and change AboutView's body property to the following:

```
var body: some View {
  VStack {
    Text("🎯 Bullseye 🎯")
    Text("This is Bullseye, the game where you can win points
and earn fame by dragging a slider.")
    Text("Your goal is to place the slider as close as possible
to the target value. The closer you are, the more points you
score.")
    Text("Enjoy!")
  }
}
```

In case you've forgotten, the keyboard command to enter emojis is **control+⌘+space**. You can then find the 🎯 character by typing **bullsey**e into the emoji pop-up's search text field.

➤ Run the app and press **Info**. `AboutView`now contains the proper text, but the formatting needs work:

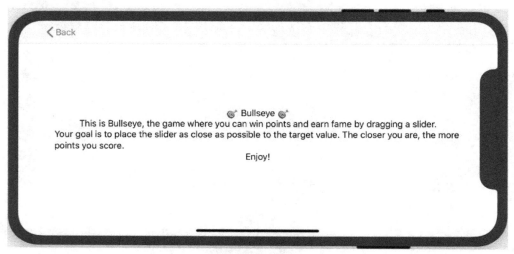

AboutView, with text

Let's improve the formatting with a couple of `ViewModifiers`. We'll make one for the heading, and one for the body text beneath it.

➤ Add the following between `AboutView` and `AboutView_Previews`:

```swift
// View modifiers
// ===============

struct AboutHeadingStyle: ViewModifier {
  func body(content: Content) -> some View {
    content
      .font(Font.custom("Arial Rounded MT Bold", size: 30))
      .foregroundColor(Color.black)
      .padding(.top, 20)
      .padding(.bottom, 20)
  }
}

struct AboutBodyStyle: ViewModifier {
  func body(content: Content) -> some View {
    content
      .font(Font.custom("Arial Rounded MT Bold", size: 16))
      .foregroundColor(Color.black)
      .padding(.leading, 60)
      .padding(.trailing, 60)
      .padding(.bottom, 20)
  }
}
```

These are similar to the `ViewModifiers` in `ContentView`. The only significant difference is that these include some padding for spacing between the heading and paragraphs.

Now that there are some `ViewModifiers`, it's time to apply them to the text.

➤ Change `AboutView`'s body property to the following:

```
var body: some View {
  VStack {
    Text("◎ˣ Bullseye ◎ˣ")
      .modifier(AboutHeadingStyle())
    Text("This is Bullseye, the game where you can win points
and earn fame by dragging a slider.")
      .modifier(AboutBodyStyle())
    Text("Your goal is to place the slider as close as possible
to the target value. The closer you are, the more points you
score.")
      .modifier(AboutBodyStyle())
    Text("Enjoy!")
      .modifier(AboutBodyStyle())
  }
}
```

➤ Run the app and press **Info**. You'll see this:

AboutView, with styled text

There are only a couple of tasks left. We need to create a plain beige background for the text, and behind that, we'll use the same background image as `ContentView`.

The first step is to create a custom beige color. It's like creating the midnight blue color, just with different values for red, green, and blue.

➤ Add the following to AboutView *above* the body property:

```
// Constants
let beige = Color(red: 1.0,
                  green: 0.84,
                  blue: 0.70)
```

Now that we have the beige color defined, let's make it the background of the VStack that holds all the Text views.

➤ Change AboutView's body property to the following:

```
var body: some View {
  VStack {
    Text("🎯 Bullseye 🎯")
      .modifier(AboutHeadingStyle())
    Text("This is Bullseye, the game where you can win points
and earn fame by dragging a slider.")
      .modifier(AboutBodyStyle())
      .lineLimit(nil)
    Text("Your goal is to place the slider as close as possible
to the target value. The closer you are, the more points you
score.")
      .modifier(AboutBodyStyle())
    Text("Enjoy!")
      .modifier(AboutBodyStyle())
  }
  .background(beige)
}
```

➤ Run the app and press **Info**. The VStack is now visible as a beige rectangle. It's large enough to accommodate the views it contains, complete with padding:

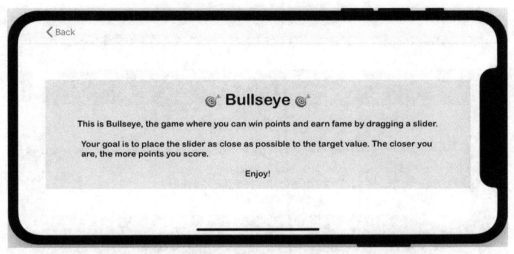

AboutView, with the beige VStack

We now need some kind of view whose only purpose is to act as a container for the background image. There's a type of `View` called `Group`, and it's used to group views together. It also expands to fill the view which contains it, which would be the entire screen. Let's put the `VStack` inside a `Group`, and then set the `Group`'s background to the background image.

➤ Change the body property so that the `VStack` it contains is inside a `Group` view. It should end up looking like this:

```
var body: some View {
  Group {
    VStack {
      Text("◎ Bullseye ◎")
        .modifier(AboutHeadingStyle())
      Text("This is Bullseye, the game where you can win points
and earn fame by dragging a slider.")
        .modifier(AboutBodyStyle())
      Text("Your goal is to place the slider as close as
possible to the target value. The closer you are, the more
points you score.")
        .modifier(AboutBodyStyle())
      Text("Enjoy!")
        .modifier(AboutBodyStyle())
    }
    .background(beige)
  }
  .background(Image("Background"))
}
```

➤ Run the app and press **Info**. It looks like we've made it:

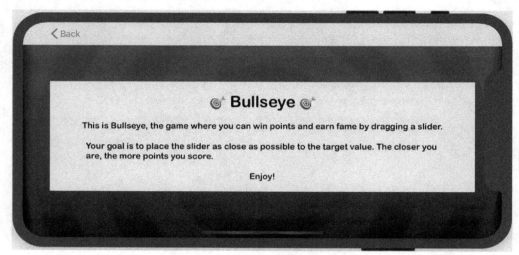

The final AboutView

Congrats! This completes the game. All the functionality is there and – as far as I can tell – there are no bugs to spoil the fun.

You can find the project files for the finished app under **07 - The New Look** in the Source Code folder.

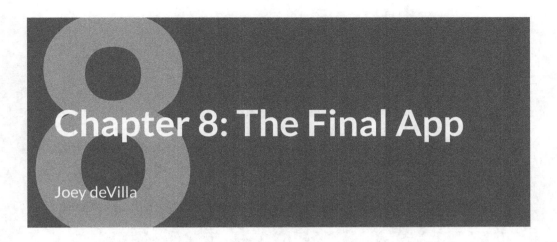

Chapter 8: The Final App

Joey deVilla

You might be thinking, "Okay, *Bullseye* is now done and I can move on to the next app!" If you were, I'm afraid that you're in for some disappointment — there's just a teensy bit more to do in the game.

"But the task list is complete!" you might say, and you'd be right. It's just that software has a way of finding more things for you to do. In this chapter, we'll add a few more touches to Bullseye to make it truly polished. One of these touches is absolutely necessary for apps to be published in the App Store. And finally, there's the matter of trying out *Bullseye* on a real device instead of the Simulator.

Don't worry; you're almost done!

Here are the specific items covered in this chapter:

- **Including animation**: Add some animation to make the start of a new round or game a bit more dynamic.

- **Adding an icon**: Giving the app its own distinctive icon, replacing the default blank one.

- **Display name**: Set the display name — the one users see on the home screen — for the app.

- **Running the app on a device**: How to configure everything to run your app on an actual device.

Adding a title to the navigation bar

The NavigationView object that *Bullseye* uses to take the user from the main screen to the "About" screen and back adds a translucent navigation bar that runs across the top of the screen. This bar gives the user a visual hint that the app has more than one screen and also provides a place for navigation controls, such as the **Back** button that automatically appears on the "About" screen:

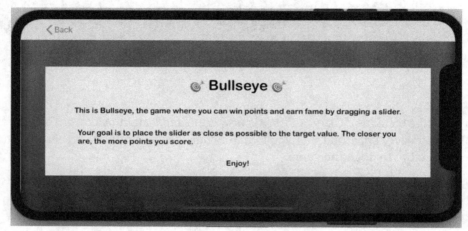

The 'About' screen, with the navigation bar displaying a 'Back' button

The navigation bar seems a little less useful on the main screen. There, it's an empty translucent strip that gives the user the impression that the developer — that's *you*! — didn't quite finish working on the user interface:

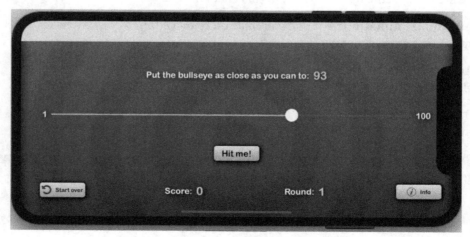

The main screen with a blank navigation bar

We can solve this problem and do a little app marketing at the same time by putting a title into the navigation bar when it's on the main screen. We can do this with a method available to any view object called navigationBarTitle(), which accepts a Text object to set text that appears in the center of the navigation bar.

The navigationBarTitle() method can be called from any view inside the NavigationView. To make it easy to see that the NavigationView is getting a title, we'll call navigationBarTitle() from the first Spacer in the main screen's NavigationView.

➤ Change the start of ContentView's body variable to the following:

```
var body: some View {
    NavigationView {
        VStack {
            Spacer().navigationBarTitle("◎ˢ Bullseye ◎ˢ")
```

➤ Run the app. You should see a title in the formerly blank navigation bar:

The main screen with a navigation bar with a title

When you navigate away from a page with navigation bar title, the "Back" button on the destination page displays the name of the page you just left:

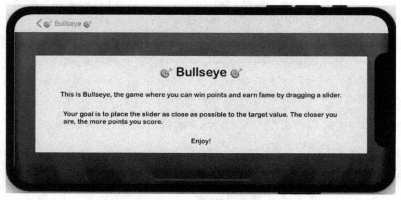

The 'About' screen with a 'Bullseye' back button in the navigation bar

We can also add a navigation bar title to the "About" page. Once again, it's a matter of calling the `navigationBarTitle()` method from any of its views. We'll call it from the first `Text` element on that screen.

➤ Change the start of `AboutView`'s body variable to the following:

```
var body: some View {
  Group {
    VStack {
      Text("@ Bullseye @")
        .modifier(AboutHeadingStyle())
        .navigationBarTitle("About Bullseye")
```

➤ Run the app and press the **Info** button. The "About" page will now have a title:

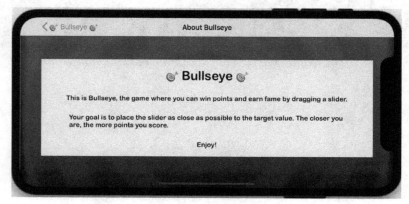

The 'About' screen with a navigation bar title

Including animation

There's one last improvement that you can add to the app: Animation. iOS contains a technology called Core Animation that makes it very easy to add animation effects to your app's views. With Core Animation, you can get several different kinds of animation with very little code. SwiftUI gives you access to Core Animation's power and, with it, you can add subtle animations (with an emphasis on *subtle!*) that can make your app a delight to use.

Right now, when a new round or game begins, the slider simply snaps to its randomly-determined position. You'll add an animation to the slider so that it *slides* to that randomly-determined position instead.

➤ In the *Slider row* section of ContentView's body property, change the line that defines the slider to look like this:

```
Slider(value: $sliderValue, in: 1...100)
    .accentColor(Color.green)
    .animation(.easeOut)
```

➤ Run the app. You can either play a few rounds or, if you're feeling impatient, you can simply press the **Start over** button over and over again. Either way, you'll see the slider slide to its new random position.

The call to the slider's animation() method added the animation effect to the slider. It takes a parameter that specifies the kind of animation that should be used. In this case, you provided a parameter called .easeOut, which is an "ease out" animation. "Ease out" means that as the slider approaches its destination it slows down a little, making its motion look more natural.

The animation() method is called whenever the app changes the position of the slider, which in turn happens when the app changes the value of the sliderValue property. This means that the animation takes place whenever the game starts, at the start of a new round, and at the start of a new game.

Adding an icon

You're almost done with the app, but there are still a few loose ends to tie up. You may have noticed that the app has a really boring white icon. That won't do!

➤ Open the asset catalog (**Assets.xcassets**) and select **AppIcon**:

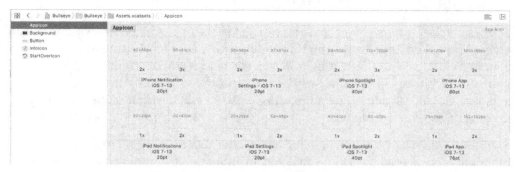

The AppIcon group in the asset catalog

It turns out that there isn't just one icon for an app, but 18 of them, to account for various device screen resolutions and different uses. They range in size from a minuscule 20 by 20 pixels for use in notifications to an enormous 1024 by 1024 pixels for the App Store.

Importing icons is like importing images — it's a drag-and-drop process.

➤ In Finder, open the **Resources** folder for this book and then open the **Icon** folder. Drag the **Icon-40.png** file into the **2x** slot in the area marked **iPhone Notification / iOS 7 - 13 / 20pt**:

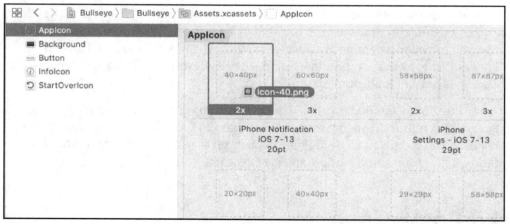

Dragging the icon into the asset catalog

You've probably figured out that the numbers in the filenames in the **Icon** folder indicate their dimensions in pixels. The **Icon-40.png** file is a 40-pixel by 40-pixel icon. So why are you dragging the **Icon-40.png** file into the slot marked **20pt** and not **Icon-20.png**?

The reason is that the filenames specify the icon size in *pixels* and the slots specify the icon size in points. On pre-Retina iPhones, one point was equal to one pixel. Retina iPhones and iPads have twice the pixel density. So, on those devices, one point is equal to *two* pixels. The Retina HD iPhones — the X, XS, XS Max, and any iPhone with a "+" in its name — have three times the pixel density. For them, one point is equal to *three* pixels.

Also, if you look at each of the slots, they've conveniently put the pixel dimensions in each one.

➤ Drag the **Icon-60.png** file into the **3x** slot next to it. This is for the iPhone Plus devices with their 3x resolution.

➤ For the **iPhone / Settings - iOS 7 - 13 / 29pt** slots, drag the **Icon-58.png** file into the **2x** slot and **Icon-87.png** into the **3x** slot. What, you don't know your times table for 29?

➤ For the **iPhone Spotlight / iOS 7 - 13 / 40pt** slots, drag the **Icon-80.png** file into the **2x** slot and **Icon-120.png** into the **3x** slot.

➤ For the **iPhone App / iOS 7 - 13 / 60pt** slots, drag the **Icon-120.png** file into the **2x** slot and **Icon-180.png** into the **3x** slot.

That's four icons in two different sizes. Phew!

The other AppIcon groups are mostly for the iPad.

➤ Drag the specific icons — based on size — into the proper slots for iPad. Notice that the iPad icons need to be supplied in 1x and 2x sizes but not 3x. You can either do the math to match pixel and point sizes or use the points specified in each slot to figure out which icons need to go in which iPad slots.

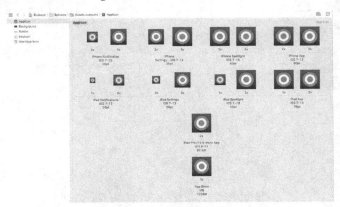

The full set of icons for the app

➤ Run the app and close it. You'll see that the icon has changed on the Simulator's springboard. If not, remove the app from the Simulator and try again (sometimes the Simulator keeps using the old icon and re-installing the app will fix this).

The icon on the Simulator's springboard

Display name

The text below the app's icon on the Home screen is its *display name*. It can be different from the project name, and it often *has* to be — there's a limited amount of space under any app's icon, and display names can be only one line long.

You the project with the name **Bullseye**. Xcode automatically used it as the app's display name. Sometimes, as you work on a project, you'll come up with a better one. Let's pretend that this happened, and in a fit of inspiration, you decided to change the name of the app to **Bullseye**?? (note the "bullseye" emoji added at the end).

➤ Go to the **Project Settings** screen. The very first option is **Display Name**. Change this to **Bullseye**??:

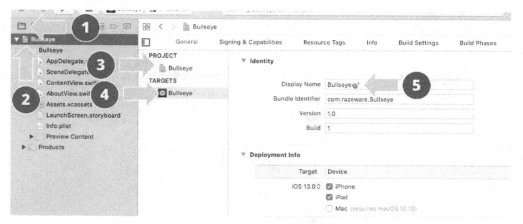

Changing the display name of the app

In case you've forgotten, you access the macOS emoji keyboard by pressing **ctrl + ⌘ + space**.

As with many of your project's settings, you can also find the display name in the app's **Info.plist** file. Let's take a look.

➤ From the **Project navigator**, select **Info.plist**.

The display name of the app in Info.plist

The row **Bundle display name** contains the new name you've just entered.

Note: If **Bundle display name** is not present, the app will use the value from the field **Bundle name**. That has the special value "$(PRODUCT_NAME)", meaning Xcode will automatically put the project name, BullsEye, in this field when it adds the Info.plist to the application bundle. By providing a **Bundle display name** you can override this default name and give the app any name you want.

➤ Run the app and quit it to see the new name under the icon.

The bundle display name setting changes the name under the icon

Guess what — your very first app is complete!

You can find the project files for the finished app under **08 - The Final App** in the **Source Code** folder.

Running the app on a device

So far, you've run the app on the Simulator. That's nice, but you probably didn't take up learning iOS development simply to make apps for pretend devices. You want to make apps that run on real iPhones and iPads and even distribute them in the App Store! There's hardly anything more satisfying than seeing an app that you made running on your own device — except showing off the fruits of your labor to other people!

Don't get me wrong: Developing your apps on the Simulator works very well. When developing, it's very convenient to spend most of your time with the Simulator and only test the app on a device every so often.

However, you *do* need to run your creations on a real device in order to test them properly. There are some things the Simulator simply can't do. For example, if your app needs the iPhone's accelerometer, you have no choice but to test that functionality on an actual device. You can't just sit there and shake your Mac! (Well, you *can*, but it'll have no effect.)

In the past, you needed a paid Developer Program account to run apps on your iPhone. These days, you can do it for free. All you need is an Apple ID, and the latest Xcode makes it easier than ever before.

Configuring your device for development

➤ Connect your iPhone, iPod touch or iPad to your Mac using a USB cable.

➤ From the Xcode menu bar select **Window ▸ Devices and Simulators** to open the **Devices and Simulators** window. Yours will look similar to the one shown below:

The Devices and Simulators window

The left column contains a list of devices that are currently connected to your Mac and which can be used for development.

➤ Click on a device name in the left column to select it.

If this is the first time you're using the selected device with Xcode, the window will show a message that says something like: "iPhone is not paired with your computer." To pair the device with Xcode, you'll need to unlock the device first. Once you've unlocked it, an alert will pop up on the device asking you to trust the computer you're trying to pair with. Tap on **Trust** to continue.

Xcode will now refresh the page and let you use the device for development. Give it a few minutes and see the progress bar in the main Xcode window. If it takes too long, you may need to unplug the device and plug it back in.

At this point it's possible you may get the error message: "An error was encountered while enabling development on this device." You'll need to unplug the device and reboot it. Make sure to restart Xcode before you reconnect the device.

Also, note the checkbox that says **Connect via network**? That checkbox (gasp!) allows you to deploy and debug code on your iPhone over WiFi!

That takes care of deploying to your device — cool!

Adding your developer account to Xcode

The next step is setting up your Apple ID with Xcode. It's okay to use the same Apple ID that you're already using with iTunes and your iPhone for hobby projects. However, if you run a business you might want to create a new Apple ID strictly for that purpose. Of course, if you've already registered for a paid Developer Program account, you should use that Apple ID.

➤ Open the **Accounts** pane in the Xcode Preferences window:

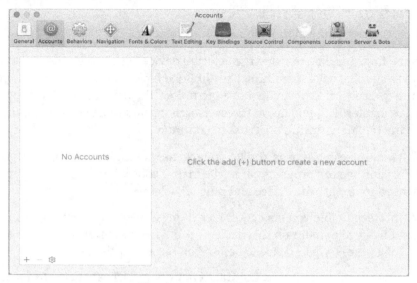

The Accounts preferences

➤ Click the + button at the bottom, select **Add Apple ID** from the list of options and click **Continue**:

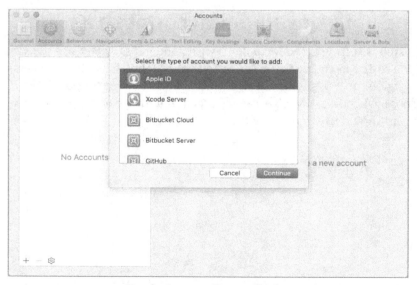

Xcode Account Type selection

Xcode will ask for your Apple ID:

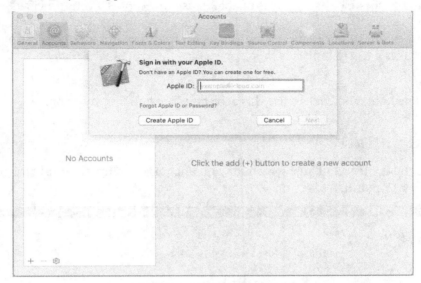

Adding your Apple ID to Xcode

➤ Type your Apple ID username and click **Next**.

Xcode will ask for your Apple ID password:

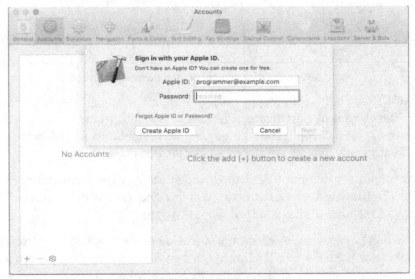

Entering your Apple ID password

Xcode verifies your account details and adds it to the stored list of accounts.

Note: It's possible that Xcode is unable to use the Apple ID your provided. For example, if it has been used with a Developer Program account in the past that is now expired. The simplest solution is to make a new Apple ID. It's free and only takes a few minutes. appleid.apple.com

You still need to tell Xcode to use this account when building your app.

Code signing

➤ Go to the **Project Settings** screen for your app target. In the **General** tab go to the **Signing & Capabilities** section.

The Signing options in the Project Settings screen

In order to allow Xcode to put an app on your device, the app must be *digitally signed* with your **Development Certificate**. A *certificate* is an electronic document that identifies you as an iOS application developer and is valid only for a specific amount of time. Creating and using a development certificate is free.

Apps that you want to submit to the App Store must be signed with another certificate, the **Distribution Certificate**. To create and use a distribution certificate, you must be a member of the paid Developer Program.

In addition to a having a valid certificate, you also need a **Provisioning Profile** for each app you make. Xcode uses this profile to sign the app for use on your particular device or devices. The specifics don't really matter. just know that you need a provisioning profile or the app won't be installed on your device.

Making the certificates and provisioning profiles used to be a really frustrating and error-prone process. Fortunately, those days are over: Xcode now makes it really easy. When the **Automatically manage signing** option is enabled, Xcode will take care of all this business with certificates and provisioning profiles and you don't have to worry about a thing.

➤ Click on **Team** to select your Apple ID.

Xcode will now automatically register your device with your account, create a new Development Certificate and download and install the Provisioning Profile on your device. These are all steps you had to do by hand in the past, but now Xcode takes care of all that.

You could get some signing errors like these:

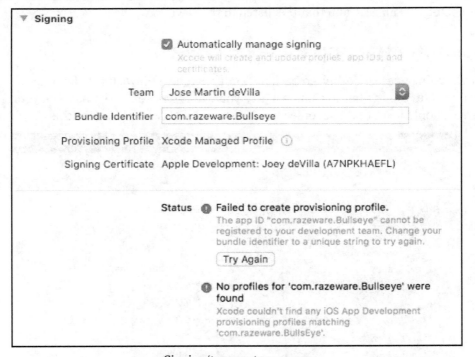

Signing/team set up errors

The app's **Bundle Identifier** must be unique. If another app is already using that identifier, your app can't use it. That's why it's suggested that you start the Bundle ID with your own domain name. The fix is easy: change the Bundle Identifier field to something else and try again.

It's also possible you get this error (or something similar):

No devices registered

Xcode must know about the device that you're going to run the app on. That's why you were told to connect your device first. Double-check that your device is still connected to your Mac and that it is listed in the Devices window.

Running the app on your device

If everything goes smoothly, go back to Xcode's main window and click on the dropdown in the toolbar to change where you will run the app. The name of your device should be in that list somewhere. It should look something like this:

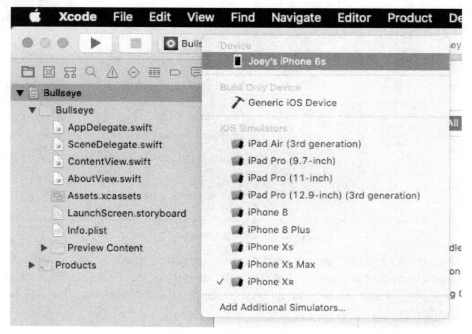

Setting the active device

You're all set and ready to go!

➤ Tap **Run** to launch the app.

At this point, you may get a pop-up with the question: "Codesign wants to sign using key... in your keychain." If so, answer with **Always Allow**. This is Xcode trying to use the new Development Certificate you just created — you just need to give it permission first.

Does the app work? Awesome! If not, read on...

When things go wrong...

There are a few things that can go wrong when you try to put the app on your device, especially if you've never done this before, so don't panic if you run into problems.

The device is not connected

Make sure your iPhone, iPod touch or iPad is connected to your Mac. The device must be listed in Xcode's Devices window and there should not be a yellow warning icon.

The device does not trust you

You might get this warning:

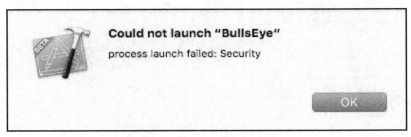

Quick, call security!

On the device itself, there will be a pop-up with the text: "Untrusted Developer. Your device management settings do not allow using apps from developer..."

If this happens, open the Settings app on the device and go to **General ▸ Profile**. Your Apple ID should be listed in that screen. Tap it, followed by the **Trust button**. Then, try running the app again.

The device is locked

If your phone locks itself with a passcode after a few minutes, you might get this warning:

The app won't run if the device is locked

Simply unlock your device by holding the home button, typing in the 4-digit passcode or using FaceID and tap **Run** again.

Signing certificates

If you're curious about these certificates, then open the **Preferences** window and go to the **Accounts** tab. Select your account and click the **Manage Certificates...** button in the bottom-right corner.

This brings up another panel, listing your signing certificates:

The Manage Certificates panel

When you're done, close the panel and go to the **Devices and Simulators** window. You can see the provisioning profiles that are installed on your device by right-clicking the device name and choosing **Show Provisioning Profiles**.

The provisioning profiles on your device

The "iOS Team Provisioning Profile" is the one that allows you to run the app on your device. By the way, they call it the "team" profile because often there is more than one developer working on an app and they can all share the same profile.

You can have more than one certificate and provisioning profile installed. This is useful if you're on multiple development teams or if you prefer to manage the provisioning profiles for different apps by hand.

To see how Xcode chooses which profile and certificate to sign your app with, go to the **Project Settings** screen and switch to the **Build Settings** tab. There are a lot of settings in this list, so filter them by typing **signing** in the search box. Also make sure **All** is selected, not Basic.

The screen will look something like this:

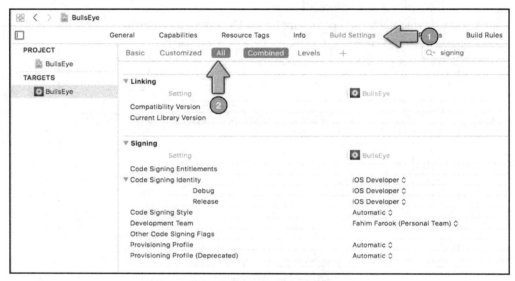

The Code Signing settings

Under **Code Signing Identity** it says **iOS Developer**. This is the certificate that Xcode uses to sign the app. If you click on that line, you can choose another certificate. Under **Provisioning Profile** you can change the active profile. Most of the time, you won't need to change these settings but at least you know where to find them now.

And that concludes everything you need to know about running your app on an actual device.

The end... or the beginning?

It's been a bit of a journey to get to this point — if you're new to programming, you've had to get a lot of new concepts into your head. I hope your brain didn't explode! At the very least, you should have gotten some insight into what it takes to develop an app.

I don't expect you to totally understand everything that you did, especially not the parts that involved writing Swift code and the finer points of building a user interface with SwiftUI. It is perfectly fine if you didn't, as long as you're enjoying yourself and you sort of get the basic concepts of objects, methods and variables. If you were able to follow along and do the exercises, you're in good shape!

I encourage you to play around with the code a bit more. The best way to learn programming is to do it, and that includes making mistakes and messing things up. I hereby grant you full permission to do so! Maybe you can add some cool new features to the game (and if you do, please let me know).

In the **Source Code** folder for this book, you can find the complete source code for the *Bullseye* app. If you're still unclear about anything you did between the start of the project and this finished product, it might be a good idea to look at this cleaned up source code.

If you're interested in how the graphics for *Bullseye* were made, take a peek at the Photoshop files in the Resources folder. The wood background texture was made by Atle Mo from subtlepatterns.com.

If you're feeling exhausted after all that coding, pour yourself a drink and put your feet up for a bit. You've earned it! On the other hand, if you just can't wait to get coding again, let's move on to our next app!

Section 2: Checklists

In this section, you'll build *Checklists*. As you may have gathered from the name, it's a TODO app that lets the user create, manage, and track items in one or more lists. Lists are a key part of many apps, and the lessons you'll learn while building Checklists will serve you well when you start coding your creations.

You'll make a multi-screen app, which will teach you the concepts of navigating from screen to screen, and sharing information between screens. You'll see how SwiftUI makes it easy to display lists of data. You'll also learn about data models (how data is represented in a program) and data persistence (saving data). And finally, you'll use local notifications to present the user with timely reminders and important messages that appear at the top of the screen. By the end of this section, you'll be able to write some basic (but useful) productivity apps.

This section contains the following chapters:

9. List Views: It's time to start your next iOS project. Are you ready for the challenge? In this chapter, we will commence our next app using SwiftUI, Checklists. Prepare for NavigationView, Arrays, Loops and removing items from the list.

10. A "Checkable" List: A Checklist app without being able to tick off the items? In this chapter, you will add the toggle for a Checklist item.

11. The App Structure: You have eagerly made great progress on creating a TODO list app by adding the checked status. In this chapter, you will start adding more features and start thinking about iOS design patterns.

12. Adding Items to the List: Your goal in this chapter is to start adding new items to your TODO list app. It also included learning about CRUD (Create, report, update and delete).

13. Editing Checklist Items: Congratulations! You can now add new items to your TODO list app, in this chapter, it's time to start editing your list and changing the text.

14. Saving & Loading: In this final chapter for your TODO list app, you will learn about data persistence. Right now all the items are hardcoded so it's time to persist and go!

Chapter 9: List Views

Joey deVilla

Ready to get started on your next app? Here you go!

To-do list apps are one of the most popular types of app on the App Store. Do a search on the web for "iOS to-do list apps" and you'll see reviews of dozens of list apps, even though iOS comes bundled with the **Reminders** app. From pilots to busy parents to surgeons to Santa Claus, many people need to have a good checklist.

Building a to-do list app is a rite of passage for budding iOS developers. It's the kind of app that's so useful that it has its own category. Making one will teach you to master code features and functionality that you'll end up using in so many other apps. It makes sense for you to create one as well.

Your own to-do list app, **Checklist**, will look like this when you're finished:

The finished Checklist app

This app lets you organize to-do items into a list with various priority levels. You can check off the items once you've completed them.

As far as to-do list apps go, *Checklist* is very basic, but don't let that fool you. Even a simple app such as this has a lot of complexity behind the scenes. In building it, you'll learn many different programming concepts. You're going to continue to use SwiftUI, the brand new way to build iOS apps, to build Checklist.

This chapter will cover:

- **NavigationView and List views**: You'll quickly review NavigationView, then you'll learn to use List. You'll also see how both views are often used together in apps that you probably use every day. Finally, you'll build an app that displays a basic list.

- **Arrays**: Just as Lists organize arrange views in a row, arrays organize data in the same way. Arrays are so useful that they're the most common data structure that programmers use.

- **Loops**: One of the reasons that computers are so useful is that they're very good at doing the same thing over and over again, no matter how tedious it is. How do they do this? With loops. You'll learn how to make your first dynamic list using List, arrays and loops.

- **Deleting items from the list**: At this point, you've filled the onscreen list with items. You'll then learn how to give the user the power to delete any item with a swipe of their finger.

- **Moving list items**: Deleting items is pretty cool, but giving the user the ability to rearrange the items on the list is even more impressive. It's amazing how few lines of code this takes.

- **Key points**: A quick review of what you've learned in this chapter.

NavigationView and List views

In the previous app, **Bullseye**, you learned to use `NavigationView`. `NavigationView` acts as a container for screens and makes it possible to navigate between them by creating a **navigation hierarchy** that's similar to how you navigate the web.

Embedding Bullseye's main screen, `ContentView`, inside a `NavigationView` lets users navigate to other screens by stacking those screens on top of `ContentView`. You did this by using a `NavigationLink` as the **Info** button. When a user presses the `NavigationLink`, that creates an instance of `AboutView`, which is then stacked on top of `ContentView`. Since `AboutView` is on top of the stack contained within `NavigationView`, the user sees that screen:

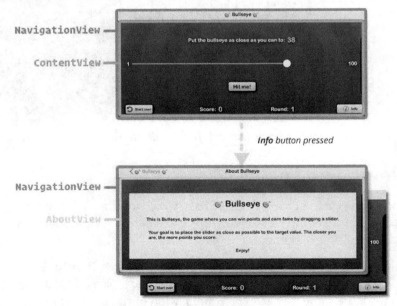

A basic list with five 'to-do' items

When the stack within a `NavigationView` is two or more screens deep, the navigation bar displays a "Back" button with the title of the screen just below. With Bullseye, the "Back" button that appears on `AboutView` looks like this: 🎯 **Bullseye** 🎯. Pressing the "Back" button removes `AboutView` from the stack of screens within the `NavigationView`, which makes `ContentView` visible again:

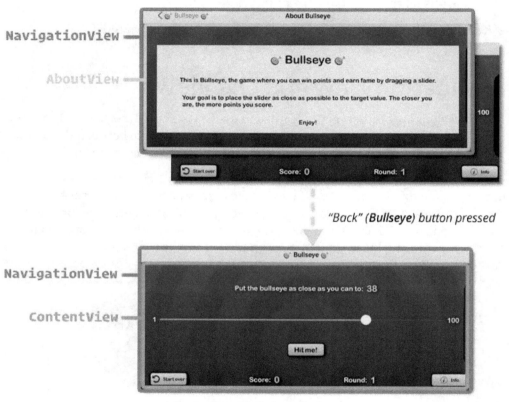

A basic list with five 'to-do' items

List views

As its name implies, a `List` view displays lists, which are rows of data arranged in a single column. This user interface element is extremely versatile, the most important one to master in iOS development.

Take a look at the apps that come with your iPhone – **Notes**, **Reminders**, **Music**, **Mail** and **Settings**. You'll notice that even though they look slightly different, all these apps work the same way, using a combination of Navigation and List views.

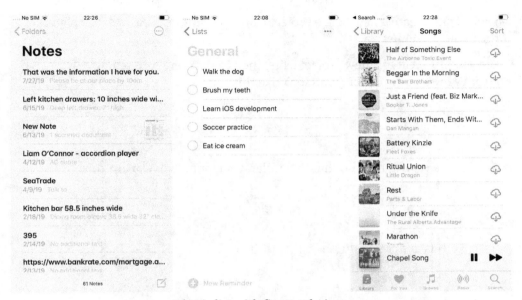

A basic list with five 'to-do' items

The **Music** app also has a tab bar at the bottom, which you'll learn about later on in this book.

If you want to learn how to program iOS apps in SwiftUI, you need to master these views as they make an appearance in almost every app. That's exactly what you'll focus on in this section of the book. You'll also learn how to pass data from one screen to another, a very important topic that often puzzles beginners.

A basic list

Start with a **static list**, which is one where the items and their order don't change. You might use this sort of list when you want to present the user with several choices or a table of contents.

This first app will simply display the following "to do" items in a list:

- Walk the dog.

- Brush my teeth.

- Learn iOS development.

- Soccer practice.

- Eat ice cream.

Go ahead and create a new Xcode Project using the **Single View App** template. Give it the name **Checklist**.

Since you just created a new project using the **Single View App** template, ContentView's body property will look like this:

```
var body: some View {
   Text("Hello World")
}
```

➤ Replace Text with List so that the declaration for body looks like this:

```
var body: some View {
  List {
    Text("Walk the dog")
    Text("Brush my teeth")
    Text("Learn iOS development")
    Text("Soccer practice")
    Text("Eat ice cream")
  }
}
```

➤ Build and run the app in the Simulator. You'll see the "to do" items in a list form:

A basic list with five 'to-do' items

Lists are often used as the "master" part of a **master-detail interface**. In these interfaces, the user sees a **master list** of items, where each item in the list contains the item's name and a couple of details about it. The user can select an item in the master list, which takes them to the **detail view** for the item, which displays all its information.

Many apps that come with your iOS device, like Calendar, Messages, Notes, Contacts, Mail and Settings, use a master-detail interface. For example, Mail has a master list showing each incoming email's sender and subject line along with a short excerpt. Selecting an email from the master list takes you to a screen that displays the full email.

On the iPhone, you construct master-detail interfaces by putting a List inside a Navigation. List functions as the master list and Navigation makes it possible to navigate to the detail view and back.

Now, put the List you just created into a Navigation view.

➤ Change ContentView's body so that Navigation now contains List. The result should be the following:

```
var body: some View {
  NavigationView {
    List {
      Text("Walk the dog")
      Text("Brush my teeth")
      Text("Learn iOS development")
      Text("Soccer practice")
      Text("Eat ice cream")
    }
  }
}
```

➤ Run the app. You'll see that List no longer takes up the whole screen:

The list, now contained within a navigation view

Navigation is a container that lets you build a hierarchy of screens that lead from one screen to another. It adds a navigation bar at the top, which can hold a title and some controls that allow the user to navigate between screens and perform edits on the screen that Navigation contains.

At the moment, the navigation bar is empty, which makes the app look like it's missing something. Fix that by adding a title to the navigation bar using navigationBarTitle().

➤ Add a call to navigationBarTitle() to the List view so that the declaration for body becomes:

```
var body: some View {
  NavigationView {
    List {
      Text("Walk the dog")
      Text("Brush my teeth")
      Text("Learn iOS development")
      Text("Soccer practice")
      Text("Eat ice cream")
    }
    .navigationBarTitle("Checklist")
  }
}
```

➤ Run the app. It now has a title:

The app with a title in the navigation bar

Lists with sections

There are two styles of List: **plain** and **grouped**. Right now, the app's List uses the plain style.

Use the plain style for lists where all the items in the list are similar to one another, yet independent. One example is an email app, where each item in the List represents an email.

Use the grouped style when you can organize the items in the list by a particular attribute, like genre categories for a list of books. You could also use the grouped style table to show related information that doesn't necessarily have to go together, like a contact's address, contact information, and e-mail.

Lists default to the plain style. Using the grouped style requires the following:

1. Using List's listStyle() to specify that the list should use the grouped style.

2. Adding a Section inside the List for each group, which appears as a separate sublist within the list. Sections can contain their own headers.

Now, change the list to the grouped style. You'll split the list into two groups using two Section views: One for high-priority and one for low-priority tasks. The first three items in the list will be high-priority, and the last two will be low-priority.

➤ Change the declaration for body to the following:

```
var body: some View {
  NavigationView {
    List {
      Section(header: Text("High priority")) {
        Text("Walk the dog")
        Text("Brush my teeth")
        Text("Learn iOS development")
      }
      Section(header: Text("Low priority")) {
        Text("Soccer practice")
        Text("Eat ice cream")
      }
    }
    .listStyle(GroupedListStyle())
    .navigationBarTitle("Checklist")
  }
}
```

➤ Run the app to see the grouped list in action:

The app with a grouped style list

The limits of views

Most people who use checklists have more than just five to-do items. At this point, make a more realistic list by adding more items so that both the high-priority and low-priority groups each have ten to-do items.

➤ Add more items to each Section so that the declaration for body looks like this:

```
var body: some View {
  NavigationView {
    List {
      Section(header: Text("High priority")) {
        Text("Walk the dog")
        Text("Brush my teeth")
        Text("Learn iOS development")
        Text("Make dinner")
        Text("Do laundry")
        Text("Pay bills")
        Text("Finish homework")
        Text("Change internet provider")
        Text("Read Raywenderlich.com")
        Text("Clean the kitchen")
      }
      Section(header: Text("Low priority")) {
        Text("Soccer practice")
        Text("Eat ice cream")
        Text("Take vocal lessons")
```

```
            Text("Record hit single")
            Text("Learn every martial art")
            Text("Design costume")
            Text("Design crime-fighting vehicle")
            Text("Come up with superhero name")
            Text("Befriend space raccoon")
            Text("Save the world")
        }
      }
      .listStyle(GroupedListStyle())
      .navigationBarTitle("Checklist")
    }
  }
```

Make a note of the number of Texts inside each Section: Ten. This number will become important shortly.

➤ Run the app. Even on the largest iPhones, you'll need to scroll to see the entire list:

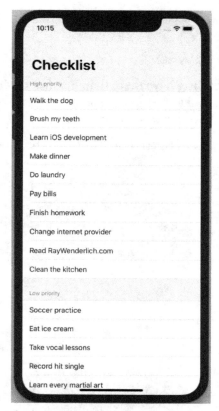

The list with ten items in each section

Now, add one more item to the high-priority group in the list, making for eleven
`Texts` inside the first `Section`.

➤ Add one more item to the first `Section` so that the declaration for body looks like
this:

```
var body: some View {
  NavigationView {
    List {
      Section(header: Text("High priority")) {
        Text("Walk the dog")
        Text("Brush my teeth")
        Text("Learn iOS development")
        Text("Make dinner")
        Text("Do laundry")
        Text("Pay bills")
        Text("Finish homework")
        Text("Change internet provider")
        Text("Read RayWenderlich.com")
        Text("Clean the kitchen")
        Text("Wash the car")
      }
      Section(header: Text("Low priority")) {
        Text("Soccer practice")
        Text("Eat ice cream")
        Text("Take vocal lessons")
        Text("Record hit single")
        Text("Learn every martial art")
        Text("Design costume")
        Text("Design crime-fighting vehicle")
        Text("Come up with superhero name")
        Text("Befriend space raccoon")
        Text("Save the world")
      }
    }
    .listStyle(GroupedListStyle())
    .navigationBarTitle("Checklist")
  }
}
```

Shortly after you add that item, Xcode will respond with a cryptic complaint:
Argument passed to call that takes no arguments:

```
struct ContentView: View {
  var body: some View {
    NavigationView {
      List {
        Section(header: Text("High priority")) {
          Text("Walk the dog")      🔴 Argument passed to call that takes no arguments
          Text("Brush my teeth")
          Text("Learn iOS development")
          Text("Make dinner")
          Text("Do laundry")
          Text("Pay bills")
          Text("Finish homework")
          Text("Change internet provider")
          Text("Read RayWenderlich.com")
          Text("Clean the kitchen")
          Text("Wash the car")
        }
```

The 'Argument passed to call that takes no arguments' error message

This is one of those technically correct, but ultimately unhelpful error messages that Xcode will surprise you with from time to time. Rather than bore you with the internal details of how SwiftUI builds user interfaces based on a View's body, I'll keep it simple. You've just run into a big limit of working with Views: They're limited to holding a maximum of ten Views.

In a static list, the simplest way to get around this limitation is to use a Group. Its sole purpose is to provide a way for you to treat a group of two to ten views as a single view.

➤ In body's first List, put the first six Text views into a Group, then do the same for the last five. You should end up with a body that looks like this:

```
var body: some View {
  NavigationView {
    List {
      Section(header: Text("High priority")) {
        Group {
          Text("Walk the dog")
          Text("Brush my teeth")
          Text("Learn iOS development")
          Text("Make dinner")
          Text("Do laundry")
          Text("Pay bills")
        }
        Group {
          Text("Finish homework")
          Text("Change internet provider")
          Text("Read RayWenderlich.com")
          Text("Clean the kitchen")
          Text("Wash the car")
        }
      }
      Section(header: Text("Low priority")) {
```

```
        Text("Soccer practice")
        Text("Eat ice cream")
        Text("Take vocal lessons")
        Text("Record hit single")
        Text("Learn every martial art")
        Text("Design costume")
        Text("Design crime-fighting vehicle")
        Text("Come up with superhero name")
        Text("Befriend space raccoon")
        Text("Save the world")
      }
    }
    .listStyle(GroupedListStyle())
    .navigationBarTitle("Checklist")
  }
}
```

➤ Run the app. It should work now because the first List now contains only *two* views, which is well under the limit of ten.

The limits of static lists

Static lists have their uses, but they're missing a lot of features that a checklist app needs. The user needs to be able to add and delete items from the list, edit existing items and change their order in the list.

So far, you've seen only one way to change the contents of a list: By changing the contents of the List view during the programming process. You lock in these changes at **compile time** — that is, when you compile your code into an app that the device can run. What you need is a way to change the list at **run time**, which is while the app is running.

This is what you'll do next, but before you can, you'll need to become acquainted with arrays.

Arrays

Up to this point, you've been working with **scalar** variables and constants. These are variables and constants that hold one value at any given time. You used several scalar variables and constants in the Bullseye app. Each one acted as a container for one value, such as the score, the round, the value of the target and the message that the user received based on their score.

Not all data return a single value. A lot of data come as an ordered series of values, such as the mid-day temperature of a given location for the past month, the grades for every student in a given course... or the items in a checklist. Most programming languages, Swift included, have a data type called an **array**, which can hold many values at the same time.

If you think of scalar variables and constants as boxes that hold one value, think of an array as a *collection* of boxes. Each box holds one value, and the boxes are numbered in ascending order starting with 0. The numbering scheme lets you point to the contents of a specific box ("What's inside box 5?") or to put a value into a specific box ("Put the value **42** into box 3").

In an array, you call these boxes **elements**.

Scalar values		Array values	
Hold only one value at a time		Hold multiple values at a time	
score		**checklistItems**	
327	index 0	Walk the dog	
round	index 1	Brush my teeth	
5	index 2	Learn iOS development	
title	index 3	Soccer practice	
Perfect!	index 4	Eat ice cream	

Scalar values and array values

In Swift, arrays can grow by having more elements added to them; they can also shrink by having elements removed from them. You'll use this ability, coupled with arrays' ability to hold many values, to store information about the checklist in this app.

The key to mastering programming is to learn by doing, especially when you're dealing with arrays and other concepts that you don't use outside of coding. So put this knowledge into practice by setting up the app to make use of an array to store list items.

Creating an array

Your next step is to create an array to hold the checklist items. Enter the following, immediately after the start of ContentView (the `struct ContentView: View { ` line):

```
var checklistItems = ["Walk the dog", "Brush my teeth", "Learn
iOS development", "Soccer practice", "Eat ice cream"]
```

To walk through this line of code:

- The `var checklistItems` says "This is a variable named `checklistItems`. It's not followed by a colon (:), which means that it's up to Swift to infer what kind of variable `checklistItems` is.

- The = in Swift stands for "takes the following value". You should read `var checklistItems =` as "This is a variable named `checklistItems` and it takes the following value."

- The simplest way to define an array is to take a list of values separated by commas (`,`) and surround them with square brackets, which is what appears on the right side of the =. This value is an array of the five strings that made up our original set of checklist items.

Accessing array elements

The name `checklistItems` refers to the entire array. When you need to provide the entire array to an object or method, as you'll need to do shortly, you'll use that.

To access a specific element of an array, you use the array's name followed by the number of the element you want to access in square brackets. For example, if you wanted to access element 2 of the `checklistItems` array, you'd use this syntax:

```
checklistItems[2]
```

The number inside the square bracket specifies its location in the array; it's called the **index**. The combination of the square brackets and the number inside is called the **subscript**. In the case of `checklistItems[2]`:

- `checklistItems[2]` is an **element** of `checklistItems`.

- 2 is the **index** that specifies the third element. Remember, the first array index is **0**, not **1**.

- `[2]` is the **subscript** that specifies that you want a specific element of the array and not the whole thing.

Now that you know how to access individual array elements, it's time to put that knowledge to use.

➤ Change the body property to the following:

```
var body: some View {
  NavigationView {
    List {
      Text(checklistItems[0])
      Text(checklistItems[1])
      Text(checklistItems[2])
      Text(checklistItems[3])
      Text(checklistItems[4])
    }
```

```
        .navigationBarTitle("Checklist")
    }
}
```

Just so that there isn't any confusion at this point, the complete code for ContentView should look like this:

```
struct ContentView: View {

    var checklistItems = ["Walk the dog", "Brush my teeth", "Learn
iOS development", "Soccer practice", "Eat ice cream"]

    var body: some View {
        NavigationView {
            List {
                Text(checklistItems[0])
                Text(checklistItems[1])
                Text(checklistItems[2])
                Text(checklistItems[3])
                Text(checklistItems[4])
            }
            .navigationBarTitle("Checklist")
        }
    }
}
```

➤ Before we get into a discussion about array syntax, run the app to see what the new code does. You should see this:

The list, using an array

Changing array elements and responding to taps on list items

Changing an array element is simple: You put the array element you want to change on the left side of an = and the value you want to change it to on the right side. For example, to change the contents of the first item in checklistItems to "Take the dog to the vet", you'd use this code:

```
checklistItems[0] = "Take the dog to the vet"
```

Now, change the list so that tapping on the first item in the list, **Walk the dog**, changes the item to **Take the dog to the vet**. You'll take advantage of a method built into every view object: onTapGesture(), which causes code to be executed whenever a user taps the view.

➤ Update body so that it looks like this:

```
var body: some View {
  NavigationView {
    List {
      Text(checklistItems[0])
        .onTapGesture {
          self.checklistItems[0] = "Take the dog to the vet"
        }
      Text(checklistItems[1])
      Text(checklistItems[2])
      Text(checklistItems[3])
      Text(checklistItems[4])
    }
    .navigationBarTitle("Checklist")
  }
}
```

Note that you use self.checklistItems[0] instead of just plain checklistItems[0]. That's because the code in the braces after .onTapGesture is a closure — a self-contained bit of code that you can pass around as if it were a value like an integer or a string. That means it needs to use the self keyword to refer to checklistItems.

Even with the use of `self`, Xcode still reports an error: **Cannot assign through subscript: 'self' is immutable**...

```
11   struct ContentView: View {
12
13     var checklistItems = ["Walk the dog", "Brush my teeth", "Learn iOS development",
         "Soccer practice", "Eat ice cream"]
14
15     var body: some View {
16       NavigationView {
17         List {
18           Text(checklistItems[0])
19             .onTapGesture {
20               self.checklistItems[0] = "Take the dog to the vet"
21             }                     ● Cannot assign through subscript: 'self' is immutable      ⊗
22           Text(checklistItems[1])
23           Text(checklistItems[2])
24           Text(checklistItems[3])
25           Text(checklistItems[4])
26         }
27         .navigationBarTitle("Checklist")
28       }
29     }
30   }
```

The 'self is immutable' error message

Oh look, it's another technically correct but not-so-helpful message from Xcode! What does it mean?

To keep things simple here, just remember that *by default*, code inside a `struct` object is not allowed to change the values of that `struct`'s properties. *Normally*, only code outside the `struct` is allowed to do that.

Note the emphasized words in the previous paragraph: *by default* and *normally*. There *are* a couple of ways for code inside a `struct` to change the values of that `struct`'s own properties — and better yet, you've already used one of them!

That way is the `@State` attribute, which marks a property as a state variable. Remember, state variables determine what happens in the app, and the user's actions often affect them, and the view must respond to those changes. Marking a property with `@State` makes it exempt from the rule that code inside a `struct` can't change that `struct`'s own properties.

So go ahead and add the `@State` attribute to the declaration of `checklistItems`. While you're at it, reformat `checklistItems` so that it's easier to read and change.

➤ Update the declaration of `checklistItems` to the following:

```
@State var checklistItems = [
  "Walk the dog",
  "Brush my teeth",
  "Learn iOS development",
  "Soccer practice",
  "Eat ice cream",
]
```

`checklistItems` is now different in a couple of ways:

1. It's now marked as a state variable. That makes it exempt from the "`structs` can't modify their own properties" rule. As a result, the `onTapGesture()` code can now change the value inside `checklistItems[0]`, which means that "`self` is immutable error message will disappear.

2. Its contents have been arranged as a list. This doesn't change the contents of the array or how it works, but it *does* make it easier to edit and update.

Note the new formatting, which makes the `checklistItems` array is easier to read. It's also easier to get a sense of how many items are in the array. Swift ignores most "white space" — spaces, tabs, new lines and so on — which allows you to format the code for maximum legibility.

Note that the last item, **Eat ice cream**, has a **,** after it, even though it's not followed by another item. That's not an error; that's a deliberate addition that makes it easy to add another item after it, should it become necessary. Good code is code that's easy to update.

➤ Run the app and tap the "Walk the dog" item in the list. By default, SwiftUI is a little fussy and won't register the tap unless you tap right on the **Walk the dog** text. When tapped, the item should change to "Take the dog to the vet":

The list, with the first item changed to 'Take the dog to the vet' after the user tapped on it

The limits of the current approach

Suppose you added an additional item — "Learn every martial art" — to checklistItems:

```
@State var checklistItems = [
  "Walk the dog",
  "Brush my teeth",
  "Learn iOS development",
  "Soccer practice",
  "Eat ice cream",
  "Learn every martial art",
]
```

If you were to run the app, it wouldn't display the newly-added item. That's because List in the body is currently set to display Text views for checklistItems[0] through checklistItems[4]:

```
List {
  Text(checklistItems[0])
    .onTapGesture {
      self.checklistItems[0] = "Take the dog to the vet"
    }
  Text(checklistItems[1])
  Text(checklistItems[2])
  Text(checklistItems[3])
  Text(checklistItems[4])
}
```

What you need is a way for the list to display the complete contents of checklistItems without having to make any changes to body as the array changes. To help you do that, it's time to introduce a concept that goes hand-in-hand with arrays (and many other aspects of programming): loops.

Loops

Up to this point, you've experienced two different kinds of **flow control**, or ways of executing your code. Let's look at them, and then you'll learn a new kind of flow control: **Looping**.

Flow control

The first kind of flow control that you've seen is **sequence**, which is simply performing instructions in the order in which they appear.

Here's an example from Bullseye:

```
func startNewGame() {
  score = 0
  round = 1
  resetSliderAndTarget()
}
```

In `startNewGame()`, the code performs its instructions in order. First, the value of `score` is set to 0, then the value of `round` is set to 1 and finally, it executes `resetSliderAndTarget()`.

You've also seen the second kind of flow control: **Branching**, which some computer science people also like to call **selection**. This is the "decision-making" flow control, which offers two or more courses of action, depending on some kind of test. Here's an example from Bullseye:

```
func alertTitle() -> String {
  let title: String
  if sliderTargetDifference == 0 {
    title = "Perfect!"
  } else if sliderTargetDifference < 5 {
    title = "You almost had it!"
  } else if sliderTargetDifference <= 10 {
    title = "Not bad."
  } else {
    title = "Are you even trying?"
  }
  return title
}
```

In `alertTitle()`, the code performs different instructions based on the value of `sliderTargetDifference`. Each of these instructions is a branch in a structure of multiple choices called a **decision tree**.

It's time to introduce a third kind of flow control: **Looping**, which some computer science people also call **iteration**. This is the "repetition" flow control, where instructions are performed over and over again, either indefinitely or until some condition is met.

You're going to use looping to go through the elements in `checklistItems`, one at a time, in order, to display each one onscreen. You can also call this process **looping through** or **iterating through** each element.

for loops

You'll start by displaying all the elements in `checklistItems` in Xcode's debug console. Another way of saying this is "For every item in `checklistItems`, print its name," which is pretty close to the way you'd code it in Swift:

```
for item in checklistItems {
  print(item)
}
```

The code above goes through every item in `checklistItems`, starting with the item in index 0 and ending after the last item in the array. `item` is a temporary variable that exists only as long as we're still in the loop. The first time through the loop, `item` is set to the first item in the array, "Walk the dog".

The code inside the loop is then executed: It's `print(item)`, which prints "Walk the dog" in Xcode's debug console. This completes the first iteration of the loop.

The program returns to the beginning of the loop, and there are still more items in `checklistItems` to go through. `item` is set to the next item in the array, "Brush my teeth", after which the code in the loop executes, printing "Brush my teeth" in Xcode's debug console. The second iteration of the loop is now complete.

The program returns to the beginning of the loop, and the cycle repeats until it's gone through every item in `checklistItems`.

You can see this process in action.

➤ First, make sure that `checklistItems` has the original five items:

```
@State var checklistItems = [
  "Walk the dog",
  "Brush my teeth",
  "Learn iOS development",
  "Soccer practice",
  "Eat ice cream",
]
```

Take the loop code shown earlier and put it inside a method.

➤ Enter the following method after the end of body:

```
func printChecklistContents() {
  for item in checklistItems {
    print(item)
  }
}
```

Finally, you need to do two things with body:

1. Since you won't be displaying the contents of checklistItems onscreen yet, you'll simplify the list that appears onscreen.

2. You'll also use onAppear(), which is built into every view, to call howChecklistContents() when the list is first drawn onscreen.

➤ Change body to the following:

```
var body: some View {
  NavigationView {
    List {
      Text("Nothing to see here...yet!")
    }
    .navigationBarTitle("Checklist")
    .onAppear() {
      self.printChecklistContents()
    }
  }
}
```

With all the changes you made, ContentView should look like this:

```
struct ContentView: View {

  @State var checklistItems = [
    "Walk the dog",
    "Brush my teeth",
    "Learn iOS development",
    "Soccer practice",
    "Eat ice cream"
  ]

  var body: some View {
    NavigationView {
      List {
        Text("Nothing to see here...yet!")
      }
      .navigationBarTitle("Checklist")
      .onAppear() {
        self.printChecklistContents()
      }
    }
  }

  func printChecklistContents() {
    for item in checklistItems {
      print(item)
    }
  }
}
```

```
}
```

➤ Run the app but don't bother looking at the simulator. All the action is happening in the Xcode window, in the debug console:

```
88  <  >   Checklist 〉 Checklist 〉 ContentView.swift 〉 No Selection                        ≡
11  struct ContentView: View {
12
13    @State var checklistItems = ["Walk the dog",
14                                 "Brush my teeth",
15                                 "Learn iOS development",
16                                 "Soccer practice",
17                                 "Eat ice cream",]
18
19    var body: some View {
20      NavigationView {
21        List {
22          Text("Nohing to see here...yet!")
23        }
24        .navigationBarTitle("Checklist")
25        .onAppear() {
26          self.showChecklistContents()
27        }
28      }
29    }
30
31    func showChecklistContents() {
32      for item in checklistItems {
33        print(item)
34      }
35    }
36
37  }
```

```
▽  ▶  ‖  ⬆  ⬇  ⬆  ⬚  ⅋  ▤  ◁  Checklist
                                    Walk the dog
                                    Brush my teeth
                                    Learn iOS development
                                    Soccer practice
                                    Eat ice cream
Auto ⌄  ⊚ ⓘ          Filter          All Output ⌄      Filter          🗑
```

The Xcode window, with the contents of checklistItems displayed in the debug console

When List first appears on the screen, its onAppear() is called, which then calls printChecklistContents(). printChecklistContents() goes through checklistItems in order, printing each item's value in the debug console.

As you've seen before, printing to the debug console doesn't affect the user interface; it's only for the benefit of the programmer. How do you show the contents of the checklist to the user?

The ForEach view

SwiftUI has a view called ForEach that takes a collection of data, such as an array, and generates views based on that data. This is one of those cases where "Show, don't tell" is the better approach, so take a look at ForEach in action first, then you'll look at it in more detail afterward.

➤ Change body to the following:

```
var body: some View {
  NavigationView {
    List {
      ForEach(checklistItems, id: \.self) { item in
        Text(item)
      }
    }
    .navigationBarTitle("Checklist")
    .onAppear() {
      self.printChecklistContents()
    }
  }
}
```

➤ Run the app. You'll see this:

The original five-element array displayed using 'ForEach'

For the user, there's no difference between an app that uses ForEach and one that simply uses a Text view for every item in checklistItems. The benefit of ForEach becomes clear when you make changes to checklistItems.

➤ Change the declaration of checklistItems to the items on the following page, which has no items in common with the original list.

```
@State var checklistItems = [
    "Take vocal lessons",
    "Record hit single",
    "Learn every martial art",
    "Design costume",
    "Design crime-fighting vehicle",
    "Come up with superhero name",
    "Befriend space raccoon",
    "Save the world",
    "Star in blockbuster movie",
]
```

➤ Run the app to see this all-new list:

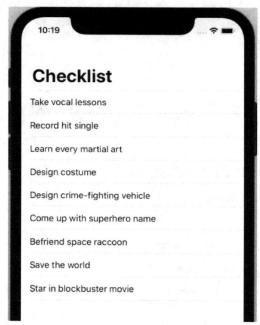

A completely different list displayed using 'ForEach'

With ForEach, you don't have to make any changes to the user interface to change the items in the checklist. You only have to change the underlying data.

Take a closer look at ForEach, which you added to body:

```
ForEach(checklistItems, id: \.self) { item in
    Text(item)
}
```

There are four key parts here:

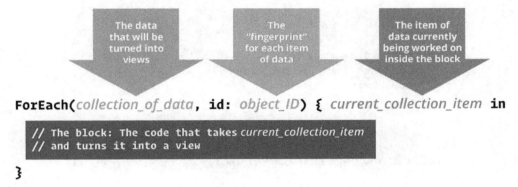

A completely different list displayed using 'ForEach'

First, there's the **collection of data** that you're using ForEach to display in a view. In this case, that collection of data is checklistItems.

Next is a **"digital fingerprint"** that uniquely identifies each element in the collection of data provided to ForEach. That's what id: is for. SwiftUI uses it to update the views that ForEach creates when a user moves or deletes elements in the collection, and when they add new ones. For this parameter, you use \.self, which means: "Use the item's value as its identifier."

Then there's the value representing the **current collection item**, which lets you refer to that item in the code in the ForEach block. If you're using the most recent version of checklistItems, this value will be ""Eat ice cream" during the first pass through ForEach, then "Take vocal lessons", then "Record hit single" and so on, until you hit the final item, "Star in blockbuster movie".

And finally, there's the block, which contains the code that specifies the views that will display the collection of data. In this case, it's a Text view that contains the current collection item.

The similarity between for and ForEach is intentional, especially the way the values represent the collection of data that you pass to them and the value that represents the item in the collection that you're currently working on.

The diagram below shows how the two relate to each other:

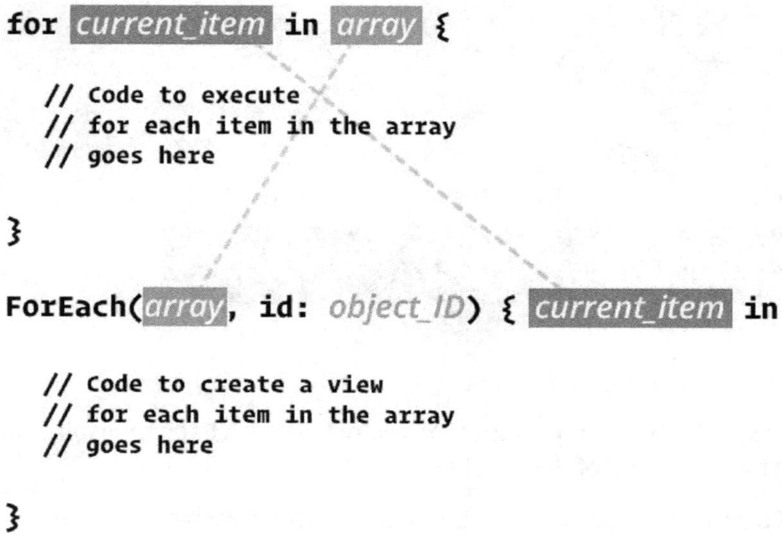

```
for current_item in array {

    // Code to execute
    // for each item in the array
    // goes here

}


ForEach(array, id: object_ID) { current_item in

    // Code to create a view
    // for each item in the array
    // goes here

}
```

The similarities between 'for' and 'ForEach'

Deleting items from the list

Now that the list is based on an array and is no longer a "hardwired" part of the user interface, changing the array's contents can change the list's contents.

Adding items to the end of an array (and the checklist)

Since arrays are ordered lists of items, and lists often grow by adding items to the end, arrays have an append() method, which lets you add new items to the end of the array.

Suppose you have an array named myArray that contains the following items:

• This is an item.

• This is another item.

• Third item!

If you wanted to add another item, "One more item!!!" to the array, you'd use the append() method this way:

```
append("One more item!!!")
```

Once that code executes, myArray would contain:

- This is an item.

- This is another item.

- Third item!

- One more item!!!

You'd be able to access this new item with myArray[3]. Remember, array indexes begin at 0, so the fourth item is at index 3.

Now, try out append() in the app. Now that List is connected to checklistItems, which is a state variable, adding an item to the end of the array will add an item to the end of the List.

You'll change the app so that tapping on a checklist item will add a copy of that item to the end of the list. You'll use onTapGesture() to respond to the user's taps.

➤ Start by changing checklistItems back to its original contents:

```
@State var checklistItems = [
  "Walk the dog",
  "Brush my teeth",
  "Learn iOS development",
  "Soccer practice",
  "Eat ice cream",
]
```

➤ Change body to the following:

```
var body: some View {
  NavigationView {
    List {
      ForEach(checklistItems, id: \.self) { item in
        Text(item)
          .onTapGesture {
            self.checklistItems.append(item)
            self.printChecklistContents()
          }
      }
    }
    .navigationBarTitle("Checklist")
```

```
        .onAppear() {
          self.printChecklistContents()
        }
      }
    }
```

Take a look at the `ForEach` view, which contains the lines of code you just added:

```
ForEach(checklistItems, id: \.self) { item in
  Text(item)
    .onTapGesture {
      self.checklistItems.append(item)
      self.printChecklistContents()
    }
}
```

You added a call to the `Text` view's `onTapGesture()`, which contains code that does two things:

- It uses `append()` to add `item` to the end of `checklistItems`. This means that tapping on the "Walk the dog" list item adds a new "Walk the dog" item to the end of `checklistItems`, which in turn causes a new "Walk the dog" item to appear at the end of the list onscreen.

- It calls `printChecklistContents()` so that you can look at Xcode's debug console to confirm that a new item was added to `checklistItems`.

➤ Run the app and tap the **Walk the dog** item. You'll see a new **Walk the dog** item at the end of the list...

Adding a new item to the end of the list

If you look at Xcode's debug console, you'll see the output of
`printChecklistContents()`, which shows that `checklistItems` contains the
following items in the given order:

- Walk the dog.

- Brush my teeth.

- Learn iOS development.

- Soccer practice.

- Eat ice cream.

- Walk the dog.

Later on, you'll change the app so that the user will be able to add new items of their
choice instead of simply adding duplicates of existing items. The underlying
principle will still be the same, however: You'll use `append()` to add the new, user-
provided item to the end of `checklistItems`.

Removing items from an array (and the checklist)

There are several methods that remove an element from an array. You'll try two of
them out in your app.

Removing items using remove(at:)

The simplest one is `remove(at:)`, which removes the element at the given index. For
example, if you wanted to remove the first element of `checklistItems`, you'd use
the code `checklistItems.remove(at: 0)`.

Now, use that code by changing the app so that tapping a list item removes the first
item from the list. Do this by replacing this line in `onTapGesture()`:

```
self.checklistItems.append(item)
```

with this:

```
self.checklistItems.remove(at: 0)
```

➤ Incorporate this change by changing body to:

```
var body: some View {
  NavigationView {
    List {
      ForEach(checklistItems, id: \.self) { item in
        Text(item)
          .onTapGesture {
            self.checklistItems.remove(at: 0)
            self.printChecklistContents()
          }
      }
    }
    .navigationBarTitle("Checklist")
    .onAppear() {
      self.printChecklistContents()
    }
  }
}
```

➤ Run the app and start tapping on list items. The list will shrink from the top, with the first item in the list disappearing with each tap until the list is empty:

An empty checklist

Using remove(atOffsets:) to remove list items

Another way to remove list items is `remove(atOffsets:)`. This is a bulk version of `remove(at:)`, which removes a specific range of elements from an array. You specify the starting index and ending index of the items you want to remove using

IndexSet. To see it in action, change the app so that tapping a list item removes the elements from index 0 through index 4. You do this by replacing this line in the onTapGesture() method:

```
self.checklistItems.remove(at: 0)
```

with this:

```
let indexesToRemove = IndexSet(integersIn: 0...4)
self.checklistItems.remove(atOffsets: indexesToRemove)
```

➤ Incorporate this change by changing body to:

```
var body: some View {
  NavigationView {
    List {
      ForEach(checklistItems, id: \.self) { item in
        Text(item)
          .onTapGesture {
            let indexesToRemove = IndexSet(integersIn: 0...4)
            self.checklistItems.remove(atOffsets:
indexesToRemove)
            self.printChecklistContents()
          }
      }
    }
    .navigationBarTitle("Checklist")
    .onAppear() {
      self.printChecklistContents()
    }
  }
}
```

➤ Run the app and tap on any list item. That will call the onTapGesture() method, which will remove elements 0 through to 4 of checklistItems. This will empty the array, which in turn will empty the list.

Now that you know how to remove items from an array, it's time to learn how to respond to the "swipe to delete" gesture.

Responding to the "swipe to delete" gesture

Even though many apps use the list control that comes standard with iOS, many people still don't know the standard "swipe to delete" gesture.

In many apps, you can put your finger on a list item and drag it slightly to the left to reveal a **Delete** button:

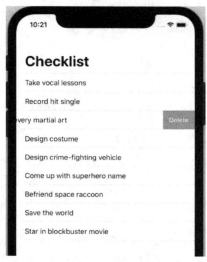

The 'Delete' button that appears when you 'slide to delete' a list item

To delete the list item, you can either tap the **Delete** button or continue swiping to the left. As your finger moves leftward, the list item gets moved offscreen and the **Delete** button grows wider until it's half the width of the list.

At that point, it expands to fill the entire width and deletes the list item:

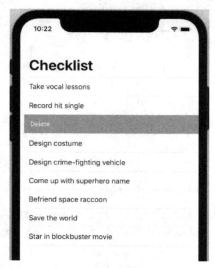

The 'Delete' button at full width

The user can cancel the delete action either by swiping to the right or by tapping on the list item.

Your next step is to add this "swipe to delete" capability to the app. Do this by using ForEach's onDelete(perform:), which is called whenever the user completes the "swipe to delete" gesture.

onDelete(perform:) has one parameter, perform:, where you specify the name of a method that deletes the data behind the list item that the user just swiped. onDelete(perform:) will pass this method an IndexSet that starts and ends with the list item's index, so that it knows which data to delete.

It's time to write this method, which you'll call deleteListItem.

➤ Add this method after printChecklistContents():

```
func deleteListItem(whichElement: IndexSet) {
    checklistItems.remove(atOffsets: whichElement)
    printChecklistContents()
}
```

The method removes the item whose index is contained in index, then prints the contents of checklistItems in Xcode's debug console.

Now, add onDelete(perform:) to ForEach, which will enable "swipe to delete" for the user. You'll also remove onTapGesture() from the Text in ForEach, just to keep things simple.

➤ Change body to the following:

```
var body: some View {
  NavigationView {
    List {
      ForEach(checklistItems, id: \.self) { item in
        Text(item)
      }
      .onDelete(perform: deleteListItem)
    }
    .navigationBarTitle("Checklist")
    .onAppear() {
      self.printChecklistContents()
    }
  }
}
```

➤ Run the app, then swipe a list item to delete it. Check `printChecklistContents()`'s output in Xcode's debug console to confirm that the item you swiped no longer exists in `checklistItems`.

Now the user can delete items from the checklist!

Moving list items

Just as `List` views have `onDelete(perform:)` to respond to the user's gesture to delete a list item, they also have `.onMove(perform:)` to respond to the user's gesture to move a list item.

Unlike deleting items from a `List`, you can only move list items when the list is in "Edit" mode. To make "Edit" mode available to the user, you need to add the button that enables it to the navigation bar using `navigationBarItems()`.

➤ Change body to the following:

```
var body: some View {
  NavigationView {
    List {
      ForEach(checklistItems, id: \.self) { item in
        Text(item)
      }
      .onDelete(perform: deleteListItem)
    }
    .navigationBarItems(trailing: EditButton())
    .navigationBarTitle("Checklist")
    .onAppear() {
      self.printChecklistContents()
    }
  }
}
```

Here, you've added `navigationBarItems()` to `List`. Its parameter adds an **Edit** button to the "trailing" side of the navigation bar. In languages like English, which read from left to right, the trailing side is the right side.

➤ Run the app. There's now an **Edit** button in the navigation bar:

The app with an 'Edit' button in the navigation bar

➤ Tap the **Edit** button to switch to edit mode. The screen will look like this:

The app in edit mode, showing 'Delete' buttons

In edit mode, each list item has a **Delete** button, which looks like a minus sign in a red circle, on its left side. You can tap the button to delete the item. There's still no visual indicator for moving list items, because you haven't made use of `.onMove(perform:)` yet.

Like onDelete(perform:), .onMove(perform:) has a perform: parameter, where you specify the name of a method that moves the data behind the list item that the user just moved. .onMove(perform:) will pass this method an IndexSet that starts and ends with the list item's index, so that it knows which data to move and an Int that indicates where to move it to. Now, write this method, which you'll call moveListItem.

➤ Add this method after deleteListItem():

```
func moveListItem(whichElement: IndexSet, destination: Int) {
  checklistItems.move(fromOffsets: whichElement, toOffset:
destination)
  printChecklistContents()
}
```

The first line of moveListItem(whichElement:destination:) uses an array method you haven't seen yet: move(fromOffsets:, toOffset:), which moves one or more array elements within the array. You put the indexes of the starting and ending elements that you want to move in fromOffsets:, and the index of the place to move them to in toOffset:.

The second line displays the newly-rearranged contents of checklistItems so that you can confirm that the array element moved correctly.

Now, make use of moveListItem in .onMove.

➤ Change body to the following:

```
var body: some View {
  NavigationView {
    List {
      ForEach(checklistItems, id: \.self) { item in
        Text(item)
      }
      .onDelete(perform: deleteListItem)
      .onMove(perform: moveListItem)
    }
    .navigationBarItems(trailing: EditButton())
    .navigationBarTitle("Checklist")
    .onAppear() {
      self.printChecklistContents()
    }
  }
}
```

➤ Run the app and tap the **Edit** button. This time, when you enter edit mode, you see the **Delete** buttons on the left side of each list item and **move handles** on the right side:

The app in edit mode, showing 'Delete' buttons and move handles

➤ Press down on the move handle of any list item and drag it to a new location:

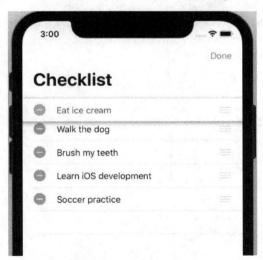

Dragging 'Eat ice cream' to the top of the list

When you let go of the item, it "snaps" to the closest "slot", changing the order of the list. You can confirm that checklistItems reflects the onscreen changes by checking the output of printChecklistContents() in Xcode's debug console.

Key points

In this chapter, you did the following:

- You started with a static list of items that were "hard-wired" into the user interface, using both plain and grouped styles.

- You learned about arrays, the most-used data structure, and loops, one of the key means of flow control in programs.

- You applied your newly-gained knowledge about arrays and loops, as well as ForEach, to build a dynamic list. The contents of that list aren't hard-wired into the user interface; underlying data determine the contents.

- With your dynamic list, you used the power of SwiftUI to give the user the ability to delete items from the list and rearrange the list's items.

Phew! That was a lot of new stuff to take in, so I hope you're still with me. If not, then take a break and start at the beginning again. You're learning a whole bunch of new concepts all at once, and that can be overwhelming.

But don't worry, it's OK if everything doesn't make perfect sense yet. As long as you get the gist of what's going on, you're good to go.

If you want to check your work up to this point, you can find the project files for the app under **09 - List Views** in the Source Code folder.

Chapter 10: A "Checkable" List

Joey deVilla

Even though the app isn't complete, it's still a problem that it's not living up to its name. It displays a list of items, but it doesn't show if they're checked or not. It doesn't even track if an item is checked or not. And it most certainly doesn't let the user check or uncheck items!

In this chapter, the goal is to fix these problems by:

- **Creating checklist item objects**: Swift is an object-oriented programming language, which means that sooner or later, you're going to have to "roll your own" objects. And by "sooner or later," I mean *now*. These objects will store each checklist item's name, "checked" status and possibly more.

- **Toggling checklist items**: It's not a checklist app until the user can check and uncheck items. It's time to make this app live up to its name!

- **Key points**: A quick review of what you've learned in this chapter.

Creating checklist item objects

Arrays: A review

In its current state, the app stores the checklist items in an array named `checklistItems`. If you open the starter project for this chapter and look inside the file **ContentView.swift**, you'll see this at the start of `ContentView`:

```
@State var checklistItems = [
  "Walk the dog",
  "Brush my teeth",
  "Learn iOS development",
  "Soccer practice",
  "Eat ice cream",
]
```

You may notice that `checklistItems`'s last element, "Eat ice cream," has a comma , after it. Swift will ignore it, but that trailing comma makes it easier for you to add additional elements to the array in the future. It's a good idea to use tricks like this that make your programs easy to update.

Arrays are ordered lists of objects, and `checklistItems` is a specific array instance that contains the five items that the checklist contains when the app is launched:

checklistItems

index 0	Walk the dog
index 1	Brush my teeth
index 2	Learn iOS development
index 3	Soccer practice
index 4	Eat ice cream

The checklistItems array with its current contents

checklistItems is missing information. It stores the name of each item, but it doesn't store each item's "checked" status — that is, is the item checked or not? What we need is a checklistItems array where each element stores a checklist item's name and "checked" status:

checklistItems

	name	isChecked
index 0	Walk the dog	false
index 1	Brush my teeth	false
index 2	Learn iOS development	true
index 3	Soccer practice	false
index 4	Eat ice cream	true

The checklistItems array with each element holding two values

While an array can hold many items, its individual elements are like regular variables: They can hold only one item at a time.

What we need is a single package for each checklist item that we can use to hold its name, its "checked" status and any other data.

That package, being a single item, could be put into an array element or ordinary variable. Using these packages, the checklistItems array would look like this:

checklistItems

The checklistItems array with each element holding a single package containing all the value for a checklist item

Here's the good news: These things exist, and you've already been using them. They're objects or, more accurately, instances of structs.

structs vs. objects or instances

Until now, I've been referring to structs as *objects* to keep things simple. This isn't technically correct, but it was good enough to get you started. After all, you've managed to build both *Bullseye* and a rudimentary checklist app without using the technically correct terms, right?

An analogy that gets used all the time in object-oriented programming is the "blueprint and houses" analogy. A blueprint is a set of drawings that describes a house.

The blueprint is used to build one or more houses. The houses based on the same blueprint are identical in structure. They're made with the same number of rooms with the same dimensions, but each house is a unique instance and will hold different people, furniture and other possessions.

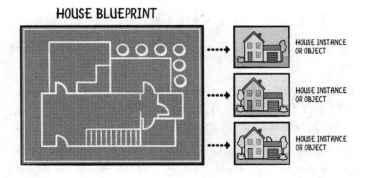

You should think of a struct as the *blueprint* for objects. Just as you don't live in a blueprint, your app doesn't create structs to be components in your program. Instead, your program creates *objects* or *instances* based on the information in the struct.

For this app, you'll code a struct named ChecklistItem that will be the blueprint for checklist item objects. When the app runs, instances of ChecklistItem will be created for each item in the list: "Walk the dog," "Brush my teeth," "Learn iOS development" and so on.

Each of these objects will hold two pieces of data: The checklist item's name and its "checked" status.

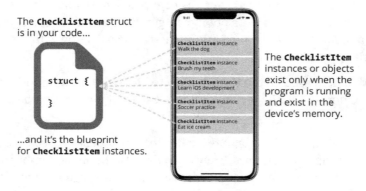

A struct and its object instances

Creating a struct for checklist items

Let's define the ChecklistItem struct. It will specify that its instances will have two properties:

- The name of the checklist item, which we'll call name. Since this will contain text data, this will be a String property. The user should be able to change the name of checklist items, so this should be a variable, which we specify with the var keyword.

- The "checked" status of the checklist item. This is a true/false value, so it will be a Bool (Boolean) property. Since it's a Boolean property, we'll follow the convention of giving this property a name that begins with the word "is": isChecked. The user should be able to check and uncheck checklist items, so this should also be a variable.

When someone adds an item to our checklist, we'll assume the item is incomplete. After all, that's why checklists exist in the first place. We should set up ChecklistItem so that unless otherwise indicated, its initial "checked" status should be "unchecked."

With this criteria, there's enough information to define the ChecklistItem struct.

> Note that ChecklistItem starts with an uppercase "C." In programming, things that act like blueprints typically have names that begin with uppercase

letters. Meanwhile, objects based on those blueprints usually have names that start with lowercase letters. It's a convention that programmers use to make their code easier to understand.

➤ Add the following to `ContentView`, just after the `import SwiftUI` line and before the `struct ContentView: View {` line:

```
struct ChecklistItem {
  var name: String
  var isChecked: Bool = false
}
```

The declaration for the `name` property simply says that it's a `String` property. The declaration for `isChecked` ends with `= false`, which means that `isChecked` has a default value of `false`.

Now that you've defined the `ChecklistItem` blueprint, you can create objects based on it. There are a couple of ways you can refer to this process: Creating `ChecklistItem` objects, creating `ChecklistItem` instances or instantiating `ChecklistItem` objects or instances. Any of these are correct. They all describe making a new thing based on a design for that thing.

To create an object or instance of a `struct`, use the `struct`'s name followed by parentheses containing the `struct`'s properties and the values for those properties. For example, to create a `ChecklistItem` object for "Learn iOS development" that is checked, you'd write this line of code:

```
ChecklistItem(name: "Learn iOS development", isChecked: true)
```

For a `ChecklistItem` object for "Walk the dog" that is unchecked, you can initialize it a couple of ways. First, there's the complete way:

```
ChecklistItem(name: "Walk the dog", isChecked: false)
```

Since `isChecked` has a default value of `false`, you can simply just provide a value for the `name` parameter and skip providing a value for `isChecked`, which will cause it to default to `false`:

```
ChecklistItem(name: "Walk the dog")
```

When you're creating a new instance of a `struct`, Xcode will try to help you by showing you the options. Here's what it will show you when you're making a `ChecklistItem` object:

```
ChecklistItem(|
  M ChecklistItem (name: String)
  M ChecklistItem (name: String, isChecked: Bool)
```

Xcode will try to help you when you're instantiating an object

Let's update the `checklistItems` array by replacing the `Strings` that currently fill it with `ChecklistItem` instances. We want the same item names, and they should have these "checked" statuses:

- Walk the dog — *unchecked*

- Brush my teeth — *unchecked*

- Learn iOS development — *checked*

- Soccer practice — *unchecked*

- Eat ice cream — *checked*

➤ Edit `checklistItems` so that it looks like this:

```
@State var checklistItems = [
  ChecklistItem(name: "Walk the dog"),
  ChecklistItem(name: "Brush my teeth"),
  ChecklistItem(name: "Learn iOS development", isChecked: true),
  ChecklistItem(name: "Soccer practice"),
  ChecklistItem(name: "Eat ice cream", isChecked: true),
]
```

Showing an item's "checked" status

Now that the `checklistItems` array is filled with `checklistItem` instances instead of `Strings`, we need to update the way that `ContentView` displays checklist items. Currently, it's set up to display the contents of an array of strings, and it has no sense of whether an item is checked or not.

Here's the part of `ContentView`'s body property that displayed the contents of `checklistItems` when it was an array of strings:

```
List {
  ForEach(checklistItems, id: \.self) { item in
    Text(item)
  }
  .onDelete(perform: deleteListItem)
  .onMove(perform: moveListItem)
}
```

We need to change the contents of the `ForEach` view so that it displays both the name and checked" status of each checklist item. The name should appear on the left side of the row, while the checkmark should appear on the right side. This sounds like a job for an `HStack`, a couple of `Text` views and a `Spacer` between them, arranged like this:

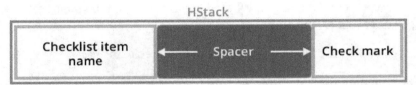

The HStack containing the items in a checklist row

➤ Change the `ForEach` view in body to the following:

```
ForEach(checklistItems, id: \.self) { checklistItem in
  HStack {
    Text(checklistItem.name)
    Spacer()
    if checklistItem.isChecked {
      Text("☑")
    } else {
      Text("☐") }
  }
}
.onDelete(perform: deleteListItem)
.onMove(perform: moveListItem)
```

To get the ☑️ emoji, type **control+⌘+space** to get the emoji selector and enter **check** into the **Search** text field. To get the ⬜️ character, enter **square** into the emoji selector's **Search** text field and scroll through the results to find it.

You're almost ready to run the app and see the results of the changes you made. But first, there's the matter of this error message:

```
ForEach(checklistItems, id: \.self) { checklistItem in
  HStack {
    Text(checklistItem          ● Referencing initializer 'init(_:id:content:)' on 'ForEach' requires that    ⊗
    Spacer()                       'ChecklistItem' conform to 'Hashable'
```

What does this error message mean?

Hooray for cryptic error messages! What Xcode is trying to tell you is that it's running into trouble on this line:

```
ForEach(checklistItems, id: \.self) { checklistItem in
```

The part of the line where it's running into trouble is id: \.self. The id parameter of ForEach tells SwiftUI how to identify each element in the data provided to it, which in this case is checklistItems. When checklistItems was an array of strings, we told ForEach to simply use the value of the string as a way of distinguishing one element from another, and it worked. Now that checklistItems is an array of ChecklistItem instances, \.self refers to a whole ChecklistItem instance, which is a blob of data.

We can fix this by changing the id parameter so that SwiftUI distinguishes between each ChecklistItem instance by its name property.

➤ Change the ForEach line to the following:

```
ForEach(checklistItems, id: \.self.name) { checklistItem in
```

This revised line of code says "loop through all the items in checklistItems, using each item's name property to uniquely identify it, and within each loop through checklistItems, put the current item inside the checklistItem variable."

You should notice that Xcode's cryptic error message has disappeared. Will the app compile and run? There's an easy way to find out:

➤ Run the app. Items in the list now have a checked and unchecked status:

The app now displays items' "checked" status

What happens when two checklist items have the same name?

Let's look at the ForEach line again:

```
ForEach(checklistItems, id: \.self.name) { checklistItem in
```

As I said earlier, setting the id parameter to \.self.name tells ForEach to use each item's name property as a way of uniquely identifying it. What happens if two or more items have the same name? Let's find out.

➤ Change the declaration of checklistItems so that "Walk the dog" appears three times, with two of them checked:

```
@State var checklistItems = [
  ChecklistItem(name: "Walk the dog"),
  ChecklistItem(name: "Brush my teeth"),
  ChecklistItem(name: "Walk the dog", isChecked: true),
  ChecklistItem(name: "Soccer practice"),
  ChecklistItem(name: "Walk the dog", isChecked: true),
]
```

Before you run the app, try to guess what this change will do.

➤ Run the app. You'll see this:

The checklist, with multiple "Walk the dog" items, all unchecked

The checklist has three "Walk the dog" items in the right places, but they're all unchecked. That's because the app is identifying items by name, and the first "Walk the dog" item it saw was the unchecked one. It thinks that the second and third instances, both of which are supposed to be checked, are the same instance as the first one, so it thinks they're all unchecked.

If you've ever been in a situation with someone with the same name as you and someone called out your name, you know this sort of confusion.

A better identifier for checklist items

There's a simple fix for this, and it involves giving each CchecklistItem instance a unique "fingerprint" so that it can be distinguished from other instances, even those with identical name and isChecked properties.

➤ Change the declaration of ChecklistItem so that it looks like this:

```swift
struct ChecklistItem: Identifiable {
  let id = UUID()
  var name: String
  var isChecked: Bool = false
}
```

You just made two changes to `ChecklistItem`. The first is in the first line:

```
struct ChecklistItem: Identifiable {
```

The line still defines a `struct` named `ChecklistItem`. The addition to the end of the line says that `ChecklistItem` is also a kind of `Identifiable`. Remember, in most cases in Swift, the ":" character means "is a kind of."

You're probably wondering what `Identifiable` is. It's a protocol, which in case you've forgotten, is an agreement for an object blueprint to provide some kind of feature or service by including specific properties and methods. The `Identifiable` protocol is an agreement that an object blueprint *adopts* or *conforms to* to guarantee that all its instances can be uniquely identified — hence the name "Identifiable."

`Identifiable` is a simple protocol. For an object blueprint to adopt it, it needs to do only one thing: Include an `id` property whose value is guaranteed to be different for every object. Luckily, Apple operating systems have a built-in `struct` called `UUID`, which generates a universally unique value (a UUID, short for "universally unique identifier") every time it's called. And I'm not kidding. By *universally unique*, I mean that if you took billions of UUID generators and had them generate billions of UUIDs a day for billions of years, the odds of any two of them generating the same UUID would still be practically zero.

This brings us to the second change to `ChecklistItem`, which is the addition of this line:

```
let id = UUID()
```

This adds a property named `id` to `ChecklistItem`. The `let` makes it a constant, which means its value can be set only once when the object is created. `UUID()` creates a new instance of `UUID`, which creates a new universally unique identifier value. This value is put into `id`.

`id` is a constant, and its value is set when the `ChecklistItem` instance is created. This means that you don't have to set it when creating a new `ChecklistItem` instance.

You won't even get the opportunity to set its value. As this Xcode screenshot shows, there won't be an option to set id's value during instantiation:

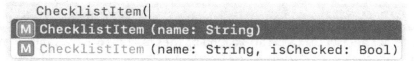

There's no option to set a predefined constant of a struct during instantiation

With these changes, we've upgraded ChecklistItem so it now comes with a "fingerprint" in the form of the id property that uniquely identifies every instance. With this change comes a bonus: You no longer have to tell the ForEach view how to uniquely identify instances of ChecklistItem anymore, because they now conform to the Identifiable protocol.

➤ Change the ForEach line to the following:

```
ForEach(checklistItems) { checklistItem in
```

Note the change: It's now ForEach(checklistItems) instead of ForEach(checklistItems, id: \.self.name) because each ChecklistItem now has the ability to uniquely identify itself to ForEach.

➤ Run the app. Now that each ChecklistItem instance has its own unique identifier, the app can properly distinguish between items, even if they have the same name:

The checklist with properly identified multiple "Walk the dog" items

Using a little less code with the ternary conditional operator

Here's the code in the ForEach view that determines whether the checked or unchecked emoji is displayed for a checklist item:

```
if checklistItem.isChecked {
  Text("✅")
} else {
  Text("⬜")
}
```

The pattern — "if this condition is met, use this value; otherwise use this other value" — is one you'll often use in programming. In fact, it's used so often that Swift and many other programming languages use a special shorthand that condenses this sort of decision down to a single line. Using this shorthand, replace the code above with the following:

```
Text(checklistItem.isChecked ? "✅" : "⬜")
```

This shorthand is called the *ternary conditional operator*, or *ternary operator*. "Ternary" refers to the fact that it has three parts:

- A condition that is evaluated as either true or false. This is the part that comes before the ?.

- The "true" outcome. This is the output if the condition evaluates to true, and it appears between the ? and the :.

- The "false" outcome. This is the output if the condition evaluates to false, and it appears after :.

With the ternary operator, what once took five lines of code now takes just one. When you look at others' code, which is a great way to learn, you'll find that many programmers prefer to use the ternary operator whenever possible.

A quick check before moving on

With *Checklist* now able to track the "checked" status of checklist items, you're a little closer to a working checklist app.

Before moving to the next step — giving the user the ability to check and uncheck items — let's restore the checklist and review the code. Remember, it has some duplicate items right now.

Restoring the checklist

➤ Change the declaration for the `ChecklistItems` array back to the original:

```
@State var checklistItems = [
  ChecklistItem(name: "Walk the dog", isChecked: false),
  ChecklistItem(name: "Brush my teeth", isChecked: false),
  ChecklistItem(name: "Learn iOS development", isChecked: true),
  ChecklistItem(name: "Soccer practice", isChecked: false),
  ChecklistItem(name: "Eat ice cream", isChecked: false),
]
```

Reviewing the code

The code in **ContentView.swift**, minus the comments at the start, should look like this:

```
import SwiftUI

struct ChecklistItem: Identifiable {
  let id = UUID()
  var name: String
  var isChecked: Bool = false
}


struct ContentView: View {

  // Properties
  // ==========

  @State var checklistItems = [
    ChecklistItem(name: "Walk the dog", isChecked: false),
    ChecklistItem(name: "Brush my teeth", isChecked: false),
    ChecklistItem(name: "Learn iOS development", isChecked:
true),
    ChecklistItem(name: "Soccer practice", isChecked: false),
    ChecklistItem(name: "Eat ice cream", isChecked: true),
  ]

  // User interface content and layout
  var body: some View {
    NavigationView {
      List {
```

```
        ForEach(checklistItems) { checklistItem in
          HStack {
            Text(checklistItem.name)
            Spacer()
            Text(checklistItem.isChecked ? "✅" : "⬜")
          }
          .onTapGesture {
            print("checklistitem name: \(checklistItem.name)")
          }
        }
        .onDelete(perform: deleteListItem)
        .onMove(perform: moveListItem)
      }
      .navigationBarItems(trailing: EditButton())
      .navigationBarTitle("Checklist")
      .onAppear() {
        self.printChecklistContents()
      }
    }
  }


  // Methods
  // =======

  func printChecklistContents() {
    for item in checklistItems {
      print(item)
    }
  }

  func deleteListItem(whichElement: IndexSet) {
    checklistItems.remove(atOffsets: whichElement)
    printChecklistContents()
  }

  func moveListItem(whichElement: IndexSet, destination: Int) {
    checklistItems.move(fromOffsets: whichElement, toOffset:
destination)
    printChecklistContents()
  }
}


// Preview
// =======

struct ContentView_Previews: PreviewProvider {
    static var previews: some View {
        ContentView()
    }
}
```

If you're new to programming in general, this may look like a lot of code. You might be surprised to discover that a checklist app that can do as much as this one, even in its incomplete state, would require considerably more code if you did it using UIKit (the previous way of writing iOS apps), on Android or various web application frameworks.

Checking the Canvas

If you haven't been looking at the app in the Canvas lately, now's a good time! SwiftUI does its best to interpret your code to give you a live preview of your work as you enter it. If you don't see the Canvas, show it by selecting it in the menu in the upper right corner of the editor:

Showing the Canvas

Press the **Resume** button, and you should see your app:

Looking at the code and the Canvas

Toggling checklist items

Finding out when the user tapped a list item

The app now tracks each item's "checked" status and can display it to the user. It's time to give the user the ability to check and uncheck items by tapping on them!

Let's look at the ForEach view inside body:

```
ForEach(checklistItems) { checklistItem in
  HStack {
```

```
    Text(checklistItem.name)
    Spacer()
    Text(checklistItem.isChecked ? "☑" : "☐")
  }
  .onTapGesture {
    print("checklistitem name: \(checklistItem.name)")
  }
}
.onDelete(perform: deleteListItem)
.onMove(perform: moveListItem)
```

For every item in the bundle of data that you pass to ForEach, which in this case is checkListItems, it creates a view as defined by the stuff in the braces that follow the ForEach keyword, which is this code:

```
{ checklistItem in
  HStack {
    Text(checklistItem.name)
    Spacer()
    Text(checklistItem.isChecked ? "☑" : "☐")
  }
  .onTapGesture {
    print("checklistitem name: \(checklistItem.name)")
  }
}
```

The checklistItem at the start of this block of code contains the current checklist item. The first time through the loop, checklistItem contains the "Walk the dog" checklist item.

The second time, it contains the "Brush my teeth" item, and so on. As a result, each item in the checklist gets its own view: An HStack containing two Text views that show the item's name and "checked" status, and a Spacer between them.

There are also calls to methods at the end of the ForEach view:

```
.onDelete(perform: deleteListItem)
.onMove(perform: moveListItem)
```

These attach instructions to each item in the List for when the user opts to delete and move list items, and we wrote those instructions in the previous chapter.

If there are methods for responding to events where the user deletes or moves a list item, there must be one for responding to the user tapping a list item.

There is, and it's called `onTapGesture()`, and it's a method that all `Views` have. Here's how we'll use it:

```
.onTapGesture {
    // Code to perform when the user taps a list item goes here
}
```

Let's start with something simple: We'll print "The user tapped a list item!" to Xcode's debug console whenever the user taps an item.

➤ Update body so that it looks like this:

```
var body: some View {
  NavigationView {
    List {
      ForEach(checklistItems) { checklistItem in
        HStack {
          Text(checklistItem.name)
          Spacer()
          Text(checklistItem.isChecked ? "✅" : "⬜")
        }
      }
      .onDelete(perform: deleteListItem)
      .onMove(perform: moveListItem)
      .onTapGesture {
        print("The user tapped a list item!")
      }
    }
    .navigationBarItems(trailing: EditButton())
    .navigationBarTitle("Checklist")
    .onAppear() {
      self.printChecklistContents()
    }
  }
}
```

The change you made was adding a call to `onTapGesture()` immediately after the call to `onMove()`:

```
.onTapGesture {
  print("The user tapped a list item!")
}
```

➤ Run the app and tap some list items. Look at the debug console in Xcode. You should see "The user tapped a list item!" for every time you tapped a list item:

```
44              .onTapGesture {
45                  print("The user tapped a list item!")
46              }
47          }
48          .navigationBarItems(trailing: EditButton())
49          .navigationBarTitle("Checklist")
50          .onAppear() {
51              self.printChecklistContents()
52          }
53      }
54  }
55
```

```
The user tapped a list item!
The user tapped a list item!
The user tapped a list item!
The user tapped a list item!
```

The user tapped a list item

Finding out which item the user tapped

It's good to know that the user tapped a list item, but it's even better to know *which* item.

The `checklistItem` variable inside the `ForEach` view contains the current list item, so we should be able to use it to identify the tapped item.

➤ Change `onTapGesture()` so that its `print` function displays the name of the current item:

```
.onTapGesture {
  print("The user tapped \(checklistItem.name).")
}
```

Xcode will complain, showing you an error message that says "Use of unresolved identifier 'checklistItem'":

```
.onTapGesture {
  print("The user tapped \(checklistItem.name).")      ⓘ  Use of unresolved identifier 'checklistItem'
}
```

Xcode says that checklistItem is unresolved

This is Xcode's terribly technical way of saying, "I have no idea what you mean by `checklistItem`." If your response is "But it's *right there!*," I feel your pain.

If you take a closer look at the code, you'll see the reason behind Xcode's confusion. A variable, constant, or method that is defined within a set of braces is "visible" — or as programmers say, *in scope* — only to code within the same set of braces. checklistItem's visibility or *scope* is limited to the ForEach braces:

```
ForEach(checklistItems) { checklistItem in
  HStack {
    Text(checklistItem.name)
    Spacer()
    Text(checklistItem.isChecked ? "☑" : "☐")
  }
}
.onDelete(perform: deleteListItem)
.onMove(perform: moveListItem)
.onTapGesture {
  print("The user tapped \(checklistItem.name).")
}
```

checklistItem is in scope within these braces.

checklistItem is in out of scope here.

⊘ Use of unresolved identifier 'checklistItem'

checklistItem's scope

The onTapGesture() method call lives outside the braces where checklistItem is in scope. If we want to know which item the user tapped, we'll need to use onTapGesture() somewhere inside those braces.

The HStack that makes up a list row is a View, which means that it has an onTapGesture() method. Better still, it's inside the braces where checklistItem is in scope. Let's move the call to onTapGesture() there!

➤ Update body so that it looks like this:

```
var body: some View {
  NavigationView {
    List {
      ForEach(checklistItems) { checklistItem in
        HStack {
          Text(checklistItem.name)
          Spacer()
          Text(checklistItem.isChecked ? "☑" : "☐")
        }
        .onTapGesture {
          print("The user tapped \(checklistItem.name).")
        }
      }
      .onDelete(perform: deleteListItem)
      .onMove(perform: moveListItem)
    }
    .navigationBarItems(trailing: EditButton())
    .navigationBarTitle("Checklist")
    .onAppear() {
      self.printChecklistContents()
```

```
      }
    }
  }
```

Note the change: The call to `onTapGesture()` is now attached to the `HStack` view instead of the `ForEach` view. `onTapGesture` is called whenever the user taps one of the `HStacks` in the list. Don't take my word for it, though — try it out for yourself!

➤ Run the app, tap some list items, and look at Xcode's debug console, which shows you which item the user tapped.

```
var body: some View {
  NavigationView {
    List {
      ForEach(checklistItems) { checklistItem in
        HStack {
          Text(checklistItem.name)
          Spacer()
          Text(checklistItem.isChecked ? "✅" : "⬜")
        }
        .onTapGesture {
          print("The user tapped \(checklistItem.name).")
        }
      }
```

```
The user tapped Soccer practice.
The user tapped Learn iOS development.
The user tapped Brush my teeth.
The user tapped Walk the dog.
```

Seeing which item the user tapped

Now that you know which item the user tapped, it's time to check or uncheck it.

Checking and unchecking a checklist item

Tapping an item in the list should change its "checked" status. If the item is unchecked, tapping it should change it to checked. Conversely, tapping a checked item should uncheck it.

The `isChecked` property determines a checklist item's "checked" status. Setting it to `true` checks the item, and setting it to `false` unchecks it. With that in mind, we could code `onTapGesture()` like so:

```
.onTapGesture {
  if checklistItem.isChecked {
```

```
      checklistItem.isChecked = false
    } else {
      checklistItem.isChecked = true
    }
  }
```

However, there's a better, shorter way. Boolean (Bool) values have a method called toggle() which does the same thing, toggling the value from true to false and vice versa. This reduces all those lines of the if statement above to a single line. Lets use that instead.

➤ Change the call to onTapGesture() so that it uses toggle() to change the item's isChecked property:

```
.onTapGesture {
  checklistItem.isChecked.toggle()
}
```

Once again, Xcode has an issue with what you just did. Lets have a look at what the issue is this time.

```
.onTapGesture {
  checklistItem.isChecked.toggle()|
}
}
.onDelete(perform: deleteListItem)      ● Type of expression is ambiguous without more context        ⊗
.onMove(perform: moveListItem)          ⚠ Result of call to function returning '_' is unused
```

Two errors appear when you change the call to onTapGesture()

checklistItem is a constant, and Xcode's two error messages, "Type of expression is ambiguous without more context," and "Result of call to function returning '_' is unused," are a result of you trying to change one of its properties. You can't change the properties of a constant — you can only *read* them.

You'll often run into situations like this when programming. You'll come up with a solution that you think *should* work, but when you code it, the compiler throws this kind of seemingly intractable obstacle in your way. This is the time to step back, look at the code, and see if it provides you with another solution.

First, think about what we *can* do with checklistItem. We can read its properties, which are:

- id: The automatically generated universally unique identifier for the item.

- name: The name of the item. We used this earlier to print the name of the tapped item in the Xcode console.

- isChecked: The "checked" status of the item.

Then you should ask yourself: Is there another way to access a given checklist item? There might be, by way of the array of checklist items, checklistItems. The entire ContentView struct is its scope.

It's declared as a var property, which means it's a variable, and so are its contents. Accessing a given element of checklistItems is done using *array notation*: checklistItems[0] is the first element of the array, checklistItems[1] is the second, checklistItems[2] is the third, and so on.

Let's test this idea by changing onTapGesture() so that when the user taps a list item, the first item in the list — checklistItems[0] — is toggled.

➤ Change the call to onTapGesture() to the following:

```
.onTapGesture {
  self.checklistItems[0].isChecked.toggle()
}
```

➤ Run the app and tap any list item. The first item in the list, "Walk the dog," should toggle between checked and unchecked.

Now we're getting somewhere. We now know that if you know the index (the element number, which starts at 0) of the item in checklistItems, you can change the item's "checked" status. The problem is that there's no such information inside the single checklistItem we get inside the ForEach view. All we have are checklistItems properties.

Look again at checklistItem's properties. That first one, id, uniquely identifies it. Couldn't we use it as a "search term" to scan through the items in the checklistItems array to find the matching item, and then toggle that item's isChecked property?

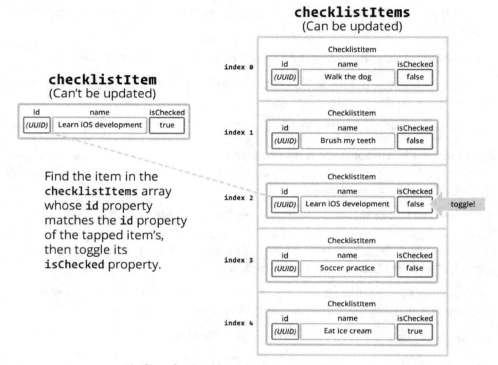

Finding the matching item in checklistItems

Fortunately, the answer is "yes," and there's a way to do it in a couple of lines of code.

Swift arrays have many built-in methods for all sorts of purposes, including inspecting their contents, accessing one or more of their elements, adding and removing elements and *finding* specific elements. This final method is the most important for our immediate needs. One of these methods is firstIndex(of:), which gives you the index of the first element in the array that matches the given criteria. Remember, an array index is the number that specifies an element in an array.

Suppose we had an array named myList that was defined this way:

```
let myList = [
  "Alpha",
  "Bravo",
  "Charlie",
  "Delta",
]
```

If you wanted to find the index of "Charlie" in myList, you'd use this code:

```
let charlieIndex = myList.firstIndex(of: "Charlie")
```

"Charlie" is the third item in myList, which means its index is **2**, so the value of charlieIndex is set to 2. As a reminder, array elements begin at **0**.

What happens if you search for an item that *isn't* in the array, say "Egbert?"

```
let egbertIndex = myList.firstIndex(of: "Egbert")
```

Since "Egbert" isn't in myList, it doesn't have an index. When this happens, firstIndex(of:) returns a value called nil, and that's the value put into egbertIndex.

In case you were wondering how I knew about firstIndex(of:), I didn't spring forth from the womb as a fully-formed Swift programmer. Instead, I looked at the *Arrays* section of Apple's Swift documentation, located at developer.apple.com/documentation/swift/array. If you ever have a question about a Swift language feature, the developer docs are an excellent place to start.

Introducing nil and its friend, if let

nil is a special value, and it means "no value." nil doesn't mean **0**, because **0** is a value. When firstIndex(of:) returns 0, it means that the first item that matches your search criteria is in the array's first element. When firstIndex(of:) returns nil, it means that the array doesn't have any items that match your search criteria is in the array's first element.

> You'll learn more about nil and optional types later on.

You'll often find yourself writing code that follows this pattern: "If an operation produced a result with a value, do something with that result." In many programming languages, you'd have to write this sort of code this way:

```
let result = someOperation()
if result != nil {
  // Do something with result
}
```

In case you were wondering, != means "is not equal to."

In the code above, we're calling someOperation(), which returns a result. If that result is *not* nil, the code inside the braces with the "Do something with result" comment is executed. If the result is nil, the code inside the braces is skipped entirely.

Swift has the if let construct, which makes this sort of code a little more concise. Here's how you'd rewrite the code above using if let:

```
if let result = someOperation() {
  // Do something with result
}
```

Just like the code before it, this code calls someOperation() and puts its result in the variable result. If result's value is not nil, the code inside the braces with the "Do something with result" comment is executed. Otherwise, the code inside the braces is skipped.

We're going to use if let to toggle the "checked" status of a checklist item in checklistItems if one whose id matches the id of the tapped item is found by a close cousin of the firstIndex(of:) method.

Finding a specific item in checklistItems

The firstIndex(of:) method is good for doing simple matches. Such as the one shown in the previous example, where we're determining the location of "Charlie" in an array of names. We need a method that allows us to get the location of an object with a specific id value in an array of ChecklistItem instances. That method is the firstIndex(where:) method.

The firstIndex(where:) method follows this format:

result = firstIndex(where: { *Code for search criteria that produces a* true *or* false *result goes here* })

Where firstIndex(of:) is useful for finding the first exact match in an array, firstIndex(where:) lets you get *really* specific. In a really fancy checklist app, you could use it to search for the first checklist item in the list that is checked, entered on a Tuesday, marked as high priority and features a cat picture. In this checklist app, you'll use it to find the first item in the list with a specific id value.

Using firstIndex(where:) is another one of those cases where showing it in action first is better than telling you how to use it. So, that's just what I'll do:

➤ Change the call to `onTapGesture()` to this:

```
.onTapGesture {
  if let matchingIndex = self.checklistItems.firstIndex(where: {
$0.id == checklistItem.id }) {
    self.checklistItems[matchingIndex].isChecked.toggle()
  }
  self.printChecklistContents()
}
```

➤ Run the app. Tap on any of the item names or checkboxes to check and uncheck them. You might notice that the blank space between the name and checkbox doesn't respond to taps — we'll fix that shortly.

You can confirm that the items' `isChecked` properties are being updated by looking at Xcode's debug console:

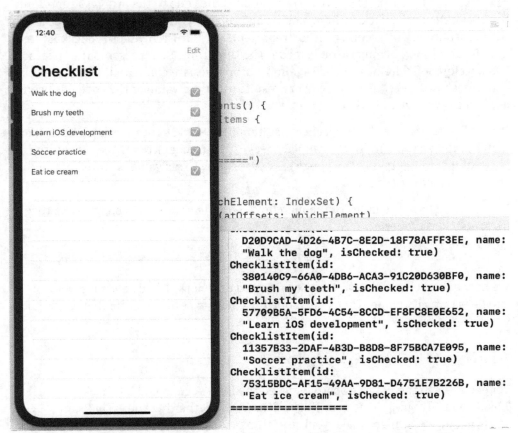

A working checklist, as seen in the Simulator and debug console

Now that it's possible for the user to check and uncheck items, let's look at the code that made it possible. Here's the first line of the new code:

```
if let matchingIndex = self.checklistItems.firstIndex(where:
{ $0.id == checklistItem.id }) {
```

Let's take a closer look at funny-looking part of that line, namely:

```
{ $0.id == checklistItem.id }
```

You provide `firstIndex(where:)` with the code in the braces — in case you've forgotten, it's called a *closure* — and it goes through the array, applying that code to each element. The `$0` is shorthand for "the first parameter passed to the closure," which is the current array element.

The first time that `firstIndex(where:)` applies the code to the array, `$0` represents the "Walk the dog" checklist item, and its `id` property compared to the `id` property of the tapped item. The second time, `$0` represents the "Brush my teeth" checklist item, and the `id` property comparison is made. The third time, `$0` represents the "Learn iOS development" item, and once again, `id` properties are compared. This cycle continues until the code in the closure results in a `true` value or the code has been applied to every element in the array.

If `firstIndex(where:)` finds a checklist item in `checklistItems` whose `id` property matches the `id` property of the tapped checklist item (`checklistItem`), it returns the index of matching item in the `checklistItems` array. This value is stored in the constant `matchingIndex`.

Now that we have the index of the matching item in `checklistItems`, we can toggle its `isChecked` property:

```
self.checklistItems[matchingIndex].isChecked.toggle()
```

We now have a checklist that the user can actually check! It's always nice when an app lives up to its name. There's just one little user experience issue that we should fix.

Fixing the "dead zone"

For each row in the list, the space between the item's name and its checkbox is a "dead zone." Tapping on it doesn't check or uncheck the checkbox. That's an annoying quirk. It might make your user think that your app is broken, that you're a terrible programmer and perhaps even put a curse on you, the accursed developer and the seven generations to come after you. Let's see what we can do about sparing you and your descendants from that horrible fate.

The solution was the result of some experimenting and guessing. Rather than drag you through my experimentation and guesswork, let me simply give you the summary.

Do you know how you can make the whole row tappable, rather than just the visible parts? *Give it a background color.*

I decided to set the row's background color to white, which I did by adding this method call to the HStack that defines each row:

```
.background(Color.white) // This makes the entire row clickable
```

With this change, the body property should look like this:

```
var body: some View {
  NavigationView {
    List {
      ForEach(checklistItems) { checklistItem in
        HStack {
          Text(checklistItem.name)
          Spacer()
          Text(checklistItem.isChecked ? "✅" : "⬜")
        }
        .background(Color.white) // This makes the entire row
clickable
        .onTapGesture {
          if let matchingIndex =
            self.checklistItems.firstIndex(where: { $0.id ==
checklistItem.id }) {

self.checklistItems[matchingIndex].isChecked.toggle()
          }
          self.printChecklistContents()
        }
      }
      .onDelete(perform: deleteListItem)
      .onMove(perform: moveListItem)
    }
    .navigationBarItems(trailing: EditButton())
    .navigationBarTitle("Checklist")
    .onAppear() {
      self.printChecklistContents()
    }
  }
}
```

Why does this work? It's because, in its default state, list rows are transparent. The white color of a default list row is actually the white color of the view that contains the whole user interface.

The standard for most user interfaces — not just iOS' — is that transparent objects aren't tappable or clickable. Giving the row a color means that its pixels are clickable, and giving it the same color as the background view makes the whole under interface seamless.

As you gain more experience programming, you'll find that your ability to come up with these flashes of insight will improve. Practice, to twist the expression slightly, makes programmer.

Key points

In this chapter, you did the following:

- You created your first `struct`, and in the process, learned the difference between `struct`s and objects or instances.

- You updated the user interface to show each checklist item's name and "checked" status.

- You learned about the ternary operator.

- You used the `onTapGesture` method that `View`s have to detect when the user tapped on a row.

- You learned about methods for finding the first occurrence of an item in an array that met specific criteria.

- You got a look into the sort of problem-solving that goes hand in hand with writing programs. As you do more programming, you'll get better at it!

As always, you can find the project files for the app at this stage under **10 - Checkable List** in the Source Code folder.

In the next chapter, we'll handle the next big piece of missing functionality: Adding and editing checklist items. *Checklist* is beginning to look like a real app, isn't it?

Chapter 11: The App Structure

Joey deVilla

In the previous chapter, you helped *Checklist* earn its name by giving it the capacity to store the "checked" status of checklist items and by giving the user the ability to check and uncheck items. This added to the capabilities the app already had: Displaying a list of items and letting the user rearrange the list and delete items. Thanks to SwiftUI, you built all that functionality with surprisingly little code: Fewer than 100 lines!

However, the app's still missing some very important functionality. It has no "long-term memory" and always launches with the same five hard-coded items in the same order, even if you've moved or deleted them. There's no way for the user to add new items or edit existing ones.

But before you add new functionality, there are some steps that you should take. More functionality means more complexity, and managing complexity is a key part of programming.

Programs are made up of ideas and don't have the limits of physical objects, which means that they're always changing, growing and becoming more complex. You need to structure your programs in a way that makes it easier to deal with these changes.

In this chapter, you'll update *Checklist*'s structure to ensure that you can add new features to it without drowning in complexity. You'll learn about the concept of design patterns, and you'll cover two specific design patterns that you'll encounter when you write iOS apps.

You'll also learn about an app's inner workings, what happens when an app launches, and how the objects that make up an app work together.

Design patterns: MVC and MVVM

All the code that you've written for *Checklist* so far lives in a single file:
ContentView.swift. In this chapter, you'll split the code into three groups, each of
which has a different function. This will make your code easier to maintain in the
future. Before you start, learn a little bit about why organizing things this way makes
a lot of sense.

Different parts of the code do different things. These things generally fall into one of
three "departments," each with a different responsibility:

- **Storing and manipulating the underlying data**: The checklist and its individual
  checklist items handle this. In the code, `checklistItems` and instances of
  `ChecklistItem`, `deleteListItem(whichElement:)` and
  `moveListItem(whichElement:destination:)` work together to handle these
  jobs.

- **Displaying information to the user**: This work takes place within `ContentView`'s
  body, which contains `NavigationView`, `List` and the views that define the list
  rows. Each of these includes each item's name and checkbox.

- **Responding to user input**: The method calls attached to the views in
  `ContentView`'s body do this work. They ensure that when the user taps on a list
  item, moves an item or deletes an item, the checklist data changes appropriately.

Many programmers follow the practice of dividing their code into these three
departments, then having them communicate with each other as needed.

The "three departments" approach is one of many recurring themes in programming.
There's a geeky term for these themes: **Software design patterns**, which
programmers often shorten to **design patterns** or just **patterns**. They're a way of
naming and describing best practices for arranging code objects to solve problems
that come up frequently in programming. Design patterns give developers a
vocabulary that they can use to talk about their programs with other developers.

> **Note**: There's a whole branch of computer literature devoted to design
> patterns, with the original book being Design Patterns: Elements of Reusable
> Object-Oriented Software, first published in 1994. Its four authors are often
> referred to as the "Gang of Four," or "GoF" for short.

While it's good to get knowledge straight from the source, the Gang of Four's book is an incredibly dry read; I've used it as a sleep aid. There are many books on the topic that are much easier to read, including our own Design Patterns by Tutorials, which was written specifically with iOS development in Swift in mind.

The Model-View-Controller (MVC) pattern

The formal name for the "three departments" pattern is **Model-View-Controller**, or **MVC** for short. Each name represents a category of object:

- **Models**: These objects contain your data and any operations on that data. For example, if you're writing a cookbook app, the model would consist of the recipes. In a game, it would be the design of the levels, the player score and the positions of the monsters.

Models can interact with each other, and the way in which they interact — the **business rules** or the **domain logic** — is also determined by the models. In a game, the player and opponent models determine how the players and their various opponents interact.

In *Checklist*, the checklists along with their to-do items and the "move" and "delete" operations form the data model. Models are the keepers of the knowledge in the system.

- **Views**: These are the visual part of the app: Text, images, buttons, lists and their rows and so on. In a game, the views form the visual representation of the game world, such as the monster animations or a frag counter.

A view can draw itself and respond to user input, but it shouldn't handle any app logic. It should be "dumb" in the sense that it only knows how to show data to the user, without knowing anything about that data or making any decisions about what it's displaying. Many different apps can all use views like Lists, because they're not tied to a specific data model.

- **Controllers**: A controller is an object that connects your data model objects to the views. It listens to taps on the views, makes the data model objects do calculations in response, and updates the views to reflect the new state of your model.

Here's how model, view and controller objects fit together:

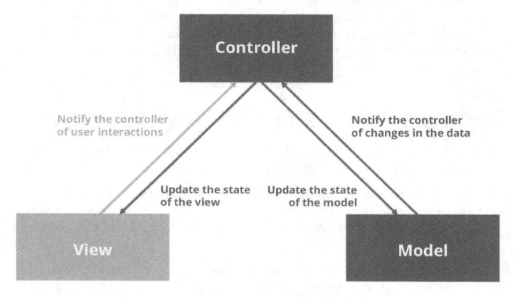

How the Model, View and Controller in MVC fit together

The flow of activity in MVC is circular. The user taps a button or enters information in the view, then the view notifies the controller. The controller interprets the user interaction and then contacts the model for the information it needs to complete the request. The model provides the information to the controller, which relays it to the view, which shows it to the user.

The Model-View-Controller pattern has been around since the 1970s. Most desktop, web and mobile apps that you use are built on this pattern, or something similar to it. That's because it does a good job of separating the various aspects of an app into more manageable chunks. This pattern makes life easier for both the solo developer, who has to manage a lot of code alone and developer teams, who have to work on the same app without getting in each other's way.

You'll use the Model-View-Controller pattern later in this book, when you build apps with the UIKit framework. SwiftUI uses a slightly different pattern, called MVVM.

Model-View-ViewModel (MVVM)

Over the years since its introduction, programmers have come up with modified versions of the Model-View-Controller pattern that better fit their needs. One of these is **Model-View-ViewModel**, which is often shortened to *MVVM*.

Like Model-View-Controller, its name suggests that it has three different object categories:

- **Models**: MVVM models, like MVC models, contain the data for the app.

- **Views**: As with MVC, MVVM views present data to the user and accept user input. Unlike MVC, there's very little code in an MVVM view, since they focus on the user interface and nothing else.

- **ViewModels**: "ViewModel" is a clumsy name, but since the brightest minds in computer science haven't come up with a better one, we're stuck with it. The ViewModel gives the view the data and functionality it needs from the model, and nothing more. You can think of the ViewModel as the model's "customer service representative" and the view as the "customer."

Here's how model, view and ViewModel objects fit together:

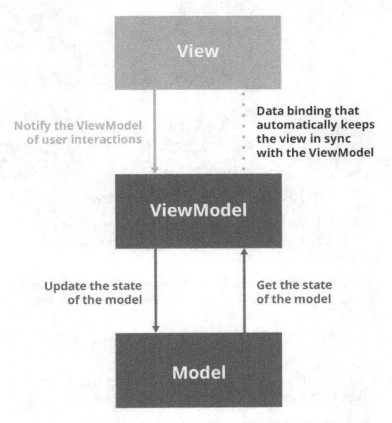

How the Model, View and ViewModel in MVVM fit together

The flow of activity in MVVM is often described as more linear than in MVC. In MVC, the Controller acts as a central hub and has to know about both the view and the model. In MVVM, the view knows only about the ViewModel, and the ViewModel knows only about the model.

This linear arrangement of one-way relationships makes it easier to maintain, modify and even swap out components. The flexibility that MVVM offers is one reason why it's popular with Windows and web app developers, and it's why Apple adopted this approach for the SwiftUI framework.

Using MVVM with Checklist

Here's how you'll split up *Checklist*'s code:

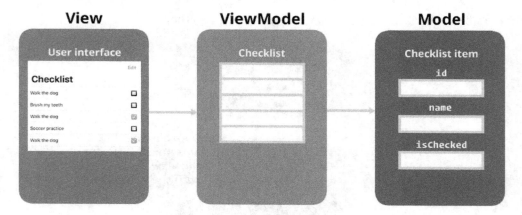

The model, view and ViewModel in Checklist

- The existing ContentView already acts as the app's view. To adopt MVVM for *Checklist*, you'll extract the code that makes up the ViewModel and the model and put each set of code into its own file.

- The ViewModel is an object that contains the properties and methods that the view needs to show data to the user and to respond to the user's actions. You'll extract the list of items and the methods that manipulate the list from ContentView and put them into their own ViewModel object, which will live in its own file.

- The model is an object representing individual checklist items. You'll extract ChecklistItem from ContentView and put it into its own file.

The end result will be an app that appears the same to the user, but to programmers, it'll be better organized and easier to maintain and to add features to.

Along the way, you'll learn about breaking up a project into easier-to-manage pieces, dive deeper into how objects work and learn what happens "under the hood" when the user launches an app.

There's a lot to do in this chapter, so go ahead and get started!

Renaming the view

Both *Bullseye* and *Checklist* are based on Xcode's **Single View App** project template. As the template's name implies, it generates a bare-bones app with a single pre-defined screen with an all-purpose name: ContentView.

It's a good enough name for an app with a single screen, but a bit too generic for an app that will have multiple screens.

Since you're in the process of rearranging the app to fit the Model-View-ViewModel pattern, give the app's main view a more fitting name: ChecklistView.

You can do this manually, by searching for ContentView throughout the project's files and renaming the **ContentView.swift** file itself, but that's a tedious and error-prone process. Instead, you'll rename it automatically using Xcode's refactoring tools.

➤ Open **ContentView.swift**. Find the opening line of ContentView. Select ContentView and right-click or control-click it. Select **Refactor** from the menu that appears, then select **Rename...** from the next menu:

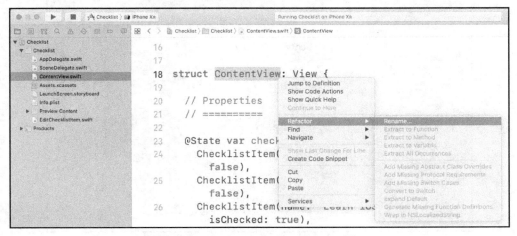

The first step in renaming ContentView

Xcode will scan all the project files for any occurrence of the name `ContentView`. It will then display all these occurrences in the Editor pane so you can easily rename them.

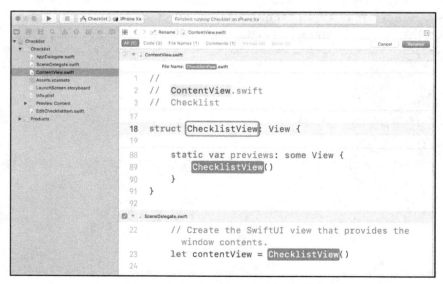

Xcode shows you all the instances of the name ContentView

➤ Type `ChecklistView`. This change will be reflected in most of the instances of `ContentView`:

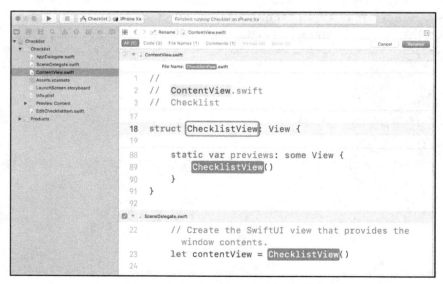

Changing ContentView's name to ChecklistView

➤ Click **Rename**. All the instances of `ContentView` that matter — in the code and in filenames — will be changed to `ChecklistView`.

There's a bug in Xcode's refactoring that causes it to fail to update the one instance of `ContentView` that appears in the comments. It won't affect the app, but you should change that instance manually, if only to be consistent.

➤ Build and run to reassure yourself that you didn't break anything during the name change.

Adding a file for the model

Creating a file for the model

Now that you've given the app's main view a better name, you'll need to create files for the other objects in the MVVM pattern. You'll start by creating a file for the model's code.

➤ Add a new file to the project by right-clicking or control-clicking on the **Checklist** folder in Xcode's Project Explorer. Select **New File...** from the menu that appears:

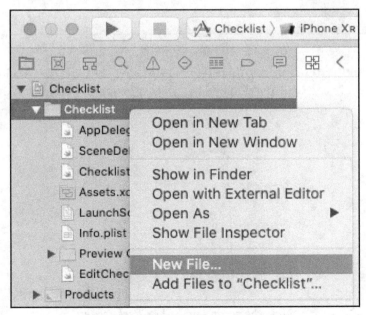

Add the second new file to the project

This time, you don't want to add a new view to the app, but rather to a class. This calls for adding a different kind of file to the project.

➤ In the window that appears, make sure that you've selected **iOS** then select **Swift File**, and *not* **SwiftUI View**. Unlike the SwiftUI View template, which comes with code to generate a simple "Hello World!" screen, this option gives you a mostly empty file. Click **Next**:

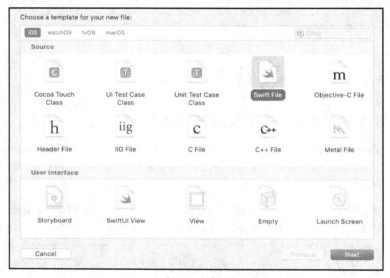

Select Swift File

➤ Enter **ChecklistItem** into the **Save As:** field. Make sure that you've selected **ChecklistItem** in the **Group** menu and in the **Targets** menu, then click **Create**:

Name the second new file 'ChecklistItem'

The project now has a new file named **ChecklistItem.swift**.

Moving the model code to the file

Now that you have a new file for the model, it's time to move its code there. Luckily, this is a simple process.

➤ Open **ChecklistView.swift** and cut the declaration of ChecklistItem:

```
struct ChecklistItem: Identifiable {
  let id = UUID()
  var name: String
  var isChecked: Bool = false
}
```

➤ Then paste it into **ChecklistItem.swift** so that the code in the file looks like this:

```
import Foundation

struct ChecklistItem: Identifiable {
  let id = UUID()
  var name: String
  var isChecked: Bool = false
}
```

➤ Build and run the app. It still works because you haven't changed any code; you merely relocated the definition of ChecklistItem into its own file.

That takes care of the model code. It's now time to tackle the ViewModel!

Adding a file for the ViewModel

Your next step is to create a file for the ViewModel.

➤ Add another new file to the project by right-clicking or control-clicking the **Checklist** folder in Xcode's Project Explorer. Select **New File...** from the menu:

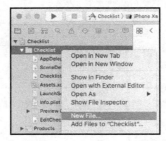

Add the first new file to the project

➤ Once again, make sure that you've selected **iOS** in the new window, then select **Swift File** and click **Next**:

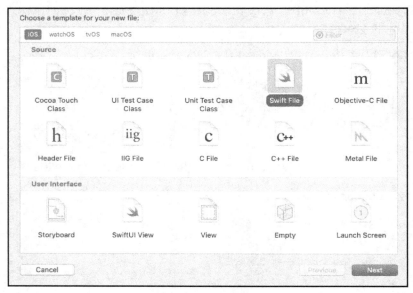

Select Swift File

➤ Enter **Checklist** into the **Save As:** field. Make sure that you've selected **Checklist** in the **Group** menu and in the **Targets** menu, then click **Create**:

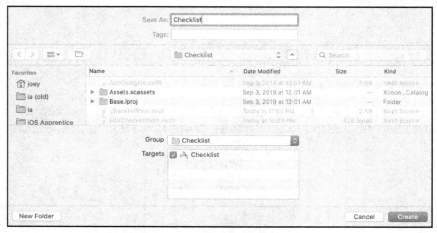

Name the first new file 'Checklist'

The project now has a new file named **Checklist.swift**. You just need to add the ViewModel code to it.

Moving the ViewModel code to the file

Add the following to **Checklist.swift**, just after the import Foundation line:

```
class Checklist: ObservableObject {

}
```

A class is another kind of blueprint for objects. Like a struct, it has properties and methods and you can create class instances. In the spirit of "show, don't tell," continue with moving the ViewModel code into this class and see how it works in action before getting into a deeper discussion about classes.

You may not know much about classes yet, but you should have enough of a grasp of Swift syntax to know that you just added the definition of a class named Checklist and that it's a kind of ObservableObject.

ObservableObject is a protocol, and as its name implies, when you use it on an object, another object can observe it for changes. That other object is called an observer.

In the MVVM pattern, the view observes the ViewModel. This observer/observed relationship binds the view and ViewModel so that when data that's displayed to the user is updated in the ViewModel, the view updates itself automatically.

The ViewModel should contain all the functionality that the view needs to present information to the user. So far, that functionality is:

1. Displaying the checklist items.

2. Deleting an item.

3. Moving an item.

4. Toggling an item between "checked" and "unchecked".

Start by moving the code for the first item on that list: Displaying the checklist items. The checklist items are stored in checklistItems in ChecklistView.

➤ Open **ChecklistView.swift**. Cut checklistItems in ChecklistView:

```
@State var checklistItems = [
  ChecklistItem(name: "Walk the dog", isChecked: false),
```

```
    ChecklistItem(name: "Brush my teeth", isChecked: false),
    ChecklistItem(name: "Learn iOS development", isChecked: true),
    ChecklistItem(name: "Soccer practice", isChecked: false),
    ChecklistItem(name: "Eat ice cream", isChecked: true),
  ]
```

Xcode will show some error messages. Ignore them for now.

➤ Paste `checklistItems` into `Checklist` in **Checklist.swift**. Change `@State` to `@Published`.

The class should now look like this:

```
class Checklist: ObservableObject {

  @Published var checklistItems = [
    ChecklistItem(name: "Walk the dog", isChecked: false),
    ChecklistItem(name: "Brush my teeth", isChecked: false),
    ChecklistItem(name: "Learn iOS development", isChecked:
true),
    ChecklistItem(name: "Soccer practice", isChecked: false),
    ChecklistItem(name: "Eat ice cream", isChecked: true),
  ]

}
```

Marking a property in an `ObservableObject` as `@Published` means that making changes to that property notifies any observing objects. By marking `checklistItems` as `@Published`, any changes to it — toggling an item, deleting an item or moving an item — will update any views that are observing the ViewModel.

That takes care of all the ViewModel properties. It's time to move the ViewModel methods into `Checklist`.

➤ Open **ChecklistView.swift**. Cut the methods from `ChecklistView`:

```
func printChecklistContents() {
  for item in checklistItems {
    print(item)
  }
}

func deleteListItem(whichElement: IndexSet) {
  checklistItems.remove(atOffsets: whichElement)
  printChecklistContents()
}

func moveListItem(whichElement: IndexSet, destination: Int) {
  checklistItems.move(fromOffsets: whichElement, toOffset:
```

```
destination)
   printChecklistContents()
}
```

➤ Then go back to **Checklist.swift** and paste the methods into Checklist, just after the checklistItems.

Checklist should now look like this:

```
class Checklist: ObservableObject {

  @Published var checklistItems = [
    ChecklistItem(name: "Walk the dog", isChecked: false),
    ChecklistItem(name: "Brush my teeth", isChecked: false),
    ChecklistItem(name: "Learn iOS development", isChecked:
true),
    ChecklistItem(name: "Soccer practice", isChecked: false),
    ChecklistItem(name: "Eat ice cream", isChecked: false),
  ]

  func printChecklistContents() {
    for item in checklistItems {
      print(item)
    }
  }

  func deleteListItem(whichElement: IndexSet) {
    checklistItems.remove(atOffsets: whichElement)
    printChecklistContents()
  }

  func moveListItem(whichElement: IndexSet, destination: Int) {
    checklistItems.move(fromOffsets: whichElement, toOffset:
destination)
    printChecklistContents()
  }
}
```

The ViewModel, Checklist, now has the following:

• A property called checklistItems, which contains the checklist items.

These methods are all that the view currently needs to present information to the user and respond to the user's actions – exactly what a ViewModel provides to a view.

At this point, you have a file for the model that includes its object blueprint, **ChecklistItem.swift**, `ChecklistItem`, a file for the ViewModel with its object blueprint, **Checklist.swift** and `Checklist`. You put these together from bits and pieces extracted from **ChecklistView.swift** and `ChecklistView`.

Now, take a look at what's left of the view file and its object blueprint.

➤ Open **ChecklistView.swift** and look at `ChecklistView`. There's a lot less code and a few more errors:

```swift
struct ChecklistView: View {

  // Properties
  // ==========

  // User interface content and layout
  var body: some View {
    NavigationView {
      List {
        ForEach(checklistItems) { checklistItem in     ❶ Use of unresolved identifier 'checklistItems'
          HStack {
            Text(checklistItem.name)
            Spacer()
            Text(checklistItem.isChecked ? "✅" : "◻️")
          }
          .background(Color.white) // This makes the entire row clickable
          .onTapGesture {
            if let matchingIndex =
              self.checklistItems.firstIndex(where: { $0.id == checklistItem.id }) {
              self.checklistItems[matchingIndex].isChecked.toggle()
            }
            self.printChecklistContents()
          }
        }
        .onDelete(perform: deleteListItem)       ❶ Use of unresolved identifier 'deleteListItem'
        .onMove(perform: moveListItem)           ❶ Use of unresolved identifier 'moveListItem'
      }
      .navigationBarItems(trailing: EditButton())
      .navigationBarTitle("Checklist")
      .onAppear() {
        self.printChecklistContents()
      }
    }
  }
}
```

ChecklistView's code and error messages

It appears that the view will need a little tweaking before *Checklist*'s new MVVM setup will work. The problem is that there isn't a connection between the view, `ChecklistView` and the ViewModel, `Checklist`.

You'll establish that connection in a while, after you learn a little more about objects.

Structs and classes

Until this chapter, the only kind of object blueprint you've worked with was a struct. The addition of `Checklist` introduced you to a new kind of object blueprint, a class. How are classes and structs the same, and how are they different?

Both are used to create instances or objects. Both have properties, which are what the objects know, and methods, which are what the objects do.

They also differ in a few ways, the most notable one being that structs are **value types** and classes are **reference types**. Rather than give you a dry technical definition of what these are, or confuse you with an analogy, your next step is to play with them using an Xcode feature called **playgrounds**.

Starting a new playground

A playground is a type of Xcode project that lets you experiment with Swift code and see the results immediately. Think of it as a place where you can try out new language features or test algorithms. Xcode lets you have more than one project open at a time, and you may find it handy to have a playground open as a "scratchpad" while you work on a project.

➤ In Xcode's **File** menu, select **New...**, and then **Playground**.

You'll see a pop-up where you select options for the playground you want to create:

Options for creating a new playground

I've found that the best kind of playground for playing with Swift language features is the blank macOS playground. That's because it doesn't load all the extra material that iOS and tvOS programming require, and it crashes less often. Here are the options to choose to create this kind of playground.

➤ In the pop-up, select **macOS**, highlight the **Blank** playground type, then click **Next**. You'll see a **Save As:** dialog;

Choosing a place to save the playground

➤ Enter a name for the playground; I used **Structs and classes**. In the **Add to:** menu, select **Don't add to any project or workspace**. Once you've done that, click the **Create** button.

Xcode will create a new playground, which will look like this:

The newly-created Xcode playground

You can see what all the code up to and including a particular line in the playground does by moving the cursor over its line number and pressing the "Play" button that appears. The results will appear in the live view column on the right.

➤ Move the cursor over the number for line 3 in the playground and click the "Play" button:

Running a line of code in the playground

You should see "Hello, playground" appear in the live view column. That's the value that was assigned to the variable `str`.

➤ Add the following line to the playground:

```
print("str contains: \(str)")
```

➤ Move the cursor over the line number of the line you just entered and click the "Play" button. You should see this:

Printing in the playground

`print()` works in playgrounds just like it does in iOS projects: It prints to the debug console.

Now that you've covered playgrounds and their basics, it's time to use yours to learn about value types.

Value types

A "value type" is a type of data where each instance keeps its own copy. In Swift, numbers are value types. Play with a couple of numbers so you can see what this means.

➤ Add the following to the playground, after the code you entered previously:

```
var firstNumber = 5
var secondNumber = firstNumber
print("firstNumber contains \(firstNumber) and secondNumber
contains \(secondNumber)")
```

➤ Move the cursor over the line number for the last line and click the "Play" button.

The debug console should show the text: "firstNumber contains 5 and secondNumber contains 5". This makes sense; the line var secondNumber = firstNumber copies the contents of firstNumber into secondNumber.

➤ Add the following to the playground, after the code you entered previously:

```
secondNumber = 10
print("firstNumber contains \(firstNumber) and secondNumber
contains \(secondNumber)")
```

➤ Move the cursor over the line number for the last line and click the "Play" button.

The debug console should show the text "firstNumber contains 5 and secondNumber contains 10". Changing the value of secondNumber did not change the value of firstNumber. This is what "each instance keeps its own copy" means.

Structs are also **value types**. Next, you'll define a simple struct and play with it, like you just did with numbers.

➤ Add the following to the playground, after the code you entered previously:

```
struct PetValueType {
  var name: String = ""
  var species: String = ""
}
```

Now, create an instance of `PetValueType` and a copy of that instance.

➤ Add the following to the playground, after the code you entered previously:

```
var pet1 = PetValueType()
pet1.name = "Fluffy"
pet1.species = "cat"
var pet2 = pet1
print("pet1: \(pet1.name) is a \(pet1.species)")
print("pet2: \(pet2.name) is a \(pet2.species)")
```

➤ Move the cursor over the line number for the last line and click the "Play" button.

The output in the debug console shows that both `pet1` and `pet2`'s `name` properties are set to "Fluffy", and their `species` properties are both set to "cat".

➤ Add the following to the playground after the code you entered previously:

```
pet2.name = "Spot"
pet2.species = "dog"
print("pet1: \(pet1.name) is a \(pet1.species)")
print("pet2: \(pet2.name) is a \(pet2.species)")
```

➤ Move the cursor over the line number for the last line and click the "Play" button.

From the output in the debug console, you should see that `pet1`'s `name` and `species` properties are still "Fluffy" and "cat", but `pet2`'s `name` and `species` properties are now "Spot" and "dog". `pet1` and `pet2` are two separate values. Use value types for data where each instance is guaranteed to be its own thing and independent of any other instance. The individual checklist items in your app should be separate entities, which is why the `ChecklistItem` object blueprint is a value type — a struct.

Reference types

Classes are **reference types**. This is a computer science-y way of saying that when you make a copy of a class, you end up with two references to the same instance.

Once again, take a look at a code example. Define an object blueprint with the same properties as `PetValueType`, but as a `class` rather than a `struct`.

➤ Add the following to the playground, after the code you entered previously:

```
class PetReferenceType {
  var name: String = ""
  var species: String = ""
}
```

Now, create an instance of PetValueType and a copy of that instance.

➤ Add the following to the playground after the code you entered previously:

```
var pet3 = PetReferenceType()
pet3.name = "Tonkatsu"
pet3.species = "pot-bellied pig"
var pet4 = pet3
print("pet3: \(pet3.name) is a \(pet3.species)")
print("pet4: \(pet4.name) is a \(pet4.species)")
```

➤ Move the cursor over the line number for the last line and click the "Play" button.

In the debug console, you'll see that both pet3 and pet4's name properties are set to "Tonkatsu", and their species properties are set to "pot-bellied pig".

Now, check what happens when you change the values for pet4.

➤ Add the following to the playground, after the code you entered previously:

```
pet4.name = "Sashimi"
pet4.species = "goldfish"
print("pet3: \(pet3.name) is a \(pet3.species)")
print("pet4: \(pet4.name) is a \(pet4.species)")
```

Note the output in the debug console: "pet3: Sashimi is a goldfish" and "pet4: Sashimi is a goldfish". Both pet3 and pet4 are references to the same thing, which means that changing one changes the other.

Use reference types for data that different parts of an app share, or if the data needs the features that only a class offers.

The array of checklist items in your app is a shared resource that different screens will use. For this reason, the Checklist object blueprint is a reference type — a class.

It's time to switch away from the playground and turn your attention to the last component of your app's Model-View-ViewModel pattern: The view.

Connecting the view to the ViewModel

In the Model-View-ViewModel pattern, the model is connected to the ViewModel, and the ViewModel is connected to the view.

➤ To see the connection between the model and ViewModel, open **Checklist.swift** and look at the `checklistItems` array.

The connection between model and ViewModel is `checklistItems`, which is a property of `Checklist`, the ViewModel. Each element of `checklistItems` contains an instance of `ChecklistItem`, the model object.

I've mentioned it before, but we've been going over so much new material that it's worth repeating: The key to connecting the ViewModel to the view is in the first line of `Checklist`:

```
class Checklist: ObservableObject {
```

And in the first line of the declaration of `checklistItems`:

```
@Published var checklistItems = [
```

`Checklist` adopts the `ObservableObject` protocol, which means that an observer can constantly watch its `@Published` properties and be notified if their values change. Now, you need to set up the view, `ChecklistView`, as an observer of `Checklist`.

➤ Open **ChecklistView.swift**. Here's what the code for `ChecklistView` should look like:

```
struct ChecklistView: View {

  // Properties
  // ==========

  // User interface content and layout
  var body: some View {
    NavigationView {
      List {
        ForEach(checklistItems) { checklistItem in
          HStack {
            Text(checklistItem.name)
            Spacer()
            Text(checklistItem.isChecked ? "✅" : "⬜")
          }
          .background(Color.white) // This makes the entire row
  clickable
          .onTapGesture {
            if let matchingIndex =
              self.checklistItems.firstIndex(where: { $0.id ==
  checklistItem.id }) {

  self.checklistItems[matchingIndex].isChecked.toggle()
```

```
            }
            self.printChecklistContents()
          }
        }
      }
      .onDelete(perform: deleteListItem)
      .onMove(perform: moveListItem)
    }
    .navigationBarItems(trailing: EditButton())
    .navigationBarTitle("Checklist")
    .onAppear() {
      self.printChecklistContents()
    }
  }
}


  // Methods
  // =======

}
```

You've reduced ChecklistView to a single property, body, which describes the user interface. This is typical for views in SwiftUI — they contain only those things which define the user interface, and that's done entirely with properties.

Back when the entire app lived in this file, the List view that displayed the checklist items got its data from checklistItems, an array that was both a @State and a property of the original ContentView. That array still exists; it's a @Published property of Checklist, which is an ObservableObject.

You need the view to create an instance of Checklist and then observe it.

Add this line to ChecklistView, after the "Properties" comment and before the declaration for body:

```
@ObservedObject var checklist = Checklist()
```

This adds a new property to ChecklistView named checklist. The = sign means "put whatever is on the right side of me into checklist," and Checklist() means "create a new instance of Checklist." This is ChecklistView's connection to Checklist — the view's connection to the ViewModel. As an @ObservedObject, checklist will always keep the view up-to-date with any changes to its @Published properties.

Now that you've made the connection to Checklist, you just need to update body so that it refers to its required properties and methods in the ViewModel.

The array that body used to refer to, `checklistItems`, is now the `checklistItems` property of the `checklist` instance. Next, you'll use Xcode's "Find and Replace" feature to replace any occurrence of `checklistItems` in `ChecklistView` with `checklist.checklistItems`.

➤ In the **Find** menu, select **Find and Replace....** You can also use the keyboard shortcut, **Command+Option+F**.

The "Find and Replace" function will appear at the top of the editor:

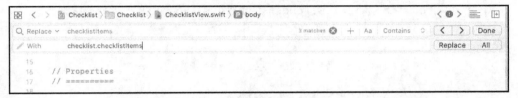

'Find and Replace' at the top of the editor

➤ Enter **checklistItems** into the **Replace** field and **checklist.checklistItems** into the **With** field, then click the **All** button.

There are also a couple of calls to `printChecklistContents()`, which was also moved to `Checklist`. Once again, "Find and Replace" will fix this.

➤ Enter **printChecklistContents()** into the **Replace** field and **checklist.printChecklistContents()** into the **With** field, then click the **All** button.

➤ Change the line:

```
.onDelete(perform: deleteListItem)
```

to:

```
.onDelete(perform: checklist.deleteListItem)
```

➤ Change the line:

```
.onMove(perform: moveListItem)
```

to:

```
.onMove(perform: checklist.moveListItem)
```

The last of the error messages will disappear, and the code for `ChecklistView` should look like this:

```
struct ChecklistView: View {

  // Properties
  // ==========

  @ObservedObject var checklist = Checklist()

  // User interface content and layout
  var body: some View {
    NavigationView {
      List {
        ForEach(checklist.checklistItems) { checklistItem in
          HStack {
            Text(checklistItem.name)
            Spacer()
            Text(checklistItem.isChecked ? "☑" : "☐")
          }
          .background(Color.white) // This makes the entire row
clickable
          .onTapGesture {
            if let matchingIndex =
              self.checklist.checklistItems.firstIndex(where:
{ $0.id == checklistItem.id }) {

self.checklist.checklistItems[matchingIndex].isChecked.toggle()
            }
            self.checklist.printChecklistContents()
          }
        }
        .onDelete(perform: checklist.deleteListItem)
        .onMove(perform: checklist.moveListItem)
      }
      .navigationBarItems(trailing: EditButton())
      .navigationBarTitle("Checklist")
      .onAppear() {
        self.checklist.printChecklistContents()
      }
    }
  }


  // Methods
  // =======

}
```

➤ Build and run. It works as before, but it'll be easier to maintain and upgrade now that it's been neatly divided into model, ViewModel, and view components.

Refactoring once more

You still have one more change to the code to make...

checklistItems's name comes from the time when it was a property of the old ContentView. Now that it's a property of Checklist, the code in ChecklistView accesses it using the unnecessarily wordy checklist.checklistItems.

Let's change Checklist's checklistItems property's name to items.

➤ In **Checklist.swift**, select `checklistItems`, right-click or control-click on it, select **Refactor** ➤ and then **Rename…**:

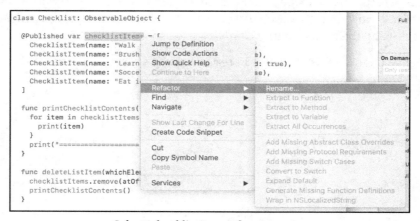

Select 'checklistItems' for renaming

➤ Type **items** and click the **Rename** button to rename the property across all the code in the project:

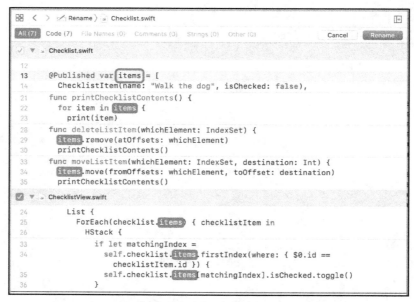

Renaming 'checklistItems' to "items

➤ Build and run to confirm that this change didn't break it.

What happens when you launch an app?

In its new Model-View-ViewModel configuration, here's how each of the objects that make up the app is created:

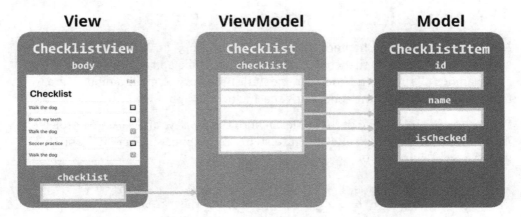

The View, ViewModel, and Model creation order

When the app launches, the view object, `checklistView`, is created first. The view has two properties: body, which defines the user interface, and `checklist`, which is the connection to the ViewModel.

The `Checklist()` part of this line in `ChecklistView`:

```
@ObservedObject var checklist = Checklist()
```

creates an instance of `Checklist`, which brings the app's ViewModel into existence.

In `Checklist`, the declaration of the array you renamed to `items`:

```
@Published var items = [
    ChecklistItem(name: "Walk the dog", isChecked: false),
    ChecklistItem(name: "Brush my teeth", isChecked: false),
    ChecklistItem(name: "Learn iOS development", isChecked: true),
    ChecklistItem(name: "Soccer practice", isChecked: false),
    ChecklistItem(name: "Eat ice cream", isChecked: true),
]
```

Creates an instance of `ChecklistItem` for each instance of an item in the list.

Simply put, an instance of `ChecklistView` creates an instance of `Checklist`, which in turn creates a number of instances of `ChecklistItem`.

But what starts the process? What creates the instance of `ChecklistView`?

The app delegate and scene delegate

As you learned back in Chapter 2, "The One-Button App," an Xcode project includes a number of source files that contain code to support the app you're writing. This code handles all the behind-the-scenes details necessary to make a mobile app work, freeing you to focus on the code that's specific to your app.

You may have noticed two of these files in both the *Bullseye* and *Checklist* projects: **AppDelegate.swift** and **SceneDelegate.swift**. They appear in every iOS app that uses the SwiftUI framework.

> **Note**: When you switch to building apps with the UIKit framework later in this book, you'll only see **AppDelegate.swift**. UIKit predates SwiftUI, and all its startup code lives in **AppDelegate.swift**. With SwiftUI, the Apple developers decided to separate that code into two separate files, where **AppDelegate.swift** contains code for managing the overall app and **SceneDelegate.swift** is the place for code that manages the app's individual windows, or scenes.

Every program, regardless of programming language and platform, has an **entry point**. It's the start of the program — the first set of instructions that execute when the program launches. For iOS apps, the entry point is in **app delegate** whose code is in **AppDelegate.swift**.

You can think of the app delegate as your app's "root object." It manages your app at the system level, which includes initializing your app's user interface.

➤ Open **AppDelegate.swift**. The code inside may look incomprehensible to you right now, but you should take note of a few things. The first one is this line:

```
class AppDelegate: UIResponder, UIApplicationDelegate {
```

You should interpret this line as "this is a class named `AppDelegate`, and it's a kind of `UIResponder` and `UIApplicationDelegate`".

In case you're wondering, a `UIApplicationDelegate` defines what an app delegate does and a `UIResponder` is an object that responds to user interface events such as the user tapping the screen or wiggling their phone.

Here's `AppDelegate`'s first method:

```
func application(_ application: UIApplication,
didFinishLaunchingWithOptions launchOptions:
[UIApplication.LaunchOptionsKey: Any]?) -> Bool {
  // Override point for customization after application launch.
  return true
}
```

This method's name is `application(_:didFinishLaunchingWithOptions:)`. It performs some tasks when the app has finished launching. One of those tasks is to put your app's user interface on the screen, which it does by creating a **scene delegate** whose code is defined in **SceneDelegate.swift**.

On Apple platforms, a **scene** is an instance of an app's user interface. On a macOS desktop app, which can have multiple windows, each window is contained within a scene. iOS apps have only one window, and therefore have only one scene.

Each scene has a scene delegate, which manages what happens to the scene under different circumstances. Take a look at those circumstances now.

➤ Open **SceneDelegate.swift**. As with **AppDelegate.swift**, the details of the code might not be clear to you, but you should note a few things.

First, it defines a class named `SceneDelegate`, which is a kind of `UIResponder` and `UIWindowSceneDelegate`. `UIWindowSceneDelegate` defines what an app delegate does and, like the app delegate, also responds to user interface events.

It also has a number of methods, whose names mostly begin with different circumstances that could arise while an app is running. These include **sceneWillEnterForeground** and **sceneDidEnterBackground**. Most of these methods contain nothing but comments; they're there for advanced programmers to add code for custom behaviors to handle different circumstances.

However, the first method in the class *does* contain code:

```
func scene(_ scene: UIScene, willConnectTo session:
UISceneSession, options connectionOptions:
UIScene.ConnectionOptions) {
  // Use this method to optionally configure and attach the
UIWindow `window` to the provided UIWindowScene `scene`.
  // If using a storyboard, the `window` property will
automatically be initialized and attached to the scene.
```

```
    // This delegate does not imply the connecting scene or
session are new (see
`application:configurationForConnectingSceneSession` instead).

    // Create the SwiftUI view that provides the window contents.
    let contentView = ContentView()

    // Use a UIHostingController as window root view controller.
    if let windowScene = scene as? UIWindowScene {
        let window = UIWindow(windowScene: windowScene)
        window.rootViewController = UIHostingController(rootView:
contentView)
        self.window = window
        window.makeKeyAndVisible()
    }
}
```

Remember: A scene is a container for a window in your app. In iOS apps, there's only one window and it takes up the entire screen. This method determines which view is the first screen your app shows, and it does so with this code:

```
// Create the SwiftUI view that provides the window contents.
let contentView = ChecklistView()
```

Now, look at this code in detail. The first thing it does is declare a constant called contentView. As a constant, you can fill it with a value only once. Once filled, you can't change it to another value as long as the app is running.

The = specifies that you're going to fill contentView with a value, and that value is the thing that follows. In this case, it's ChecklistView().

As a reminder, a capitalized name followed by parentheses, (), typically means that you're creating an object or instance. That's what's happening with ChecklistView(): It tells Swift to create a new instance of ChecklistView, which is defined inside the **ChecklistView.swift** file. This new instance is stored inside contentView.

Note: The convention is that names for constants, variables, methods and functions start with lowercase letters, and names for data types and object blueprints like structs and classes start with uppercase letters.

Now that `contentView` has been defined as an instance of a `ChecklistView` screen, the next bit of code puts the contents of `contentView` into the scene's window:

```
// Use a UIHostingController as window root view controller.
if let windowScene = scene as? UIWindowScene {
    let window = UIWindow(windowScene: windowScene)
    window.rootViewController = UIHostingController(rootView:
contentView)
    self.window = window
    window.makeKeyAndVisible()
}
```

Here's the line in the code above that matters:

```
window.rootViewController = UIHostingController(rootView:
contentView)
```

This line makes `contentView` the first screen that the app displays. Since `contentView` contains an instance of `ChecklistView`, that first screen is your list of to-do items!

Now that you know about the app delegate and the scene delegate, here's a more complete view of the objects in the app and how they're created:

The app's objects

Changing the app's first screen

Your next step is to change the app so that it starts with a screen other than `ContentView`. The app will need a couple of additional screens anyway, so add a screen that you'll eventually use to edit items in the list.

➤ Add a new file by right-clicking or control-clicking on the **Checklist** folder in Xcode's Project Explorer. Select **New File...** from the menu that appears:

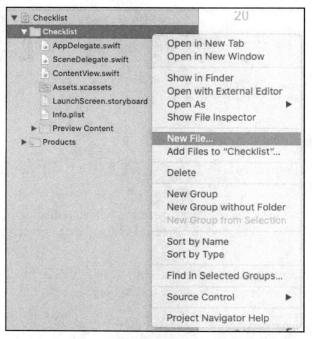

Creating a new file

➤ You want to add a new view to the app. So in the window that appears, make sure you've selected **iOS**, then select **SwiftUI View** and click **Next**:

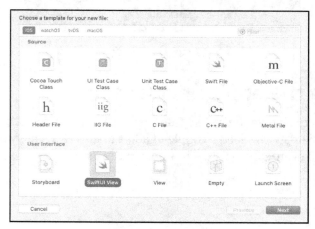

Selecting SwiftUI View

➤ Enter the name of the new view, **EditChecklistItemView**, into the **Save As:** field. Make sure that you've selected **Checklist** in the **Group** menu and in the **Targets** menu, then click **Create**:

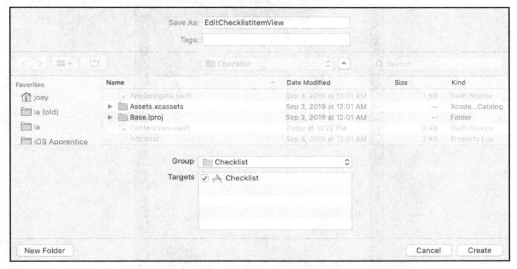

Save the file as 'EditChecklistItemView'

The project now has a new file, **EditChecklistItemView.swift**. If you open it, you'll see the code for a new view, EditChecklistItemView. Here's the interesting part of the file:

```swift
struct EditChecklistItemView: View {
    var body: some View {
        Text("Hello World!")
    }
}
```

You've seen this before — this is the default content for a new view created by Xcode, which is an empty screen with the text "Hello World!" in the center. Your next step is to change SceneDelegate so that the app opens with it, instead.

➤ Open **SceneDelegate.swift** and find this line in scene(_:willConnectTo:options:):

```swift
let contentView = ChecklistView()
```

➤ Change the line to the following:

```swift
let contentView = EditChecklistItemView()
```

➤ Build and run. Instead of seeing the checklist, you'll see the "Hello World!" screen from `EditChecklistItemView`:

The initial EditChecklistItem screen

You actually want `ChecklistView` to be the app's first screen, so change the code back to what it was.

➤ Find this line:

```
let contentView = EditChecklistItemView()
```

➤ And change it back to this:

```
let contentView = ChecklistView()
```

➤ Build and run to confirm that `ChecklistView` is the screen that the app shows when it launches.

Congratulations! You've learned a lot about how your app works, and made some improvements to it along the way, including how best to utilise design patterns to better structure your code.

Key points

In this chapter, you did the following:

- You learned about design patterns in general, and specifically about two key patterns that you'll use as an iOS developer: Model-View-Controller (MVC) and Model-View-ViewModel (MVVM).

- You renamed the app's view from the default `ContentView` to one that better fits this project: `ChecklistView`.

- You changed the architecture of the app so that all the code no longer lives in a single file, but in a model file, a ViewModel file and a view file.

- You learned about the app and scene delegate objects and about what happens when an app launches.

You'll find the project files for the app at this stage under **11 - App Structure** in the Source Code folder.

In the next chapter, you'll add the next major feature: Adding and editing checklist items.

Chapter 12: Adding Items to the List

Joey deVilla

Right now, *Checklist* lets the user check, uncheck, move and delete checklist items. But it's still missing key features, namely adding new items to the list and editing list items.

Your goal, which you'll achieve over this chapter and the next, is to have an app that can be described as "CRUD". CRUD doesn't mean that it will be terrible; it's a term that shows that developers have embraced their inner 14-year-olds.

CRUD is shorthand for the tasks that most record-keeping apps perform. It's made up of the first letters of those tasks:

- **Create** a new record. For *Checklist*, this means creating a new checklist item. You'll add this capability to the app in this chapter.

- **Report** all records. Your app already does this by presenting the list of all items.

- **Update** an existing record. In *Checklist*, this is the ability to edit an existing checklist item. The app can't do this yet, but it will by the end of the chapter.

- **Delete** a record. The app already has this capability.

Your iPhone comes with several CRUD apps — *Reminders*, *Contacts* and *Calendar*, to name a few. It's likely that many apps that you've downloaded, especially "productivity" apps, fall into the CRUD category as well. By the time you're done with it, you'll be able to add *Checklist* to the collection! In this chapter, you'll enable the "C" in CRUD: creating a new checklist item.

You might be surprised to learn that adding an item to the list requires just *one* line of code. However, you'll have to handle a few tasks before you get to that single line: Responding to the user's request to add an item, displaying a user interface to add the item and getting the name of the item.

Setting up the user interface

To add an item to the list, the user should be able to indicate that they want to add an item. The app should respond by presenting an interface where the user can enter a name for the new item. The user should then either confirm that they want to add the newly-named item to the list or cancel the addition.

The property that starts the process

If you think back to those long-ago days when you were coding *Bullseye*, you might remember that an alert pop-up appears when the user presses the **Hit me!** button:

The Bullseye app displays its alert pop-up

alert(isPresented:) made this possible. It defines an alert pop-up complete with a title, a message and a button to dismiss the alert. It also makes use of a Boolean property that determines whether the pop-up is visible.

For *Checklist*, you'll use the same technique to present the user with a pop-up where they can enter the name of the item that they want to add, then either confirm the addition or cancel it.

Now, you'll create that Boolean property for the checklist view, name it newChecklistItemViewIsVisible and add it to ChecklistView.

➤ Open **ChecklistView.swift** and add the following line to ChecklistView's **Properties** section, just after the checklist property and before the body property:

```
@State var newChecklistItemViewIsVisible = false
```

This property, when true, will cause the **Add item** pop-up to appear. You don't want the pop-up to appear until the user presses the **Add item** button, which is why its initial value is false. When the user wants to add an item to the list, they'll perform an action that changes the property's value to true. Once they've added an item, something should happen to cause the value to revert to false.

Now that we have the property, it's time to give the user a way to change it.

Adding the "Add item" button

What should the user do to create a new item in *Checklist*?

It's a good idea to look at other people's apps for inspiration, especially if those apps do something similar to the one you're writing. You'll often get good user interface ideas, learn from other developers' design mistakes and get insight into the kinds of features and functionality that users expect from an app.

Look at how users add new items to lists in iOS' built-in checklist app. Here's a list from the iOS 13 version of *Reminders*:

The Reminders app on iOS 13

To add a new item to a list in *Reminders*, the user presses the **New Reminder** button located at the bottom of the screen. You'll use a similar button in *Checklist*.

On any given list screen in *Reminders*, the navigation bar is already fully occupied with controls on either side: the **Back** button on the left and a button for options on the right. That's why the **New Reminder** button is at the bottom of the screen.

Now, look at *Checklist*'s user interface:

Where the navigation bar buttons go

Only the right-hand side of the navigation bar contains a control: the **Edit** button. The left side is available, and that's where you'll put the **Add item** button. It will follow the same format as the **New Reminder** button in *Reminders*: a "plus" sign in a circle and some text that explains the button. Our text will say: "Add item."

Before you add a new button to the navigation bar, check to see how you added the one that's already there. You put it there with this call to one of List's methods — a modifier — attached to end of the List in the Checklist view's body property:

```
.navigationBarItems(trailing: EditButton())
```

This line of code adds an EditButton, a built-in user interface element, to the *trailing* side of the navigation bar. When the device's language is set to a left-to-right language, such as English, the *right* side is the trailing side. In a right-to-left language like Hebrew, the *left* side is the trailing side.

The opposite of the trailing side is the **leading** side, which is on the left for devices set to a left-to-right language. We'll put the **Add item** button there.

➤ Open **ChecklistView.swift** and update the navigationBarItems modifier to this:

```
.navigationBarItems(
  leading: Button(action: { self.newChecklistItemViewIsVisible =
true }) {
    HStack {
      Image(systemName: "plus.circle.fill")
      Text("Add item")
    }
  },
  trailing: EditButton()
)
```

The modifier now has *two* parameters: leading:, for the button on the leading side of the navigation bar, and trailing:, for the button on the trailing side. The button on the trailing side remains the same.

This code defines the **Add item** button on the leading side:

```
Button(action: { self.newChecklistItemViewIsVisible = true }) {
  HStack {
    Image(systemName: "plus.circle.fill")
    Text("Add item")
  }
}
```

This code creates a button based on two parameters:

• The action: parameter, which contains code that defines what should happen when a user presses the button. This code sets the value contained in the newChecklistItemViewIsVisible property to true.

• The parameter within the { and } characters, which contains View objects that define what the button looks like. These objects could be Text, Image or any other object that's a kind of View.

In this case, you'll use an HStack to create a button appearance that's a combination of an Image view followed by Text, just like the **New Reminder** button in *Reminders*.

You probably noticed that you used a slightly different method, Image(systemName:), to create the icon for the **Add item** button. This method makes an image based on **SF Symbols**, a pre-defined set of over 1,500 symbols that you can use in any app running on iOS 13 or later. Image(systemName:) lets you call up any of the symbols' images by name. The symbol named "plus.circle.fill" is a + sign drawn in a filled circle.

> **Note:** You can browse the complete set of SF Symbols in the SF Symbols desktop app, which is available at Apple's Developer site.

It's time to see the button in action!

➤ Run the app. You should now see the **Add item** button on the left, or leading, side of the navigation bar. You can try pressing it, but nothing will happen... yet!

The app, now featuring the 'Add item' button

Displaying a pop-up

In *Bullseye,* when the user presses the **Hit me!** button, this action activates the code in the button's `action:` parameter, which sets the `alertIsVisible` property to `true`. `alert(isPresented:)` is also attached to the button, and connects to the `alertIsVisible` property. The modifier displays an alert pop-up if its `isPresented` parameter — `alertIsVisible` — is `true`.

Here's the code for the modifier:

```
.alert(isPresented: self.$alertIsVisible) {
  Alert(title: Text(alertTitle()),
      message: Text(scoringMessage()),
      dismissButton: .default(Text("Awesome!")) {
        self.startNewRound()
```

```
        }
    )
}
```

You're going to do something similar with the **Add item** button. You've already done some of the work: You've added a Boolean property that will control the appearance of a pop-up screen, and you've added a button that controls the value in the Boolean property. The next step is to create a pop-up window that the Boolean property controls.

An `Alert` pop-up would be a little too small:

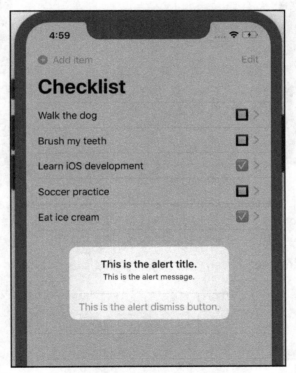

The app, displaying an 'Alert' pop-up

Whatever kind of pop-up you use should provide lots of space — not just enough space for the user to enter a name for the new checklist item, but enough space for additional information that you might decide to include with an item in later editions of the app.

That kind of pop-up is called a sheet. It's much larger than an alert; in fact, it takes up nearly the entire screen. Here's an example of a sheet in action:

The app, displaying an 'Sheet' pop-up

Next, you'll write the code to display a basic sheet with the message, "New item screen coming soon!" when the newChecklistItemViewIsVisible property is true, which happens when the user presses the **Add item** button.

➤ Add the following code after NavigationView's closing brace:

```
.sheet(isPresented: $newChecklistItemViewIsVisible) {
  Text("New item screen coming soon!")
}
```

The sheet(isPresented:) method takes two arguments:

• isPresented: displays the sheet if its value is true.

• The second argument, which you'll find within the brackets, is a view defining the content of the sheet. The code above sets that content to a Text view displaying the text "New item screen coming soon!".

➤ Run the app and press the **Add item** button. You'll see this:

The app, displaying a sheet that says 'New item screen coming soon!'

➤ Swipe down on the sheet. This will dismiss it, returning you to the checklist view.

Defining the sheet

Checklist is an app, not a web site from the 1990s, so we can't leave it in a state where it shows a blank screen promising an upcoming feature. Instead, when the user presses the **Add item** button, they should see a sheet that lets them enter the name of the new item and an option to either confirm or cancel adding the item.

You'll set up the sheet so that it displays the following:

- The title "Add new item".

- A text field where the user can enter the name of the new item.

- A button that the user can press to confirm that they want to add the new item to the list.

- A text prompt that tells the user to swipe down to cancel adding an item to the list.

You'll define this screen in its own view, NewChecklistItemView, which will live in its own file, **NewChecklistItemView.swift**.

➤ Add a new file to the project by right-clicking or control-clicking on the **Checklist** folder in Xcode's Project Explorer. Select **New File...** from the menu that appears:

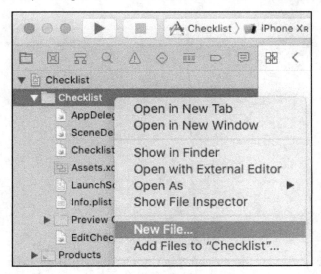

Add a new file to the project

➤ In the window that appears, make sure that you've selected **iOS** then select **SwiftUI View**. Click **Next**:

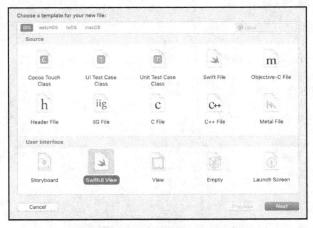

Select the 'SwiftUI View' template

➤ Enter **NewChecklistItemView** into the **Save As:** field. Make sure that you've selected **ChecklistItem** in the **Group** menu and in the **Targets** menu, then click **Create**:

Name the file 'NewChecklistItemView'

The project now has a new file named **NewChecklistItemView.swift**.

➤ Open **NewChecklistItemView.swift**. Its body defines the default "Hello World!" view:

```
var body: some View {
  Text("Hello World!")
}
```

➤ Update NewChecklistItemView's body to the following:

```
var body: some View {
  VStack {
    Text("Add new item")
    Text("Enter item name")
    Button(action: {
    }) {
      HStack {
        Image(systemName: "plus.circle.fill")
        Text("Add new item")
      }
    }
    Text("Swipe down to cancel.")
  }
}
```

To see your new screen, you need to change the line of code that defines the content of the sheet that appears when the user presses the **Add item** button on the checklist screen.

➤ Open **ChecklistView.swift** and change the code that opens the sheet to the following:

```
.sheet(isPresented: $newChecklistItemViewIsVisible) {
  NewChecklistItemView()
}
```

➤ Run the app and press the **Add item** button. You'll see this:

The 'Add new item' sheet

That's not quite the look you're going for. Next, you'll try to fix it.

Fixing the sheet's layout

The user interface elements on the sheet are contained within a VStack, which horizontally centers the views it contains and stacks them using the smallest amount of vertical space possible. It then vertically centers itself. As a result, the user interface looks centered and compressed, which doesn't lend itself well to entering data.

You could use Spacer views to fix this user interface, just as you did with *Bullseye*, but it's worth looking at a couple of other approaches.

The List view organizes the views it contains into a vertical stack, just as a VStack does. Let's put the **Enter item name** text and **Add new item** button into a List and see what happens.

➤ Update the body property to the following:

```
var body: some View {
  VStack {
    Text("Add new item")
    List {
      Text("Enter item name")
      Button(action: {
      }) {
        HStack {
          Image(systemName: "plus.circle.fill")
          Text("Add new item")
        }
      }
    }
    Text("Swipe down to cancel.")
  }
}
```

➤ Run the app and press **Add item**. You'll see this:

The 'Add new item' sheet, using a List

A List aligns the views it contains to the leading side, which is the left side for left-to-right languages such as English. Unlike the VStack, which takes only the vertical space it needs, the List expands to take as much vertical space as possible, filling it with empty cells.

A List is a better container for the **Enter item name** text and **Add new item** button than a VStack, but it's still not quite right. The empty cells at the bottom of the list suggest that the screen might present more information, but that's not the case.

It's time to introduce a new SwiftUI view: the Form. The official documentation describes it as, "A container for grouping controls used for data entry, such as in settings or inspectors." Rather than comment on this description, change your List view into a Form and see what happens.

➤ Update body to the following:

```
var body: some View {
  VStack {
    Text("Add new item")
    Form {
      Text("Enter item name")
      Button(action: {
      }) {
        HStack {
          Image(systemName: "plus.circle.fill")
          Text("Add new item")
        }
      }
    }
    Text("Swipe down to cancel.")
  }
}
```

➤ Run the app and press **Add item**. You'll see this:

The 'Add new item' sheet, using a Form

Form was designed with data entry in mind. The way it separates itself from the views above and below it is a visual hint to the user that says, "You're going to enter information here." It aligns the views appropriately based on the user's language settings, making it easier for them to enter information. It also provides clear divisions between the views it contains, clearly showing the user each piece of information they must provide, and subtly giving them an idea of how much information they're expected to enter.

Some views, when put into a Form, adapt themselves for data entry. For example, the Button view expands its tappable area to take up the full width of the form:

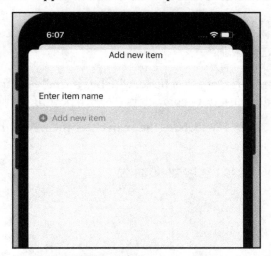

Buttons expand their tappable areas when inside a Form

For these reasons, you'll use Form as the view to contain the **Enter item name** text and the **Add new item** button.

Collecting user input

Now that you've settled on the layout of the **Add new item** sheet, you can make it functional.

➤ Run the app and press **Add item**. Try tapping on **Enter item name** to enter the name of an item to add to the list.

Nothing happens, because you tapped on a Text view. It's a view that only *outputs* data. In order to collect data from the user, you'll need to use a different view.

You've already used a view that allows the user to input data: the Slider view in *Bullseye*. You also created a property to store the slider's current position and set up a two-way binding between the slider and the property. With the binding in effect, the property updated whenever the user moved the slider, and any changes made to the property updated the slider's position.

You'll do something similar to get the name of the item to add to the list. You'll set a TextField view where the user can enter the name and a property to store the name. You'll also bind the two together so that changes to the property will change the content of the text field and changes to the text field will change the content of the property.

Now, go ahead and create the property to store the name.

➤ Add the following to NewChecklistItemView, before body:

```
@State var newItemName = ""
```

This creates a new property, newItemName, which is initially set to an empty string — that's what the two double-quote characters (") with nothing between them means.

Now, give the user a TextField where they can enter the new item name and connect it to newItemName.

➤ Find the following line in the body property:

```
Text("Enter item name")
```

And change it to this:

```
TextField("Enter new item name here", text: $newItemName)
```

This line initializes a new TextField. It takes two arguments:

• Some **hint text**: Light-colored text that tells the user what the text field is for or what information to enter into it. This tutorial uses the text, "Enter new item name here" for the hint text, but feel free to customize it however you like.

• A **binding**: A two-way connection to a property. This tutorial sets this value to $newItemName, which connects the text field to newItemName. Remember: newItemName refers to the value stored in the property, and $newItemName is a two-way connection to that value.

As the user changes text inside the text field, the value stored in newItemName will change to match. Conversely, if code changes the values stored in newItemName, the contents inside the text field will change to match.

With the changes you just made, the code for `NewChecklistItemView` should now look like this:

```
struct NewChecklistItemView: View {

  @State var newItemName = ""

  var body: some View {
    VStack {
      Text("Add new item")
      Form {
        TextField("Enter new item name here", text:
$newItemName)
        Button(action: {
        }) {
          HStack {
            Image(systemName: "plus.circle.fill")
            Text("Add new item")
          }
        }
      }
      Text("Swipe down to cancel.")
    }
  }

}
```

Now it's time to see these changes in action!

➤ Run the app and press **Add item**. You should see this:

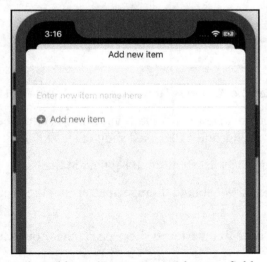

The 'Add new item' screen with a text field

As promised, the `TextField` displays the hint text. Now, you can try entering some text.

➤ Tap the text field and try typing in it. You can now type a name for a new checklist item:

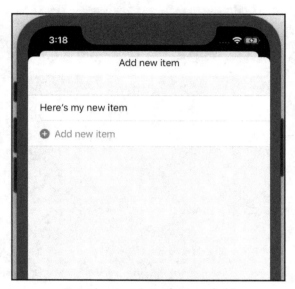

Entering text into the text field

If you also pressed the **Add new item** button, you saw that nothing happened. You'll take care of that next.

Adding a new item to the list

When the user presses the **Add new item** button, the following should happen:

1. The app should create a new checklist item. Its name should be whatever the user typed into the text field, and `isChecked` should be the default value, `false`.

2. The newly-created checklist item should appear in the list.

3. The **Add new item** sheet should disappear, returning the user to the checklist view.

Before you write the code that performs these tasks, check out where it will go.

Take a look at the code in body that defines the **Add new item** button:

```
Button(action: {
}) {
  HStack {
    Image(systemName: "plus.circle.fill")
    Text("Add new item")
  }
}
```

There's code that defines what the button *looks like*:

```
HStack {
  Image(systemName: "plus.circle.fill")
  Text("Add new item")
}
```

And there's a place where you'll add code to define what the button *does* when pressed — the Button's action: parameter:

```
Button(action: {
})
```

Start by adding the code to perform the first task: creating the new checklist item.

Creating a new checklist item

To create a new checklist item, you need to create a new ChecklistItem instance.

You may not realize it, but you've been creating new instances for some time now. You've been doing it by using the **initializer** of the struct or class that you wanted to instantiate, which is a special method that creates a new instance of a struct or class and can also set values for that instance's properties.

When you define a new struct or class, Swift automatically defines at least one initializer for it. You can also define your own additional initializers to set up instances in very specific ways.

An initializer takes its name from struct or class that it initializes. Whenever you see a capitalized name followed by parentheses (the (and) characters), you're probably looking at an initializer. If you look at the body of any view you've worked on so far, you'll see that it's full of calls to initializers: things like Text and Button.

Now, you'll use ChecklistItem's initializer to create a new checklist item.

➤ Add a line to the Button's action: parameter so that the part of body that defines the button looks like this:

```
Button(action: {
  let newChecklistItem = ChecklistItem(name: self.newItemName)
}) {
  HStack {
    Image(systemName: "plus.circle.fill")
    Text("Add new item")
  }
}
```

As you typed in the new line to create a new ChecklistItem instance, Xcode suggested a couple of initializers:

```
Button(action: {
  var newChecklistItem = ChecklistItem(
}) {                    M  ChecklistItem (name: String)
  HStack {              M  ChecklistItem (name: String, isChecked: Bool)
    Image(systemName: "plus.circle.fill")
    Text("Add new item")
  }
}
```

Xcode suggests initializers for ChecklistItem

That's because ChecklistItem has not one, but *two* initializers:

• **ChecklistItem(name:)**: Creates a new ChecklistItem instance, given only a name for the new item.

• **ChecklistItem(name:isChecked:)**: Also creates a new ChecklistItem instance, but requires that you specify both a name for the new item and whether it's checked or not.

ChecklistItem has two initializers because its isChecked property has a default value of false. Swift detected this default value and automatically created two initializers: One where you don't have to provide a value for isChecked, and one where you do. Since you're treating all new checklist items as unchecked, you'll use the initializer that doesn't require a value for isChecked.

The new line declares a new variable named newChecklistItem and assigns a new ChecklistItem instance to it. The item's name is set to the contents of NewChecklistItemView's newItemName. newItemName is bound to the text field, so its contents are the text field's contents. With this single line, you've taken care of the first step of adding a new item to the list.

Now that you have a new checklist item, it's time to add it to the list.

Getting access to the checklist

You can't add the item to the list without accessing the list. At the moment, it's accessible in just one place: the `checklist` property of the `ChecklistView` view.

To work with the list from within `NewChecklistItemView`, you'll need to do a couple of things:

• Set up a property within `NewChecklistItemView` that will hold the list.

• Have `ChecklistView` give the list to `NewChecklistItemView`, which will store the list inside the property mentioned above.

Now, go ahead and set up the property.

➤ Add the following line of code just before the line where you declare `newItemName`.

```
var checklist: Checklist
```

This new line of code is pretty straightforward. It declares a property named `checklist` that can hold `Checklist` instances.

Moments after you add this new line of code, Xcode will show an error message in the code that generates the preview:

```
struct NewChecklistItemView_Previews: PreviewProvider {
    static var previews: some View {
        NewChecklistItemView()     ⊗  Missing argument for parameter 'checklist' in call
    }
}
```

A new error message appears

Adding the `checklist` property to `NewChecklistItemView` changed its initializer. It now has a parameter, `checklist:`, which you'll use to pass the checklist from `ChecklistView` to `NewChecklistItemView`. The preview is making a call to the old initializer, `NewChecklistItemView()`, which no longer exists.

To fix the problem, you'll change the call so that it passes the value of `checklist` to the preview.

➤ Change the preview code to the following:

```
struct NewChecklistItemView_Previews: PreviewProvider {
    static var previews: some View {
        NewChecklistItemView(checklist: Checklist())
    }
}
```

The code on the previous page tells the preview that its content is an instance of NewChecklistItemView and that it should use a new instance of Checklist for its checklist. Xcode then uses this information to generate the preview. [I changed this sentence from passive to active voice. Is Xcode the correct actor.]

Now that you've fixed the error in the preview, you can return to the task of passing the checklist from ChecklistView to NewChecklistItemView.

➤ Open **ChecklistView.swift** and change the code in ChecklistView's body that displays the sheet to the following:

```swift
.sheet(isPresented: $newChecklistItemViewIsVisible) {
  NewChecklistItemView(checklist: self.checklist)
}
```

The complete body should now look like this:

```swift
var body: some View {
  NavigationView {
    List {
      ForEach(checklist.items) { checklistItem in
        HStack {
          Text(checklistItem.name)
          Spacer()
          Text(checklistItem.isChecked ? "✅" : "⬜️")
        }
        .background(Color.white) // This makes the entire row
clickable
        .onTapGesture {
          if let matchingIndex =
            self.checklist.items.firstIndex(where: { $0.id ==
checklistItem.id }) {

self.checklist.items[matchingIndex].isChecked.toggle()
          }
          self.checklist.printChecklistContents()
        }
      }
      .onDelete(perform: checklist.deleteListItem)
      .onMove(perform: checklist.moveListItem)
    }
    .navigationBarItems(
      leading: Button(action:
{ self.newChecklistItemViewIsVisible = true }) {
        HStack {
          Image(systemName: "plus.circle.fill")
          Text("Add item")
        }
      },
      trailing: EditButton()
```

```
      )
    .navigationBarTitle("Checklist")
    .onAppear() {
      self.checklist.printChecklistContents()
    }
  }
  .sheet(isPresented: $newChecklistItemViewIsVisible) {
    NewChecklistItemView(checklist: self.checklist)
  }
}
```

➤ Run the app and press the **Add item** button. It appears to work as before, but under the hood, NewChecklistItemView has information that it didn't have before: It now has access to the checklist data.

A quick reminder: Checklist is a class

It's time for a quick reminder about Checklist, which uses a slightly different kind of object blueprint.

➤ Open **Checklist.swift**. Near the top of the file you'll see this line:

```
class Checklist: ObservableObject {
```

Unlike most of the other object blueprints in the project, Checklist is a class and not a struct. I covered this in the previous chapter, but rather than make you look back, I'll provide a quick refresher.

A struct is a **value type**, where each instance keeps its own copy. Think of value types as being like a spreadsheet file that you email to your co-workers:

A value type is like a spreadsheet file

With this arrangement, each co-worker has their own copy of the spreadsheet. Any change that a co-worker makes to their spreadsheet will appear only in that co-worker's spreadsheet and nowhere else.

On the other hand, a class is a **reference type**, where all instances refer to the same copy. Think of reference types as being like a Google Docs spreadsheet that you share with your co-workers:

A reference type is like a Google doc

In this scenario, every co-worker is working on the same copy of the doc. Any change that a co-worker makes to the doc will be seen by every other co-worker, since they're all viewing the same thing.

By declaring Checklist as a class, you made it possible for different views to access the same checklist. When ChecklistView passes the checklist to NewChecklistItemView, it's giving NewChecklistItemView access to the same checklist that it uses. That's what makes it possible for NewChecklistItemView to add an item to the checklist.

Adding the new item to the list

Now that you've gone through all that setup, plus a quick review of value and reference types, it's time to add the newly-created checklist item to the list!

➤ In **NewChecklistItemView.swift**, add a couple of lines to the Button's action: parameter so that the part of body that defines the button looks like this:

```
Button(action: {
  let newChecklistItem = ChecklistItem(name: self.newItemName)
  self.checklist.items.append(newChecklistItem)
  self.checklist.printChecklistContents()
}) {
```

```
    HStack {
      Image(systemName: "plus.circle.fill")
      Text("Add new item")
    }
  }
```

As I mentioned near the start of the chapter, it takes a single line of code to add a new item to the checklist. It's this line:

```
self.checklist.items.append(newChecklistItem)
```

Remember that `items` is a property of the checklist and that it's an array that holds all its items. `append()` is an array method that takes a given object, adds an element to the array and puts the object in the new element. `append(newChecklistItem)` adds `newChecklistItem` to the checklist.

To confirm that the app is really adding newly-created objects to the checklist, you included this line of code:

```
self.checklist.printChecklistContents()
```

This uses the `printChecklistContents()` method in `Checklist` to display what's in the checklist.

Now, try adding items to the list!

➤ Run the app. Press the **Add item** button, which will display the **Add new item** sheet.

➤ Type something into the text field and press the **Add new item** button:

Entering the first new checklist item

Look at Xcode's debug console; you should see that the item has been added to the list:

```
ChecklistItem(id: F7F60F48-13C9-405C-9FE1-84752849DB58,
  name: "Walk the dog", isChecked: false)
ChecklistItem(id: C58F4509-A903-40A1-892F-56B1F5242639,
  name: "Brush my teeth", isChecked: false)
ChecklistItem(id: 74ADC696-23BC-4C91-A143-F13AF26F1143,
  name: "Learn iOS development", isChecked: true)
ChecklistItem(id: 3132033D-6FE6-4926-9538-6AB581716AA1,
  name: "Soccer practice", isChecked: false)
ChecklistItem(id: 0E57C488-0CB1-4417-B806-7D4B9393810E,
  name: "Eat ice cream", isChecked: true)
ChecklistItem(id: 32994B78-024B-4A1F-8355-AD6B6495FD16,
  name: "This is the first new checklist item!", isChecked:
  false)
====================
```

The new checklist item in the Xcode console

➤ Swipe down on the **Add new item** sheet. It will disappear, revealing the checklist screen, which will contain the newly-added item:

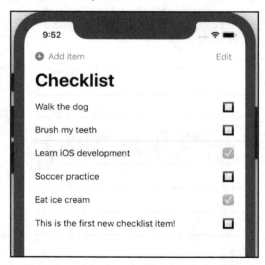

The checklist with the newly-added checklist item

It works! The user can now add items to the checklist, bringing you one step closer to having a fully-CRUD app. (Don't forget, in this case, CRUD is a good thing. :])

Dismissing the Add new item sheet automatically

The user should only swipe down on the **Add new item** sheet to cancel adding an item. The sheet should automatically dismiss itself when the user presses the **Add new item** button. With just two lines of code, you can make this happen.

The first line of code will create a property that allows you to control the way the current view presents itself.

➤ Add the following just below the line where you declared the `newItemName` property:

```
@Environment(\.presentationMode) var presentationMode
```

While you may not know exactly what this line of code does, you've probably seen enough Swift syntax to know that it creates a variable property named `presentationMode`, which is a kind of `@Environment(\.presentationMode)`, whatever that is.

In Swift, anything that begins with the @ character is a hint to the operating system that it's something special that it needs to pay particular attention to.

You've already seen something that begins with the @ character: `@State`. In *Checklist*, you used it in both `ChecklistView` and `NewChecklistItemView` to mark certain properties as state properties. In `ChecklistView`, you marked the `checklist` property as a `@State` property so that changes to `checklist` would be immediately and automatically reflected in the `List` view. In `NewChecklistItemView`, you marked the `newItemName` property so that its contents would be reflected in the "Add new item" text field and vice versa.

`@Environment` marks a property as one that can access a specific system setting related to the operating system *environment*, hence the name. It lets you find useful settings, such as whether the user's language is left-to-right or right-to-left, which calendar system is appropriate for the user's locale settings, the current color scheme and other system-wide settings.

The content of the parentheses (the (and) characters) that follow `@Environment` specifies the kind of setting to access. In this case, you're accessing a setting called `presentationMode`. It's an object that has a method that dismisses the current view.

Now that you have the `presentationMode` property, you can call on one of the methods nestled deep within it to dismiss the sheet when the user presses the **Add new item** button.

➤ In **NewChecklistItemView.swift**, add a new line of code to the `Button`'s `action:` parameter so that the part of the body property that defines the button looks like this:

```
Button(action: {
  let newChecklistItem = ChecklistItem(name: self.newItemName)
  self.checklist.items.append(newChecklistItem)
  self.checklist.printChecklistContents()
  self.presentationMode.wrappedValue.dismiss()
}) {
  HStack {
    Image(systemName: "plus.circle.fill")
    Text("Add new item")
  }
}
```

➤ Run the app. Press the **Add item** button, which will display the **Add new item** sheet. Enter a name for a new item and press the **Add new item** button.

The sheet will dismiss itself and you'll return to the checklist, which is the way the app should work.

Dealing with a SwiftUI bug

The perils of new platforms

Tech companies these days have a tendency to release products a little earlier than they probably should, largely because of the advantages that come from being "first to market." Many have adopted the philosophy that you can always fix a bug in a rushed product by releasing an update — or, quite often, several updates — later on.

This "release early, release often" approach is doubly true for developer tools and platforms. Unlike consumer products, which usually have a small set of use cases, developers use their tools in many different ways, and there's no way to predict how they'll use any given feature. The vendors who make developer tools often find it more practical to treat their users as "gamma testers" — in the Greek alphabet, gamma is the next letter after beta — and rely on their feedback to find out where the bugs are.

SwiftUI is a brand-new platform, and as one of the earliest developers to use it, you should expect to encounter some bugs. If you've been playing with the app, you may have already encountered the one that you're about to deal with next.

Fixing the navigation bar button bug

➤ Run the app. Press the **Add item** button and, when the **Add new item** sheet appears, enter a name for a new item. Press the **Add new item** button, which will return you to the checklist. So far, so good:

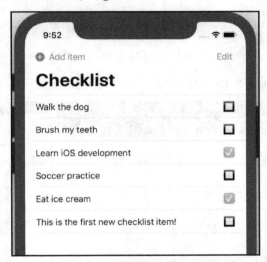

The checklist with a newly-added checklist item

The bug becomes apparent when you try to add another item.

➤ On the checklist screen, press the **Add item** button again. This time, it doesn't respond to your touch, nor does it take you to the **Add new item** sheet. If you press the **Edit** button, you'll find that it also doesn't work.

I struggled with this bug for a few minutes and discovered that checking or unchecking any item in the list un-sticks the buttons in the navigation bar:

➤ Tap on any item in the checklist to check or un-check it. Then try pressing the **Add item** or **Edit** button. You'll see that they work now.

I looked at the code that defined the buttons in the navigation bar and the code that dismissed the **Add new item** sheet after the user added a new item and couldn't see anything that would cause this strange behavior.

With the help of Adam Rush, the technical editor for this book, I found a strange workaround. For some reason, changing the style of the title in the navigation bar fixes the bug:

➤ Open **ChecklistView.swift**. In the body of ChecklistView, change the line that defines the navigation bar title from this:

```
.navigationBarTitle("Checklist")
```

To this:

```
.navigationBarTitle("Checklist", displayMode: .inline)
```

Want to see what this change does? Run the app and find out.

➤ Run the app. The checklist screen will look like this:

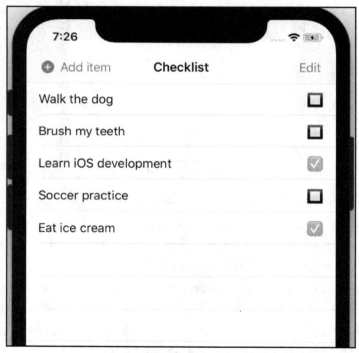

The checklist with an inline navigation bar title

This alteration to the code changes the style of the navigation bar title from the default style...

Navigation bar with the default style title

...to the **inline** style, where the navigation bar's title is on the same line as its buttons:

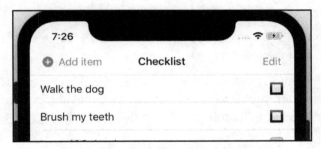

Navigation bar with the inline style title

While I prefer the default style, I prefer a properly-working app even more.

Apple will eventually address this bug with an iOS update, and when that happens, this fix will no longer be necessary.

How to deal with SwiftUI bugs on your own

Just as developer tool vendors often rely on the developer community to find bugs, you can also rely on the developer community to help you find ways around them. Programming has a strong tradition of sharing information, and you'll find that iOS programmers are generally an energetic and friendly bunch. They're quick to discover bugs in iOS, figure out solutions or workarounds and publish their findings. If you frequent their online hangouts, you're quite likely to find answers to your questions.

Whenever you find yourself stuck while working on a project in *The iOS Apprentice*, the first place you should go for help is the online forum for this book. It's the perfect place to ask questions if anything we've written has you confused or isn't working for you. A team of moderators keeps an eye on the forums, ensuring when you ask a question, you're not just screaming into the void. When they see a new question, they alert the authors — Yours Truly included — and we'll gladly help out.

> **Note**: We'll update this edition of *The iOS Apprentice* when Apple updates iOS 13 and makes fixes, and those updates are included in the cost of the book! Make sure that you check this book's page on the raywenderlich.com site for new versions.

There are other places online that you may find useful — not just for dealing with SwiftUI bugs, but also for getting answers for your iOS programming questions and learning about other aspects of iOS programming. Here are some good starting points:

- raywenderlich.com's forums: These cover not just iOS topics, but Android, Unity and Flutter development as well.

- Stack Overflow: This is the best-known of all the developer forum sites out there. If you're a programmer, you'll eventually end up here looking for (or possibly dispensing) answers. You'll probably peruse the questions tagged iOS, Swift, and SwiftUI often.

- Reddit's iOSProgamming subreddit: The biggest collection of forums online has one dedicated to iOS programming. It's so active that collectively, its readers have filed over 60,000 "radars" — that's Apple's term for bug reports and requests for features or enhancements.

Improving the user interface

Before closing out this chapter, make one more improvement to *Checklist*'s user interface that will make it more usable.

Disabling the "Add new item" button

Here's a question: What happens if you create a new checklist item without providing a name? It's time to be empirical and try it out.

➤ Run the app. Press the **Add item** button, which will display the **Add new item** sheet. *Without* entering a name for a new item, press the **Add new item** button.

Here's what you'll see when the **Add new item** sheet dismisses itself:

The checklist with an unnamed item

As you can see, the app currently lets the user add items without names to the list. The app shouldn't allow this; each item should have at least one character in its name.

You can fix this easily by using one of `Button`'s methods: `disabled`, which accepts a single Boolean parameter. Setting this parameter to `true` disables the button so pressing it has no effect. Use it now to disable the button when the text field in the **Add new item** sheet is empty.

➤ Open **NewChecklistItemView.swift** and update `NewChecklistItemView`'s body to this:

```
var body: some View {
  VStack {
    Text("Add new item")
    Form {
      TextField("Enter new item name here", text: $newItemName)
      Button(action: {
        let newChecklistItem = ChecklistItem(name:
self.newItemName)
        self.checklist.items.append(newChecklistItem)
        self.checklist.printChecklistContents()
        self.presentationMode.wrappedValue.dismiss()
      }) {
        HStack {
          Image(systemName: "plus.circle.fill")
          Text("Add new item")
```

```
            }
          }
        .disabled(newItemName.count == 0)
      }
      Text("Swipe down to cancel.")
    }
  }
}
```

In making the change, you added one line to the end of the section that defines the button:

```
.disabled(newItemName.count == 0)
```

This line disables the button if newItemName's count property is equal to zero. newItemName is a string property, and for properties that contain strings, the count property contains the number of characters in that string. An empty string — that is, a string that doesn't contain any characters — has a count of zero.

> **Note**: To determine if one value is equal to another, use the "double-equals" operator, ==. Don't use the "single-equals", =, which is for assigning values to constants and variables.

➤ Run the app. Press the **Add item** button, which will display the **Add new item** sheet. Note that the **Add new item** button is disabled:

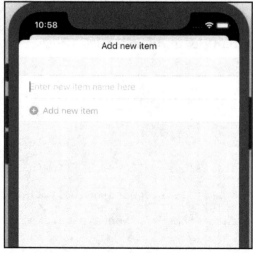

The 'Add new item' sheet, with an empty text field and a disabled button

➤ Enter some text — any text — into the text field. The **Add new item** button will enable:

The 'Add new item' sheet, with a non-empty text field and an enabled button

If you delete all the text from the text field, the button will be disabled again. This has the effect you want: The user won't be able to add an item to the list unless it has at least one character in its name.

With *Checklists* now able to add new items to the list, you're one step closer to a fully-CRUD app!

Key points

- You learned about CRUD apps, and what CRUD stands for: Create, Report, Update and Delete.

- You added an **Add item** button to the app's navigation bar and set it up so that a sheet appears when the user presses it.

- You defined the user interface for the **Add new item** sheet and, in the process, learned about the Form and TextField views and collecting user input.

- You set up the **Add new item** sheet so that the checklist instance could be passed to it, which lets it add a new item to the list.

- You had a quick review of value and reference types.

- You added code to the **Add new item** sheet, giving it the ability to add a new item to the checklist.

- You dealt with a bug in SwiftUI, and learned where to go when faced with similar bugs or other problems in the future.

- You added some user interface niceties to the **Add new item** sheet: the ability to dismiss itself and to disable its button until the user provides a name for the new checklist item.

You'll find the project files for the app at this stage under **12 – Adding Items** in the Source Code folder.

In the next chapter, you'll make *Checklists* fully-CRUD and give it the ability to edit checklist items.

Chapter 13: Editing Checklist Items

Joey deVilla

In the previous chapter, you added a key feature to *Checklist*: The ability to add items to the list. You're no longer stuck with the five default items.

However, you still can't fully edit an item. You can change its status from checked to unchecked, and vice versa, but you can't change its name.

In this chapter, we'll make checklist items fully editable, allowing the user to change both their names and checked status.

Changing how the user changes checklist items

Right now, when the user taps on a checklist item to toggle the item's checked status. Tapping an unchecked item checks it, and tapping on a checked item unchecks it:

Tapping on a checklist item toggles its checked status

We're going to give the user the ability to change either the name of a checklist item or its checked status. This will require making changes to how the app works.

Let's look at the *Reminders* app that Apple includes on every iOS device as an example.

Here, tapping on an item's name allows you to edit the name, while tapping on an item's checkbox toggles its checked status:

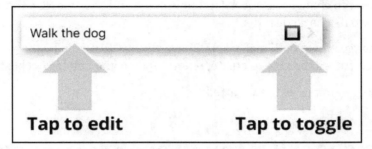

Ideally, the user would tap on an item's name to edit it, and tap on its checkbox to check or uncheck it

Building this kind of user interface, as nice as it is, adds more complexity than an introductory tutorial should have. It would require changing the code in ChecklistView to support both showing the contents of the checklist and editing any given checklist item.

Instead, when the user taps a checklist item, we'll take them to an edit screen that allows them to edit both its name and checked status:

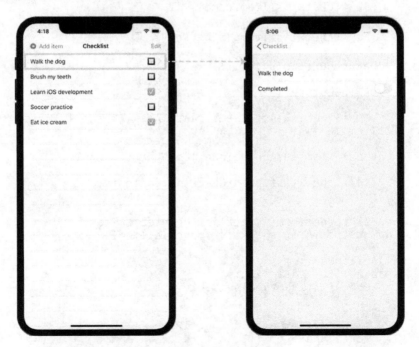

Tapping on a checklist item will take the user to an edit screen

The edit screen, which you'll code in this chapter, will contain a Form view similar to the one you included in the **Add new item** screen. This Form will contain a view that allows the user to change the checklist item's name and another view that allows the user to change its checked status.

With the changes that you'll make, you'll have a fully CRUD app by the end of this chapter. *Checklist* will be able to create, report, update and delete checklist items.

With that goal in mind, let's get started!

Giving checklist rows their own view

First, we should look at the way that ChecklistView draws the list of checklist items onscreen. Here's ChecklistView's body property:

```
// User interface content and layout
var body: some View {
  NavigationView {
    List {
      ForEach(checklist.items) { checklistItem in
        HStack {
          Text(checklistItem.name)
          Spacer()
          Text(checklistItem.isChecked ? "✅" : "⬜")
        }
        .background(Color.white) // This makes the entire row
clickable
        .onTapGesture {
          if let matchingIndex =
            self.checklist.items.firstIndex(where: { $0.id ==
checklistItem.id }) {

self.checklist.items[matchingIndex].isChecked.toggle()
          }
          self.checklist.printChecklistContents()
        }
      }
      .onDelete(perform: checklist.deleteListItem)
      .onMove(perform: checklist.moveListItem)
    }
    .navigationBarItems(
      leading: Button(action:
{ self.newChecklistItemViewIsVisible = true
      }) {
        HStack {
          Image(systemName: "plus.circle.fill")
          Text("Add item")
```

```
        }
      },
      trailing: EditButton()
    )
    .navigationBarTitle("Checklist", displayMode: .inline)
    .onAppear() {
      self.checklist.printChecklistContents()
    }
  }
  .sheet(isPresented: $newChecklistItemViewIsVisible) {
    NewChecklistItemView(checklist: self.checklist)
  }
}
```

There's a lot going on in this property. It:

- Draws each checklist item, including its name and checked status.

- Responds to presses on checklist items.

- Responds to the user moving a checklist item.

- Responds to the user deleting a checklist item.

- Draws the navigation bar and its items, including the **Add item** button, the **Edit** button, and the title.

- Responds to the user pressing the **Add item** button.

That's already a lot of responsibilities in one place, and that means a lot of complexity.

Consider a term I used a couple of times in Section 1 of this book: **Functional decomposition**. It's a fancy academic term that means "breaking down a big complex task into a set of smaller, simpler tasks." We're going to apply this principle to ChecklistView to simplify it. We'll do this by splitting ChecklistView's set of responsibilities into two groups:

We'll do this by defining a new view that will be responsible for drawing individual checklist rows. We'll then call on this view from ChecklistView.

Defining the new row view

We'll call this new view RowView, and we'll put it in its own file, **RowView.swift**.

➤ Add a new file to the project by right-clicking or control-clicking on the **Checklist** folder in Xcode's Project Explorer. Select **New File...** from the menu that appears:

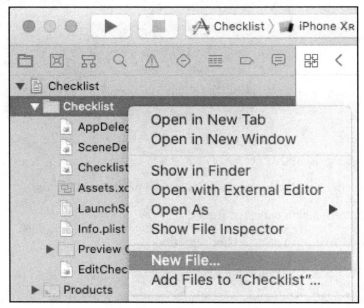

Add a new file to the project

➤ In the window that appears, make sure that you've selected **iOS**, then select **SwiftUI View** and click **Next**:

Select the 'SwiftUI View' template

➤ Enter **RowView** into the **Save As:** field. Make sure that you've selected **ChecklistItem** in the **Group** menu and in the **Targets** menu, then click **Create**:

Name the file 'RowView'

The project now has a new file named **RowView.swift**.

➤ Open **RowView.swift** and change the definition of RowView to the following:

```swift
struct RowView: View {

  @State var checklistItem: ChecklistItem

  var body: some View {
    HStack {
      Text(checklistItem.name)
      Spacer()
      Text(checklistItem.isChecked ? "✅" : "⬜")
    }
  }
}
```

As soon as you make this change, Xcode will report an error: **Missing argument for parameter 'checklistItem' in call**...

```swift
struct RowView_Previews: PreviewProvider {
    static var previews: some View {
        RowView()          🔴 Missing argument for parameter 'checklistItem' in call
    }
}
```

An error appears in the preview code

Let's fix the error first, then look at why it came up.

➤ In **RowView.swift**, change the preview section of the code to the following:

```
struct RowView_Previews: PreviewProvider {
  static var previews: some View {
    RowView(checklistItem: ChecklistItem(name: "Sample item"))
  }
}
```

With this change, the error message will disappear. Let's find out why.

Initializing structs

If you look through the `structs` that make up the app, you'll see that most of them have pre-defined properties. Let's look at the first `struct` that you defined for this app.

➤ Open **ChecklistView.swift** and look at its properties: `checklist`, `newChecklistItemViewIsVisible` and `body`. You'll see this. For brevity's sake, only the first few lines of `body` are shown:

```
@ObservedObject var checklist = Checklist()
@State var newChecklistItemViewIsVisible = false

// User interface content and layout
var body: some View {
  NavigationView {
    List {
      ...
```

All three of `ChecklistView`'s properties have initial values assigned to them:

• `checklist` is assigned the value `Checklist()`, which returns a new instance of `Checklist`.

• `newChecklistItemViewIsVisible` is assigned the value `false`.

• `body` is assigned a `NavigationView` that defines the user interface of the checklist screen.

Now, let's look at the app's newest `struct`: `RowView`.

➤ Open **RowView.swift** and look at its property: `checklistItem`:

```
@State var checklistItem: ChecklistItem
```

In this case, the property **doesn't** have a value assigned to it. `checklistItem` is declared as a variable that holds instances of `ChecklistItem`, but it doesn't have an initial value. It sits there, waiting for one.

With that observation, let's now take a look at the change to the preview section of **RowView.swift** that made the error disappear. It was a change from this:

```
struct RowView_Previews: PreviewProvider {
  static var previews: some View {
    RowView()
  }
}
```

To this:

```
struct RowView_Previews: PreviewProvider {
  static var previews: some View {
    RowView(checklistItem: ChecklistItem(name: "Sample item"))
  }
}
```

More precisely, you changed this line of code, which simply says, "Create a new instance of RowView":

```
RowView()
```

To this:

```
RowView(checklistItem: ChecklistItem(name: "Sample item"))
```

This line also creates a new instance of RowView. It also specifies a value to be assigned the new RowView instance's checklistItem property: A new instance of ChecklistItem, with name property set to "Sample item."

Since RowView doesn't assign an initial value to its checklistItem property, you have to provide an initial value whenever you create a new instance. That's why RowView() results in an error, but RowView(checklistItem: ChecklistItem(name: "Sample item")) doesn't.

This isn't the first time you've assigned values to struct instances while creating them. You also did it when you created the initial set of items for the checklist.

➤ Open **Checklist.swift** and look at its items property:

```
@Published var items = [
  ChecklistItem(name: "Walk the dog", isChecked: false),
  ChecklistItem(name: "Brush my teeth", isChecked: false),
  ChecklistItem(name: "Learn iOS development", isChecked: true),
  ChecklistItem(name: "Soccer practice", isChecked: false),
```

```
    ChecklistItem(name: "Eat ice cream", isChecked: true),
]
```

To create each of the checklist items in `items`, use
`ChecklistItem(name:isChecked:)` to create a new instance of `ChecklistItem` and
specify both its `name` and `isChecked` properties. For example, the line:

```
ChecklistItem(name: "Walk the dog", isChecked: false)
```

Says, "Create a new `ChecklistItem` whose `name` property is 'Walk the dog' and
whose `isChecked` property is `false`."

Since we're instantiating `ChecklistItem` instances, let's take a look at its properties.

➤ Open **ChecklistItem.swift** and look at its properties:

```
let id = UUID()
var name: String
var isChecked: Bool = false
```

Note the following:

- The first property, `id`, is assigned an initial value using the `let` keyword instead of
  a `var`. This means that it is a constant, and its value can't be changed. It's what's
  called a **read-only** property; its value can be read, but not rewritten. You can't
  assign a value to this property.

- The second property, `name`, isn't given an initial value, which means you must
  provide one when creating an instance of this `struct`.

- The third property, `isChecked`, is assigned an initial value of `false` using the `var`
  keyword. This means that the value of `isChecked` can be changed — either when
  creating the instance, or at a later time.

How `ChecklistItem`'s properties are defined means that you have a couple of
options when creating `ChecklistItem` instances. You can provide a value for the
`name` property:

```
ChecklistItem(name: "Sweep the floor")
```

This creates a new `ChecklistItem` instance whose name value is "Sweep the floor" and whose `isChecked` value is the default value, `false`.

You can also provide values for both the `name` and `isChecked` properties:

```
ChecklistItem(name: "Clean the bathroom", isChecked: true)
```

This creates a new `ChecklistItem` instance whose name value is "Clean the bathroom" and whose `isChecked` value is `true`.

Going back to `RowView` and its property, remember that this line defines it:

```
@State var checklistItem: ChecklistItem
```

The property allows another object to specify which checklist item the row should represent. By not giving the property an initial value, the checklist item has to be specified when the row generates. You'll see this in action in the next part, where we finally make use of this new view.

Updating ChecklistView to use RowView

Our goal was to make each checklist row responsible to drawing itself. Now that we've defined the view that lets rows do just that, let's update `ChecklistView`.

➤ Open **ChecklistView.swift** and in the body property of `ChecklistView`, change the lines of the `ForEach` view from this:

```
ForEach(checklist.items) { checklistItem in
  HStack {
    Text(checklistItem.name)
    Spacer()
    Text(checklistItem.isChecked ? "☑" : "☐")
  }
  .background(Color.white) // This makes the entire row
clickable
  .onTapGesture {
    if let matchingIndex =
self.checklist.items.firstIndex(where: { $0.id ==
checklistItem.id }) {
        self.checklist.items[matchingIndex].isChecked.toggle()
    }
    self.checklist.printChecklistContents()
  }
}
```

To this:

```
ForEach(checklist.items) { checklistItem in
  RowView(checklistItem: checklistItem)
}
```

➤ Run the app. It will appear to run as before, which means that we've successfully moved the responsibility of drawing individual rows from ChecklistItem to RowView.

Let's see what happens if you tap on a row.

➤ Tap on any item in the list. You'll see that it no longer checks or unchecks items.

Don't worry; we'll give individual rows the ability to respond to taps shortly.

In the meantime, since the code in ChecklistView that responds to taps on the list no longer works, let's remove it.

➤ Update the body property in ChecklistView by removing the code for handling taps on the list. The result should look like this:

```
var body: some View {
  NavigationView {
    List {
      ForEach(checklist.items) { checklistItem in
        RowView(checklistItem: checklistItem)
      }
      .onDelete(perform: checklist.deleteListItem)
      .onMove(perform: checklist.moveListItem)
    }
    .navigationBarItems(
      leading: Button(action:
{ self.newChecklistItemViewIsVisible = true }) {
        Image(systemName: "plus")
      },
      trailing: EditButton()
    )
    .navigationBarTitle("Checklist")
    .onAppear() {
      self.checklist.printChecklistContents()
    }
  }
  .sheet(isPresented: $newChecklistItemViewIsVisible) {
    NewChecklistItemView(checklist: self.checklist)
  }
}
```

➤ Run the app to confirm that the changes you made didn't create any errors.

Just as we made each row responsible for drawing itself by moving the row-drawing code to RowView, we'll also make each row responsible for responding to user taps by moving the tap-response code to the same place.

Making rows respond to taps

Instead of checking or unchecking the corresponding item, tapping a row should take the user to a screen where they can edit both the item's name and checked status:

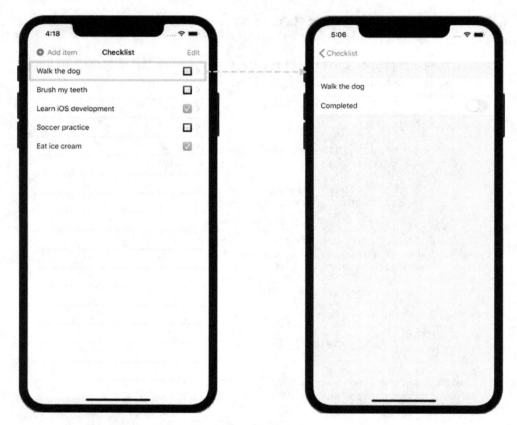

Tapping on a checklist item will take the user to an edit screen

You already have experience navigating between screens in a SwiftUI app. You used the NavigationLink view to provide the user a link that, when tapped, takes them to another screen. We'll use the same kind of view to take the user to an "Edit item" screen when they tap a checklist item.

➤ Open **RowView.swift** and update the body property of RowView to the following:

```swift
var body: some View {
  NavigationLink(destination: EditChecklistItemView()) {
    HStack {
      Text(checklistItem.name)
      Spacer()
      Text(checklistItem.isChecked ? "✅" : "⬜")
    }
  }
}
```

You just took the HStack that defined a checklist row and put it inside a NavigationLink. This makes the entire row respond to taps from the user, and it will respond by taking the user to the view specified in the destination: parameter: A new instance of the EditChecklistItemView view.

> Reminder: You created EditChecklistItemView and its file, **EditChecklistItemView.swift**, back in Chapter 11. Right now, EditChecklistItemView defines a mostly empty screen that says, "Hello World."

➤ Run the app. Tap on any item in the list. You'll see the following:

The initial "Edit checklist item" screen

Now that tapping on a checklist item takes you to `EditChecklistItemView`, it's time to define that screen.

Defining EditChecklistItemView

Remember, when the user taps on a checklist item, we want them to see an "Edit" screen that looks like this:

The initial "Edit checklist item" screen

This screen should have the following:

- A TextField view containing the name of the selected checklist item. The user should be able to change the name of the checklist item by changing the text in this view. You used this control when creating the **Add new item** sheet in the previous chapter.

- A control that displays the current checked status of the checklist item. The user should be able to change the checked status of the item by toggling this control. We'll use a Toggle view to create this control.

Just as we did with NewChecklistItemView, we'll put these into a Form view that will organize and display them in a way that is most suitable for gathering user input.

➤ Open **EditChecklistItemView.swift** and change all the code below the 'Import SwiftUI' with the following:

```swift
struct EditChecklistItemView: View {

  // Properties
  // ==========

  @State var checklistItem: ChecklistItem

  // User interface content and layout
  var body: some View {
    Form {
      TextField("Name", text: $checklistItem.name)
      Toggle("Completed", isOn: $checklistItem.isChecked)
```

```
      }
    }
  }

  // Preview
  // ========

  struct EditChecklistItemView_Previews: PreviewProvider {
    static var previews: some View {
      EditChecklistItemView(checklistItem: ChecklistItem(name:
  "Sample item"))
    }
  }
```

You might be tempted to run the app right now to see how the EditChecklistItemView screen looks, but you won't be able to just yet. This new code has caused an error to pop up in RowView.

➤ Open **RowView.swift**. Look at RowView's body property, and you'll see a familiar error: **Missing argument for parameter 'checklistItem' in call**...

The "Missing argument" error in RowView

Before you read on, ask yourself: How did you fix this error the last time you saw it?

The reason that the NavigationLink line now has an error is because of a key change you made in EditChecklistItem. You gave it a property that doesn't have an initial value: checklistItem. It's there so that the NavigationLink can do more than just bring up the "Edit item" screen. It can also tell the "Edit item" screen which item it's editing.

Since EditChecklistItem's checklistItem property doesn't have an initial value, we need to provide that value when creating the EditChecklistItemView view. Let's do that.

➤ In **RowView.swift**, update the body property of RowView to the following:

```swift
var body: some View {
  NavigationLink(destination:
EditChecklistItemView(checklistItem: checklistItem)) {
    HStack {
      Text(checklistItem.name)
      Spacer()
      Text(checklistItem.isChecked ? "☑" : "☐")
    }
  }
}
```

With this change, the error should vanish. Let's see the "Edit item" screen in action now!

➤ Run the app:

The checklist before attending to edit the 'Walk the dog' item

Let's try editing the **Walk the dog** item.

➤ Tap the **Walk the dog** row. The "Edit item" screen will appear, containing the item's current name and checked status.

➤ Change "Walk the dog" to "Walk the cat" and moved the **Completed** toggle from the "off" to the "on" position:

Editing a checklist item

➤ Now that you've made those edits, tap the **< Checklist** button in the Navigation Bar to return to the checklist. Here's what you'll see:

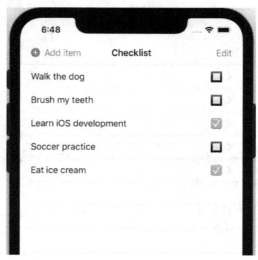

The checklist after attending to edit the 'Walk the dog' item

Your changes vanished! The first checklist item's name is still "Walk the dog" instead of "Walk the cat," and it remains unchecked instead of checked.

What happened?

Retracing our steps so far

As you progress as a developer, you're going to have more of these experiences where you're coding away, and everything seems fine when suddenly, you run into an unexpected problem. Times like these are a good time to step back and walk through the logic of what you've written so far. Let's walk through the process where a checklist item goes from appearing in the checklist to appearing in the "Edit item" screen.

➤ Open **ChecklistView.swift** and look at its body property. Here's the part of body that draws all the items in the checklist:

```
ForEach(checklist.items) { checklistItem in
  RowView(checklistItem: checklistItem)
}
```

The ForEach view goes through checklist.items, the array containing all the items in the checklist. For each item in that array, it creates a new RowView instance and, in doing so, sets that RowView instance's checklistItem property to the current checklist item.

Each checklist item is an instance of ChecklistItem, which is a struct. That means that when you set a RowView instance's checklistItem property, you're giving the RowView instance its own copy of the checklist item.

➤ Open **RowView.swift** and look at its body property. Here's the line in body that determines what happens when the user taps the row:

```
NavigationLink(destination: EditChecklistItemView(checklistItem:
  checklistItem)) {
```

The NavigationLink, when tapped, takes the user to the view specified in its destination: parameter. In this case, the destination is a new EditChecklistItemView view. In creating the new EditChecklistItemView, we set its checklistItem property to the checklist item used by RowView.

Once again, the checklist item that we're passing to EditChecklistItemView is a struct, which means that we're giving the EditChecklistItemView instance its own copy of the checklist item, which in turn is a copy of the checklist item from ChecklistView.

Here's what you should take from all this retracing: When you're editing a checklist item in `EditChecklistItemView`, you're editing a copy of a copy of an item in the checklist. That's why your changes to the "Walk the dog" item don't appear in the checklist after you dismiss the "Edit item" window.

What we need is a way to pass a connection to the actual checklist item from `ChecklistView` to `RowView` to `EditChecklistItemView` instead of a mere copy. That way, any changes made in `EditChecklistItemView` will be made in the checklist.

@Binding properties

Luckily for us, there *is* a way to pass a connection to a checklist item rather than a copy. Let's make use of it by starting with `EditChecklistItemView`.

Updating EditChecklistItemView

➤ Open **EditChecklistItemView.swift**. Change the line that defines the `checklistItem` property from this:

```
@State var checklistItem: ChecklistItem
```

To this:

```
@Binding var checklistItem: ChecklistItem
```

You've just changed `checklistItem` from a `@State` property to a `@Binding` property. As a `@State` property, `checklistItem` was a property that belonged to `EditChecklistItemView`. When a `RowView` instance passes a checklist item to an `EditChecklistItemView` instance via the `checklistItem` item property, it makes a copy of `RowView`'s checklist item. Any changes made to the checklist item in `EditChecklistItemView` aren't reflected in the matching checklist item in `RowView`, which is what we want.

As a `@Binding` property, `checklistItem` is a connection to another object's property. Now, when a `RowView` instance passes a checklist item to an `EditChecklistItemView` via the `checklistItem` item property, any changes made to the checklist item in `EditChecklistItemView` will be reflected in the matching checklist item in `RowView`.

This change will cause an error in the preview code, whose code is trying to pass put a checklist item into a property that now expects a binding to a checklist item:

The error message that appears in the preview section

➤ Update the preview code in EditChecklistItemView to the following:

```
struct EditChecklistItemView_Previews: PreviewProvider {
  static var previews: some View {

EditChecklistItemView(checklistItem: .constant(ChecklistItem(nam
e: "Sample item")))
  }
}
```

Wrapping ChecklistItem(name: "Sample item") inside the .constant function creates a binding to a checklist item, which is the kind of value that the checklistItem property expects.

This completes all the changes we need to make to EditChecklistItemView. It's time to edit the blueprint for objects that pass checklist items to EditChecklistItemView: RowView.

Updating RowView

➤ Open **RowView.swift**. Change the line that defines the checklistItem property from:

```
@State var checklistItem: ChecklistItem
```

To:

```
@Binding var checklistItem: ChecklistItem
```

This should give you a sense of *déjà vu*, and with good reason. You made the exact same changes in EditChecklistItemView! The connection to a checklist item that EditChecklistItemView receives from RowView is, in fact, a connection that RowView will receive from ChecklistItemView.

Since RowView will not be passing a checklist item to EditChecklistItemView, but a **binding** to a checklist item, we need to specify that.

➤ Change the `NavigationLink` line in RowView's body property from:

```
NavigationLink(destination: EditChecklistItemView(checklistItem:
checklistItem)) {
```

To:

```
NavigationLink(destination: EditChecklistItemView(checklistItem:
$checklistItem)) {
```

The change is so subtle that you might have missed it. Instead of setting
`EditChecklistItemView`'s checklistItem property to checklistItem, you're now
setting it to $checklistItem. The $ makes the difference: checklistItem is a
checklist item, and $checklistItem is a **binding** to a checklist item.

Just as with `EditChecklistItemView`, changing RowView's checklistItem property
into a @Binding created an error in the preview code. Once again, it's a matter of
changing its code so that it passes a binding to a checklist item and not just a
checklist item to RowView.

➤ Update the preview code in RowView to the following:

```
struct RowView_Previews: PreviewProvider {
  static var previews: some View {
    RowView(checklistItem: .constant(ChecklistItem(name: "Sample
item")))
  }
}
```

We're done making the necessary changes to RowView. But, there's one more object
blueprint to edit: ChecklistView.

Updating ChecklistView

Just as RowView passes a binding to its checklist item to `EditChecklistItemView`,
we want ChecklistView to pass bindings to checklist items to RowView. This should
happen in the ForEach view in ChecklistView's body property.

➤ Open **ChecklistView.swift** and look at the ForEach view in the body property:

```
ForEach(checklist.items) { checklistItem in
  RowView(checklistItem: checklistItem)
}
```

Since the `checklistItem` property of RowView now holds bindings to checklist items instead of checklist items, the current code causes Xcode to display an error message:

The error message that appears in ChecklistView

This should easily be fixed by changing the value we put into `RowView`'s `checklistItem` property from a checklist item into a binding to a checklist item by prefacing it with a $ character.

➤ Change the `ForEach` view in the body property to the following:

```
ForEach(checklist.items) { checklistItem in
  RowView(checklistItem: $checklistItem)
}
```

That won't work either:

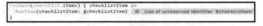

The resulting error message in ChecklistView

The error message, **Use of unresolved identifier '$checklistItem'**, is Xcode's way of saying: "I have no idea what you mean by "$checklistItem." The problem is that you can only create a binding to a `@State` or `@Binding` variable, and the `checklistItem` inside `ForEach`'s braces is neither.

The perils of new platforms, again

IIn the previous chapter, we worked around a bug that caused strange behavior in the navigation bar buttons. You've just run into another rough edge that comes with working with a brand new platform like SwiftUI. There **is** a workaround, but it requires learning about another Swift feature.

Introducing extensions

Sometimes a struct or class gives you *almost* all the functionality you need. If it's one that you wrote or have the source code for, you can add that missing functionality by writing more properties and methods. But what do you do when you didn't write the struct or class, and you don't have the source code?

That's when you use **extensions**. They're a way for you to say: "Here's some extra code that I'd like to add to the struct or class."

Making a simple extension

The best way to understand extensions is to see them in action, and the simplest way to do that is to start another Xcode playground session!

➤ In Xcode's **File** menu, select **New** ➤ and then **Playground....** The **Choose a template for you new playground** window will appear. Select **macOS** and **Blank**, then click **Next**.

Options for creating a new playground

➤ The **Save as:** window will appear. Enter a name for the playground. I used **Extensions**. In the **Add to:** menu, select **Don't add to any project or workspace**. Once you've done that, click the **Create** button:

Choosing a place to save the playground

➤ Replace the code in the playground with the following:

```
print(true.asYesOrNo)
print(false.asYesOrNo)
```

Soon after you enter the code, you'll see the following error messages:

```
print(true.asYesOrNo)          ❶  Value of type 'Bool' has no member 'asYesOrNo'
print(false.asYesOrNo)         ❶  Value of type 'Bool' has no member 'asYesOrNo'
```

The 'Bool' types doesn't have an 'asYesOrNo' property...yet

That's because `true` and `false` are both instances of the `Bool` type, which doesn't have a property called `asYesOrNo`. `Bool` *is* a `struct`, which means that we can add a property to it using an extension.

The property we'll add will be called `asYesOrNo`, and it will return the string "Yes" if the `Bool`'s value is `true` and the string "No" if the `Bool`'s value is `false`.

➤ Change the contents of the playground to the following:

```
extension Bool {

  var asYesOrNo: String {
    if self {
      return "Yes"
    } else {
      return "No"
    }
  }

}

print(true.asYesOrNo)
print(false.asYesOrNo)
```

Let's test the extension.

➤ Move the cursor over the number for the last line of code in the playground and click the "Play" button that appears in the margin:

```
1    extension Bool {
2
3      var asYesOrNo: String {
4        if self {
5          return "Yes"
6        } else {
7          return "No"
8        }
9      }
10
11   }
12
13   print(true.asYesOrNo)
 ▶   print(false.asYesOrNo)
```

Testing the extension in the playground

The debug console will show the output of both the print statements: "Yes" for
true.asYesOrNo and "No" for false.asYesOrNo.

That's the power of extensions — they let you add functionality to objects, even if
you don't have access to their source code.

Adding extensions to Checklist

Let's get back to the issue that we currently have with *Checklist*.

We need a way for ChecklistView to go through each item in the checklist and give
RowView a binding to each item. SwiftUI doesn't have a built-in way to do this, but
we've written some extensions that make up for this shortcoming.

➤ Open the **Resources** folder that comes with this book, and then open the
Checklist subfolder. Inside that folder, you'll find a folder named **Extensions**. Drag
this folder onto the yellow **Checklist** folder in the Xcode project.

➤ When the **Choose options for adding these files:** window appears, make sure that the **Copy items if needed** checkbox is checked, the **Create groups** option is selected and that the **Checklist** item in the **Add to targets** menu is checked:

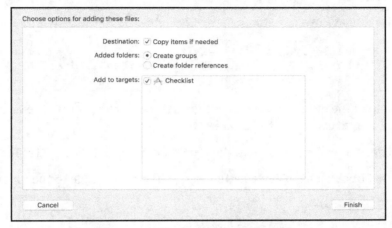

Choose options for adding these files

The project should look similar to this in Xcode's Project Navigator:

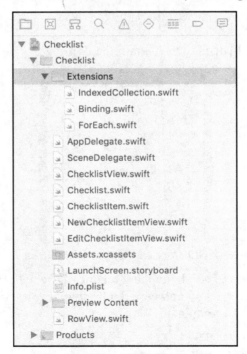

The extensions folder in Xcode

Updating EditChecklistItemView

Now that the project has the necessary extensions, let's make use of them!

➤ Open **ChecklistView.swift**. Change the ForEach view in the body property to:

```
ForEach(checklist.items) { index in
  RowView(checklistItem: self.$checklist.items[index])
}
```

With the help of the extensions, this code goes through checklist.items and passes a binding to each item to RowView.

You'll also need to make a change to the preview code in EditChecklistItemView.

➤ Open **EditChecklistItemView.swift**. Change its preview code to the following:

```
struct EditChecklistItemView_Previews: PreviewProvider {
  static var previews: some View {

EditChecklistItemView(checklistItem: .constant(ChecklistItem(nam
e: "Sample item")))
  }
}
```

➤ Run the app. It should display the default list of items:

The checklist before editing the 'Walk the dog' item

➤ Select a checklist item to edit by tapping on one of them. In this example, I tapped on the first item, "Walk the dog" and edited it by changing its name to "Walk the cat" and changing its status to completed:

Editing a checklist item

➤ Tap on the **< Checklist** button in the upper left-hand corner of the screen to return to the checklist. You'll see that this time, your edits remain!

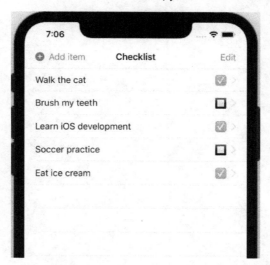

The checklist after editing the 'Walk the dog' item

Congratulations — *Checklist* is now CRUD!

Key points

In this chapter, you:

- Created a new view, allowing rows to draw themselves and respond to taps independently.

- Learned more about initializing `structs` and their properties.

- Updated *Checklist*'s user interface to support both checking items and editing their names.

- Defined the "Edit item" screen.

- Learned about how `@Bindings` can be used to shared properties among screens.

- Learned about extensions and how to use them to extend the functionality of objects.

- Used extensions to get around a rough edge in SwiftUI.

- Brought the app to the point where it can list checklist items, create a new checklist item, edit an existing checklist item and delete checklist items. You have a full CRUD app now!

In the next chapter, we'll add a much-needed capability to checklist: The ability to remember list items between sessions.

Chapter 14: Saving and Loading

Joey deVilla

Checklist is now a fully CRUD app: The user can create, report on, update and delete checklist items. It would be a fully-functional basic checklist app if not for two issues. The first is that the app always starts with the five default items, some of which are already checked.

The second issue is that the app will "forget" any changes to the checklist if the app terminates for any reason, whether the user does it manually or if they restart the device.

It's time to make some changes so that the app behaves in the following ways:

- When the user launches *Checklist* for the first time, they'll start with an empty checklist instead of the five default checklist items that the app's had since the beginning.

- The app will remember the state of its checklist after it terminates. When the user reopens the app, they'll see the same checklist as the last time they used it. The contents of the checklist should *persist* over time.

In this chapter, you'll cover the following topics:

- **Data persistence**: In most cases, apps need to remember something from the last time you used them.

- **The Documents folder**: Each app has its own place where it can store data. You'll learn how to find this place and use it to store checklist items.

- **Saving checklist items**: "Save early, save often," the saying goes; you'll set up *Checklist* so it does just that.

- **Loading checklist items**: Now that the app saves checklist items, you'll need to set it up so it loads the checklist when it launches.

Data persistence

Modern smartphone operating systems are technological wonders. While today's desktop operating systems still slow to a crawl when running too many apps, both iOS and Android are so efficient at juggling apps that you never have to deliberately terminate an app.

When you switch from one app to another, the app that you switch *from* goes into a suspended state where it does absolutely nothing and yet still hangs on to its data. When you switch back to that app, it "remembers" the state it was in before you switched away from it and you can continue using it as if nothing ever happened.

However, it's not a perfect world, and sometimes an app will terminate. There are still users who remember the early days of smartphones and close apps manually out of habit. Apps and operating systems can also crash, requiring a restart. And sometimes a device will run out of power before you can recharge it.

Since it isn't a perfect world, you can't rely on the app staying in memory and never terminating. Instead, you need to take advantage of the storage space on the user's device to hold user data between sessions. It's not just for cat pictures and videos!

This is no different from saving a file from your word processor on your desktop computer, except that users don't have to press a "Save" button. Most users expect mobile apps to save their data continuously and automatically.

Saving data between app launches is called **data persistence**. You'll add this feature to *Checklist* in this chapter.

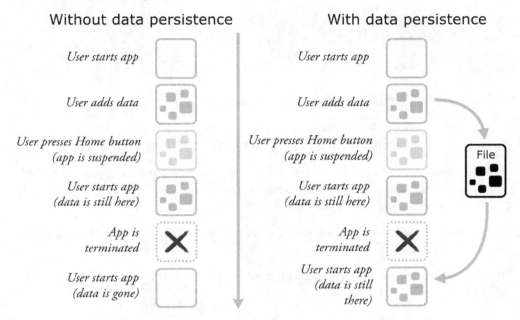

Apps need to persist data just in case the app is terminated

If you were working on a traditional desktop app, implementing data persistence might take a fair bit of code. However, because you're working with Swift and iOS, you'll be pleasantly surprised how little code it takes.

It's time to start working on that data persistence functionality! The first step is to figure out *where* you'll store the data.

The Documents directory

Unlike desktop apps, which mostly have unfettered access to the computer's hard drive, each iOS app goes into a **sandbox** when installed. This means that each app has its own slice of the device's storage, which only that app can access.

This is a security measure designed to prevent malicious software from doing any serious damage. If an app can change only its own files, it can't modify or mess with any other part of the system.

Think of the sandbox as your app's very own hard drive. Within that hard drive is the **Documents** directory, which is the designated place for your app to store data.

> **Note**: If you're unfamiliar with the term "directory", it's just the more computer science-y term for "folder."

The **Documents** folder has a couple of benefits:

- **Automatic backup**: When the user syncs their device with their computer or iCloud, the system also backs up the **Documents** directories for their apps.

- **Persistence between updates**: When you release a new version of your app, the update doesn't touch the app's **Documents** directory. Any saved data in this directory persists between updates.

With its security features and benefits, the **Documents** folder is the perfect place to store your app's data files.

Now that you know about the **Documents** folder, it's time to find it so that you can put it to use.

Finding the Documents directory to save checklist data

➤ Add the following methods to **Checklist.swift** after the moveListItem(whichElement:destination:) method:

```
func documentsDirectory() -> URL {
  let paths = FileManager.default.urls(for: .documentDirectory,
                                        in: .userDomainMask)
  return paths[0]
}

func dataFilePath() -> URL {
  return
documentsDirectory().appendingPathComponent("Checklist.plist")
}
```

The first method, documentsDirectory(), returns the location of the app's **Documents** directory. It does this by using the built-in FileManager.default object, which is the preferred way to access the file system in an app's sandbox.

`FileManager.default` has a method called `urls(for:in:)`, which lets you specify a kind of directory to look for — in this case, the **Documents** directory — and returns an array containing one or more URLs where you may find them. Even though each app has just one **Documents** directory, `urls(for:in:)` returns an array of results. The path for the **Documents** directory is in that array's first and only element, which is what `documentsDirectory()` returns.

The second method, `dataFilePath()`, uses the result of `documentsDirectory()` to construct the full path to the file that will store the checklist items. This file is named **Checklist.plist** and it will live inside the **Documents** folder.

Notice that both methods return a URL object. You may think of a URL as a "web address", but it's really just a path for a given directory or file, which can be either online or on the local system. iOS uses URLs to refer to files in its file system. When a URL begins with `http://` or `https://`, it refers to a directory or file on the web. When it refers to a local file, a URL will begin with `file://`.

> **Note**: Double check to make sure your code says `.documentDirectory` and not `.documentationDirectory`. Xcode's autocomplete can easily trip you up here!

Now that you have these methods, go ahead and put them to use.

➤ Still in **Checklist.swift**, add the following method to the start of the `Methods` section, immediately after the "Methods" comment:

```
init() {
  print("Documents directory is: \(documentsDirectory())")
  print("Data file path is: \(dataFilePath())")
}
```

`init()` is a method that you haven't seen before. Its name comes from the term "initializer." It's a special method built into `struct`s and `class`es that are automatically called when a new instance is created.

You use Initializers to set up or *initialize* an object at the moment when it's created, and you can also use them to perform tasks at that moment.

Right now, you're using the `init()` method to print the paths of the **Documents** directory and the file where you'll save the checklist to Xcode's debug console. Later on, you'll use it to restore the saved checklist when the app starts up.

➤ Run the app and look at Xcode's debug console. It will display the file paths of the **Documents** directory and where the app will eventually save **Checklist.plist**.

The full names of the file paths will differ from device to device. When I run the app on the Simulator on my computer. the Xcode debug console displays this:

```
Documents directory is:
   file:///Users/joey/Library/Developer/CoreSimulator/Devices/C74A344A-0
   9BB-4E7E-8A24-882C58C421A1/data/Containers/Data/Application/43286A9D-
   86D5-4DAC-A546-E892EA375F41/Documents/
Data file path is:
   file:///Users/joey/Library/Developer/CoreSimulator/Devices/C74A344A-0
   9BB-4E7E-8A24-882C58C421A1/data/Containers/Data/Application/43286A9D-
   86D5-4DAC-A546-E892EA375F41/Documents/Checklists.plist
```

Console output showing Documents folder and data file locations

If you run the app on your iPhone, your path will look slightly different. Here's what mine says:

```
Documents directory is: file:///var/mobile/Containers/Data/
Application/5F4CB154-1CAD-4F54-8673-4ADCCEF98D78/Documents/
Data file path is: file:///var/mobile/Containers/Data/
Application/5F4CB154-1CAD-4F54-8673-4ADCCEF98D78/Documents/
Checklist.plist
```

As you'll notice, the sandbox's directory name is a set of random characters that are determined when you install the app. Anything inside that directory, such as the **Documents** directory, is part of the app's sandbox.

Browsing the Documents directory

For the rest of this chapter, run the app on the simulator instead of a device. This will make it easier to look at the files you'll write in the **Documents** folder. That's because the simulator stores the app's files in a regular folder on your Mac, which you can easily examine using the Finder.

➤ Run the app in the simulator. When the path for the **Documents** directory appears in Xcode's debug console, copy it. Don't include the **file://** bit — the path starts with / **Users/yourname/…**.

➤ Open a new Finder window by clicking on the Desktop and typing **Command+N** or by clicking the Finder icon in your dock, if you have one. Then press **Command+Shift+G** or select **Go ‣ Go to Folder…** from the menu.

You'll see a dialog box that says **Go to the folder:**

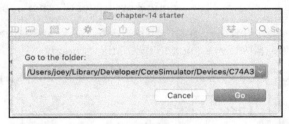

The 'Go to the folder:' dialog box

➤ Paste the full path of the **Documents** folder into the text field in the dialog box and click the **Go** button:

The 'Go to the folder:' dialog box with the 'Documents' directory pasted in

The Finder window shows you the contents of that folder.

Keep this window open; you'll want to be able to verify that **Checklist.plist**, the file containing the checklist data, is actually created when the time comes.

The app's directory structure in the Simulator

Note: If you want to navigate to the simulator's app directory by traversing your folder structure, you should know that the **Library** folder, which is in your home folder, is normally hidden. If you can't see the **Library** folder, hold down the **Alt/Option** key and click on Finder's **Go** menu (or hold down the **Alt/Option** key while the **Go** menu is open). This should reveal a shortcut to the **Library** folder on the **Go** menu, if it wasn't visible before.

You can see several folders inside the app's sandbox folder:

- The **Documents** folder, where the app will put its data files. It's currently empty.

- The **Library** folder has cache files and preferences files. The operating system manages the contents of this folder.

- The **SystemData** folder is for the operating system to use to store any system-level information relevant to the app.

- The **tmp** folder is for temporary files. Sometimes, apps need to create files for temporary use. You don't want these to clutter up your Documents folder, so tmp is a good place to put them. iOS will clear out this folder from time to time.

You can also get an overview of the **Documents** folder of other apps on your device.

➤ On your device, open **Settings** and then select **General** ▸ **iPhone Storage**. Scroll down to the list of installed apps and tap the name of an app.

You'll see the size of its Documents folder, but not the actual content:

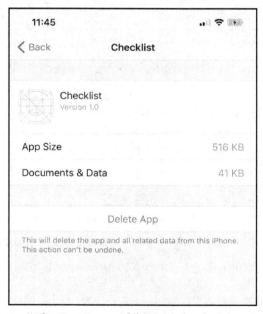

The Documents folder on the device

Now that you have a good understanding of where you'll save your app's information, it's time to move on to implementing your save functionality.

Saving checklist items

For your next step, you'll write the code that will save the list of to-do items. These items will save to a file named **Checklist.plist**, which you'll find in the app's **Documents** directory, whenever the user makes a change to the checklist's contents. Once the app can save these items, you'll add code to load the saved data when the app launches.

.plist files

You probably looked at the name of the checklist data file, **Checklist.plist** and wondered, "What's a **.plist** file?"

You've already seen a file named **Info.plist** back when you were working on *Bullseye*. All apps, *Checklist* included, have such a file, which you can see if you look at its files in Xcode's Project navigator. **Info.plist** contains information about the app for iOS to use, such as what name to display under the app's icon on the home screen.

".plist" is short for **Property List**. It's an XML file format that stores app settings and their corresponding values. In iOS, .plist files are often used for storing app data, as they're simple to read for both apps and their human programmers.

The Codable protocol, encoding, and decoding

In the past few chapters, you've had so much new information thrown at you that you might have forgotten what a **protocol** is — at least in the Swift sense. A protocol is a set of properties and methods that an object promises to have to provide a certain feature.

For the app to save its checklist items, you'll use the Codable protocol, which gives objects the ability to save their data to and load their data from the file system.

The beauty of Codable is that it insulates you from having to know much about the format of the files it writes. In this case, Codable will save the checklist item data in a .plist file. You won't have to work with the file directly. All you care about is that the data is stored as a file in the app's **Documents** folder, and Codable will do most of the work.

The name `Codable` captures the two kinds of tasks it will perform, namely:

- **Encoding**, which is converting an object's data from its form in system RAM into a form that you can write to "disk"… or, in this case, the device's flash drive. Think of encoding as saving a file in a word processor.

- **Decoding**, which is reading data stored on "disk" and converting it back into a form that an app's object can use. Think of decoding like loading a file in a word processor.

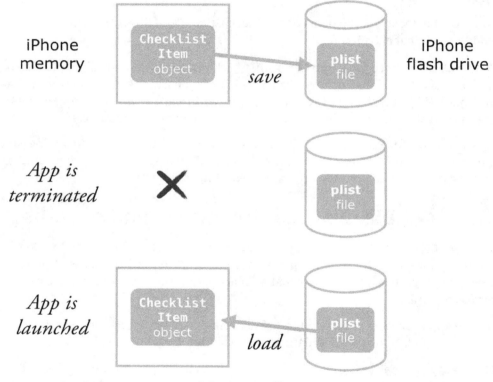

Memory vs. plist

The process of converting objects to files and back again is known as **serialization**. It's a big topic in software engineering.

Programmers use all sorts of metaphors for serialization, and many of them revolve around food preservation techniques. Some programmers think of serialization like taking a living object and freezing it, preserving it and suspending it in time. You store that frozen object in a file on the device's flash drive, where it will spend some time in cryostasis. Later, you can read that file into memory and defrost the object, bringing it back to life again.

Saving data to a file

Now that you have a method that determines *where* the app will write **Checklist.plist**, it's time to write a method to save that file.

➤ Add the following method to **Checklist.swift**:

```
func saveListItems() {
  // 1
  let encoder = PropertyListEncoder()
  // 2
  do {
    // 3
    let data = try encoder.encode(items)
    // 4
    try data.write(to: dataFilePath(),
                   options: Data.WritingOptions.atomic)
  // 5
  } catch {
    // 6
    print("Error encoding item array: \
(error.localizedDescription)")
  }
}
```

This method takes the contents of the items array, converts it to a block of binary data and then writes this data to the **Checklist.plist** file in the app's **Documents** directory.

In order to understand this code, go through the commented lines step-by-step:

1. First, the method creates an instance of PropertyListEncoder, a type of object that Apple operating systems use to encode the data stored in an app's objects into a property list.

2. The do keyword, which you haven't encountered before, sets up the first of two blocks of code, which are Swift's way of catching errors that might come up when the program is running.

```
do {
```

Code that attempts to do something
that has a chance of failing or resulting in an error

```
} catch {
```

Code that will be executed if the code
in the do block fails or results in an error

```
}
```

'do' and 'catch blocks, illustrated'

The do block contains code that might fail or result in a error — or, as you say in programming, *throw* an error. Under normal circumstances, this would cause the app to come to a crashing halt. The do block changes all that: It lets you mark lines of code that might fail with the try keyword, and if any of those lines throw an error, the code in the catch block takes over.

3. Here, you call the encoder's encode() method to encode the items array. The method could fail. It throws an error if it's unable to encode the data for some reason: Perhaps it's not in the expected format, or it's corrupted, or the device's flash drive is unavailable.

The try keyword indicates that the call to encode can fail and if that happens, that it will throw an error. The try keyword is mandatory when calling methods that throw errors; in fact, if you remove the try keyword that comes before encoder.encode(items), Xcode will display an error message.

If the call to encode() fails, execution will immediately jump to the catch block instead of proceeding to the next line.

4. If the call to encode() succeeds, data now contains the contents of the items array in encoded form. This line attempts to write this encoded data to a file using the file path returned by a call to dataFilePath(). The write() method, like many file operations, can fail for many reasons and throw an error. Once again, you have to make use of a try statement, so the catch block can handle the case where write() fails.

5. This is the start of the catch block, which contains the code to execute if any line of code in the do block threw an error.

6. This is the code that executes if code in the do block throws an error. If you were planning to sell this app in the App Store, you might do all kinds of things with

this code to deal with cases where encoding the data or writing it to the device's file system fails. In this case, you'll simply print out an error message to Xcode's console.

You might notice that the `print()` statement references an `error` variable. Where did that come from?

When you create a pair of `do` — `catch` code blocks, you can explicitly check for specific types of errors. This chapter won't get into that. All you need to know is that if you have a `catch` block, Swift will automatically create a local variable named `error`. It will contain the error thrown by the code within the do block. You can refer to that `error` variable within the `catch` block, which is handy for printing out a descriptive error message that indicates the error's source.

You'll notice that Xcode is showing one of its cryptic error messages: "Referencing instance method 'encode' on 'Array' requires that 'ChecklistItem' conform to 'Encodable'". This is because any object encoded or decoded by a `PropertyListEncoder` — or for that matter, any of the other encoders and decoders compatible with the `Codable` protocol — must support the `Codable` protocol.

A closer look at the Codable protocol

Swift arrays — as well as most other standard Swift objects and data types — already conform to the `Codable` protocol. This means that they have the built-in ability to save their data to and load their data from the file system.

The `items` property of `Checklist` is an array, so it conforms to `Codable`. However, the objects contained within the `items` array must also support `Codable` in order for the array to be serialized. The question becomes: Is your `ChecklistItem` class `Codable` compliant? Apparently not...

> **Note**: Sometimes when working with code dealing with `Codable` support, you'll see error messages or references to `Encodable` or `Decodable` protocols. So, it might be good to know that `Codable` is actually a protocol which combines these two other protocols, `Encodable` and `Decodable` — one for each side of the serialization process.

➤ Switch to **ChecklistItem.swift** and modify the `struct` line as follows:

```
struct ChecklistItem: Identifiable, Codable {
```

In the above code, you're telling Swift that `ChecklistItem` is not just a kind of `Identifiable`, but also a kind of `Codable`. This tells the compile that `ChecklistItem` conforms to the `Codable` protocol. That's all you need to do!

"Now, hold on," you might say. "In *Bullseye*, I had to write additional code to support the `ViewModifier` protocol. How come I don't have to do that here?"

In case you've forgotten, you used the `ViewModifier` protocol to style different parts of *Bullseye's* user interface in Chapter 7, "The New Look." To make use of it, you had to add a body property to objects that adopted it.

That's because protocols can have default implementations, which means that objects that adopt them don't need any additional code. It's often useful for a protocol to have a default implementation that provides functionality that makes things easier or covers a lot of standard scenarios.

In this case, all of the properties of `ChecklistItem` — `id`, `name` and `isChecked` — are standard Swift types that conform to the `Codable` protocol. As a result, Swift already knows how to encode and decode them. So, you can simply piggyback on existing functionality without having to write any code of your own to implement encoding or decoding in `ChecklistItem`. Handy, eh?

Putting saveListItems() to use

Now that you have the `saveListItems()` method, you need to be able to call it from the places in the code where the user can modify the list of items.

> **Challenge**: Before continuing, ask yourself: Where in the source code would you call `saveListItems()`?

You should call `saveListItems()` when any of the following happens:

- The user adds a new item to the checklist.

- The user changes an existing item in the checklist, either by changing its name or its checked status.

- The user deletes an item from the checklist.

- The user moves an item to a different location within the checklist.

The code for deleting and moving checklist items is in `Checklist`, so you'll add calls to `saveListItems()` to handle those cases first.

➤ Open **Checklist.swift** and add calls to saveListItems() to the end of deleteListItem(whichElement:) and moveListItem(whichElement:). They should end up looking like this:

```
func deleteListItem(whichElement: IndexSet) {
  items.remove(atOffsets: whichElement)
  printChecklistContents()
  saveListItems()
}

func moveListItem(whichElement: IndexSet, destination: Int) {
  items.move(fromOffsets: whichElement, toOffset: destination)
  printChecklistContents()
  saveListItems()
}
```

The code for creating a new checklist item is in NewChecklistItemView, so another call to saveListItems() should go there.

➤ Switch to **NewChecklistItemView.swift**. In body, add a call to saveListItems() in the Button's action: parameter so that the lines defining the button look like this:

```
Button(action: {
  var newChecklistItem = ChecklistItem(name: self.newItemName)
  self.checklist.items.append(newChecklistItem)
  self.checklist.printChecklistContents()
  self.checklist.saveListItems()
  self.presentationMode.wrappedValue.dismiss()
}) {
```

There's one more situation where you need to call saveListItems(): When the user makes a change to a checklist item. This happens in EditChecklistItemView.

➤ Open **EditChecklistItemView.swift** and look at the code that defines the view:

```
struct EditChecklistItemView: View {

  @Binding var checklistItem: ChecklistItem

  var body: some View {
    Form {
      TextField("Name", text: $checklistItem.name)
      Toggle("Completed", isOn: $checklistItem.isChecked)
    }
  }

}
```

There's a problem here: Unlike `NewChecklistItemView`, `EditChecklistItemView` doesn't have a property that contains a reference to the checklist. Without access to the checklist object, there's no way to call its `saveListItems()`.

This is a good time to step back and take a look at what happens the user edits a checklist item:

- The user taps on a checklist item.

- The app responds by displaying the "Edit checklist item" screen.

- The user has the option of changing the item's name, checked status or both. The user can also opt to *not* change anything.

- The user returns to the checklist screen by pressing the **Checklist** button located in the upper-left corner of the "Edit checklist item" screen.

- The app responds by displaying the checklist screen.

That last event in the list — "The app responds by displaying the checklist screen" — always happens after the user closes the "Edit checklist item" screen, whether they have made any changes to the item or not. The checklist screen has access to the checklist object, which means that the call to `saveListItems()` should be made when the "Edit checklist item" screen closes and the checklist screen appears.

Take a look at the checklist screen's code.

➤ Switch to **ChecklistView.swift**. Look near the end of `ChecklistView`'s body and you'll see `onAppear()`:

```
.onAppear() {
  self.checklist.printChecklistContents()
}
```

Add a call to `saveListItems()` to `onAppear()`, which causes the app to save the checklist any time the checklist displays:

```
.onAppear() {
  self.checklist.printChecklistContents()
  self.checklist.saveListItems()
}
```

This takes care of all the cases where the checklist or one of its items changes. Next, you'll confirm that our calls to `saveListItems()` works.

Verifying the saved file

➤ Run the app now and do something that results in a save. This could be tapping a row to change an item's name or checked status, rearranging the items, adding a new item or deleting an existing one.

The updated checklist

Remember to run the app in the simulator. You'll need access to the simulator's file system, which is easy to view on your Mac.

In my case, I made the following changes to the checklist items:

- Edited the name of the "Walk the dog" item, changing it to "Walk the cat."

- Deleted the "Brush my teeth' item.

- Checked the "Soccer practice" item.

- Rearranged the items so that "Eat ice cream" comes before "Soccer practice."

➤ Go to the Finder window that has the app's **Documents** directory open:

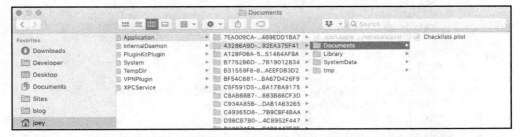

The Documents directory now contains a Checklist.plist file

There's now a **Checklist.plist** file in the Documents folder, which contains the items from the list.

You can look inside this file if you want. What you see depends on which app you use to open it. If you use a general-purpose text editor, the file's contents won't make much sense. Here's what it looks like in *Visual Studio Code* on my computer:

```
bplist00ÖÖRidTnameVisChecked_$FA9D1B56-7BB9-4233-83AC-8761C9F7A19E\Wa
lk the catÖ
_$3C397BFB-575E-4B84-912A-379F5CB1DD98_Learn iOS development  Ö
_$5279F8E8-F25D-46FB-85DD-B5DD7FF0B69F]Eat ice cream
Ö_$23395DAA-F08C-468B-AED2-771534ADB308_Soccer practice  ÖÖ
ÖÖÖ&ÖmÖzÖ[ÖbÖÖÖÖÖÖÖÖÖÖÖÖÖÖ
ÖÖÖÖÖÖÖÖÖÖÖÖÖÖÖÖÖÖÖÖÖÖÖÖÖÖÖÖ
```

The plist file, as seen in Visual Studio Code

Even though it's XML, the .plist file is stored in a binary format, which is why it looks so garbled in *Visual Studio Code*.

Some text editors, especially those designed specifically for macOS, support this file format and can read it as if it were text. *TextWrangler* is a good option, and it's a free download from the Mac App Store. Here's what **Checklist.plist** looks like when you view it in one of these editors:

```xml
<?xml version="1.0" encoding="UTF-8"?>
<!DOCTYPE plist PUBLIC "-//Apple//DTD PLIST 1.0//EN" "http://
www.apple.com/DTDs/PropertyList-1.0.dtd">
<plist version="1.0">
<array>
    <dict>
        <key>id</key>
        <string>FA9D1B56-7BB9-4233-83AC-8761C9F7A19E</string>
        <key>isChecked</key>
        <false/>
        <key>name</key>
        <string>Walk the cat</string>
    </dict>
    <dict>
        <key>id</key>
        <string>3C397BFB-575E-4B84-912A-379F5CB1DD98</string>
        <key>isChecked</key>
        <true/>
        <key>name</key>
        <string>Learn iOS development</string>
    </dict>
    <dict>
        <key>id</key>
        <string>5279F8E8-F25D-46FB-85DD-B5DD7FF0B69F</string>
        <key>isChecked</key>
        <true/>
        <key>name</key>
        <string>Eat ice cream</string>
```

```
    </dict>
    <dict>
        <key>id</key>
        <string>23395DAA-F08C-468B-AED2-771534ADB308</string>
        <key>isChecked</key>
        <true/>
        <key>name</key>
        <string>Soccer practice</string>
    </dict>
</array>
</plist>
```

Checklist.plist is considerably readable in this form. You can even see how it corresponds to the items in the app's checklist.

Naturally, you can also open the plist file with Xcode, which displays the contents of plist files in an even more user-friendly way.

➤ Right-click the **Checklist.plist** file and choose **Open With ▸ Xcode**.

You'll see the following window appear:

The plist file with the items closed, as seen in Xcode

To see the contents of the checklist items, expand each item by clicking on its disclosure triangle. You'll see each item's ID value, name and checked status:

The plist file with the items closed, as seen in Xcode

You'll also see that the contents of the plist file correspond to the current state of the checklist in the app. This confirms that the checklist data is saving properly.

It's now time to take care of loading the data.

Loading the file

Saving is all well and good, but it's only half of what the app needs. It also needs to load the data from the **Checklist.plist** file.

Fortunately, loading saved data is very straightforward. You're going to do the same thing you just did for encoding the items array — but in *reverse*.

Reading data from a file

➤ Open **Checklist.swift** and add the following new method, just after saveListItems():

```
func loadListItems() {
  // 1
  let path = dataFilePath()
  // 2
  if let data = try? Data(contentsOf: path) {
    // 3
    let decoder = PropertyListDecoder()
    do {
      // 4
      items = try decoder.decode([ChecklistItem].self,
                                 from: data)
      // 5
    } catch {
      print("Error decoding item array: \
(error.localizedDescription)")
    }
  }
}
```

As you did with saveListItems(), go through the commented lines in loadListItems() step-by-step:

1. First, you store the results of dataFilePath() — the path to the **Checklist.plist** file — in a temporary constant named path.

2. The method tries to load the contents of **Checklist.plist** into a new Data object. The try? command attempts to create the Data object, but returns nil — Swift's

way of saying "no result" — if it fails. That's why you put it in an if let statement.

Why would it fail? If there is no **Checklist.plist** file, then there are obviously no ChecklistItem objects to load. This happens when the app starts up for the very first time. In that case, you'll skip the rest of this method.

Notice that this is another way to use the try statement. Instead of enclosing the try statement within a do block, as you did previously, you have a try? statement that indicates that the try could fail. If it does, it will return nil. Whether you use the do block approach or this one is completely up to you.

3. When the app does find a **Checklist.plist** file, the method creates an instance of PropertyListDecoder.

4. The method loads the saved data back into items using the decoder's decode method. The only item of interest here is the first parameter passed to decode. The decoder needs to know what type of data the result of the decode operation will be. You let it know that it will be an array of ChecklistItem objects.

This populates the array with exact copies of the ChecklistItem objects that you froze into the **Checklist.plist** file.

5. This is the start of the catch block, which contains the code that executes if any line of code in the do block throws an error.

As with saveListItems(), if this were an app that would go into the App Store, this code might do all sorts of things to deal with cases where decoding the data or reading it from the device's file system fails. Once again, you'll simply print out an error message to Xcode's console.

Putting loadListItems() to use

You now have the loadListItems() method, which restores the app's data from **Checklist.plist**.

Challenge: Before continuing, ask yourself: Where in the source code would you call the saveListItems() method?

There's only one time when you need to load the saved checklist data: when the app launches, or more specifically, at the moment when the Checklist instance is created. This is where Checklist's init() method — its initializer — comes in handy. It's called at that very moment, making it the perfect place to put the call to loadListItems().

➤ Open **Checklist.swift** and add a call to loadListItems() at the end of its init() method. init() should look like this:

```
init() {
  print("Documents directory is: \(documentsDirectory())")
  print("Data file path is: \(dataFilePath())")
  loadListItems()
}
```

It's time to test loadListItems() by seeing if the app "remembers" changes to the checklist after the user closes and reopens it.

➤ Run the app and make some changes to the checklist.

In my case, I made the same changes that I made when testing saveListItems():

• Edited the name of the "Walk the dog" item, changing it to "Walk the cat."

• Deleted the "Brush my teeth' item.

• Checked the "Soccer practice" item.

• Rearranged the items so that "Eat ice cream" comes before "Soccer practice."

After these changes, my checklist looked like this:

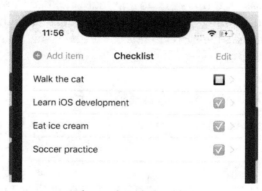

The updated checklist

➤ Close the app. You can do this by clicking the **Stop** button in Xcode or by terminating the app in the simulator.

➤ Restart the app. Instead of the five default checklist items, you should see the checklist as it was when you quit the app.

In my case, the newly-launched app showed this checklist:

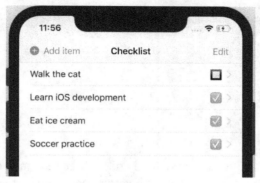

The updated checklist

Before you make the final change to the app, take a closer look at the `init()` method where you placed `loadListItems()`.

A closer look at initializers

Methods named `init` are special in Swift. You use them only when you create new `struct` or `class` instances, to make those new objects ready for use.

Think of it like buying new clothes. The clothes are in your possession (the memory for the object is allocated) but they're still in the bag. You need to put the new clothes on (initialization) before you're ready to go out and party.

When you write the following to create a new object:

```
let checklist = Checklist()
```

Swift first allocates a chunk of memory big enough to hold the new object and then calls `Checklist`'s `init()` method with no parameters.

Every object blueprint has a built-in `init()` method with no parameters. If you don't write your own object blueprint, Swift simply uses the built-in one, which just creates a new instance.

It's pretty common for objects to have more than one init method. Which one the app uses depends on the circumstances.

Consider `ChecklistItem`. Here's its code:

```
struct ChecklistItem: Identifiable, Codable {

  // Properties
  // ===========

  let id = UUID()
  var name: String
  var isChecked: Bool = false

}
```

It has two properties that can be set: `name` and `isChecked`. `name` doesn't have a value assigned to it, which means that it must be assigned a value when the `ChecklistItem` instance is created. `isChecked` can also be assigned a value when the instance is created, but it has a default value of `false`. This means that setting its value at instance creation is optional.

As a result, `ChecklistItem` has two `init()` methods:

- `ChecklistItem(name:)`, which you call when you want to create a `ChecklistItem` instance and specify just its name. Its `isChecked` property will take the default value of `false`.

- `ChecklistItem(name:isChecked)`, which you call when you want to create a `ChecklistItem` instance and specify both its name and its checked status.

Now, consider the case of `Checklist`, where you defined your own `init()` method:

```
init() {
  print("Documents directory is: \(documentsDirectory())")
  print("Data file path is: \(dataFilePath())")
  loadListItems()
}
```

By writing this method, you're **overriding** the built-in `init()`, which means that you're replacing the default initializer with one of your own. You did this because you wanted to do more than simply creating a `Checklist` instance. You also wanted to perform some tasks as the instance was being created.

Note that unlike other methods, `init` does not have the `func` keyword.

Sometimes, you'll see it written as `override init` or `required init?`. That's necessary when you're adding the `init` method to an object that's a subclass of some other object. Much more about that later.

You use the version with the question mark when `init?` can potentially fail and return a `nil` value instead of a real object. Decoding an object can fail if not enough information is present in the plist file.

Inside the `init` method, you first need to make sure that all your instance variables and constants have a value. Recall that in Swift, all variables must always have a value, except for optionals.

When you declare an instance variable, you can give it an initial value (or initialize it), like so:

```
var checked = false
```

It's also possible to write just the variable name and its type (or declare the variable), but not give the variable a value yet:

```
var checked: Bool
```

In the latter case, you have to give this variable a value in your `init` method:

```
init() {
   checked = false
}
```

You must use one of these approaches. If you don't give the variable a value at all, Swift considers this an error. The only exception is optionals, which don't need to have a value. If they don't, they are `nil`. You'll learn more about optionals later in this book.

Swift's rules for initializers can be a bit complicated but fortunately, the compiler will remind you if you forget to provide an `init` method.

Removing the default checklist items

Since *Checklist* now remembers its checklist items between sessions, it no longer needs its default checklist items.

You want the app to behave this way:

- If the app has been launched before, it should contain the same checklist items from the previous session when it launches again.

- If the user has just installed the app and has never used it, the app should display an empty checklist at launch.

This change in behavior is easy to accomplish.

➤ Switch to **Checklist.swift** and change the definition of the `items` property from this:

```
@Published var items = [
  ChecklistItem(name: "Walk the dog", isChecked: false),
  ChecklistItem(name: "Brush my teeth", isChecked: false),
  ChecklistItem(name: "Learn iOS development", isChecked: true),
  ChecklistItem(name: "Soccer practice", isChecked: false),
  ChecklistItem(name: "Eat ice cream", isChecked: true),
]
```

To this:

```
@Published var items: [ChecklistItem] = []
```

Now, test the effect of this change. You'll need to run the app as if it were freshly installed and never used, which requires getting rid of the existing **Checklist.plist** file.

➤ Go to the Finder window displaying **Checklist.plist** file. Delete the file.

➤ Run the app. You should now see an empty checklist, ready for you to fill it:

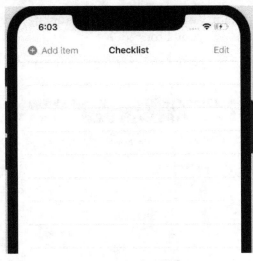

An empty checklist

Next, make sure that everything in the app works properly.

➤ Tap the **Add item** button, enter a name for the new item, and tap the **Add new item** button. You'll return to the checklist, which will display the newly-created item:

The checklist with a newly-created item

➤ Close the app. Once again, you can do this by clicking the **Stop** button in Xcode or by terminating theÏapp in the simulator.

➤ Run the app again. You'll see that the checklist is the same as when you closed the app:

The saved checklist reappears when you restart the app

With this final change, *Checklist* is complete! You have a fully-functional checklist app that remembers its contents between sessions.

This is a good time to go back and repeat those parts you're still a bit fuzzy about. Don't rush through these chapters — there are no prizes for finishing first. Rather than going fast, take your time to truly understand what you're doing.

As always, feel free to change the app and experiment. Here at iOS Apprentice Academy, we not only allow breaking things — we encourage it! You can find the project files for the app up to this point under **14 – Saving and Loading** in the **Source Code** folder.

Next steps

iOS should start to make sense by now. You've written an entire app from scratch! Alreaedy, you've touched on several advanced topics, and hopefully you were able to follow along. Kudos for sticking with it until the end!

It's okay if you're still a bit fuzzy on the details. Sleep on it for a bit and keep tinkering with the code. Programming requires its own way of thinking, and you won't learn that overnight. Don't be afraid to create this app again from the start — it will make more sense the second time around!

The first two sections of this book focused mainly on the SwiftUI framework, which is the newest way of building iOS apps. The next sections of this book will introduce you to UIKit, the framework that iOS developers have been using since the beginning of the iPhone, and which many will continue to use for some time.

The next section will also take a step back and cover more details about the Swift language. Pay particular attention, as it's helpful not just for understanding the code in your upcoming projects... it'll also give you a better understanding of the code in the projects you've already completed.

Section 3: Getting Started with UIKit

In this section, you'll learn about UIKit, which is an alternative way to build the UI of your app. UIKit has been around since the first iOS and is currently powering all of the existing iOS apps in the App Store. UIKit is the foundation on which most of SwiftUI is built upon.

You're about to create Bullseye again but this time using UIKit so you can see the differences between using SwiftUI and UIKit. We feel like SwiftUI is the future of iOS development but we truly think a programmer learning iOS you should have a good grasp of both.

You'll start by creating a basic view to understand how UIKit works, how it places UI elements on the screen and how to interact with them. You'll also read about the most common design pattern used when building apps using UIKit. You'll then go on to create Bullseye!

This section contains the following chapters:

15. UIKit & The One-Button App: You've built two apps using SwiftUI, yay!. In this chapter, you will start building Bullseye using UIKit, Apple's existing way of building UI for iOS apps.

16. Sliders & Labels: Congratulations, you have a UIButton on the screen. It's time to start adding the UISlider which will be fundamental to the game.

17. Outlets: You'll be well on your way of noticing the differences between building an app using SwiftUI and now UIKit. In this chapter you will deal with random numbers, adding rounds to the game and calculating the points scored.

18. Polish: In this chapter, we will add some UIKit polish to the app and show an alert to the user.

19. The New Look: Bullseye is looking great! The gameplay is now complete but it's time to make it look pretty. In this chapter, we will add some graphics and create an about screen to display the rules of the game.

20. TableView: TableViews are fundamental in the UIKit toolbox. In this chapter, you will learn about data sources, delegates, and general TableView best practices. Be sure to take this knowledge in your future iOS career.

21. The Data Model: A TableView is no good without real data. It's time to create the data model that will hold the high score data.

22. Navigation Controllers: UINavigationControllers are super important in an iOS app. In this chapter, you will learn about adding a NavigationController, which will help present the high scores view. You will also add the functionality to delete rows from the TableView.

23. Edit High Score Screen: Now that you have the navigation flow sorted, it's time to implement the edit high score functionality. In this chapter, we will add a static TableViewCell and read the contents from the UITextField.

24. Delegates & Protocols: You now have an edit high score screen but how do we get this data back to the high score screen? In this chapter, you will learn about Delegates and how best to use them.

25. The Final App: Phew! You have successfully created Bullseye using UIKit. In this final chapter of this section you will learn about supporting different device sizes and add some beautiful animations.

Chapter 15: UIKit and The One-Button App

Eli Ganim

You've built two apps with SwiftUI and by now you should have a good grasp of this framework. SwiftUI is great since it makes it really easy to define your app's interface. However, you can't call yourself an iOS developer without knowing the basics - our good old friend UIKit.

UIKit is an alternative way to build the UI of your app. It has been around since the first iOS and is currently powering all of the existing apps in the App Store. Actually, it's the foundation on which SwiftUI is built.

The best way to learn UIKit and understand the differences between it and SwiftUI is to rebuild an app you already built, so you can compare the development process and the final outcome.

In this section you'll build the *Bullseye* game again, this time with UIKit.

This chapter covers the following:

- **The *Bullseye* game**: A reminder of the game you already built in Section 1.

- **The one-button app**: Creating a simple one-button app in which the button can take an action based on a tap on the button.

- **The anatomy of an app**: A brief explanation as to the inner-workings of an app.

The Bullseye game

As a reminder, this is what the *Bullseye* game will look like when you're finished:

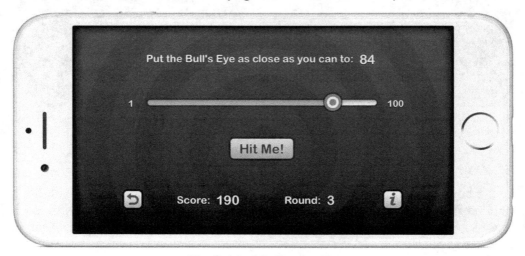

The finished Bullseye game

As you probably remember, the objective of the game is to put the bullseye, which is on a slider that goes from 1 to 100, as close to a randomly chosen target value as you can. In the screenshot above, the aim is to put the bullseye at 84. Because you can't see the current value of the slider, you'll have to "eyeball" it.

When you're confident of your estimate, you press the "Hit Me!" button and a pop-up will tell you what your score is. The closer to the target value you are, the more points you score. After you dismiss the alert pop-up, a new round begins with a new random target. The game repeats until the player presses the "Start Over" button, which resets the score to 0.

Making a programming to-do list

Just like in Section 1, you'll follow this to-do list to get the job done:

- Put a button on the screen and label it "Hit Me!"

- When the player presses the Hit Me! button, the app has to show an alert pop-up to inform the player how well he or she did. Somehow, you have to calculate the score and put that into this alert.

- Put text on the screen, such as the "Score:" and "Round:" labels. Some of this text changes over time; for example, the score, which increases when the player scores points.

- Put a slider on the screen with a range between the values 1 and 100.

- Read the value of the slider after the user presses the Hit Me! button.

- Generate a random number at the start of each round and display it on the screen. This is the target value.

- Compare the value of the slider to that random number and calculate a score based on how far off the player is. You show this score in the alert pop-up.

- Put the Start Over button on the screen. Make it reset the score and put the player back to the first round.

- Put the app in landscape orientation.

- Make it look pretty.

The one-button app

Start at the top of the list and make an extremely simple first version of the game that just displays a single button. When you press the button, the app pops up an alert message. That's all you are going to do for now. Once you have this working, you can build the rest of the game on this foundation.

The app will look like this:

The app contains a single button (left) that shows an alert when pressed (right)

Creating a new project

➤ Launch Xcode.

➤ Choose **Create a new Xcode project**.

➤ Select **Single View Application** and press **Next**.

➤ Fill out these options as follows:

• Product Name: **Bullseye**.

• Team: **None** or your team.

• Organization Name: Your name or the name of your company.

- Organization Identifier: Your own identifier in reverse domain notation.

- Language: **Swift**

- Make sure the three options at the bottom — Use Core Data, Include Unit Tests, and Include UI Tests — are *not* selected. You won't use those in this project.

- Most importantly: Uncheck the **Use SwiftUI** checkbox! This is how you tell Xcode you're going to create a UIKit based app.

➤ Press **Next**.

You can ignore the "Create Git repository on My Mac" checkbox for now. You'll learn about the Git version control system later on.

➤ Press **Create** to finish.

When it is done, the screen should look something like this:

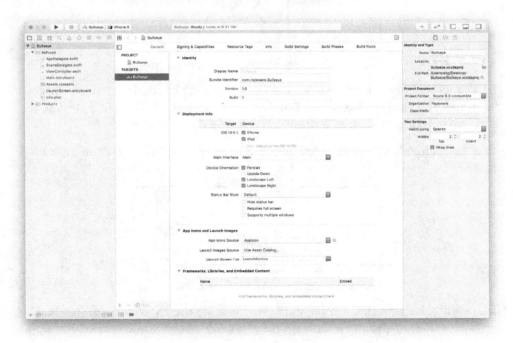

The main Xcode window at the start of your project

This is very similar to what you saw when you created your first SwiftUI app, but there are some minor differences which you'll learn about later on.

Adding a button

➤ In the **Project navigator**, find the item named **Main.storyboard** and click it once to select it:

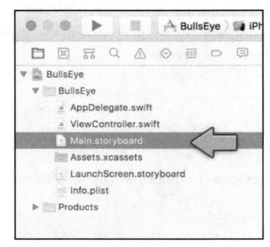

The Project navigator lists the files in the project

Like a superhero changing his or her clothes in a phone booth, the main editing pane now transforms into the **Interface Builder**. This tool lets you drag-and-drop user interface components such as buttons to create the UI of your app.

➤ If it's not already blue, click the **Hide or Show the Inspectors** button in Xcode's toolbar.

Click this button to show the Utilities pane

These toolbar buttons in the top-right corner change the appearance of Xcode. This one in particular opens a new pane on the right side of the Xcode window.

Your Xcode should now look something like this:

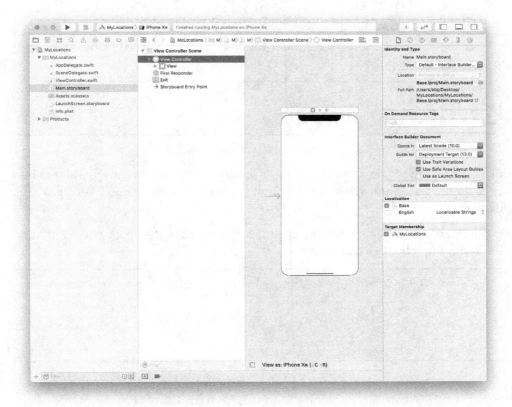

Editing Main.storyboard in Interface Builder

This is the *storyboard* for your app. The storyboard contains the designs for all of your app's screens and shows the navigation flow in your app from one screen to another.

Currently, the storyboard contains just a single screen or *scene*, represented by a rectangle in the middle of the Interface Builder canvas.

Note: If you don't see the rectangle labeled "View Controller" but only an empty canvas, then use your mouse or trackpad to scroll the storyboard around a bit. Trust me, it's in there somewhere! Also make sure your Xcode window is large enough. Interface Builder takes up a lot of space...

The scene currently is probably set to the size of an iPhone XR. To keep things simple, you will first design the app for the iPhone 8, which has a smaller screen. Later, you'll also make the app fit on the larger iPhone models.

➤ At the bottom of the Interface Builder window, click **View as: iPhone XR** to open up the following panel:

Choosing the device type

Select the **iPhone 8**, thus resizing the preview UI you see in Interface Builder to be set to that of an iPhone 8. You'll notice that the scene's rectangle now becomes a bit smaller.

Do note that depending on the size of your Xcode window, the above panel might also look something like this:

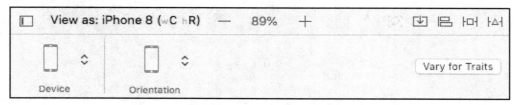

Choosing the device type - compact view

If you get this screen, just select the **iPhone 8** from the list of choices you get when you click on **Device**.

➤ In the Xcode toolbar, make sure it says **Bullseye > iPhone 8** (next to the Stop button). If it doesn't, then click it and pick iPhone 8 from the list.

Now, when you run the app, it will run on the iPhone 8 Simulator (try it out!).

Back to the storyboard.

➤ The first button on the top right toolbar shows the **Library** panel when you click it:

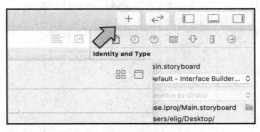

The Object Library

Scroll through the items in the Object Library list until you see **Button**. Alternatively, you can type the word "button" in to the search/filter box at the top.

➤ Click on **Button** and drag it onto the working area, on top of the scene's rectangle.

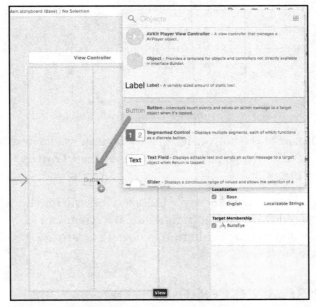

Dragging the button on top of the scene

That's how easy it is to add most new UI items — just drag and drop. You'll do a lot of this, so take some time to get familiar with the process.

Drag and drop a few other controls, such as labels, sliders, and switches, just to get the hang of it. Once you are done, delete everything except for the first button you added.

This should give you some idea of the UI controls that are available in iOS. Notice that the Interface Builder helps you to lay out your controls by snapping them to the edges of the view and to other objects. It's a very handy tool!

➤ Double-click the button to edit its title. Call it Hit Me!

The button with the new title

It's possible that your button might have a border around it:

The button with a bounds rectangle

This border is not part of the button, it's just there to show you how large the button is. You can turn these borders on or off using the **Editor ▸ Canvas ▸ Show Bounds Rectangles** menu option.

When you're done playing with Interface Builder, press the Run button from Xcode's toolbar. The app should now appear in the simulator, complete with your "Hit Me!" button. However, when you tap the button, it doesn't do anything yet. For that, you'll have to write some Swift code!

Using the source code editor

A button that doesn't do anything when tapped is of no use to anyone. So let's make it show an alert pop-up. In the finished game, the alert will display the player's score; for now, you will limit yourself to a simple text message (the traditional "Hello, World!").

➤ In the **Project navigator**, click on **ViewController.swift**.

The Interface Builder will disappear and the editor area now contains a bunch of brightly colored text. This is the Swift source code for your app.

➤ Add the following lines directly **above** the very last } bracket in the file:

```
@IBAction func showAlert() {
}
```

The source code for **ViewController.swift** should now look like this:

```
import UIKit

class ViewController: UIViewController {
  override func viewDidLoad() {
    super.viewDidLoad()
    // Do any additional setup after loading the view.
  }

  @IBAction func showAlert() {
  }
}
```

View controllers

You've edited the **Main.storyboard** file to build the user interface of the app. It's only a button on a white background, but a user interface nonetheless. You also added source code to **ViewController.swift**.

These two files — the storyboard and the Swift file — together form the design and implementation of a *view controller*. A lot of the work in building iOS apps is making view controllers. The job of a view controller, generally, is to manage a single screen in your app.

Take a simple cookbook app, for example. When you launch the cookbook app, its main screen lists the available recipes.

Tapping a recipe opens a new screen that shows the recipe in detail with an appetizing photo and cooking instructions.

Each of these screens is managed by a view controller.

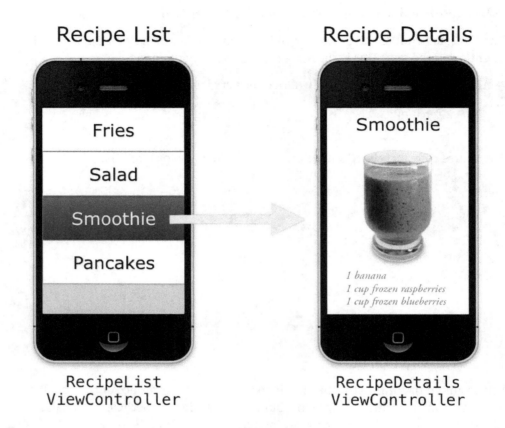

Recipe List   Recipe Details

RecipeList   RecipeDetails
ViewController   ViewController

The view controllers in a simple cookbook app

What these two screens do is very different. One is a list of several items; the other presents a detail view of a single item.

That's why you need two view controllers: One that knows how to deal with lists and another that can handle images and cooking instructions. One of the design principles of iOS is that each screen in your app gets its own view controller.

Currently, *Bullseye* has only one screen (the white one with the button) and thus only needs one view controller. That view controller is simply named "ViewController," and the storyboard and Swift file work together to implement it.

If you are curious, you can check the connection between the screen and the code for it by switching to the Identity inspector on the right sidebar of Xcode in the storyboard view. The Class value shows the current class associated with the storyboard scene.

Simply put, the Main.storyboard file contains the design of the view controller's user interface, while ViewController.swift contains its functionality — the logic that makes the user interface work, written in the Swift language.

Because you used the Single View Application template, Xcode automatically created the view controller for you. Later, you will add a second screen to the game and you will create your own view controller for that.

Making connections

The two lines of source code you just added to ViewController.swift lets Interface Builder know that the controller has a "showAlert" action, which presumably will show an alert pop-up. You will now connect the button on the storyboard to that action in your source code.

➤ Click **Main.storyboard** to go back into Interface Builder.

In Interface Builder, there should be a second pane on the left, next to the navigator area, called the **Document Outline**, that lists all the items in your storyboard. If you do not see that pane, click the small toggle button in the bottom-left corner of the Interface Builder canvas to reveal it.

The button that shows the Document Outline pane

➤ Click the **Hit Me button** once to select it.

With the Hit Me button selected, hold down the **Control** key, click on the button and drag up to the **View Controller** item in the Document Outline. You should see a blue line going from the button up to View Controller.

Please note that, instead of holding down Control, you can also right-click and drag, but don't let go of the mouse button before you start dragging.

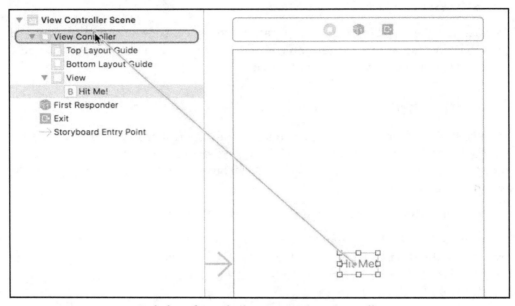

Ctrl-drag from the button to View Controller

Once you're on View Controller, let go of the mouse button and a small menu will appear. It contains several sections: "Action Segue," "Sent Events," and "Non-Adaptive Action Segue," with one or more options below each. You're interested in the **showAlert** option under Sent Events.

The Sent Events section shows all possible actions in your source code that can be hooked up to your storyboad — **showAlert** is the name of the action that you added earlier in the source code of **ViewController.swift**.

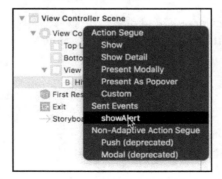

The pop-up menu with the showAlert action

➤ Click on **showAlert** to select it. This instructs Interface Builder to make a connection between the button and the line `@IBAction func showAlert()`.

From now on, whenever the button is tapped the `showAlert` action will be performed. That is how you make buttons and other controls do things: You define an action in the view controller's Swift file and then you make the connection in Interface Builder. You can see that the connection was made by going to the **Connections inspector** in the Utilities pane on the right side of the Xcode window. You should have the button selected when you do this.

➤ Click the small arrow-shaped button at the top of the pane to switch to the Connections inspector:

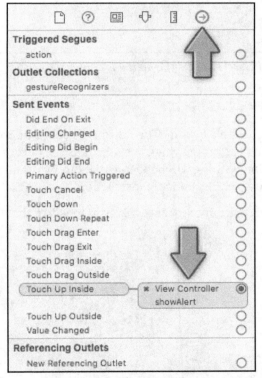

The inspector shows the connections from the button to any other objects

In the Sent Events section, the "Touch Up Inside" event is now connected to the showAlert action. You should also see the connection in the Swift file.

➤ Select **ViewController.swift** to edit it.

Notice how, to the left of the line with @IBAction func showAlert(), there is a solid circle? Click on that circle to reveal what this action is connected to.

```
30
31     class ViewController: UIViewController {
32
33       override func viewDidLoad() {
34         super.viewDidLoad()
35         // Do any additional setup after loading the
36       }
37
       ⊚  📄 Main.storyboard — B  Hit Me!          {
39
40     }
41
```

A solid circle means the action is connected to something

Acting on the button

You now have a screen with a button. The button is hooked up to an action named showAlert that will be performed when the user taps the button. Currently, however, the action is empty and nothing will happen (try it out by running the app again, if you like). You need to give the app more instructions.

➤ In **ViewController.swift**, modify showAlert to look like the following:

```
@IBAction func showAlert() {
  let alert = UIAlertController(title: "Hello, World",
                                  message: "This is my first
app!",
                                  preferredStyle: .alert)

  let action = UIAlertAction(title: "Awesome", style: .default,
                             handler: nil)

  alert.addAction(action)

  present(alert, animated: true, completion: nil)
}
```

The code in showAlert creates an alert with a title "Hello, World," a message that states, "This is my first app!" and a single button labeled "Awesome.".

➤ Click the **Run** button from Xcode's toolbar. If you didn't make any typos, your app should launch in iOS Simulator and you should see the alert box when you tap the button.

The alert pop-up in action

Congratulations, you've just written your first UIKit app!

You can strike off the first two items from the to-do list already: Putting a button on the screen and showing an alert when the user taps the button.

The anatomy of an app

It might be good at this point to get some sense of what goes on behind the scenes of an app.

An app is essentially made up of **objects** that can send messages to each other. Many of the objects in your app are provided by iOS; for example, the button is a UIButton object and the alert pop-up is a UIAlertController object. Some objects you will have to program yourself, such as the view controller.

These objects communicate by passing messages to each other. For example, when the user taps the Hit Me button in the app, that UIButton object sends a message to your view controller. In turn, the view controller may message more objects.

On iOS, apps are *event-driven*, which means that the objects listen for certain events to occur and then process them.

As strange as it may sound, an app spends most of its time doing... absolutely nothing. It just sits there waiting for something to happen. When the user taps the screen, the app springs to action for a few milliseconds, and then it goes back to sleep again until the next event arrives.

Your part in this scheme is that you write the source code for the actions that will be performed when your objects receive the messages for such events.

In the app, the button's Touch Up Inside event is connected to the view controller's showAlert action. So when the button recognizes it has been tapped, it sends the showAlert message to your view controller.

Inside showAlert, the view controller sends another message, addAction, to the UIAlertController object. And to show the alert, the view controller sends the present message.

Your whole app will be made up of objects that communicate in this fashion.

Maybe you have used PHP or Ruby scripts on your web site. This event-based model is different from how a PHP script works. The PHP script will run from top-to-bottom, executing the statements one-by-one until it reaches the end and then it exits.

Apps, on the other hand, don't exit until the user terminates them (or they crash!). They spend most of their time waiting for input events, then handle those events and go back to sleep.

Input from the user, mostly in the form of touches and taps, is the most important source of events for your app, but there are other types of events as well. For example, the operating system will notify your app when the user receives an incoming phone call, when it has to redraw the screen, when a timer has counted down, etc.

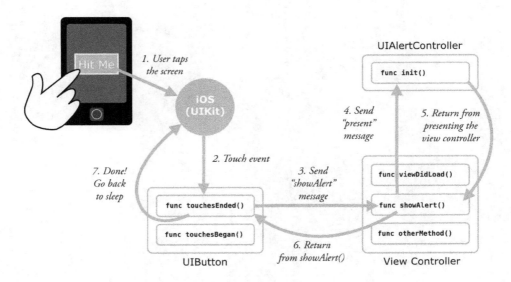

The general flow of events in an app

Everything your app does is triggered by some event.

You can find the project files for the app up to this point under **15-The One-Button App** in the Source Code folder.

Chapter 16: Slider & Labels

Eli Ganim

Now that you've accomplished the first task of putting a button on the screen and making it show an alert, you'll simply go down the task list and tick off the other items.

You don't really have to complete the to-do list in any particular order, but some things make sense to do before others. For example, you cannot read the position of the slider if you don't have a slider yet.

Now add the rest of the controls — the slider and the text labels — and turn this app into a real game!

When you're done, the app will look like this:

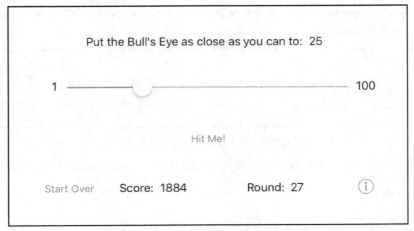

The game screen with standard UIKit controls

Similarly to what you did in the SwiftUI version of Bullseye, you'll start off with a barebone version of the app and add graphics later.

In this chapter, you'll cover the following:

- **Portrait vs. landscape**: Switch your app to landscape mode.

- **Objects, data and methods**: A quick primer on the basics of object-oriented programming.

- **Adding the other controls**: Add the rest of the controls necessary to complete the user interface of your app.

Portrait vs. landscape

Just like in SwiftUI, your app can be displayed in landsapce or portrait orientation. Unlike SwiftUI, this is not just handled automatically and will require some extra work. You'll take care of that now.

Converting the app to landscape

To switch the app from portrait to landscape, you have to do two things:

1. Make the view in **Main.storyboard** landscape instead of portrait.

2. Change the **Supported Device Orientations** setting of the app.

➤ Open **Main.storyboard**. In Interface Builder, in the **View as: iPhone 8** panel, change **Orientation** to landscape:

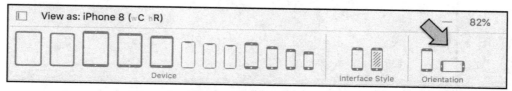

Changing the orientation in Interface Builder

This changes the dimensions of the view controller. It also puts the button off-center.

➤ Move the button back to the center of the view because an untidy user interface just won't do in this day and age.

The view in landscape orientation

That takes care of the view layout.

➤ Run the app on iPhone 8 Simulator. Note that the screen does not show up as landscape yet, and the button is no longer in the center.

➤ Choose **Hardware** ▸ **Rotate Left** or **Rotate Right** from Simulator's menu bar at the top of the screen, or hold ⌘ and press the left or right Arrow keys on your keyboard. This will flip the simulator around.

Now, everything will look as it should.

Notice that in landscape orientation the app no longer shows the iPhone's status bar. This gives apps more room for their user interfaces.

To finalize the orientation switch, you should block the Portrait and Upside Down device orientations, just like you did when you built *Bullseye* in SwiftUI.

➤ Click the blue **Bullseye** project icon at the top of the **Project navigator**. The editor pane of the Xcode window now reveals a bunch of settings for the project.

➤ Make sure that the **General** tab is selected:

The settings for the project

In the **Deployment Info** section, there is an option for **Device Orientation**.

➤ Check only the **Landscape Left** and **Landscape Right** options and leave the Portrait and Upside Down options unchecked.

Run the app again and it properly launches in the landscape orientation right from the start.

Understanding objects, data and methods

Time for some programming theory. No, you can't escape it.

Swift is a so-called "object-oriented" programming language, which means that most of the stuff you do involves objects of some kind. I already mentioned a few times that an app consists of objects that send messages to each other.

When you write an iOS app, you'll be using objects that are provided for you by the system, such as the UIButton object from UIKit, and you'll be making objects of your own, such as view controllers.

Objects

So what exactly *is* an object? Think of an object as a building block of your program. Programmers like to group related functionality into objects. *This* object takes care of parsing a file, *that* object knows how to draw an image on the screen, and *that* object over there can perform a difficult calculation.

Each object takes care of a specific part of the program. In a full-blown app, you will have many different types of objects (tens or even hundreds).

Even your small starter app already contains several different objects. The one you have spent the most time with so far is `ViewController`. The Hit Me! button is also an object, as is the alert pop-up. And the text values that you put on the alert — "Hello, World" and "This is my first app!" — are also objects.

The project also has an object named `AppDelegate` — you're going to ignore that for the moment, but feel free to look at its source if you're curious. These object thingies are everywhere!

Data and methods

An object can have both *data* and *functionality*:

- An example of data is the Hit Me! button that you added to the view controller earlier. When you dragged the button into the storyboard, it actually became part of the view controller's data. Data *contains* something. In this case, the view controller contains the button.

- An example of functionality is the `showAlert` action that you added to respond to taps on the button. Functionality *does* something.

The button itself also has data and functionality. Examples of button data are the text and color of its label, its position on the screen, its width and height and so on. The button also has functionality: It can recognize that the user tapped on it and it will trigger an action in response.

The thing that provides functionality to an object is commonly called a *method*. Other programming languages may call this a "procedure" or "subroutine" or "function." You will also see the term function used in Swift; a method is simply a function that belongs to an object.

Your `showAlert` action is an example of a method. You can tell it's a method because the line says `func` (short for "function") and the name is followed by parentheses:

All method definitions start with the word func and have parentheses

If you look through the rest of **ViewController.swift**, you'll see another method, viewDidLoad(). It currently doesn't do much; the Xcode template placed it there for your convenience. It's a method that's often used by view controllers, so it's likely that you will need to add some code to it at some point.

> **Note**: These additional methods added by an Xcode template are known as "boilerplate code." If you don't need to add functionality to these boilerplate methods, feel free to remove them — it'll make your code cleaner and more compact.
>
> There's a caveat though; sometimes, the boilerplate code is needed in order not to get a compiler error. You will see this later on when we start using more complex view controllers. So if you remove the boilerplate code and get a compiler error, restore the code and try removing the code selectively until you figure out what is needed and what is not.

The concept of methods may still feel a little weird, so here's an example:

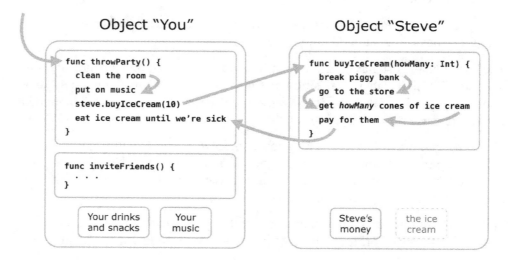

Every party needs ice cream!

You (or at least an object named "You") want to throw a party, but you forgot to buy ice cream. Fortunately, you have invited the object named Steve who happens to live next door to a convenience store. It won't be much of a party without ice cream so, at some point during your party preparations, you send object Steve a message asking him to bring some ice cream.

The computer now switches to object Steve and executes the commands from his `buyIceCream()` method, one by one, from top to bottom.

When the `buyIceCream()` method is done, the computer returns to your `throwParty()` method and continues with that, so you and your friends can eat the ice cream that Steve brought back with him.

The Steve object also has data. Before he goes to the store, he has money. At the store, he exchanges this money data for other, much more important, data: ice cream! After making that transaction, he brings the ice cream data over to the party (if he eats it all along the way, your program has a bug).

Messages

"Sending a message" sounds more involved than it really is.

It's a good way to think conceptually of how objects communicate, but there really aren't any pigeons or mailmen involved. The computer simply jumps from the `throwParty()` method to the `buyIceCream()` method and back again.

Often the terms "calling a method" or "invoking a method" are used instead. That means the exact same thing as sending a message: The computer jumps to the method you're calling and returns to where it left off when that method is done.

The important thing to remember is that objects have methods (the steps involved in buying ice cream) and data (the actual ice cream and the money to buy it with).

Objects can look at each other's data (to some extent anyway, just like Steve may not approve if you peek inside his wallet) and can ask other objects to perform their methods.

That's how you get your app to do things. But not all data from an object can be inspected by other objects and/or code — this is an area known as access control and you'll learn about this later.

Adding the other controls

Your app already has a button, but you still need to add the rest of the UI controls, also known as "views." Here is the screen again, this time annotated with the different types of views:

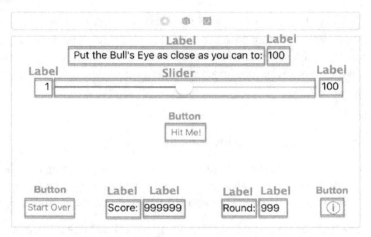

The different views in the game screen

As you can see, you'll add placeholder values in some of the labels (for example, "999999"). That makes it easier to see how the labels will fit on the screen when they're actually used. The score label could potentially hold a large value, so you'd better make sure the label has room for it.

➤ Try to re-create the above screen on your own by dragging the various controls from the Object Library onto your scene. You'll need a few new Buttons, Labels and a Slider. You can see in the screenshot above how big the items should (roughly) be. It's OK if you're a few points off.

> **Note**: It might seem a little annoying to use the Library panel since it goes away as soon as you drag an item from it. You then have to tap the icon on the toolbar to show the Library panel again to select another item. If you are placing multiple components, just hold down the Alt/Option key (⌥) as you drag an item from the Library panel — the Library panel will remain open, allowing you to select another item.

To tweak the settings of these views, you use the **Attributes inspector**. You can find this inspector in the right-hand pane of the Xcode window:

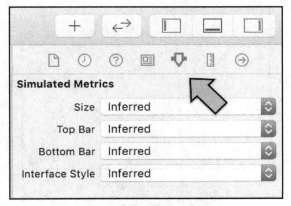

The Attributes inspector

The inspector area shows various aspects of the item that is currently selected. The Attributes inspector, for example, lets you change the background color of a label or the size of the text on a button. You've already seen the Connections inspector that showed the button's actions. As you become more proficient with Interface Builder, you'll be using all of these inspector panes to configure your views.

➤ Hint: The ⓘ button is actually a regular button, but its **Type** is set to **Info Light** in the Attributes inspector:

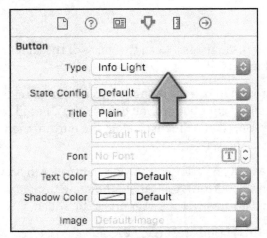

The button type lets you change the look of the button

➤ Also use the Attributes inspector to configure the **slider**. Its minimum value should be 1, its maximum 100, and its current value 50.

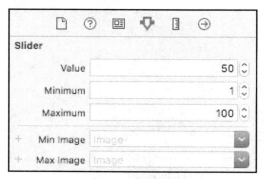

The slider attributes

When you're done, you should have 12 user interface elements in your scene: one slider, three buttons and a whole bunch of labels. Excellent!

➤ Run the app and play with it for a minute. The controls don't really do much yet (except for the button that should still pop up the alert), but you can at least drag the slider around.

You can now tick a few more items off the to-do list, all without much programming! That is going to change really soon, because you will have to write Swift code to actually make the controls do something.

The slider

The next item on your to-do list is: "Read the value of the slider after the user presses the Hit Me! button."

If, in your messing around in Interface Builder, you did not accidentally disconnect the button from the showAlert action, you can modify the app to show the slider's value in the alert pop-up. (If you did disconnect the button, then you should hook it up again first. You know how, right?)

Remember how you added an action to the view controller in order to recognize when the user tapped the button? You can do the same thing for the slider. This new action will be performed whenever the user drags the slider.

The steps for adding this action are largely the same as before.

➤ First, go to **ViewController.swift** and add the following at the bottom, just before the final closing curly bracket:

```
@IBAction func sliderMoved(_ slider: UISlider) {
  print("The value of the slider is now: \(slider.value)")
}
```

➤ Second, go to the storyboard and Control-drag from the slider to View controller in the Document Outline. Let go of the mouse button and select **sliderMoved**: from the pop-up. Done!

Just to refresh your memory, the Document Outline sits on the left-hand side of the Interface Builder canvas. It shows the View hierarchy of the storyboard. Here, you can see that the View controller contains a view (succinctly named View), which, in turn, contains the sub-views you've added: the buttons and labels.

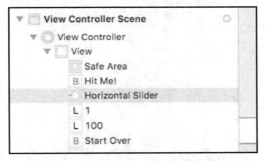

The Document Outline shows the view hierarchy of the storyboard

Remember, if the Document Outline is not visible, click the little icon at the bottom of the Xcode window to reveal it:

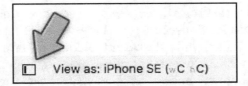

This button shows or hides the Document Outline

When you connect the slider, make sure to Control-drag to View controller (the yellow circle icon), not View controller Scene at the very top. If you don't see the yellow circle icon, then click the arrow in front of View controller scene (called the "disclosure triangle") to expand it.

If all went well, the `sliderMoved:` action is now hooked up to the slider's Value Changed event. This means the `sliderMoved()` method will be called every time the user drags the slider to the left or right, changing its value.

You can verify that the connection was made by selecting the slider and looking at the **Connections inspector**:

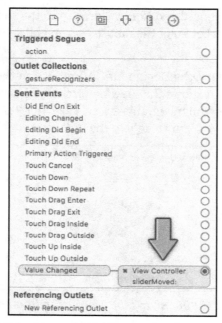

The slider is now hooked up to the view controller

> **Note**: Did you notice that the `sliderMoved:` action has a colon in its name but `showAlert` does not? That's because the `sliderMoved()` method takes a single parameter, `slider`, while `showAlert()` does not have any parameters. If an action method has a parameter, Interface Builder adds a : to the name. You'll learn more about parameters and how to use them soon.

➤ Run the app and drag the slider.

As soon as you start dragging, the Xcode window should open a new pane at the bottom, the **Debug area**, showing a list of messages:

```
@IBAction func sliderMoved(_ slider: UISlider) {
    print("The value of the slider is now: \(slider.value)")
  }
}
```

BullsEye

```
The value of the slider is now: 37.9439
The value of the slider is now: 32.8732
The value of the slider is now: 29.4927
The value of the slider is now: 27.8024
The value of the slider is now: 25.9915
The value of the slider is now: 24.422
The value of the slider is now: 24.0598
The value of the slider is now: 24.0598
```

Auto ⌄   Filter   All Output ⌄   Filter

Printing messages in the Debug area

Note: If, for some reason, the Debug area does not show up, you can always show (or hide) the Debug area by using the appropriate toolbar button on the top right corner of the Xcode window. You will notice from the above screenshot that the Debug area is split into two panes. You can control which of the panes is shown/hidden by using the two blue square icons shown above in the bottom-right corner.

Show Debug area

If you swipe the slider all the way to the left, you should see the value go down to 1. All the way to the right, the value should stop at 100.

The print() function is a great way to show you what is going on in the app. Its entire purpose is to write a text message to the **Console** — the right-hand pane in the Debug area. Here, you used print() to verify that you properly hooked up the action to the slider and that you can read the slider value as the slider is moved.

Developers often use print() to make sure their apps are doing the right thing before they add more functionality. Printing a message to the Console is quick and easy.

> **Note**: You may see a bunch of other messages in the Console, too. This is debug output from UIKit and iOS Simulator. You can safely ignore these messages.

Creating a variable and functions

Printing information with `print()` to the Console is very useful during the development process, but it's absolutely useless to users because they can't see the Console when the app is running on a device.

You're going to improve this by showing the value of the slider in the alert pop-up. So how do you get the slider's value?

When you read the slider's value in sliderMoved(), that piece of data disappears when the action method ends. It would be handy if you could remember this value until the user taps the Hit Me! button.

➤ Open **ViewController.swift** and add the following at the top, directly below the line that says `class ViewController`:

```
var currentValue: Int = 0
```

➤ Change the contents of the `sliderMoved()` method in **ViewController.swift** to the following:

```
@IBAction func sliderMoved(_ slider: UISlider) {
  currentValue = lroundf(slider.value)
}
```

You removed the `print()` statement and replaced it with this line:

```
currentValue = lroundf(slider.value)
```

➤ Now change the `showAlert()` method to the following:

```
@IBAction func showAlert() {
  let message = "The value of the slider is: \(currentValue)"

  let alert = UIAlertController(title: "Hello, World",
                                 message: message,     // changed
                          preferredStyle: .alert)

  let action = UIAlertAction(title: "OK",              // changed
                             style: .default,
                           handler: nil)
```

```
    alert.addAction(action)

    present(alert, animated: true, completion: nil)
}
```

As before, you create and show a UIAlertController, except this time its message says: "The value of the slider is: X," where X is replaced by the contents of the currentValue variable (a whole number between 1 and 100).

Suppose currentValue is 34, which means the slider is about one-third to the left. The new code above will convert the string "The value of the slider is: \ (currentValue)" into "The value of the slider is: 34" and put that into a new object named message.

The old print() did something similar, except that it printed the result to the Console. Here, however, you do not wish to print the result but show it in the alert pop-up. That is why you tell the UIAlertController that it should now use this new string as the message to display.

➤ Run the app, drag the slider and press the button. Now, the alert should show the actual value of the slider.

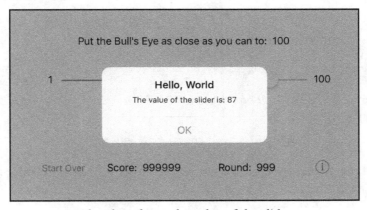

The alert shows the value of the slider

Cool. You have used a variable, currentValue, to remember a particular piece of data, the rounded-off position of the slider, so that it can be used elsewhere in the app — in this case in the alert's message text.

If you tap the button again without moving the slider, the alert will still show the same value. The variable keeps its value until you put a new one into it.

Your first bug

There is a small problem with the app, though. Maybe you've noticed it already. Here is how to reproduce the problem:

➤ Press the Stop button in Xcode to completely terminate the app, then press Run again. Without moving the slider, immediately press the Hit Me! button.

The alert now says: "The value of the slider is: 0". But the slider is obviously at the center, so you would expect the value to be 50. You've discovered a bug!

> **Exercise**: Think of a reason why the value would be 0 in this particular situation (start the app, don't move the slider, press the button).

Answer: The clue here is that this only happens when you don't move the slider. Of course, without moving the slider the sliderMoved() message is never sent and you never put the slider's value into the currentValue variable.

The default value for the currentValue variable is 0, and that is what you are seeing here.

➤ To fix this bug, change the declaration of currentValue to:

```
var currentValue: Int = 50
```

Now the starting value of currentValue is 50, which should be the same value as the slider's initial position.

➤ Run the app again and verify that the bug is fixed.

You can find the project files for the app up to this point under **16-Slider and Labels** in the Source Code folder.

Chapter 17: Outlets

Eli Ganim

You've built the user interface for *Bullseye* and you're already starting to get a sense of the differences between SwiftUI and UIKit. This chapter takes care of a few items from the to-do list and covers the following:

- **Improve the slider**: Set the initial slider value (in code) to be whatever value was set in the storyboard instead of assuming an initial value.

- **Generate the random number**: Generate the random number to be used as the target by the game.

- **Add rounds to the game**: Add the ability to start a new round of the game.

- **Display the target value**: Display the generated target number on screen.

- **Calculating the points scored**: Determine how many points to award to the player, based on how closely they positioned the slider to the target value.

Improving the slider

You completed storing the value of the slider into a variable and showing it via an alert. That's great, but you can still improve on it a little.

What if you decide to set the initial value of the slider in the storyboard to something other than 50 — say, 1 or 100? Then currentValue would be wrong again because the app always assumes it will be 50 at the start. You'd have to remember to also fix the code to give currentValue a new initial value.

Take it from me — that kind of thing is hard to remember, especially when the project becomes bigger and you have dozens of view controllers to worry about, or when you haven't looked at the code for weeks.

Getting the initial slider value

To fix this issue once and for all, you're going to do some work inside the viewDidLoad() method in **ViewController.swift**. That method currently looks like this:

```
override func viewDidLoad() {
  super.viewDidLoad()
  // Do any additional setup after loading the view.
}
```

The viewDidLoad() message is sent by UIKit immediately after the view controller loads its user interface from the storyboard file. At this point, the view controller isn't visible yet, so this is a good place to set instance variables to their proper initial values.

➤ Change viewDidLoad() to the following:

```
override func viewDidLoad() {
  super.viewDidLoad()
  currentValue = lroundf(slider.value)
}
```

The idea is that you take whatever value is set on the slider in the storyboard (whether it is 50, 1, 100 or anything else) and use that as the initial value of currentValue.

Recall that you need to round off the number, because currentValue is an Int and integers cannot take decimal (or fractional) numbers.

Unfortunately, Xcode immediately complains about these changes even before you try to run the app.

```
33  class ViewController: UIViewController {
34    var currentValue: Int = 50
35
36    override func viewDidLoad() {
37      super.viewDidLoad()
38      currentValue = lroundf(slider.value)        🔵 Use of unresolved identifier 'slider'
39    }
```

Xcode error message about missing identifier

> **Note**: Xcode tries to be helpful and it analyzes the program for mistakes as you're typing. Sometimes, you may see temporary warnings and error messages that will go away when you complete the changes that you're making.
>
> Don't be too intimidated by these messages; they are only short-lived while the code is in a state of flux.

The above happens because viewDidLoad() does not know of anything named slider.

Then why did this work earlier, in sliderMoved()? Let's take a look at that method again:

```
@IBAction func sliderMoved(_ slider: UISlider) {
  currentValue = lroundf(slider.value)
}
```

Here, you do the exact same thing: You round off slider.value and put it into currentValue. So why does it work here but not in viewDidLoad()?

The difference is that, in the code above, slider is a *parameter* of the sliderMoved() method. Parameters are the things inside the parentheses following a method's name. In this case, there's a single parameter named slider, which refers to the UISlider object that sent this action message.

Action methods can have a parameter that refers to the UI control that triggered the method. This is convenient when you wish to refer to that object in the method, just as you did here (the object in question being the UISlider).

When the user moves the slider, the UISlider object basically says, "Hey, View controller! I'm a slider object and I just got moved. By the way, here's my phone number so you can get in touch with me."

The slider parameter contains this "phone number," but it is only valid for the duration of this particular method.

In other words, slider is *local*; you cannot use it anywhere else.

Locals

When you first learned about variables, it was mentioned that each variable has a certain lifetime, known as its *scope*. The scope of a variable depends on where in your program you defined that variable.

There are three possible scope levels in Swift:

1. **Global scope**: These objects exist for the duration of the app and are accessible from anywhere.

2. **Instance scope**: This is for variables such as currentValue. These objects are alive for as long as the object that owns them stays alive.

3. **Local scope**: Objects with a local scope, such as the slider parameter of sliderMoved(), only exist for the duration of that method. As soon as the execution of the program leaves this method, the local objects are no longer accessible.

Let's look at the top part of showAlert():

```swift
@IBAction func showAlert() {
  let message = "The value of the slider is: \(currentValue)"

  let alert = UIAlertController(title: "Hello, World",
                                message: message,
                         preferredStyle: .alert)

  let action = UIAlertAction(title: "OK", style: .default,
                             handler: nil)
  . . .
```

Because the message, alert, and action objects are created inside the method, they have local scope. They only come into existence when the showAlert() action is performed and they cease to exist when the action is done.

As soon as the showAlert() method completes, i.e., when there are no more statements for it to execute, the computer destroys the message, alert, and action objects and their storage space is cleared out.

The `currentValue` variable, however, lives on forever... or at least for as long as the `ViewController` does, which is until the user terminates the app. This type of variable is named an *instance variable*, because its scope is the same as the scope of the object instance it belongs to.

In other words, you use instance variables if you want to keep a certain value around, from one action event to the next.

Setting up outlets

So, with this newly gained knowledge of variables and their scopes, how do you fix the error that you encountered?

The solution is to store a reference to the slider as a new instance variable, just like you did for `currentValue`. Except that this time, the data type of the variable is not `Int`, but `UISlider`. And you're not using a regular instance variable but a special one called an *outlet*.

➤ Add the following line to **ViewController.swift**:

```
@IBOutlet weak var slider: UISlider!
```

It doesn't really matter where this line goes, just as long as it is somewhere inside the brackets for `class ViewController`. It's common to put outlets with the other instance variables — at the top of the class implementation.

This line tells Interface Builder that you now have a variable named `slider` that can be connected to a `UISlider` object. Just as Interface Builder likes to call methods *actions*, it calls these variables *outlets*. Interface Builder doesn't see any of your other variables, only the ones marked with `@IBOutlet`.

Don't worry about weak or the exclamation point for now. Why these are necessary will be explained later on. For now, just remember that a variable for an outlet needs to be declared as `@IBOutlet weak var` and has an exclamation point at the end. (Sometimes you'll see a question mark instead; all this hocus pocus will be explained in due time.)

Once you add the `slider` variable, you'll notice that the Xcode error goes away. Does that mean that you can run your app now? Try it and see what happens.

The app crashes on start with an error similar to the following:

```
BullsEye 〉 BullsEye 〉 ViewController.swift 〉 ViewController
29  import UIKit
30
31  class ViewController: UIViewController {
○    @IBOutlet weak var slider: UISlider!
33    var currentValue: Int = 50
34
35    override func viewDidLoad() {
36      super.viewDidLoad()
37      currentValue = lroundf(slider.value)    Thread 1: Fatal error: Unexpectedly found nil while unwrapping an Optional value
38    }
```

App crash when outlet is not connected

So, what happened?

Remember that an outlet has to be *connected* to something in the storyboard. You defined the variable, but you didn't actually set up the connection yet. So, when the app ran and `viewDidLoad()` was called, it tried to find the matching connection in the storyboard and could not — and crashed.

Let's set up the connection in storyboard now.

➤ Open the storyboard. Hold **Control** and click on the **slider**. Don't drag anywhere, though — a menu should pop up that shows all the connections for this slider. (Instead of Control-clicking, you can also right-click once.)

This pop-up menu works exactly the same as the Connections inspector. It just an alternative approach.

➤ Click on the open circle next to **New Referencing Outlet** and drag to **View controller**:

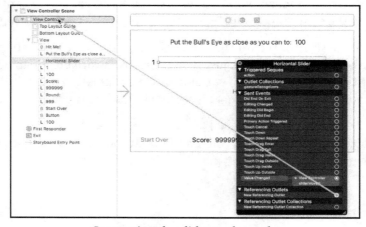

Connecting the slider to the outlet

➤ In the pop-up that appears, select **slider**.

This is the outlet that you just added. You have successfully connected the slider object from the storyboard to the view controller's s lider outlet.

Now that you have done all this set up work, you can refer to the slider object from anywhere inside the view controller using the s lider variable.

With these changes in place, it no longer matters what you choose for the initial value of the slider in Interface Builder. When the app starts, currentValue will always correspond to that setting.

➤ Run the app and immediately press the Hit Me! button. It correctly says: "The value of the slider is: 50." Stop the app, go into Interface Builder and change the initial value of the slider to something else — say, 25. Run the app again and press the button. The alert should read 25, now.

> **Note**: When you change the slider value — or the value in any Interface Builder field — remember to tab out of field when you make a change. If you make the change but your cursor remains in the field, the change might not take effect. This is something which can trip you up often.

Put the slider's starting position back to 50 when you're done playing.

> **Exercise**: Give currentValue an initial value of 0 again. Its initial value is no longer important — it will be overwritten in viewDidLoad() anyway — but Swift demands that all variables always have some value and 0 is as good as any.

Generating the random number

You already read in section 1 how to generate random numbers, so you'll jump straight to the code:

➤ Add a new variable at the top of **ViewController.swift**, with the other variables:

```
var targetValue = 0
```

You might wonder why we didn't specify the type of the targetValue variable, similar to what we'd done earlier for currentValue. This is because Swift is able to *infer* the type of variables if it has enough information to work with. Here, for example, you initialize targetValue with 0 and, since 0 is an integer value, the compiler knows that targetValue will be of type Int.

It should be clear why you made targetValue an instance variable: You want to calculate the random number in one place – like in viewDidLoad() — and then remember it until the user taps the button in showAlert() when you have to check this value against the user selection.

Next, you need to generate the random number. A good place to do this is when the game starts.

➤ Add the following line to viewDidLoad() in **ViewController.swift**:

```
targetValue = Int.random(in: 1...100)
```

The complete viewDidLoad() should now look like this:

```
override func viewDidLoad() {
  super.viewDidLoad()
  currentValue = lroundf(slider.value)
  targetValue = Int.random(in: 1...100)
}
```

Displaying the random number

➤ Change showAlert() to the following:

```
@IBAction func showAlert() {
  let message = "The value of the slider is: \(currentValue)" +
                "\nThe target value is: \(targetValue)"

  let alert = . . .
}
```

Tip: Whenever you see . . . in a source code listing, this is a shorthand for: This part didn't change. Don't go replacing the existing code with actual ellipsis!

You've simply added the random number, which is now stored in targetValue, to the message string. This should look familiar to you by now: The \(targetValue) placeholder is replaced by the actual random number.

The \n character sequence is new. It means that you want to insert a special "new line" character at that point, which will break up the text into two lines so the message is a little easier to read. The + is also new but is simply used here to combine two strings. We could just as easily have written it as a single long string, but it might not have looked as good to the reader.

➤ Run the app and try it out!

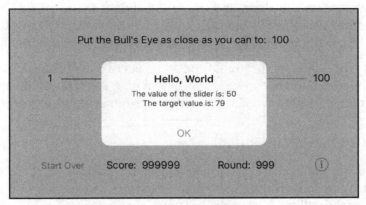

The alert shows the target value on a new line

Note: Earlier, you used the + operator to add two numbers together (just like how it works in math) but, here, you're also using + to glue different bits of text into one big string.

Swift allows the use of the same operator for different tasks, depending on the data types involved. If you have two integers, + adds them up. But with two strings, + concatenates, or combines, them into a longer string.

Programming languages often use the same symbols for different purposes, depending on the context. After all, there are only so many symbols to go around!

Adding rounds to the game

If you press the Hit Me! button a few times, you'll notice that the random number never changes. I'm afraid the game won't be much fun that way. This happens because you generate the random number in viewDidLoad() and never again afterwards.

The viewDidLoad() method is only called once when the view controller is created during app startup. The item on the to-do list actually said: "Generate a random number *at the start of each round*". Let's talk about what a round means in terms of this game.

When the game starts, the player has a score of 0 and the round number is 1. You set the slider halfway (to value 50) and calculate a random number. Then you wait for the player to press the Hit Me! button. As soon as they do, the round ends.

You calculate the points for this round and add them to the total score. Then you increment the round number and start the next round. You reset the slider to the halfway position again and calculate a new random number. Rinse, repeat.

Starting a new round

Whenever you find yourself thinking something along the lines of, "At this point in the app we have to do such and such," then it makes sense to create a new method for it. This method will nicely capture that functionality in a self-contained unit of its own.

➤ With that in mind, add the following new method to **ViewController.swift**:

```
func startNewRound() {
  targetValue = Int.random(in: 1...100)
  currentValue = 50
  slider.value = Float(currentValue)
}
```

It doesn't really matter where you put the code, as long as it is inside the ViewController implementation (within the class curly brackets), so that the compiler knows it belongs to the ViewController object.

It's not very different from what you did before, except that you moved the logic for setting up a new round into its own method, startNewRound(). The advantage of doing this is that you can execute this logic from more than one place in your code.

Using the new method

First, you'll call this new method from viewDidLoad() to set up everything for the very first round. Recall that viewDidLoad() happens just once when the app starts up, so this is a great place to begin the first round.

➤ Change viewDidLoad() to:

```
override func viewDidLoad() {
  super.viewDidLoad()
  startNewRound()  // Replace previous code with this
}
```

Note that you've removed some of the existing statements from viewDidLoad() and replaced them with just the call to startNewRound().

You will also call startNewRound() after the player pressed the Hit Me! button, from within showAlert().

➤ Make the following change to showAlert():

```
@IBAction func showAlert() {
  . . .

  startNewRound()
}
```

The call to startNewRound() goes at the very end, right after present(alert, …).

Until now, the methods from the view controller have been invoked for you by UIKit when something happened: viewDidLoad() is performed when the app loads, showAlert() is performed when the player taps the button, sliderMoved() when the player drags the slider, and so on. This is the event-driven model we talked about earlier.

It is also possible to call methods directly, which is what you're doing here. You are sending a message from one method in the object to another method in that same object.

In this case, the view controller sends the startNewRound() message to itself in order to set up the new round. Program execution will then switch to that method and execute its statements one-by-one. When there are no more statements in the method, it returns to the calling method and continues with that — either viewDidLoad(), if this is the first time, or showAlert() for every round after.

Calling methods in different ways

Sometimes, you may see method calls written like this:

```
self.startNewRound()
```

That does the exact same thing as startNewRound() without self. in front. Recall you read that the view controller sends the message to itself. Well, that's exactly what self means.

To call a method on an object, you'd normally write:

```
receiver.methodName(parameters)
```

The receiver is the object you're sending the message to. If you're sending the message to yourself, then the receiver is self. But because sending messages to self is very common, you can also leave this special keyword out for many cases.

This isn't exactly the first time you've called methods. addAction() is a method on UIAlertController and present() is a method that all view controllers have, including yours.

When you write Swift apps, a lot of what you do is calling methods on objects, because that is how the objects in your app communicate.

The advantages of using methods

It's very helpful to put the "new round" logic into its own method. If you didn't, the code for viewDidLoad() and showAlert() would look like this:

```
override func viewDidLoad() {
  super.viewDidLoad()

  targetValue = Int.random(in: 1...100)
  currentValue = 50
  slider.value = Float(currentValue)
}

@IBAction func showAlert() {
  . . .

  targetValue = Int.random(in: 1...100)
  currentValue = 50
  slider.value = Float(currentValue)
}
```

Can you see what is going on here? The same functionality is duplicated in two places. Sure, it is only three lines of code but, often, the code you duplicate could be much larger.

And what if you decide to make a change to this logic (as you will shortly)? Then you will have to make the same change in two places.

You might be able to remember to do so if you recently wrote this code and it is still fresh in memory, but, if you have to make that change a few weeks down the road, chances are that you'll only update it in one place and forget about the other.

Code duplication is a big source of bugs. So, if you need to do the same thing in two different places, consider making a new method for it instead of duplicating code.

Naming methods

The name of the method also helps to make it clear as to what it is supposed to be doing. Can you tell at a glance what the following does?

```
targetValue = Int.random(in: 1...100)
currentValue = 50
slider.value = Float(currentValue)
```

You probably have to reason your way through it: "It is calculating a new random number and then resets the position of the slider, so I guess it must be the start of a new round."

Some programmers will use a comment to document what is going on (and you can do that too), but, in my opinion, the following is much clearer than the above block of code with an explanatory comment:

```
startNewRound()
```

This line practically spells out for you what it will do. And if you want to know the specifics of what goes on in a new round, you can always look up the startNewRound() method implementation.

Well-written source code speaks for itself!

➤ Run the app and verify that it calculates a new random number between 1 and 100 after each tap on the button.

You should also have noticed that, after each round, the slider resets to the halfway position. That happens because startNewRound() sets currentValue to 50 and then tells the slider to go to that position. That is the opposite of what you did before (you used to read the slider's position and put it into currentValue), but it would work better in the game if you start from the same position in each round.

> **Exercise**: Just for fun, modify the code so that the slider does not reset to the halfway position at the start of a new round.

Type conversion

By the way, you may have been wondering what Float(…) does in this line:

```
slider.value = Float(currentValue)
```

Swift is a *strongly typed* language, meaning that it is really picky about the shapes that you can put into the boxes. For example, if a variable is an Int, you cannot put a Float, or a non-whole number, into it, and vice versa.

The value of a UISlider happens to be a Float — you've seen this when you printed out the value of the slider — but currentValue is an Int. So the following won't work:

```
slider.value = currentValue
```

The compiler considers this an error. Some programming languages are happy to convert the Int into a Float for you, but Swift wants you to be explicit about such conversions.

When you say Float(currentValue), the compiler takes the integer number that's stored in currentValue and converts it into a new Float value that it can pass on to the UISlider.

Because Swift is stricter about this sort of thing than most other programming languages, it is often a source of confusion for newcomers to the language. Unfortunately, Swift's error messages aren't always very clear about what part of the code is wrong or why.

Just remember, if you get an error message saying, "Cannot assign value of type 'something' to type 'something else'," then you're probably trying to mix incompatible data types. The solution is to explicitly convert one type to the other — if conversion is allowed, of course — as you've done here.

Displaying the target value

Great, you figured out how to calculate the random number and how to store it in an instance variable, targetValue, so that you can access it later.

Now, you are going to show that target number on the screen. Without it, the player won't know what to aim for and that would make the game impossible to win.

Setting up the storyboard

When you set up the storyboard, you added a label for the target value (top-right corner). The trick is to put the value from the targetValue variable into this label. To do that, you need to accomplish two things:

1.   Create an outlet for the label so you can send it messages.

2.   Give the label new text to display.

This will be very similar to what you did with the slider. Recall that you added an @IBOutlet variable so you could reference the slider anywhere from within the view controller. Using this outlet variable you could ask the slider for its value, through slider.value. You'll do the same thing for the label.

➤ In **ViewController.swift**, add the following line below the other outlet declaration:

```
@IBOutlet weak var targetLabel: UILabel!
```

➤ In **Main.storyboard**, click to select the correct label — the one at the very top that says "100."

➤ Go to the **Connections inspector** and drag from **New Referencing Outlet** to the yellow circle at the top of your view controller in the central scene.

You could also drag to the **View Controller** in the Document Outline — there are many ways to do the same thing in Interface Builder.

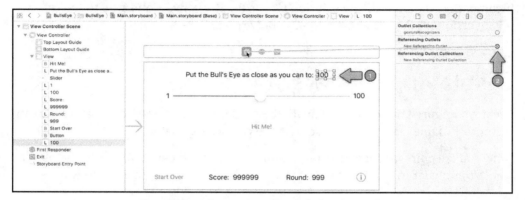

Connecting the target value label to its outlet

➤ Select **targetLabel** from the pop-up, and the connection is made.

Displaying the target value via code

➤ Add the following method below startNewRound() in **ViewController.swift**:

```
func updateLabels() {
  targetLabel.text = String(targetValue)
}
```

You're putting this logic in a separate method because it's something you might use from different places.

The name of the method makes it clear what it does: It updates the contents of the labels. Currently it's just setting the text of a single label, but later on you will add code to update the other labels as well (total score, round number).

The code inside updateLabels() should have no surprises for you, although you may wonder why you cannot simply do:

```
targetLabel.text = targetValue
```

The answer again is that you cannot put a value of one data type into a variable of another type — the square peg just won't go in the round hole.

The `targetLabel` outlet references a `UILabel` object. The `UILabel` object has a `text` property, which is a `String` object. So, you can only put `String` values into `text`, but `targetValue` is an `Int`. A direct assignment won't fly because an `Int` and a `String` are two very different types.

So, you have to convert the `Int` into a `String`, and that is what `String(targetValue)` does. It's similar to what you've done before with `Float(…)`.

Just in case you were wondering, you could also convert `targetValue` to a `String` by using string interpolation, like you've done before:

```
targetLabel.text = "\(targetValue)"
```

Which approach you use is a matter of taste. Either approach will work fine.

Notice that `updateLabels()` is a regular method — it is not attached to any UI controls as an action — so it won't do anything until you actually call it. You can tell because it doesn't say `@IBAction` before `func`.

Action methods vs. normal methods

So what is the difference between an action method and a regular method?

Answer: Nothing.

An action method is really just the same as any other method. The only special thing is the `@IBAction` attribute, which allows Interface Builder to see the method so you can connect it to your buttons, sliders and so on.

Other methods, such as `viewDidLoad()`, don't have the `@IBAction` specifier. This is good because all kinds of mayhem would occur if you hooked these up to your buttons.

This is the simple form of an action method:

```
@IBAction func showAlert()
```

You can also ask for a reference to the object that triggered this action, via a parameter:

```
@IBAction func sliderMoved(_ slider: UISlider)
@IBAction func buttonTapped(_ button: UIButton)
```

But the following method cannot be used as an action from Interface Builder:

```
func updateLabels()
```

That's because it is not marked as @IBAction and as a result, Interface Builder can't see it. To use updateLabels(), you will have to call it yourself.

Calling the method

The logical place to call updateLabels() would be after each call to startNewRound(), because that is where you calculate the new target value. So, you could always add a call to updateLabels() in viewDidLoad() and showAlert(), but there's another way, too!

What is this other way, you ask? Well, if updateLabels() is always (or at least in your current code) called after startNewRound(), why not call updateLabels() directly from startNewRound() itself? That way, instead of having two calls in two separate places, you can have a single call.

➤ Change startNewRound() to:

```
func startNewRound() {
    targetValue = Int.random(in: 1...100)
    currentValue = 50
    slider.value = Float(currentValue)
    updateLabels()  // Add this line
}
```

You should be able to type just the first few letters of the method name, like **upd**, and Xcode will show you a list of suggestions matching what you typed.

Press **Enter** (or **Tab**) to accept the suggestion (if you are on the right item — or scroll the list to find the right item and then press Enter)

```
64   func startNewRound() {
65       targetValue = Int.random(in: 1...100)
66       currentValue = 50
67       slider.value = Float(currentValue)
68       up
    Void updateLabels()
mach_port_t upl_t
    Void updateFocusIfNeeded()
    Void updateViewConstraints()
    Void updateUserActivityState(activity: NSUserActivity)
    upl_t UPL_NULL
    Int32 IFF_UP
    UIPress UIPress
```

Xcode autocomplete offers suggestions

Also worth noting is that you don't have to start typing the method (or property) name you're looking from the beginning — Xcode uses fuzzy search and typing "dateL" or "label" should help you find "updateLabels" just as easily.

➤ Run the app and you'll actually see the random value on the screen. That should make it a little easier to aim for.

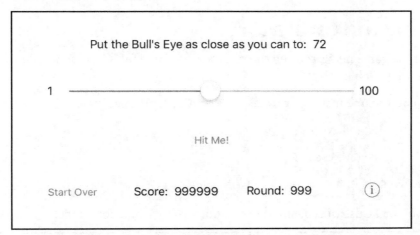

The label in the top-right corner now shows the random value

Calculating the points scored

Now that you have both the target value (the random number) and a way to read the slider's position, you can calculate how many points the player scored. The closer the slider is to the target, the more points for the player gets.

➤ Make this change to showAlert():

```
@IBAction func showAlert() {
  let difference = abs(targetValue - currentValue)
  let points = 100 - difference

  let message = "You scored \(points) points"
    . . .
}
```

Showing the total score

In this game you want to show the player's total score on the screen. After every round, the app should add the newly scored points to the total and then update the score label.

Storing the total score

Because the game needs to keep the total score around for a long time, you will need an instance variable.

➤ Add a new `score` instance variable to **ViewController.swift**:

```
class ViewController: UIViewController {

    var currentValue: Int = 0
    var targetValue = 0
    var score = 0                    // add this line
```

Again, you make use of type inference to not specify a type for `score`.

Discover the inferred type for a variable

Updating the total score

Now, `showAlert()` can be amended to update this `score` variable.

➤ Make the following changes:

```
@IBAction func showAlert() {
    let difference = abs(targetValue - currentValue)
    let points = 100 - difference

    score += points              // add this line

    let message = "You scored \(points) points"
    . . .
}
```

Nothing too shocking here. You just added the following line:

```
score += points
```

This adds the points that the user scored in this round to the total score. You could also have written it like this:

```
score = score + points
```

Displaying the score

To display your current score, you're going to do the same thing that you did for the target label: hook up the score label to an outlet and put the score value into the label's text property.

> **Exercise**: See if you can do the above by yourself. You've already done these things before for the target value label, so you should be able to repeat those steps for the score label.

Done? You should have added this line to **ViewController.swift**:

```
@IBOutlet weak var scoreLabel: UILabel!
```

Then, you connect the relevant label on the storyboard (the one that says 999999) to the new scoreLabel outlet.

Unsure how to connect the outlet? There are several ways to make connections from user interface objects to the view controller's outlets:

- Control-click on the object to get a context-sensitive pop-up menu. Then, drag from New Referencing Outlet to View controller (you did this with the slider).

- Go to the Connections Inspector for the label. Drag from New Referencing Outlet to View controller (you did this with the target label).

- Control-drag **from** View controller to the label (give this one a try now) — doing it the other way, Control-dragging from the label to View controller, won't work.

Great, that gives you a scoreLabel outlet that you can use to display the score. Now, where in the code can you do that? In updateLabels(), of course.

➤ Back in **ViewController.swift**, change `updateLabels()` to the following:

```
func updateLabels() {
  targetLabel.text = String(targetValue)
  scoreLabel.text = String(score)      // add this line
}
```

Nothing new, here. You convert the score — which is an `Int` — into a `String` and then pass that string to the label's `text` property. In response to that, the label will redraw itself with the new score.

➤ Run the app and verify that the points for this round are added to the total score label whenever you tap the button.

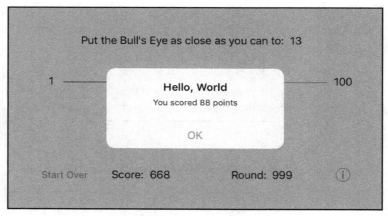

The score label keeps track of the player's total score

One more round...

Speaking of rounds, you also have to increment the round number each time the player starts a new round.

Exercise: Keep track of the current round number (starting at 1) and increment it when a new round starts. Display the current round number in the corresponding label. I may be throwing you into the deep end here, but if you've been able to follow the instructions so far, then you've already seen all the pieces you will need to pull this off. Good luck!

If you guessed that you had to add another instance variable, then you are right. You should add the following line (or something similar) to **ViewController.swift**:

```
var round = 0
```

It's also OK if you included the name of the data type, even though that is not strictly necessary:

```
var round: Int = 0
```

Also, add an outlet for the label:

```
@IBOutlet weak var roundLabel: UILabel!
```

As before, you should connect the label to this outlet in Interface Builder.

Note: Don't forget to make those connections.

Forgetting to make the connections in Interface Builder is an often-made mistake, especially by yours truly.

It happens to me all the time that I make the outlet for a button and write the code to deal with taps on that button but, when I run the app, it doesn't work. Usually, it takes me a few minutes and some head scratching to realize that I forgot to connect the button to the outlet or the action method.

You can tap on the button all you want but, unless that connection exists, your code will not respond.

Finally, updateLabels() should be modified like this:

```
func updateLabels() {
   targetLabel.text = String(targetValue)
   scoreLabel.text = String(score)
   roundLabel.text = String(round)      // add this line
}
```

Did you also figure out where to increment the round variable?

I'd say the startNewRound() method is a pretty good place. After all, you call this method whenever you start a new round. It makes sense to increment the round counter there.

➤ Change `startNewRound()` to:

```
func startNewRound() {
    round += 1              // add this line
    targetValue = ...
}
```

Note that, when you declared the `round` instance variable, you gave it a default value of 0. Therefore, when the app starts up, `round` is initially 0. When you call `startNewRound()` for the very first time, it adds 1 to this initial value and, as a result, the first round is properly counted as round 1.

Run the app and try it out. The round counter should update whenever you press the Hit Me! button.

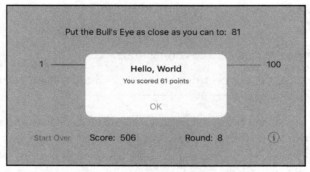

The round label counts how many rounds have been played

You're making great progress; well done!

You can find the project files for the app up to this point under **17-Outlets** in the Source Code folder.

Chapter 18: Polish

Eli Ganim

At this point, your game is fully playable. The gameplay rules are all implemented and the logic doesn't seem to have any big flaws, but there's still some room for improvement.

This chapter will cover the following:

- **Tweaks**: Small UI tweaks to make the game look and function better.

- **The alert**: Updating the alert view functionality so that the screen updates *after* the alert goes away.

- **Start over**: Resetting the game to start afresh.

Tweaks

Obviously, the game is not very pretty yet — you will get to work on that soon. In the mean time, there are a few smaller tweaks you can make.

The alert title

Unless you already changed it, the title of the alert still says "Hello, World!" You could give it the name of the game, *Bullseye*, but there's a better idea. What if you change the title depending on how well the player did?

If the player put the slider right on the target, the alert could say: "Perfect!" If the slider is close to the target but not quite there, it could say, "You almost had it!" If the player is way off, the alert could say: "Not even close..."

And so on. This gives the player a little more feedback on how well they did.

You already did that in Section 1, so without further ado here's the updated showAlert() method:

```swift
@IBAction func showAlert() {
  let difference = abs(targetValue - currentValue)
  let points = 100 - difference
  score += points

  // add these lines
  let title: String
  if difference == 0 {
    title = "Perfect!"
  } else if difference < 5 {
    title = "You almost had it!"
  } else if difference < 10 {
    title = "Pretty good!"
  } else {
    title = "Not even close..."
  }

  let message = "You scored \(points) points"

  let alert = UIAlertController(title: title,  // change this
                            message: message,
                       preferredStyle: .alert)

  let action = UIAlertAction(title: "OK", style: .default,
                            handler: nil)
  alert.addAction(action)
  present(alert, animated: true, completion: nil)
```

```
    startNewRound()
}
```

You create a new string constant named `title`, which will contain the text that is set for the alert title. Initially, this `title` doesn't have any value. We'll discuss the `title` variable and how it is set up a bit more in detail just a little further on.

To decide which title text to use, you look at the difference between the slider position and the target:

- If it equals 0, then the player was spot-on and you set `title` to "Perfect!"

- If the difference is less than 5, you use the text, "You almost had it!"

- A difference less than 10 is "Pretty good!"

- However, if the difference is 10 or greater, then you consider the player's attempt "Not even close..."

Can you follow the logic, here? It's just a bunch of `if` statements that consider the different possibilities and choose a string in response.

When you create the `UIAlertController` object, you now give it this `title` string instead of some fixed text.

Constant initialization

In the above code, did you notice that `title` was declared explicitly as being a `String` constant? And did you ask yourself why type inference wasn't used there instead? Also, if `title` is a constant, how do we have code which sets its value in multiple places?

The answer to all of these questions lies in how constants (or `let` values, if you prefer) are initialized in Swift.

You could certainly have used type inference to declare the type for `title` by setting the initial declaration to:

```
let title = ""
```

But do you see the issue there? Now you've actually set the value for `title` and since it's a constant, you can't change the value again. So, the following lines where the `if` condition logic sets a value for `title` would now throw a compiler error since you are trying to set a value to a constant which already has a value. (Go on, try it out for yourself! You know you want to...)

One way to fix this would be to declare `title` as a variable rather than a constant. Like this:

```
var title = ""
```

The above would work great, and the compiler error would go away. But you've got to ask yourself, do you really need a variable there? Or, would a constant do? It's preferable to use constants where possible since they have less risk of unexpected side-effects because the value was accidentally changed in some fashion — for example, because one of your team members changed the code to use a variable that you had originally depended on being unchanged. That is why the code was written the way it was. However, you can go with whichever option you prefer since either approach would work.

But if you do declare `title` as a constant, how is it that your code above assigns multiple values to it?

The secret is in the fact that while there are indeed multiple values being assigned to `title`, only one value would be assigned per each call to `showAlert` since the branches of an `if` condition are mutually exclusive.

So, since `title` starts out without a value (the `let title: String` line only assigns a type, not a value), as long as the code ensures that `title` would always be initialized to a value before the value stored in `title` is accessed, the compiler will not complain.

Again, you can test this by removing the `else` condition in the block of code where a value is assigned to `title`.

Since an `if` condition is only one branch of a test, you need an `else` branch in order for the tests (and the assignment to `title`) to be exhaustive.

So, if you remove the `else` branch, Xcode will immediately complain with an error like: "Constant 'title' used before being initialized."

```
59      let title: String
60      if difference == 0 {
61        title = "Perfect!"
62      } else if difference < 5 {
63        title = "You almost had it!"
64      } else if difference < 10 {
65        title = "Pretty good!"
66  //    } else {
67  //      title = "Not even close..."
68      }
69
70      let message = "You scored \(points) points"
71
72      let alert = UIAlertController(title: title,       ● Constant 'title' used before being initialized
73                          message: message,
74                          preferredStyle: .alert)
```

A constant needs to be initialized exhaustively

Run the app and play the game for a bit. You'll see that the title text changes depending on how well you're doing. That `if` statement sure is handy!

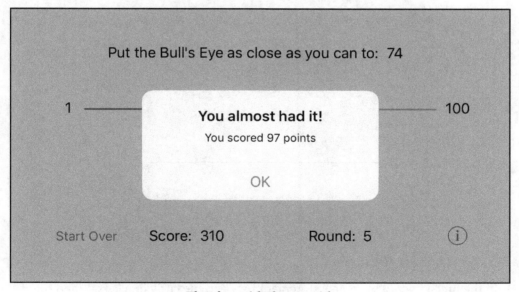

The alert with the new title

Bonus points

Exercise: Give players an additional 100 bonus points when they get a perfect score. This will encourage players to really try to place the bullseye right on the target. Otherwise, there isn't much difference between 100 points for a perfect score and 98 or 95 points if you're close but not quite there.

Now there is an incentive for trying harder — a perfect score is no longer worth just 100 but 200 points! Maybe you can also give the player 50 bonus points for being just one off.

➤ Here's how you can make these changes:

```
@IBAction func showAlert() {
  let difference = abs(targetValue - currentValue)
  var points = 100 - difference        // change let to var

  let title: String
  if difference == 0 {
    title = "Perfect!"
    points += 100                      // add this line
  } else if difference < 5 {
    title = "You almost had it!"
    if difference == 1 {               // add these lines
      points += 50                     // add these lines
    }                                  // add these lines
  } else if difference < 10 {
    title = "Pretty good!"
  } else {
    title = "Not even close..."
  }
  score += points                      // move this line here from
the top
    . . .
}
```

You should notice a few things:

- In the first if you'll see a new statement between the curly brackets. When the difference is equal to zero, you now not only set title to "Perfect!" but also award an extra 100 points.

- The second if has changed, too. There is now an if inside another if. Nothing wrong with that! You want to handle the case where difference is 1 in order to give the player bonus points. That happens inside the new if statement.

After all, if the difference is more than 0 but less than 5, it could be 1 (but not necessarily all the time). Therefore, you perform an additional check to see if the difference truly is 1, and if so, add 50 extra points.

- Because these new `if` statements add extra points, `points` can no longer be a constant; it now needs to be a variable. That's why you change it from `let` to `var`.

- Finally, the line `score += points` has moved below the `if`s. This is necessary because the app updates the `points` variable inside those `if` statements (if the conditions are right) and you want those additional points to count towards the final score.

If your code is slightly different, then that's fine too, as long as it works! There is often more than one way to program something, and if the results are the same, then any approach is equally valid.

➤ Run the app to see if you can score some bonus points!

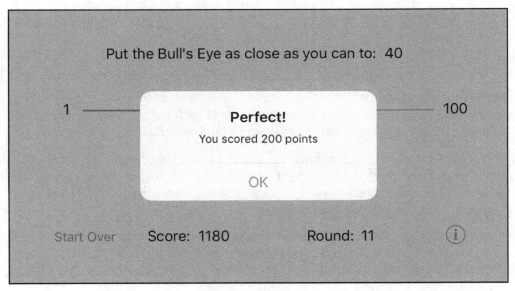

Raking in the points...

The alert

One annoying thing about the app is that as soon as you tap the Hit Me! button and the alert pops up, the slider immediately jumps back to its center position, the round number increments, and the target label already gets the new random number.

What happens is that the new round has already begun while you're still watching the results of the last round. That's a little confusing (and annoying).

It would be better to wait on starting the new round until *after* the player has dismissed the alert pop-up. Only then is the current round truly over.

Asynchronous code execution

Maybe you're wondering why this isn't already happening? After all, in showAlert() you only call startNewRound() after you've shown the alert pop-up:

```
@IBAction func showAlert() {
    . . .
    let alert = UIAlertController(. . .)
    let action = UIAlertAction(. . .)
    alert.addAction(action)

    // Here you make the alert visible:
    present(alert, animated: true, completion: nil)

    // Here you start the new round:
    startNewRound()
}
```

Contrary to what you might expect, present(alert:animated:completion:) doesn't hold up execution of the rest of the method until the alert pop-up is dismissed. That's how alerts on other platforms tend to work, but not on iOS.

Instead, present(alert:animated:completion:) puts the alert on the screen and immediately returns control to the next line of code in the method. The rest of the showAlert() method is executed right away, and the new round starts before the alert pop-up has even finished animating.

In programmer-speak, alerts work *asynchronously*. We'll talk much more about that in a later chapter, but what it means for you right now is that you don't know in advance when the alert will be done. But you can bet it will be well after showAlert() has finished.

Alert event handling

So, if your code execution can't wait in showAlert() until the pop-up is dismissed, then how do you wait for it to close?

The answer is simple: events! As you've seen, a lot of the programming for iOS involves waiting for specific events to occur — buttons being tapped, sliders being moved, and so on. This is no different. You have to wait for the "alert dismissed" event somehow. In the mean time, you simply do nothing.

Here's how it works:

For each button on the alert, you have to supply a `UIAlertAction` object. This object tells the alert what the text on the button is — "OK" — and what the button looks like (you're using the default style, here):

```
let action = UIAlertAction(title: "OK", style: .default,
  handler: nil)
```

The third parameter, `handler`, tells the alert what should happen when the button is pressed. This is the "alert dismissed" event you've been looking for! Currently `handler` is `nil`, which means nothing happens. In case you're wondering, a `nil` in Swift indicates "no value." You will learn more about `nil` values later on.

You can however, give the `UIAlertAction` some code to execute when the OK button is tapped. When the user finally taps OK, the alert will remove itself from the screen and jump to your code. That's your cue to start a new round. This is also known as the *callback* pattern. There are several ways this pattern manifests on iOS. Often you'll be asked to create a new method to handle the event. But here you'll use a *closure*.

➤ Change the bottom bit of `showAlert()` to:

```
@IBAction func showAlert() {
  . . .
  let alert = UIAlertController(. . .)

  let action = UIAlertAction(title: "OK", style: .default,
                             handler: { _ in
                                        self.startNewRound()
                             })

  alert.addAction(action)
  present(alert, animated: true, completion: nil)
}
```

Two things have happened here:

1. You removed the call to `startNewRound()` from the bottom of the method. (Don't forget this part!)

2. You placed it inside a block of code that you gave to UIAlertAction's handler parameter.

    Such a block of code is called a *closure*. You can think of it as a method without a name. This code is not performed right away. Rather, it's performed only when the OK button is tapped. This particular closure tells the app to start a new round (and update the labels) when the alert is dismissed.

➤ Run the app and see for yourself.

Start over

No, you're not going to throw away the source code and start this project all over! This part is about the game's "Start Over" button. This button is supposed to reset the score and start over from the first round.

One use of the Start Over button is for playing against another person. The first player does ten rounds, then the score is reset and the second player does ten rounds. The player with the highest score wins.

> **Exercise**: Try to implement the Start Over button on your own. You've already seen how you can make the view controller react to button presses, and you should be able to figure out how to change the score and round variables.

How did you do? If you got stuck, then follow the instructions below.

The new method

First, add a method to **ViewController.swift** that starts a new game. You should put it near startNewRound() because the two are conceptually related.

➤ Add the new method:

```
func startNewGame() {
  score = 0
  round = 0
  startNewRound()
}
```

This method resets score and round to zero, and starts a new round as well.

Notice that you set round to 0 here, not to 1. You use 0 because incrementing the value of round is the first thing that startNewRound() does. If you were to set round to 1, then startNewRound() would add another 1 to it and the first round would actually be labeled round 2.

So, you begin at 0, let startNewRound() add one and everything works great.

It's probably easier to figure this out from the code than from my explanation. This should illustrate why we don't program computers in English.

You also need an action method to handle taps on the Start Over button. You could write a new method like the following:

```
@IBAction func startOver() {
    startNewGame()
}
```

But you'll notice that this method simply calls the previous method that you added. So, why not cut out the middleman? You can simply change the method you added previously to be an action instead, like this:

```
@IBAction func startNewGame() {
    score = 0
    round = 0
    startNewRound()
}
```

You could follow either of the above approaches since both are equally valid. Having less code means there's less stuff to maintain (and less of a chance of screwing something up). Sometimes, there could also be legitimate reasons for having a seperate action method which calls your own method, but in this particular case, it's better to keep things simple.

Just to keep things consistent, in viewDidLoad() you should replace the call to startNewRound() with startNewGame().

Because score and round are already 0 when the app starts, it won't really make any difference to how the app works, but it does make the intention of the source code clearer. If you wonder whether you can call an IBAction method directly instead of hooking it up to an action in the storyboard, yes, you certainly can do so.

➤ Make this change:

```
override func viewDidLoad() {
  super.viewDidLoad()
  startNewGame()          // this line changed
}
```

Connect the outlet

Finally, you need to connect the Start Over button to the action method.

➤ Open the storyboard and Control-drag from the **Start Over** button to View controller. Let go of the mouse button and pick **startNewGame** from the pop-up if you opted to have startNewGame() as the action method. Otherwise, pick the name of your action method .

That connects the button's Touch Up Inside event to the action you have just defined.

➤ Run the app and play a few rounds. Press Start Over and the game puts you back at square one.

Tip: If you're losing track of what button or label is connected to what method, you can click on View controller in the storyboard to see all the connections that you have made so far.

You can either right-click on View controller to get a pop-up, or simply view the connections in the **Connections inspector**.

This shows all the connections for the view controller.

Now your game is pretty polished and your task list has gotten really short.

You can find the project files for the current version of the app under **18-Polish** in the Source Code folder.

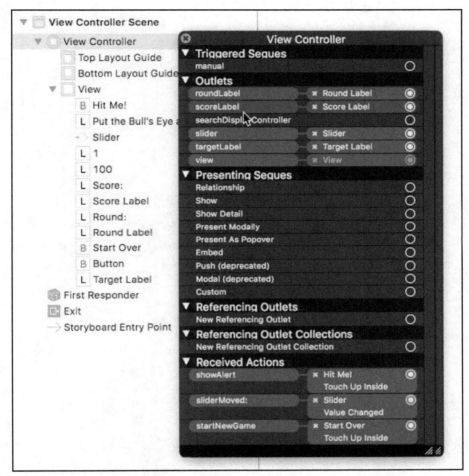

All the connections from View Controller to the other objects

Chapter 19: The New Look

By Eli Ganim

Bullseye is looking good! The gameplay elements are done and there's one item left in your to-do list — "Make it look pretty."

You have to admit the game still doesn't look great. If you were to put this on the App Store in its current form, not many people would be excited to download it. Fortunately, iOS makes it easy for you to create good-looking apps, so let's give *Bullseye* a makeover and add some visual flair.

This chapter covers the following:

- **Landscape orientation revisited**: Project changes to make landscape orientation support work better.

- **Spice up the graphics**: Replace the app UI with custom graphics to give it a more polished look.

- **The about screen**: Add an about screen to the app and make it look spiffy.

Landscape orientation revisited

Just like you did in the SwiftUI version of Bullseye - you'll need to hide the status bar.

Apps in landscape mode do not display the iPhone status bar, unless you tell them to. That's great for your app — games require a more immersive experience and the status bar detracts from that.

➤ Go to the **Project Settings** screen and scroll down to **Deployment Info**. Under **Status Bar Style**, check **Hide status bar**.

This will ensure that the status bar is hidden during application launch.

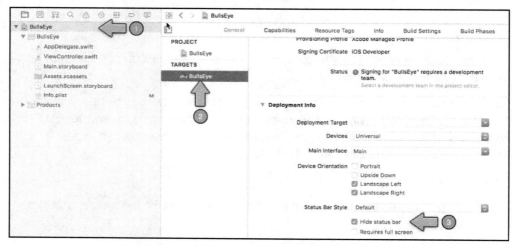

Hiding the status bar when the app launches

➤ That's it. Run the app and you'll see that the status bar is history.

Spicing up the graphics

Getting rid of the status bar is only the first step. You want to go from this:

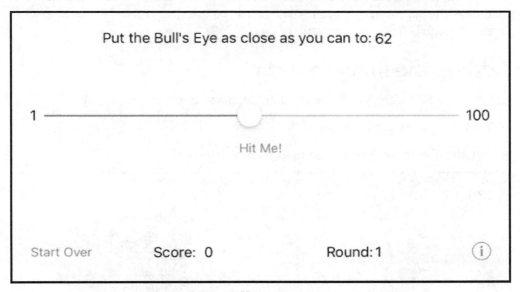

Yawn...

To something that's more like this:

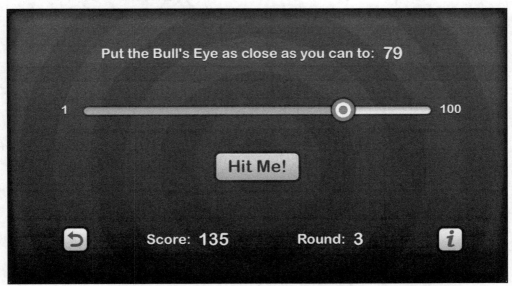

The actual controls won't change. You'll simply be using images to smarten up their look, and you will also adjust the colors and typefaces.

You can put an image in the background, on the buttons, and even on the slider, to customize the appearance of each. The images you use should generally be in PNG format, though JPG files would work too.

Adding the image assets

Just like you did before, you'll need to add the image assets to the project.

➤ Open the **Assets.xcassets** file.

➤ Drag the files in the provided **Images** folder to the project.

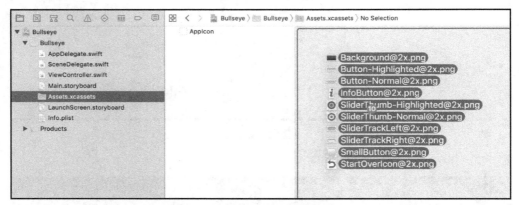

Choose Import to put existing images into the asset catalog

Putting up the wallpaper

You'll begin by changing the drab white background in *Bullseye* to something more fancy.

➤ Open **Main.storyboard**, open the **Library** panel (via the top toolbar) and locate an **Image View**.

The Image View control in the Objects Library

➤ Drag the image view on top of the existing user interface. It doesn't really matter where you put it, as long as it's inside the Bullseye view controller.

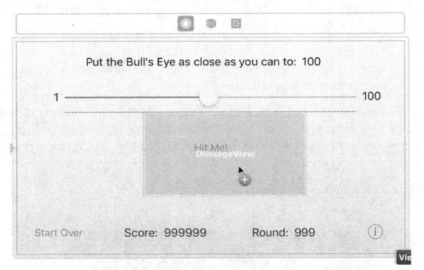

Dragging the Image View into the view controller

➤ With the image view still selected, go to the **Size inspector** (that's the one next to the Attributes inspector) and set X and Y to 0, Width to 667 and Height to 375.

This will make the image view cover the entire screen.

➤ Go to the **Attributes inspector** for the image view. At the top there is an option named **Image**. Click the downward arrow and choose **Background** from the list.

➤ Change **Mode** to **Scale To Fill**

This will put the image named "Background" from the asset catalog into the image view.

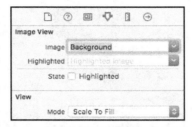

Setting the background image on the Image View

There is only one problem: the image now covers all the other controls. There is an easy fix for that; you have to move the image view behind the other views.

➤ With the image view selected, in the **Editor** menu in Xcode's menu bar at the top of the screen, choose **Arrange** ▸ **Send to Back**.

Sometimes Xcode gives you a hard time with this and you might not see the Send to Back item enabled. If so, try de-selecting the Image View and then selecting it again. Now the menu item should be available.

Alternatively, pick up the image view in the Document Outline and drag it to the top of the list of views, just below Safe Area. The items in the Document Outline view are listed so that the backmost item is at the top of the list and the frontmost one is at the bottom.

Your interface should now look something like this:

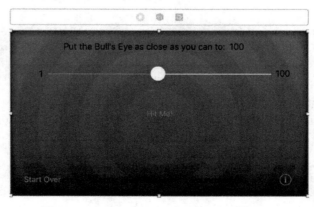

The game with the new background image

That takes care of the background. Run the app and marvel at the new graphics.

Changing the labels

Because the background image is quite dark, the black text labels have become hard to read. Fortunately, Interface Builder lets you change label color. While you're at it, you might change the font as well.

➤ Still in the storyboard, select the label at the top, open the **Attributes inspector** and click on the **Color** item to show a dropdown for color values. Select **Custom...** at the bottom of the list.

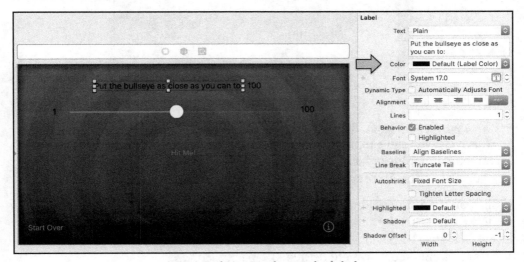

Setting the text color on the label

This opens the Color Picker, which has several ways to select colors. You'll use the sliders (second tab).

If all you see is a gray scale slider, then select **RGB Sliders** from the picker at the top.

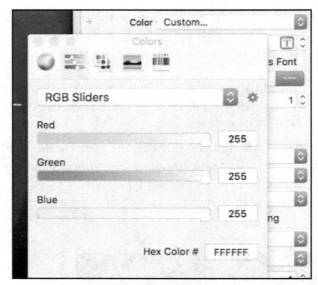

The Color Picker

➤ Pick a pure white color, Red: 255, Green: 255, Blue: 255, Opacity: 100%. Alternatively, you can simply pick **White Color** from the initial dropdown instead of opening the Color Picker at all, but it's good to know that the Color Picker is there in case you want to do custom colors.

➤ Click on the **Shadow** item from the Attributes inspector. This lets you add a subtle shadow to the label. By default this color is transparent (also known as "Clear Color") so you won't see the shadow. Using the Color Picker, choose a pure black color that is half transparent, Red: 0, Green: 0, Blue: 0, Opacity: 50%.

➤ Change the **Shadow Offset** to Width: 0, Height: 1. This puts the shadow below the label.

The shadow you've chosen is very subtle. If you're not sure that it's actually visible, then toggle the height offset between 1 and 0 a few times. Look closely and you should be able to see the difference. As I said, it's very subtle.

➤ Click on the **[T]** icon of the **Font** attribute. This opens the Font Picker.

By default, the System font is selected. That uses whatever is the standard system font for the user's device. The system font is nice enough but we want something more exciting for this game.

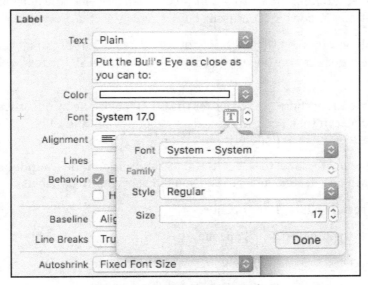

Font picker with the System font

➤ Choose **Font: Custom**. That enables the Family field. Choose **Family: Arial Rounded MT Bold**. Set the Size to 16.

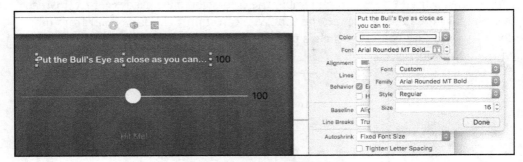

Setting the label's font

➤ The label also has an attribute **Autoshrink**. Make sure this is set to **Fixed Font Size**.

If enabled, Autoshrink will dynamically change the size of the font if the text is larger than will fit into the label. That is useful in certain apps, but not in this one. Instead, you'll change the size of the label to fit the text rather than the other way around.

➤ With the label selected, press ⌘= on your keyboard, or choose **Size to Fit Content** from the **Editor** menu.

If the Size to Fit Content menu item is disabled, then de-select the label and select it again. Sometimes Xcode gets confused about what is selected. Poor thing.

The label will now become slightly larger or smaller so that it fits snugly around the text. If the text got cut off when you changed the font, now all the text will show again.

You don't have to set these properties for the other labels one by one; that would be a big chore. You can speed up the process by selecting multiple labels and then applying these changes to that entire selection.

➤ Click on the **Score**: label to select it. Hold ⌘ and click on the **Round**: label. Now both labels will be selected. Repeat what you did above for these labels:

• Set Color to pure white, 100% opaque.

• Set Shadow to pure black, 50% opaque.

• Set Shadow Offset to width 0, height 1.

• Set Font to Arial Rounded MT Bold, size 16.

• Make sure Autoshrink is set to Fixed Font Size.

Tip: Xcode is smart enough to remember the colors you have used recently. Instead of going into the Color Picker all the time, you can simply choose a color from the Recently Used Colors menu which is part of the dropdown you get when you click on any color option:

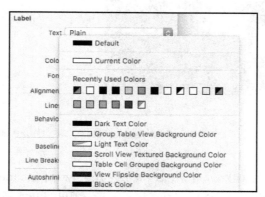

Quick access to recently used colors and several handy presets

Exercise: You still have a few labels to go. Repeat what you just did for the other labels. They should all become white, have the same shadow and have the same font. However, the two labels on either side of the slider (1 and 100) will have font size 14, while the other labels (the ones that will hold the target value, the score and the round number) will have font size 20 so they stand out more.

Because you've changed the sizes of some of the labels, your carefully constructed layout may have been messed up a bit. You may want to clean it up a little.

At this point, the game screen should look something like this:

What the storyboard looks like after styling the labels

All right, it's starting to look like something now. By the way, feel free to experiment with the fonts and colors. If you want to make it look completely different, then go right ahead. It's your app!

The buttons

Changing the look of the buttons works very much the same way.

➤ Select the **Hit Me!** button. In the **Size inspector** set its Width to 100 and its Height to 37.

➤ Center the position of the button on the inner circle of the background image.

➤ Go to the **Attributes inspector**. Change **Type** from System to **Custom**.

A "system" button just has a label and no border. By making it a custom button, you can style it any way you wish.

➤ Still in the **Attributes inspector**, press the arrow on the **Background** field and choose **Button-Normal** from the list.

➤ Set the **Font** to **Arial Rounded MT Bold**, size 20.

➤ Set the **Text Color** to red: 96, green: 30, blue: 0, opacity: 100%. This is a dark brown color.

➤ Set the **Shadow Color** to pure white, 50% opacity. The shadow offset should be Width 0, Height 1.

Blending in

Setting the opacity to anything less than 100% will make the color slightly transparent (with opacity of 0% being fully transparent). Partial transparency makes the color blend in with the background and makes it appear softer.

Try setting the shadow color to 100% opaque pure white and notice the difference.

This finishes the setup for the Hit Me! button in its "default" state:

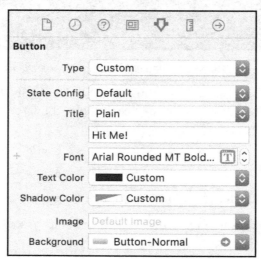

The attributes for the Hit Me! button in the default state

Buttons can have more than one state. When you tap a button and hold it down, it should appear "pressed down" to let you know that the button will be activated when you lift your finger. This is known as the *highlighted* state and is an important visual cue to the user.

➤ With the button still selected, click the **State Config** setting and pick **Highlighted** from the menu. Now the attributes in this section reflect the highlighted state of the button.

➤ In the **Background** field, select **Button-Highlighted**.

➤ Make sure the highlighted **Text Color** is the same color as before (red 96, green 30, blue 0, or simply pick it from the Recently Used Colors menu). Change the **Shadow Color** to half-transparent white again.

➤ Check the **Reverses On Highlight** option. This will give the appearance of the label being pressed down when the user taps the button.

You could change the other properties too, but don't get too carried away. The highlight effect should not be too jarring.

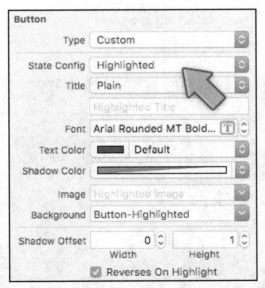

The attributes for the highlighted Hit Me! button

To test the highlighted look of the button in Interface Builder you can toggle the **Highlighted** box in the **Control** section, but make sure to turn it off again or the button will initially appear highlighted when the screen is shown.

That's it for the Hit Me! button. Styling the Start Over button is very similar, except you will replace its title text with an icon.

➤ Select the **Start Over** button and change the following attributes:

• Set Type to Custom.

• Remove the text "Start Over" from the button.

• For Image choose **StartOverIcon**.

• For Background choose **SmallButton**.

• Set Width and Height to 32.

You won't set a highlighted state on this button — let UIKit take care of this. If you don't specify a different image for the highlighted state, UIKit will automatically darken the button to indicate that it is pressed.

➤ Make the same changes to the ⓘ button, but this time choose **InfoButton** for the image.

The user interface is almost done. Only the slider is left...

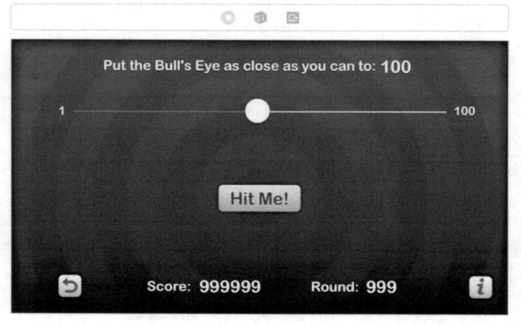

Almost done!

The slider

Unfortunately, you can only customize the slider a little bit in Interface Builder. For the more advanced customization that this game needs – putting your own images on the thumb and the track – you have to resort to writing code.

Do note that everything you've done so far in Interface Builder you could also have done in code. Setting the color on a button, for example, can be done by sending the setTitleColor() message to the button. (You would normally do this in viewDidLoad.)

However, I find that doing visual design work is much easier and quicker in a visual editor such as Interface Builder than writing the equivalent source code. But for the slider you have no choice.

➤ Go to **ViewController.swift**, and add the following to viewDidLoad():

```
let thumbImageNormal = UIImage(named: "SliderThumb-Normal")!
slider.setThumbImage(thumbImageNormal, for: .normal)

let thumbImageHighlighted = UIImage(named: "SliderThumb-
Highlighted")!
slider.setThumbImage(thumbImageHighlighted, for: .highlighted)

let insets = UIEdgeInsets(top: 0, left: 14, bottom: 0, right:
14)

let trackLeftImage = UIImage(named: "SliderTrackLeft")!
let trackLeftResizable =
                trackLeftImage.resizableImage(withCapInsets:
insets)
slider.setMinimumTrackImage(trackLeftResizable, for: .normal)

let trackRightImage = UIImage(named: "SliderTrackRight")!
let trackRightResizable =
                trackRightImage.resizableImage(withCapInsets:
insets)
slider.setMaximumTrackImage(trackRightResizable, for: .normal)
```

This sets four images on the slider: two for the thumb and two for the track. (And if you're wondering what the "thumb" is, that's the little circle in the center of the slider, the one that you drag around to set the slider value.)

The thumb works like a button so it gets an image for the normal (un-pressed) state and one for the highlighted state.

The slider uses different images for the track on the left of the thumb (green) and the track to the right of the thumb (gray).

➤ Run the app. You have to admit it looks fantastic now!

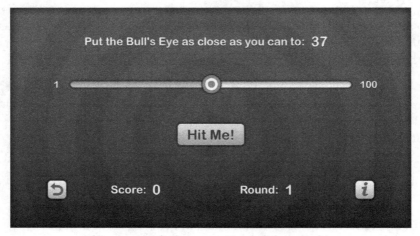

The game with the customized slider graphics

To .png or not to .png

If you recall, the images that you imported into the asset catalog had filenames like **SliderThumb-Normal@2x.png** and so on.

When you create a UIImage object, you don't use the original filename but the name that is listed in the asset catalog, **SliderThumb-Normal**.

That means you can leave off the **@2x** bit and the **.png** file extension.

The About screen

Just like in the previous version of Bullseye, you'll add an About screen to the app. This new screen contains a *text view* with the gameplay rules and a button to close the screen.

Most apps have more than one screen, even very simple games. So, this is as good a time as any to learn how to add additional screens to your apps.

In UIKit each screen in your app will have its own view controller. If you think "screen," think "view controller."

Xcode automatically created the main ViewController object for you, but you'll have to create the view controller for the About screen yourself.

Adding a new view controller

➤ Go to Xcode's **File** menu and choose **New ▸ File...** In the window that pops up, choose the **Cocoa Touch Class** template (if you don't see it then make sure **iOS** is selected at the top).

Click **Next**. Xcode gives you some options to fill out:

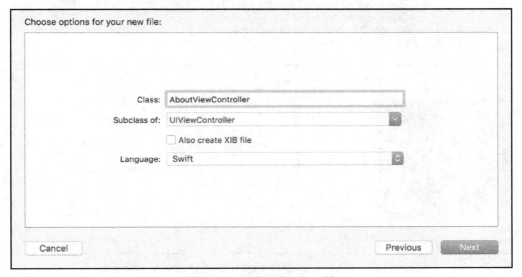

The options for the new file

Choose the following:

• Class: **AboutViewController**.

• Subclass of: **UIViewController**.

• Also create XIB file: Leave this box unchecked.

• Language: **Swift**.

Click **Next** and then **Create**.

Xcode will create a new file and add it to your project. As you might have guessed, the new file is **AboutViewController.swift**.

Designing the view controller in Interface Builder

To design this new view controller, you need to pay a visit to Interface Builder.

➤ Open **Main.storyboard**. There is no scene representing the About view controller in the storyboard yet. So, you'll have to add this first.

➤ From the **Library**, choose **View Controller** and drag it on to the canvas, to the right of the main View controller.

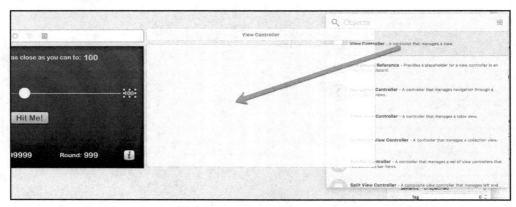

Dragging a new View Controller from the Objects Library

This new view controller is totally blank. You may need to rearrange the storyboard so that the two view controllers don't overlap. Interface Builder isn't very tidy about where it puts things.

➤ Drag a new **Button** on to the screen and give it the title **Close**. Put it somewhere around the bottom center of the view (use the blue guidelines to help with positioning).

➤ Drag a **Text View** on to the view and make it cover most of the space above the button.

You can find these components in the Library. If you don't feel like scrolling, you can filter the components by typing in the field at the top:

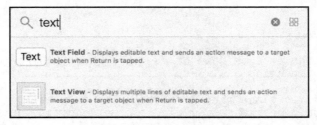

Searching for text components

Note that there is also a Text Field, which is a single-line text component — that's not what you want. You're looking for Text View, which can contain multiple lines of text.

After dragging both the text view and the button on to the canvas, it should look something like this:

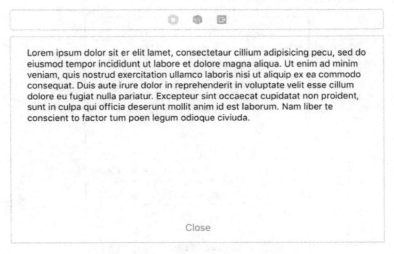

The About screen in the storyboard

➤ Double-click the text view to edit its content. By default, the Text View contains a bunch of Latin placeholder text (also known as "Lorem Ipsum"). Replace the text with this:

```
*** Bullseye ***

Welcome to the awesome game of Bullseye where you can win points
and fame by dragging a slider.

Your goal is to place the slider as close as possible to the
target value. The closer you are, the more points you score.
Enjoy!
```

You can also enter that text into the Attributes inspector's **Text** property for the text view if you find that easier.

➤ Make sure to uncheck the **Editable** checkbox in the Attribute Inspector. Otherwise, the user can actually type into the text view and you don't want that.

The design of the screen is done for now.

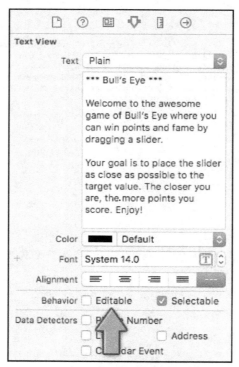

The Attributes inspector for the text view

Showing the new view controller

So how do you open this new About screen when the user presses the ⓘ button?

Storyboards have a neat trick for this: *segues* (pronounced "seg-way" like the silly scooters). A segue is a transition from one screen to another. They are really easy to add.

➤ Click the ⓘ button in the **View controller** to select it. Then hold down **Control** and drag over to the **About** screen.

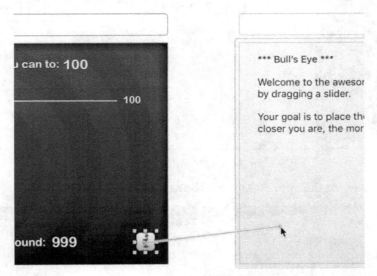

Control-drag from one view controller to another to make a segue

➤ Let go of the mouse button and a pop-up appears with several options. Choose **Present Modally**.

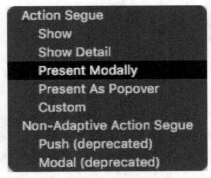

Choosing the type of segue to create

Now an arrow will appear between the two screens. This arrow represents the segue from the main scene to the About scene.

➤ Click the arrow to select it. Segues also have attributes. In the **Attributes inspector**, choose **Transition, Flip Horizontal**. That is the animation that UIKit will use to move between these screens.

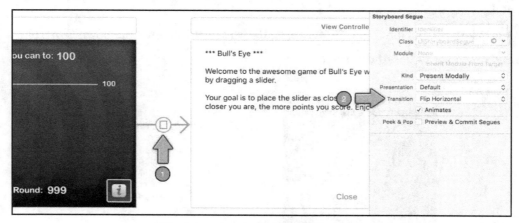

Changing the attributes for the segue

➤ Now you can run the app. Press the ⓘ button to see the new screen.

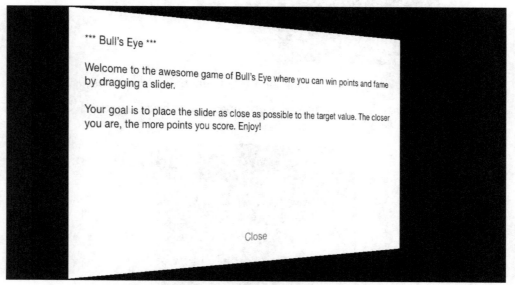

The About screen appears with a flip animation

The About screen should appear with a neat animation. Good, that seems to work.

Dismissing the About view controller

Did you notice that there's an obvious issue here? Tapping the Close button seems to have no effect. Once the user enters the About screen they can never leave... that doesn't sound like good user interface design, does it?

The problem with segues is that they only go one way. To close this screen, you have to hook up some code to the Close button. As a budding iOS developer you already know how to do that: use an action method!

This time you will add the action method to AboutViewController instead of ViewController, because the Close button is part of the About screen, not the main game screen.

➤ Open **AboutViewController.swift** and replace its contents with the following:

```swift
import UIKit

class AboutViewController: UIViewController {
  @IBAction func close() {
    dismiss(animated: true, completion: nil)
  }
}
```

The code in the close() action method tells UIKit to close the About screen with an animation.

If you had said dismiss(animated: false, ...), then there would be no page flip and the main screen would instantly reappear. From a user experience perspective, it's often better to show transitions from one screen to another via an animation.

That leaves you with one final step, hooking up the Close button's Touch Up Inside event to this new close action.

➤ Open the storyboard and Control-drag from the **Close** button to the About scene's View Controller. Hmm, strange, the **close** action should be listed in this pop-up, but it isn't. Instead, this is the same pop-up you saw when you made the segue:

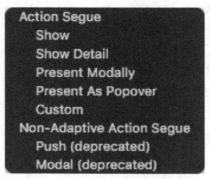

The "close" action is not listed in the pop-up

> **Exercise**: Bonus points if you can spot the error. It's a very common – and frustrating! – mistake.

The problem is that this scene in the storyboard doesn't know yet that it is supposed to represent the AboutViewController.

Setting the class for a view controller

You first added the **AboutViewController.swift** source file, and then dragged a new view controller on to the storyboard. But, you haven't told the storyboard that the design for this new view controller belongs to AboutViewController. That's why in the Document Outline it just says View Controller and not About View controller. That's the design of the screen done for now. ➤ Fortunately, this is easily remedied. In Interface Builder, select the About scene's **View controller** and go to the **Identity inspector** (that's the tab/icon to the left of the Attributes inspector).

➤ Under **Custom Class**, enter **AboutViewController**.

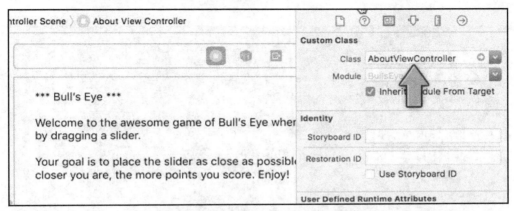

The Identity inspector for the About screen

Xcode should auto-complete this for you once you type the first few characters. If it doesn't, then double-check that you really have selected the View controller and not one of the views inside it. (The view controller should also have a blue border on the storyboard to indicate it is selected.)

Now you should be able to connect the Close button to the action method.

➤ Control-drag from the **Close** button to **About View controller** in the Document Outline (or to the yellow circle at the top of the scene in the storyboard). This should be old hat by now. The pop-up menu now does have an option for the **close** action (under Sent Events). Connect the button to that action.

➤ Run the app again. You should now be able to return from the About screen.

OK, that does get us a working About screen, but it does look a little plain doesn't it? What if you added some of the design changes you made to the main screen?

> **Exercise**: Add a background image to the About screen. Also, change the Close button on the About screen to look like the Hit Me! button and play around with the Text View properties in the Attribute Inspector. **Tip**: The background color of the TextView is white by default and will hide whatever is behind it.
>
> You should be able to do this by yourself now. Piece of cake! Refer back to the instructions for the main screen if you get stuck.

When you are done, you should have an About screen which looks something like this:

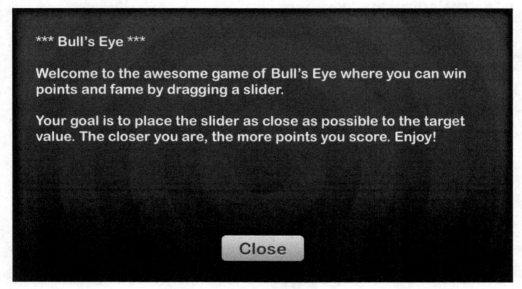

The new and improved About screen

That looks good, but it could be better. So how do you improve upon it?

Using a web view for HTML content

➤ Now select the **text view** and press the **Delete** key on your keyboard. (Yep, you're throwing it away, and after all those changes, too! But don't grieve for the Text View too much, you'll replace it with something better.)

➤ Put a **WebKit View** in its place (as always, you can find this view in the Objects Library). There are two web view options — an older Web View, which is deprecated, or ready to be retired, and the WebKit View. Make sure that you select the WebKit View.

This view can show web pages. All you have to do is give it the URL to a web site or the name of a file to load. The WebKit View object is named WKWebView.

For this app, you will make it display a static HTML page from the application bundle, so it won't actually have to go online and download anything.

➤ Go to the **Project navigator** and right-click on the **Bullseye** group (the yellow folder). From the menu, choose **Add Files to "Bullseye"**...

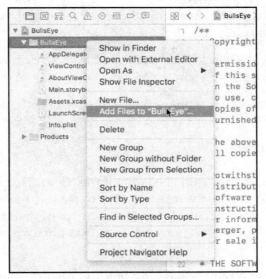

Using the right-click menu to add existing files to the project

➤ In the file picker, select the **Bullseye.html** file from the Resources folder. This is an HTML5 document that contains the gameplay instructions.

Make sure that **Copy items if needed** is selected and that under **Add to targets**, there is a checkmark in front of **Bullseye**. (If you don't see these options, click the Options button at the bottom of the dialog.)

➤ Press **Add** to add the HTML file to the project.

➤ In **AboutViewController.swift**, add an outlet for the web view:

```
class AboutViewController: UIViewController {
  @IBOutlet weak var webView: WKWebView!
  . . .
}
```

Xcode will complain soon after you add the above line. The error should look something like this:

```
30  import UIKit
31
32  class AboutViewController: UIViewController {
      @IBOutlet weak var webView: WKWebView!          Use of undeclared type 'WKWebView'
34
      @IBAction func close() {
36        dismiss(animated: true, completion: nil)
37    }
38  }
39
```

Xcode complains about WKWebView

What does this error mean? It means that Xcode, or rather the compiler, does not know what WKWebView is.

But how can that be? We selected the component from Xcode's own Objects Library and so it should be supported, right?

The answer to this lies with this line of code at the top of both your view controller source files:

```
import UIKit
```

I'm sure you saw this line and wondered what it was about. That statement tells the compiler that you want to use the objects from a framework named UIKit. Frameworks, or libraries if you prefer, bundle together one or more objects which perform a particular type of task (or tasks). The UIKit library provides all the UI components for iOS.

So why does UIKit not contain WKWebView, you ask? That's because the previously mentioned deprecated WebView is the one which is included with UIKit. The newer (and improved) WKWebView comes from a different framework called WebKit.

➤ Click on your **Bullseye**'s' project file

➤ Go the the **Build Phases** tab and expand the **Link Binary With Libraries** category.

➤ Click on the little + button and search for **WebKit.framework** and click **Add**.

Xcode complains about WKWebView

Now you have access to all the wonders of the WebKit framework. All that's left to do is actually use it.

➤ Add the following code at the top of **AboutViewController.swift**, right below the existing `import` statement:

```
import WebKit
```

That tells the compiler that we want to use objects from the WebKit framework and since now the compiler knows about all the objects in the WebKit framework, the Xcode error will go away.

➤ In the storyboard file, connect the WKWebView to this new outlet. The easiest way to do this is to Control-drag from **About View controller** (in the Document Outline) to the **Web View**.

➤ In **AboutViewController.swift**, add a `viewDidLoad()` implementation:

```
override func viewDidLoad() {
  super.viewDidLoad()

  if let url = Bundle.main.url(forResource: "Bullseye",
                              withExtension: "html") {
    let request = URLRequest(url: url)
    webView.load(request)
  }
}
```

This displays the HTML file using the web view.

The code first gets the URL (Uniform Resource Locator) for the **Bullseye.html** file in the application bundle. A URL, as you might be familiar with from the Interwebs, is a way to identify the location of a resource, like a web page. Here, the URL provides the location of the HTML file in your application bundle.

It then creates a URLRequest using that URL since that's one of the easiest ways to send a load request to the web view.

Finally, the code asks the web view to load the contents specified by the URL request.

➤ Run the app and press the info button. The About screen should appear with a description of the gameplay rules, this time in the form of an HTML document:

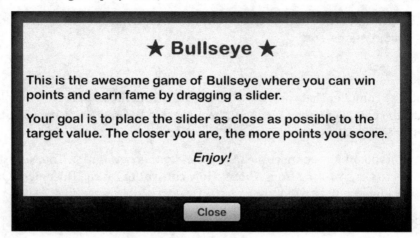

The About screen in all its glory

Well done! You've created an (almost) identical version of the Bullseye game both in SwiftUI and in UIKIt. In the next chapters of this section you'll improve the Bullseye game even further, by adding an high-scores screen.

You can find the project files under **19-The New Look** in the Source Code folder.

Chapter 20: Table Views

By Eli Ganim

Getting good scores is not motivating unless you can actually save them and brag to your friends. In this chapter you'll learn how to save the high scores and present them.

This is how the screen will look like when you're finished:

The reader of this book	50000
Manda	10000
Joey	5000
Adam	1000
Eli	500

This is how the screen would look at the end of this chapter

This chapter covers the following:

- **Table views and navigation controllers**: A basic introduction to navigation controllers and table views.

- **Add a table view**: Create your first UIKit table view and add a prototype cell to display data.

- **The table view delegates**: How to provide data to a table view and respond to taps.

Table views and navigation controllers

This screen will introduce you to two of the most commonly used UI elements in iOS apps: the table view and the navigation controller.

A **table view** is UIKit's equivalent of SwiftUI's **List**. This component is extremely versatile and the most important one to master in iOS development.

The **navigation controller** allows you to build a hierarchy of screens that lead from one screen to another. It adds a navigation bar at the top with a title and a back button.

In this screen, tapping an entry slides in the screen containing the information about the high score, like who made it and when it was achieved. Navigation controllers and table views are often used together.

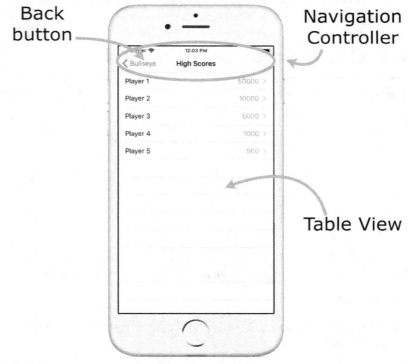

The grey bar at the top is the navigation bar. The list of items is the table view.

Adding a table view

As table views are so important, you will start out by examining how they work.

Because smart developers split up the workload into small, simple steps, this is what you're going to do in this chapter:

1. Put a table view on the app's screen.

2. Put data into that table view.

3. Allow the user to tap a row in the table to show when that high score was reached.

Once you have these basics up and running, you'll keep adding new functionality over the next few chapters until you end up with a fully working high scores screen.

Creating a new screen

➤ Go to Xcode's **File** menu and choose **New ▸ File…**

➤ Choose the **Cocoa Touch Class** template. Click **Next**. Call the file **HighScoresViewController** and make it a subclass of **UITableViewController**.

A **table view controller** is a special type of view controller that makes working with table views easier.

➤ Click on **Main.storyboard** to open Interface Builder and drag a new **Table View Controller** from the Objects Library into the storyboard.

➤ Select the **View Controller** of the new scene you just added. Open the **Identity Inspector** from the right pane and update the class name to **HighScoresViewController**.

The name of the scene in the Document Outline on the left should change to "High Scores View Controller Scene". As its name implies, and as you can see in the storyboard, the view controller contains a Table View object. We'll go into the difference between controllers and views soon, but for now, remember that the controller is the whole screen while the table view is the object that actually draws the list.

Connecting the new view controller

Right now there's no way to reach the new screen you just added. In order to fix that, you'll add a new button to the main screen of the game.

➤ Open the storyboard and add a new button to the main screen, just above the *about* button.

➤ Use this settings for the button. **Type**: Custom; **Background**: SmallButton.

➤ Change the text inside the button to be a trophy symbol: 🏆. You can find it under **Edit ▸ Emoji & Symbol**s and then search for the word 'Trophy'.

➤ Set the button size to be 32x32.

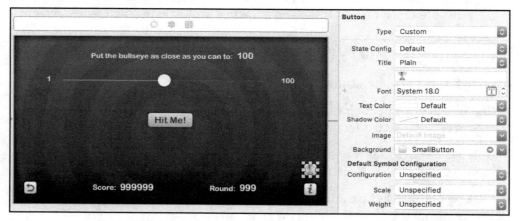

The arrow points at the initial view controller

Now you're going to hook this button up to the high scores screen.

➤ Click the 🏆 button to select it. Then hold down **Control** and drag over to the **High Score**s screen.

➤ Let go of the mouse button and a pop-up appears with several options. Choose **Show**.

➤ Run the app on the Simulator and click on the trophy button.

You should see an empty list. This is the table view. You can drag the list up and down but it doesn't contain any data yet.

By the way, it doesn't really matter which Simulator you use. Table views resize themselves to fit the dimensions of the device, and the app will work equally well on the small iPhone 8 or the huge iPhone X.

> **Note**: When you build the app, Xcode gives the warning "Prototype table cells must have reuse identifiers." Don't worry about this for now, you'll fix it soon.

The anatomy of a table view

First, let's talk a bit more about table views. A UITableView object displays a list of items.

There are two styles of tables: "plain" and "grouped." They work mostly the same, but there are a few small differences. The most visible difference is that rows in the grouped style table are placed into boxes (the groups) on a light gray background.

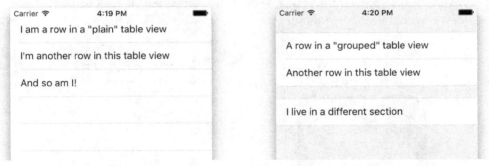

A plain-style table (left) and a grouped table (right)

> **Note**: I'm not sure why it's named a *table*, because a table is commonly thought of as a spreadsheet-type object that has multiple rows and multiple columns, whereas the UITableView only has rows. It's more of a list than a table, but I guess we're stuck with the name now. UIKit also provides a UICollectionView object that works similar to a UITableView but allows for multiple columns.

The plain style is used for rows that all represent something similar, such as contacts in an address book where each row contains the name of one person.

The grouped style is used when the items in the list can be organized by a particular attribute, like book categories for a list of books. The grouped style table could also be used to show related information which doesn't necessarily have to stand together — like the address information, contact information, and e-mail information for a contact.

You will use both table styles in the upcoming chapters.

The data for a table comes in the form of **rows**. You can potentially have many rows (even tens of thousands) but that kind of design isn't recommended. Most users will find it incredibly annoying to scroll through ten thousand rows to find the one they want. And who can blame them?

Tables display their data in **cells**. A cell is related to a row but it's not exactly the same. A cell is a view that shows a row of data that happens to be visible at that moment. If your table can show 10 rows at a time on the screen, then it only has 10 cells, even though there may be hundreds of rows of actual data.

Whenever a row scrolls off the screen and becomes invisible, its cell will be re-used for a new row that becomes visible.

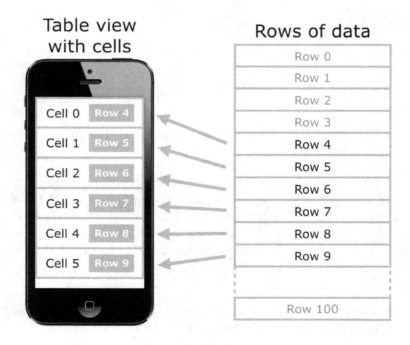

Cells display the contents of rows

Adding a prototype cell

Xcode has a very handy feature named *prototype cells* that lets you design your cells visually in Interface Builder.➤ Open the storyboard and click the empty cell (the white row below the Prototype Cells label) to select it.

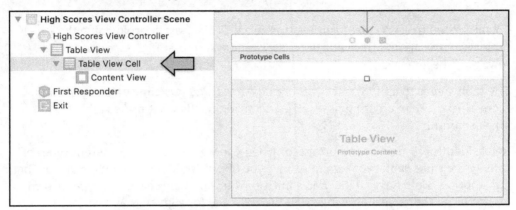

Selecting the prototype cell

Sometimes it can be hard to see exactly what is selected, so keep an eye on the Document Outline to make sure you've picked the right thing. (Or use the Document Outline to select the cell directly.)

➤ Drag a **Label** from the Objects Library on to the white area in the table view representing the cell. Make sure the label spans from the left edge (with a small margin) until the middle of the cell.

➤ Drag another **Label** and place it next to the previous label, so it spans from it's right edge to the cell's right edge.

➤ In the **Attributes inspector**, change the alignment to **Right**.

The result should look similar to this:

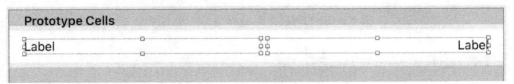

Adding the label to the prototype cell

> **Note**: If you simply drag the label on to the table view, it might not work. You need to drag the label on to the cell itself. You can check where the label ended up using the Document Outline. It has to be inside the Content View for the table view cell.

You also need to set a *reuse identifier* on the cell. This is an internal name that the table view uses to find free cells to reuse when rows scroll off the screen and new rows must become visible.

The table needs to assign cells for those new rows, and recycling existing cells is more efficient than creating new cells. This technique is what makes table views scroll smoothly.

Reuse identifiers are also important for when you want to display different types of cells in the same table. For example, one type of cell could have an image and a label and another could have a label and a button. You would give each cell type its own identifier, so the table view can assign the right cell for a given row type.

This screen has only one type of cell but you still need to give it an identifier.

➤ Type **HighScoreItem** into the Table View Cell's **Identifier** field (you can find this in the **Attributes inspector**).

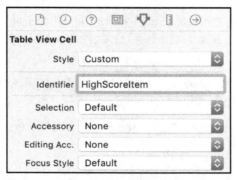

Giving the table view cell a reuse identifier

Compiler warnings

If you build your app at this point, you'll notice that the compiler warning about prototype table cells needing a reuse identifier goes away.

But... you've got a new warning — one about views without any layout constraints clipping or overlapping other views. Sounds familiar?

Yes, this is the same warning you saw previously when you had views without any Auto Layout constraints! And you know how to find the affected views now, right?

➤ In the storyboard, click on the yellow warning circle for the table view to see the list of views with issues. It is the new label you just added to the prototype table cell.

That's simple enough to fix, right? Simply select the label, select the **Add New Constraints** icon at the bottom of the Interface Builder window, and add 4 constraints for the left, top, right, and bottom of the label. (You can go with the current defaults as long as you have the label positioned correctly.)

➤ Run the app and you'll see... nothing — exactly the same as before. The table is still empty.

This is because you only added a cell design to the table, not actual data. Remember that the cell is just the visual representation of the row, not the actual data. To add data to the table, you have to write some code.

The table view delegates

➤ Switch to **HighScoresViewController.swift** and add the following methods just before the closing bracket at the bottom of the file:

```swift
// MARK:- Table View Data Source
override func tableView(_ tableView: UITableView,
      numberOfRowsInSection section: Int) -> Int {
  return 1
}

override func tableView(_ tableView: UITableView,
            cellForRowAt indexPath: IndexPath) ->
            UITableViewCell {
  let cell = tableView.dequeueReusableCell(
                      withIdentifier: "HighScoreItem",
                                 for: indexPath)
  return cell
}
```

These methods look a bit more complicated than the ones you've seen in *Bullseye*, but that's because each takes two parameters and returns a value to the caller. Other than that, they work the same way as the methods you've dealt with before.

Protocols

The above two methods are part of UITableView's **data source** protocol.

The data source is the link between your data and the table view. Usually, the view controller plays the role of data source and implements the necessary methods. So, essentially, the view controller is acting as a delegate on behalf of the table view. (This is the delegate pattern that we've talked about before — where an object does some work on behalf of another object.)

The table view needs to know how many rows of data it has and how it should display each of those rows. But you can't simply dump that data into the table view's lap and be done with it. You don't say: "Dear table view, here are my 100 rows, now go show them on the screen."

Instead, you say to the table view: "This view controller is now your data source. You can ask it questions about the data anytime you feel like it."

Once it is hooked up to a data source – i.e. your view controller – the table view sends a numberOfRowsInSection message to find out how many data rows there are.

And when the table view needs to draw a particular row on the screen it sends a cellForRowAt message to ask the data source for a cell.

You see this pattern all the time in iOS: one object does something on behalf of another object. In this case, the HighScoresViewController works to provide the data to the table view, but only when the table view asks for it.

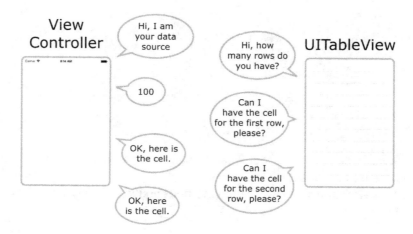

The dating ritual of a data source and a table view

Your implementation of tableView(_:numberOfRowsInSection:) – the first method that you added – returns the value 1. This tells the table view that you have just one row of data.

The return statement is very important in Swift. It allows a method to send data back to its caller. In the case of tableView(_:numberOfRowsInSection:), the caller is the UITableView object and it wants to know how many rows are in the table.

The statements inside a method usually perform some kind of computation using instance variables and any data received through the method's parameters. When the method is done, return says, "Hey, I'm done. Here is the answer I came up with." The return value is often called the *result* of the method.

For tableView(_:numberOfRowsInSection:) the answer is really simple: there is only one row, so return 1. Now that the table view knows it has one row to display, it calls the second method you added – tableView(_:cellForRowAt:) – to obtain a cell for that row. This method grabs a copy of the prototype cell and gives that back to the table view, again with a return statement.

Inside tableView(_:cellForRowAt:) is also where you would normally put the row data into the cell, but the app doesn't have any row data yet.

➤ Run the app and go to the high scores screen. You'll see there is a single cell in the table:

The table now has one row

Method signatures

In the above text, you might have noticed some special notation for the method names, like tableView(_:numberOfRowsInSection:) or tableView(_:cellForRowAt:). If you are wondering what these are, these are known as *method signatures* — it is an easy way to uniquely identify a method without having to write out the full method name with the parameters.

The method signature identifies where each parameter would be (and the parameter name, where necessary) by separating out the parameters with a colon.

In the method for `tableView(_:numberOfRowsInSection:)` for example, you might notice an underscore for the first parameter — that means, that method does not need to have the parameter name specified when calling the method — it is simply a convenience in Swift where the parameter can generally be inferred from the method name. You might have more questions about this — but we'll come back to that later.

If you are not sure about the signature for a method, take a look at the Xcode **Jump bar** (the tiny toolbar right above the source editor) and click on the last item of the file path elements to get a list of methods (and properties) in the current source file.

```
ne 8                                      Running Bullse
  <  >   Bullseye  ⟩  Bullseye  ⟩   HighScoresViewController.s

 33        override func viewDidLoad() {
 34            super.viewDidLoad()
 35            // Do any additional setup a
 36        }
 37
 38    // MARK:- Table View Data Source
 39    override func tableView(_ tableView: UITableView,
 40            numberOfRowsInSection section: Int) -> Int {
 41        return 5
 42    }
 43
 44    override func tableView(_ tableView: UITableView,
 45                cellForRowAt indexPath: IndexPath)
 46                -> UITableViewCell {
 47        let cell = tableView.dequeueReusableCell(
 48                        withIdentifier: "HighScoreItem",
 49                                    for: indexPath)
```

Jump bar popup:
```
 C  HighScoresViewController
 M  viewDidLoad()

 ▤  Table View Data Source
 M  tableView(_:numberOfRowsInSection:)
 M  tableView(_:cellForRowAt:)
```

The Jump Bar shows the method signatures

Also, do note that in the above examples, `tableView` is not the method name — or rather, `tableView` by itself is not the method name. The method name is the `tableView` plus the parameter list — everything up to the closing bracket for the parameter list. That's how you get multiple unique methods such as `tableView(_:numberOfRowsInSection:)` and `tableView(_:cellForRowAt:)` even though they all look as if they are methods called `tableName` — the complete signature uniquely identifies the method.

Special comments

You might have noticed the following line in the code you just added:

```
// MARK:- Table View Data Source
```

If you were wondering what that was for, here's the scoop. Of course, you already know that line is a comment, because the line begins with //, but it's not *just* a comment. As the keyword at the beginning of the comment line, MARK, indicates, it is a marker. But a marker for what?

It's a marker to organize the code and for you to find a section of code (for example, a set of related methods, like for the table view data source) via the Xcode Jump Bar.

Take a look at the previous screenshot showing the Xcode Jump Bar. Do you notice the separator line in the middle of the list of methods? Do you notice the bolded text title right after? Does that title seem familiar?

The text you provide after the MARK: keyword defines how the section title is displayed in the menu. If you put in a hyphen (-), you get a separator line followed by any text after the hyphen as the section title.

If you don't provide a hyphen but provide some text, then you simply get a section title but no separator. If you provide neither, then you just get a section icon with no text and no separator. (Try these out.)

There are a couple of other comment tags besides MARK: that you can use in your Swift files. These are TODO: and FIXME:. The first is generally used to indicate portions of your code that need to be completed, while the latter is used to mark portions of code that need re-writing or fixing.

Consider using these tags to organize your code better. When you are in a hurry and need to find that particular bit of code in a long source file, they come in handy. I certainly use them all the time in my own code.

Testing the table view data source

Exercise: Modify the app so that it shows five rows.

That shouldn't have been too hard:

```
override func tableView(_ tableView: UITableView,
      numberOfRowsInSection section: Int) -> Int {
  return 5
}
```

If you were tempted to go into the storyboard and duplicate the prototype cell five times, then you were confusing cells with rows.

When you make tableView(_:numberOfRowsInSection:) return the number 5, you tell the table view that there will be five rows.

The table view then sends the cellForRowAt message five times, once for each row. Because tableView(_:cellForRowAt:) currently just returns a copy of the prototype cell, your table view will show five identical rows:

Label		Label
Label		Label
Label		Label
Label		Label
Label		Label

The table now has five identical rows

There are several ways to create cells in tableView(_:cellForRowAt:), but by far the easiest approach is what you've done here:

1. Add a prototype cell to the table view in the storyboard.

2. Set a reuse identifier on the prototype cell.

3. Call tableView.dequeueReusableCell(withIdentifier:for:). This makes a new copy of the prototype cell if necessary, or, recycles an existing cell that is no longer in use.

Once you have a cell, you should set it up with the data from the corresponding row and give it back to the table view. That's what you'll do in the next section.

Putting row data into the cells

Currently, the rows (or rather the cells) all contain the placeholder text "Label." Let's add some unique text for each row.

➤ Open the storyboard and select the left **Label** inside the table view cell. Go to the **Attributes inspector** and set the **Tag** field to 1000.

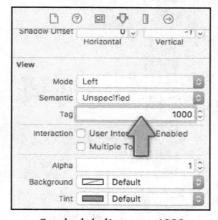

Set the label's tag to 1000

A *tag* is a numeric identifier that you can give to a user interface control in order to uniquely identify it later. Why the number 1000? No particular reason. It should be something other than 0, as that is the default value for all tags. 1000 is as good a number as any.

➤ Do the same for the right label, but use 2000 as the tag instead.

Double-check to make sure you set the tag on the *Labels*, not on the Table View Cell or its Content View. It's a common mistake to set the tag on the wrong view and then the results won't be what you expected!

➤ In **HighScoresViewController.swift**, change `tableView(_:cellForRowAt:)` to the following:

```
override func tableView(_ tableView: UITableView,
            cellForRowAt indexPath: IndexPath)
            -> UITableViewCell {
  let cell = tableView.dequeueReusableCell(
                   withIdentifier: "HighScoreItem",
```

```
                                      for: indexPath)
  // Add the following code
  let nameLabel = cell.viewWithTag(1000) as! UILabel
  let scoreLabel = cell.viewWithTag(2000) as! UILabel

  if indexPath.row == 0 {
    nameLabel.text = "The reader of this book"
    scoreLabel.text = "50000"
  } else if indexPath.row == 1 {
    nameLabel.text = "Manda"
    scoreLabel.text = "10000"
  } else if indexPath.row == 2 {
    nameLabel.text = "Joey"
    scoreLabel.text = "5000"
  } else if indexPath.row == 3 {
    nameLabel.text = "Adam"
    scoreLabel.text = "1000"
  } else if indexPath.row == 4 {
    nameLabel.text = "Eli"
    scoreLabel.text = "500"
  }
  // End of new code block

  return cell
}
```

You've already seen the first line. It gets a copy of the prototype cell — either a new one or a recycled one — and puts it into a local constant named cell. (Recall that this is a constant because it's declared with let, not var. It is local because it's defined inside a method.)

The first new line that you've just added is:

```
let nameLabel = cell.viewWithTag(1000) as! UILabel
```

Here you ask the table view cell for the view with tag 1000. That is the tag you just set on the label in the storyboard. So, this returns a reference to the corresponding UILabel. Using tags is a handy trick to get a reference to a UI element without having to make an @IBOutlet variable for it.

Exercise: Why can't you simply add an @IBOutlet variable to the view controller and connect the cell's label to that outlet in the storyboard? After all, that's how you created references to the labels in *Bullseye*... so why won't that work here?

Answer: There will be more than one cell in the table and each cell will have its own label. If you connected the label from the prototype cell to an outlet on the view controller, that outlet could only refer to the label from *one* of these cells, not all of them. Since the label belongs to the cell and not to the view controller as a whole, you can't make an outlet for it on the view controller. Confused? We'll circle around to this topic soon, so don't worry about it for now. Back to the code. What is this indexPath thing?

IndexPath is simply an object that points to a specific row in the table. When the table view asks the data source for a cell, you can look at the row number inside the indexPath.row property to find out the row for which the cell is intended.

> **Note**: As was mentioned before, it is also possible for tables to group rows into sections. In an address book app you might sort contacts by last name. All contacts whose last name starts with "A" are grouped into their own section, all contacts whose last name starts with "B" are in another section, and so on.
>
> To find out which section a row belongs to, you'd look at the indexPath.section property. This app has no need for this kind of grouping, so you'll ignore the section property of IndexPath for now.

Now that you know about indexPath, the following code should make sense to you:

```
if indexPath.row == 0 {
  nameLabel.text = "The reader of this book"
  scoreLabel.text = "50000"
} else if indexPath.row == 1 {
  nameLabel.text = "Manda"
  scoreLabel.text = "10000"
} else if indexPath.row == 2 {
  nameLabel.text = "Joey"
  scoreLabel.text = "5000"
} else if indexPath.row == 3 {
  nameLabel.text = "Adam"
  scoreLabel.text = "1000"
} else if indexPath.row == 4 {
  nameLabel.text = "Eli"
  scoreLabel.text = "500"
}
```

You have seen this if − else if − else structure before. It simply looks at the value of indexPath.row, which contains the row number, and changes the label's text accordingly. The cell for the first row gets the player name "The reader of this book" and the scores next to it would be "50000". The cell for the second row gets the player name "Manda" with scores of "10000", and so on. Look at that, you're already ranked the highest!

> **Note**: Computers generally start counting at 0 for lists of items. If you have a list of 4 items, they are counted as 0, 1, 2 and 3. It may seem a little silly at first, but that's just the way programmers do things.
>
> For the first row in the first section, indexPath.row is 0. The second row has row number 1, the third row is row 2, and so on.
>
> Counting from 0 may take some getting used to, but after a while it becomes second nature and you'll start counting at 0 even when you're out for groceries.

➤ Run the app — it now has five rows, each with its own high score:

The reader of this book	50000
Manda	10000
Joey	5000
Adam	1000
Eli	500

The rows in the table now have their own text

That is how you write the tableView(_:cellForRowAt:) method to provide data to the table. You first get a UITableViewCell object and then change the contents of that cell based on the row number of the indexPath.

Tapping on the rows

When you tap on a row, the cell color changes to indicate it is selected. The cell remains selected till you tap another row. You are going to change this behavior so that when you lift your finger the row is deselected.

The reader of this book	50000
Manda	10000
Joey	5000
Adam	1000
Eli	500

A tapped row stays gray

Taps on rows are handled by the table view's **delegate**. Remember you read before that in iOS you often find objects doing something on behalf of other objects? The data source is one example of this, but the table view also depends on another little helper, the table view delegate.

The concept of delegation is very common in iOS. An object will often rely on another object to help it out with certain tasks. This *separation of concerns* keeps the system simple, as each object does only what it is good at and lets other objects take care of the rest. The table view offers a great example of this.

Because every app has its own requirements for what its data looks like, the table view must be able to deal with lots of different types of data. Instead of making the table view very complex, or requiring that you modify it to suit your own apps, the UIKit designers have chosen to delegate the duty of providing the cells to display to another object, the data source.

The table view doesn't really care who its data source is or what kind of data your app deals with, just that it can send the `cellForRowAt` message and receive a cell in return. This keeps the table view component simple and moves the responsibility for handling the data to where it belongs: your code.

Likewise, the table view knows how to recognize when the user taps a row, but what it should do in response depends on the app. In this app, you'll transition to a different view controller; another app will likely do something totally different.

Using the delegation system, the table view can simply send a message that a tap occurred and let the delegate sort it out.

Usually, components will have just one delegate. But the table view splits up its delegate duties into two separate helpers: the `UITableViewDataSource` for putting rows into the table, and the `UITableViewDelegate` for handling taps on the rows and several other tasks.

➤ To see this, open the storyboard and **Control-click** on the table view to bring up its connections.

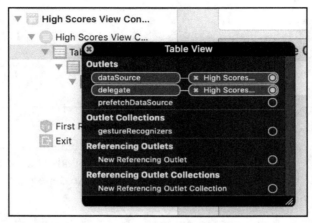

The table's data source and delegate are hooked up to the view controller

You can see that the table view's data source and delegate are both connected to the view controller. That is standard practice for a UITableViewController. (You can also use table views in a basic UIViewController but then you'll have to connect the data source and delegate manually.)

➤ Add the following method to **HighScoresViewController.swift**:

```
// MARK:- Table View Delegate
override func tableView(_ tableView: UITableView,
          didSelectRowAt indexPath: IndexPath) {
  tableView.deselectRow(at: indexPath, animated: true)
}
```

The tableView(_:didSelectRowAt:) method is one of the table view delegate methods and gets called whenever the user taps on a cell. Run the app and tap a row – the cell briefly turns gray and then becomes de-selected again.

Currently the high scores are hard-coded and never update. You need some way to keep track of new high scores. That means it's time to expand the data source and make it use a proper *data model*, which is the topic of the next section.

Methods with multiple parameters

Most of the methods you used in the *Bullseye* app took only one parameter or did not have any parameters at all, but these new table view data source and delegate methods take two:

```
override func tableView(
        _ tableView: UITableView,              // parameter 1
        numberOfRowsInSection section: Int)    // parameter 2
        -> Int {                               // return value
    . . .
}
override func tableView(
        _ tableView: UITableView,              // parameter 1
        cellForRowAt indexPath: IndexPath)     // parameter 2
        -> UITableViewCell {                   // return value
    . . .
}
override func tableView(
        _ tableView: UITableView,              // parameter 1
        didSelectRowAt indexPath: IndexPath) { // parameter 2
    . . .
}
```

The first parameter is the UITableView object on whose behalf these methods are invoked. This is done for convenience, so you won't have to make an @IBOutlet in order to send messages back to the table view.

For numberOfRowsInSection the second parameter is the section number. For cellForRowAt and didSelectRowAt it is the index-path.

Methods are not limited to just one or two parameters, they can have many. But for practical reasons two or three is usually more than enough, and you won't see many methods with more than five parameters.

In other programming languages a method typically looks like this:

```
Int numberOfRowsInSection(UITableView tableView, Int section) {
    . . .
}
```

In Swift we do things a little differently, mostly to be compatible with the iOS frameworks, which are all written in the Objective-C programming language. Let's take a look again at numberOfRowsInSection:

```
override func tableView(_ tableView: UITableView,
        numberOfRowsInSection section: Int) -> Int {
    . . .
}
```

The method signature for the above method, as discussed before, is tableView(_:numberOfRowsInSection:). If you say that out loud (without the underscores and colons, of course), it actually makes sense. It asks for the number of rows in a particular section of a particular table view.

The first parameter looks like this:

```
_ tableView: UITableView
```

The name of this parameter is `tableView`. The name is followed by a colon and the parameter's type, `UITableView`.

The second parameter looks like this:

```
numberOfRowsInSection section: Int
```

This one has two names, `numberOfRowsInSection` and `section`.

You use the first name, `numberOfRowsInSection`, when calling the method. This is the *external* parameter name. Inside the method itself you use the second name, `section`, known as the *local* parameter name. The data type of this parameter is `Int`.

The _ underscore is used when you don't want a parameter to have an external name. You'll often see the _ on the first parameter of methods that come from Objective-C frameworks. With such methods the first parameter only has one name but the other parameters have two. Strange? Yes.

It makes sense if you've ever programmed in Objective-C, but no doubt it looks weird if you're coming from another language. Once you get used to it, you'll find that this notation is actually quite readable.

Sometimes people with experience in other languages get confused because they think that HighScoresViewController.swift contains three functions that are all named `tableView()`. But that's not how it works in Swift: the names of the parameters are part of the full method name. That's why these three methods are actually named:

```
tableView(_:numberOfRowsInSection:)
tableView(_:cellForRowAt:)
tableView(_:didSelectRowAt:)
```

By the way, the return type of the method is at the end, after the –> arrow. If there is no arrow, as in `tableView(_:didSelectRowAt:)`, then the method is not supposed to return a value.

Phew! That was a lot of new stuff to take in, so I hope you're still with me. If not, then take a break and start at the beginning again. You're being introduced to a whole bunch of new concepts all at once and that can be overwhelming.

But don't worry, it's OK if everything doesn't make perfect sense yet. As long as you get the gist of what's going on, you're good to go.

If you want to check your work up to this point, you can find the project files for the app under **20-Table Views** in the Source Code folder.

Chapter 21: The Data Model

By Eli Ganim

In the previous chapter, you created a table view for the high scores and got it to display rows of items. However, this was all done using hard-coded, fake data. This would not do for a real high score screen since your users want to see their own real high scores up there.

To manage and display this information efficiently, you need a data model that allows you to store (and access) the high scores easily. That's what you're going to do in this chapter.

This chapter covers the following:

- **Model-View-Controller**: A quick explanation of the MVC fundamentals that are central to iOS programming.

- **The data model**: Creating a data model to hold the high scores data.

Model-View-Controller

First, a tiny detour into programming-concept-land so that you understand some of the principles behind using a data model. No book on programming for iOS can escape an explanation of **Model-View-Controller**, or MVC for short.

MVC is one of the three fundamental design patterns of iOS. You've already seen the other two: *Delegation*, making one object do something on behalf of another, and *target-action*, connecting events such as button taps to action methods.

The Model-View-Controller pattern states that the objects in your app can be split into three groups:

- **Model objects**: These objects contain your data and any operations on the data. For example, if you were writing a cookbook app, the model would consist of the recipes. In a game, it would be the design of the levels, the player score and the positions of the monsters.

  The operations that the data model objects perform are sometimes called the *business rules* or the *domain logic*. For the high score screen, the high scores themselves form the data model.

- **View objects**: These make up the visual part of the app: Images, buttons, labels, text fields, table view cells and so on. In a game, the views form the visual representation of the game world, such as the monster animations and a frag counter.

  A view can draw itself and responds to user input, but it typically does not handle any application logic. Many views, such as UITableView, can be re-used in many different apps because they are not tied to a specific data model.

- **Controller objects**: The controller is the object that connects your data model objects to the views. It listens to taps on the views, makes the data model objects do some calculations in response and updates the views to reflect the new state of your model. The controller is in charge. On iOS, the controller is called the "view controller."

Conceptually, this is how these three building blocks fit together:

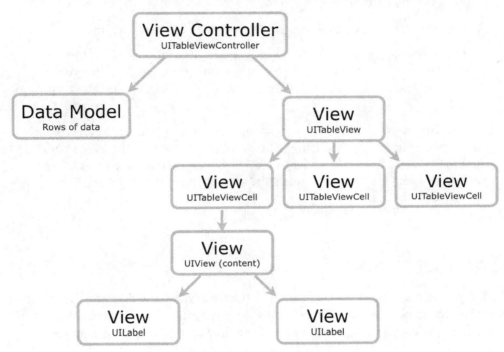

How Model-View-Controller works

The view controller has one main view, accessible through its view property, that contains a bunch of subviews. It is not uncommon for a screen to have dozens of views all at once. The top-level view usually fills the whole screen. You design the layout of the view controller's screen in the storyboard.

In the high score screen, the main view is the UITableView and its subviews are the table view cells. Each cell also has several subviews of its own, namely the text labels.

Generally, a view controller handles one screen of the app. If your app has more than one screen, each of these is handled by its own view controller and has its own views. Your app flows from one view controller to another.

You will often need to create your own view controllers. However, iOS also comes with ready-to-use view controllers, such as the image picker controller for photos, the mail compose controller that lets you write an email and, of course, the table view controller for displaying lists of items.

Views vs. view controllers

Remember that a view and a view controller are two different things.

A view is an object that draws something on the screen, such as a button or a label. The view is what you see. The view controller is what does the work behind the scenes. It is the bridge that sits between your data model and the views.

A lot of beginners give their view controllers names such as `FirstView` or `MainView`. That is very confusing! If something is a view controller, its name should end with "ViewController," not "View." I sometimes wish Apple had left the word "view" out of "view controller" and just called it "controller" as that is a lot less misleading.

The data model

So far, you've put a bunch of fake data into the table view. The data consists of a text string and a number. As you saw in the previous chapter, you cannot use the cells to remember the data as cells get re-used all the time and their old contents get overwritten.

Table view cells are part of the view. Their purpose is to display the app's data, but that data actually comes from somewhere else: The data model. Remember this well: The rows are the data, the cells are the views.

The table view controller is the thing that ties them together through the act of implementing the table view's data source and delegate methods.

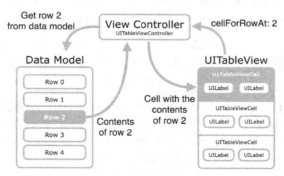

The table view controller (data source) gets the data from the model and puts it into the cells

The data model for this app will be a list of high score items. Each of these items will get its own row in the table.

For each high score, you need to store two pieces of information: The name of the high scorer (Like "Manda", "Adam", etc) and the score.

That is two pieces of information per row, so you need two variables for each row.

The first iteration

First, you'll see the cumbersome way to program this. It will work, but it isn't very smart. Even though this is not the best approach, you should still follow along and copy-paste the code into Xcode and run the app so that you understand how this approach works.

Understanding why this approach is problematic will help you appreciate the proper solution better.

➤ In **HighScoresViewController.swift**, add the following constants right after the `class HighScoresViewController` line:

```swift
class HighScoresViewController: UITableViewController {
  let row0name = "The reader of this book"
  let row1name = "Manda"
  let row2name = "Joey"
  let row3name = "Adam"
  let row4name = "Eli"
  let row0score = 50000
  let row1score = 10000
  let row2score = 5000
  let row3score = 1000
  let row4score = 500
  . . .
```

These constants are defined outside of any method, they are not "local", so they can be used by all of the methods in `HighScoresViewController`.

➤ Change the data source methods to:

```swift
override func tableView(_ tableView: UITableView,
      numberOfRowsInSection section: Int) -> Int {
  return 5
}

override func tableView(_ tableView: UITableView,
                      cellForRowAt indexPath: IndexPath)
-> UITableViewCell {
  let cell = tableView.dequeueReusableCell(
```

```
      withIdentifier: "HighScoreItem",
      for: indexPath)
  let nameLabel = cell.viewWithTag(1000) as! UILabel
  let scoreLabel = cell.viewWithTag(2000) as! UILabel

  if indexPath.row == 0 {
    nameLabel.text = row0name
    scoreLabel.text = String(row0score)
  } else if indexPath.row == 1 {
    nameLabel.text = row1name
    scoreLabel.text = String(row1score)
  } else if indexPath.row == 2 {
    nameLabel.text = row2name
    scoreLabel.text = String(row2score)
  } else if indexPath.row == 3 {
    nameLabel.text = row3name
    scoreLabel.text = String(row3score)
  } else if indexPath.row == 4 {
    nameLabel.text = row4name
    scoreLabel.text = String(row4score)
  }
  return cell
}
```

➤ Run the app. It still shows the same five rows as originally.

What have you done here? For every row, you have added 2 constants with the name and score for that row. Together, these constants are your data model. You could have used variables instead of constants, but since the values won't change for this particular example, it's better to use constants.

In `tableView(_:cellForRowAt:)` you look at `indexPath.row` to figure out which row to display and put the text from the corresponding constant into the cell.

Simplifying the code

Let's combine the name and score into a new object of your own!

The object

➤ Select the **Bullseye** group in the project navigator and right-click it. Choose **New File...** from the pop-up menu.

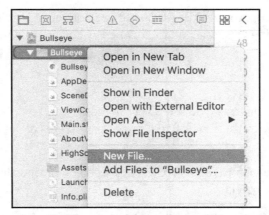

Adding a new file to the project

Under the **Source** section, choose **Swift File**.

Click **Next** to continue. Save the new file as **HighScoreItem**. You don't really need to add the **.swift** file extension since it will be automatically added for you.

Click **Create** to add the new file to the project.

➤ Add the following to the new **HighScoreItem.swift** file, below the import line:

```swift
class HighScoreItem {
  var name = ""
  var score = 0
}
```

The name property will store the name of the high scorer, the text that will appear in the table view cell's label, and the score property will store the score.

> **Note**: You may be wondering what the difference is between the terms *property* and *instance variable* — we've used both to refer to an object's data items. You'll be glad to hear that these two terms are interchangeable.
>
> In Swift terminology, a property is a variable or constant that is used in the context of an object. That's exactly what an instance variable is.
>
> In Objective-C, properties and instance variables are closely related but not quite the same thing. In Swift, they are the same.

That's all for **HighScoreItem.swift** for now. The HighScoreItem object currently only serves to combine the name and the score variables into one object. Later you'll do more with it.

Using the object

Before you try using an array, you'll replace the name and score instance variables in the view controller with these new HighScoreItem objects to see how that approach would work.

➤ In **HighScoresViewController.swift**, remove the old properties and replace them with HighScoreItem objects:

```
class HighScoresViewController: UITableViewController {
    var row0item = HighScoreItem()
    var row1item = HighScoreItem()
    var row2item = HighScoreItem()
    var row3item = HighScoreItem()
    var row4item = HighScoreItem()
```

These replace the row0name, row0score, etc. instance variables.

Wait a minute though... We've had variable declarations with a type, or with explicit values like an empty string or a number, but what are these? These variables are being assigned with what looks like a method!

And you are right about the method. It's a special method that all classes have called an *initializer* method. An initializer method creates a new instance of the given object, in this case HighScoreItem. This creates an empty instance of HighScoreItem with the default values you defined when you added the class implementation — an empty string ("") for name and 0 for score.

Instead of the above, you could have used what's known as a *type annotation* to simply indicate the type of row0Item like this:

```
var row0item: HighScoreItem
```

If you did that, row0item won't have a value yet, it would just be an empty container for a HighScoreItem object. And you'd still have to create the HighScoreItem instance later in your code. For example, in viewDidLoad.

The way you've done the code now, you initialize the variables above immediately with an empty instance of HighScoreItem and let Swift's type inference do the work in letting the compiler figure out the type of the variables. Handy, right?

Just to clarify the above a bit more, the data type is like the brand name of a car. Just saying the words "Porsche 911" out loud doesn't magically get you a new car. You actually have to go to the dealer to buy one.

The parentheses ( ) behind the type name are like going to the object dealership to buy an object of that type. The parentheses tell Swift's object factory: "Build me an object of the type HighScoreItem."

It is important to remember that just declaring that you have a variable does not automatically make the corresponding object for you. The variable is just the container for the object. You still have to instantiate the object and put it into the container. The variable is the box and the object is the thing inside the box.

Until you order an actual HighScoreItem object from the factory and put that into row0item, the variable is empty. And empty variables are a big no-no in Swift.

Fixing existing code

Because some methods in the view controller still refer to the old variables, Xcode will throw up multiple errors at this point. Before you can run the app again, you need to fix these errors. So, let's do that now.

> **Note:** I generally encourage you to type in the code from this book by hand, instead of copy-pasting, because that gives you a better feel for what you're doing, but in the following instances it's easier to just copy-paste from the PDF.
>
> Unfortunately, copying from the PDF sometimes adds strange or invisible characters that confuse Xcode. It's best to first paste the copied text into a plain text editor such as TextMate and then copy-paste from the text editor into Xcode.
>
> Of course, if you're reading the print edition of this book, copy-pasting from the book isn't going to work. But you can still use copy-paste to save yourself some effort. Make the changes on one line and then copy that line to create the other lines. Copy-paste is a programmer's best friend, but don't forget to update the lines you pasted to use the correct variable names!

➤ In tableView(_:cellForRowAt:), replace the if statements with the following:

```
if indexPath.row == 0 {
  nameLabel.text = row0item.name
```

```
    scoreLabel.text = String(row0item.score)
} else if indexPath.row == 1 {
    nameLabel.text = row1item.name
    scoreLabel.text = String(row1item.score)
} else if indexPath.row == 2 {
    nameLabel.text = row2item.name
    scoreLabel.text = String(row2item.score)
} else if indexPath.row == 3 {
    nameLabel.text = row3item.name
    scoreLabel.text = String(row3item.score)
} else if indexPath.row == 4 {
    nameLabel.text = row4item.name
    scoreLabel.text = String(row4item.score)
}
```

Basically, all of the above changes do one thing. Instead of using the separate row0name and row0score variables, you now use row0item.name and row0item.score.

That takes care of all of the errors and you can even build and run the app. But if you do, you'll notice that you get a table with 5 zeros in it.

So what went wrong?

Setting up the objects

Remember how the new row0item etc. variables are initialized with empty instances of HighScoreItem? That means that the text for each variable is empty. You still need to set up the values for these new variables!

➤ Modify viewDidLoad in **HighScoreViewController.swift** as follows:

```
override func viewDidLoad() {
  super.viewDidLoad()

  // Add the following lines
  row0item.name = "The reader of this book"
  row0item.score = 50000
  row1item.name = "Manda"
  row1item.score = 10000
  row2item.name = "Joey"
  row2item.score = 5000
  row3item.name = "Adam"
  row3item.score = 1000
  row4item.name = "Eli"
  row4item.score = 500
}
```

This code simply sets up each of the new HighScoreItem variables that you created.

Essentially, it's doing the same thing as before. Except, this time, the name and score variables are not separate instance variables of the view controller. Instead, they are properties of a HighScoreItem object.

➤ Run the app just to make sure that everything works now.

Putting the name and score properties into their own HighScoreItem object already improved the code, but it is still a bit unwieldy.

Using arrays

With the current approach, you need to keep around a HighScoreItem instance variable for each row. That's not ideal, especially if you want more than just a handful of rows.

Time to bring that array into play!

➤ In **HighScoresViewController.swift**, remove all of the instance variables and replace them with a single array variable named items:

```
class HighScoresViewController: UITableViewController {
  var items = [HighScoreItem]()
```

Instead of five different instance variables, one for each row, you now have just one variable for the array.

This looks similar to how you declared the previous variables but this time there are square brackets around HighScoreItem. Those square brackets indicate that the variable is going to be an array containing HighScoreItem objects. And the brackets at the end () simply indicate that you are creating an instance of this array. It will create an empty array with no items in the array.

➤ Modify viewDidLoad as follows:

```
override func viewDidLoad() {
   super.viewDidLoad()

   // Replace previous code with the following
   let item1 = HighScoreItem()
   item1.name = "The reader of this book"
   item1.score = 50000
   items.append(item1)

   let item2 = HighScoreItem()
   item2.name = "Manda"
   item2.score = 10000
   items.append(item2)
```

```
    let item3 = HighScoreItem()
    item3.name = "Joey"
    item3.score = 5000
    items.append(item3)

    let item4 = HighScoreItem()
    item4.name = "Adam"
    item4.score = 1000
    items.append(item4)

    let item5 = HighScoreItem()
    item5.name = "Eli"
    item5.score = 500
    items.append(item5)
}
```

This is not that different from before, except that you now have to first create — or *instantiate* — each HighScoreItem object and add each instance to the array. Once the above code completes, the items array contains five HighScoreItem objects. This is your new data model.

Simplifying the code — again

Now that you have all your rows in the items array, you can simplify the table view data source and delegate methods once again.

➤ Change this methods:

```
override func tableView(_ tableView: UITableView,
            cellForRowAt indexPath: IndexPath)
            -> UITableViewCell {
  let cell = tableView.dequeueReusableCell(
                    withIdentifier: "HighScoreItem",
                                for: indexPath)

  let item = items[indexPath.row]        // Add this

  let nameLabel = cell.viewWithTag(1000) as! UILabel
  let scoreLabel = cell.viewWithTag(2000) as! UILabel

  // Replace everything after the above line with the following
  nameLabel.text = item.name
  scoreLabel.text = String(item.score)
  return cell
}
```

That's a lot simpler than what you had before! This method is now only a handful of lines long.

The most important part is the line:

```
let item = items[indexPath.row]
```

This asks the array for the `HighScoreItem` object at the index that corresponds to the row number. Once you have that object, you can simply look at its `name` and `score` properties and do whatever you need to do.

If the user were to add 100 high score items to this list, none of this code would need to change. It works equally well with five items as with a hundred (or a thousand).

Speaking of the number of items, you can now change `numberOfRowsInSection` to return the actual number of items in the array, instead of a hard-coded number.

➤ Change the `tableView(_:numberOfRowsInSection:)` method to:

```
override func tableView(_ tableView: UITableView,
      numberOfRowsInSection section: Int) -> Int {
  return items.count
}
```

Not only is the code a lot shorter and easier to read, it can now also handle an arbitrary number of rows. That is the power of arrays!

➤ Run the app and see for yourself. It should still work exactly the same as before, but the internal structure of the code is way better.

Exercise: Add a few more rows to the table. You should only have to change `viewDidLoad` for this to work.

If you want to check your work, you can find the project files for the current version of the app in the folder **21-The Data Model** in the Source Code folder.

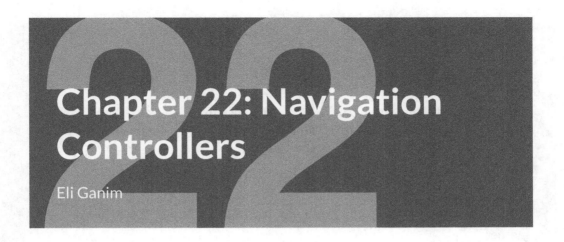

Chapter 22: Navigation Controllers

Eli Ganim

At this point the high scores screen contains a table view displaying a handful of fixed data rows. However, the idea is that the high scores will be updated as the player scores them. Therefore, you need to implement the ability to add items.

In this chapter you'll expand the app to have a **navigation bar** at the top. Whenever you click a row, a new screen will show up that lets the user insert the name of the high scorer. When you tap Done, the new item will be added to the list.

This chapter covers the following:

- **Navigation controller**: Add a navigation controller to the app to allow navigation between screens.

- **Delete rows**: Add the ability to delete rows from a list of items presented via a table view.

- **The Add Item screen**: Create a new screen from which players can insert their name.

Navigation controller

First, let's add the navigation bar. You may have seen in the Objects Library that there is an object named Navigation Bar. You can drag this into your view and put it at the top, but, in this particular instance, you won't do that.

Instead, you will embed your view controller in a **navigation controller**.

Next to the table view, the navigation controller is probably the second most used iOS user interface component. It is the thing that lets you go from one screen to another:

A navigation controller in action

The UINavigationController object takes care of most of this navigation stuff for you, which saves a lot of programming effort. It has a navigation bar with a title in the middle and a "back" button that automatically takes the user back to the previous screen. You can put a button (or several buttons) of your own on the right.

Adding a navigation controller

Adding a navigation controller is really easy.

➤ Open **Main.storyboard** and select the **View Controller Scene**.

➤ From the menu bar at the top of the screen, choose **Editor ▸ Embed In ▸ Navigation Controller**.

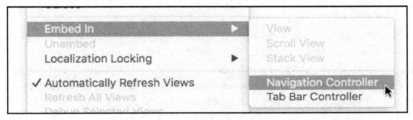

Putting the view controller inside a navigation controller

Several things have happened in Interface Builder now:

1. Interface Builder has added a new **Navigation Controller Scene** and made a relationship between it and the main view controller.

2. There's a navigation bar at the top of the main screen (just like in the SwiftUI version of *Bullseye*)

3. The **High Scores View Controller** also has a navigation bar with a Back button.

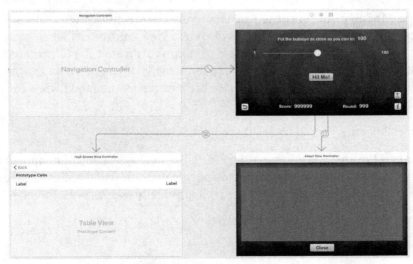

The navigation controller is now linked with your view controller

Why was a navigation bar added to the **High Scores View Controller Scene**, but not to **About View Controller Scene**? When you connected the main view controller to the *About screen* a few chapters ago, you chose the *Present Modally* segue. When you connected the *High Scores Screen*, you chose *Show*.

Segue types

What are the possible Segues and what do they mean? Here is a brief explanation of each type of segue:

- **Show**: Pushes the new view controller onto the navigation stack so that the new view controller is at the top of the navigation stack. It also provides a back button to return to the previous view controller. If the view controllers are not embedded in a navigation controller, then the new view controller will be presented modally (see Present Modally in the list below as to what this means).

  Example: Navigating folders in the *Mail* app

- **Show Detail**: For use in a split view controller (you'll learn more about those when developing the last app in this book). The new view controller replaces the detail view controller of the split view when in an expanded two-column interface. Otherwise, if in single-column mode, it will push in a navigation controller.

  Example: In *Messages*, tapping a conversation will show the conversation details — replacing the view controller on the right when in a two-column layout, or push the conversation when in a single column layout

- **Present Modally**: Presents the new view controller to cover the previous view controller — most commonly used to present a view controller that covers the entire screen on iPhone, or on iPad it's common to present it as a centered box that darkens the presenting view controller. Usually, if you had a navigation bar at the top or a tab bar at the bottom, those are covered by the modal view controller too.

  Example: Selecting Touch ID & Passcode in *Settings*

- **Present as Popover**: When run on an iPad, the new view controller appears in a popover, and tapping anywhere outside of this popover will dismiss it. On an iPhone, will present the new view controller modally over the full screen.

  Example: Tapping the + button in *Calendar*

- **Custom**: Allows you to implement your own custom segue and have control over its behavior. (You will learn more about this in a later chapter.)

➤ Run the app and try it out. Navigate to the About screen and then to the High Score screen and witness the difference between the two segue types.

Setting the navigation bar title

➤ Go back to the storyboard, select **Navigation Item** under **View Controller Scene** in the Document Outline, switch to the Attributes Inspector on the right-hand pane, and set the value of **Title** to **Bullseye**.

Changing the title in the navigation bar

What you're doing here is changing a **Navigation Item** object that was automatically added to the view controller when you chose the **Embed In** command.

The Navigation Item object contains the title and buttons that appear in the navigation bar when this view controller becomes active. Each embedded view controller has its own Navigation Item that it uses to configure what shows up in the navigation bar.

If you run the app now, you'll see that the title in the navigation controller of the main screen is now *Bullseye*. However, if you open the high scores screen you'll see it has no title.

When the navigation controller slides a new view controller in, it replaces the contents of the navigation bar with the new view controller's Navigation Item. You'll add a **Navigation Item** to the high scores view controller and set its title.

➤ Go to the storyboard and select the High Scores scene

➤ Drag a **Navigation Item** from the object library into the scene

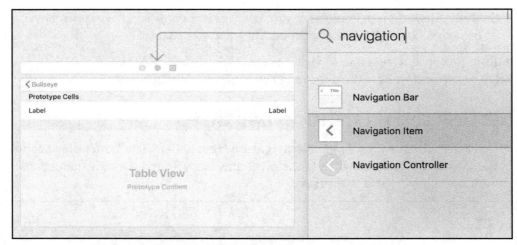

Add a navigation item to the view controller

➤ Change the Navigation Item's title to "High Scores".

Run the app, open the high scores screen and verify the title was indeed updated:

‹ Bullseye	High Scores	
The reader of this book		50000
Manda		10000
Joey		5000

Navigation bar with title

Deleting rows

Imagine you let a friend enjoy the amazing Bullseye game on your iPhone and he reaches a high score you can't beat. That would be really annoying!

For that purpose you need a way to delete high scores from the list. A common way to do this in iOS apps is "swipe-to-delete." You swipe your finger over a row and a Delete button slides into view. A tap on the Delete button confirms the removal, tapping anywhere else will cancel.

‹ Bullseye	**High Scores**	
The reader of this book		50000
	10000	Delete
Joey		5000
Adam		1000

Swipe-to-delete in action

Swipe-to-delete

Swipe-to-delete is very easy to implement.

➤ Add the following method to **HighScoresViewController.swift**. You should put this with the other table view delegate methods, to keep things organized.

```
override func tableView(
            _ tableView: UITableView,
        commit editingStyle: UITableViewCell.EditingStyle,
          forRowAt indexPath: IndexPath) {
  // 1
  items.remove(at: indexPath.row)

  // 2
  let indexPaths = [indexPath]
  tableView.deleteRows(at: indexPaths, with: .automatic)
}
```

When the `commitEditingStyle` method is present in your view controller (it is a method defined by the table view data source protocol), the table view will automatically enable swipe-to-delete. All you have to do is:

1. Remove the item from the data model.

2. Delete the corresponding row from the table view.

➤ Run the app to try it out!

Adding a navigation button

Now that you can remove items from the list, it would be useful to also have a way to reset the high scores list to its initial state. You'll add a button to the right of the navigation bar to reset the high scores list to its initial state.

➤ Open the storyboard.

➤ Go to the Objects Library and look for **Bar Button Item**. Drag it into the right-side slot of the navigation bar. (Be sure to use the navigation bar on the High Scores View Controller, not the one from the navigation controller!)

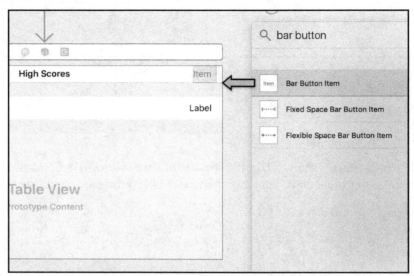

Dragging a Bar Button Item into the navigation bar

By default, this new button is named "Item". Let's rename it to "Reset".

➤ In the **Attributes inspector** for the bar button item, update the title to Reset.

OK, that gives us a button. If you open the high scores screen, the navigation bar should look like this:

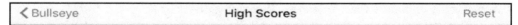

The app with the reset button

Making the navigation button do something

If you tap on your new reset button, it doesn't actually do anything. That's because you haven't hooked it up to an action. You got plenty of exercise with this for *Bullseye*, so it should be child's play for you by now.

➤ Add a new action method to **HighScoresViewController.swift**:

```
// MARK:- Actions
```

```
@IBAction func resetHighScores() {
}
```

You're leaving the method empty for the moment, but it needs to be there so you have something to connect the button to.

➤ Open the storyboard and connect the Reset button to this action. To do this, **Control-drag** from the reset button to the yellow circle in the bar above the view (this circle represents the High Scores View Controller):

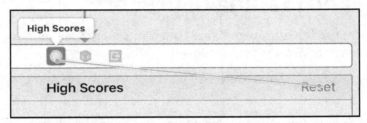

Control-drag from Reset button to High Scores View Controller

Actually, you can Control-drag from the Add button to almost anywhere in the same scene to make the connection.

➤ After dragging, pick **resetHighScores** from the pop-up (under **Sent Actions**):

➤ Let's give resetHighScores() something to do. Back in **HighScoresViewController.swift**, move all the **HighScoreItem** initialization code from viewDidLoad() to resetHighScores() and call it from viewDidLoad(). The final code should look like this (some items were removed for brevity:

```
override func viewDidLoad() {
  super.viewDidLoad()
  resetHighScores()
}

// MARK:- Actions
@IBAction func resetHighScores() {
  items = [HighScoreItem]()
  let item1 = HighScoreItem()
  item1.name = "The reader of this book"
  item1.score = 50000
  items.append(item1)

  . . .

  let item5 = HighScoreItem()
  item5.name = "Eli"
  item5.score = 500
  items.append(item5)
```

```
    tableView.reloadData()
  }
```

Note that at the beginning you clear the items array by assinging it an empty array. You then add the default 5 items and eventually call reloadData on the table view, so that it will be refreshed.

Saving and loading high scores

You probably noticed that the high scores data resets every time you restart the app. That's because you're not saving or loading the data.

First, you need to make **HighScoreItem** conform to Codable so that you can write it to a file.

➤ Open **HighScoreItem.swift** and update the class definition to this:

```
class HighScoreItem : Codable
```

Next, you'll create a helper class to save and load the data and use it to fetch items when the high scores screen loads.

➤ Create a new Swift file and name it **PersistencyHelper.swift**. Put this content in the new file:

```
class PersistencyHelper {
  static func saveHighScores(_ items: [HighScoreItem]) {
    let encoder = PropertyListEncoder()
    do {
      let data = try encoder.encode(items)
      try data.write(to: dataFilePath(), options:
Data.WritingOptions.atomic)
    } catch {
      print("Error encoding item array: \
(error.localizedDescription)")
    }
  }

  static func loadHighScores() -> [HighScoreItem] {
    var items = [HighScoreItem]()
    let path = dataFilePath()
    if let data = try? Data(contentsOf: path) {
      let decoder = PropertyListDecoder()
      do {
        items = try decoder.decode([HighScoreItem].self, from:
data)
```

```
        } catch {
          print("Error decoding item array: \
(error.localizedDescription)")
        }
    }
    return items
  }

  static func dataFilePath() -> URL {
    let paths =
FileManager.default.urls(for: .documentDirectory,
                                  in: .userDomainMask)
    return paths[0].appendingPathComponent("HighScores.plist")
  }
}
```

This should all be familiar to you, since you've done exactly the same thing in *Checklists*. You have one method to save the high scores to file and one that loads them from the file. The third method simply creates the path to the plist as a URL.

Now it's time to use these methods. First, you want to load the high scores.

➤ Open **HighScoresViewController.swift** and add loadHighScores() to viewDidLoad(). If there's no high scores file (or if loading fails for any reason), you fallback to the default list of high scores:

```
override func viewDidLoad() {
  super.viewDidLoad()
  items = PersistencyHelper.loadHighScores()
  if (items.count == 0) {
    resetHighScores()
  }
}
```

Next, you want to save the high scores whenever an item is deleted or the list is reset.

➤ Add PersistencyHelper.saveHighScores(items) at the end of resetHighScores() and tableView(_:commit:forRowAt:).

Adding new high scores

There's one piece missing: How do you add new high scores to the list? Obviously, it needs to happen when a game ends.

In Bullseye everyone's a winner. Even if your score is really low - you still make it to the high scores list (albeit at the bottom of the list).

> **Exercise**: Where's the right place to detect when a game ends, and how would you add the new high score?

The score needs to be added when a game ends, which is right before a new game starts.

➤ Open **ViewController.swift** and add this at the top of the method `startNewGame()`:

```
@IBAction func startNewGame() {
    addHighScore(score)
    . . .
}
```

Next, you need to implement the new method.

➤ Add this code somewhere in **ViewController.swift**:

```
func addHighScore(_ score:Int) {
  // 1
  guard score > 0 else {
    return;
  }

  // 2
  let highscore = HighScoreItem()
  highscore.score = score
  highscore.name = "Unknown"

  // 3
  var highScores = PersistencyHelper.loadHighScores()
  highScores.append(highscore)
  highScores.sort { $0.score > $1.score }
  PersistencyHelper.saveHighScores(highScores)
}
```

Here's what this piece of code is doing:

1. Make sure the score is higher than 0, since you don't want to store games in which the player didn't score any points.

2. Create a new `HighScoreItem` with the score and set the player name to "Unknown".

3. Load the high scores from the file, add the new score, sort the list and save it back to the file.

Run the app and give it a try. Play a game, click on the "Start Over" button to end the game and head over to the high scores screen to see your score.

The Edit High Score screen

You've learned how to add new high scores, but all of them contain the same player name - "Unknown". You will need to provide a way to change the name. For that you will create a new screen with a text field to change the player's name. It will look like this:

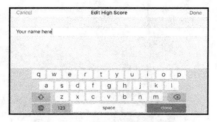

The Edit High score screen

Adding a new view controller to the storyboard

➤ Go to the Objects Library and drag a new **Table View Controller** (not a regular view controller) on to the storyboard canvas.

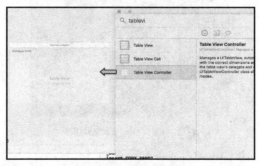

Dragging a new Table View Controller into the canvas

You may need to zoom out to fit everything properly. Right-click on the canvas to get a pop-up with zoom options, or use the - **100%** + controls at the bottom of the Interface Builder canvas. (You can also double-click on an empty spot in the canvas to zoom in or out. Or, if you have a Trackpad, simply pinch with two fingers to zoom in or out.)

➤ With the new view controller in place, select **Table View** and change its view's background to **Group Table View Background**.

➤ Select the prototype cell from the High Scores View Controller. **Control-drag** to the new view controller. It might be difficult to capture the correct object here, so instead you can control-drag from **HighScoreItem** in the outline to the left.

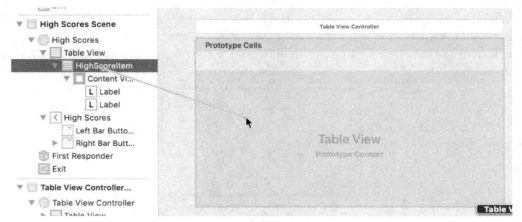

Control-drag from the Add button to the new table view controller

Let go of the mouse and a list of options pops up.

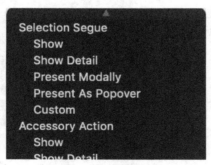

The Action Segue popup

➤ Choose **Show** from the menu.

The segue is represented by the arrow between the two view controllers:

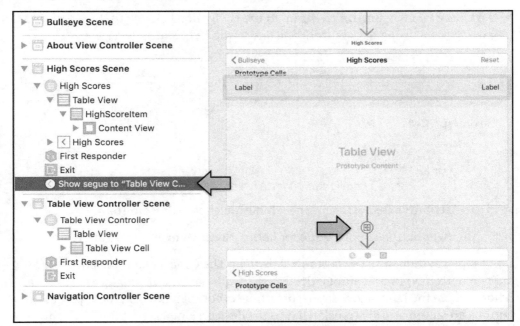

A new segue is added between the two view controllers

➤ Run the app to see what it does.

When you press any of the cells, a new empty table view slides in from the right. You can press the back button – the one that says "High Scores" – at the top to go back to the previous screen.

Note: Xcode may be giving you the warning, "Prototype table cells must have reuse identifiers". You might remember this issue from before — you will fix this issue soon.

Customizing the navigation bar

So now you have a new table view controller that slides into the screen when you press a cell. However, this screen is empty. Data input screens usually have a navigation bar with a Cancel button on the left and a Done button on the right. In some apps the button on the right is called Save or Send. Pressing either of these buttons will close the screen, but only Done will save your changes.

➤ First, drag a **Navigation Item** from the Objects Library on to the new scene.

➤ Next, drag two **Bar Button Items** on to the navigation bar, one to the left slot (removing the existing back button) and one to the right slot.

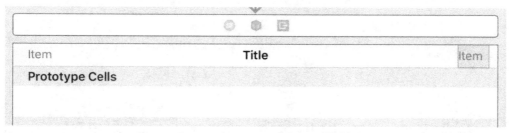

The navigation bar items for the new screen

➤ In the **Attributes inspector** for the left button choose **System Item: Cancel**.

➤ For the right button choose **Done** for both **System Item** and **Style** attributes.

Don't type anything into the button's Title field. The Cancel and Done buttons are built-in button types that automatically use the proper text. If your app runs on an iPhone where the language is set to something other than English, these predefined buttons are automatically translated into the device's language.

➤ Double-click the navigation bar for the new table view controller to edit its title and change it to **Edit High Score**. You can also change this via the Attributes inspector as you did before.

➤ Run the app, click on the high scores button, tap any cell and you'll see that your new screen has Cancel and Done buttons.

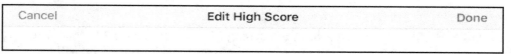

The Cancel and Done buttons in the app

Making your own view controller class

You created a custom view controller for the About screen. Do you remember how to do it on your own? If not, here are the steps:

➤ Right-click on the Bullseye group (the yellow folder) in the project navigator and choose **New File...** Choose the **Cocoa Touch Class** template.

➤ In the next dialog, set the Class to **EditHighScoreViewController** and Subclass to **UITableViewController** (when you change the subclass, the class name will automatically change — so either set the subclass first or change the class name back after the change). Leave the language at **Swift** (or change it back if it is not set to Swift).

➤ Save the file to your project folder, which should be the default location.

➤ The file should have a lot of source and commented code — this is known as *boilerplate code*, or code that is generally always needed. In this particular case, you don't need most of it. So remove everything except for viewDidLoad (and remove the comments from inside viewDidLoad as well) so that your code looks like this:

```
import UIKit

class EditHighScoreViewController: UITableViewController {
  override func viewDidLoad() {
    super.viewDidLoad()
  }
}
```

This tells Swift that you have a new object for a table view controller that goes by the name of EditHighScoreViewController. You'll add the rest of the code soon. First, you have to let the storyboard know about this new view controller.

➤ In the storyboard, select the Edit High Score Scene and go to the **Identity inspector**. Under **Custom Class**, type **EditHighScoreViewController**.

This tells the storyboard that the view controller from this scene is actually your new EditHighScoreViewController object.

Make sure that it is really the view controller that is selected before you change the fields in the Identity inspector (the scene needs to have a blue border). A common mistake is to select the table view and change that.

Making the navigation buttons work

There's still one issue — the Cancel and Done buttons ought to close the Add Item screen and return the app to the main screen, but tapping them has no effect yet.

> **Exercise**: Do you know why the Cancel and Done buttons do not return you to the main screen?

Answer: Because those buttons have not yet been hooked up to any actions!

You will now implement the necessary action methods in
EditHighScoreViewController.swift.

➤ Add these new `cancel()` and `done()` action methods:

```
// MARK:- Actions
@IBAction func cancel() {
  navigationController?.popViewController(animated: true)
}

@IBAction func done() {
  navigationController?.popViewController(animated: true)
}
```

This tells the navigation controller to close the Add Item screen with an animation
and to go back to the previous screen, which in this case is the main screen.

You still need to hook up the Cancel button to the `cancel()` action and the Done
button to the `done()` action.

➤ Open the storyboard and find the Add Item View controller. **Control-drag** from
the bar buttons to the yellow circle icon and pick the proper action from the pop-up
menu.

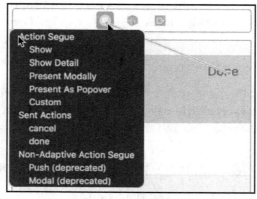

Control-dragging from the bar button to the view controller

➤ Run the app to try it out. The Cancel and Done buttons now return the app to the
main screen.

What do you think happens to the `EditHighScoreViewController` object when you
dismiss it? After the view controller disappears from the screen, its object is
destroyed and the memory it was using is reclaimed by the system.

Every time the user opens the Edit High Score screen, the app makes a new instance of it. This means a view controller object is only alive for the duration that the user is interacting with it; there is no point in keeping it around afterwards.

Container view controllers

You've read that one view controller represents one screen, but here you actually have two view controllers for each screen: a Table View controller that sits inside a navigation controller.

The navigation controller is a special type of view controller that acts as a container for other view controllers. It comes with a navigation bar and has the ability to easily go from one screen to another, by sliding them in and out of sight. The container essentially "wraps around" these screens.

The navigation controller is just the frame that contains the view controllers that do the real work, which are known as the "content" controllers. Here, the `HighScoresViewController` provides the content for the first screen; the content for the second screen comes from the `EditHighScoreViewController`.

Another often-used container is the Tab Bar controller, which you'll see in the next app.

On the iPad, container view controllers are even more commonplace. View controllers on the iPhone are full-screen but on the iPad they often occupy only a portion of the screen, such as the content of a popover or one of the panes in a split-view.

This completes the implementation of the navigation functionality for your app. If at any point you got stuck, you can refer to the project files for the app from the **22-Navigation Controllers** folder in the Source Code folder.

Chapter 23: Edit High Score Screen

Eli Ganim

Now that you have the navigation flow from your main screen to the Edit High Score screen working, it's time to actually implement the edit functionality for this screen!

Let's change the look of the Edit screen. Currently, it is an empty table with a navigation bar on top — but it's going to look like this:

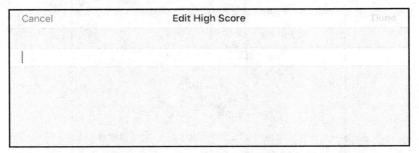

What the Add Item screen will look like when you're done

This chapter covers the following:

- **Static table cells**: Add a static table view cell to the table to display the text field for data entry.

- **Read from the text field**: Access the contents of the text field.

- **Polish it up**: Improve the look and functionality of the Edit High Score screen.

Static table cells

First, you need to add a table view cell to handle the data input for the Edit High Score screen. As is generally the case with UI changes, you start with the storyboard.

Storyboard changes

➤ Open the storyboard and select the **Table View** object inside the Edit High Score scene.

➤ In the **Attributes inspector**, change the **Content** setting from Dynamic Prototypes to **Static Cells**.

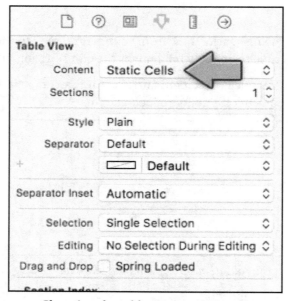

Changing the table view to static cells

You use static cells when you know beforehand how many sections and rows the table view will have. This is handy for screens that require the user to enter data, such as the one you're building here. With static cells, you can design the rows directly in the storyboard. For a table with static cells, you don't need to provide a data source and you can hook up the labels and other controls from the cells directly to outlets on the view controller.

As you can see in the Document Outline, the table view now has a table view section object under it and three table view Cells in that section. You may need to expand the table view item first by clicking the disclosure triangle.

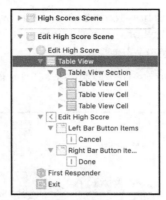

The table view has a section with three static cells

➤ Select the bottom two cells and delete them by pressing the **delete** key on your keyboard. You only need one cell for now.

➤ Select the table view again and in the **Attributes inspector** set its **Style** to **Grouped**.

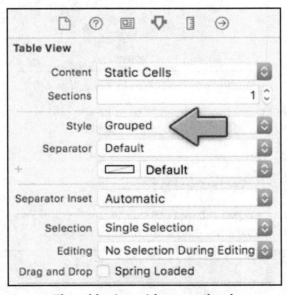

The table view with grouped style

Next up, you'll add a text field component inside the table view cell that lets the user type text.

➤ Drag a **text field** object into the cell and size it up nicely. You might want to add left, top, right and bottom Auto Layout constraints to the text field if you don't want any Xcode warnings. You know how to do that on your own, right? Hint: use the **Add New Constraints** button at the bottom of the Interface Builder screen after you've sized/positioned the field as you want.

➤ In the **Attributes inspector** for the text field, set the **Border Style** to **no border** by selecting the dotted box:

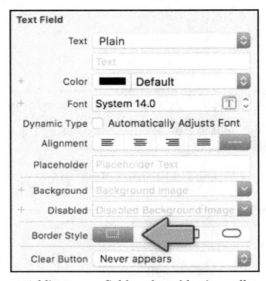

Adding a text field to the table view cell

➤ Run the app and click on any high score to open the Edit High Score screen. Tap on the cell with the text field and you'll see the keyboard slide in from the bottom of the screen.

Disabling cell selection

Look what happens when you tap just outside of the text field's area but still in the cell. Try tapping in the margins that surround the text field:

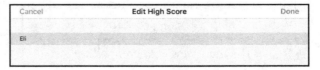

Whoops, that looks a little weird

The row turns gray because you selected it. Oops, that's not what you want. You should disable selections for this row. You can do this easily via code by adding the following table view delegate method to **EditHighScoreViewController.swift**:

```
// MARK:- Table View Delegates
override func tableView(_ tableView: UITableView,
          willSelectRowAt indexPath: IndexPath)
          -> IndexPath? {
   return nil
}
```

When the user taps on a cell, the table view sends the delegate a willSelectRowAt message that says: "Hi delegate, I am about to select this particular row."

By returning the special value nil, the delegate answers: "Sorry, but you're not allowed to!"

The tableView(_:willSelectRowAt:) method is supposed to return an IndexPath object. However, you can also make it return nil, indicating no value/object.

That's what the ? behind IndexPath is for. The question mark tells the Swift compiler that you can also return nil from this method. Note that returning nil from a method is only allowed if there is a question mark (or exclamation point) behind the return type. A type declaration with a question mark behind it is known as an *optional*. You'll learn more about optionals in the next chapter.

The special value nil represents "no value" but it's used to mean different things throughout the iOS SDK. Sometimes it means "nothing found" or "don't do anything." Here it means that the row should not be selected when the user taps it.

How do you know what nil means for a certain method? You can find that in the documentation of the method in question.

In the case of willSelectRowAt, the iOS documentation says:

Return Value: An indexPath object that confirms or alters the selected row. Return an IndexPath object other than IndexPath if you want another cell to be selected. Return nil if you don't want the row selected.

This means you can either:

1. Return the same IndexPath you were given. This confirms that this row can be selected.

2. Return another IndexPath to select a different row.

3. Return nil to prevent the row from being selected, which is what you did.

Working with the text field

You have a text field in a table view cell that the user can type into. How do you populate it with the current name from the HighScoreItem? And how do you read the text that the user has typed?

Adding an outlet for the text field

You already know how to refer to controls from within your view controller: Use an outlet. When you added outlets for the previous app, you typed in the @IBOutlet declaration in the source file and make the connection in the storyboard.

You're going to see a trick now that will save you some typing. You can let Interface Builder do all of this automatically by control-dragging from the control in question directly into your source code file!

➤ First, go to the storyboard and select the **Edit High Score View Controller**. Then, open the **Assistant editor** using the toolbar button on the top right.

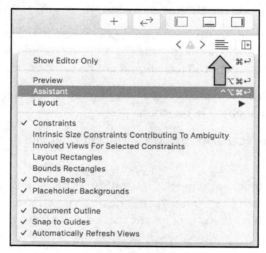

Click the toolbar button to open the Assistant editor

This may make the screen a little crowded. — there might now be up to five horizontal panels open. If you're running out of space, you might want to close the Project navigator, the Utilities pane and/or the Document Outline using the relevant toolbar buttons.

The Assistant editor opens a new pane on the right of the screen by default. It might give you horizontal split views instead if you have changed your default view settings.

In the Jump Bar, below the toolbar, it should say **Automatic** and the Assistant editor should be displaying the **EditHighScoreViewController.swift** file:

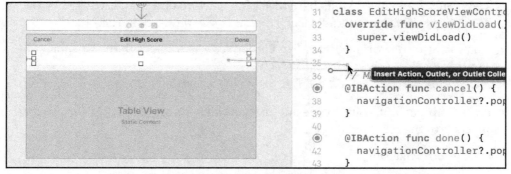

The Assistant editor

"Automatic" means the Assistant editor tries to figure out what other file is related to the one you're currently editing. When you're editing a storyboard, the related file is generally the selected view controller's Swift file.

Sometimes Xcode can be a little dodgy here. If it shows you something other than **EditHighScoreViewController.swift**, then click in the Jump Bar and manually select the correct file.

➤ With the storyboard and the Swift file side-by-side, select the text field. Then, **Control-drag** from the text field into the Swift file.

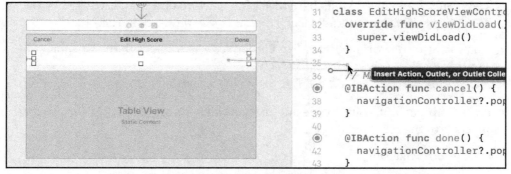

Control-dragging from the text field into the Swift file

When you let go, a pop-up appears:

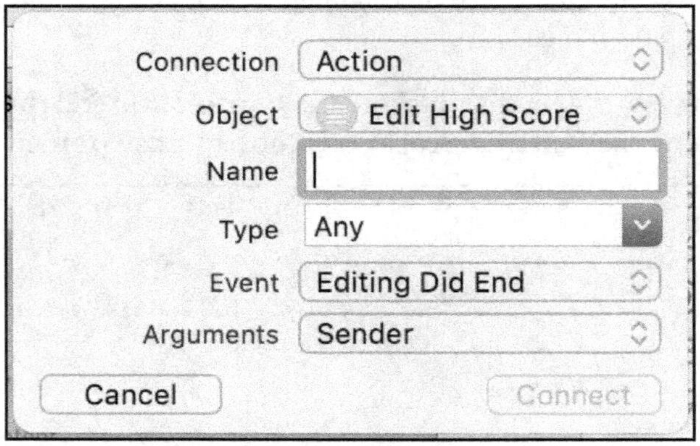

The pop-up that lets you add a new outlet

➤ Choose the following options:

- Connection: Outlet
- Name: **textField**
- Type: UITextField
- Storage: Weak

> **Note**: If "Type" does not say UITextField, but instead says UITableViewCell or UIView, then you selected the wrong thing.
>
> Make sure you're control-dragging from the text field inside the cell, not the cell itself. Granted, it's kinda hard to see being white on white. If you're having trouble selecting the text field, click that area several times in succession.
>
> You can also control-drag from "No Border Style Text Field" in the Document Outline.

➤ Press **Connect** and, voila, Xcode automatically inserts an @IBOutlet for you and connects it to the text field object.

In code it looks like this:

```
@IBOutlet weak var textField: UITextField!
```

Just by dragging, you have successfully hooked up the text field object with a new property named textField. How easy was that?

Reading from the text field

Now, you'll modify the done() action to write the contents of this text field to the Xcode Console, the pane at the bottom of the screen where print() messages show up. This is a quick way to verify that you can actually read what the user typed.

➤ In **EditHighScoreViewController.swift**, change done() to:

```
@IBAction func done() {
  // Add the following line
  print("Contents of the text field: \(textField.text!)")

  navigationController?.popViewController(animated: true)
}
```

You can make these changes directly inside the Assistant editor. It's very handy that you can edit the source code and the storyboard side-by-side.

➤ Run the app, go to the high scores screen, click on any high score to navigate to the Edit High Score screen and type something in the text field. When you press Done, the Edit High Score screen should close and Xcode should reveal the Debug pane with a message like this:

```
Contents of the text field: Hello, world!
```

Great, so that works! print() should be an old friend by now. It's one of the faithful debugging companions.

> **Note:** Because the iOS Simulator already outputs a lot of debug messages of its own, it may be a bit hard to find your print() messages in the Console. Luckily, there is a filter box at the bottom that lets you search for your own messages — just type in what you're looking for into the filter box.

Polishing it up

Before you write the code to take the text and update the high score item, let's improve the design and workings of the Edit High Score screen a little.

Giving the text field focus on-screen opening

For instance, it would be nice if you didn't have to tap on the text field to bring up the keyboard. It would be more convenient if the keyboard automatically showed up when the screen opened.

➤ To accomplish this, add a new method to **EditHighScoreViewController.swift**.

```
override func viewWillAppear(_ animated: Bool) {
  super.viewWillAppear(animated)
  textField.becomeFirstResponder()
}
```

The view controller receives the `viewWillAppear()` message just before it becomes visible. That is a perfect time to make the text field active. You do this by sending it the `becomeFirstResponder()` message.

If you've done programming on other platforms, this is often called "giving the control focus." In iOS terminology, the control becomes the *first responder*.

➤ Run the app and go to the Edit High Score screen. You can start typing right away.

Again, note that the keyboard may not appear on the Simulator. Press ⌘+K to bring it up. The keyboard will always appear when you run the app on an actual device, though.

It's often little features like these that make an app a joy to use. Having to tap on the text field before you can start typing gets old really fast. In this fast-paced age, using their phones on the go, users don't have the patience for that. Such minor annoyances may be reason enough for users to switch to a competitor's app. I always put a lot of effort into making my apps as frictionless as possible.

Styling the text field

With that in mind, let's style the input field a bit.

➤ Open the storyboard and select the text field. Go to the **Attributes inspector** and set the following attributes:

- Placeholder: **High scorer name**

- Font: System 17

- Adjust to Fit: Uncheck this

- Capitalization: Sentences

• Return Key: Done

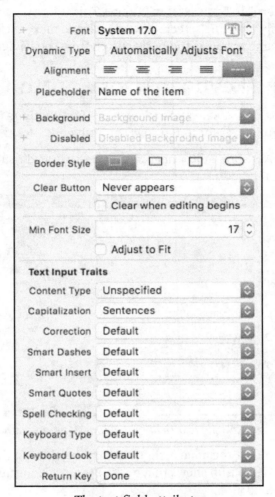

The text field attributes

There are several options here that let you configure the keyboard that appears when the text field becomes active.

If this were a field that only allowed numbers, for example, you would set the Keyboard Type to Number Pad. If it were an email address field, you'd set it to E-mail Address. For our purposes, the Default keyboard is appropriate.

You can also change the text that is displayed on the keyboard's "Return" key. By default, it says "Return" but you set it to "Done." This is just the text on the button, it doesn't automatically close the screen. You still have to make the keyboard's Done button trigger the same action as the Done button from the navigation bar.

Handling the keyboard Done button

➤ Make sure the text field is selected and open the **Connections inspector**. Drag from the **Did End on Exit** event to the view controller and pick the **done** action.

If you still have the Assistant editor open, you can also drag directly to the source code for the done() method.

Connecting the text field to the done() action method

To see the connections for the done action, click on the circle in the gutter next to the method name. The pop-up shows that done() is now connected to both the bar button and the text field:

Viewing the connections for the done() method

➤ Go to the Edit High Score screen. Pressing Done on the keyboard will now close the screen and print the text to the debug area.

The keyboard now has a big blue Done button

Disallowing empty input

Now that you have user input working, It's always good to validate what the user entered to make sure that the input is acceptable. For instance, what should happen if the user taps the Done button on the Edit High Score screen without entering any text?

Having a high score that has no name is not very useful. So, to prevent this, you should disable the Done button when no text has been typed yet.

Of course, you have two Done buttons to take care of: One on the keyboard and one in the navigation bar. Let's start with the Done button from the keyboard as this is the simplest one to fix.

➤ On the **Attributes inspector** for the text field, check **Auto-enable Return Key**.

That's it. Now, when you run the app, the Done button on the keyboard is disabled when there is no text in the text field. Try it out!

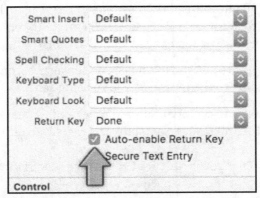

The Auto-enable Return Key option disables the return key when there is no text

For the Done button in the navigation bar, you have to do a little more work. You have to check the contents of the text field after every keystroke to see if it is now empty or not. If it is, then you disable the button.

The user can always press Cancel, but Done only works when there is text.to listen to changes to the text field — which may come from taps on the keyboard but also from cut/paste — you need to make the view controller a delegate for the text field.

The text field will send events to its delegate to let it know what is going on. The delegate, which will be the EditHighScoreViewController, can then respond to these events and take appropriate actions.

A view controller is allowed to be the delegate for more than one object. The EditHighScoreViewController is already a delegate, and data source, for the UITableView because it is a UITableViewController). Now, it will also become the delegate for the text field object: UITextField.

These are two different delegates and you make the view controller play both roles. Later on, you'll add even more delegates for this app.

Becoming a delegate

Delegates are used everywhere in the iOS SDK, so it's good to remember that it always takes three steps to become a delegate:

1. You declare yourself capable of being a delegate. To become the delegate for UITextField you need to include UITextFieldDelegate in the class line for the view controller. This tells the compiler that this particular view controller can actually handle the notification messages that the text field sends to it.

2. You let the object in question, in this case the UITextField, know that the view controller wishes to become its delegate. If you forget to tell the text field that it has a delegate, it will never send you any notifications.

3. Implement the delegate methods. It makes no sense to become a delegate if you're not responding to the messages you're being sent!

Often, delegate methods are optional, so you don't need to implement all of them. For example, UITextFieldDelegate actually declares seven different methods but you only care about textField(_:shouldChangeCharactersIn:replacementString:) for this app.

➤ In **EditHighScoreViewController.swift**, add `UITextFieldDelegate` to the class declaration:

```
class EditHighScoreViewController: UITableViewController,
UITextFieldDelegate {
```

The view controller now says: "I can be a delegate for text field objects."

You also have to let the text field know that you have a delegate for it.

➤ Go to the storyboard and select the text field.

There are several different ways in which you can hook up the text field's delegate outlet to the view controller. One way is to go to its **Connections inspector** and drag from **delegate** to the view controller's little yellow icon:

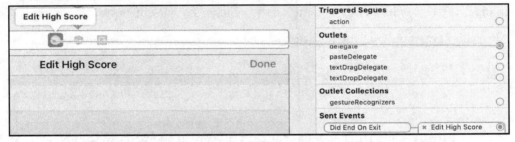

Drag from the Connections inspector to connect the text field delegate

Configuring the Done button

You also have to add an outlet for the Done bar button item so you can send it messages from within the view controller to enable or disable it.

➤ Open the **Assistant editor** and make sure **EditHighScoreViewController.swift** is visible in the assistant pane.

➤ **Control-drag** from the Done bar button into the Swift file and let go. Name the new outlet `doneBarButton`.

This adds the following outlet:

```
@IBOutlet weak var doneBarButton: UIBarButtonItem!
```

➤ Add the following to **EditHighScoreViewController.swift**, at the bottom and before the final curly brace:

```
// MARK:- Text Field Delegates
```

```
func textField(_ textField: UITextField,
               shouldChangeCharactersIn range: NSRange,
               replacementString string: String) -> Bool {

  let oldText = textField.text!
  let stringRange = Range(range, in: oldText)!
  let newText = oldText.replacingCharacters(in: stringRange,
                                            with: string)
  if newText.isEmpty {
    doneBarButton.isEnabled = false
  } else {
    doneBarButton.isEnabled = true
  }
  return true
}
```

This is one of the UITextField delegate methods. It is invoked every time the user changes the text, whether by tapping on the keyboard or via cut/paste.

First, you figure out what the new text will be:

```
let oldText = textField.text!
let stringRange = Range(range, in:oldText)!
let newText = oldText.replacingCharacters(in: stringRange, with:
string)
```

The textField(_:shouldChangeCharactersIn:replacementString:) delegate method doesn't give you the new text, only which part of the text should be replaced (the range) and the text it should be replaced with (the replacement string). You need to calculate what the new text will be by taking the text field's text and doing the replacement yourself. This gives you a new string object that you store in the newText constant.

NSRange vs. Range and NSString vs. String

In the above code, you get a parameter as NSRange and you convert it to a Range value. If you're wondering what a range is, the clue is in the name. A range object gives you a range of values. Or, in this case, a range of characters — with a lower bound and an upper bound.

So, why did we convert the original NSRange value to a Range value, you ask? NSRange is an Objective-C structure whereas Range is its Swift equivalent. They are similar, but not exactly the same.

So, while an NSRange parameter is used by the UITextField — which internally and historically is Objective-C based — in its delegate method, in our Swift code, if we wanted to do any String operations, such as `replacingCharacters`, then we need a Range value instead. Swift methods generally use Range values and do not understand NSRange values. This is why we converted the NSRange value to a Swift-understandable Range value.

There was a different way to approach this problem as well, though it might not be as "Swift-y." We could have converted the Swift `String` value into its Objective-C equivalent: `NSString`. Since Swift is still young, its `String` handling methods aren't as good ... but they are getting better. `NSString` is considered by some to be more powerful and often easier to use than Swift's own `String`.

`String` and `NSString` are "bridged," meaning that you can use `NSString` in place of `String`. `NSString` too has a `replacingCharacters(in:with:)` method and that method takes an `NSRange` as a parameter!

So, you could have simply converted the `String` value to an `NSString` value and then used the `NSString` `replacingCharacters(in:with:)` method with the passed in range value instead of the above code. But personally, I prefer to use Swift types and classes in my code as much as possible. So, I opted to go with the solution above.

By the way, `String` isn't the only object that is bridged to an Objective-C type. Another example is `Array` and its Objective-C counterpart `NSArray`. Because the iOS frameworks are written in a different language than Swift, sometimes these little Objective-C holdovers pop up when you least expect them. Once you have the new text, you check if it's empty and enable or disable the Done button accordingly:

```
if newText.isEmpty {
  doneBarButton.isEnabled = false
} else {
  doneBarButton.isEnabled = true
}
```

However, you could simplify the above code even further. Since `newText.isEmpty` returns a `true` or `false` value, you can discard the `if` condition and use the value returned by `newText.isEmpty` to decide whether the Done button should be enabled or not.

```
doneBarButton.isEnabled = !newText.isEmpty
```

Basically, if the text is not empty, enable the button. Otherwise, don't enable it. That's much more compact and concise, right?

Remember this trick: Whenever you see code like this:

```
if some condition {
  something = true
} else {
  something = false
}
```

You can write it simply as:

```
something = (some condition)
```

In practice, it doesn't really matter which version you use. I prefer the shorter one. That's what the pros do. Just remember that comparison operators such as == and > always return `true` or `false`, so the extra `if` really isn't necessary.

➤ Run the app and type some text into the text field. Now, remove that text and you'll see that the Done button in the navigation bar properly gets disabled when the text field becomes empty.

You can find the project files for the app up to this point under **23-Edit High Score Screen** in the Source Code folder.

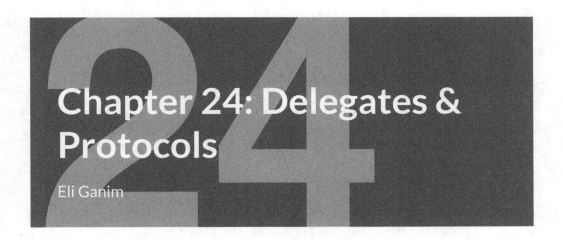

Chapter 24: Delegates & Protocols

Eli Ganim

You now have an Edit High Score screen showing a keyboard that lets the user enter text. The app also properly validates the input so that you'll never end up with text that's empty.

But how do you get this text into HighScoreItem and add it to items on the High Scores screen? That's the topic that this chapter will explore.

Updating HighScoreItem

For editing to work, you'll have to get the Edit High Score screen to notify the High Scores View Controller of the updated `HighScoreItem`. This is one of the fundamental tasks that every iOS app needs to do: Send messages from one view controller to another.

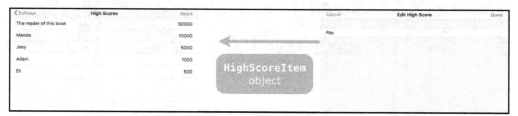

Sending a HighScoreItem object to the screen with the items array

The messy way

> **Exercise**: How would you tackle this problem? `done()` needs to update `HighScoreItem` with the text from the text field, which is easy, then update it in the Table view in `HighScoreViewController`, which is not so easy.

Maybe you came up with something like this:

```
class EditHighScoreViewController: UITableViewController, . . .
{
  // This variable refers to the other view controller
  var highScoresViewController: HighScoresViewController

  @IBAction func done() {
    highScoreItem.name = textField.text!

    // Directly call a method from HighScoresViewController
    highScoresViewController.update(item)
  }
}
```

In this scenario, `EditHighScoreViewController` has a variable that refers to the `HighScoresViewController`, and `done()` calls its `update()` method with the new `HighScoreItem`. This will work, but it's not the iOS way.

The big downside to this approach is that it shackles these two view controller objects together. As a general principle, if screen A launches screen B then you don't want screen B to know too much about the screen that invoked it, A. The less B knows of A, the better.

Giving `EditHighScoreViewController` a direct reference to `HighScoresViewController` prevents you from opening the Edit High Score screen from somewhere else in the app. It can only ever talk back to `HighScoresViewController`. That's a big disadvantage.

You won't need to do this in **Bullseye**, but in many apps, it's common for one screen to be accessible from multiple places. Examples include a login screen that appears after the app has logged a user out for inactivity, or a details screen that shows more information about a tapped item no matter where that item is in the app. You'll see an example of this in the next app.

Therefore, it's best if `EditHighScoreViewController` doesn't know anything about `HighScoresViewController`. But if that's the case, how can you make the two communicate?

The solution is to make your own **delegate**.

The delegate way

You've already seen delegates in a few different places: The Table view has a delegate that responds to taps on the rows. The text field has a delegate that you used to validate the length of the text. The app also has something named the `AppDelegate` (see the project navigator).

It seems like you can't turn a corner in this place without bumping into a delegate. The delegate pattern is commonly used to handle the situation you find yourself in: Screen A opens screen B. At some point screen B needs to communicate back to screen A, usually when it closes. The solution is to make screen A the delegate of screen B so that B can send its messages to A whenever it needs to.

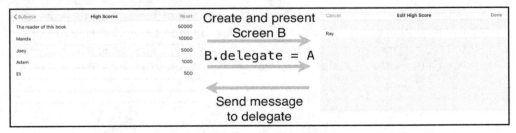

Screen A launches screen B and becomes its delegate

The cool thing about the delegate pattern is that screen B doesn't really know anything about screen A. It knows that *some* object is its delegate, but it doesn't really care who that is. Just like how UITableView doesn't really care about your view controller, only that it delivers Table view cells when the Table view asks for them.

This principle, where screen B is independent of screen A and yet can still talk to it, is called **loose coupling** and is good software design practice.

You'll use the delegate pattern to let the EditHighScoreViewController send notifications back to the HighScoresViewController without it having to know anything about the latter. Delegates go hand-in-hand with **protocols**, a prominent feature of the Swift language.

The delegate protocol

➤ At the top of **EditHighScoreViewController.swift**, add the following after the import line but before the class line — it's not part of the EditHighScoreViewController object:

```
protocol EditHighScoreViewControllerDelegate: class {
  func editHighScoreViewControllerDidCancel(
    _ controller: EditHighScoreViewController)
  func editHighScoreViewController(
    _ controller: EditHighScoreViewController,
    didFinishEditing item: HighScoreItem)
}
```

This defines EditHighScoreViewControllerDelegate. You should recognize that the lines inside protocol { ... } block as method declarations, but unlike the previous methods you've seen, they don't have any source code in them. The protocol just lists the names of the methods.

Think of the delegate protocol as a contract between screen B, or the Edit High Score View Controller in this case, and any screens that wish to use it.

Are you wondering why you have the keyword class after the colon in the protocol name? You might have noticed that the syntax for the protocol declaration looks similar to the one you've used to declare classes previously, giving the name of your class followed by a colon and then specifying the class your class inherited from.

You're seeing exactly the same thing here with protocols: You can have one protocol inherit from another protocol, but you can also specify a particular type of object to adopt your protocol. The `class` keyword identifies that you want to limit `EditHighScoreViewControllerDelegate` to class types.

If you're asking why that is, it's because you mark any references to this protocol as weak. To have weak references, you need a protocol that can only be used with a **reference type**.

You'll read about weak references a bit further along in this chapter; this might all become a little bit clearer at that point.

Protocols [TODO: delete me?]

In Swift, a **protocol** has nothing to do with computer networks or meeting royalty, it's simply a name for a group of methods.

A protocol doesn't usually implement any of the methods it declares. It just says: Any object that conforms to this protocol must implement methods X, Y and Z. There are special cases where you might want to provide a default implementation for a protocol, but that's an advanced topic that you don't need to get into right now.

The two methods listed in `EditHighScoreViewControllerDelegate` are:

- `editHighScoreViewControllerDidCancel(_:)`
- `editHighScoreViewController(_:didFinishAdding:)`

Delegates often have very long method names!

The first method is for when the user presses **Cancel**, while the second is for when they press **Done**. In the latter case, `didFinishAdding` passes along the updated `HighScoreItem`.

For `HighScoresViewController` to conform to this protocol, it must provide implementations for these two methods. From then on, you can refer to `HighScoresViewController` using the protocol name instead of the class name.

If you've programmed in other languages, you may recognize protocols as being very similar to **interfaces**.

In `EditHighScoreViewController`, you can use the following to refer back to `HighScoresViewController`:

```
var delegate: EditHighScoreViewControllerDelegate
```

The variable `delegate` is nothing more than a reference to *some* object that implements the methods of `EditHighScoreViewControllerDelegate`. You can send messages to the object that the `delegate` variable references without knowing what kind of object it really is.

Of course, *you* know the object referenced by `delegate` is the `HighScoresViewController`, but `EditHighScoreViewController` doesn't need to be aware of that. All it sees is some object that implements its delegate protocol.

If you wanted, you could make some other object implement the protocol; `EditHighScoreViewController` would be perfectly fine with that. That's the power of delegation: You have removed – or **abstracted** away – the dependency between the `EditHighScoreViewController` and the rest of the app.

It may seem a little overkill for a simple app such as this, but delegates are one of the cornerstones of iOS development. The sooner you master them, the better!

Notifying the delegate

You're not done in **EditHighScoreViewController.swift** yet. The view controller needs a property that it can use to refer to the delegate; you'll take care of that now.

➤ Add this inside the `EditHighScoreViewController` class, below the outlets:

```
weak var delegate: EditHighScoreViewControllerDelegate?
```

It looks like a regular instance variable declaration, with two differences: `weak` and the question mark.

Delegates are usually declared as being **weak**. This is not a statement of their moral character, but rather a way to describe the relationship between the view controller and its delegate. Delegates are also **optional**, as indicated by the question mark, which you learned a bit about in the previous chapter.

You'll learn more about what that means in a moment.

➤ Add this below the `delegate` declaration:

```
var highScoreItem: HighScoreItem!
```

You'll use this to store the item you're editing.

➤ Replace the `cancel()` and `done()` actions with the following:

```
@IBAction func cancel() {
  delegate?.editHighScoreViewControllerDidCancel(self)
}

@IBAction func done() {
  highScoreItem.name = textField.text!

  delegate?.editHighScoreViewController(self, didFinishEditing:
highScoreItem)
}
```

Now, look at the changes you made. When the user taps the Cancel button, you send the `editHighScoreViewControllerDidCancel(_:)` message back to the delegate.

You do something similar for the Done button, except that the message is `editHighScoreViewController(_:didFinishEditing:)` and you pass along `HighScoreItem`, which has the text string from the text field.

Note: It's customary for the delegate methods to have a reference to their owner as the first (or only) parameter.

Doing this is not required, but it's a good idea. For example, in the case of Table views, an object may be a delegate or data source for more than one Table view. In that case, you'll need to be able to distinguish between those Table views. To allow for this, the Table view delegate methods have a parameter for the `UITableView` that sent the notification. Having this reference also saves you from having to make an `@IBOutlet` for the Table view.

That explains why you pass `self` to your delegate methods. Recall that `self` refers to the object itself: `EditHighScoreViewController`, in this case. It's also why all the delegate method names start with `editHighScoreViewController`.

➤ Run the app and try the Cancel and Done buttons. They no longer work!

Hopefully, you're not too surprised! The Edit High Score screen now depends on a delegate to make it close, but you haven't told it who its delegate is yet.

That means the `delegate` property has no value and the messages aren't being sent to anyone – there is no one listening for them.

Optionals

You read a few times before that variables and constants in Swift must always have a value. In other programming languages, the special symbol nil or NULL is often used to indicate that a variable has no value. Swift doesn't allow this for normal variables.

The problem with nil and NULL is that they frequently cause apps to crash. If an app attempts to use a variable that is nil when you expect it to have a value, the app will crash. This is the dreaded **null pointer dereference** error.

Swift avoids these crashes by preventing you from using nil with regular variables.

However, sometimes a variable does need to have "no value." In that case, you can make it an **optional**. You mark something as optional in Swift using either a question mark ? or an exclamation point !.

Only variables that are optional can have a nil value.

You've already seen the question mark used with IndexPath?, the return type of tableView(_:willSelectRowAt:). Returning nil from this method is a valid response; it means that the table should not select a particular row.

The question mark tells Swift that it's OK for the method to return nil instead of an actual IndexPath object.

Variables that refer to a delegate are usually marked as optional, too. You can tell because there's a question mark behind the type:

```
weak var delegate: EditHighScoreViewControllerDelegate?
```

Thanks to the ?, it's perfectly acceptable for a delegate to be nil.

You may be wondering why the delegate would ever be nil. Doesn't that negate the idea of having a delegate in the first place? Well, there are two reasons.

Often, delegates are truly optional; a UITableView works fine even if you don't implement any of its delegate methods, although you do need to provide at least some of its data source methods.

More importantly, when you load EditHighScoreViewController from the storyboard and instantiate it, it won't know right away who its delegate is. Between the time the view controller is loaded and the delegate is assigned, the delegate variable will be nil. And variables that can be nil, even if only temporarily, must be optionals.

When delegate is nil, you don't want cancel() or done() to send any of the messages. Doing that would crash the app because there is no one to receive the messages. Swift has a handy shorthand for skipping the work when delegate is not set:

```
delegate?.editHighScoreViewControllerDidCancel(self)
```

Here the ? tells Swift not to send the message if delegate is nil. You can read this as, "Is there a delegate? Then send the message." This practice is called **optional chaining** and it's used a lot in Swift.

In this app, delegate should never be nil – that would get users stuck on the Edit High Score screen. However, Swift doesn't know that, so you'll have to pretend that it can happen anyway and use optional chaining to send messages to the delegate.

Optionals aren't common in other programming languages, so they may take some getting used to. I find that optionals do make programs clearer – most variables never have to be nil, so it's good to prevent them from becoming nil and avoid potential sources of bugs. Remember, if you see ? or ! in a Swift program, you're dealing with optionals. In the course of this app, I'll come back to this topic a few more times and explain the finer points of using optionals in more detail.

Conforming to the delegate protocol

Before you can give EditHighScoreViewController its delegate, you need to make HighScoresViewController suitable to play the role of a delegate.

➤ In **HighScoresViewController.swift**, change the class line to the following (this all goes on one line):

```
class HighScoresViewController: UITableViewController,
EditHighScoreViewControllerDelegate {
```

This tells the compiler that HighScoresViewController now promises to follow the EditHighScoreViewControllerDelegate protocol. Or, in programming terminology, that it **conforms** to the EditHighScoreViewControllerDelegate protocol.

Xcode should now throw up an error: "Type HighScoresViewController does not conform to protocol EditHighScoreViewControllerDelegate."

```
class HighScoresViewController: UITableViewController,
  EditHighScoreViewControllerDelegate| {
  var items = [HighScoreItem](  ⊙  Type 'HighScoresViewController' does not conform to protocol  ⊗
                                   'EditHighScoreViewControllerDelegate'
  override func viewDidLoad()
    super.viewDidLoad()           Do you want to add protocol stubs?                              Fix
```

Xcode warns about not conforming to protocol

That is correct: You still need to add the methods that are listed in
EditHighScoreViewControllerDelegate. With the latest version of Xcode, there's
an easy way to get started fixing this issue — see that **Fix** button? Simply click it.

Xcode will add in the stubs, or the bare minimum code, for the missing methods.
You'll have to add in the actual implementation for each method, of course.

➤ Add the implementations for the protocol methods to
HighScoresViewController:

```
// MARK:- Edit High Score ViewController Delegates
func editHighScoreViewControllerDidCancel(
                    _ controller:
  EditHighScoreViewController) {
  navigationController?.popViewController(animated:true)
}
func editHighScoreViewController(
               _ controller: EditHighScoreViewController,
       didFinishEditing item: HighScoreItem) {
  navigationController?.popViewController(animated:true)
}
```

Currently, both methods simply close the Edit High Score screen, which is what the
EditHighScoreViewController used to do with its cancel() and done() actions.
You've simply moved that responsibility to the delegate. You haven't added the code
that updates the HighScoreItem object in the Table view yet. You'll do that in a
moment, but there's something else you need to do first.

5.

You've done the first four steps, so there's just one more thing you need to do — step
5: tell EditHighScoreViewController that HighScoresViewController is its
delegate.

The proper place to do that is in the prepare(for:sender:) method, also known as
prepare-for-segue.

UIKit invokes `prepare(for:sender:)` right before it performs a segue from one screen to another. Remember that the segue is the arrow between two view controllers in the storyboard.

Using prepare-for-segue allows you to pass data to the new view controller before displaying it. You'll usually do this by setting one or more of the new view controller's properties.

➤ Add this method to **HighScoresViewController.swift**:

```
// MARK:- Navigation
override func prepare(for segue: UIStoryboardSegue,
                      sender: Any?) {
  // 1
  let controller = segue.destination as!
EditHighScoreViewController
  // 2
  controller.delegate = self
  // 3
  if let indexPath = tableView.indexPath(for: sender as!
UITableViewCell) {
    controller.highScoreItem = items[indexPath.row]
  }
}
```

This is what the above code does, step by step:

1. You find the new view controller that you want to display in `segue.destination`. `destination` is of type `UIViewContoller`, since the new view controller could be any view controller subclass.

    To handle that issue, you **cast** `destination` to `EditHighScoreViewController` to get a reference to an object with the right type. The `as!` keyword is known as a **type cast** or a **force downcast** since you are casting an object of one type to a different type.

    Do note that if you downcast objects of completely different types, you might get a `nil` value. Casting works here because `EditHighScoreViewController` is a sub-class of `UIViewContoller`.[TODO: FPE: Is this spacing OK? I can't see how it renders, so I can't verify.]

2. Once you have a reference to `EditHighScoreViewController`, you set its `delegate` property to `self`. This tells `EditHighScoreViewController` that from now on, the object identified as `self` is its delegate. But what is "self" here? Well, since you're editing **HighScoresViewController.swift**, `self` refers to `HighScoresViewController`.

3. The parameter `sender` contains a reference to the control that triggered the segue. In this case, it refers to the Table view cell which you tapped.

    You use that `UITableViewCell` object to find the Table view row number by looking up the corresponding index path using `tableView.indexPath(for:)`.

    The return type of `indexPath(for:)` is `IndexPath?`, an optional, meaning it could return `nil`. That's why you need to unwrap this optional value with `if let` before you can use it.

    Once you have the index path, you obtain the `HighScoreItem` object to edit and you assign it to `EditHighScoreViewController`'s `highScoreItem` property.

Excellent! `HighScoresViewController` is now the delegate of `EditHighScoreViewController`. It took some work, but you're almost set now.

Now that you have a reference to the item you're editing, you can make the screen actually show the name of the current high scorer before you edit it.

➤ Open **EditHighScoreViewController.swift** and add this to `viewDidLoad()`:

```
textField.text = highScoreItem.name
```

➤ Run the app, click on any high score and see that the edit item screen now has the current name already in the text field.

Updating the table view

If you change the name and click **Done**, you'll update the item itself, but the Table view will still show the old value. That's because you didn't tell the Table view to refresh the cell after the data changed. Time to fix it!

➤ Change the implementation of the `didFinishEditing` delegate method in **HighScoresViewController.swift** to the following:

```
func editHighScoreViewController(_ controller:
EditHighScoreViewController,
                                 didFinishEditing item:
HighScoreItem) {
  // 1
  if let index = items.firstIndex(of: item) {
    // 2
    let indexPath = IndexPath(row: index, section: 0)
    let indexPaths = [indexPath]
    // 3
    tableView.reloadRows(at: indexPaths, with: .automatic)
```

```
    }
    // 4
    PersistencyHelper.saveHighScores(items)
    navigationController?.popViewController(animated:true)
}
```

Here's what this new code does:

1. To update the cell, you need the `IndexPath` of that cell. The cell index is the same as the index of `HighScoreItem` in the `items` array. You can use `firstIndex(of:)` to return that index.

   Now, it won't happen here, but it's possible that you could use `index(of:)` on an object that's not actually in the array. To account for that possibility, `index(of:)` doesn't return a normal value, it returns an optional. If the object is not part of the array, the returned value is `nil`.

   That's why you need to use `if let` here to unwrap the return value from `index(of:)`.

2. You create a new array of `IndexPath` objects to update. In this case, there's only one cell you want to update so you create an array with a single index path.

3. You tell the Table view to update that specific cell. Keep in mind that, should you ever need to, you can also use `insertRows(at:with:)` and `deleteRows(at:with:)`.

4. Eventually, you save the updated list of high scores and pop [TODO: FPE: Is "pop" right word? Should it be "populate" instead?] the view controller

➤ Try to build the app. Oops, Xcode has found another reason to complain:

```
if let index = items.firstIndex(of: item) {
    let indexPath = IndexP  ⓘ  Argument type 'HighScoreItem' does not conform to expected type   ⊗
    let indexPaths = [inde      'Equatable'
    tableView.reloadRows(a...........................................
```

New Xcode error

Xcode displays this error because you can't use `firstIndex(of:)` on just any array, or collection of objects. An object has to be "equatable" if you are to use `firstIndex(of:)` on an array of that object type.

That's because `firstIndex(of:)` needs a way to compare the object that you're looking for against the objects in the array, to see if they are equal.

Your `HighScoreItem` object does not have any functionality for that yet. There are a few ways you can fix this, but in this case, you[1]ll use the easy one.

➤ In **HighScoreItem.swift**, change the class line to:

```
class HighScoreItem : NSObject, Codable {
```

If you've programmed in Objective-C before, you'll be familiar with NSObject.

Almost all objects in Objective-C programs are based on NSObject. It's the most basic building block that iOS provides, and it offers a bunch of useful functionality that standard Swift objects don't have.

You can write many Swift programs without having to resort to NSObject but in times like these, it comes in handy.

Building HighScoreItem on top of NSObject is enough to satisfy the "equatable" requirement. In case you're interested, the other way to do this would have been to specify that HighScoreItem conforms to the Equatable protocol. But then you'd have to implement an additional method to indicate how the comparison of two HighScoreItem instances would happen. So going with NSObject conformance is easier, for the time being.

➤ Build and run the app again and verify that editing items works now. Excellent!

Weak

I promised you an explanation of the weak keyword. Relationships between objects can be weak or strong. You use weak relationships to avoid an **ownership cycle**.

When object A has a strong reference to object B, and at the same time object B also has a strong reference back to A, then these two objects are involved in a dangerous kind of romance: An ownership cycle.

Normally, you destroy, or **deallocate**, an object when there are no more strong references to it. But because A and B have strong references to each other, they keep each other alive.

The result is a potential **memory leak**, where an object isn't destroyed, even though it should be, and the memory for its data is never reclaimed. With enough such leaks, iOS will run out of available memory and your app will crash. I told you it was dangerous!

Due to the strong references between them, A owns B and at the same time, B also owns A:

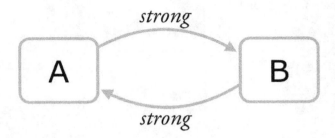

To avoid ownership cycles you can make one of these references weak.

In the case of a view controller and its delegate, screen A usually has a strong reference to screen B, but B only has a weak reference back to its delegate, A.

Because of the weak reference, B no longer owns A:

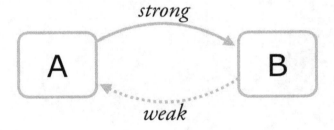

Now there is no ownership cycle.

Such cycles can occur in other situations, too, but they are most common with delegates. Therefore, you should always make delegates weak.

There is another relationship type that is similar to weak and that you can also use delegates: unowned. The difference is that weak variables can be nil. However, you don't need to worry about that right now.

Usually, you also declare @IBOutlets with the weak keyword. This isn't done to avoid an ownership cycle, but to make it clear that the view controller isn't really the owner of the views from the outlets.

In the course of this book, you'll learn more about weak, strong, optionals and the relationships between objects. These are important concepts in Swift, but they may take a while to make sense. If you don't understand them immediately, don't lose any sleep over it!

You can find the project files for the app up to this point under **24-Delegates and Protocols** in the Source Code folder.

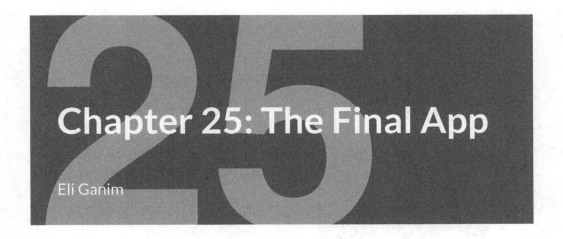

Chapter 25: The Final App

Eli Ganim

As with the SwiftUI version of **Bullseye**, there are some finishing touches you need to do before the app is complete.

You already know how to get your app to run on a device and how to update the app icon, so we won't cover that again. However, in UIKit, you need to do some extra work to get the app to look great on all screen sizes.

You've been developing and testing for a 4.7" screen like those found on devices such as the iPhone 8. But what about other iPhones such as the 5.5-inch iPhone Plus or the 5.8-inch iPhone X, which have bigger screens? Or the iPad with its various screen sizes? Will the game work correctly on all these different screen sizes?

This chapter covers the following:

- **Supporting different screen sizes**: Ensuring that the app will run correctly on all the different iPhone and iPad screen sizes.

- **Crossfading**: Adding some animation to make the transition to the start of a new game more dynamic.

Supporting different screen sizes

First, check if there is, indeed, an issue running Bullseye on a device with a larger screen.

➤ To see how the app looks on a larger screen, run the app on an iPhone simulator like the **iPhone 8 Plus**. You can switch between simulators using the selector at the top of the Xcode window:

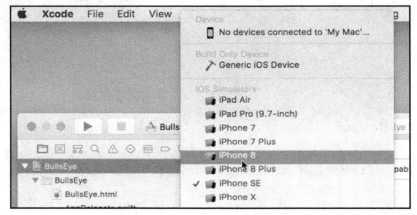

Using the scheme selector to switch to the iPhone 8 simulator

The result might not be what you expected:

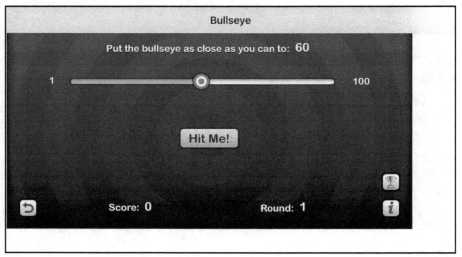

On the iPhone 8 simulator, the app doesn't fill the entire screen

Obviously, this won't do. Not everybody is going to be using a 4.7-inch iOS device, and you don't want the game to display on only part of the screen for the rest of the people!

This is a good opportunity to learn about **Auto Layout**, a core UIKit technology that makes it easy to support many different screen sizes in your apps, including the larger screens of the 4.7-inch, 5.5-inch and 5.8-inch iPhones as well as the iPad.

Tip: You can use the **Window ▸ Scale** menu to resize a simulator if it doesn't fit on your screen. Some of those simulators, like the one for the iPad, can be monsters! Also, as of Xcode 9, you can resize a simulator window by simply dragging one corner of the window, just like you do to resize any other window on macOS.

Interface Builder has a few handy tools to help you make the game fit on any screen.

The background image

➤ Go to **Main.storyboard**. Open the **View as**: panel at the bottom and choose the **iPhone 8 Plus** device. You may need to change the orientation back to landscape.

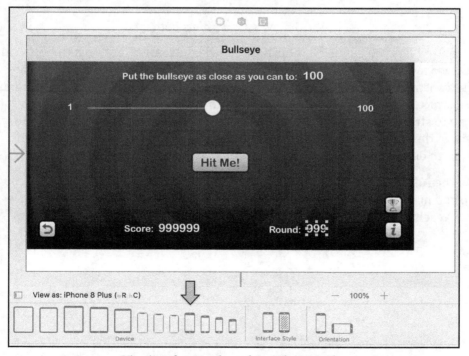

Viewing the storyboard on iPhone 8 Plus

The storyboard should look like your screen from the iPhone 8 Plus simulator. This shows you how changes on the storyboard affect the bigger iPhone screens.

First, let's fix the background image. At its normal size, the image is too small to fit on the larger screens.

This is where Auto Layout comes to the rescue.

➤ In the storyboard, select the **Background image view** on the main **view controller** and click the small **Add New Constraints** button at the bottom of the Xcode window:

The Add New Constraints button

This button lets you define relationships, called **constraints**, between the currently-selected view and other views in the scene. When you run the app, UIKit evaluates these constraints and calculates the final layout of the views. This probably sounds a bit abstract, but you'll soon see how it works in practice. In order for the background image to stretch from edge to edge on the screen, the left, top, right and bottom edges of the image should be flush against the screen's edges. You can use Auto Layout to do this.

➤ In the **Add New Constraints** menu, set the **left**, **top**, **right** and **bottom** spacing to zero and make sure that you've enabled the red I-beam markers next to (or above/below) each item.

The red I-beams indicate which constraints you've enabled when adding new constraints:

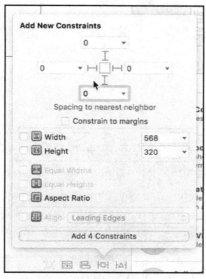

Using the Add New Constraints menu to position the background image

➤ Press **Add 4 Constraints** to finish. The background image will now cover the view fully. Press **Undo** and **Redo** a few times to see the difference.

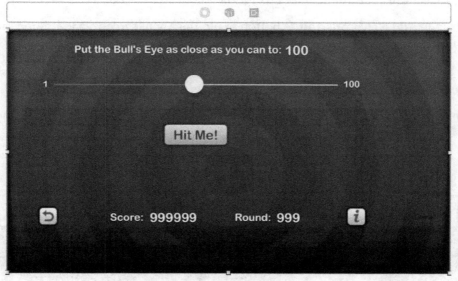

The background image now covers the whole view

You might have also noticed that the Document Outline now has a new item called **Constraints**:

The new Auto Layout constraints appear in the Document Outline

There should be four constraints listed there, one for each edge of the image.

➤ Run the app again on the iPhone 8 Plus Simulator and also on the iPhone 8 Simulator. In both cases, the background should display correctly now. Of course, the other controls are still off-center, but you'll fix that soon.

If you use the **View as** panel to switch the storyboard back to the iPhone 8, the background should display correctly there, too.

The About screen

Let's repeat the background image fix for the About screen, too.

➤ Use the **Add New Constraints** button to pin the About screen's background image view to the parent view.

The background image is now fine. Of course, the Close button and web view are still completely off.

➤ In the storyboard, drag the **Close** button so that it snaps to the center of the view as well as to the bottom guide.

Interface Builder shows a handy guide, the dotted blue line, near the edges of the screen. This is useful for aligning objects by hand.

The dotted blue lines are guides that help position your UI elements

You want to create a centering constraint that keeps the Close button in the middle of the screen, regardless of how wide the screen is.

➤ Click the **Close** button to select it. From the **Align** menu, which is to the left of the Add New Constraints button, choose **Horizontally in Container** and click **Add 1 Constraint**.

The Align menu

Interface Builder now draws a blue bar to represent the constraint. It draws a red box around the button as well.

The Close button has red borders

That's a problem: The red box indicates that something is wrong with the constraints, which usually means that there aren't enough of them. The thing to remember is this: For each view, there must always be enough constraints to define both its position and its size.

The Close button already knows its size – you typed it into the Size inspector earlier.

But for its position, there's only a constraint for the X-coordinate (the alignment in the horizontal direction). You also need to add a constraint for the Y-coordinate.

As you've noticed, there are different types of constraints — there are alignment constraints and spacing constraints, like the ones you added via the Add New Constraints button. In this case, you want to add a spacing constraint. [TODO: FPE: I added this last sentence, please verify it's OK --editor]

➤ With the **Close** button still selected, click on the **Add New Constraints** button.

You want the Close button to always sit at a distance of 20 points from the bottom of the screen.

➤ In the **Add New Constraints** menu, in the **Spacing to nearest neighbor** section, set the bottom spacing to **20** and make sure that you've enabled the I-beam above the text box.

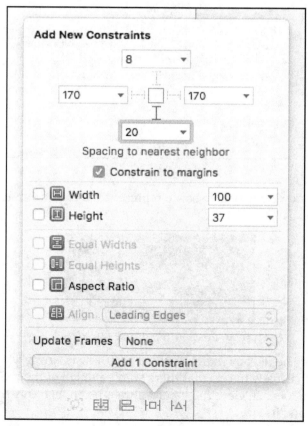

The red I-beams determine the sides that you have pinned down

➤ Click **Add 1 Constraint** to finish.

The red border will now turn blue, meaning that everything is OK:

The constraints on the Close button are valid

If you see orange bars instead of blue ones at this point, then something's still wrong with your Auto Layout constraints:

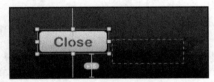

The views are not positioned according to the constraints

This happens when the constraints are valid (otherwise some, or all, of the bars or borders would be red) but the view is not in the right place in the scene. The dashed orange box off to the side is where Auto Layout has calculated the view should be, based on the constraints you have given it.

To fix this issue, select the **Close** button again and click the **Update Frames** button at the bottom of the Interface Builder canvas.

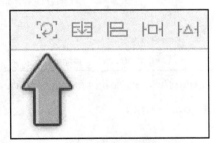

The Update Frames button

You can also use the **Editor ▸ Resolve Auto Layout Issues ▸ Update Frames** item from the menu bar.

The Close button should always be perfectly centered now, regardless of the device's screen size.

Note: What happens if you don't add any constraints to your views? In that case, Xcode will automatically add constraints when it builds the app. That's why you didn't need to bother with any of this before.

However, these default constraints may not always do what you want. For example, they will not automatically resize your views to accommodate larger (or smaller) screens. If you want that to happen, then it's up to you to add your own constraints. After all, Auto Layout can't read your mind!

As soon as you add just one constraint to a view, Xcode will no longer add any other automatic constraints to that view. From then on, you're responsible for adding enough constraints so that UIKit always knows what the position and size of the view will be.

There's one thing left to fix in the About screen: The web view.

➤ Select the **Web View** and open the **Add New Constraints** menu. First, make sure you've unchecked **Constrain to margins**. Click all four I-beam icons so they become solid red and then set their spacing to 20 points, except the bottom one which should be 8 points:

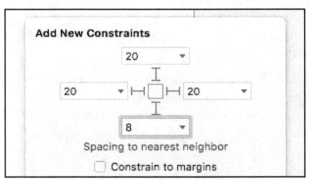

Creating the constraints for the web view

➤ Finish by clicking **Add 4 Constraints**.

There are now four constraints on the web view, indicated by the blue bars on each side:

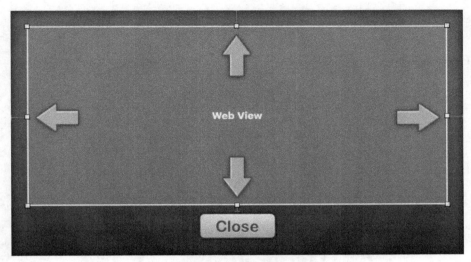

The four constraints on the web view

Three of these constraints pin the Web view to the Main view, so that they always resize together, while one connects the Web view to the Close button. This is enough to determine the size and position of the web view in any scenario.

Fixing the rest of the main scene

Back to the main game scene, which still needs some work.

The game now looks a bit lopsided on bigger screens. You'll fix that by placing all the labels, buttons and the slider into a new "Container" view. Using Auto Layout, you'll center that Container view in the screen, regardless of how big the screen is.

➤ Select all the labels, the buttons and the slider. You can hold down **Command** and click them individually, but an easier method is to go to the **Document Outline**, click on the first view (for me that's the "Put the Bullseye as close as you can to:" label) and then hold down Shift and click on the last view.

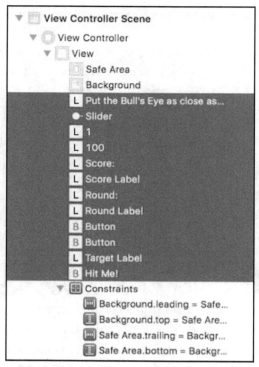

Selecting the views from the Document Outline

You should have selected everything but the background image view.

➤ From Xcode's menu bar, choose **Editor ▸ Embed In ▸ View**. This places the selected views inside a new container view:

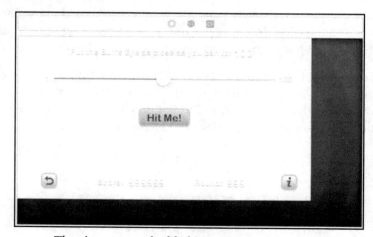

The views are embedded in a new container view

This new view is completely white. You'll want to change this eventually, but for now, it makes it easier to add the constraints.

➤ Select the newly-added **container view** and open the **Add New Constraints** menu. Check the boxes for **Width** and **Height** to make constraints for them and leave the width and height at the values specified by Interface Builder. Click **Add 2 Constraints** to finish.

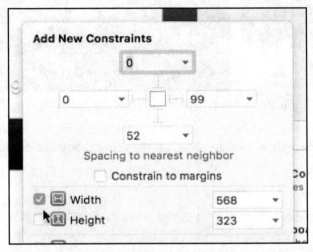

Pinning the width and height of the container view

Interface Builder now draws several bars around the view that represent the Width and Height constraints that you just made... but they're red. Don't panic! It only means that there aren't enough constraints yet. No problem, you'll add the missing constraints next.

➤ With the container view still selected, open the **Align menu**. Check the **Horizontally in Container** and **Vertically in Container** options, then click **Add 2 Constraints**.

All of the Auto Layout bars should be blue now, and the view is perfectly centered.

➤ Finally, change the **Background** color of the container view to **Clear Color** – in other words, 100% transparent.

You now have a layout that works correctly on any iPhone display! Try it out:

The game running on 4-inch and 5.5-inch iPhones

Auto Layout may take a while to get used to. Adding constraints in order to position UI elements is a little less obvious than just dragging them into place.

But this also buys you a lot of power and flexibility, which you need when you're dealing with devices that have different screen sizes.

You'll learn more about Auto Layout in the other parts of **The iOS Apprentice**.

Exercise: As you try the game on different devices, you might notice something — the controls for the game are always centered on screen, but they do not take up the whole area of the screen on bigger devices!

This is because you set the container view for the controls to be a specific size. If you want the controls to change position and size depending on how much screen space is available, then you have to remove the container view or set it to resize depending on screen size. You then need to set up the Auto Layout constraints for each control separately.

Are you up to the challenge of doing this on your own?

Compiler warning

There's a compiler warning about views without any layout constraints that's been there since from almost the first time you created the main game view.

But where are these views without constraints? The Issue navigator certainly does not give you any clue! You have to go to a different screen to find the list of affected views.

If you look at the Document Outline, you'll notice that there's a small yellow circle with an arrow inside it next to the View Controller Scene — an indication that there are some warnings (not errors). If you click this circle, it will bring you to a list of Auto Layout issues in the scene:

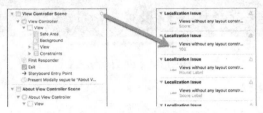

List of Auto Layout issues for your scene

You'll notice that all the controls inside the container view have warnings. This is because none of those views have any Auto Layout constraints, so they'll remain at their original positions when the view displays.

So how do you fix these warnings? Simple enough — add some constraints for each view so that Auto Layout can determine the view's size and position when it displays. Of course, you have the necessary knowledge at this point to do that yourself. So I'll leave it to you to tackle as a personal challenge.

If you get stuck, check out the final project provided for this chapter — that should show you how I fixed the issues.

Testing on iPhone X

So it looks as if you got the app working correctly for all devices, right?

Well... not quite!

Try running the app on the iPhone X simulator. You should see something like this:

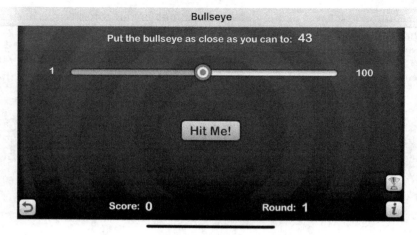

The game on iPhone X

Whoa! What happened?

In Xcode 9, Apple introduced a new mechanism to go along with Auto Layout for the iPhone X screen. Since the iPhone X has a notch at the top, you don't want your app to display its content beneath the notch, since that content would not display properly.

So, Xcode 9 has **safe layout guides** that define where it's safe to display content. If you take a look at the Auto Layout constraints for the background image on the main scene (or even the About scene, for that matter), you will notice that the background image aligns to the safe area.

Just to be clear, this is the correct behavior for most apps — you want your content to stick to the safe area. However, in the case of a game like **Bullseye** where you have a custom background, you want the background to cover the entire screen.

So how do you fix it? Simple enough... just change the image constraints so that they align with the superview, which is the main view for the scene.

➤ Select the background image in the main scene and switch to the **Size inspector**. It should show the four constraints set on the image:

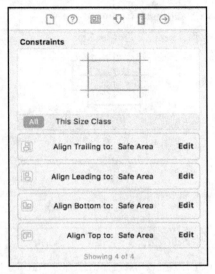

Auto Layout constraints for your image

➤ Double-click the first one. You should get a detailed editor for that Auto Layout constraint:

Auto Layout constraint editor

➤ Click the drop-down for **First Item** and change it from **Safe Area** to **Superview**. Also, if the **Constant** field has a non-zero value, change it to 0.

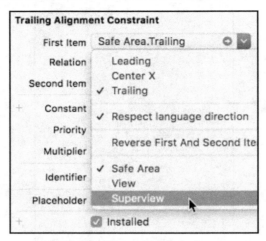

Edit Auto Layout constraints

➤ Do the same for the other three constraints. Note that for two of the constraints, Safe Area will be the Second Item and not the First Item. So change either one based on which one specifies Safe Area.

➤ Build and run your app on both the iPhone X simulator and at least one of the other simulators, like the iPhone 8 Plus, to make sure that your changes work correctly on all devices.

Crossfade

There's one final bit of knowledge I want to impart before calling the game complete — Core Animation. This technology makes it easy to create really sweet animations in your apps with just a few lines of code. Adding subtle animations (with the emphasis on subtle!) can make your app a delight to use.

So next, you'll add a simple crossfade after the user presses the **Start Over**, so the transition back to round one won't seem so abrupt.

➤ In **ViewController.swift**, change startNewGame() to:

```
@IBAction func startNewGame() {
  ...
  startNewRound()
  // Add the following lines
```

```
    let transition = CATransition()
    transition.type = CATransitionType.fade
    transition.duration = 1
    transition.timingFunction = CAMediaTimingFunction(name:
                                CAMediaTimingFunctionName.easeOut)
    view.layer.add(transition, forKey: nil)
}
```

I'm not going to go into too much detail here. Suffice it to say you're setting up an animation that crossfades from what is currently on the screen to the changes you're making in startNewRound(). You reset the slider to center position and reset the values of the labels.

➤ Run the app and move the slider so that it's no longer in the center. Press the **Start Over** button and you should see a subtle crossfade animation.

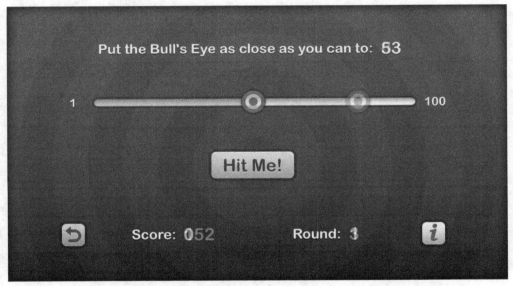

The screen crossfades between the old and new states

UIKit knowledge unlocked!

You're now familiar with SwiftUI and UIKit. Well done!

In the Source Code folder for this book, you can find the complete source code for the UIKit version of the **Bullseye** app. If you're still unclear about something in this chapter, it's a good idea to look at this cleaned-up source code.

If you're feeling exhausted after all that coding, pour yourself a drink and put your feet up for a bit. You've earned it! On the other hand, if you just can't wait to get to grips with more code, go ahead and move on to the next app!

Section 4: My Locations

With this fourth section and the MyLocations app, you get into Swift programming in earnest.

Sure you've already done coding in the previous sections, but this section starts with a good review of all the Swift coding principles you've learned so far and added to it by introducing some new concepts, too. In addition to that, you learn about using GPS coordinates, displaying data on maps, and using the iOS image picker to take photos using your camera or to pick existing images from your photo album. There's a lot of valuable general information on Swift development as well as specific information about building location-aware apps.

This section contains the following chapters:

26. Swift Review: You have made great progress. You have built your first app using UIKit which is some achievement. Whilst we have been writing the apps using Swift, you will need some additional theory to level up your knowledge. In this chapter, we will go into details about some of the Swift language, such as Variables, Constants, Types, Methods & Functions, Loops, and Objects.

27. Get Location Data: Are you ready for the final app challenge? In this chapter, you will commence the final app MyLocations. It's all about using the Core Location framework and displaying using MapKit.

28. Use Location Data: You've learned about getting GPS coordinate information. Now it's time to deal with GPS errors, improving GPS results and testing on real devices to mimic real-world scenarios.

29. Objects vs. Classes: This question will most likely crop up in your next iOS interview. It's time to put the toolbox down and learn some theory. Expect to learn about classes, inheritance, overriding methods and casting an object.

30. The Tag Location Screen: In this chapter, you will be picking up the toolbox again and building our tag location screen. This involves building out some TableViewCells, displaying location info and adding a category picker.

31. Adding Polish: Who doesn't love adding a bit of polish? It's time to start making it look more like an app ready for the App Store. We will improve the experience of the app and add a loading 'HUD'.

32. Saving Locations: At this point, you have an app that obtains GPS coordinates and allows the user to tag the location. We're going to be deep-diving into Core Data, the object persistence framework for iOS apps.

33. The Locations Tab: Now that you can persist the data to Core Data, we're going to explore displaying this data in the TableView. Learn about TableView sections, NSFetchedResults and add functionality to delete tagged locations.

34. Maps: Showing a list of locations is great, but not very visually appealing. In this chapter, you will learn about MapKit, the awesome map view control giving in the iOS toolbox.

35. Image Picker: UIKit comes with a built-in view controller, UIImagePickerController that lets users take new photos or select existing ones. In this chapter explore this controller and how best to display the image on the screen.

36. Polishing the App: You have made it this far! It's time to give MyLocations a complete makeover. Prepare your pixel paintbrush for this chapter and let's get your creative flair at the ready. In this chapter you will cover the map screen improvements by adding icons, polishing the main screen and adding some cool effects to the app.

Print Book Edition

You're reading the print edition of *iOS Apprentice*. This edition contains all of sections 1—3 and the first half of Section 4. Due to print size limitations, the final chapters are available to you as part of the downloadable source code materials.

You can download the source code materials here: https://store.raywenderlich.com/products/ios-apprentice-source-code.

Chapter 26: Swift Review

Eli Ganim

You have made great progress! You've learned the basics of Swift programming and created two applications from scratch, one of them in SwiftUI and the other in UIKit. You are on the threshold of creating your next app.

A good building needs a good foundation. And in order to strengthen the foundations of your Swift knowledge, you first need some additional theory. There is still a lot more to learn about Swift and object-oriented programming!

In the previous chapters, you saw a fair bit of the Swift programming language already, but not quite everything. Previously, it was good enough if you could more-or-less follow along, but now is the time to fill in the gaps in the theory. So, here's a little refresher on what you've learned so far.

In this chapter, you will cover the following:

- **Variables, constants and types**: the difference between variables and constants, and what a type is.

- **Methods and functions**: what are methods and functions — are they the same thing?

- **Making decisions**: an explanation of the various programming constructs that can be used in the decision making process for your programs.

- **Loops**: how do you loop through a list of items?

- **Objects**: all you ever wanted to know about Objects — what they are, their component parts, how to use them, and how not to abuse them.

- **Protocols**: the nitty, gritty details about protocols.

Variables, constants and types

A **variable** is a temporary container for a specific type of value:

```
var count: Int
var shouldRemind: Bool
var text: String
var list: [ChecklistItem]
```

The **data type**, or just **type**, of a variable determines what kind of values it can contain. Some variables hold simple values such as Int or Bool, others hold more complex objects such as String or Array.

The basic types you've used so far are: Int for whole numbers, Float for numbers with decimals (also known as *floating-point* numbers), and Bool for boolean values (true or false).

There are a few other fundamental types as well:

• Double. Similar to a Float but with more precision. You will use Doubles later on for storing latitude and longitude data.

• Character. Holds a single character. A String is a collection of Characters.

• UInt. A variation on Int that you may encounter occasionally. The U stands for *unsigned*, meaning the data type can hold positive values only. It's called unsigned because it cannot have a negative sign (-) in front of the number. UInt can store numbers between 0 and 18 quintillion, but no negative numbers.

• Int8, UInt8, Int16, UInt16, Int32, UInt32, Int64, UInt64. These are all variations on Int. The difference is in how many bytes they have available to store their values. The more bytes, the bigger the values they can store. In practice, you almost always use Int, which uses 8 bytes for storage on a 64-bit platform (a fact that you may immediately forget) and can fit positive and negative numbers up to about 19 digits. Those are big numbers!

• CGFloat. This isn't really a Swift type but a type defined by the iOS SDK. It's a decimal point number like Float and Double. For historical reasons, this is used throughout UIKit for floating-point values. (The "CG" prefix stands for the **Core Graphics** framework.)

Swift is very strict about types, more so than many other languages. If the type of a variable is Int, you cannot put a Float value into it. The other way around also won't work: an Int won't go into a Float.

Even though both types represent numbers of some sort, Swift won't automatically convert between different number types. You always need to convert the values explicitly.

For example:

```
var i = 10
var f: Float
f = i          // error
f = Float(i)   // OK
```

You don't always need to specify the type when you create a new variable. If you give the variable an initial value, Swift uses **type inference** to determine the type:

```
var i = 10            // Int
var d = 3.14          // Double
var b = true          // Bool
var s = "Hello, world" // String
```

The integer value 10, the floating-point value 3.14, the boolean true and the string "Hello, world" are named **literal constants** or just **literals**.

Note that using the value 3.14 in the example above leads Swift to conclude that you want to use a Double here. If you intended to use a Float instead, you'd have to write:

```
var f: Float = 3.14
```

The : Float bit is called a **type annotation**. You use it to override the guess made by Swift's type inference mechanism, since it doesn't always get things right.

Likewise, if you wanted the variable i to be a Double instead of an Int, you'd write:

```
var i: Double = 10
```

Or a little shorter, by giving the value 10 a decimal point:

```
var i = 10.0
```

These simple literals such as 10, 3.14, or "Hello world", are useful only for creating variables of the basic types — Int, Double, String, and so on. To use more complex types, you'll need to **instantiate** an object first.

When you write the following,

```
var item: ChecklistItem
```

it only tells Swift you want to store a ChecklistItem object into the item variable, but it does not create that ChecklistItem object itself. For that you need to write:

```
item = ChecklistItem()
```

This first reserves memory to hold the object's data, followed by a call to init() to properly set up the object for use. Reserving memory is also called **allocation**; filling up the object with its initial value(s) is **initialization**.

The whole process is known as **instantiating** the object — you're making an object **instance**. The instance is the block of memory that holds the values of the object's variables (that's why they are called "instance variables," get it?).

Of course, you can combine the above into a single line:

```
var item = ChecklistItem()
```

Here you left out the : ChecklistItem type annotation because Swift is smart enough to realize that the type of item should be ChecklistItem.

However, you can't leave out the () parentheses — this is how Swift knows that you want to make a new ChecklistItem instance.

Some objects allow you to pass **parameters** to their init method. For example:

```
var item = ChecklistItem(text: "Charge my iPhone", checked:
false)
```

This calls the corresponding init(text:checked:) method to prepare the newly allocated ChecklistItem object for usage.

You've seen two types of variables: **local variables,** whose existence is limited to the method they are declared in, and **instance variables** (also known as "ivars," or properties) that belong to the object and therefore can be used from within any method in the object.

The lifetime of a variable is called its **scope**. The scope of a local variable is smaller than that of an instance variable. Once the method ends, any local variables are destroyed.

```
class MyObject {
  var count = 0        // an instance variable

  func myMethod() {
    var temp: Int      // a local variable
    temp = count       // OK to use the instance variable here
  }

  // the local variable "temp" doesn't exist outside the method
}
```

If you have a local variable with the same name as an instance variable, then it is said to **shadow** (or **hide**) the instance variable. You should avoid these situations as they can lead to subtle bugs where you may not be using the variable that you think you are:

```
class MyObject {
  var count = 7        // an instance variable

  func myMethod() {
    var count = 42     // local variable "hides" instance variable
    print(count)       // prints 42
  }
}
```

Some developers place an underscore in front of their instance variable names to avoid this problem: _count instead of count. An alternative is to use the keyword self whenever you want to access an instance variable:

```
func myMethod() {
  var count = 42
  print(self.count)    // prints 7
}
```

Constants

Variables are not the only code elements that can hold values. A variable is a container for a value that is allowed to *change* over the course of the app being run.

For example, in a note-taking app, the user can change the text of the note. So, you'd place that text into a String variable. Every time the user edits the text, the variable is updated.

Sometimes, you'll just want to store the result of a calculation or a method call into a temporary container, after which this value will never change. In that case, it is better to make this container a **constant** rather than a variable.

The following values cannot change once they've been set:

```
let pi = 3.141592
let difference = abs(targetValue - currentValue)
let message = "You scored \(points) points"
let image = UIImage(named: "SayCheese")
```

If a constant is local to a method, it's allowed to give the constant a new value the next time the method is called. The value from the previous method invocation is destroyed when that method ends, and the next time the app enters that method you're creating a new constant with a new value (but with the same name). Of course, for the duration of that method call, the constant's value must remain the same.

Tip: My suggestion is to use let for everything — that's the right solution 90% of the time. When you get it wrong, the Swift compiler will warn that you're trying to change a constant. Only then should you change it to a var. This ensures you're not making things variable that don't need to be.

Value types vs. reference types

When working with basic values such as integers and strings — which are **value types** — a constant created with let cannot be changed once it has been given a value:

```
let pi = 3.141592
pi = 3                  // not allowed
```

However, with objects that are **reference types**, it is only the reference that is constant. The object itself can still be changed:

```
let item = ChecklistItem()
item.text = "Do the laundry"
item.checked = false
item.dueDate = yesterday
```

But this is not allowed:

```
let anotherItem = ChecklistItem()
item = anotherItem    // cannot change the reference
```

So how do you know what is a reference type and what is a value type?

Objects defined as `class` are reference types, while objects defined as `struct` or `enum` are value types. In practice, this means most of the objects from the iOS SDK are reference types but things that are built into the Swift language, such as `Int`, `String`, and `Array`, are value types. (More about this important difference later.)

Collections

A variable stores only a single value. To keep track of multiple objects, you can use a **collection** object. Naturally, I'm talking about arrays (`Array`) and dictionaries (`Dictionary`), both of which you've seen previously.

An **array** stores a list of objects. The objects it contains are ordered sequentially and you retrieve them by index.

```
// An array of ChecklistItem objects:
var items: Array<ChecklistItem>

// Or, using shorthand notation:
var items: [ChecklistItem]

// Making an instance of the array:
items = [ChecklistItem]()

// Accessing an object from the array:
let item = items[3]
```

You can write an array as `Array<Type>` or `[Type]`. The first one is the official version, the second is "syntactic sugar" that is a bit easier to read. (Unlike other languages, in Swift you don't write `Type[]`. The type name goes inside the brackets.)

A **dictionary** stores key-value pairs. An object, usually a string, is the key that retrieves another object.

```
// A dictionary that stores (String, Int) pairs, for example a
// list of people's names and their ages:
var ages: Dictionary<String, Int>

// Or, using shorthand notation:
var ages: [String: Int]

// Making an instance of the dictionary:
ages = [String: Int]()

// Accessing an object from the dictionary:
var age = dict["Jony Ive"]
```

The notation for retrieving an object from a dictionary looks very similar to reading from an array — both use the [ ] brackets. For indexing an array, you always use a positive integer, but for a dictionary you typically use a string.

There are other sorts of collections as well, but array and dictionary are the most common ones.

Generics

Array and Dictionary are known as **generics**, meaning that they are independent of the type of thing you want to store inside these collections.

You can have an Array of Int objects, but also an Array of String objects — or an Array of any kind of object, really (even an array of other arrays).

That's why you have to specify the type of object to store inside the array, before you can use it. In other words, you cannot write this:

```
var items: Array  // error: should be Array<TypeName>
var items: []     // error: should be [TypeName]
```

There should always be the name of a type inside the [ ] brackets or following the word Array in < > brackets. (If you're coming from Objective-C, be aware that the < > mean something completely different there.)

For Dictionary, you need to supply two type names: one for the type of the keys and one for the type of the values.

Swift requires that all variables and constants have a value. You can either specify a value when you declare the variable or constant, or by assigning a value inside an init method.

Optionals

Sometimes, it's useful to have a variable that can have no value, in which case you need to declare it as an **optional**:

```
var checklistToEdit: Checklist?
```

You cannot use this variable immediately; you must always first test whether it has a value or not. This is called **unwrapping** the optional:

```
if let checklist = checklistToEdit {
  // "checklist" now contains the real object
```

```
} else {
  // the optional was nil
}
```

The age variable from the dictionary example in the previous section is actually an optional, because there is no guarantee that the dictionary contains the key "Jony Ive." Therefore, the type of age is Int? instead of just Int.

Before you can use a value from a dictionary, you need to unwrap it first using if let:

```
if let age = dict["Jony Ive"] {
  // use the value of age
}
```

If you are 100% sure that the dictionary contains a given key, you can also use **force unwrapping** to read the corresponding value:

```
var age = dict["Jony Ive"]!
```

With the ! you tell Swift, "This value will not be nil. I'll stake my reputation on it!" Of course, if you're wrong and the value *is* nil, the app will crash and your reputation is down the drain. Be careful with force unwrapping!

A slightly safer alternative to force unwrapping is **optional chaining**. For example, the following will crash the app if the navigationController property is nil:

```
navigationController!.delegate = self
```

But this won't:

```
navigationController?.delegate = self
```

Anything after the ? will simply be ignored if navigationController does not have a value. It's equivalent to writing:

```
if navigationController != nil {
  navigationController!.delegate = self
}
```

It is also possible to declare an optional using an exclamation point instead of a question mark. This makes it an **implicitly unwrapped** optional:

```
var dataModel: DataModel!
```

Such a value is potentially unsafe because you can use it as a regular variable without having to unwrap it first. If this variable has the value `nil` when you don't expect it — and don't they always — your app will crash.

Optionals exist to guard against such crashes, and using ! undermines the safety of using optionals.

However, sometimes using implicitly unwrapped optionals is more convenient than using pure optionals. Use them when you cannot give the variable an initial value at the time of declaration, nor in `init()`.

But once you've given the variable a value, you really ought not to make it `nil` again. If the value can become `nil` again, it's better to use a true optional with a question mark.

Methods and functions

You've learned that objects, the basic building blocks of all apps, have both data and functionality. Instance variables and constants provide the data, **methods** provide the functionality.

When you call a method, the app jumps to that section of the code and executes all the statements in the method one-by-one. When the end of the method is reached, the app jumps back to where it left off:

```
let result = performUselessCalculation(314)
print(result)

. . .

func performUselessCalculation(_ a: Int) -> Int {
  var b = Int(arc4random_uniform(100))
  var c = a / 2
  return (a + b) * c
}
```

Methods often return a value to the caller, usually the result of a computation or looking up something in a collection. The data type of the result value is written after the -> arrow. In the example above, it is `Int`. If there is no -> arrow, the method does not return a value (also known as returning `Void`).

Methods are **functions** that belong to an object, but there are also standalone functions such as `print()`.

Functions serve the same purpose as methods — they bundle functionality into small re-usable units — but live outside of any objects. Such functions are also called *free* functions or *global* functions.

These are examples of methods:

```
// Method with no parameters, no return a value.
override func viewDidLoad()

// Method with one parameter, slider. No return a value.
// The keyword @IBAction means that this method can be connected
// to a control in Interface Builder.
@IBAction func sliderMoved(_ slider: UISlider)

// Method with no parameters, returns an Int value.
func countUncheckedItems() -> Int

// Method with two parameters, cell and item, no return value.
// Note that the first parameter has an extra label, for,
// and the second parameter has an extra label, with.
func configureCheckmarkFor(for cell: UITableViewCell,
                           with item: ChecklistItem)

// Method with two parameters, tableView and section.
// Returns an Int. The _ means the first parameter does not
// have an external label.
override func tableView(_ tableView: UITableView,
        numberOfRowsInSection section: Int) -> Int

// Method with two parameters, tableView and indexPath.
// The question mark means it returns an optional IndexPath
// object (may also return nil).
override func tableView(_ tableView: UITableView,
        willSelectRowAt indexPath: IndexPath) -> IndexPath?
```

To call a method on an object, you write `object.method(parameters)`. For example:

```
// Calling a method on the lists object:
lists.append(checklist)

// Calling a method with more than one parameter:
tableView.insertRows(at: indexPaths, with: .fade)
```

You can think of calling a method as *sending a message* from one object to another: "Hey `lists`, I'm sending you the append message for this `checklist` object."

The object whose method you're calling is known as the *receiver* of the message.

It is very common to call a method from the same object. Here, `loadChecklists()` calls the `sortChecklists()` method. Both are members of the `DataModel` object.

```
class DataModel {
  func loadChecklists() {
    . . .
    sortChecklists()  // this method also lives in DataModel
  }

  func sortChecklists() {
    . . .
  }
}
```

Sometimes, this is written as:

```
func loadChecklists() {
  . . .
  self.sortChecklists()
}
```

The self keyword makes it clear that the DataModel object itself is the receiver of this message.

> **Note**: In this book, the self keyword is left out for method calls, because it's not necessary to have it. Objective-C developers are very attached to self, so you'll probably see it used a lot in Swift too. It is a topic of heated debate in developer circles, but except for a few specific scenarios, the compiler doesn't really care whether you use self or not.

Inside a method, you can also use self to get a reference to the object itself:

```
@IBAction func cancel() {
  delegate?.itemDetailViewControllerDidCancel(self)
}
```

Here, cancel() sends a reference to the object (i.e. self) along to the delegate, so the delegate knows who sent this itemDetailViewControllerDidCancel() message.

Also note that the use of **optional chaining** here. The delegate property is an optional, so it can be nil. Using the question mark before the method call will ensure nothing bad happens if delegate is not set.

Parameters

Often methods have one or more **parameters**, so they can work with multiple data items. A method that is limited to a fixed set of data is not very useful or reusable. Consider sumValuesFromArray(), a method that has no parameters:

```
class MyObject {
  var numbers = [Int]()

  func sumValuesFromArray() -> Int {
    var total = 0
    for number in numbers {
      total += number
    }
    return total
  }
}
```

Here, numbers is an instance variable. The sumValuesFromArray() method is tied closely to that instance variable, and is useless without it.

Suppose you add a second array to the app that you also want to apply this calculation to. One approach is to copy-paste the above method and change the name of the variable to that of the new array. That certainly works, but it's not smart programming!

It is better to give the method a parameter that allows you to pass in the array object that you wish to examine. Then, the method becomes independent from any instance variables:

```
func sumValues(from array: [Int]) -> Int {
  var total = 0
  for number in array {
    total += number
  }
  return total
}
```

Now you can call this method with any [Int] (or Array<Int>) object as its parameter.

This doesn't mean methods should never use instance variables, but if you can make a method more general by giving it a parameter, then that is usually a good idea.

Often methods use two names for their parameters, the **external label** and the **internal label**. For example:

```
func downloadImage(for searchResult: SearchResult,
              withTimeout timeout: TimeInterval,
                andPlaceOn button: UIButton) {
  . . .
}
```

This method has three parameters: `searchResult`, `timeout`, and `button`. Those are the internal parameter names you'd use in the code inside the method.

The external labels become part of the method name. The full name for the method is `downloadImage(for:withTimeout:andPlaceOn:)` — method names in Swift are often quite long!

To call this method, you'd use the external labels:

```
downloadImage(for: result, withTimeout: 10,
                     andPlaceOn: imageButton)
```

Sometimes you'll see a method whose first parameter does not have an external label, but has an _ underscore instead:

```
override func tableView(_ tableView: UITableView,
      numberOfRowsInSection section: Int) -> Int
```

This is often the case with delegate methods. It's a holdover from the Objective-C days, where the label for the first parameter was embedded in the first part of the method name. For example, in Objective-C the `downloadImage()` method example above would be named `downloadImageForSearchResult()`. These kinds of names should become less and less common in the near future.

Swift is pretty flexible with how it lets you name your methods, but it's smart to stick to the established conventions.

Inside a method you can do the following things:

• Create local variables and constants.

• Do basic arithmetic with mathematical operators such as +, −, *, /, and %.

• Put new values into variables (both local and instance variables).

• Call other methods.

• Make decisions with `if` or `switch` statements.

- Perform repetitions with the for or while statements.

- Return a value to the caller.

Let's look at the if and for statements in more detail.

Making decisions

The if statement looks like this:

```
if count == 0 {
  text = "No Items"
} else if count == 1 {
  text = "1 Item"
} else {
  text = "\(count) Items"
}
```

The expression after if is called the **condition**. If a condition is true then the statements in the following { } block are executed. The else section gets performed if none of the conditions are true.

Comparison Operators

You use **comparison operators** to perform comparisons between two values:

==   equal to

!=   not equal

\>   greater than

\>=   greater than or equal

<   less than

<=   less than or equal

```
let a = "Hello, world"
let b = "Hello," + " world"
print(a == b)            // prints true
```

When you use the == operator, the contents of the objects are compared. The above code only returns true if a and b have the same value:

This is different from Objective-C, where == is only true if the two objects are the exact same instance in memory. However, in Swift == compares the values of the objects, not whether they actually occupy the same spot in memory. (If you need to do that use ===, the identity operator.)

Logical Operators

You can use **logical** operators to combine two expressions:

a && b is true if both a *and* b are true

a || b is true when either a *or* b is true (or both)

There is also the logical **not** operator, !, that turns true into false, and false into true. (Don't confuse this with the ! that is used with optionals.)

You can group expressions with ( ) parentheses:

```
if ((this && that) || (such && so)) && !other {
  // statements
}
```

This reads as:

```
if ((this and that) or (such and so)) and not other {
  // statements
}
```

Or if you want to see clearly in which order these operations are performed:

```
if (
      (this and that)
           or
      (such and so)
   )
   and
      (not other)
```

Of course, the more complicated you make it, the harder it is to remember exactly what you're doing!

switch statement

Swift has another very powerful construct in the language for making decisions, the `switch` statement:

```
switch condition {
  case value1:
    // statements

  case value2:
    // statements

  case value3:
    // statements

  default:
    // statements
}
```

It works the same way as an `if` statement with a bunch of `else` `if`s. The following is equivalent:

```
if condition == value1 {
  // statements
} else if condition == value2 {
  // statements
} else if condition == value3 {
  // statements
} else {
  // statements
}
```

In such a situation, the `switch` statement would be more convenient to use. Swift's version of `switch` is much more powerful than the one in Objective-C. For example, you can match on ranges and other patterns:

```
switch difference {
  case 0:
    title = "Perfect!"
  case 1..<5:
    title = "You almost had it!"
  case 5..<10:
    title = "Pretty good!"
  default:
    title = "Not even close..."
}
```

The ..< is the **half-open range** operator. It creates a range between the two numbers, but the top number is exclusive. So the half-open range 1..<5 is the same as the **closed range** 1...4.

You'll see the switch statement in action a little later on.

return statement

Note that if and return can be used to return early from a method:

```
func divide(_ a: Int, by b: Int) -> Int {
  if b == 0 {
    print("You really shouldn't divide by zero")
    return 0
  }
  return a / b
}
```

This can even be done for methods that don't return a value:

```
func performDifficultCalculation(list: [Double]) {
  if list.count < 2 {
    print("Too few items in list")
    return
  }

  // perform the very difficult calculation here
}
```

In this case, return simply means: "We're done with the method." Any statements following the return are skipped and execution immediately returns to the caller.

You could also have written it like this:

```
func performDifficultCalculation(list: [Double]) {
  if list.count < 2 {
    print("Too few items in list")
  } else {
    // perform the very difficult calculation here
  }
}
```

Which approach you use is up to you. The advantage of an early return is that it avoids multiple nested blocks of code with multiple levels of indentation — the code just looks cleaner.

For example, sometimes you see code like this:

```swift
func someMethod() {
  if condition1 {
    if condition2 {
      if condition3 {
        // statements
      } else {
        // statements
      }
    } else {
      // statements
    }
  } else {
    // statements
  }
}
```

This can become very hard to read. You could restructure that kind of code as follows:

```swift
func someMethod() {
  if !condition1 {
    // statements
    return
  }

  if !condition2 {
    // statements
    return
  }

  if !condition3 {
    // statements
    return
  }

  // statements
}
```

Both do exactly the same thing, but the second one is easier to understand. (Note that the conditions now use the ! operator to invert their meaning.)

Swift even has a dedicated feature, guard, to help write this kind of code. It looks like this:

```swift
func someMethod() {
  guard condition1 else {
    // statements
    return
```

```
    }
  guard condition2 else {
    // statements
    return
  }
  . . .
```

As you become more experienced, you'll start to develop your own taste for what looks good and what is readable code.

Loops

You've seen the `for...in` statement for looping through an array:

```
for item in items {
  if !item.checked {
    count += 1
  }
}
```

Which can also be written as:

```
for item in items where !item.checked {
  count += 1
}
```

This performs the statements inside the `for...in` block once for each object from the `items` array matching the condition provided by the `where` clause.

Note that the scope of the variable `item` is limited to just this `for` statement. You can't use it outside this statement, so its lifetime is even shorter than a local variable.

Looping through number ranges

Some languages, including Swift 2, have a `for` statement that looks like this:

```
for var i = 0; i < 5; ++i {
  print(i)
}
```

When you run this code, it should print:

```
0
1
2
3
4
```

However, as of Swift 3.0 this kind of `for` loop was removed from the language. Instead, you can loop over a range. This has the same output as above:

```
for i in 0...4 {    // or 0..<5
  print(i)
}
```

By the way, you can also write this loop as:

```
for i in stride(from: 0, to: 5, by: 1) {
  print(i)
}
```

The `stride()` function creates a special object that represents the range 0 to 5 in increments of 1. If you wanted to show just the even numbers, you could change the by parameter to 2. You can even use `stride()` to count backwards if you pass the by parameter a negative number.

while statement

The `for` statement is not the only way to perform loops. Another very useful looping construct is the `while` statement:

```
while something is true {
  // statements
}
```

The `while` loop keeps repeating the statements until its condition becomes false. You can also write it as follows:

```
repeat {
  // statements
} while something is true
```

In the latter case, the condition is evaluated after the statements have been executed at least once.

You can rewrite the loop that counts the `ChecklistItems` as follows using a `while` statement:

```
var count = 0
var i = 0
while i < items.count {
  let item = items[i]
  if !item.checked {
    count += 1
  }
  i += 1
}
```

Most of these looping constructs are really the same, they just look different. Each of them lets you repeat a bunch of statements until some ending condition is met.

Still, using a `while` is slightly more cumbersome than "for item in items," which is why you'll see `for...in` used most of the time.

There really is no significant difference between using a `for`, `while`, or `repeat...while` loop, except that one may be easier to read than the others, depending on what you're trying to do.

> **Note**: `items.count` and `count` in this example are two different things with the same name. The first `count` is a property on the `items` array that returns the number of elements in that array; the second `count` is a local variable that contains the number of unchecked to-do items counted so far.

Just like you can prematurely exit from a method using the `return` statement, you can exit a loop at any time using the `break` statement:

```
var found = false
for item in array {
  if item == searchText {
    found = true
    break
  }
}
```

This example loops through the array until it finds an `item` that is equal to the value of `searchText` (presumably both are strings). Then it sets the variable `found` to `true` and jumps out of the loop using `break`. You've found what you were looking for, so it makes no sense to look at the other objects in that array — for all you know there could be hundreds of items.

There is also a `continue` statement that is somewhat the opposite of `break`. It doesn't exit the loop but immediately skips to the next iteration. You use `continue` to say, "I'm done with the current item, let's look at the next one."

Loops can often be replaced by *functional programming* constructs such as `map`, `filter`, or `reduce`. These are known as *higher order functions* and they operate on a collection, performing some code for each element, and return a new collection (or single value, in the case of `reduce`) with the results.

For example, using `filter` on an array will return items that satisfy a certain condition. To get a list of all the unchecked `ChecklistItem` objects, you'd write:

```
var uncheckedItems = items.filter { item in !item.checked }
```

That's a lot simpler than writing a loop. Functional programming is an advanced topic so we won't spend too much time on it here.

Objects

Objects are what it's all about. They combine data with functionality into coherent, reusable units — that is, if you write them properly!

The data is made up of the object's instance variables and constants. We often refer to these as the object's **properties**. The functionality is provided by the object's methods.

In your Swift programs you will use existing objects, such as `String`, `Array`, `Date`, `UITableView`, and you'll also make your own.

To define a new object, you need a bit of code that contains a `class` section:

```
class MyObject {
  var text: String
  var count = 0
  let maximum = 100

  init() {
    text = "Hello world"
  }

  func doSomething() {
    // statements
  }
}
```

Inside the brackets for the class, you add properties (the instance variables and constants) and methods.

Properties

There are two types of properties:

• **Stored properties** are the usual instance variables and constants.

• **Computed properties** don't store a value, but perform logic when you read from, or write to, their values.

This is an example of a computed property:

```
var indexOfSelectedChecklist: Int {
  get {
    return UserDefaults.standard.integer(
              forKey: "ChecklistIndex")
  }
  set {
    UserDefaults.standard.set(newValue,
                                forKey: "ChecklistIndex")
  }
}
```

The indexOfSelectedChecklist property does not store a value like a normal variable would. Instead, every time someone uses this property, it performs the code from the get or set block.

The alternative would be to write separate setIndexOfSelectedChecklist() and getIndexOfSelectedChecklist() methods, but that doesn't read as nicely.

If a property name is preceded by the keyword @IBOutlet, that means that the property can refer to a user interface element in Interface Builder, such as a label or button. Such properties are usually declared weak and optional.

Similarly, the keyword @IBAction is used for methods that will be performed when the user interacts with the app.

Methods

There are three kinds of methods:

- Instance methods

- Class methods

- Init methods

As mentioned previously, a method is a function that belongs to an object. To call such a method you first need to have an instance of the object:

```
let myInstance = MyObject()    // create the object instance
. . .
myInstance.doSomething()       // call the method
```

You can also have **class methods**, which can be used without an object instance. In fact, they are often used as "factory" methods, to create new object instances:

```
class MyObject {
  . . .

  class func makeObject(text: String) -> MyObject {
    let m = MyObject()
    m.text = text
    return m
  }
}

let myInstance = MyObject.makeObject(text: "Hello world")
```

Init methods, or **initializers**, are used during the creation of new object instances. Instead of the above factory method, you might as well use a custom `init` method:

```
class MyObject {
  . . .

  init(text: String) {
    self.text = text
  }
}

let myInstance = MyObject(text: "Hello world")
```

The main purpose of an `init` method is to set up (or, initialize) the object's properties. Any instance variables or constants that do not have a value yet must be given one in the `init` method.

Swift does not allow variables or constants to have no value (except for optionals), and `init` is your last chance to make this happen.

Objects can have more than one `init` method; which one you use depends on the circumstances.

A `UITableViewController`, for example, can be initialized either with `init?(coder:)` when automatically loaded from a storyboard, with `init(nibName:bundle:)` when manually loaded from a nib file, or with `init(style:)` when constructed without a storyboard or nib — sometimes you use one, sometimes the other. You can also provide a `deinit` method that gets called just before the object is destroyed.

By the way, `class` isn't the only way to define an object in Swift. It also supports other types of objects such as `structs` and `enums`. You'll learn more about these later in the book.

Protocols

Besides objects, you can also define **protocols**. A protocol is simply a list of method names (and possibly, properties):

```
protocol MyProtocol {
  func someMethod(value: Int)
  func anotherMethod() -> String
}
```

A protocol is like a job ad. It lists all the things that a candidate for a certain position in your company should be able to do.

But the ad itself doesn't do the job — it's just words printed in the careers section of the newspaper. So, you need to hire an actual employee who can get the job done. That would be an object.

Objects need to indicate that they conform to a protocol:

```
class MyObject: MyProtocol {
  . . .
}
```

This object now has to provide an implementation for the methods listed in the protocol. (If not, it's fired!)

From then on, you can refer to this object as a MyObject (because that is its class name) but also as a MyProtocol object:

```
var m1: MyObject = MyObject()
var m2: MyProtocol = MyObject()
```

To any part of the code using the m2 variable, it doesn't matter that the object is really a MyObject under the hood. The type of m2 is MyProtocol, not MyObject.

All your code sees is that m2 is *some* object conforming to MyProtocol, but it's not important what sort of object that is.

In other words, you don't really care that your employee may also have another job on the side, as long as it doesn't interfere with the duties you've hired him, or her, for.

Protocols are often used to define **delegates**, but they come in handy for other uses as well, as you'll find out later on.

This concludes the quick recap of what you've seen so far of the Swift language. After all that theory, it's time to write some code!

Chapter 27: Get Location Data

Eli Ganim

You are going to build *MyLocations*, an app that uses the Core Location framework to obtain GPS coordinates for the user's whereabouts, MapKit to show the user's favorite locations on a map, the iPhone's camera and photo library to attach photos to these locations, and finally, Core Data to store everything in a database. Phew, that's a lot of stuff!

The finished app looks like this:

The MyLocations app

MyLocations lets you keep a list of spots that you find interesting. Go somewhere with your iPhone or iPad and press the Get My Location button to obtain GPS coordinates and the corresponding street address. Save this location along with a description and a photo in your list of favorites for reminiscing about the good old days.

Think of this app as a "location album" instead of a photo album.

To make the workload easier to handle, you'll split the project up into smaller chunks:

1. You will first figure out how to obtain GPS coordinates from the Core Location framework and how to convert these coordinates into an address, a process known as **reverse geocoding**. Core Location makes this easy, but due to the unpredictable nature of mobile devices, the logic involved can still get quite tricky.

2. Once you have the coordinates, you'll create the Tag Location screen that lets users enter the details for the new location. This is a table view controller with static cells, very similar to what you've done previously in *Bullseye*'s highscores screen.

3. You'll store the location data into a Core Data store. For the last app you saved app data into a .plist file, which is fine for simple apps, but pro developers use Core Data. It's not as scary as it sounds!

4. Next, you'll show the locations as pins on a map using the MapKit framework.

5. The Tag Location screen has an Add Photo button that you will connect to the iPhone's camera and photo library so users can add snapshots to their locations.

6. Finally, you'll make the app look good using custom graphics. You will also add sound effects and some animations to the mix.

Of course, you are not going to do all of that at once. In this chapter, you will do the following:

• **Get GPS Coordinates**: Create a tab bar based app and set up the UI for the first tab.

• **CoreLocation**: Use the CoreLocation framework to get the user's current location.

• **Display coordinates**: Display location information on screen.

When you're done with this chapter, the app will look like this:

The first screen of the app

Get GPS coordinates

First, you'll create the *MyLocations* project in Xcode and then use the Core Location framework to find the latitude and longitude of the user's location.

Creating the project

➤ Fire up Xcode and make a new project. Choose the **Tabbed App** template.

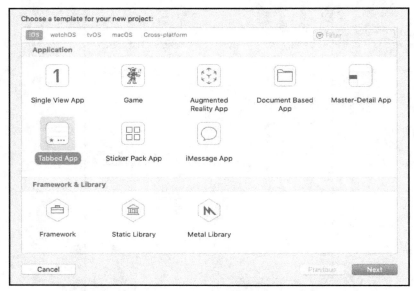

Choosing the Tabbed Application template

➤ Fill in the options as follows:

• Product Name: **MyLocations**

• Organization Name: Your name or the name of your company

• Organization Identifier: Your own identifier in reverse domain notation

• Language: **Swift**

• Include Unit Tests and Include UI Tests: unchecked

• Use SwiftUI: unchecked

➤ Save the project.

If you run the app, it looks like this:

The app from the Tabbed Application template

The app has a tab bar along the bottom with two tabs: First and Second.

Even though it doesn't do much yet, the app already employs three view controllers:

1. The *root controller* is a UITabBarController that contains the tab bar and performs the switching between the different screens.

2. A view controller for the First tab.

3. A view controller for the Second tab.

The two tabs each have their own view controller. By default, the Xcode template names them FirstViewController and SecondViewController.

At this point, the storyboard looks like this:

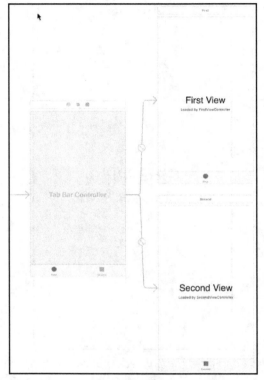

The storyboard from the Tabbed Application template

It's zoomed out to fit the whole thing on the screen. Storyboards are great, but they sure take up a lot of space!

As before, you'll be editing the storyboard using the iPhone 8 dimensions. Later, if necessary, you'll make some adjustments to get the app to work on other screen sizes as well.

➤ In the **View as**: pane at the bottom, choose **iPhone 8**.

The first tab

In this chapter, you'll be working with the first tab only. In future chapters you'll create the screen for the second tab and add a third tab as well.

Let's give `FirstViewController` a better name.

Remember the refactoring trick you learned previously? That's what you'll use here since that renames both the file and any references to it anywhere in the project.

➤ Open **FirstViewController.swift**, hover your mouse cursor over the word `FirstViewController` in the `class` line, right-click (or Control-click) and select **Refactor > Rename...** from the context menu.

➤ Change the name to **CurrentLocationViewController**. This changes the file name, the class name and the reference to the class in the storyboard, all at once! Nifty, eh?

➤ Go to the **Project Settings** screen and de-select the Landscape Left and Landscape Right settings under **Deployment Info — Device Orientation**. Now the app is portrait-only. (You can enable **Upside Down** at the same time if you like, since this would enable both portrait modes on iPad.)

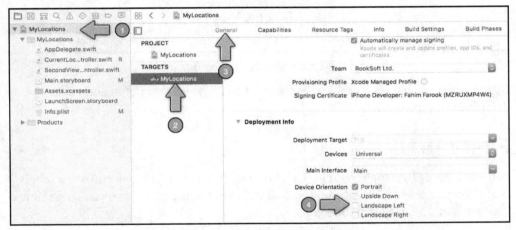

The app only works in portrait

➤ Run the app again just to make sure everything still works.

Whenever you change how things are hooked up in the storyboard, it's useful to run the app and verify that the change was successful — it's way too easy to forget a step and you want to catch such mistakes right away.

And if you are wondering where you changed things in the storyboard, remember how you renamed the `FirstViewController`? That change modified the storyboard, too.

A view controller that sits inside a navigation controller has a Navigation Item object that allows it to configure the navigation bar. Tab bars work the same way. Each view controller that represents a tab has a Tab Bar Item object.

➤ Open the storyboard, select the **Tab Bar Item** object from the **First Scene** (this is the Current Location View Controller) and go to the **Attributes inspector**. Change the **Title** to **Tag**.

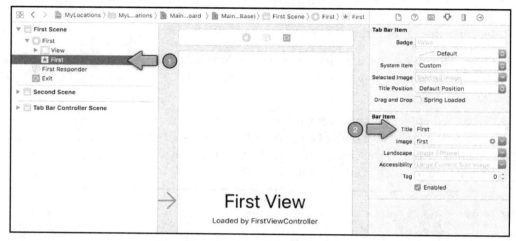

Changing the title of the Tab Bar Item

Later on, you'll also set a new image for the Tab Bar Item too; it currently uses the default image from the template.

First tab UI

You will now design the screen for this first tab. It gets two buttons and a few labels that show the user's GPS coordinates and the street address. To save you some time, you'll add all the outlets in one go.

➤ Add the following to the class in **CurrentLocationViewController.swift**, just after the class definition and before viewDidLoad():

```
@IBOutlet weak var messageLabel: UILabel!
@IBOutlet weak var latitudeLabel: UILabel!
@IBOutlet weak var longitudeLabel: UILabel!
@IBOutlet weak var addressLabel: UILabel!
@IBOutlet weak var tagButton: UIButton!
@IBOutlet weak var getButton: UIButton!
```

➤ Still in **CurrentLocationViewController.swift**, add this just before the last curly brackets:

```
// MARK:- Actions
@IBAction func getLocation() {
```

```
    // do nothing yet
  }
```

Now open the storyboard, remove the existing labels and design the UI to look something like this — always make use of the positioning guides that Interface Builder provides to place controls since this gives you nice, even spacing:

The design of the Current Location screen

➤ The **(Message Label)** at the top should span the whole width of the screen. You'll use this label for status messages while the app is obtaining the GPS coordinates. Set the **Alignment** attribute to centered and connect the label to the `messageLabel` outlet.

➤ Once you've positioned the **(Message Label)**, set its Auto Layout constraints for left, top and right so that it aligns with the Safe Area. In case you're wondering, you don't have to explicitly select the Safe Area.

If you set up the constraints as below, most of the time the constraints should be set correctly for you.

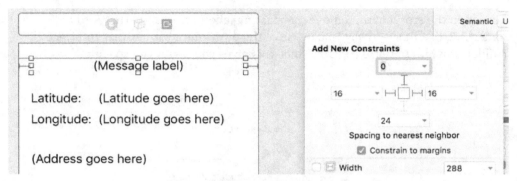

The (Message Label) constraints

➤ Make the **(Latitude goes here)** and **(Longitude goes here)** labels right-aligned and connect them to the latitudeLabel and longitudeLabel outlets respectively.

➤ Set up **left**, **top**, **right** and **bottom** Auto Layout constraints for the **Latitude**: label. You can use your judgement with regards to the top spacing — here 24 points is the value used — or you can use the suggested spacing of 8 points. It's totally up to you, but feels like there should be a bit more spacing between the message and the latitude, longitude grouping.

➤ Then, set up **left**, **right** and **bottom** constraints for the **Longitude**: label — you don't need a top constraint since the bottom constraint of the **Latitude**: label acts as the top constraint for this one.

Again, you can use your judgement with regards to the bottom spacing since that determines how far away the **(Address goes here)** label is from the **Longitude**: label. It probably should have the same amount of spacing as there was at the top to the **(Message Label)** and so 24 points make sense.

➤ Add **top**, **right** and **bottom** constraints for **(Latitude goes here)** and **right** and **bottom** constraints for **(Longitude goes here)**.

Do note that as you add constraints, the positions of some of the labels might shift. So you might need to adjust positioning again — for example, position the **(Longitude goes here)** label so that it stretches to the right edge of the screen — to set things up as they originally were.

➤ You will get some Auto Layout constraint issues at this point. This is due to none of the labels in the latitude and longitude grouping having specific widths or heights. It's hard for Xcode to determine what the actual sizes should be.

We know that the longer of the two left labels is **Longitude**: So let's try setting both labels on the left to be the same size as the **Longitude**: label — Control-drag from the **Longitude**: label to the **Latitude**: label and select **Equal Widths** from the pop-up.

Hmm... that made things worse! Why?

Because you had an existing trailing space from the **Latitude**: label to the **(Latitude goes here)** label and that spacing is now incorrect. Select the **(Latitude goes here)** label, switch to the **Size inspector** and remove the leading constraint to the **Latitude**: label.

➤ The **(Latitude goes here)** label will resize to fit its contents again. Add a leading constraint between it and the **Latitude**: label, but make the spacing greater than or equal to 8 points to match what's there for the longitude label set.

Why greater than or equal to when all the other constraints are set to equal to? Because if you set it to equal to, you'll get another set of red constraints.

➤ The **(Address goes here)** label spans the whole width of the screen and should be **50** points high so it can fit two lines of text. Set its **Lines** attribute to **0** (that means it can display a variable number of lines). Connect this label to the addressLabel outlet.

➤ Set **left**, **right** and **bottom** constraints on the **(Address goes here)** label. Make the bottom constraint be 24 points to match the top spacing previously set, or, whatever value you set/like. It's your choice.

➤ The **Tag Location** button doesn't do anything yet, but should be connected to the tagButton outlet.

➤ Set **left** and **right** constraints of 16 points on the **Tag Location** button so that it stretches from side to side.

➤ Connect the **Get My Location** button to the getButton outlet and its Touch Up Inside event to the getLocation action.

➤ Set **left**, **right** and **bottom** constraints on the **Get My Location** button so that it stretches from side to side and is at least 16 points from the bottom of the screen — you can use your judgement as to the actual positioning you think is good.

➤ Run the app to see the new design in action.

If you think the positioning of some element is off, feel free to adjust the Auto Layout constraints till the layout looks right. There is no right or wrong here, it's all a matter of how it looks to you.

So far, nothing special. With the exception of the tab bar, this is stuff you've seen and done before. Time to add something new: Let's play with Core Location!

Core Location

Most iOS devices have a way to let you know exactly where you are on the globe, either through communication with GPS satellites, or Wi-Fi and cell tower triangulation. The Core Location framework puts that power in your own hands.

An app can ask Core Location for the user's current latitude and longitude. For devices with a compass, it can also give the heading — you won't be using that for this app. Core Location can also provide continuous location updates while you're on the move.

Get your current location

Getting a location from Core Location is pretty easy, but there are some pitfalls that you need to avoid. Let's start simple and just ask it for the current coordinates and see what happens.

➤ At the top of **CurrentLocationViewController.swift**, add an import statement:

```
import CoreLocation
```

That is all you have to do to add the Core Location framework to your project.

Core Location, like many other parts of the iOS SDK, works via a delegate, so you should make the view controller conform to the CLLocationManagerDelegate protocol.

➤ Add CLLocationManagerDelegate to the view controller's class line:

```
class CurrentLocationViewController: UIViewController,
                                    CLLocationManagerDelegate {
```

➤ Also add a new property:

```
let locationManager = CLLocationManager()
```

The CLLocationManager is the object that will give you GPS coordinates. You're putting the reference to this object in a constant — using let, not a variable (var). Once you have created the location manager object, the value of locationManager will never have to change.

The new CLLocationManager object doesn't give you GPS coordinates right away. To begin receiving coordinates, you have to call its startUpdatingLocation() method first.

Unless you're doing turn-by-turn navigation, you don't want your app to continuously receive GPS coordinates. That requires a lot of power and will quickly drain the battery. For this app, you only turn on the location manager when you want a location fix and turn it off again when you've received a usable location.

You'll implement that logic in a minute — it's more complex than you'd think. For now, you're only interested in receiving something from Core Location, just so you know that it works.

➤ Change the getLocation() action method to the following:

```
@IBAction func getLocation() {
  locationManager.delegate = self
  locationManager.desiredAccuracy =
                 kCLLocationAccuracyNearestTenMeters
  locationManager.startUpdatingLocation()
}
```

This method is hooked up to the **Get My Location** button. It tells the location manager that the view controller is its delegate and that you want to receive locations with an accuracy of up to ten meters. Then you start the location manager. From that moment on, the CLLocationManager object will send location updates to its delegate, i.e., the view controller.

➤ Speaking of the delegate, add the following code:

```
// MARK: - CLLocationManagerDelegate
func locationManager(_ manager: CLLocationManager,
       didFailWithError error: Error) {
  print("didFailWithError \(error.localizedDescription)")
}

func locationManager(_ manager: CLLocationManager,
  didUpdateLocations locations: [CLLocation]) {
  let newLocation = locations.last!
  print("didUpdateLocations \(newLocation)")
}
```

These are the delegate methods for the location manager. For the time being, you'll simply output a print() message to the Console. Also, do note the error.localizedDescription bit which, instead of simply printing out the contents of the error variable, outputs a human readable version of the error (if possible) based on the device's current locale (or language setting).

➤ Run the app in the simulator and press the **Get My Location** button.

Hmm… nothing seems to be happening. That's because you need to ask for permission before accessing location information.

Ask for permission

➤ Add the following lines to the top of getLocation():

```
let authStatus = CLLocationManager.authorizationStatus()
if authStatus == .notDetermined {
  locationManager.requestWhenInUseAuthorization()
  return
}
```

This checks the current authorization status. If it is .notDetermined — meaning that this app has not asked for permission yet — then the app will request "When In Use" authorization. That allows the app to get location updates while it is open and the user is interacting with it.

There is also "Always" authorization, which permits the app to check the user's location even when it is not active. That's useful for a navigation app, for example. For most apps, including *MyLocations*, when-in-use is what you want to ask for.

Just adding these lines of code is not enough. You also have to add a special key to the app's Info.plist.

➤ Open **Info.plist** file. Right-click somewhere inside Info.plist and choose **Add Row** from the menu.

Adding a new row to Info.plist

➤ For the key, type **NSLocationWhenInUseUsageDescription** (or choose **Privacy — Location When In Use Usage Description** from the list).

➤ Type the following text in the Value column:

This app lets you keep track of interesting places. It needs access to the GPS coordinates for your location.

This description tells the user what the app wants to use the location data for.

Adding the new item to Info.plist

➤ Run the app again and press the **Get My Location** button.

Core Location will pop up the following alert, asking the user for permission:

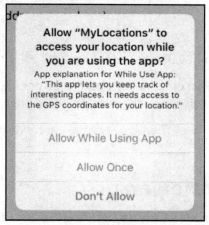

Users have to allow your app to use their location

If a user denies the request with the Don't Allow button, then Core Location will never give your app location coordinates. If the user chooses "Allow Once", then location services will only be available during this session and the app will request access again next time.

➤ Press the **Don't Allow** button. Now press Get My Location again.

Xcode's debug area should now show the following message (or something similar):

```
didFailWithError The operation couldn't be completed.
(kCLErrorDomain error 1.)
```

This comes from the `locationManager(_:didFailWithError:)` delegate method. It's telling you that the location manager wasn't able to obtain a location. The reason why is described by an `Error` object, which is the standard object that the iOS SDK uses to convey error information. You'll see it in many other places in the SDK since there are plenty of places where things can go wrong!

This `Error` object has a *domain* and a *code*. The domain in this case is `kCLErrorDomain` meaning the error came from Core Location (CL). The code is 1, also identified by the symbolic name `CLError.denied`, which means the user did not allow the app to obtain location information.

> **Note**: The k prefix is often used by the iOS frameworks to signify that a name represents a constant value — maybe whoever came up with this prefix thought it was spelled "konstant." This is an old convention and you won't see it used much in new frameworks or in Swift code, but it still pops up here and there.

➤ Stop the app from within Xcode and run it again.

When you press the Get My Location button, the app does not ask for permission anymore but immediately gives you the same error message.

Let's make this a bit more user-friendly, because a normal user would never see that `print()` output.

Handle permission errors

➤ Add the following method to **CurrentLocationViewController.swift**:

```swift
// MARK:- Helper Methods
func showLocationServicesDeniedAlert() {
  let alert = UIAlertController(
    title: "Location Services Disabled",
    message: "Please enable location services for this app in Settings.",
    preferredStyle: .alert)

  let okAction = UIAlertAction(title: "OK", style: .default,
                               handler: nil)
  alert.addAction(okAction)

  present(alert, animated: true, completion: nil)
}
```

This pops up an alert with a helpful hint. This app is pretty useless without access to the user's location, so it should encourage the user to enable location services. (It's not necessarily the user of the app who has denied access to the location data; a systems administrator or parent could also have restricted location access.)

➤ To show this alert, add the following lines to getLocation(), just before you set the locationManager's delegate:

```
if authStatus == .denied || authStatus == .restricted {
    showLocationServicesDeniedAlert()
    return
}
```

This shows the alert if the authorization status is denied or restricted. Notice the use of || here, the "logical or" operator. showLocationServicesDeniedAlert() will be called if either of those two conditions is true.

➤ Try it out. Run the app and tap **Get My Location**. You should now get the Location Services Disabled alert:

The alert that pops up when location services are not available

Fortunately, users can change their minds and enable location services for your app again. This is done from the device's Settings app.

➤ Open the **Settings** app in the simulator and go to **Privacy ▸ Location Services**.

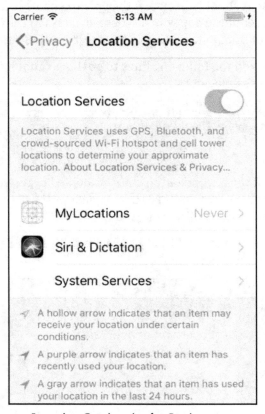

Location Services in the Settings app

➤ Click **MyLocations** and then **While Using the App** to enable location services again. Switch back to the app (or run it again from Xcode) and press the **Get My Location** button.

If you try it, the following message will appear in Xcode's debug area:

```
didFailWithError The operation couldn't be completed.
(kCLErrorDomain error 0.)
```

Again there is an error message but with a different code, 0. This is "location unknown" which means Core Location was unable to obtain a location for some reason.

That is not so strange, as you're running this from the simulator, which obviously does not have a real GPS. Your Mac may have a way to obtain location information through Wi-Fi but this is not built into the simulator. Fortunately, there is a way to fake it!

Fake location on the simulator

➤ With the app running, from the simulator's menu bar at the top of the screen, choose **Debug ▸ Location ▸ Apple**.

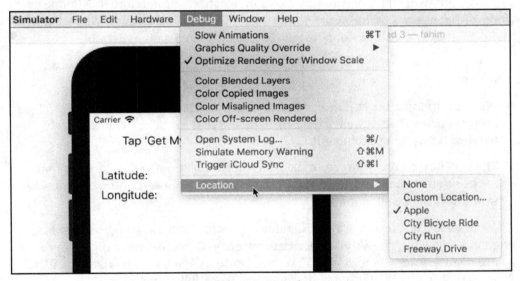

The simulator's Location menu

You should now see messages like these in the debug area:

```
didUpdateLocations <+37.33259552,-122.03031802> +/- 500.00m
(speed -1.00 mps / course -1.00) @ 6/30/17, 8:19:11 AM Israel
Daylight Time
didUpdateLocations <+37.33241211,-122.03050893> +/- 65.00m
(speed -1.00 mps / course -1.00) @ 6/30/17, 8:19:13 AM Israel
Daylight Time
didUpdateLocations <+37.33240901,-122.03048800> +/- 65.00m
(speed -1.00 mps / course -1.00) @ 6/30/17, 8:19:14 AM Israel
Daylight Time
```

It keeps going on and on, giving the app a new location every second or so. These particular coordinates point at the Apple headquarters in Cupertino, California.

Look carefully at the coordinates the app is receiving. The first one says "+/- 500.00m," the second one "+/- 65.00m," a little further on "+/- 50.00m" etc. This number keeps getting smaller and smaller until it stops at about "+/- 5.00m."

This is the accuracy of the measurement, expressed in meters. What you see is the simulator imitating what happens when you ask for a location on a real device.

If you go out with an iPhone and try to obtain location information, the iPhone uses three different ways to find your coordinates. It has onboard cellular, Wi-Fi and GPS radios that each give it location information at different levels of detail:

- Cell tower triangulation will always work if there is a signal but it's not very precise.

- Wi-Fi positioning works better, but that is only available if there are known Wi-Fi routers nearby. This system uses a big database that contains the locations of wireless networking equipment.

- The very best results come from the GPS (**G**lobal **P**ositioning **S**ystem), but that needs satellite communication and is therefore is the slowest of the three. It also won't work very well indoors.

So, your device has several ways of obtaining location data, ranging from fast but inaccurate (cell towers, Wi-Fi) to accurate but slow (GPS). And none of these are guaranteed to work. Some devices don't even have a GPS or cellular radio at all and have to rely on just Wi-Fi. Suddenly obtaining a location seems a lot trickier.

Fortunately for us, Core Location does all of the hard work of turning the location readings from its various sources into a useful number. Instead of making you wait for the definitive results from the GPS — which may never come — Core Location sends location data to the app as soon as it gets it, and then follows up with more and more accurate readings.

> **Exercise**: If you have an iPhone, iPod touch or iPad nearby, try the app on your device and see what kind of readings it gives you. If you have more than one device, try the app on all of them and note the differences.

Asynchronous operations

Obtaining a location is an example of an **asynchronous** process.

Sometimes apps need to do things that may take a while. After you start an operation, you have to wait until it gives you the results. If you're unlucky, those results may never come at all!

In the case of Core Location, it can take a second or two before you get the first location reading and then quite a few seconds more to get coordinates that are accurate enough for your app to use.

Asynchronous means that after you start such an operation, your app will continue on its merry way. The user interface is still responsive, new events are being sent and handled, and the user can still tap on things.

The asynchronous process is said to be operating "in the background." As soon as the operation is done, the app is notified through a delegate so that it can process the results.

The opposite is **synchronous** (without the a). If you start an operation that is synchronous, the app won't continue until that operation is done. In effect, the app freezes up.

In the case of CLLocationManager that would cause a big problem: your app would be totally unresponsive for the couple of seconds that it takes to get a location fix. Those kinds of "blocking" operations are often a bad experience for the user.

For example, *MyLocations* has a tab bar at the bottom. If the app blocked while getting the location, switching to another tab during that time would have no effect. The user expects to always be able to change tabs, but now it appears that the app is frozen, or worse, has crashed.

The designers of iOS decided that such behavior is unacceptable and therefore operations that take longer than a fraction of a second should be performed in an asynchronous manner.

For the next app, you'll see more asynchronous processing in action when we talk about network connections and downloading stuff from the Internet.

By the way, iOS has something called a *watchdog timer*. If your app is unresponsive for too long, then under certain circumstances, the watchdog timer will kill your app without mercy — so don't do anything that freezes your UI!

The take-away is this: any operation that takes long enough to be noticeable by the user should be done asynchronously, in the background.

Displaying coordinates

The `locationManager(_:didUpdateLocations:)` delegate method gives you an array of `CLLocation` objects that contain the current latitude and longitude coordinates of the user. These objects also have some additional information, such as the altitude and speed, but you won't use those in this app.

You'll take the last `CLLocation` object from the array — because that is the most recent update — and display its coordinates in the labels that you added to the screen earlier.

➤ Add a new instance variable to **CurrentLocationViewController.swift**:

```
var location: CLLocation?
```

You will store the user's current location in this variable. This needs to be an optional, because it is possible to *not* have a location, for example, when you're stranded out in the Sahara desert somewhere and there are no cell towers or GPS satellites in sight (it happens).

But even when everything works as it should, the value of `location` will still be `nil` until Core Location reports back with a valid `CLLocation` object, which as you've seen, may take a few seconds. So an optional it is.

➤ Change `locationManager(_:didUpdateLocations:)` to:

```
func locationManager(_ manager: CLLocationManager,
    didUpdateLocations locations: [CLLocation]) {
  let newLocation = locations.last!
  print("didUpdateLocations \(newLocation)")

  location = newLocation       // Add this
  updateLabels()               // Add this
}
```

You store the `CLLocation` object that you get from the location manager into the instance variable and call a new `updateLabels()` method.

Keep the `print()` in there because it's handy for debugging.

➤ Add the `updateLabels()` method:

```
func updateLabels() {
  if let location = location {
    latitudeLabel.text = String(format: "%.8f",
                                location.coordinate.latitude)
```

```
      longitudeLabel.text = String(format: "%.8f",
                              location.coordinate.longitude)
      tagButton.isHidden = false
      messageLabel.text = ""
   } else {
      latitudeLabel.text = ""
      longitudeLabel.text = ""
      addressLabel.text = ""
      tagButton.isHidden = true
      messageLabel.text = "Tap 'Get My Location' to Start"
   }
 }
```

Because the `location` instance variable is an optional, you use the `if let` syntax to unwrap it.

Note the *shadowing* of the original `location` variable by the unwrapped variable. Inside the `if` statement, `location` now refers to an actual `CLLocation` object that is not `nil`.

If there is a valid location object, you convert the latitude and longitude, which are values with type `Double`, into strings and put them into the labels.

You've seen *string interpolation* before to put values into strings, so why doesn't this code simply do the following?

```
latitudeLabel.text = "\(location.coordinate.latitude)"
```

That would certainly work, but it doesn't give you any control over how the latitude value appears. For this app, you want both latitude and longitude to be shown with 8 digits behind the decimal point.

For that sort of control, you need to use a *format string*.

Format strings

Like string interpolation, a format string uses placeholders that will be replaced by the actual value during runtime. These placeholders, or *format specifiers*, can be quite intricate.

To create the text for the latitude label you do this:

```
String(format: "%.8f", location.coordinate.latitude)
```

This creates a new `String` object using the format string `"%.8f"` and the value to replace in that string, `location.coordinate.latitude`.

Placeholders always start with a percent (%) sign. Examples of common placeholders are: %d for integer values, %f for floating-point and %@ for objects.

Format strings are very common in Objective-C code, but less so in Swift because string interpolation is much simpler (but less powerful).

The %.8f format specifier does the same thing as %f: it takes a decimal number and puts it in the string. The .8 means that there should always be 8 digits behind the decimal point.

➤ Run the app, select a location to simulate from the simulator's **Debug** menu and tap the **Get My Location** button. You'll now see the latitude and longitude appear on the screen.

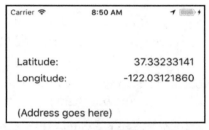

The app shows the GPS coordinates

When the app starts up, it has no location object (location is still nil) and therefore ought to show the "Tap 'Get My Location' to Start" message at the top as a hint to the user. But it doesn't do that yet since the app doesn't call updateLabels() until it receives the first coordinates.

➤ To fix this, also call updateLabels() from viewDidLoad():

```
override func viewDidLoad() {
  super.viewDidLoad()
  updateLabels()
}
```

➤ Run the app. Initially, the screen should now say, Tap 'Get My Location' to Start, and the latitude and longitude labels are empty.

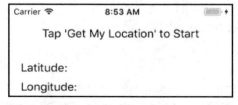

What the app looks like when you start it

You can find the project files for this chapter under **27 - Get Location Data** in the Source Code folder.

Chapter 28: Use Location Data

By Eli Ganim

You've learned how to get GPS coordinate information from the device and to display the information on screen.

In this chapter, you will learn the following:

- **Handle GPS errors**: Receiving GPS information is an error-prone process. How do you handle the errors?

- **Improve GPS results**: How to improve the accuracy of the GPS results you receive.

- **Reverse geocoding**: Getting the address for a given set of GPS coordinates.

- **Testing on device**: Testing on device to ensure that your app handles real-world scenarios.

- **Support different screen sizes**: Setting up your UI to work on iOS devices with different screen sizes.

Handling GPS errors

Getting GPS coordinates is error-prone. You may be somewhere where there is no clear line-of-sight to the sky — such as inside or in an area with lots of tall buildings — blocking your GPS signal.

There may not be many Wi-Fi routers around you, or they haven't been catalogued yet, so the Wi-Fi radio isn't much help getting a location fix either.

And of course your cellular signal might be so weak that triangulating your position doesn't offer particularly good results either.

All of that is assuming your device actually has a GPS or cellular radio. I just went out with my iPod touch to capture coordinates and get some pictures for this app. In the city center it was unable to obtain a location fix. My iPhone did better, but it still wasn't ideal.

The moral of this story is that your location-aware apps had better know how to deal with errors and bad readings. There are no guarantees that you'll be able to get a location fix, and if you do, then it might still take a few seconds.

This is where software meets the real world. You should add some error handling code to the app to let users know about problems getting those coordinates.

The error handling code

➤ Add these two instance variables to **CurrentLocationViewController.swift**:

```
var updatingLocation = false
var lastLocationError: Error?
```

➤ Change `locationManager(_:didFailWithError:)` to the following:

```
func locationManager(_ manager: CLLocationManager,
        didFailWithError error: Error) {
  print("didFailWithError \(error.localizedDescription)")

  if (error as NSError).code ==
      CLError.locationUnknown.rawValue {
    return
  }
  lastLocationError = error
  stopLocationManager()
  updateLabels()
}
```

The location manager may report errors for a variety of scenarios. You can look at the code property of the Error object to find out what type of error you're dealing with. (You do need to cast to NSError first since that is the subclass of Error that actually contains the code property.)

Some of the possible Core Location errors:

- CLError.locationUnknown — the location is currently unknown, but Core Location will keep trying.

- CLError.denied — the user denied the app permission to use location services.

- CLError.network — there was a network-related error.

There are more (having to do with the compass and geocoding), but you get the point. Lots of reasons for things to go wrong!

> **Note**: These error codes are defined in the CLError enumeration. Recall that an enumeration, or enum, is a list of values and names for these values.
>
> The error codes used by Core Location have simple integer values. Rather than using the values 0, 1, 2 and so on in your program, Core Location has given them symbolic names using the CLError enum. That makes these codes easier to understand and you're less likely to pick the wrong one.
>
> To convert these names back to an integer value you ask for the rawValue.

In your updated locationManager(_:didFailWithError:), you do:

```
if (error as NSError).code == CLError.locationUnknown.rawValue {
    return
}
```

The CLError.locationUnknown error means the location manager was unable to obtain a location right now, but that doesn't mean all is lost. It might just need another second or so to get an uplink to the GPS satellite. In the mean time, it's letting you know that, for now, it could not get any location information.

When you get this error, you will simply keep trying until you do find a location or receive a more serious error.

In the case of a more serious error, you store the error object into a new instance variable, lastLocationError:

```
lastLocationError = error
```

That way, you can look up later what kind of error you were dealing with. This comes in useful in updateLabels(). You'll be modifying that method shortly to show the error to the user because you don't want to leave them in the dark about such things.

Exercise: Can you explain why lastLocationError is an optional?

Answer: When there is no error, lastLocationError will not have a value. In other words, it can be nil, and variables that can be nil must be optionals in Swift.

Finally, the update to locationManager(_:didFailWithError:) adds a new method call:

```
stopLocationManager()
```

Stopping location updates

If obtaining a location appears to be impossible for wherever the user currently is on the globe, then you need to tell the location manager to stop. To conserve battery power, the app should power down the iPhone's radios as soon as it doesn't need them anymore.

If this was a turn-by-turn navigation app, you'd keep the location manager running even in the case of a network error, because who knows, a couple of meters ahead you might get a valid location.

For this app, the user will simply have to press the Get My Location button again if they want to try in another spot.

➤ Add the stopLocationManager() method:

```
func stopLocationManager() {
  if updatingLocation {
    locationManager.stopUpdatingLocation()
    locationManager.delegate = nil
    updatingLocation = false
  }
}
```

There's an `if` statement that checks whether the boolean instance variable `updatingLocation` is `true` or `false`. If it is `false`, then the location manager isn't currently active and there's no need to stop it.

The reason for having this `updatingLocation` variable is that you are going to change the appearance of the Get My Location button and the status message label when the app is trying to obtain a location fix, to let the user know the app is working on it.

➤ Put some extra code in `updateLabels()` to show the error message:

```swift
func updateLabels() {
  if let location = location {
    . . .
  } else {
    . . .
    // Remove the following line
    messageLabel.text = "Tap 'Get My Location' to Start"
    // The new code starts here:
    let statusMessage: String
    if let error = lastLocationError as NSError? {
      if error.domain == kCLErrorDomain &&
         error.code == CLError.denied.rawValue {
        statusMessage = "Location Services Disabled"
      } else {
        statusMessage = "Error Getting Location"
      }
    } else if !CLLocationManager.locationServicesEnabled() {
      statusMessage = "Location Services Disabled"
    } else if updatingLocation {
      statusMessage = "Searching..."
    } else {
      statusMessage = "Tap 'Get My Location' to Start"
    }
    messageLabel.text = statusMessage
  }
}
```

The new code determines what to put in the `messageLabel` at the top of the screen. It uses a bunch of `if` statements to figure out what the current status of the app is. If the location manager gave an error, the label will show an error message.

The first error it checks for is `CLError.denied` in the error domain `kCLErrorDomain`, which means Core Location errors. In that case, the user has not given this app permission to use the location services. That sort of defeats the purpose of this app but it can happen, and you have to check for it anyway.

If the error code is something else, then you simply say "Error Getting Location" as this usually means there was no way of obtaining a location fix.

Even if there was no error, it might still be impossible to get location coordinates if the user disabled Location Services completely on their device (instead of just for this app). You check for that situation with the `locationServicesEnabled()` method of `CLLocationManager`.

Suppose there were no errors and everything works fine, then the status label will say "Searching..." before the first location object has been received.

If your device can obtain the location fix quickly, then this text will be visible only for a fraction of a second, but often, it might take a short while to get that first location fix. No one likes waiting, so it's nice to let the user know that the app is actively looking up their location. That is what you're using the `updatingLocation` boolean for.

> **Note**: You put all this logic into a single method because that makes it easy to change the screen when something has changed. Received a location? Simply call `updateLabels()` to refresh the contents of the screen. Received an error? Let `updateLabels()` sort it out...

Starting location updates

➤ Also add a new `startLocationManager()` method — I suggest you put it right above `stopLocationManager()`, to keep related functionality together:

```
func startLocationManager() {
  if CLLocationManager.locationServicesEnabled() {
    locationManager.delegate = self
    locationManager.desiredAccuracy =
                    kCLLocationAccuracyNearestTenMeters
    locationManager.startUpdatingLocation()
    updatingLocation = true
  }
}
```

Starting the location manager used to happen in the `getLocation()` action method. However, because you now have a `stopLocationManager()` method, it makes sense to move the start code into a method of its own, `startLocationManager()`, just to keep things symmetrical.

The only difference from before is that this checks whether the location services are enabled and you set the variable `updatingLocation` to `true` if you did indeed start location updates.

➤ Change getLocation() to:

```
@IBAction func getLocation() {
  . . .
  if authStatus == .denied || authStatus == .restricted {
    . . .
  }
  // New code below, replacing existing code after this point
  startLocationManager()
  updateLabels()
}
```

There is one more small change to make. Suppose there was an error and no location could be obtained, but then you walk around for a bit and a valid location comes in. In that case, it's a good idea to remove the old error code.

➤ At the bottom of locationManager(_:didUpdateLocations:), add the following line just before calling updateLabels():

```
lastLocationError = nil
```

This clears out the old error state. After receiving a valid coordinate, any previous error you may have encountered is no longer applicable.

➤ Run the app. While the app is waiting for incoming coordinates, the label at the top should say "Searching…" until it finds a valid coordinate or encounters a fatal error.

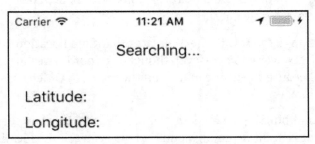

The app is waiting to receive GPS coordinates

Play around with the Simulator's location settings for a while and see what happens when you choose different locations.

Note that changing the Simulator's location to None isn't an error anymore. This still returns the .locationUnknown error code but you ignore that because it's not a fatal error.

Tip: You can also simulate locations from within Xcode. If your app uses Core Location, the bar at the top of the debug area gets an arrow icon. Click on that icon to change the simulated location:

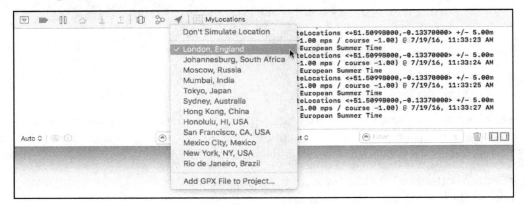

Simulating locations from within the Xcode debugger

Ideally, you should not just test in the Simulator but also on your device, as you're more likely to encounter real errors that way.

Improving GPS results

Cool, you know how to obtain a CLLocation object from Core Location and you're able to handle errors. Now what?

Well, here's the thing: You saw in the Simulator that Core Location keeps giving you new location objects over and over, even though the coordinates may not have changed. That's because the user could be on the move, in which case their GPS coordinates *do* change.

However, you're not building a navigation app. So, for *MyLocations* you just want to get a location that is accurate enough and then you can tell the location manager to stop sending updates.

This is important because getting location updates costs a lot of battery power as the device needs to keep its GPS/Wi-Fi/cellular radios powered up for this. This app doesn't need to ask for GPS coordinates all the time, so it should stop when the location is accurate enough.

The problem is that you can't always get the accuracy you want, so you have to detect this. When the last couple of coordinates you received aren't increasing in accuracy then that is probably as good as it's going to get, and you should let the radio power down.

Getting results for a specific accuracy level

➤ Change `locationManager(_:didUpdateLocations:)` to the following:

```
func locationManager(_ manager: CLLocationManager,
  didUpdateLocations locations: [CLLocation]) {
  let newLocation = locations.last!
  print("didUpdateLocations \(newLocation)")

  // 1
  if newLocation.timestamp.timeIntervalSinceNow < -5 {
    return
  }

  // 2
  if newLocation.horizontalAccuracy < 0 {
    return
  }

  // 3
  if location == nil || location!.horizontalAccuracy >
                        newLocation.horizontalAccuracy {

    // 4
    lastLocationError = nil
    location = newLocation

    // 5
    if newLocation.horizontalAccuracy <=
       locationManager.desiredAccuracy {
      print("*** We're done!")
      stopLocationManager()
    }
    updateLabels()
  }
}
```

Let's take these changes one by one:

1. If the time at which the given location object was determined is too long ago — 5 seconds in this case — then this is a *cached* result.

    Instead of returning a new location fix, the location manager may initially give you the most recently found location under the assumption that you might not have moved much in the last few seconds — obviously, this does not take into consideration people with jet packs.

    You'll simply ignore these cached locations if they are too old.

2. To determine whether new readings are more accurate than previous ones, you'll use the `horizontalAccuracy` property of the location object. However, sometimes locations may have a `horizontalAccuracy` that is less than 0. In which case, these measurements are invalid and you should ignore them.

3. This is where you determine if the new reading is more useful than the previous one. Generally speaking, Core Location starts out with a fairly inaccurate reading and then gives you more and more accurate ones as time passes. However, there are no guarantees — so, you cannot assume that the next reading truly is always more accurate.

    Note that a larger accuracy value means *less* accurate — after all, accurate up to 100 meters is worse than accurate up to 10 meters. That's why you check whether the previous reading, `location!.horizontalAccuracy`, is greater than the new reading, `newLocation.horizontalAccuracy`.

    You also check for `location == nil`. Recall that `location` is an optional instance variable that stores the `CLLocation` object that you obtained in a previous call to `didUpdateLocations`. If `location` is `nil`, then this is the very first location update you're receiving and in that case you should continue.

    So, if this is the very first location reading (`location` is `nil`) or the new location is more accurate than the previous reading, you continue to step 4. Otherwise you ignore this location update.

4. You've seen this part before. It clears out any previous error and stores the new `CLLocation` object into the `location` variable.

5. If the new location's accuracy is equal to or better than the desired accuracy, you can call it a day and stop asking the location manager for updates. When you started the location manager in `startLocationManager()`, you set the desired accuracy to 10 meters (`kCLLocationAccuracyNearestTenMeters`), which is good enough for this app.

Short circuiting

Because `location` is an optional object, you cannot access its properties directly — you first need to unwrap it. You could do that with `if let`, but if you're sure that the optional is not `nil` you can also *force unwrap* it with `!`.

That's what you are doing in this line:

```
if location == nil || location!.horizontalAccuracy >
                      newLocation.horizontalAccuracy {
```

You wrote `location!.horizontalAccuracy` with an exclamation point instead of just `location.horizontalAccuracy`.

But what if `location == nil`, won't the force unwrapping fail then? Not in this case, because the force unwrap is never performed.

The `||` operator (logical or) tests whether either of the two conditions is true. If the first one is true (`location is nil`), it will not evaluate the second condition. That's called *short circuiting*. There is no need for the app to check the second condition if the first one is already true.

So, the app will only look at `location!.horizontalAccuracy` when `location` is guaranteed to be non-`nil`. Blows your mind, eh?

➤ Run the app. First set the Simulator's location to None, then press Get My Location. The screen now says "Searching…"

➤ Switch to location Apple (but don't press Get My Location again). After a brief moment, the screen is updated with GPS coordinates as they come in.

If you check the Xcode Console, you'll get about 10 location updates before it says "*** We're done!" and the location updates stop.

> **Note:** It's possible the above steps won't work for you. If the screen does not say "Searching…" but shows an old set of coordinates instead, then the Simulator is holding on to old location data. This seems to happen when you pick a location from within Xcode (using the arrow in the debug area) instead of the Simulator's Debug menu.
>
> The quickest way to fix this is to quit the Simulator and run the app again — this launches a new Simulator. If you can't get it to work, no worries, it's not that important. Just be aware that the Simulator can be finicky sometimes.

You, as the developer, can tell from the Console when the location updates stop, but obviously, the user won't see this.

The Tag Location button becomes visible as soon as the first location is received so the user can start saving this location to their library right away, but at this point the location may not be accurate enough yet. So it's nice to show the user when the app has found the most accurate location.

Updating the UI

To make this clearer, you are going to toggle the Get My Location button to say "Stop" when the location grabbing is active and switch it back to "Get My Location" when it's done. That gives a nice visual clue to the user. Later on, you'll also show an animated activity spinner that makes this even more obvious.

To change the state of the button, you'll add a configureGetButton() method.

➤ Add the following method to **CurrentLocationViewController.swift**:

```
func configureGetButton() {
  if updatingLocation {
    getButton.setTitle("Stop", for: .normal)
  } else {
    getButton.setTitle("Get My Location", for: .normal)
  }
}
```

It's quite simple: if the app is currently updating the location, then the button's title becomes Stop, otherwise it is Get My Location.

You need to now call configureGetButton() from several different places in your code. If you look closely, you'll notice that wherever you call updateLabels(), you also need to call the new method. So might as well call the new method from within updateLabels(), right?

➤ Add a call to configureGetButton() at the end of updateLabels():

```
func updateLabels() {
  . . .
  configureGetButton()
}
```

➤ Run the app again and perform the same test as before. The button changes to Stop when you press it. When there are no more location updates, it switches back.

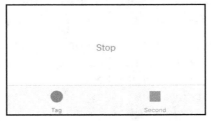

The stop button

When a button says "Stop," you naturally expect to be able to press it so you can interrupt the location updates. This is especially so when you're not getting any coordinates at all. Eventually Core Location may give an error, but as a user, you may not want to wait for that.

Currently, however, pressing Stop doesn't stop anything. You have to change `getLocation()` for this, as any taps on the button call this method.

➤ In `getLocation()`, replace the line with the call to `startLocationManager()` with the following:

```
if updatingLocation {
   stopLocationManager()
} else {
   location = nil
   lastLocationError = nil
   startLocationManager()
}
```

Again, you're using the `updatingLocation` flag to determine what state the app is in.

If the button is pressed while the app is already doing the location fetching, you stop the location manager.

Note that you also clear out the old location and error objects before you start looking for a new location.

➤ Run the app. Now pressing the Stop button will put an end to the location updates. You should see no more updates in the Console after you press Stop.

> **Note**: If the Stop button doesn't appear long enough for you to click it, set the location back to None first, tap Get My Location a few times, and then select the Apple location again.

Reverse geocoding

The GPS coordinates you've dealt with so far are just numbers. The coordinates 37.33240904, -122.03051218 don't really mean that much, but the address 1 Infinite Loop in Cupertino, California does.

Using a process known as **reverse geocoding**, you can turn a set of coordinates into a human-readable address. (Regular or "forward" geocoding does the opposite: it turns an address into GPS coordinates. You can do both with the iOS SDK, but for *MyLocations* you only do the reverse one.)

You'll use the CLGeocoder object to turn the location data into a human-readable address and then display that address on screen.

It's quite easy to do this but there are some rules. You're not supposed to send out a ton of these reverse geocoding requests at the same time. The process of reverse geocoding takes place on a server hosted by Apple and it costs them bandwidth and processor time to handle these requests. If you flood their servers with requests, Apple won't be happy.

MyLocations is only supposed to be used occasionally. So theoretically, its users won't be spamming the Apple servers, but you should still limit the geocoding requests to one at a time, and once for every unique location. After all, it makes no sense to reverse geocode the same set of coordinates over and over.

Reverse geocoding needs an active Internet connection and anything you can do to prevent unnecessary use of the iPhone's radios is a good thing for your users.

The implementation

➤ Add the following properties to **CurrentLocationViewController.swift**:

```
let geocoder = CLGeocoder()
var placemark: CLPlacemark?
var performingReverseGeocoding = false
var lastGeocodingError: Error?
```

These mirror what you did for the location manager. CLGeocoder is the object that will perform the geocoding and CLPlacemark is the object that contains the address results.

The placemark variable needs to be an optional because it will have no value when there is no location yet, or when the location doesn't correspond to a street address — I don't think it will respond with "Sahara desert, Africa," but to be fair, I haven't had the chance to try.

You set performingReverseGeocoding to true when a geocoding operation is taking place, and lastGeocodingError will contain an Error object if something went wrong, or, nil if there is no error.

➤ You'll put the geocoder to work in `locationManager(didUpdateLocations)`. Add these lines right under the call to `updateLabels()`:

```
if !performingReverseGeocoding {
  print("*** Going to geocode")

  performingReverseGeocoding = true

  geocoder.reverseGeocodeLocation(newLocation,
                                  completionHandler: {
    placemarks, error in
    if let error = error {
      print("*** Reverse Geocoding error: \
(error.localizedDescription)")
      return
    }
    if let places = placemarks {
      print("*** Found places: \(places)")
    }
  })
}
```

The app should only perform a single reverse geocoding request at a time. So, first you check whether it is busy by looking at the `performingReverseGeocoding` variable. Then you start the geocoder.

The code looks straightforward enough, right? If you are wondering what the `completionHandler` bit is, harken back to chapter 6 when you used a similar construct to handle a `UIAlertController` action — it's a *closure*.

Closures

Unlike the location manager, `CLGeocoder` does not use a delegate to return results from an operation. Instead, it uses a closure. Closures are an important Swift feature and you can expect to see them all over the place — for Objective-C programmers, a closure is similar to a "block."

Closures can have parameters too and here, the parameters for the closure are `placemarks` and `error`, both of which are optionals because either one or the other can be `nil` depending on the situation.

So, while all the code inside the closure does is print out either the list of places or the error, you do have to unwrap each optional before you do that to be sure that you have a value there.

Unlike the rest of the code in `locationManager(_:didUpdateLocations:)`, the code in the closure is not performed right away. After all, you can only print the geocoding results once the geocoding completes, and that may be several seconds later.

The closure is kept for later use by the CLGeocoder object and is only performed after CLGeocoder finds an address or encounters an error.

So why does CLGeocoder use a closure instead of a delegate?

The problem with using a delegate to provide feedback is that you need to write one or more separate methods. For example, for CLLocationManager there are the locationManager(_:didUpdateLocations:) and locationManager(_:didFailWithError:) methods.

By creating separate methods, you move the code that deals with the response away from the code that makes the request. With closures, on the other hand, you can put that handling code in the same place. That makes the code more compact and easier to read. Some APIs do both, and you have a choice between using a closure or becoming a delegate.

So when you write,

```
geocoder.reverseGeocodeLocation(newLocation, completionHandler:
{ placemarks, error in
  // put your statements here
}
```

you're telling the CLGeocoder object that you want to reverse geocode the location, and that the code in the block following completionHandler: should be executed as soon as the geocoding is completed.

The closure itself is:

```
{ placemarks, error in
    // put your statements here
}
```

The items before the in keyword — placemarks and error — are the parameters for this closure and they work just like parameters for a method or a function.

When the geocoder finds a result for the location object that you gave it, it invokes the closure and executes the statements within. The placemarks parameter will contain an array of CLPlacemark objects that describe the address information, and the error variable contains an error message in case something went wrong.

Closures are basically the same principle as using delegate methods, except you're not putting the code into a separate method but in a closure.

It's OK if closures have got you scratching your head right now. You'll see them used many more times in the upcoming chapters.

➤ Run the app and pick a location. As soon as the first location is found, you can see in the Console that the reverse geocoder has kicked in (give it a second or two):

```
didUpdateLocations <+37.33233141,-122.03121860> +/- 379.75m
(speed -1.00 mps / course -1.00) @ 7/1/17, 10:31:15 AM Israel
Daylight Time
*** Going to geocode
*** Found places: [Apple Inc., Apple Inc., 1 Infinite Loop,
Cupertino, CA  95014, United States @
<+37.33233141,-122.03121860> +/- 100.00m, region
CLCircularRegion (identifier:'<+37.33233140,-122.03121860>
radius 141.73', center:<+37.33233140,-122.03121860>,
radius:141.73m)]
```

If you choose the Apple location, you'll see that some location readings are duplicates; the geocoder only does the first of those. Only when the accuracy of the reading improves does the app reverse geocode again. Nice!

Note: Several readers have reported that if you are in China and are trying to reverse geocode an address that is outside of China, you may get an error and `placemarks` will be `nil` — try a location inside China instead.

Handling reverse geocoding errors

➤ Replace the contents of the geocoding closure with the following:

```
self.lastGeocodingError = error
if error == nil, let p = placemarks, !p.isEmpty {
  self.placemark = p.last!
} else {
  self.placemark = nil
}

self.performingReverseGeocoding = false
self.updateLabels()
```

Just as with the location manager, you store the error object so you can refer to it later — you do use a different instance variable this time, `lastGeocodingError`.

The next line does something you haven't seen before:

```
if error == nil, let p = placemarks, !p.isEmpty {
```

You know that if let is used to unwrap optionals. Here, placemarks is an optional, so it needs be unwrapped before you can use it or you risk crashing the app when placemarks is nil. The unwrapped placemarks array gets the temporary name p.

The !p.isEmpty bit says that we should only enter this if statement if the array of placemark objects is not empty.

You should read this line as:

```
if there's no error and the unwrapped placemarks array is not
empty {
```

Of course, Swift doesn't speak English, so you have to express this in terms that Swift understands.

You could also have written this as three different, nested if statements:

```
if error == nil {
   if let p = placemarks {
      if !p.isEmpty {
```

But it's just as easy to combine all of these conditions into a single if.

You're doing a bit of **defensive programming** here: you specifically check first whether the array has any objects in it. If there is no error, then it should have at least one object, but you're not going to trust that it always will. Good developers are paranoid!

If all three conditions are met — there is no error, the placemarks array is not nil, and there is at least one CLPlacemark inside this array — then you take the last of those CLPlacemark objects:

```
self.placemark = p.last!
```

The last property refers to the last item from an array. It's an optional because there is no last item if the array is empty. As an alternative, you can also write placemarks[placemarks.count − 1] but that's not as tidy.

Usually there will be only one CLPlacemark object in the array, but there is the odd situation where one location coordinate may refer to more than one address. This app can only handle one address at a time. So, you'll just pick the last one, which usually is the only one.

If there was an error during geocoding, you set `self.placemark` to `nil`. Note that you did not do that for the locations. If there was an error there, you kept the previous location object because it may actually be correct (or good enough) and it's better than nothing. But for the address that makes less sense.

You don't want to show an old address, only the address that corresponds to the current location or no address at all.

In mobile development, nothing is guaranteed. You may get coordinates back or you may not, and if you do, they may not be very accurate. The reverse geocoding will probably succeed if there is some type of network connection available, but you also need to be prepared to handle the case where there is none.

And remember, not all GPS coordinates correspond to actual street addresses — there is no corner of 52nd and Broadway in the Sahara desert.

> **Note**: Did you notice that inside the `completionHandler` closure you used `self` to refer to the view controller's properties and methods? This is a Swift requirement.
>
> Closures are said to *capture* all the variables they use and `self` is one of them. You can forget about that immediately, if you like; just know that Swift requires that all captured variables are explicitly mentioned.
>
> As you've seen, outside a closure, you can use `self` to refer to properties and methods, but it's not a requirement. However, you do get a compiler error if you leave out `self` inside a closure. So you don't have much choice there.

Displaying the address

Let's show the address to the user.

➤ Modify `updateLabels()` like this:

```
func updateLabels() {
   if let location = location {
      . . .
      // Add this block
      if let placemark = placemark {
        addressLabel.text = String(from: placemark)
      } else if performingReverseGeocoding {
        addressLabel.text = "Searching for Address..."
      } else if lastGeocodingError != nil {
        addressLabel.text = "Error Finding Address"
```

```
      } else {
         addressLabel.text = "No Address Found"
      }
      // End new code
   } else {
      . . .
   }
}
```

Because you only do the address lookup once the app has a valid location, you just have to change the code inside the first if branch. If you've found an address, you show that to the user, otherwise you show a status message.

The code to format the CLPlacemark object into a string is placed in its own method, just to keep the code readable.

➤ Add the string(from) method:

```
func string(from placemark: CLPlacemark) -> String {
   // 1
   var line1 = ""

   // 2
   if let s = placemark.subThoroughfare {
      line1 += s + " "
   }

   // 3
   if let s = placemark.thoroughfare {
      line1 += s
   }

   // 4
   var line2 = ""

   if let s = placemark.locality {
      line2 += s + " "
   }
   if let s = placemark.administrativeArea {
      line2 += s + " "
   }
   if let s = placemark.postalCode {
      line2 += s
   }

   // 5
   return line1 + "\n" + line2
}
```

Let's look at this in detail:

1. The address will be two lines of text — create a new string variable for the first line of text.

2. If the placemark has a subThoroughfare, add it to the string. This is an optional property, so you unwrap it with if let first. Just so you know, subThoroughfare is a fancy name for house number.

3. Adding the thoroughfare (or street name) is done similarly. Note that you put a space between it and subThoroughfare so they don't get glued together.

4. The same logic goes for the second line of text. This adds the locality (the city), administrative area (the state or province), and postal code (or zip code), with spaces between them where appropriate.

5. Finally, the two lines are concatenated (added together) with a newline character in between. The \n adds the line break (or newline) to the string.

➤ In getLocation(), clear out the placemark and lastGeocodingError variables to start with a clean slate. Put this just above the call to startLocationManager():

```
placemark = nil
lastGeocodingError = nil
```

➤ Run the app again. Seconds after a location is found, the address label should be filled in as well.

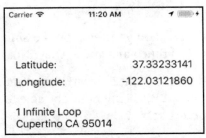

Reverse geocoding finds the address for the GPS coordinates

It's fairly common that street numbers or other details are missing from the address. The CLPlacemark object may contain incomplete information, which is why its properties are all optionals. Geocoding is not an exact science!

Exercise: If you pick the City Bicycle Ride or City Run locations from the Simulator's Debug menu, you should see in the Console that the app jumps

> through a whole bunch of different coordinates — it simulates someone moving from one place to another. However, the coordinates on the screen and the address label don't change nearly as often. Why is that?

Answer: The logic for *MyLocations* was designed to find the most accurate set of coordinates for a stationary position. You only update the `location` variable when a new set of coordinates comes in that is more accurate than previous readings. Any new readings with a higher — or the same — `horizontalAccuracy` value are simply ignored, regardless of what the actual coordinates are.

With the City Bicycle Ride and City Run options, the app doesn't receive the same coordinates with increasing accuracy but a series of completely different coordinates. That means this app doesn't work very well when you're on the move — unless you press Stop and try again —, but that's also not what it was intended for.

> **Note**: If you're playing with different locations in the Simulator or from the Xcode debugger menu and you get stuck, then the quickest way to get unstuck is to reset the Simulator. Sometimes it just doesn't want to move to a new location even if you tell it to, and then you have to show it who's the boss!

Testing on device

When I first wrote this code, I had only tested it on the Simulator. It worked fine there. Then, I put it on my iPod touch and guess what? Not so good.

The problem with the iPod touch is that it doesn't have GPS, so it relies only on Wi-Fi to determine the location. But Wi-Fi might not be able to give you accuracy up to ten meters; I got +/- 100 meters at best.

Right now, you only stop the location updates when the accuracy of the reading falls within the `desiredAccuracy` setting — something that will never actually happen on my iPod touch.

That goes to show that you can't always rely on the Simulator to test your apps. You need to put them on your device and test them in the wild, especially when using device-dependent functionality like location-based APIs. If you have more than one device, then test on all of them! In order to deal with this situation, you will improve upon the `didUpdateLocations` delegate method.

First fix

➤ Change `locationManager(_:didUpdateLocations:)` to:

```swift
func locationManager(_ manager: CLLocationManager,
  didUpdateLocations locations: [CLLocation]) {
  . . .

  if newLocation.horizontalAccuracy < 0 {
    return
  }

  // New section #1
  var distance = CLLocationDistance(
      Double.greatestFiniteMagnitude)
  if let location = location {
    distance = newLocation.distance(from: location)
  }
  // End of new section #1
  if location == nil || location!.horizontalAccuracy >
                        newLocation.horizontalAccuracy {

    . . .
    if newLocation.horizontalAccuracy <=
       locationManager.desiredAccuracy {

      . . .
      // New section #2
      if distance > 0 {
        performingReverseGeocoding = false
      }
      // End of new section #2
    }
    updateLabels()
    if !performingReverseGeocoding {
      . . .
    }

  // New section #3
  } else if distance < 1 {
    let timeInterval = newLocation.timestamp.timeIntervalSince(
                                       location!.timestamp)

    if timeInterval > 10 {
      print("*** Force done!")
      stopLocationManager()
      updateLabels()
    }
    // End of new sectiton #3
  }
}
```

It's a pretty long method now, but only the three highlighted sections were added. This is the first one:

```
var distance = CLLocationDistance(
    Double.greatestFiniteMagnitude)
if let location = location {
  distance = newLocation.distance(from: location)
}
```

This calculates the distance between the new reading and the previous reading, if there was one. We can use this distance to measure if our location updates are still improving.

If there was no previous reading, then the distance is Double.greatestFiniteMagnitude. That is a built-in constant that represents the maximum value that a Double value can have. This little trick gives it a gigantic distance if this is the very first reading. You're doing that so any of the following calculations still work even if you weren't able to calculate a true distance yet.

You also add an if statement later where you stop the location manager:

```
if distance > 0 {
  performingReverseGeocoding = false
}
```

This forces a reverse geocoding for the final location, even if the app is already currently performing another geocoding request.

You absolutely want the address for that final location, as that is the most accurate location you've found. But if some previous location was still being reverse geocoded, this step would normally be skipped.

Simply by setting performingReverseGeocoding to false, you always force the geocoding to be done for this final coordinate.

(Of course, if distance is 0, then this location is the same as the location from a previous reading, and you don't need to reverse geocode it anymore.)

The real improvement is found in the final new section:

```
} else if distance < 1 {
  let timeInterval = newLocation.timestamp.timeIntervalSince(
                                        location!.timestamp)
  if timeInterval > 10 {
    print("*** Force done!")
    stopLocationManager()
    updateLabels()
```

```
    }
  }
```

If the coordinate from this reading is not significantly different from the previous reading and it has been more than 10 seconds since you've received that original reading, then it's a good point to hang up your hat and stop.

It's safe to assume you're not going to get a better coordinate than this and you can stop fetching the location.

This is the improvement that was necessary to make my iPod touch stop scanning after some time. It wouldn't give me a location with better accuracy than +/- 100 meters, but it kept repeating the same one over and over.

A time limit of 10 seconds seems to give good results.

Note that you don't just say:

```
} else if distance == 0 {
```

The distance between subsequent readings is never exactly 0. It may be something like 0.0017632. Rather than checking for equals to 0, it's better to check for less than a certain distance, in this case one meter.

By the way, did you notice how you used `location!` to unwrap it before accessing the timestamp property? When the app gets inside this `else-if`, the value of `location` is guaranteed to be non-`nil`, so its safe to force unwrap the optional.

➤ Run the app and test that everything still works. It may be hard to recreate this situation on the Simulator, but try it on your device inside the house and see what output you see in the Console.

There is another improvement you can make to increase the robustness of this logic, and that is to set a time-out on the whole thing. You can tell iOS to perform a method one minute from now. If by that time the app hasn't found a location yet, you stop the location manager and show an error message.

Second fix

➤ First add a new instance variable:

```
var timer: Timer?
```

➤ Then change `startLocationManager()` to:

```
func startLocationManager() {
  if CLLocationManager.locationServicesEnabled() {
    . . .
    timer = Timer.scheduledTimer(timeInterval: 60, target: self,
                selector: #selector(didTimeOut), userInfo: nil,
                repeats: false)
  }
}
```

The new lines set up a timer object that sends a `didTimeOut` message to `self` after 60 seconds; `didTimeOut` is the name of a method.

A *selector* is the term that Objective-C uses to describe the name of a method, and the `#selector()` syntax is how you create a selector in Swift.

➤ Change `stopLocationManager()` to:

```
func stopLocationManager() {
  if updatingLocation {
    . . .
    if let timer = timer {
      timer.invalidate()
    }
  }
}
```

You have to cancel the timer in case the location manager is stopped before the time-out fires. This happens when an accurate enough location is found within one minute after starting, or when the user taps the Stop button.

➤ Finally, add the `didTimeOut()` method:

```
@objc func didTimeOut() {
  print("*** Time out")
  if location == nil {
    stopLocationManager()
    lastLocationError = NSError(
                    domain: "MyLocationsErrorDomain",
                    code: 1, userInfo: nil)
    updateLabels()
```

```
      }
   }
```

There's something new about this method — there's a new @objc attribute before func — whatever could it be?

Remember how how #selector is an Objective-C concept? (How could you forget, it was just a few paragraphs ago, right?) So, when you use #selector to identify a method to call, that method has to be accessible not only from Swift, but from Objective-C as well. The @objc attribute allows you to identify a method (or class, or property, or even enumeration) as being accessible from Objective-C.

So, that's what you've done for didTimeOut — declared it as being accessible from Objective-C.

didTimeOut() is always called after one minute, whether you've obtained a valid location or not — unless stopLocationManager() cancels the timer first.

If after that one minute there still is no valid location, you stop the location manager, create your own error code, and update the screen.

By creating your own NSError object and putting it into the lastLocationError instance variable, you don't have to change any of the logic in updateLabels().

However, you do have to make sure that the error's domain is not kCLErrorDomain because this error object does not come from Core Location but from within your own app.

An error domain is simply a string, so MyLocationsErrorDomain will do. For the code I picked 1. The value of the code doesn't really matter at this point because you only have one custom error, but you can imagine that when an app becomes bigger, you might need multiple error codes.

Note that you don't always have to use an NSError object; there are other ways to let the rest of your code know that an error occurred. In this case updateLabels() was already using an NSError anyway, so having your own error object just made sense.

➤ Run the app. Set the Simulator location to None and press **Get My Location**.

After a minute, the debug area should say "*** Time out" and the Stop button reverts to Get My Location. There should also be an error message on the screen:

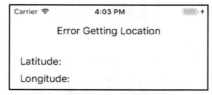

The error after a time out

Just getting a simple location from Core Location and finding the corresponding street address turned out to be a lot more hassle than it looked. There are many different situations to handle. Nothing is guaranteed, and everything can go wrong — iOS development sometimes requires nerves of steel!

To recap, the app either:

- Finds a location with the desired accuracy,

- Finds a location that is not as accurate as you'd like and you don't get any more accurate readings,

- Doesn't find a location at all,

- Or, takes too long finding a location.

The code now handles all these situations, but I'm sure it's not perfect yet. No doubt the logic could be tweaked more, but it will do for the purposes of this book.

I hope it's clear that if you're releasing a location-based app, you need to do a lot of field testing!

Required device capabilities

The **Info.plist** file has a key, **Required device capabilities**, that lists the hardware that your app needs in order to run. This is the key that the App Store uses to determine whether a user can install your app on their device.

The default value is **armv7**, which is the CPU architecture of the iPhone 3GS and later models. If your app requires additional features, such as Core Location to retrieve the user's location, you should list them here.

➤ Add a new item with the value **location-services** to **Info.plist**:

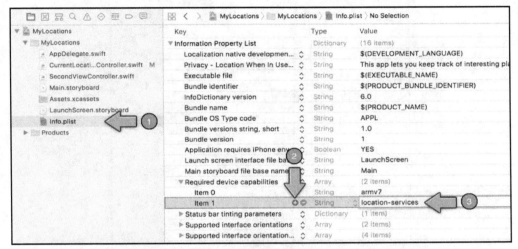

Adding location-services to Info.plist

You could also add the item **gps**, in which case the app requires a GPS receiver. But if you did, users won't be able to install the app on an iPod touch or on certain iPads.

For the full list of possible device capabilities, see the *App Programming Guide for iOS* on the Apple Developer website.

P.S. You can now take the print() statements out of the app (or simply comment them out). You might want to keep them in there as they're handy for debugging. In an app that you plan to upload to the App Store, you'll definitely want to remove the print() statements when development's complete.

Attributes and properties

Most of the attributes in Interface Builder's inspectors correspond directly to properties on the selected object. For example, a UILabel has the following attributes:

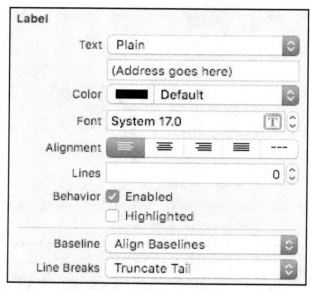

These are directly related to the following properties:

```
Text          label.text
Color         label.textColor
Font          label.font
Alignment     label.textAlignment
Lines         label.numberOfLines
Enabled       label.isEnabled
Baseline      label.baselineAdjustment
Line Breaks   label.lineBreakMode
```

And so on... As you can see, the names may not always be exactly the same ("Lines" and numberOfLines) but you can easily figure out which property goes with which attribute.

You can find these properties in the documentation for `UILabel`. From the Xcode **Help** menu, select **Developer Documentation**. Type "uilabel" into the search field to bring up the class reference for `UILabel`:

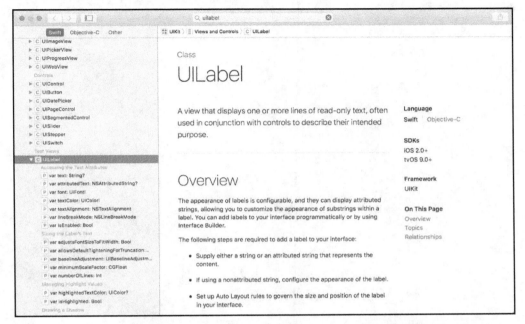

The documentation for `UILabel` does not list properties for all of the attributes from the inspectors. For example, in the Attributes inspector there is a section named "View." The attributes in this section come from `UIView`, which is the base class of `UILabel`. So if you can't find a property in the `UILabel` class, you may need to check the documentation under the "Inherits From" section (which is under the **Relationships** section) of the documentation.

You can find the project files for this chapter under **28 – Use Location Data** in the Source Code folder.

Section 5: Store Search

The final section of the book covers iPad support in more detail via the Store Search app.

Store Search shows you how to have separate custom screens both for specific orientations (landscape vs. portrait) as well as for specific platforms (iPhone vs. iPad). This section covers networking, working with remote API endpoints to fetch data needed by your app, and how to parse the fetched data. If that wasn't enough, this section also takes you through the full application life cycle — from developing the code, testing it, and all the way to submitting to Apple. So don't skip this section thinking that you know all about iOS development after the last few sections!

This section contains the following chapters:

37. Search Bar: One of the most common tasks for mobile apps is to talk to a server. In this final UIKit app you will build StoreSearch. In this chapter, you will build the first screens, add fake searches and create the data models.

38. Custom Table Cells: Before your app can search the iTunes store for real, we need to make the app look visually appealing. In this chapter, you will cover custom table view cells and nibs. Learn a little more about using git and the debugger right inside Xcode.

39. Networking: Networking you say? Start querying the iTunes web service by using HTTP requests. An introduction to JSON and best to convert them into data models and finally look at how best to sort results.

40. Asynchronous Networking: Phew! You will rarely want to block the main thread with a network request. In this chapter, we will explore asynchronous networking and finally showing an activity indicated to let the user know something is loading.

41. URLSession: The iOS toolbox and the Swift language has many tools for our disposal, including URLSession. In this chapter, we will explore URLSession and it's many benefits. Downloading the iTunes artwork and how best to merge your git changes.

42. The Detail Pop-Up: In this chapter, we will create a detail pop-up view when a user taps a row in the TableView. We don't want to display too much information now, do we?

43. Polish the Pop-Up: We're about to get the polish back out again. The detail pop-up view is working well but we can display the information better. Learn about dynamic types, gradients for the background and let's explore adding some more animations.

44. Landscape: Users expect apps to work in both portrait and landscape. They also expect the app to look great in both orientations. In this chapter, we will learn about adding a completely different user interface for landscape vs. portrait.

45. Refactoring: The final app is looking great. You should put your feet up and grab a coffee! Programming is all about building new pretty features but when you join an existing company with an existing code-base you have to learn about the best ways to refactor existing code. Let's go!

46. Internationalization: So far our app works great in English. But if you want your app to go international you must support multiple languages and formats. In this chapter, you will explore adding support for a new language and look at regional settings.

47. The iPad: Even though the app works *OK* on the iPad, but it's not exactly optimized for the iPad. In this chapter, we're going to explore universal apps, the split view controller functionality, and dark mode support.

48. Distributing the App: Are you ready to ship to the App Store? Finally, you will learn the key fundamentals on how to ship the app to the App Store, including the Apple Developer Program, beta testing using TestFlight and finally submitting to the App Store.

Print Edition

You're reading the print edition of *iOS Apprentice*. This edition contains Section 1—4. Due to print size limitations, the final section, Section 5, is available to you as part of the downloadable source code materials.

You can download the source code materials here: https://store.raywenderlich.com/products/ios-apprentice-source-code.

Conclusion

We hope you're excited about the new world of iOS development that lies before you!

By completing this book, you've given yourself the knowledge and tools to create your own iOS applications, or even start working with other developers on a team. It's up to you now to couple your creativity with the things you've learned in this book and create some impressive apps of your own!

If you have any questions or comments about the projects in this book or in your own iOS apps, please stop by our forums at http://forums.raywenderlich.com.

Thank you again for purchasing this book. Your continued support is what makes the books, tutorials, videos and other things we do at raywenderlich.com possible. We truly appreciate it!

— Matthijs, Joey, Eli and Adam

The *iOS Apprentice* team

CPSIA information can be obtained
at www.ICGtesting.com
Printed in the USA
LVHW101915250320
651171LV00017B/398